The British

BOXING Board of Control YEARBOOK 1993

Edited by
Barry J. Hugman

Published by Tony Williams Publications,
24a Queen Square, North Curry, Taunton, Somerset TA3 6LE

ISBN 1 869833 35 X

Distributed by Little Red Witch Book Distribution,
Helland Cottage, Helland, North Curry, Taunton, Somerset TA3 6DU
Telephone 0823 490080, Fax 0823 490281

Typeset by Typecast (Artwork & Design), 8 Mudford Road, Yeovil, Somerset BA21 4AA
Film Origination by Character Graphics Ltd, Rear of 56/58 Station Road, Taunton, Somerset TA1 1NS
Printed & Bound by Ian Allan Printing, Addlestone
Trade Sales, Searle Association, Telephone 0753 539295

All other sales enquiries should be referred to The Little Red Witch Book Distribution Co

Contents

Acknowledgements

Once again I am most indebted to John Morris and his team at the British Boxing Board of Control for their assistance in helping me produce this, the ninth edition of the *British Boxing Yearbook.*

From the moment I was first asked by Ray Clarke OBE to publish the *British Boxing Yearbook,* back in 1982, the Board has always been wholeheartedly behind the project. These days, since Ray retired, my dealings are with the current General Secretary, John Morris, who just like his predecessor, has always had an open door. I would like to thank John and the Assistant Secretary and Honorary Secretary of the Commonwealth Boxing Council, Simon Block, for placing all of the requisite facilities at my disposal. At the same time, I would like to express my gratitude to all the staff behind the scenes at the BBBoC, such as Paula Gibson, Peter Lane, Mary Farnan and Rod Douglas, the former British middleweight title challenger, who kept me abreast of any changes taking place during the year, applicable to the *Yearbook,* in terms of boxers, managers, promoters and other licenceholders.

Once again I would like to place on record my gratitude to my great friend and assistant editor, Ron Olver. Ron has now been involved in boxing for over 40 years and without a doubt he has been the major influence in establishing the ex-boxers' associations these past 20 odd years. A former assistant editor of *Boxing News;* former assistant editor of *Boxing World;* British correspondent for the *Ring;* author of *The Professionals;* author of the boxing section within *Encyclopedia Britannica;* author of *Boxing,* Foyles Library service; former co-editor of the *Boxing News Annual;* member of the BBBoC Benevolent Fund Grants committee; member of the British Boxing Writers' Club; Vice-President of many ex-boxers' associations and the writer of the Old Timers feature in *Boxing News* for over 20 years.

To constantly remain a viable proposition, an informative book such as the *Yearbook* has to achieve the right balance each time round and John Jarrett, Chris Kempson and Jack Mitchell have provided an excellent blend of articles for this year's edition. Two year's ago, I stated in the preface that I would eventually try to introduce a selection of international records and this has finally come to fruition. Eric Armit is to be congratulated for piecing together biographical details, along with last season's complete record for over 200 of the world's leading fighters. Also, I must not forget ABC's Bob Yalen, who kept me up-to-date with all world title bout information, when required. In the amateur section, the indispensable Chris Kempson came through yet again with a summary of the past season, while invaluable help was also given by Patrick Myler, author of the *Fighting Irish* and Bill Cowan and Frank Hendry of the Scottish ABA.

On the photographic front, the *Yearbook* continues to rely heavily on the support of people like Les Clark. Les, a real boxing nut from a fighting family, has travelled the country taking action photos at many venues, while also visiting dressing rooms and gyms for poses that can be used to good effect in the *Yearbook.* If anyone requires a copy of a picture in the book, Les can be reached at 352 Trelawney Avenue, Langley, Bucks SL3 7TS. Other poses have been supplied by Chris Bevan, Belvoir House, Moss Road, Askern, Yorkshire, while further action shots come courtesy of David Jacobs of Action Images, 74 Willoughby Lane, London N17 0SP. The majority of the photos from America come from the libraries of my very good friends in the States, Tom Casino, Chris Farina and Peter Goldfield, for which I remain indebted. Tom can be reached on (0101 201 333008), Chris (0101 702 648 5792) and Peter (0101 609 962 8132).

A book will always be judged initially by its look and in the field of production, both the publisher, Tony Williams and myself, would like to thank Bob Bickerton and Jean Bastin of Typecast (Artwork & Design) for their diligent design and typesetting contributions, respectively. Advertising also has a large part to play in publishing these days and to that end the publisher thanks John Williams of Williams Agg-Manning Marketing.

Finally, I take my hat off to the publisher, Tony Williams, whose great enthusiasm and support has made the publication of this book and others possible.

B. J. Hugman (Editor)

ANGLO/SWEDISH PROMOTIONS

INTERNATIONAL PROMOTERS, MANAGERS,

KURT SJOLIN

GREG STEENE

BENNY ROSEN

Office:

11 Whitcomb Street
London
WC2H 7HA

LICENCED BY B.B.B. OF C.

Office:

Box 6003
Gothenburg
Sweden 40060

MATCHMAKERS & AGENTS

Tel: 071-839 4532 Fax: (London) 071-839 4367

Fax: (Gothenburg) 010-46312561-69

Boxers managed by Greg Steene:

Lou Gent	Super-Middleweight. Former Southern Area Cruiserweight Champion
Roland Ericsson	Super-Middleweight
Andy Wright	Former Undefeated Southern Area Super-Middleweight Champion
Tom McCarthy	Super-Middleweight
Stan King	Middleweight
Conrad Oscar	Middleweight
Georgy Wilson	Light-Welterweight
Matt Mason	Lightweight

Also UK representative for:

Horace Fleary	German International Super-Middleweight Champion

TRAINERS:

Trevor Cattouse, Casley McCallum, Peter Cann, Dave Payne

Any boxer who wants top management

Introduction

It gives me great pleasure to introduce the ninth edition of the *British Boxing Yearbook*, now to be known as the *British Boxing Board of Control Yearbook*, produced this year in a brand new format by Tony Williams Publications. The new publisher is an old friend and I look forward to a long and prosperous association.

The reason to change the old format was taken in the light of trying to give the title a far more commercial image than previous and almost getting away from how one expects a yearbook to look. Other changes have also been made in order to keep the book alive with fresh ideas. Most notably, the decision to turn the book into a far more detailed account of the past season than ever before and to lose some of the historical data which has appeared time and again.

Another decision that was taken on board was that of giving our readers far greater details on international boxers than we had done previously. To this end, Eric Armit, the long established record collector and author of *Boxing News' World Scene* has produced an A-Z of over 200 of the world's leading fighters, including their recent records. Also, every British, Commonwealth, European and world title fight that took place over the past season has been summarised as to allow the reader an opportunity to see how their championship heroes performed at a glance. And it was also decided that the time was right to ask Ron Olver to record for posterity, the deaths of all boxing personalities that have taken place since 1990. This will now become an annual feature of the *Yearbook*.

As always we try to include interesting articles, alongside the regulars, such as Around British Rings and Highlights from the Amateur Season. This time round there is an interesting piece written by Jack Mitchell about the psychology factor appertaining to professional boxers, as opposed to other sportsmen. Another article by Chris Kempson takes into account several up-and-coming young fighters who could be tomorrow's champions.

While putting together Facts and Figures for 1991-92, I discovered that while there were nearly 50 more boxers active during the campaign, compared to 1990-91, there were also 28 less promotions than in the previous season. The disturbing sign is that while more men turn to professional boxing to supplement their incomes in these times of recession, there will be less promotions taking place to offer them the opportunity of fulfilling that need. Will we ever reach the day, one might ask, that in order to keep earning and to be in a position to choose the opponent, the boxer and his manager will become joint promoters. That situation may not be too far away as there are already partnerships such as that of Dai Gardiner and Kevin Hayde and more recently, Harry Burgess and Lester Jacobs. Certainly, the big ticket sellers would be at an advantage, but it might be the way forward for young fighters to sell themselves to their local community and to the public at large.

Finally, I would like to add my personal thanks to both Tommy Gilmour and Gus Robinson for their continued generous support of the *British Boxing Board of Control Yearbook* for the fourth year running.

Abbreviations and Definitions

PTS	Points
CO	Count Out
RSC	Referee Stopped Contest
RTD	Retired
DIS	Disqualified
NC	No Contest
ND	No Decision

Barry J. Hugman, the founder-editor of the British Boxing Board of Control Yearbook, now in its ninth year
Derek Rowe (Photos) Ltd

British Boxing Board of Control Ltd: Structure

(Members of the World Boxing Council, World Boxing Association, International Boxing Federation, World Boxing Organisation, Commonwealth Boxing Council and European Boxing Union).

PRESIDENT	Sir David Hopkin
VICE PRESIDENT	Leonard E. Read, QPM
CHAIRMAN	Sir David Hopkin
VICE CHAIRMAN	Leonard E. Read, QPM
GENERAL SECRETARY	John Morris
ADMINISTRATIVE STEWARDS	Dr Adrian Whiteson OBE Norman N. Jacobs Dr Oswald Ross William Sheeran Dennis Lockton Lincoln Crawford Dr James Shea Frank Butler, OBE Tom Pendry, MP Cliff Curvis Bill Martin Robert Graham Lord Brooks of Tremorfa Julian Critchley, MP Gerald Woolard
STEWARDS OF APPEAL*	Robin Simpson, QC John Mathew, QC Nicholas Valios Robert Harman, QC William Tudor John Geoffrey Finn Judge Brian Capstick Colin Ross Munro, QC
HONORARY CONSULTANT*	Ray Clarke, OBE
HEAD OFFICE	Jack Petersen House 52a Borough High Street London SE1 1XW Tel. 071 403 5879 Fax. 071 378 6670 Telegrams: BRITBOX, LONDON

* Not directors of the company

AREA COUNCILS - AREA SECRETARIES

AREA NO 1 (SCOTLAND)
Brian McAllister
11 Woodside Crescent, Glasgow G3 7UL
Telephone 041 332 0932

AREA NO 2 (NORTHERN IRELAND)
Dr. P. MacHugh
32 Ballinderry Road, Lisburn Co.
Antrim, Northern Ireland
Telephone 02382 79798

AREA NO 3 (WALES)
Dai Corp
113 Hill Crest, Brynna, Llanharan, Mid Glamorgan
Telephone 0443 226465

AREA NO 4 (NORTHERN)
(Northumberland, Cumbria, Durham, Cleveland, Tyne and Wear, North Yorkshire [north of a line drawn from Whitby to Northallerton to Richmond, including these towns].)
John Jarrett
5 Beechwood Avenue, Gosforth, Newcastle
Telephone 091 2856556

AREA NO 5 (CENTRAL)
(North Yorkshire [with the exception of the part included in the Northern Area - see above], Lancashire, West and South Yorkshire, Greater Manchester, Merseyside and Cheshire, Isle of Man, North Humberside.)
Harry Warner
14 St Christopher's Road,
The 18th Fairway, Ashton under Lyme, Lancashire
Telephone 061 330 4572

AREA NO 6 (SOUTHERN)
(Bedfordshire, Berkshire, Buckinghamshire, Cambridgeshire, Channel Islands, Isle of Wight, Essex, Hampshire, Kent, Hertfordshire, Greater London, Norfolk, Suffolk, Oxfordshire, East and West Sussex.)
Simon Block
British Boxing Board of Control
Jack Petersen House, 52a Borough High Street, London
SE1 1XW
Telephone 071 403 5879

AREA NO 7 (WESTERN)
(Cornwall, Devon, Somerset, Dorset, Wiltshire, Avon, Gloucestershire.)
Jim Paull
The Coach House, Clarence Court, Kent Road,
Congresbury, Bristol BS19 5BE
Telephone 0934 876036

AREA NO 8 (MIDLANDS)
(Derbyshire, Nottinghamshire, Lincolnshire, Salop, Staffordshire, Hereford and Worcestershire, Warwickshire, West Midlands, Leicestershire, South Humberside, Northamptonshire.)
Alec Kirby
105 Upper Meadow Road, Quinton, Birmingham B32
Telephone 021 421 1194

Foreword

by John Morris *(General Secretary, British Boxing Board of Control)*

YEAR NINE of the British Boxing Yearbook and it is fair to say that this hardy annual has now established itself very firmly as part of the boxing scene, not only in Britain but around the world. Editor Barry Hugman has decided to add a more international flavour to the book this year and it is a timely move as more and more boxing from Europe and the United States appears on our television screens.

But, before any further consideration of the boxing action, past, present and to come, I must look back to that sad night at White Hart Lane, Tottenham, last September and the injury that damaged Michael Watson so severely in his heroic WBO super-middleweight challenge to Chris Eubank. Michael remains in hospital and his progress is slow. Our hearts and prayers go out to him and his family and the sport is rallying round to assist him.

A fascinating event will be staged on behalf of the Board Benevolent Fund at the Grosvenor House Hotel in London on 18 April next year and this is intended to be one of the great nights for boxing people. The proceeds will go primarily to Michael and to Mark Goult, who received a brain injury before Michael that has left him handicapped. Watch your local and national media for full details and I am confident they will catch your imagination.

In the last edition of the Yearbook, I wrote with enthusiasm of the state of British boxing and despite the recession my confidence for the future has not been dented with so much talent on the British scene and so many boxers pressuring for the chance to win titles.

Whatever your views on the proliferation of world championship organisations, British boxers have been able to cash in, particularly with the World Boxing Organisation. But, the world scene, the way it is now, cannot be good for the sport in the long run in my view.

What is good is the fact that in the period under review in this book, no fewer than 24 British title contests took place. The Lonsdale Belt remains the finest individual trophy in the boxing world and at every weight contenders are queuing up.

The European Boxing Union championships have retained top rate status and both British and EBU title matches are consistently producing the title contests the public want to watch and that means the type of fight the television companies are prepared to pay out to obtain.

These are themes that I shall develop elsewhere in this book. I will simply close by congratulating Barry Hugman on once again maintaining his standard and producing a volume I feel boxing people will enjoy thoroughly.

John Morris, the General Secretary of the British Boxing Board of Control

Derek Rowe (Photos) Ltd

MATCHROOM
BOXING LIMITED
PRO BOX
Sporting Club
"The Pursuit of Excellence"

British Boxing Board of Control Awards, 1992

The Awards, inaugurated in 1984, in the form of statuettes of boxers, were originally designed by Morton T. Colver, the manufacturer of the Lonsdale Belt and the winners for 1992 were selected by an Awards committee, consisting of John Morris, Frank Butler OBE, Bill Martin, Doctor Adrian Whiteson OBE and Barry J. Hugman, the editor of the *Yearbook*.

British Boxer of the Year - Colin McMillan

Other nominations: Pat Clinton, Paul Hodkinson, Lennox Lewis and Colin McMillan.

The past season has been an outstanding one for the new WBO featherweight champion. He started 1991-92 as the British champion, having had just one defeat in 18 contests, a cut eye loss to Alan McKay in his third outing and after beating Herbie Bivalacqua in three rounds, he quickly defended the domestic title against Kevin Pritchard and Sean Murphy to secure a Lonsdale Belt in the record time of 160 days. In his very next fight, he won the vacant Commonwealth title when he defeated the extremely awkward Ghanaian, Percy Commey, on points at the Royal Albert Hall and after a warm up against Tommy Valdez his name was pencilled in for an assault on the reigning WBO champion, Maurizio Stecca. His brilliant points victory brought him much public acclaim as he showed both the live and TV audience what he could do. The Italian, Stecca, a former Olympic champion, had no answer to Colin's brilliant boxing skills and was made to look very ordinary indeed.

Where does Colin go from here? A fight against Britain's other featherweight champion, Paul Hodkinson, who currently holds the WBC version, would surely be a huge draw, but, unfortunately, with boxing politics being what they are, the two may never meet in the ring.

However, a glittering career surely awaits the man who has put the skill factor back into boxing. He is young enough to go on improving and will continue to be a great advertisement for a sport that needs to both promote and advance the art of self defence for its very survival.

Previous winners:- 1984: Barry McGuigan. 1985: Barry McGuigan. 1986: Dennis Andries. 1987: Lloyd Honeyghan. 1988: Lloyd Honeyghan. 1989: Dennis Andries. 1990: Dennis Andries. 1991: Dave McAuley.

"British Boxer of the Year", Colin McMillan, seen making the defence of his British featherweight title against Sean Murphy, which brought him a Lonsdale Belt in a record 160 days

Action Images

Best British Contest of the Year: Dennis Andries v Jeff Harding

Other nominations: Chris Eubank v Michael Watson, Wally Swift v Tony Collins, Paul Hodkinson v Marcos Villasana, John Armour v Ndaba Dube and Henry Wharton v Lou Gent.

This pairing brought together two old rivals for the third time to do battle for Andries' WBC light-heavyweight title at the Hammersmith Odeon on 11 September 1991. Their first meeting in Atlantic City in 1989 had seen the Australian hardman snatch the title at the death, before Andries recaptured his old crown with a seven round kayo victory just over a year later on Harding's home territory in Melbourne. Both fights had been pot boilers, their coming meeting was to prove no exception.

The fight is reported in some detail elsewhere within these pages and to say that the action lived up to all expectations would be an understatement. Right from the opening bell both men gave it everything they had and more. It was reported in the trade paper, "Boxing News", that for courage, determination and ferocity, it was one of the best fights seen in a British ring for many a year. Nobody would deny that.

As in the previous two contests, both men took tremendous punishment unflinchingly and after receiving a terrible hammering in the earlier rounds, Harding somehow fought his way back to hold the initiative in the closing sessions. But Andries could count himself unlucky to lose out to the majority decision as neither man deserved to be defeated.

Previous winners:- 1984: Jimmy Cable v Said Skouma. 1985: Barry McGuigan v Eusebio Pedroza. 1986: Mark Kaylor v Errol Christie. 1987: Dave McAuley v Fidel Bassa. 1988: Tom Collins v Mark Kaylor. 1989: Michael Watson v Nigel Benn. 1990: Orlando Canizales v Billy Hardy. 1991: Chris Eubank v Nigel Benn.

In one of the most memorable contests ever seen in a British ring and one that was voted the "Best British Contest of the Year", Dennis Andries (right) bombs into the new WBC light-heavyweight champion, Jeff Harding
Action Images

Best Overseas Boxer of the Year: Jeff Harding

Other nominations: Raphael del Valle and Donovan Boucher.

There was only ever going to be one winner of the award, following the magnificent Andries v Harding bout and that man was Jeff Harding. Although last year's winner, Canadian, Donovan Boucher, had once again treated British fans to his special brand of magic and Raphael del Valle had wrested the WBO bantamweight title from Duke McKenzie in just a matter of seconds, the Australian's performance last September could not be surpassed.

Harding joins a superb list of great world champions who have won the Award previously and since the Andries fight he has gone on to successfully defend the WBC light-heavyweight title against Christophe Tiozzo inside eight rounds in France.

Previous winners:- 1984: Buster Drayton. 1985: Don Curry. 1986: Azumah Nelson. 1987: Maurice Blocker. 1988: Fidel Bassa. 1989: Brian Mitchell. 1990: Mike McCullum. 1991: Donovan Boucher.

"Best Overseas Boxer of the Year", Australia's Jeff Harding
Peter Goldfield

Winner of the "Special Award" for outstanding services to British Boxing, Doctor Oswald Ross Derek Rowe (Photos) Ltd

Special Award: Doctor Oswald Ross

The Special Award goes to Doctor "Ossie" Ross for his outstanding contribution to British boxing. As the Chairman of the Southern Area Council of the British Boxing Board of Control and a Representative Steward for the Southern Area for many years, he was earlier honoured in 1992 by his appointment as an Administrative Steward of the Board.

"Ossie" Ross has been involved in boxing since before the war, having come originally from Northern Ireland where his father was both a matchmaker and timekeeper.

Following boxing all his life, he first joined the Southern Area as a medical officer in 1963. He went on to the Southern Area Council in 1969 as Deputy Medical Officer to Doctor Adrian Whiteson and together they have forged a partnership that is still going strong. Doctor Whiteson, who was the inaugural winner of this Award in 1984, has risen to become the Chief Medical Officer of the Board with Doctor Ross as his immediate deputy.

After nearly 30 years of service to boxing, "Ossie" retains all of his enthusiasm for the sport and his willingness to give up his own time to help tournaments or individual boxers.

Previous winners:- 1984: Doctor Adrian Whiteson. 1985: Harry Gibbs. 1986: Ray Clarke. 1987: Hon. Colin Moynihan. 1988: Tom Powell. 1989: Winston Burnett. 1990: Frank Bruno. 1991: Muhammad Ali.

Sportsmanship Award: Duke McKenzie

Following his dramatic defeat at the hands of Raphael del Valle and with it the loss of his coveted WBO bantamweight title he had so brilliantly won from Gaby Canizales in June 1991, Duke went away to rethink his career. There were none of the normal excuses or histrionics that one normally associates with a loser, this young man, so often used to being a winner himself, merely wished the new champion well and went back home to his family.

Having been a professional for nearly ten years, Duke has brought his own dedicated brand of "professionalism" to the sport of boxing. For years he struggled to make the flyweight limit, without complaint, before losing his IBF title to Dave McAuley. He later came back as a bantam to win another version of a world title, the first Briton ever to achieve that honour and was looking forward to eventually stepping up a weight to complete a "hat-trick" of world titles.

As in the case of the previous winners of the Award, Duke was selected not for his ability to win championships, but for setting an example to all other boxers in the field of sporting behaviour.

Previous winners:- 1986:- Frank Bruno. 1987: Terry Marsh. 1988: Pat Cowdell. 1989: Horace Notice. 1990: Rocky Kelly. 1991: Wally Swift (Junior).

Former IBF flyweight and WBO bantamweight champ, Duke McKenzie, winner of the "Sportsmanship Award" Tony Fitch

Looking Back With John Morris

General Secretary, British Boxing Board of Control

The sadness of Michael Watson must inevitably override everything in British boxing at the present time, but nothing can take away the feelings of intense pride I have found creeping through our sport over the past year, at least from my own personal viewpoint.

There is nothing like a bit of name dropping, so how about this. I was standing next to Her Majesty, The Queen, on a perfect afternoon in the garden of Buckingham Palace.

All true, at the wonderful garden party arranged by the Central Council of Physical Recreation and hosted by the Queen and Prince Philip in July 1992 for the sporting greats of her 40-year reign. It was an honour to be invited as a mere administrator and a cause of great pride to see so many of our champions and former champions amid the host of famous names.

Cooper, Conteh, Bruno, Minter, Winstone, McGuigan . . . . it really is not fair to pick out individuals, although the pleasure of seeing Eddie Thomas looking so well remains with me.

Boxing's array of heroes did the sport proud and helped me to realise just how vital it is to keep boxing strong with firm control, while still seeking the way forward to improvement on all fronts. There are times when improvements, particularly on the medical side, cost boxers more money. That cannot be avoided and the Board continues to seek ways of assisting with at least some of the costs.

But, to develop the theme of pride, I have to return to Michael Watson's head injury at Tottenham in September 1991 at the end of his great epic battle against Chris Eubank. The whole affair gave boxing's opponents, and they are ever alert for an opportunity to attack, a perfect opening, but they faced a sport resolute in defence of its very existence and united as on only very rare occasions.

I was proud indeed of our licence holders and the many supporters prepared to go public and back boxing. The fact that they included the Prime Minister, the Minister for Sport and leading opposition politicians, helped considerably. When a summit meeting between the Sports Minister, the Board and medical experts was held, two of the neurosurgeons attending went at the express invitation of the Board and are long time advisors on safety at tournaments.

The direct outcome of the meeting was a Board decision to firm safety guidelines into mandatory regulations with a few refinements added. Boxing people accepted the whole package unanimously and it seemed to me that not only did they agree the letter of the Regulations but the spirit in which they were being passed. Certainly, to the best of my knowledge, all licence holders have carried out the Regulations to the letter.

This they must continue to do. Accidents cannot be avoided, but boxing cannot afford any mistakes on the medical front. Boxers complain bitterly when a medical decision rules them out of a contest, or even ends a career, but one of my corniest adages cannot be ignored.

"Health before wealth" must be a basic fact of life for any boxing control board. Sentiment cannot allow any boxer to go ahead with "a good earner" if there are any doubts about his fitness. Although boxers do not always appreciate it, the Board acts in their interests and those of the sport.

All licence holders must remember that the BMA and the rest of the anti-lobby are just waiting to feed on any mistakes by the Board or by individuals.

One of the most heartening aspects of events over the past year has been the rock solid support of boxings' own medical officers. In adversity I have learned a great deal more about the strengths of our medics and appreciate them thoroughly.

This year the BBB of C has taken one of the most adventurous steps since its formation in 1929. The Board has at last purchased its own offices and the headquarters now lie in a quiet mews just off Borough High Street, close to London Bridge.

Naturally, the knockers within boxing went vocal at once. "There they go, wasting our money, buying themselves grand offices". Ah well, we are used to the brickbats, but this time I believe they are right off target. Finally, and much too late in the day in my view, the Board has invested for the good of professional boxing in an excellent building admirably suited to our needs.

Buying at what seems to have been rock bottom during the recession, we have picked up a bargain and in 20 years time the sport will own it instead of having to pay ever-mounting rents. We can put out an image of which boxing can be proud without lashing out on luxuries.

Disputes, arising from the boxer/manager contract, have been a recurring problem throughout the history of boxing and the situation has been made even more complicated when the manager involved has also been a promoter.

The Board has tried to solve the problem in a variety of ways and has now completely redrafted the boxer/manager contract, paying particular attention to the position that arises when the manager is a promoter.

The result is a contract that gives the boxer a far greater share in the decision making on his own career - provided both parties to the contract make it work by carrying out its requirements.

Problem solved? We must hope so, but the Board recognises the concern of boxers in this direction and has not closed the matter down. A special working party of legal experts involved with the Board is preparing a report for the Stewards on all personal service contracts in boxing.

Their report is designed to lead on to discussion at gatherings of licence holders all around the country so that everyone inside the sport will have a chance to express a view. Then the Board itself will have to decide whether to make any more changes and approach the next Annual Meeting with further specific regulations. In any case, at the end of the process, this vital matter will have been given a thorough airing.

During the past year, the Board has created a publicity committee with a particular aim - swift reaction to attacks on the sport, indeed instant response whenever boxing is under pressure. This is important, but Board members and officials need every slice of help they can get not only from licence holders but supporters as well. In time of crisis the sport must continue to close ranks.

How do you do it? The answer is, through the media both nationally and locally. To answer the criticisms, contact or perhaps write to the papers and join those radio phone-ins. Let the world see just how strong and knowledgeable the support for boxing really is. If you need any guidance on specific points then ring the Board offices or ask your local officials.

Over the past year, British boxers have figured in a whole string of "world" championships with the World Boxing Organisation particularly active here. The Board has now given official recognition to the WBO and it cannot be denied that this relatively new organisation has made its mark.

Whatever your views on the multiplicity of world championship bodies, it is obvious that the vast increase in title contests spreads the rewards available to far more boxers. But is any of this good for boxing in the long-run? How long before the public and the boxing public in particular grow weary of title tags that become more and more meaningless?

As boxing folk jostle for a slice of the cake, joining the alphabet game by creating so many world bodies (they must surely run out of letters in the end) they run more and more risk of devaluing the titles that are around and at the end of the day damaging boxing as the fans and with them the media men lose interest.

In contrast, the demand for British title contests remained high and in the period under review there were 24 British championship matches, with the magnificent Lonsdale Belt at stake on each occasion. The standard remains pretty high and at every weight there are eager candidates queuing for a chance.

In Europe the picture is excellent too. Thanks to a major reconstruction of the EBU under its Spanish President, Ruben Martinez and boxing's first top line woman administrator, General Secretary, Mrs Enza Jacoponi from Rome.

The Ratings and Championships Committee chaired by Swiss lawyer, Peter Stucki, works with authority to keep the rankings fair and to enforce the rules to keep the championships moving. Amid the ever-increasing fragmentation of the world title scene we have retained a unified European title - and the financial rewards have tumbled in.

The public and the TV companies back the EBU titles with hard cash, which is reflected in the bids submitted in purse offers. A boxer challenging for an EBU title in any of the popular weights can expect to earn perhaps 100% more as a European challenger than as a challenger for the majority of the "world" titles.

There was a case earlier in the year of a boxer going into a "world" title match as challenger knowing that victory would debar him from a Euro-match, worth nearly three times as much as the "world" chance.

The answer must be to keep British and European boxing strong and united. That is the road forward and the the way to beat the recession by creating public interest and keeping respect for boxing high. If vested interest could be set aside on the world front - which may well be simply a pious hope - more and more matches for undisputed titles would be a great boost.

Even partial unification would be a step in the right direction. Just imagine the huge interest in Britain in a confrontation between WBC featherweight champion Paul Hodkinson and WBO king Colin McMillan. That is a dream match in my book.

Despite the many major tournaments this year, the number of shows in Britain continued to drop overall. These are tough times for the smaller promoters who have no television fees to bolster them, the recession is biting and we have to find ways of keeping boxing flourishing at grass root level.

So far the number of professional boxers licenced in Britain has not started to fall and that means a great many boxers eager for work. The major promoters can help by bringing in fewer trial-horses from outside Europe and making some of the attractive domestic matches just waiting to happen.

The Board has decided to accept only first series visitors from anywhere outside of Europe in a bid to improve the standard of imported boxers. Far too often the description "journeyman" turns out to mean an opponent simply not equipped to entertain the public in a competitive contest.

Defining first series is the next obvious question and to assess each opponent put forward to box here the Board has set up a check out system that may not be infallible, but on the other hand should help to improve things.

These are critical times for boxing and a change is vital in many areas over the next few years. Better liaison with the English Amateur Boxing Association would help, but prospects are against this happening because of what seems to be a totally negative approach from the top amateur officials. The sooner they realise that boxing is one sport, the better it will be for everyone. Maybe complete unification would be wrong, but sensible co-operation, particularly in defence of boxing, must surely be the only possible way.

So many topics and much to write about and for all the problems British professional boxing remains strong. There is plenty to be proud of, but thinking back to that superb afternoon at Buckingham Palace, there was indeed one thing missing - Michael Watson's presence among that array from boxing's hall of fame.

Around British Rings During 1991-92

by John Jarrett

JULY

British and European heavyweight champion Lennox Lewis took his act to Lake Tahoe in the Nevada desert, looking for some credibility on the world scene in a bout with former WBA champ Mike Weaver. Lennox came through with a knockout, but it was a bitter-sweet victory that left ringsiders shrugging their shoulders as they wandered back to the gambling tables. At 39, Weaver had been around the block a couple of times and the six rounds the fight lasted suggested that future unveilings of his magnificent torso should be in front of artists or sculptors rather than heavyweight fighters. The knockout punch was impressive, a flashing right hand shot that dumped Weaver flat on his back 65 seconds into round six, but for five rounds Lewis gave the American far more respect than he deserved.

The new model Nigel Benn was on show at Brentwood against WBC International champion Kid Milo and he was impressive, the old punching ferocity is still there, but now there was patience along with the power, maturity channelling the mayhem. The end result was the same. Milo was all through after four rounds, battered and bloody from cuts under and over his left eye, as Benn took his record to 29-2 (27 inside schedule). As early as round one Milo was rocked by thunderous punches and cut on the left cheek and in the fourth he was dropped with a left-uppercut that ripped a gash over the left eye. The bell took him to his corner and out of the fight.

Another WBC International champion, light-middleweight Tony Collins, tried to add the British title to his collection at Reading but found Wally Swift Jnr every bit as tough and determined as his father was in the 60s, the left jab just as accurate, the chin just as dependable. Wally came out with a tight decision after a grim battle.

Much-heralded Colin McMillan made his first appearance as British featherweight champion on the Reading show against American import Herbie Bivalacqua. McMillan barely worked up a sweat and Herbie was getting a hiding when the referee stopped it in round three.

Nineteen-year veteran Roy Skeldon finally got his big chance, going against Crawford Ashley for the vacant British light-heavyweight title at Dudley Town Hall. But it was too much and too late. Cut on the left eyelid in the first round, Skeldon rarely got to grips with the rangy Leeds rasta-farian and was trailing when the referee pulled him out in round seven.

Norwich heavyweight comer Herbie Hide chalked up his twelfth straight win, all via the short route, when he hammered the resistance out of Midlands champion Michael "Tucker" Richards on the Benn-Milo card. Despite a 34-pound pull on the scales, Richards was never in the race and was rescued in round three . . . Cardiff light-heavyweight Nicky Piper, the 1989 ABA champion, remained unbeaten after eleven fights, dumping Simon Harris twice for a first round stoppage . . . Birmingham welterweight Robert McCracken took his pro log to 8-0 with easy one round wins over Marty Duke and John Smith . . . Brummie Paul Wesley tossed a shock into eleven-fight winner Neville Brown, stopping the Burton middleweight with a big right hand in round one at Alfreton, but the evening belonged to local veteran Shamus Casey, in the ring for his 100th fight! They presented him with a certificate and a statuette and the crowd gave him a standing ovation. To top it all off, Shamus won his fight!

Three years after losing his British featherweight championship to Paul Hodkinson, Swansea's Peter Harris blew his Welsh title in the Cardiff ring when local favourite Steve Robinson finished like a train to take the decision after a splendid contest . . . Midlands Area lightweight champion Peter Till had better luck than Harris, hanging on to his title by stopping Karl Taylor inside four rounds at Dudley. But the rough-and-tumble Taylor gave Peter a bumpy ride before a cut over the left eye ended his challenge.

AUGUST

Newcastle featherweight John Davison made such a good impression when fighting Fabrice Benichou to a tight decision for his European championship that French promoter Roger Ferrer asked manager Tommy Conroy to bring him back to box classy American, Richard Savage, as chief support to the Benichou-Bottiglieri title bout at Juan les Pins, hard by the Mediterranean sea. Savage was fit from three weeks sparring with Benichou which was just as well because Davison fell on him like a plague of locusts. The former WBC International champion came out a winner, the fight being stopped in round six, with Savage bleeding from a bad cut on his right eyebrow.

A week later, Conroy was back on the continent, this time in Alcamo, Italy, with Northern Area lightweight champion Paul Charters going against Antonio Renzo for his European title. The Italian southpaw had to enlist the help of the hot and humid weather to wear down the Geordie as Charters was leading on all official cards going into round eleven. Then it all caught up with Paul and he was knocked out.

Stablemate Frankie Foster was also out of luck, losing a close eight rounds decision to former European title challenger Gianni di Napoli on the supporting card. Di Napoli is no mean puncher, but Foster, the Northern Area champion from Newcastle, was never in trouble and earned praise for his performance. The British contingent had one winner on the bill, but former Midlands Area heavyweight champion Al Malcolm was probably more surprised than his previously unbeaten opponent Salvatore Inserra, who was bombed out in the opening round.

However, as usual, Italy proved a barren hunting ground for our boys and another to return home empty handed was Alfreton middleweight John Ashton. To be fair to the Midlands Area champion, he was really up against it, fighting Sumbu Kalambay for the vacant European title in Pesaro. A third or fourth choice for the job, Ashton grabbed his chance while marking time for a British title bout with Herol Graham and fought out of his skin, decking the veteran former WBA champion before being floored twice himself and stopped with a damaged eye after six rounds.

There were only two shows on the home front. At Telford, local boy makes good, Ritchie Woodhall, continued to impress as he chalked up his sixth straight victory since turning to the money ranks after taking bronze at the 1988 Olympics. Mickey Duff's light-middleweight dumped Nigel Moore with a big right and although Moore beat the count he was under pressure and the fight was stopped at two minutes and 44 seconds of round one.

Brendan Ingle has another one! At Dewsbury, big Paddy Reilly chalked up his second pro win with a repeat performance over Newcastle's John Harewood, this time stretching Harewood inside the first round. At 6' 2½" and 17 stones, Paddy (Clifton Mitchell) is the colour of Cadbury's chocolate and as Irish as Slugger O'Toole!

Two weeks before he was to celebrate his 27th birthday by fighting Mexican Mario Lozano at Sunderland, British bantamweight champion Billy Hardy called a press conference to announce his retirement. Out of action since losing his second world title challenge against IBF champ Orlando Canizales in May, Hardy said he no longer had the motivation to put himself through the punishing training routine required at top level.

And this was the month that the WBO came in from the cold, with the British Boxing Board of Control announcing the two bodies were to become formally affiliated.

SEPTEMBER

The tragic aftermath of the Chris Eubank-Michael Watson fight for the vacant WBO super-middleweight championship at White Hart Lane threw a giant shadow over the British fight scene as the new season opened. In a dramatic eleventh round, Eubank snatched victory from the jaws of defeat with a tremendous right-hand shot that virtually ended the fight and almost ended the life of Michael Watson.

It was a busy month for the champions. At Cardiff, classy Robbie Regan was unlucky to lose his British flyweight crown to Francis Ampofo when a clash of heads left him with a nasty cut over his left eye and brought the referee's intervention in round eleven . . . former British super-featherweight champion Kevin Pritchard moved up to feather but was outclassed by Colin McMillan, who put a second notch on his Lonsdale Belt with a seventh round victory. Referee John Coyle pulled Pritchard out after he had been down four times and the Liverpool man announced his retirement.

Tiny Jacob Matlala (4'9½") made the journey from Soweto to Belfast to challenge IBF flyweight king Dave McAuley for his title, but found the job too big for him and was kayoed in the tenth . . . At Wolverhampton, former British super-feather champ Hugh Forde won a second title when Commonwealth king Thunder Aryeh of Ghana found the Birmingham southpaw too much of a handful. Thunder didn't rumble at all that night in a disappointing bout.

The two-fisted action in the ring at the Hammersmith Odeon was the equal of anything ever thrown up on the giant screen as Dennis Andries - Jeff Harding III made Rocky V look like Mary Poppins. The Australian hard man outpunched the veteran from Detroit's Kronk gym to win the rubber and the WBC light-heavyweight title in a helluva fight . . . Duke McKenzie had better luck than Andries the next night when he outboxed Cesar Soto of Mexico to hang on to his WBO bantamweight title at Battersea.

In the normal run of things, a British champion makes a Lonsdale Belt his own property by defeating his next two challengers. Things are a little different in the super-featherweight division however, where not one champion has successfully defended his title since the class was re-instated in 1986. The only way to get yourself a belt was to win the title three times, and that is just what John Doherty did, beginning his third reign with a decision over Sugar Gibiliru at Stockport Town Hall.

The British super-middleweight division found a new champion as Slugger O'Toole put it all together to stop Ian Strudwick in six rounds at Basildon. The fight was stopped because of Ian's badly cut right eyebrow, but O'Toole was out in front and pulling away . . . Up in Glasgow, local favourite Donnie Hood kept warm at Shawfield football ground by chasing Rocky Commey around the ring for twelve rounds to hang on to his WBC International bantamweight bauble.

The big boys were in action at the Royal Albert Hall where former IBF, British and Commonwealth cruiserweight champion, Glenn McCrory, made his grab for the brass ring, fighting Lennox Lewis for his British and European heavyweight titles. Lewis was just too big and too strong for Glenn who was down and out inside two rounds. Commonwealth champion Derek Williams failed to impress against veteran American David Bey on the same bill, although he came out a winner, Bey quitting on his stool with a swelling over his right eye. It was a lousy fight up till then.

Welsh light-heavyweight Nicky Piper suffered his first professional defeat in twelve contests when trying to concede 9½ pounds to Manchester's Carl Thompson at York Hall. Hammered to the canvas in round three, Piper struggled up at five, but was in no condition to go on and it was stopped . . . After a year on the shelf, former British and European flyweight champion Pat Clinton swung back into action in Glasgow, taking an easy decision over Mexican workhorse Armando Tapia.

Unbeaten in his nine pro starts, Liverpool southpaw Jimmy Owens found Russell Davison too tough and experienced for him when going for the Manchester man's Central Area featherweight title. Jimmy survived a fourth round knockdown to finish on his feet . . . Two to watch in the lightweight division were Billy Schwer of Luton and Michael Ayers from Tooting. Schwer added two names to

In a cracking October 1991 defence of his Commonwealth super-middleweight title, Henry Wharton (right) scored three Knockdowns over gusty Lou Gent, but still only managed a draw Chris Bevan

his unbeaten record, outpointing southpaw Tony Foster at Hammersmith and hammering Felix Kelly in two rounds a fortnight later to make it twelve in a row. In a meeting of area champions, Ayers (Southern) had a tough one on his hands with Peter Till (Midlands) and had to get off the floor himself before stopping Till in round five with a cut eye, taking his record to eight wins, all via the short route.

OCTOBER

Plenty of action this month with Newcastle featherweight John Davison dropping into the super-bantamweight division to grab his second WBC International crown, beating tough Thai Sakda Sorpakdee. Busloads of John's supporters came down the A19 to pack Hartlepool's old Borough Hall and raise the roof as their hero hammered his way to a thrilling victory in twelve pulsating rounds. It proved a costly triumph, however, as John came out with a broken jaw that kept him out of the ring for six months. Davison's stablemate, Frankie Foster, suffered a setback to his British title aspirations on the undercard when losing his Northern Area super-featherweight title to Darren Elsdon. The local favourite pulling off a sensational win in round seven when a whistling left-hook dropped Foster and the referee stopped it when he got up.

You can tell Pat Barrett's fans by their bitten-down finger nails. Pat put them through the wringer again at Manchester when defending his European light-welterweight title against Racheed Lawal. The champion was rocking all over the place in the first round before coming on to stop his challenger in the fourth to keep his world title hopes alive. Big (6'7") Henry Akinwande knocked out Gypsy John Fury in round three of their British heavyweight title eliminator, the former two-time ABA champion taking his record to 12-0.

After two defeats going after the cruiserweight title, Lou Gent was hoping for third time lucky against Henry Wharton for the Yorkshireman's Commonwealth super-middleweight crown, but it was not to be. In a fight that almost blistered the ornate paintwork off the walls at the Leeds Town Hall, Wharton needed three knockdowns to save his title with a draw.

Two Glasgow boys in Ronnie Carroll and Joe Kelly, contested the vacant British bantamweight title right in their own midden, but after twelve rounds the division was still without a successor to Billy Hardy. Referee Dave Parris calling it a draw, much to the general disgust of the fans who saw Kelly a good winner.

British featherweight champion Colin McMillan retained his title with a runaway victory over former holder Sean Murphy at the Royal Albert Hall, making the Lonsdale Belt his own in the record time of 160 days.

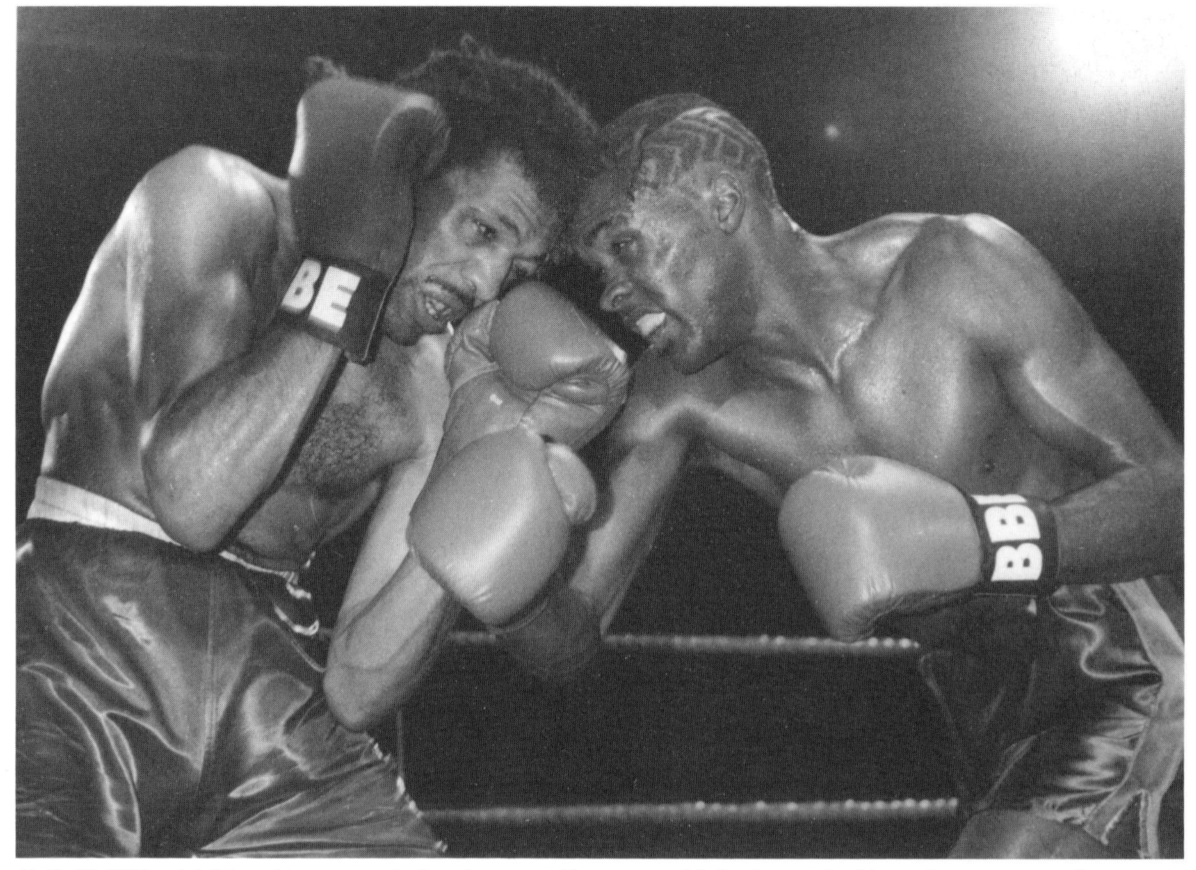

Colin McMillan (right) on his way to winning the vacant Commonwealth featherweight title against a very tough customer indeed, Percy Commey, from Ghana

Another easy winner was Derek Angol as he stopped limited Aussie Dave Russell inside four rounds to keep his Commonwealth cruiserweight title and take his record to 25-0.

Northolt milkman Andy Till showed plenty of bottle in grabbing the vacant WBC International light-middleweight championship with a split decision victory over stylish Welshman John Davies at Dudley Town Hall, while 32-year-old James Cook retained his European super-middleweight title when he forced Finland's Tarmo Uusivirta into retirement in round seven of their scrap at Battersea.

Herbie Hide was in devastating form with two quick victories, dumping a fat Eddie Gonzalez inside two rounds at Hamburg, before disposing of Welsh champion Chris Jacobs in the first at Cardiff, his fourteenth straight win. On the Hamburg bill, Michael Murray, the big Manchester heavyweight, racked up a good win when he stopped German champ Markus Bott in round seven and welter Eamonn Loughran made it a British hat-trick when he whipped Juan Carlos Ortiz over eight rounds for his 16th win against one draw.

Nigel Benn moved into the super-middleweight class with a solid victory over cagey American Lenzie Morgan at Brentwood and looked an easier winner than the 98-97½ scoreline indicated.

A rare happening at Sheffield where not only did a British champion step in as substitute, he did so within a week of winning his title! With four different opponents pulling out of a championship challenge against Herol Graham, stablemate Slugger O'Toole agreed to go back in the ring just seven days after beating Ian Strudwick to become British super-middleweight champion. Slugger was too busy for Johnny Melfah and it was called off in the seventh.

Former British light-heavyweight champion Tony Wilson received a rude shock when he returned to action after a year's layoff. With a shot at his old title pencilled in against Crawford Ashley, Wilson took a warm-up job with Glazz Campbell, who proved too hot to handle, winning a tight decision. In Glasgow, tough American import Vinnie Ponzio gave Donnie Hood a good workout over eight rounds with the WBC International bantamweight champ chalking up his eleventh straight win.

NOVEMBER

Two big names back in the heavyweight headlines, Bruno and Bugner, but the honours went to a little guy as Paul Hodkinson avenged his only defeat as a professional fighter to take the WBC featherweight championship from

Herbie Hide (Centre) burst on the heavyweight scene like a tornado last season. Here he celebrates after winning the WBC International title, following a second round destruction of the Canadian, Conroy Nelson Les Clark

Marcos Villasana in Belfast. In their first fight, 17 months previously, the lad from Liverpool hit the rock-chinned Mexican with everything but the stool, only to be stopped in eight rounds when his damaged eyes could no longer see the punches coming. This time the eyes held up and Paul punched his way to a well-deserved victory, but he had to go the full distance to vanquish the valiant Villasana.

Boxing has often been called show business with blood. Big Frank Bruno combined the two as he moved on from a farce in a London arena to a pantomime in a Bristol theatre, without breaking sweat. Bruno entered the ring at the Royal Albert Hall to a rapturous reception for his first contest following a two and a half year layoff, during which time he had surgery for a torn retina. Dutchman John Emmen was not expected to give Frank a tough test and he didn't. It was all over inside the first round with Emmen knocked down three times from Bruno's big punches.

Another big name back among the fight results was Bugner. No, big Joe was not making another comeback from his vineyard in Australia, although he did voice his disapproval at the news that his son Joe Jnr. had become a professional boxer. The big lad's debut at Milton Keynes brought the media out in force to see him outpoint veteran Denroy Bryan over four-three's. Boxing as J. A. Bugner, he stands 6'6" in his socks, weighs a solid 16 stones and has Andy Smith in his corner. Only time will tell . . .

Britain's best hope for the world heavyweight championship, Lennox Lewis, made a favourable impression on American fight fans when he stopped former contender Tyrell Biggs on the same card as Evander Holyfield's narrow escape against Bert Cooper in Atlanta. Biggs had beaten Lewis in the 1984 Olympics, but Lewis was the main man this night as he dumped Biggs three times for a third round stoppage.

On paper, young Scottish flyweight James Drummond had no chance going against Salvatore Fanni for his European title in Italy. It was the same story at the end of the fight, Drummond had no chance on the papers turned in by the three officials. Giving a fine performance, the Scot made only one mistake. In round four he knocked the Italian favourite down. He should have knocked him out! Then they might have given him the decision.

Tim Driscoll was another British visitor to Italy, jumping at the chance to challenge WBO featherweight champion Maurizio Stecca for his title. The Bermondsey boy tried to upset the odds, but was pulled out by his corner after nine rounds with his left eye cut and swollen. Stecca managed to break Tim's nose, but not his spirit.

Croydon puncher Mickey Hughes was out of luck when going after Del Bryan's British welterweight title at the York Hall. The Nottingham southpaw put the second notch on his belt when Referee Adrian Morgan stopped the fight in round three with Hughes bleeding from a badly cut right eye.

Back in the ring after a thirteen-month layoff, former British and European champion, Chris Pyatt, claimed the vacant Commonwealth light-middleweight title with a decision over Aussie Craig Trotter at Leicester's Granby Halls. Trotter climbed off the floor in the first round and gave the local a stubborn argument the rest of the way.

Another new Commonwealth champion was Ilford's Paul Harvey. In only his twelfth outing as a money fighter, Harvey racked up a chilling three rounds stoppage of super-featherweight champion Hugh Forde at Wolverhampton. The southpaw Forde, a former British champion, had struggled to make the weight and never look too happy against a lean and hungry challenger.

Mersey star Andy Holligan sent his fans into raptures as he retained his Commonwealth light-welter title against Steve Larrimore of the Bahamas at Liverpool's Central Hall. Holligan kept the pressure on all night and Larrimore was rescued by the third man in the eighth round.

Northern Area lightweight champion Paul Charters came back to the ring after his losing European title challenge, to halt light-welter Gary Barron on a fourth round cut eye stoppage at Gateshead.

In Glasgow, former British and European flyweight champion, Pat Clinton, returned to action with an easy win over Mexican Alberto Cantu . . . Willesden featherweight Alan McKay, who is the only fighter to beat British champion, Colin McMillan, albeit on a cut eye, avenged a previous defeat by Gary de Roux when he stopped the former British champion in round eight to win the Southern Area title.

DECEMBER

A few weeks after celebrating his 38th birthday and a few months after losing his world light-heavy title to Jeff Harding, Dennis Andries was back in the ring, back in America, and back in the win column, stopping Ed Neblett in four rounds at Tampa and Paul Madison in eight in Minnesota. Boxing's version of "Old Man River" just keeps rolling along.

Former British and European light-heavy champ Tom Collins was not so fortunate in his travels abroad. Now 36, Collins found the unbeaten Henry Maske too much of a handful in Dusseldorf and was running a poor second when the doctor called it off in the eighth, with Tom cut on his right eyelid.

Italy remained hostile territory so far as British fighters

were concerned, with British lightweight champion Carl Crook finding Antonio Renzo too hot to handle in their European title match at Rossano Calabro. The Englishman scored a knockdown in the first and was leading after three rounds, but Renzo is a tough guy to beat and he cut Carl's eye in the fourth, dropped him in the fifth and forced a stoppage in round six to keep his title.

Thirteen months after that stunning knockout by WBC champion Julian Jackson, Herol "Bomber" Graham returned to the ring to defend his British middleweight title against Alfreton's John Ashton at Sheffield. Waiting for Graham, John had taken a fight with Sumbu Kalambay in Italy for the vacant European title, being stopped in six rounds with a damaged eye. It was the same story against Graham, who settled down after an untidy start to force a stoppage in the sixth.

Little Francis Ampofo was not so fortunate in the first defence of the British flyweight title he took from Robbie Regan three months previously. On that occasion, a cut eye had ended Regan's reign in round eleven. This time Robbie stayed away from trouble and boxed his way back into the championship with a fine display against the willing Ampofo at Cardiff.

Nigel Benn took his big punch to Manchester's G-Mex Centre and landed it on chunky Argentine import Hector Lescano, a late replacement for fellow-countryman, Dario Matteoni. When Benn opened up in the third round, Lescano had no answer and was counted out on his second trip to the canvas. On the undercard, Paul Harvey retained his Commonwealth featherweight title with a runaway victory over former British champion Sugar Gibiliru.

It was another nail-biter for Pat Barrett's supporters at Oldham as the European light-welterweight champion played Russian roulette with American Mike Johnson. In a sensational first round, Johnson hit Barrett with practically every punch he threw, but just before the bell Pat sent him reeling with a sizzling left-hook. Halfway through round two, Pat put a smile on Mickey Duff's anguished face as he dumped the Yank with two tremendous shots and Referee Mickey Vann stopped him doing any more damage. More thrills were provided by Gary Mason's new heavyweight Billy Isaacs, who climbed off the deck to stop Larry Peart in round three of his debut.

If at first you don't succeed . . . Ian Strudwick came in second when fighting Slugger O'Toole for the vacant British super-middleweight title and when he tried for the Southern Area championship against Ray Webb at Basildon, it looked like being another night he should have stayed home watching the telly. The Stepney southpaw stuck Ian on the canvas twice and looked home and dry when Strudwick came up for the eighth, dumped Webb with a right, then knocked him out with left to claim the crown.

A couple of former British champions on the comeback trail were Steve McCarthy and Floyd Havard. McCarthy, fined and suspended for failing to go through with a defence of his British light-heavyweight title against Roy Skeldon, got his act together with a decision over John Foreman to please his local fans at Southampton. On the Regan-Ampofo bill at Cardiff, ex-super-featherweight champion Havard came out a winner when Patrick Kamy was disqualified in round five for careless headwork that left Floyd needing 17 stitches in his right eye.

Young lions in action saw Northern Area super-featherweight champion Darren Elsdon finish Scot Ian McGirr in round four at Hartlepool . . . Chatham bantamweight John Armour made it six straight when he stopped Graham O'Malley in six rounds at Bexleyheath, but plans for Eltham's Mickey Cantwell to get an early shot at the WBO light-flyweight title were put on hold after he struggled to beat Sean Norman on the same show . . . Middlesbrough featherweight comer Paul Forrest avenged his only loss when beating Colin Lynch on the Graham-Ashton bill at Sheffield . . . Henry Akinwande had no trouble beating American heavyweight Tim Bullock in Germany, a sizzling right uppercut breaking Tim's jaw and knocking him out in the third.

JANUARY

British featherweight champion Colin "Sweet C" McMillan added the vacant Commonwealth title to his collection at the Royal Albert Hall with a decision over former champion Percy Commey, but found the Ghanaian a different calibre to many of the Africans who have plied their trade here recently. With considerable height and reach advantages, Commey gave Colin a few headaches before the final bell. The London boy was cut over the left eye in round four and rocked several times throughout the fight before his skills prevailed to take his pro log to 21-1 . . . The chief supporting bout saw Commonwealth heavyweight champion Derek Williams take no chances with a triple clash looming against Lennox Lewis, bowling over inept American Tim Anderson in just 52 seconds.

One of these days, either Lewis or Williams may be facing the fierce attacks of Herbie Hide. Appearing before his hometown fans in Norwich, the 20-year-old terror blasted out his fifteenth straight win, all inside schedule, sending Canadian giant Conroy Nelson crashing to defeat in the second round. The left-hook did the job and brought Herbie his first title, the WBC International heavyweight championship.

More title action in Glasgow saw little Joe Kelly and Ronnie Carroll go at it again for the vacant British bantamweight crown. Their first contest, three months previously, resulted in a draw with most observers seeing Kelly the winner and this time there was more controversy as Referee Larry O'Connell gave it to Joe by a margin (119-116½) that infuriated Carroll's manager Tommy Gilmour. But it had been a cracking fight and Kelly looked to have done enough this time to become a British champion, after two failures as a flyweight.

The ancient city of York has a new attraction . . . watching Henry Wharton! Some 1600 fans of the Commonwealth super-middleweight champion packed the Barbican Centre to cheer Henry on to a hard-earned points win over tough American rival Nicky Walker and rack up his twelfth success against one draw.

Another American import to earn his money was

Randy Williams, who gave British light-middleweight champion Wally Swift a stubborn argument at Burton on Trent. Wally came out with the decision, but looked more like a loser, mouth and nose bleeding and both eyes swollen, shelving a proposed European title crack scheduled for 12 February in Paris.

With only one defeat on his 19-fight record, Jim Peters was hoping to bring the British light-heavyweight title back to Southampton and his local fans packed the Guildhall to cheer his challenge against Crawford Ashley. Power-puncher Ashley had other ideas and it took him only 55 seconds to get them across to Jim and retain his title. Ashley has been beaten four times, but every one of his 17 wins has come inside schedule. One guy who fancies his chance with the champion is Manchester's Maurice Coore, who chalked up his eighth win against last minute sub, heavyweight Denroy Bryan, who was stopped inside round one.

Boxing is all about taking chances. Although he was Northern Area super-featherweight champion, Darren Elsdon had a mere six fights on his card when offered the chance of a final eliminator for the British title against Michael Armstrong at Stockport. Armstrong was taking a bigger chance. He had been due to meet champion John Doherty for the title, but Doherty was forced to pull out with injury. So Michael and Darren took their chance and the gamble paid off for Armstrong when he bombed the Hartlepool boy in just 2.45 of round one. That's the fight business!

FEBRUARY

Promoter Barry Hearn threw another log on the fire he was building under Chris Eubank and Nigel Benn as he put his two super-middleweight heroes on show this month. At Birmingham, Eubank strutted his stuff in a defence of his WBO title against Sugar Boy Malinga, his first outing since the tragic bout with Michael Watson and looked somewhat jaded. In fact, one judge gave the decision to the South African, who survived a fifth round knockdown. Fortunately, for Chris, the other two officials marked him a winner. A couple of weeks later, at the Alexandra Palace, Benn busted up former Eubank victim Dan Sherry in three rounds. The Canadian had embarrassed Eubank in an untidy title bout some twelve months previously in "The Battle of the Backward Head Butt". Against Benn, however, he was never in the race. A crunching right-hand dropped Sherry in the third and when he got up Referee Larry O'Connell sent him off to the showers.

Lennox Lewis continued to blow hot and cold. Fighting in Las Vegas on "The Night of the Young Heavyweights", the British and European champion laboured to defeat Levi Billups via a ten rounds decision. Against an opponent who was never more than a willing journeyman, Lewis showed his class only in spasms, but just did enough to win.

Another heavyweight hope fighting on foreign soil was big Henry Akinwande and he remained undefeated as he pounded Young Joe Louis to defeat inside three rounds of their scrap at Issy les Moulineaux in France. The American, no longer young and certainly no "Joe Louis", became Akinwande's fourteenth victim. Back home in Peterborough, young heavyweight J. A. Bugner impressed, as he racked up Gary Railton for a smashing three rounds knockout to take his second pro victory.

Taking on an old Eubank victim, Dan Sherry, Nigel Benn bettered Chris's performance with a convincing third round stoppage win Les Clark

Some five years ago, after watching a young black fighter win his first pro fight, I queried his billing as Slugger O'Toole. The answer of course was manager Brendan Ingle. The fighter told me his real name was Fidel Castro Smith! Now, since beating Lou Gent in a defence of his British super-middleweight title at Crystal Palace, Slugger is telling everyone that his name is Fidel Castro and that is what he will be billed as in future. Whatever you call him, he is not a bad fighter, as he showed in turning back Gent's fourth attempt at becoming a champion. It went to a decision and Gent and his people didn't like it, but the champion did enough.

Having better luck in the title chase was Gary Jacobs. A former Commonwealth and WBC International welterweight champion, the Glasgow southpaw relieved Del Bryan of the British crown and the Lonsdale Belt he was hoping to make his own, via a points decision after a so-so fight in front of Gary's hometown supporters.

Another hometown boy to keep his supporters happy was British and Commonwealth light-welterweight champion, Andy Holligan, who had little difficulty turning back the challenge of former champion Tony McKenzie at Liverpool's Everton Park Sports Centre. Mac was bleeding and being hammered on the ropes when the referee stopped it in round three.

The reign of Paul Harvey as Commonwealth super-featherweight champion came to an end at Cardiff when he stepped out against Canada's elongated and elegant Tony Pep. On a previous visit, Pep had stopped Hugh Forde and he was victorious again even if he did have to travel the distance to take Harvey's title away. On the undercard, British flyweight champion Robbie Regan was in action, but not for long. Mexican Juan Bautista was no match for the Welshman, who bowled him over with a left-hook before finishing him off, a knockout after just 84 seconds of round one.

British flyweights could be forgiven for thinking that

the only way the European crown could be removed from the swarthy brow of Salvatore Fanni was by surgery! Little Danny Porter from Hitchin had already tried once, being stopped on cuts after nine rounds, but not before he floored the Italian twice. So he was back for more and this time he looked a good winner. Not, however, to the three officials scoring the fight, who managed to come up with a draw. Eat your heart out, kid!

Veteran Dennis Andries surely reached the end of a long hard road in the little French town of Beausoleil. The former three-times WBC light-heavyweight champion was trying for the vacant European cruiserweight title against a man who was bigger, stonger . . . and younger than the 38 years Dennis admits to. At the end of twelve rounds, Akim Tafer was the winner and new champion and Emmanuel Steward was telling Andries it was time to go home, for good.

MARCH

It was just like old times at Glasgow's Kelvin Hall when Pat Clinton challenged Mexican Isidro Perez for his WBO flyweight crown. The former British and European champion was hoping to become Scotland's first world title claimant since Jim Watt some ten years previously and he boxed beautifully to build an early lead. But Perez, a veteran of 57 fights, stormed back at the halfway stage and the southpaw Scot had to fight out of his skin to get his nose in front at the final bell, taking it on a split decision to the delight of his fans and the disgust of the Mexican party.

Coming in as a last minute substitute, Robert Wright (right), fresh from a convincing win over Errol McDonald, was ultimately no match for the Commonwealth welterweight champion, Donovan Boucher and although he performed bravely, he was rescued by the referee in the eleventh

Another Scot on the title trail was Donnie Hood, who travelled to Copenhagen in a bid to add the vacant European bantamweight championship to his WBC International title. Facing local idol Johnny Bredahl, Glasgow's pony-tailed puncher came up empty after sticking his man on the deck in round three. Despite the knockdown, Bredahl was always going well and stopped Donnie in the seventh after decking him twice. Defeat also meant forfeiture of the WBC crown Donnie had worn for 18 months.

Italy is a lovely place to go for a holiday, but not to fight for a title. Herol Graham became the latest in a long line of losers when he challenged former conqueror Sumbu Kalambay in Pesaro for the European middleweight championship. Bomber made a great start and floored Kalambay twice in round two, but the champ is a tough cookie and he fought back to open cuts on Herol's eyes and hang on to his title with a tight decision.

Action at the Albert Hall saw Duke McKenzie punch Puerto Rico's Wilfredo Vargas full of holes to force an eighth round stoppage and retain his WBO bantamweight crown for the second time. On the same bill, British welterweight champion Gary Jacobs eased to a second round win over American, Tommy Small, who was dumped by a left-hook before the referee intervened.

A championship tag is everything in these days of televised boxing, but as with everything else the quality goes down as the quantity goes up. Carl Crook was due to defend his Commonwealth title against an unknown African with a 5-1 pro record at the Grosvenor House. That fell through when Crook suffered a hand injury and Donovan Boucher was brought in to defend his welterweight title against Robert Wright. The Dudley boxer had just knocked out Errol McDonald seven days previously, but he found the Canadian a different class and was running a poor second when John Coyle stopped it in round eleven.

A week later at Telford, Richie Woodhall took his 8-0 record into a fight for the vacant Commonwealth middleweight championship with Australian Vito Guadiosi. Unknown here, but claiming a 13-3-2, record, Vito never got a chance to show anything but the soles of his boots as Woodhall knocked him out inside 61 seconds!

Non-title action for two other Commonwealth champions saw super-middle-weight Henry Wharton blast American Kenny Schaefer into dreamland inside 2.22 of round one at York, while light-middleweight titleholder Chris Pyatt had to go into round three before finishing another Yank, Melvin Wynn. Mark Reefer is a former Commonwealth champion, but he looked ready for the retirement home when Peter Till stopped him in three heats. Tom Collins was also reaching the end of the road when Glazz Campbell was able to beat him in their British light-heavyweight final-eliminator in Glasgow.

A trailer for a forthcoming attraction was shown at Dagenham where British and Commonwealth featherweight champion Colin "Sweet C" McMillan and Italy's Maurizio Stecca were in action. Stecca was being lined up for a defence of his WBO title against Britain's

In a return battle for the Commonwealth super-middles title, the champion, Henry Wharton (left), made no mistake with an eighth round stoppage win over Rod Carr

Chris Bevan

new golden boy and he gave food for thought as he dismantled Roy Muniz inside six rounds. McMillan also favoured round six to get rid of outclassed Mexican Tommy Valdez and the fans went home wondering if . . .

In a month when new British bantamweight champion Joe Kelly struggled to take a decision from Welshman Kevin Jenkins, former champion Billy Hardy served notice that he was back, following a short retirement, as he hammered game Chris Clarkson into submission in round five. The young lions in the heavyweight division continued feeding on easy meat as Herbie Hide chewed up a fat Percell Davis and Henry Akinwande stopped Tucker Richards.

APRIL

With the pantomime season over, big Frank Bruno returned to the prize ring for his second comback fight and this time it looked as though he might actually have a fight. Coming out of the other corner was Cuba's Jose Ribalta, a guy who stood ten rounds (almost) with Tyson and went all the way with Bonecrusher Smith and Tim Witherspoon. The fans didn't buy it, however and Wembley was barely half-full when they rang the bell. Maybe those who stayed away knew something. It lasted less than five minutes, Bruno scoring a knockout in the second round, a tremendous right-hand taking the Cuban out of a fight he was never in. Bruno did what he had to do, which is more than can be said for Jose Ribalta, who did nothing!

A week later, at the Royal Albert Hall, British and European heavyweight champion Lennox Lewis collected another title when he stripped the Commonwealth mantle from Derek Williams inside three rounds. Williams had Angelo Dundee in his corner, but it made no difference. Lewis was just too powerful, although he again came out of a fight with mixed reviews. His work before finishing Williams was somewhat sloppy. Still, the idea of a mega-fight between Lewis and Bruno filled the sports pages for a few days.

A couple of our world champions put their titles on the line and YOU could have beaten the opposition! Chris Eubank gave 35-year-old American journeyman John Jarvis a crack at his WBO super-middleweight crown and in the third round gave Jarvis a crack on the jaw that would have felled the Post Office Tower. At about the same time in Belfast and in the same round, WBC featherweight champion, Paul Hodkinson, got rid of his challenger, former WBA champ Steve Cruz. The Texan was a shadow of the fighter who whipped Barry McGuigan and had no answer to Hoko's left-hook.

The European continent was becoming a no-go area for British fighters as another two of our champions discovered. James Cook took his European super-middleweight title over to Vitrolles, a small town near Marseilles, to make his third defence against Franck Nicotra. Poor James never knew what hit him. It was the Frenchman's right-hand and it was all over in 63 seconds!

Then Wally Swift journeyed to France, hoping to add the European light-middleweight championship to his British title. Champion Jean-Claude Fontana had other ideas and topped everything Wally tried. It went twelve rounds and Swift came out with a damaged left eye and his eighth defeat.

The jinx struck again! Whenever the British super-featherweight title is on the line, the challenger always has an edge going in . . . not one champion has managed to make a successful defence. John Doherty proved no exception, but then John knew what to expect, he had already lost this title twice and when he went out there to face Michael Armstrong he would be the thirteenth champion to try the impossible. Say no more! Armstrong by a knockout in seven.

Commonwealth championship action saw Henry Wharton keep his title with an eighth round stoppage of former victim Rod Carr at Leeds. The tough Australian got off to a fine start, but couldn't stand the pace when Henry turned on the heat . . . Ndabe Dube nearly got to take the Commonwealth bantamweight title back to Zimbabwe, but John Armour kept moving forward and in the final round set up a furious attack that brought the referee diving in to stop it with a mere eleven seconds left on the clock. The 33-year-old veteran was beaten and the Chatham southpaw was the new champion . . . Chris Pyatt found James Tapisha no match at all and had no difficulty retaining his Commonwealth light-middle crown in just 2.17 of round one.

In turning back the challenge of Glazz Campbell, British light-heavyweight champion Crawford Ashley avenged a previous defeat and secured the Lonsdale Belt for a permanent position in his trophy room. Fighting on the Hodkinson bill in Belfast, Ashley took his time before ending matters in round eight . . . Preston's smart Paul Burke made his move towards the British lightweight title when he stopped Northern Area champion Paul Charters in seven rounds of their final-eliminator. Although both men weighed 9-7½, Charters seemed to have left his fight in the gym.

A sizzling young punch personality hit the British fight scene with the debut of Prince Nassem Hamed, a flyweight

Carl Crook (left) made a successful defence of his British and Commonwealth lightweight crowns against Steve Boyle, when the Scot was stopped in round seven with bad cuts Chris Bevan

with flair, who is the latest of the Brendan Ingle breed. The 18-year-old Hamed is not a prince, but he is a formidable talent, as he quickly showed, stopping Ricky Beard and Shaun Norman, both in the second round.

MAY

If you thought it was rather an ambitious project for British fighters, three world title fights inside four days, you would have been spot on. We came out of it losing two to one. Still, the one we won could be with us for a while. Colin McMillan turned loose a brilliant exhibition of boxing, make that BOXING, to take the WBO featherweight title from Italian Maurizio Stecca at London's Alexandra Palace. In twelve rounds, Stecca never did find the answer as "Sweet C" cruised to a runaway victory, a year after becoming British champion. In that time Colin had won the Lonsdale Belt outright and lifted the Commonwealth title and if boxing needs a "Golden Boy" the role fits him like a six-ounce glove.

McMillan's world title win redressed the balance as Duke McKenzie was blasted off his throne a few days previously at the Albert Hall. Puerto Rican Rafael del Valle just walked out and hit the Duke with a left and down he went. When he got up, del Valle smashed him down again and it was all over. In 116 seconds, the unknown substitute challenger was the new champ! That's the fight business. . .

On the same day that Colin McMillan lifted our hearts, cruiserweight Johnny Nelson gave us a pain somewhere else. In his second shot at the world title, the IBF version held by American James Warring, the Sheffield man showed himself to be all style and no substance as he walked through twelve boring rounds to lose a lop-sided decision. And the answer to the question, where does Nelson go from here, is another question . . . does anyone care?

Another of our lads to lose on foreign soil was Newcastle featherweight John Davison, challenging Fabrice Benichou for the European title for the second time in a year and coming second again. As usual, Davison fought his heart out . . . Johnny Nelson should be made to watch tapes of John's fights! This time around, Davison looked a winner to some observers, but the nearest he got was a draw from one of the officials. The other two saw it for Benichou.

At Cardiff, British flyweight champion Robbie Regan cost the Board of Control another Lonsdale Belt when he

Darren Dyer (right) charges into former British welterweight champion, Del Bryan, on his way to a pulsating tenth round stoppage win, following four earlier knockdowns Les Clark

turned back the challenge of James Drummond. The referee stopped the contest in round nine, a fine performance against a man who had beaten European champ Salvatore Fanni only to be robbed of the verdict . . . At Preston, Carl Crook hung on to his British and Commonwealth lightweight titles in a rough and ready tumble against former champion, Steve Boyle, the referee stopping it in round seven with the Glasgow man cut by the left eye.

The Americans used to call them Pier-Six brawls, the sort of fight Darren Dyer and former British welterweight champion Del Bryan staged at Crystal Palace. Bryan had beaten Dyer a few years back and was chasing his old title, but the latter wanted this fight more. He floored Del four times in the first four rounds and finished him off in round ten with a savage right. Bryan managed to get up, but he was too far gone and now Darren Dyer was looking for a title shot.

Nigel Benn's plan of beating up Chris Eubank's discarded victims as he waited for a rematch with the WBO super-middleweight champion, almost backfired at Birmingham, when Sugar Boy Malinga not only finished the course, but some thought he finished in front. Fortunately for Benn, Referee Paul Thomas saw enough merit in his work to award him the decision and keep him on track. But only just . . .

Glasgow bantamweight Ronnie Carroll keeps trying. When Billy Hardy was British champion, Carroll challenged twice without success. Then he fought Joe Kelly for Hardy's vacated title, managed a draw then lost the decider. He was out of luck again when going against Manchester's John Green in an eliminator, but fought well enough to keep his hopes alive.

Another Glasgow bantamweight in action was Donnie Hood, now minus his WBC International title after failing in a European championship fight with Johnny Bredahl. Hood eased back in with a comfortable points win over Pete Buckley . . . While Terry Lawless and Frank Warren went to arbitration over Derek Angol, the Commonwealth cruiserweight champion got back in the ring and knocked out Robert Clevenger (USA) in a couple of rounds . . . Wonder Boy Nassem Hamed copped his third straight win, all inside two rounds, forcing a stoppage over Andrew Bloomer on the Benn undercard.

JUNE

Kicking off at the top level, two of Britain's world champions were in action on foreign soil. Chris Eubank's billing as "Simply The Best" will have to be modified if he turns in any more performances like the one he produced against American Ronnie Essett at Quinta do Lago on the

Portugese Algarve. In retaining his WBO super-middleweight title, via a unanimous decision, Eubank posed more than he punched and with a little more effort the American could well have taken the title.

Making the sixth defence of his IBF flyweight title, Dave McAuley found things tougher in Bilbao than in Belfast, especially former opponent Rodolfo Blanco and the three officials. Dave had beaten the little Colombian challenger in their first fight, but had to climb off the deck four times to do so. Blanco's people screamed robbery after that one and it was the same thing this time, only it was McAuley and manager Barney Eastwood who swore they had been robbed as the three judges awarded the verdict and the title to Blanco after a fierce fight.

The title reign of British bantamweight champion Joe Kelly of Glasgow was indeed a short one as local rival Drew Docherty outboxed and outpunched him to force a stoppage in round five, just four months after little Joe ascended the throne. Although Docherty was having only his ninth pro fight (8 wins 1 draw), he brought an impeccable amateur pedigree to the ring and the manner of his victory pointed to a bright future.

Veteran Steve Lewsam had managed to win the Midlands Area cruiserweight title, but when he got a shot at the vacant British championship, he found Manchester's Carl Thompson wanting it more. Thompson was well on top when the referee stopped it in round eight.

Former welterweight title challenger Mickey Hughes bounced back at light-middle with an easy blowout over Andrew Furlong at Dagenham, a left-hook to the body ending matters at the 2.09 mark of round one. In action again after losing the British flyweight title back to Robbie Regan, Francis Ampofo warmed up for a crack at the European crown with a stoppage of Shaun Norman in round four.

The troubled times of Pat Barrett continued as he suffered a shoulder injury sparring in America and was forced to pull out of his European light-welterweight title defence against Valery Kayumba for the second time. The dreadlocked Mancunian not only lost a purse of £52,500, he lost the title! The EBU stripped him of the crown and handed it to Kayumba after he beat late substitute Bruno Vottero. Then they named Barrett the number one contender for the title. By that time, Pat was hoping to get Manning Galloway into the ring for a crack at his WBO welter crown, in a fight postponed from February when the American suffered a hand injury.

As things slowed down at home, many of the boys found work in Europe, with varying success. Birmingham's Paul Wesley did well to take European middleweight champ Sumbu Kalambay ten rounds in a non-title bout, losing the decision. Midlands lightweight champion Peter Till came a cropper in Randers facing Racheed Lawal and was put away inside three minutes.

Former Commonwealth super-featherweight champion Paul Harvey was another to come down with a bump as Dutch star Regilio Tuur crushed him in five rounds in Rotterdam. On the same bill, however, Sheffield light-middle Paul "Silky" Jones took a decision over Belgian's Patrick Vungbo. Big Henry Akinwande beat Kimmuel Odum at Marseille when the veteran American was thrown out in round three for "irregular boxing" . . . whatever that is!

Facts and Figures, 1991-92

There were 745 British-based boxers who were active during the period 1 July 1991 to 30 June 1992, spread over 236 tournaments held in Britain, a decrease of 28 promotions when compared against the previous season. The above figure comprised 559 boxers already holding licences, eight foreign-born boxers who had started their careers elsewhere, four British-born boxers who had begun their careers abroad and decided to return to this country and 174 new professionals. Not included is Judas Clottey, who although holding a British licence, only performed abroad during the period.

Unbeaten during season (minimum qualification: six contests) 7: Gary Delaney (1 draw), Rob Stewart (2 draws). 6: Henry Akinwande, Maurice Coore, Lee Ferrie, Kevin Lueshing, Alan McDowall, Colin McMillan, Joey Moffat, Bernard Paul, Billy Schwer, Kevin Sheeran, Ronnie Stephenson, Warren Stowe.

Most wins during season (minimum qualification: six wins) 8: John O'Johnson. 6: Henry Akinwande, Tony Booth, Maurice Coore, Gary Delaney, Lee Ferrie, Kevin Lueshing, Alan McDowall, Darren McInulty, Colin McMillan, Joey Moffat, Bernard Paul, Billy Schwer, Kevin Sheeran, Ronnie Stephenson, Warren Stowe.

Most contests during season (minimum qualification: ten contests) 15: Dean Bramhald. 14: Julian Eavis, Miguel Matthews. 12: Tony Booth. 11: Pete Buckley, Des Gargano, Carl Hook, John Kaighin, Trevor Meikle, John O'Johnson. 10: Mick Duncan, John Smith.

Most contests during career (minimum qualification: 50 contests) 124: Dean Bramhald. 108: Shamus Casey. 88: Paul Murray. 87: Des Gargano. 60: Ian Chantler, Steve Pollard, Glyn Rhodes. 58: Julian Eavis. 57: Cordwell Hylton. 53: Dennis Andries. 52: Franki Moro. 51: Newton Barnett, Sugar Gibiliru, Dave Owens. 50: Steve Gee, Miguel Matthews.

Longest unbeaten sequence (minimum qualification: ten contests) 32: Chris Eubank. 31: Pat Barrett. 26: Derek Angol. 20: Lennox Lewis. 18: Ernie Loveridge. 17: Henry Akinwande, Michael Gale (1 draw), Andy Holligan. 16: Shaun Cooper, Herbie Hide, Billy Schwer. 15: Henry Wharton (1 draw). 13: Alan Hall, Richie Wenton. 12: Glenn Campbell (1 draw), Darron Griffiths (3 draws), Ross Hale, Robbie Regan (3 draws). 11: Michael Ayers, Dean Hollington, Robert McCracken, Tony Silkstone, Martin Smith (3 draws). 10: Paul Busby, Shaun Cogan, Craig Dermody, Lester Jacobs.

Young British Prospects To Keep Your Eyes On

by Chris Kempson

The dictionary defines the word "prospect" as "a probability or chance for future success", or "a vision of the future". In this chapter we take a close look at a number of boxers who seem likely to attain championship status in the near future. In other words they are "prospects" who are likely to achieve future success, quite possibly during the 1992-93 season.

The future strength of any sport and boxing is no exception, rests with those who are striving to succeed and those who are determined to reach the top. At present, professional boxing in these islands seem to have a fairly optimistic future in most of the BBBoC standard weight divisions.

The heavyweight division is always the one which generates the most interest, excitement, anticipation and invariably the most money for its successful participants. Two unbeaten prospects, south Londoner, Henry Akinwande and Norwich's Herbie Hide, are preparing themselves to take over the current positions held by triple champion, Lennox Lewis and former European champion and double world title aspirant, Frank Bruno.

Twenty six-year-old Henry Akinwande from Lewisham is a big man in every sense of the word. He stands 6ft 7inches tall and weighs around 16 stone and made his debut in the paid ranks in October 1989 after winning the ABA heavyweight title in 1988 and 1989. He was also a losing finalist in the previous two years to underline an outstanding amateur pedigree. He has been brought along steadily by manager, Mickey Duff and his National Promotions organisation and has done all that's been asked of him since he turned pro and he is now ready for a step-up in class. He can box and he can punch too, twelve of his 17 victories have come via the short route, including a disqualification win in France in June 1992. The other "promotional nugget" for Duff is that Henry comfortably outpointed Herbie Hide in their 1989 ABA heavyweight final at the Wembley Arena, which is sure to give any "rematch" in the pro ranks that extra bit of "needle" and hopefully boost ticket sales into the bargain.

Herbie Hide was born in Nigeria on 27 August 1971 and he now lives in and fights out of Norwich where he has developed a large and enthusiastic following. He had a brief, but relatively successful amateur career in this country, culminating with the 1989 ABA final loss to Akinwande. A defeat he would dearly love to reverse!

He also made his pro debut in October 1989, teaming up with Barry Hearn's successful Matchroom Boxing organisation based in Romford. Herbie started his paid career as a cruiserweight, but moved up to heavyweight in April 1991. He stands 6ft 1½ inches tall and weighs around 14½ stone at present. Not one of Herbie's 16 opponents to date has made it through to the final bell, which proves that he has the punching power to take him to the top. He moves well and appears to have a "good chin" which should stand him in good stead as he moves steadily up the heavyweight ladder. At only 20 years of age time is certainly on Herbie's side.

Hide, however, has beaten his ABA conqueror to a "first pro title". On 21 January 1992 before his home fans at the Norwich Sports Village, Herbie knocked out the massive Canadian Conroy Nelson to smash his way to the vacant WBC International heavyweight championship. Akinwande for his part has already won a British title eliminator by knocking out John Fury in three rounds, so his potential championship credentials look good.

Akinwande and Hide are without doubt our two outstanding heavyweight prospects, but there are others who are quietly waiting in the wings to strike when the moment is right.

The son of a famous father, J. A. Bugner, made his debut last season and hopes to be a chip off the old block. Bugner (left) is seen here beating John Harewood

Les Clark

West Ham are hoping that one of their favourite sons, Gary Delaney (left), pictured destroying Nigel Rafferty, can go on to win titular honours in the pro game Les Clark

Only the Sheffield "Svengali", Brendan Ingle, could take a black heavyweight from Derby named Clifton Mitchell and "re-package" him as Paddy Reilly no less. Twenty six-year-old Reilly, a former top class amateur in the Midlands, is unbeaten in five pro starts since his debut in April 1991. His most recent and notable success was an eighth round stoppage of Central Area champion, Michael Murray, from Manchester in mid-April 1992. Paddy's manager and trainer, Brendan Ingle, says that "in twelve months time Paddy will be good enough to beat Lennox Lewis". Only time will tell Brendan.

Two other heavyweight prospects deserve a special mention. They are J. A. Bugner from St Ives and Eltham's Warren Richards. Young Joe is the son of the former British, Commonwealth and European champion who now resides comfortably in Australia. He is unbeaten in four paid outings, having made his debut in November 1991 and his mentor is his father's former manager, Andy Smith. Bugner has a large local following and is certainly big and strong enough to reach the top, although of course he is only in his professional infancy at present.

Twenty seven-year-old London born Warren Richards, a pro since April 1990, stands 6ft 3inches tall and weighs around 17 stone these days. His fierce punching power has to be reckoned with and he is beginning to make his presence felt on the domestic scene, following a successful sojourn in the United States last year. An early career loss and a recent draw against the very experienced Geordie, John Westgarth, are the only blemishes on Warren's record, which shows five victories, all inside the distance. He is certainly one to watch. As the old saying goes "a puncher always has a chance".

Manchester's 28-year-old southpaw, Carl Thompson, now rules the British cruiserweight roost and sadly there are no realistic prospects at this weight at present for us to discuss.

The light-heavyweight division throws up three potential championship contenders. First there is Maurice "Hard" Coore, the 27-year-old Mancunian, who it seems is on the verge of a British title shot. Moss Side's Maurice Coore was runner-up in the 1988 ABA light-heavyweight final and he eventually turned pro with the successful Phil Martin "Champs Camp" organisation in January 1990. Maurice stands 6ft 5inches tall and he is an exciting puncher, unbeaten now in nine pro contests. The only blemish on his record is a six round draw with Nicky Piper in May 1990, in only his third paid start. Coore seems certain to make it to the top before too long.

Michael Gale, the exciting 24-year-old unbeaten prospect from Leeds, will be looking for a British title shot in the near future. Gale has notched up 16 wins, plus one draw in 17 outings, since making his pro debut in September 1989 and is yet another of Mickey Duff's championship hopefuls. A greengrocer by day, Michael is quite adept at handing out his own brand of "cauliflower ears" by night as he hones in on the British light-heavyweight crown. He can box and punch too, ten of his victories have come inside schedule and he looks a good bet for championship honours over the next year.

Gary "The Hammer" Delaney, the unbeaten young prospect from West Ham, who is now a member of the Matchroom Organisation, will be pressing his own British title claim over the next year. Delaney a good quality amateur, who only turned pro in October 1991, has the punching power to take him to the top of the tree. His record to date is six victories (four inside the distance), with a draw being the only flaw on his record, against the very capable and durable Londoner, Simon Harris.

Cardiff's 26-year-old Nicky Piper is without a shadow of doubt, the outstanding prospect in the British super-middleweight division. Piper, the 1988 ABA runner-up at middleweight and the 1989 ABA light-heavyweight champion, is the MENSA man with the knockout punch. MENSA is an elite international society, membership of which is restricted to people whose intelligence test scores exceed those expected of 98 per cent of the population. That's some academic testimonial for the friendly Welshman who is "tops" at boxing too. Piper turned pro in September 1989 and campaigned for a couple of seasons or so as a light-heavyweight. His current record shows one defeat and one draw in 17 paid bouts. Virtually all of his successes have come via the short route. His sole reverse came in a "catchweight contest" against Carl Thompson, who is now British cruiserweight champion and the draw was against top light-heavyweight prospect, Maurice Coore. His recent move down to super-middle has suited him well and in January 1992 he convincingly outpointed Manchester's Frank Eubanks over ten rounds in an official eliminator for the British super-middleweight crown. Piper, who is managed and promoted by Frank Warren, is certainly one to watch in the coming season and can confidently be expected to challenge for the British title before long.

An "outsider" with British title aspirations is the 22-year-old Bury crowd-pleaser, Glenn Campbell, the undefeated Central Area super-middleweight champion. Glenn "packs-em-in" wherever he fights and his punching power is truly awesome. And it could just take him to the top with a little bit of luck. His unbeaten record of twelve contests, includes a draw against Carlos Christie.

The British middleweight division has for many years commanded a special place and generated genuine affection and interest among fight fans. Sadly, at present, there is little outstanding talent coming through to brighten up this "Cinderella division", with Bradford's 27-year-old southpaw, Frank "The Terminator" Grant, looking the best bet at present for championship honours.

Peckham's Lester Jacobs, unbeaten in ten contests, carries the hopes of the capital as he strives for title success. At 30 years of age, time is not really on Jacobs' side and he must surely make a positive move towards the British crown in the coming season. Lester can box and punch and seems to have a "good chin" into the bargain. He is an enterprising character, who also holds a promoter's licence and he made his debut in this capacity at the Arena Nightclub in Harringay on 17 May 1992, when he outpointed tough Marvin O'Brien of Leeds over six hard rounds.

Worcester's 26-year-old lifeguard Paul Busby, from the Matchroom stable, is also unbeaten in ten paid outings after turning pro in November 1990. He can be expected to move up in class and press his claims for a title shot in the near future. Busby had a good amateur pedigree and was an ABA semi-finalist in 1988 when he was outpointed by Nicky Piper. Paul, a neat boxer with a useful punch, is patiently working his way up the middleweight ladder and he must be considered to be a fine prospect for the new season.

Twenty six-year-old Neville Brown from Burton is another excellent prospect who is aiming for the top middleweight slot. Neville had a very successful amateur career, winning Schools, Junior ABA and NABC titles, before landing the ABA light-middleweight crown in 1987 and again in 1989.

He turned pro in November 1989 under Mickey Duff's banner and won eleven in a row, all but one inside the distance, with only Tony Booth taking him the full six rounds when they met at Alfreton in March 1991. Neville lost his unbeaten record in July 1991 when he was surprisingly stopped in a round by Paul Wesley, a defeat he has since reversed on points over eight rounds. Brown's current record is fifteen wins, with just one reverse in 16 paid outings, which certainly confirms his British title aspirations.

Unbeaten 20-year-old Rhondda southpaw, Darron Griffiths (nine wins and three draws), carries the Welsh hopes in this division and he has made good progress since turning pro in November 1990.

The brightest prospect in the light-middleweight division is 24-year-old Brummie, Robert McCracken, yet another unbeaten fighter from the Mickey Duff stable. McCracken was a fine amateur, the highlight of his career, whilst wearing the vest, was the silver medal he captured in the World Cup competition in Dublin in September 1990. He lost controversially to Alan Hall in the 1989 ABA light-welterweight final. He turned pro in January 1991 as a welterweight and soon made his presence felt with a series of quick victories. So far none of his eleven victims have gone beyond four full rounds. McCracken must be a "hot-tip" for a British title shot in the very near future.

Islington's 25-year-old Clay O'Shea, a pro since February 1990, is unbeaten in nine paid outings, with seven wins and two draws (both against Andrew Furlong) to his credit and he spearheads the capital's challenge in this division. O'Shea is a fair boxer with a good fighting brain and he also has the ability to take a man "out" with either hand. He is certainly one to watch next season.

Darlington's Charlie Moore has raced to five

Darren Dyer (left) at last shows signs of fulfilling his early potential as he stops the former British welterweight champion, Del Bryan, in the tenth Les Clark

consecutive victories since turning pro with Micky Duff in December 1991 and has looked impressive each time. It is early days yet and Duff obviously won't be looking to bring Charlie along too quickly, but will ensure he gets the experience he needs. Moore, however, is one to watch for the future.

Matchroom's Adrian Strachan, the 26-year-old southpaw from Richmond, unbeaten in six contests, is expected to make good progress over the coming year.

The welterweight division is packed with some very exciting prospects. Twenty five-year-old Darren "The Phantom" Dyer from Islington heads the list. He has accomplished 17 victories with just three losses in 20 paid outings. Dyer, a former ABA welterweight champion and Commonwealth Games gold medallist in 1986, is a devastating puncher and has become the most feared fighter in British welterweight boxing. Only one of his victims, Trevor Ambrose, has gone the full distance with him and Dyer's latest and most satisfying performance was a "revenge victory" over former British champion Del Bryan. Darren knocked Bryan out in the tenth and final round of their "gruelling war" at the National Sports Centre, Crystal Palace on 12 May 1992. Dyer, who now fights under the Matchroom banner, seems certain to be challenging for the British title next season and it is quite possible that his punching power will claim that particular prize for him.

Twenty two-year-old Eamonn Loughran, the talented Irish welterweight from Ballymena, has already been involved in a British title eliminator. He was disqualified for a headbutt delivered out of sheer frustration in the fifth round of a contest against Tony Ekubia, the former British and Commonwealth light-welterweight champion, at Bury on 10 March 1992. Loughran, a pro since December 1987, who was previously unbeaten in 17 contests, with one draw, must aim to get back quickly into title contention. He certainly has the class and ability to do so, but he will need to exercise greater self-control in future if indeed he is to reach the top.

Hard-hitting 22-year-old Michael Smyth from Barry, a former Welsh amateur champion and international, is still unbeaten in the paid ranks and carries the Principality's standard in this division. Managed and promoted by Dai Gardner, Smyth has made good progress since turning pro in May 1991 and his punching power will always give him a chance of ultimate championship success. At present, he is content to work his way steadily up the welter-weight ladder.

Promising Warley prospect Howard Clarke has now won five in a row and seems to be Midland's best long term "bet" for success, although it seems likely that he will be campaigning around the ten stone limit in future. West Ham's experienced Roy Rowland and unbeaten newcomer Kevin Lueshing, from Beckenham, cannot be overlooked either, in a generally strong and talented division.

At light-welterweight it is also pleasing to report that there is an abundance of emerging talent.

Former dual ABA champion Alan Hall from Darlington is unbeaten in thirteen professional outings and seems to be the pick of the bunch at present. Twenty two-year-old Hall, who turned pro in October 1989, is a very exciting young prospect, although periods of inactivity may have hampered his progress somewhat. He can punch, six of his victories have been inside schedule and in April 1992 he outpointed another fine prospect, Portsmouth's Michael Driscoll, over six rounds at the G-Mex Centre in Manchester. Driscoll, a former Schools and NABC champion, has been a professional since June 1988 and has a career record of eleven victories, two losses and three draws in fifteen outings. Nine of his eleven wins have come inside the distance, which clearly demonstrates Michael's fine punching power. But he was unable to do a "job" on Alan Hall, who looked a good winner in spite of the narrow margin of victory, just one round in fact, on referee Phil Cowsill's scorecard.

West Ham's Dean Hollington is now unbeaten in eleven contests and certainly looks the capital's best prospect for championship honours in this division. A top class amateur, winning Schools, Junior ABA and NABC titles, 23-year-old "Deano" has made excellent progress under trainer Jimmy Tibbs and will be looking to secure his first title, probably at Southern Area level in the first instance, in the new season. After that anything is possible as they say!

Unbeaten southpaw Ross Hale from Bristol seems to carry the hopes of the west country at this weight. Although out of action for well over a year, Ross scored two excellent stoppage victories, first over previously unbeaten Jason Matthews and then against Liverpool's very experienced John Smith, to round off the 1991-92 season on a high note. He is certainly one to watch next season and he now has twelve straight victories to his credit.

Twenty four-year-old unbeaten prospect, Shaun Cooper, from Dudley, carries the Midland's flag in this division. Cooper had a fine amateur pedigree and has made excellent progress since joining the paid ranks in May 1988. He cannot be taken lightly in this very competitive division.

Classy southpaw, Charlie Kane from Clydebank, certainly carries Scotland's hopes for championship success. Twenty three-year-old Kane, a former

Commonwealth Games gold medallist and ABA champion, is unbeaten since making his pro debut in Glasgow in March 1991, when he stopped the veteran "centurian" Dean Bramhald in six rounds. The tall Scot is now ready for a step-up in class, but needs to engage in more "regular work" if he is to fulfil his championship potential quickly.

Birmingham's stylish Tony Swift, younger brother of British light-middleweight champion, Wally, could possibly make the breakthrough into the "big time" next season. His most recent victory over Glasgow bustler Willie Beattie has clearly served notice of his championship aspirations, although this contest was in fact a welterweight championship eliminator. We are of course more accustomed to seeing Tony operate at light-welterweight and it remains to be seen if he will be "strong enough" at the higher weight to go all the way to the top.

Telford's Mark Elliot, a former dual ABA champion, is a "newcomer" to watch for next season, as is the "punching postman", Bernard Paul from Tottenham, unbeaten in eight paid contests, only three opponents having gone the distance to date. Finally, 23-year-old Liverpudlian, Carl Wright, a former top amateur star, undefeated in seven pro outings, will also be aiming to continue his way to the top.

At lightweight, we have four excellent prospects to consider. In the top spot at present is undoubtedly the 23-year-old Belfast - based Scouser, Nigel Wenton. He was an impressive amateur, winning Schools titles, a Junior ABA championship and also NABC crowns for the Window Lane Club. Although his dedication to the "hardest game" has been questioned in the past, Nigel has settled well again under the Eastwood banner since returning from an unhappy spell in the United States. He is a talented young man, who just oozes class, which is confirmed by his excellent record of 22 victories, one draw and two losses. Last time out on 25 April 1992 in Belfast, Nigel forced Miami - based Barbadian, Ed "Pit Bull" Pollard, to retire in six rounds, which proved to be a good workout for him while awaiting a possible British title challenge.

Unbeaten Luton prospect 23-year-old Billy Schwer was voted the "Best Young Boxer of the Year" by the Boxing Writers' Club in April 1992 and the accolade was just reward for his run of 16 straight victories, thirteen of which have come inside schedule. A losing ABA finalist at lightweight in 1990, Schwer turned professional in October 1990 and has made fine progress ever since under the expert guidance of manager, Mickey Duff. He is a neat and snappy boxer who possesses the ability to "read" an opponent and work out the right game-plan. He has a large and vociferous following that generate lucrative ticket sales whenever Billy fights and he certainly hopes to reward their "loyalty" with his first title success in the new season.

Another exciting unbeaten prospect is west London's Michael "Shaka" Ayers. Ayers won the ABA lightweight title in 1987, defeating Darlington's Alan Hall (now also unbeaten as a pro) in the final. Ayers turned pro in May 1989 and since then has notched up eleven straight successes. He has acquired the Southern Area title in the process and he stopped Rudy Valentino in a British title eliminator, which was also an area title defence, in February 1992 at the Alexandra Palace in London.

Billy Schwer (left), the son of a former crack amateur fighter, shows much early promise and has already been named by the Boxing Writers' Club as their "Young Fighter of the Year" Les Clark

Only one of Ayers' victims has heard the final bell. He is an explosive "pressure type" of fighter who certainly seems destined for further title honours. He is a member of the successful Matchroom Organisation and can be expected to make his "move" for a British title shot in the near future.

Scotland's 25-year-old former ABA featherweight champion Dave Anderson (he outpointed Colin McMillan no less in the final in 1988) completes our "quartet" of exciting lightweight prospects. A European bronze medallist in Athens in 1989, he won a bronze medal at the Commonwealth Games in Auckland in 1990, before discarding his vest in September of that year. Anderson is also unbeaten as a pro and can be expected to work steadily towards British title contention next season.

Unfortunately, the super-featherweight division is devoid at present of any real prospects and we will move quickly onto the featherweight division where things look much brighter.

We have an exciting "quartet" of featherweights to consider, headed-up by unbeaten Tony Silkstone from Leeds, who boxes out of the highly successful Mickey Duff stable. Twenty four-year-old Silkstone made his pro debut in April 1990 and has notched-up eleven straight wins. He is a boxer rather than a puncher - all his victories have come on points. Tony clearly has the skill to go a long way and he also showed admirable grit and determination to outscore Larkhall's Edward Cook at Leeds in April 1992.

Canning Town's Bradley Stone is another fine prospect from London's tough east-end and the 22-year-old has a current record of eleven victories and one draw in a dozen paid starts. He is a neat box-fighter and certainly looks capable of stepping up in class in the new season.

Twenty two-year-old southpaw Jimmy Clark from Tilbury, a pro since September 1988, who is equally at home campaigning at super-feather, has fourteen victories and one loss to his credit to date. Clark is a busy fighter, possessing a fine workrate and is a very accurate puncher. He should continue to make good progress next term.

Twenty six-year-old Liverpool southpaw, Jimmy Owens, is also a fine prospect and has shown some outstanding form since turning pro in January 1990. He has an excellent jab which enables him to dictate the pace and control matters effectively and it has already helped him to achieve ten victories in eleven paid outings.

The bantamweight division has some excellent talent at present as we shall now discover.

Manchester's talented 27-year-old John "Boy" Green from Phil Martin's successful "Champs Camp" is rapidly closing in on a British title shot. A pro since March 1987, the former undefeated Central Area champion possesses superb skill, coupled with terrific punching power. Still unbeaten as a bantamweight he has a career record of thirteen victories, two draws and two losses in 17 paid contests. His latest victory was clearly the most important one to date. On 29 May 1992 in Manchester, John won a British bantamweight championship eliminator when he clearly outpointed four-times challenger Ronnie Carroll, from Glasgow. Green certainly possesses championship potential and the new season should see him finally get his title chance.

Liverpool's Richie Wenton, elder brother of top lightweight prospect Nigel, is also one to watch in the bantamweight division. A pro since December 1988, 24-year-old Richie is still unbeaten as a pro and seems certain to land a title shot before too long. Richie is a clever rangy boxer with an excellent left jab and although he doesn't have brother Nigel's power, he is a tricky customer who always makes life extremely difficult for his opponents.

Glasgow's Dave Hardie, the 1991 ABA bantam-weight champion, is going well in the paid ranks and is unbeaten so far. He certainly has the pedigree to make a firm impression during the coming season.

Manchester's 22-year-old Craig Dermody is another exciting young fighter to watch. He is un-defeated with ten straight victories since making his pro debut at the end of January 1991. Craig is managed by Mickey Duff and when the time is right he will be given his title chance, make no mistake about that.

Our search for Britain's finest prospects is almost over now and finally it is the turn of the flyweights to capture our attention.

I have identified three fine "little men" who seem likely to aspire to championship potential in the coming season.

Eltham's Mickey Cantwell, the ABA light-flyweight champion in 1988 and again in 1989, is undefeated in six professional starts since discarding his vest in January 1991 and will be pressing his claim for a title shot in the new season. Cantwell is a very skilful boxer, neat and compact and although he does not posses real firepower he always makes the going tough for his opponents with his accurate and consistent punching.

Former Scottish amateur flyweight champion, Neil Armstrong from Paisley, is also unbeaten as a professional, although he has boxed a draw with Leicester's useful Shaun Norman. He made his paid debut on 31 January 1992 and stopped Kilwinning's Mark Robertson on a cut in the sixth and final round. Armstrong has a useful jab and is a workmanlike performer. He certainly needs more experience in the pro game and it will be interesting to see what progress he makes over the coming year.

To use the old show bizz expression "we have left the best 'til last". Well, certainly, the outrageous 18-year-old southpaw, "Prince" Nassem Hamed from Sheffield, would agree entirely with this assessment of his exciting championship potential. Hamed won seven national junior titles in his amateur days and he then turned pro in April 1992 under the expert guidance of his long-time mentor, Brendan Ingle.

Hamed is unbeaten in three paid starts, Ricky Beard, Shaun Norman and Andrew Bloomer, all failed to make it beyond the second round. Nas is a flashy young man, full of confidence and he is totally convinced that he will become world champion before he is 21. On the evidence so far it seems quite possible that he will fulfil his prediction. Only time will tell as they say, for Nas and all the other prospects we have reviewed. Good luck to each and every one of them.

Managing The Boxing Mind

by Jack Mitchell

In April 1991 I was part of a television panel answering questions on stress in sport from an audience of some 200 sporting people. In fact, my experience of this half hour programme was like being in the ring with Barry McGuigan, with punches coming from all angles and all directions at the speed of light! Actually, Barry himself was a member of the panel, which included our top skater Joanna Conway, an amateur. In fact, amateur sports people have an added pressure in their life until such time as they succeed on the world stage and commercial sponsors show an interest.

I was discussing the value of relaxation to sportsmen and women, but soon received a body blow from Barry who stated that relaxation was of no use to a boxer, boxers just needed aggression. Well, I am sure to be successful as a boxer you need aggression, but it is my professional opinion that a boxer and his trainer should be aware of many other mental sides to boxing performance.

The anti-boxing brigade are full of negative comments about the mental capacity of boxers. No matter what they say, boxers possess a distinct personality, temperament and an attitude to the game and are affected by their own motivation to achieve in this very tough business. It is their mind which helps them to persevere and become determined to succeed in the face of great odds.

Motivation for the game is most important. Ask yourself why you like to fight and keep asking yourself the question until you get the "right answer".

Frank Bruno told us his return to boxing was because boxing is in his blood. Larry Holmes came back at age 42 to show the world that even at that age he is still able to beat the present crop of top world heavyweights. Some can be there purely for the money.

In the past it was the "hungry fighters" who were thought to be most likely to succeed.

Throughout ten rounds of a gruelling bout, the fighter needs to concentrate on the job in hand and not be distracted. It is this mental strength which will help him win through. He needs to develop a quick reaction time to be able to counter-punch effectively against an aggressive opponent who is always coming forward. The boxer needs to develop a memory of his successes, his skills and abilities, rather than thinking about the way he lost the last fight. His self-concept or opinion about his current and future performance needs to be very positive if he is going to win through.

Emotional strength is required to cope with such tragedies as the brain damage to Michael Watson in his fight with Chris Eubank. Chris had to deal with the media as well as his own feelings of responsibility for the mental damage to poor Michael. It is at these times that the whole of the boxing

Jack Mitchell (right) pictured with Francis Ampofo, the former British flyweight champion

fraternity and their families need to rally round to support boxing. This is apparent, I understand, with the many adverts asking for donations to the Michael Watson Fund. My own attitude to the critics is that many young men join the army to learn to kill. Many die themselves, but this does not deter recruitment, neither does it stop this country, or any other in the world, from building armies.

Managing pressure is crucial, in order to survive losing a bout on points or suffering an injury, which keeps a fighter out of the game for a period of time. This is a point at which he can learn about his own mental strength and determination. I have helped boxers and other sports people to come back to top professional performance after such setbacks. The media is full of the promotion of fighters with a clean record to date, as being ideal people to fight for world titles. It is my opinion that when a fighter has lost to a real class opponent that he is now ready and able to learn far more about his craft and turn this "learning point" to his advantage at his next meeting with his opponent.

The tabloids are full of pictures of the days leading up to a world title fight of the "psyching up" and intimidating psychological strategies of various fighters. Mohammed Ali would have mentally beaten his next opponent by round five before he had got anywhere near the boxing ring. His simple slogan "Float like a Butterfly, Sting like a Bee" was firmly entrenched in his mind and he performed in this way in each fight.

Many fighters come to the ring and try to out stare their opponent. Others make abusive comments throughout the match, trying to distract them. Many observers of the Frank Bruno v Mike Tyson fight commented that Frank may have been distracted more by Mike Tyson's comments and that of the referee, rather than the pure boxing skill of Tyson.

For a boxer to go from the amateur ranks to the top of the professional world requires for him to have a very supportive family and social network. He needs looking after emotionally as well as physically. A fighter spending a couple of months away from his wife and children, could be influenced about the way he is neglecting them. If he does not have the support of his family then this is an extra pressure.

Boxer/manager conflicts can cause further mental turmoil which will affect the boxer's performance in the ring. Barry McGuigan suffered enormous mental pain during the wranglings and separation from his ex-manager, Barney Eastwood. By the time the *Yearbook* is published, a lot of fighters will have gone from manager to manager and sometimes back again. This can only have an unsettling affect on the fighter.

Recently, Nigel Benn changed his image from that of the "Dark Destroyer", when he was stopped by Chris Eubank, to a more cool fighter. I understand that he is now changing back again! Nigel, however, seems to possess great strength of character and determination to come back and wrest the world super-middleweight title back from Chris.

I would like to turn to the subject of relaxation. I don't mean that the fighter should sit in his corner, drifting off mentally from the job in hand, but that he needs to first relax in the dressing room to conserve his mental energy and to pace this over what could be twelve gruelling rounds.

At the time of writing this article, Derek Angol, our great cruiserweight hope for world fame, was stopped by American Tyrone Booth after running out of steam. Many fighters noted for their ability to "take out" the opponent early on are incapable of lasting more than eight rounds if their big punch has not been effective enough.

The fighter needs to practice pacing his mental concentration for a possible twelve rounds of action. It is, after all, the mind which tells the muscles, arms and legs to do the business, so conditioning of the mind to be prepared to last the distance will be well rewarded. I believe Frank Bruno was affected by psychological factors in a number of his fights. He had the beating of both James "Bonecrusher" Smith and Tim Witherspoon, but was unable to control his own mental and physical energies and burnt himself out before the last rounds. Unfortunately, he ended up being stopped in both of these bouts, which he could have easily won on points.

Mental coaching can be important to the fighter at every level of the game, from amateur to top professional competition. YES, physical fitness and technical ability are crucial, but without attendance to the mental side, the fighter is not going to win or stay at the top, if he ever gets there!

In my own professional practice with sportsmen, I help them to deal with all aspects of the mind, including relaxation, developing aggression, building self confidence, concentration and helping them cope with distractions. I have been particularly successful with sports people coming back from layoffs, defeat or injury. As a counsellor as well as being a psychologist, I am able to help them deal with the non-boxing side of their life, including personal worries about oneself, relationships, the pressure of money and the media, particularly in coping with success. All this information is strictly confidential and does not reach the media.

I am also mindful that many boxers are unable to stay in the game through injury or other problems. These need counselling to help them to readjust to a life outside the ring.

I hope all readers involved with the fight game are able to find something of value in this article. I would be pleased to discuss my services with anybody, including fighters, their managers, trainers, promoters and so on. If those involved in boxing consider only a couple of the factors I have highlighted in this article then it would have been of some value.

Biography:
Jack Lamport Mitchell is Director for the Centre for Sports Psychology, at 80 Grove Hill, South Woodford, London E18 2HZ.

He will be pleased to discuss how he can help boxers to achieve performance excellence in the ring, with the help of mental as well as physical and technical training. Jack possesses two Degrees in Psychology, a Masters from Birkbeck College University of London, is a member of the British Association of Sports Science, British Psychological Society and British Association of Counselling.

All professional consultations with boxers are carried out in complete confidence.

Diary of British Boxing Tournaments, 1991-92

Tournaments are listed by date, town, venue, and promoter and cover the period 1 July 1991 - 30 June 1992
Code: SC = Sporting Club

Date	Town	Venue	Promoters
03.07.91	Brentwood	International Hall	Matchroom
03.07.91	Reading	Rivermead Leisure Centre	Warren
04.07.91	Alfreton	Leisure Centre	National Promotions
18.07.91	Cardiff	National Sports Centre	Gardiner/ Hayde
25.07.91	Dudley	Town Hall	National Promotions
01.08.91	Dewsbury	Sports Centre	National Promotions
29.08.91	Oakengates	Town Hall	National Promotions
03.09.91	Cardiff	National Sports Centre	Matchroom/Gardiner/Hayde
04.09.91	Bethnal Green	York Hall	Warren
07.09.91	Belfast	Maysfield Leisure Centre	Eastwood
09.09.91	Liverpool	Devonshire House Hotel	Snagg
09.09.91	Glasgow	Forte Crest Hotel	St Andrew's SC
10.09.91	Wolverhampton	Civic Hall	Matchroom/Gray
11.09.91	Hammersmith	Odeon Cinema	National Promotions
11.09.91	Stoke	King's Hall	Stoke European SC
12.09.91	Wandsworth	Latchmere Leisure Centre	National Promotions
16.09.91	Mayfair	Grosvenor House	National Promotions
16.09.91	Cleethorpes	Winter Gardens	Gray
19.09.91	Stockport	Town Hall	Trickett
20.09.91	Manchester	Free Trade Hall	Martin
21.09.91	Tottenham	White Hart Lane Ground	Matchroom
23.09.91	Glasgow	Forte Crest Hotel	St Andrew's SC
24.09.91	Basildon	Festival Hall	Matchroom
24.09.91	Glasgow	Shawfield Stadium	Prime Promotions
26.09.91	Dunstable	Queensway Hall	National Promotions
30.09.91	Liverpool	Forte Crest Hotel	St Andrew's SC
30.09.91	Kensington	Albert Hall	Maloney
01.10.91	Bedworth	Civic Hall	Griffin
01.10.91	Sheffield	City Hall	Matchroom
02.10.91	Solihull	Civic Hall	Midland SC
02.10.91	Barking	Broadway Theatre	Robinson S./Maloney
03.10.91	Burton	Town Hall	National Promotions
07.10.91	Liverpool	Mere Lane Social Club	North-West Promotions
07.10.91	Bradford	Norfolk Gardens Hotel	Yorkshire Executive SC
07.10.91	Birmingham	Albany Hotel	Cowdell
08.10.91	Wolverhampton	Park Hall Hotel	Wolverhampton SC
09.10.91	Manchester	G-Mex Leisure Centre	National Promotions
09.10.91	Marton	Country Club	Spensley
09.10.91	Glasgow	Fort Crest Hotel	St Andrew's SC
10.10.91	Gateshead	Leisure Centre	Team Promotions
14.10.91	Manchester	Piccadilly Hotel	Trickett
15.10.91	Dudley	Town Hall	Cowdell
16.10.91	Stoke	Trentham Gardens	North Staffs SC
17.10.91	Southwark	Elephant & Castle Leisure Centre	National Promotions
17.10.91	Mossley	George Morton Hall	Tara Promotions
21.10.91	Bury	Castle Leisure Centre	Tara Promotions
21.10.91	Cleethorpes	Winter Gardens	Gray
21.10.91	Glasgow	Forte Crest Hotel	St Andrew's SC
21.10.91	Mayfair	Grosvenor House	National Promotions
22.10.91	Wandsworth	Letchmere Leisure Centre	Anglo - Swedish Promotions
22.10.91	Hartlepool	Borough Hall	Robinson G.
23.10.91	Bethnal Green	York Hall	Robinson S./Maloney

Date	Town	Venue	Promoters
23.10.91	Stoke	King's Hall	Stoke European SC
24.10.91	Dunstable	Queensway Hall	National Promotions
24.10.91	Glasgow	Hospitality Inn	Prime Promotions
24.10.91	Bayswater	Royal Lancaster Hotel	Nordoff - Robbins Trust
26.10.91	Brentwood	International Hall	Matchroom
28.10.91	Leicester	Holiday Inn	Holiday Inn Promotions
29.10.91	Kensington	Albert Hall	Warren
29.10.91	Cardiff	Star Leisure Centre	Matchroom/Gardiner/Hayde
30.10.91	Leeds	City Hall	National Promotions
31.10.91	Oakengates	Town Hall	National Promotions/Pro Sport
04.11.91	Merthyr	Rhydycar Leisure Centre	Gardiner/Hayde/Jack Solomon's SC
05.11.91	Leicester	Granby Halls	Matchroom
07.11.91	Peterborough	Mallard Park Hotel	K. K. Promotions
11.11.91	Stratford on Avon	Maot House Hotel	Brogan
11.11.91	Bradford	Norfolk Gardens Hotel	Yorkshire Executive SC
12.11.91	Wolverhampton	Civic Hall	Matchroom/Gray
12.11.91	Milton Keynes	Woughton Leisure Centre	Holland H.
13.11.91	Belfast	Maysfield Leisure Centre	Eastwood
13.11.91	Bethnal Green	York Hotel	Robinson S.
13.11.91	Liverpool	Devonshire House Hotel	Snagg
14.11.91	Bayswater	King David Suite	Philip Green Memorial Trust
14.11.91	Gateshead	Leisure Centre	Conroy
14.11.91	Edinburgh	Sheraton Hotel	St Andrew's SC
18.11.91	Manchester	Piccadilly Hotel	Trickett
18.11.91	Glasgow	Fort Crest Hotel	St Andrew's SC
19.11.91	Norwich	Sports Village	Matchroom
20.11.91	Kensington	Albert Hall	National Promotions
20.11.91	Solihull	Civic Hall	Midlands SC
20.11.91	Cardiff	Star Leisure Centre	Warren
20.11.91	Cardiff	Coal Exchange	Gardiner/Hayde
21.11.91	Stafford	Gatehouse Theatre	Gray
21.11.91	Ilkeston	Regency Rooms	Shinfield
21.11.91	Burton	Meadowside Leisure Centre	National Promotions
25.11.91	Liverpool	Forte Crest Hotel	St Andrew's SC

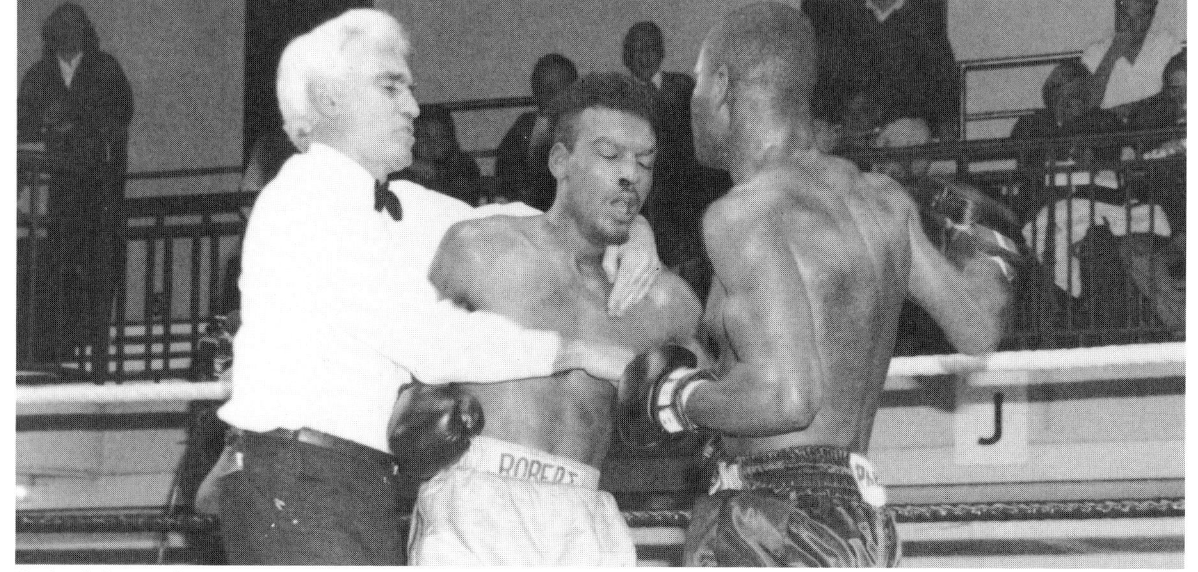

Bethnal Green - 26 November 1991: Darren Dyer (right) seen blasting Robert Wright to defeat inside three rounds

Les Clark

Date	Town	Venue	Promoters
25.11.91	Cleethorpes	Beachcomber's Club	Frater
26.11.91	Bethnal Green	York Hall	Matchroom
26.11.91	Wolverhampton	Park Hall Hotel	Wolverhampton SC
29.11.91	Marton	Country Club	Spensley
28.11.91	Evesham	Public Halls	Evesham SC
28.11.91	Hull	Grange Park Hotel	Hull & District SC
28.11.91	Glasgow	Hospitality Inn	Prime Promotions
28.11.91	Liverpool	Central Hall	National Promotions
29.11.91	Manchester	Nia Centre	Martin
02.12.91	Birmingham	Albany Hotel	Cowdell
02.12.91	Birmingham	Grand Hotel	Gray
02.12.91	Liverpool	Mere Lane Social Club	North - West Promotions
04.12.91	Stoke	Trentham Gardens	North Staffs SC
05.12.91	Oakengates	Town Hall	National Promotions/Pro Sport
05.12.91	Peterborough	Mallard Park Hotel	K. K. Promotions
05.12.91	Cannock	Chase Leisure Centre	Gray
07.12.91	Manchester	G-Mex Leisure Centre	Matchroom
09.12.91	Cleethorpes	Beachcomber's Club	Gray
09.12.91	Bradford	Norfolk Gardens Hotel	Yorkshire Executive SC
09.12.91	Brierley Hill	Civic Hall	Cowdell
10.12.91	Sheffield	City Hall	Matchroom
11.12.91	Leicester	Grand Hall	Griffin
11.12.91	Basildon	Festival Hall	Robinson S.
11.12.91	Stoke	King's Hall	Stoke European SC
12.12.91	Hartlepool	Borough Hall	Robinson G.
14.12.91	Bexleyheath	Crook Log Sports Club	Maloney
16.12.91	Southampton	Guildhall	Bishop
16.12.91	Manchester	Piccadilly Hotel	Trickett
17.12.91	Cardiff	National Ice Rink	Matchroom/Gardiner/Hayde
19.12.91	Oldham	Sports Centre	National Promotions
08.01.92	Burton	Meadowside Leisure Centre	Warren
15.01.92	Stoke	Trentham Gardens	North Staffs SC
18.01.92	Kensington	Albert Hall	Warren
20.01.92	Bradford	Norfolk Gardens Hotel	Yorkshire Executive SC
20.01.92	Coventry	Leofric Hotel	Gray
21.01.92	Norwich	Sports Village	Matchroom
21.01.92	Stockport	Town Hall	Trickett
22.01.92	Solihull	Civic Hall	Midlands SC
22.01.92	Cardiff	Star Leisure Centre	Warren
22.01.92	Stoke	King's Hall	Stoke European SC
23.01.92	York	Barbican Centre	National Promotions
27.01.92	Glasgow	Forte Crest Hotel	St Andrew's SC
28.01.92	Piccadilly	Cafe Royal	St Andrew's SC
30.01.92	Southampton	Guildhall	National Promotions
31.01.92	Manchester	Nia Centre	Martin
31.01.92	Glasgow	Hospitality Inn	Prime Promotions
01.02.92	Birmingham	National Indoor Centre	Matchroom
03.02.92	Manchester	Piccadilly Hotel	Trickett
04.02.92	Alfreton	Leisure Centre	Cowdell
06.02.92	Peterborough	Mallard Park Hotel	K. K. Promotions
09.02.92	Bradford	Maestro Night Club	Martin
10.02.92	Liverpool	Devonshire House Hotel	Snagg
11.02.92	Cardiff	National Sports Centre	Matchroom/Gardiner/Hayde
11.02.92	Wolverhampton	Park Hall Hotel	Wolverhampton SC
11.02.92	Barking	Broadway Theatre	Warren
12.02.92	Wembley	Grand Hall	National Promotions
12.02.92	Watford	Town Hall	Holland H.

Date	Town	Venue	Promoters
17.02.92	Mayfair	Grosvenor House	National Promotions
19.02.92	Muswell Hill	Alexandra Palace	Matchroom
20.02.92	Oakengates	Town Hall	Pro Sport
20.02.92	Glasgow	Scottish Exhibition Centre	National Promotions
24.02.92	Bradford	Norfolk Gardens Hotel	Yorkshire Executive SC
24.02.92	Coventry	Leofric Hotel	Gray
24.02.92	Glasgow	Forte Crest Hotel	St Andrew's SC
25.02.92	Crystal Palace	National Sports Centre	Matchroom/Anglo-Swedish Promotions
27.02.92	Liverpool	Everton Park Sports Centre	National Promotions
28.02.92	Irvine	Volunteer Rooms	St Andrew's SC

Muswell Hill - 19 February 1992: The "Dark Destroyer", Nigel Benn (left), destroyed Canada's Dan Sherry in the third round
Les Clark

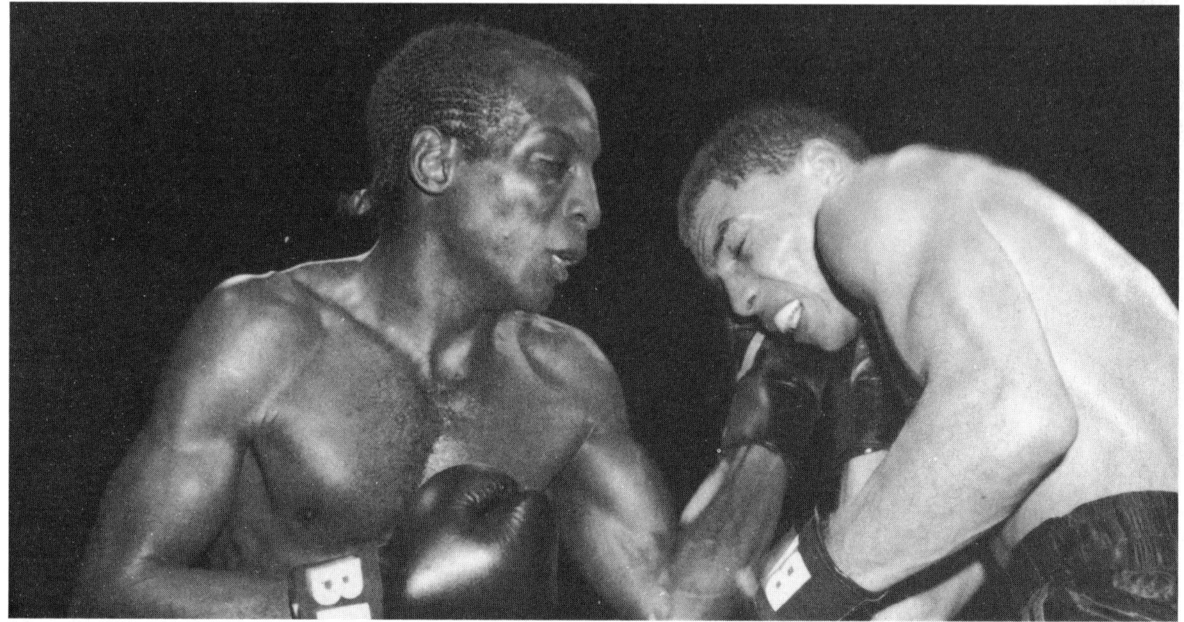

Muswell Hill - 19 February 1992: On the same bill as Benn v Sherry, the Southern Area lightweight champion, Michael Ayers (right), stopped Rudy Valentino in the seventh round of an official eliminator for the British title
Les Clark

Date	Town	Venue	Promoters
29.02.92	St Leonards	Combe Haven Holiday Park	Harris
02.03.92	Merthyr	Rhydycar Leisure Centre	Gardiner/Hayde/Jack Solomon's SC
02.03.92	Marton	Country Club	Spensley
03.03.92	Cradley Heath	Haden Hill Leisure Centre	Cowdell
03.03.92	Houghton le Spring	McEwan's Indoor Cricket School	Foster
04.03.92	Glasgow	Hospitality Inn	Prime Promotions
05.03.92	Battersea	Town Hall	Holland H.
09.03.92	Manchester	Piccadilly Hotel	Trickett
10.03.92	Bury	Castle Leisure Centre	Tara Promotions/Matchroom
11.03.92	Cardiff	Star Leisure Centre	Warren
11.03.92	Solihull	Civic Hall	Midlands SC
11.03.92	Stoke	King's Hall	Stoke European SC
11.03.92	Stoke	Trentham Gardens	North Staffs SC
12.03.92	Glasgow	Hospitality Inn	Prime Promotions
17.03.92	Mayfair	Grosvenor House	Matchroom
17.03.92	Wolverhampton	Civic Hall	Gray
18.03.92	Glasgow	Kelvin Hall	St Andrew's SC
19.03.92	York	Barbican Centre	National Promotions
24.03.92	Wolverhampton	Park Hall Hotel	Wolverhampton SC
25.03.92	Kensington	Albert Hall	National Promotions
25.03.92	Dagenham	Goresbrook Leisure Centre	Warren
25.03.92	Hinckley	Leisure Centre	Griffin
26.03.92	Telford	Ice Rink	National Promotions
26.03.92	Hull	Willoughby Manor	Hull & District SC
30.03.92	Eltham	Yorkshire Grey	Holland T.

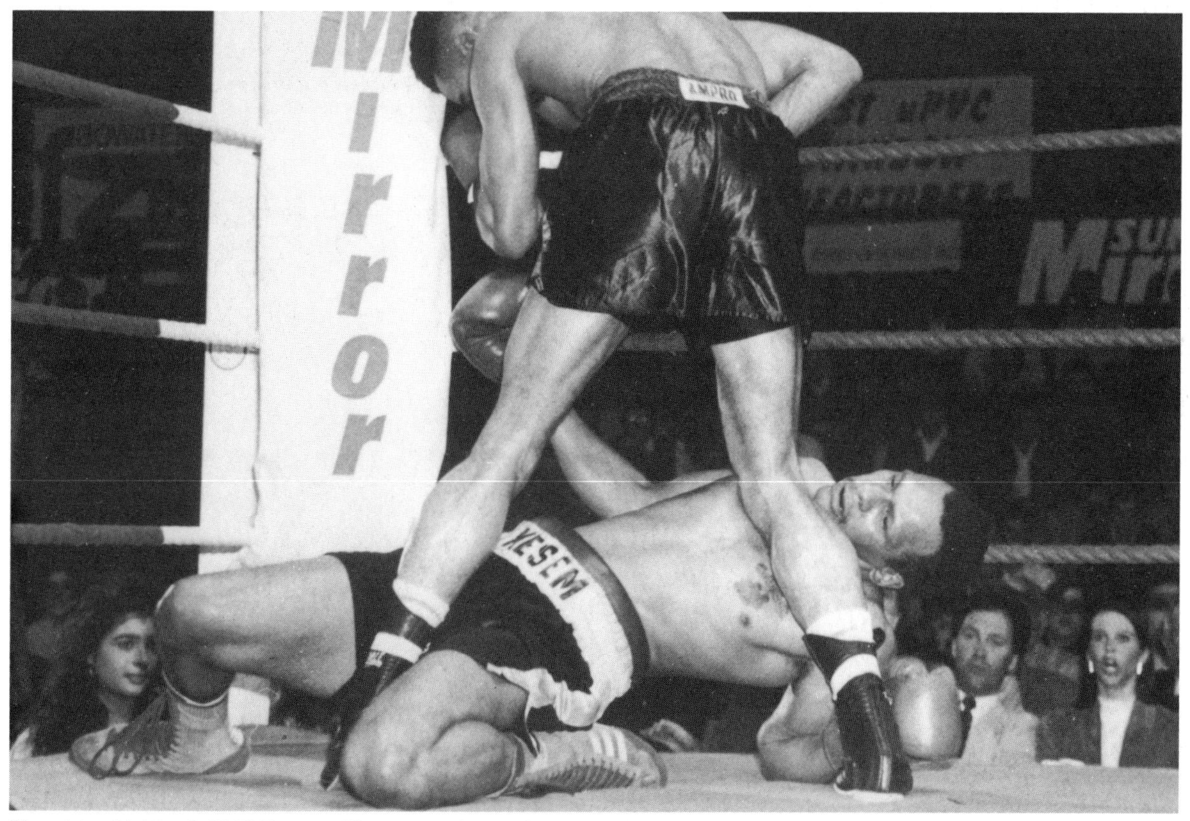

Norwich - 31 March 1992:Kessem Clayton crashes to the canvas for a fourth round defeat at the hands of Stan King

Les Clark

Date	Town	Venue	Promoters
30.03.92	Coventry	Leofric Hotel	Gray
30.03.92	Bradford	Norfolk Gardens Hotel	Yorkshire Executive SC
30.03.92	Glasgow	Forte Crest Hotel	St Andrew's SC
31.03.92	Stockport	Town Hall	Trickett
31.03.92	Norwich	Sports Village	Matchroom
02.04.92	Basildon	Festival Hall	Warren
04.04.92	Cleethorpes	Beachcomber's Club	Frater
05.04.92	Bradford	St George's Hall	Martin
06.04.92	Northampton	Moat House Hotel	Shinfield
07.04.92	Southend	Garon's Suite	Levine
08.04.92	Leeds	Town Hall	National Promotions
10.04.92	Glasgow	Hospitality Inn	Prime Promotions
13.04.92	Manchester	Piccadilly Hotel	Trickett
14.04.92	Mansfield	Leisure Centre	Matchroom
22.04.92	Wembley	The Area	National Promotions
23.04.92	Eltham	Yorkshire Grey	Holland T.
25.04.92	Belfast	Maysfield Leisure Centre	Eastwood
25.04.92	Manchester	G-Mex Leisure Centre	Matchroom
27.04.92	Glasgow	Forte Crest Hotel	St Andrew's SC
27.04.92	Bradford	Norfolk Gardens Hotel	Yorkshire Executive SC
27.04.92	Mayfair	Grosvenor House	National Promotions
28.04.92	Houghton le Sping	McEwan's Indoor Cricket School	Foster
28.04.92	Corby	Grampian Club	K. K. Promotions
28.04.92	Wolverhampton	Civic Hall	Matchroom/Gray
29.04.92	Solihull	Civic Hall	Midlands SC
29.04.92	Stoke	King's Hall	Stoke European SC
29.04.92	Liverpool	Devonshire House Hotel	Snagg
30.04.92	Kensington	Albert Hall	Maloney
30.04.92	Bayswater	Royal Lancaster Hotel	Motability Trust
30.04.92	Watford	Town Hall	Holland H.
30.04.92	Mayfair	Hilton Hotel	National Promotions
05.05.92	Preston	Guildhall	Matchroom
11.05.92	Coventry	Leofric Hotel	Gray
11.05.92	Piccadilly	Cafe Royal	Matchroom
11.05.92	Llanelli	Bulls Centre	Gardiner/Hayde
12.05.92	Crystal Palace	National Sports Centre	Matchroom/Anglo-Swedish Promotions
13.05.92	Kensington	Albert Hall	National Promotions
14.05.92	Liverpool	Central Hall	McHale
16.05.92	Muswell Hill	Alexandra Palace	Warren
17.05.92	Harringay	Arena Nightclub	Burgess
18.05.92	Barden	Stardust Club	Griffin
18.05.92	Marton	Country Club	Spensley
19.05.92	Cardiff	National Ice Rink	Matchroom/Gardiner/Hayde
21.05.92	Cradley Heath	Haden Hill Leisure Centre	Cowdell
23.05.92	Birmingham	National Indoor Centre	Matchroom
28.05.92	Gosforth	Brandling House	Fawcett
29.05.92	Glasgow	Hospitality Inn	Prime Promotions
29.05.92	Manchester	Free Trade Hall	Martin
01.06.92	Glasgow	Forte Crest Hotel	St Andrew's SC
01.06.92	Manchester	New Century Hall	Jewish Blind Society Trust
01.06.92	Solihull	Metropole Hotel	Cowdell
03.06.92	Newcastle under Lyme	Fatty Arbuckle's Club	Brogan
04.06.92	Burnley	William Thompson Centre	Tara Promotions
04.06.92	Cleethorpes	Beachcomber's Club	Frater
08.06.92	Bradford	Norfolk Gardens Hotel	Yorkshire Executive SC
12.06.92	Liverpool	State Nightspot	McHale
16.06.92	Dagenham	Goresbrook Leisure Centre	Matchroom
18.06.92	Peterborough	Mallard Park Hotel	Warren

Current British-Based Champions: Career Records

Shows the complete records of all former British champions, or British boxers, to win international championships, who have been active between 1 July 1991 to 30 June 1992. Names in brackets are real names, where they differ from ring names. The first place name given is the boxer's domicile. Minimum/maximum weights for the 1991-92 season are shown in brackets alongside weight division. The boxer's height has also been added. Boxers are either shown as self managed, denoted by a dash, or with a named manager at the time of their last contest.

Derek Angol

Camberwell. *Born* London, 28 November, 1964
Commonwealth Cruiserweight Champion. Former Undefeated British Cruiserweight Champion (13.6-14.0½) ht. 6'3½"
Manager T. Lawless

15.12.86 Gus Mendes W RSC 3 Mayfair
22.01.87 Abner Blackstock W PTS 6 Bethnal Green
12.03.87 Patrick Collins W CO 6 Piccadilly
09.04.87 Mick Cordon W RSC 4 Bethnal Green
08.10.87 Lennie Howard W RSC 5 Bethnal Green
15.02.88 Abner Blackstock W RSC 6 Mayfair
14.03.88 Alek Penarski W CO 2 Mayfair
13.04.88 Jonjo Greene W PTS 6 Bethnal Green
05.05.88 Cordwell Hylton W RSC 5 Wembly
17.10.88 Roy Smith W RSC 1 Mayfair
19.12.88 Jack Johnson W CO 1 Mayfair
18.01.89 Rick Enis W RSC 3 Kensington
08.03.89 Jamie Howe W PTS 8 Kensington
29.03.89 Teo Arvizu W RSC 3 Wembley
07.06.89 Andre Crowder W RSC 3 Wembley
04.10.89 Raymond Gonzalez W RSC 2 Kensington
30.11.89 Apollo Sweet W PTS 12 Southwark *(Commonwealth Cruiserweight Title Challenge)*
08.02.90 Eddie Smith W RSC 2 Southwark
14.03.90 Andy Straughn W CO 8 Kensington *(Commonwealth Cruiserweight Title Defence)*
04.10.90 Manfred Jassman W RSC 8 Bethnal Green
10.01.91 Dan Murphy W RSC 9 Wandsworth
13.02.91 Dave Garside W RSC 2 Wembley *(Vacant British Cruiserweight Title. Commonwealth Cruiserweight Title Defence)*
17.04.91 Yves Monsieur W RSC 2 Kensington
08.05.91 Tee Jay W RSC 3 Kensington *(British & Commonwealth Cruiserweight Title Defence)*
17.10.91 Dave Russell W RSC 4 Southwark *(Commonwealth Cruiserweight Title Defence)*
16.05.92 Robert Clevenger W CO 2 Muswell Hill

Career: 26 contests, won 26.

John Armour

Chatham. *Born* Chatham, 26 October, 1968
Commonwealth Bantamweight Champion (8.3¼-8.9) ht. 5'4¼"
Manager M. Duff

24.09.90 Lupe Castro W PTS 6 Lewisham
31.10.90 Juan Camero W RSC 4 Crystal Palace
21.01.91 Elijro Mejia W RSC 1 Crystal Palace
30.09.91 Pat Maher W CO 1 Kensington
29.10.91 Pete Buckley W PTS 6 Kensington
14.12.91 Gary Hickman W RSC 6 Bexleyheath
25.03.92 Miguel Matthews W PTS 6 Dagenham
30.04.92 Ndaba Dube W RSC 12 Kensington *(Vacant Commonwealth Bantamweight Title)*

Career: 8 contests, won 8.

John Armour Tony Fitch

Michael Armstrong (Morris)

Stoke. *Born* Moston, 18 December, 1968
British S. Featherweight Champion (9.0-9.2½) ht. 5'4"
Manager J. Trickett

27.01.88 John Hales W RSC 1 Stoke
02.03.88 Gypsy Johnny W RSC 2 Stoke
20.04.88 Pepe Webber W PTS 6 Stoke

Derek Angol (left) in action against the German, Manfred Jassman Les Clark

Michael Armstrong Chris Bevan

16.05.88 Steve Bowles W RSC 3 Manchester
13.06.88 Tony Heath W PTS 6 Manchester
09.08.88 G. G. Corbett W DIS 6 St Helier
20.09.88 Darren Weller W PTS 8 Stoke
26.10.88 Gary King DREW 8 Stoke
07.12.88 Mark Holt L PTS 8 Stoke
15.02.89 Gerry McBride W RSC 5 Stoke
19.04.89 Russell Davison W PTS 8 Stoke
24.05.89 Anthony Barcla W PTS 8 Hanley
04.09.89 Steve Pollard W PTS 8 Hull
06.12.89 Russell Davison L PTS 8 Stoke
06.03.90 Russell Davison W PTS 10 Stoke
18.09.90 Modest Napunyi L CO 9 Stoke *(Commonwealth Featherweight Title Challenge)*
14.10.91 Barrie Kelley W CO 4 Manchester
07.12.91 Mark Holt W RSC 4 Manchester
21.01.92 Darren Elsdon W RSC 1 Stockport *(Final Elim. British S. Featherweight Title)*
25.04.92 John Doherty W RSC 7 Manchester *(British S. Featherweight Title Challenge)*

Career: 20 contests, won 16, drew 1, lost 3.

(Gary) Crawford Ashley (Crawford)

Leeds. *Born* Leeds, 20 May, 1964
British L. Heavyweight Champion. Former Undefeated Central Area L. Heavyweight Champion (12.4½-12.5) ht. 6'3"
Manager B. Eastwood

26.03.87 Steve Ward W RSC 2 Merton
29.04.87 Lee Woolis W RSC 3 Stoke
14.09.87 Glazz Campbell L PTS 8 Bloomsbury
07.10.87 Joe Frater W RSC 5 Burnley
28.10.87 Ray Thomas W RSC 1 Stoke
03.12.87 Jonjo Greene W RSC 7 Leeds
04.05.88 Johnny Nelson L PTS 8 Solihull
15.11.88 Richard Bustin W CO 3 Norwich
22.11.88 Cordwell Hylton W CO 3 Basildon
24.01.89 John Foreman W RSC 4 Kings Heath
08.02.89 Lavell Stanley W CO 1 Kensington
28.03.89 Blaine Logsdon L RSC 2 Glasgow
10.05.89 Serg Fame W RTD 7 Solihull
31.10.89 Carl Thompson W RSC 6 Manchester *(Vacant Central Area L. Heavyweight Title)*
24.01.90 Brian Schumacher W RSC 3 Preston *(Central Area L. Heavyweight Title Defence)*

Crawford Ashley Les Clark

25.04.90 Dwain Muniz W RSC 1 Brighton
26.11.90 John Williams W RSC 1 Mayfair
12.02.91 Melvin Ricks W CO 1 Belfast
01.03.91 Graciano Rocchigiani L PTS 12 Dusseldorf, West Germany *(Vacant European L. Heavyweight Title)*
25.07.91 Roy Skeldon W RSC 7 Dudley *(Vacant British L. Heavyweight Title)*
30.01.92 Jim Peters W RSC 1 Southampton *(British L. Heavyweight Title Defence)*
25.04.92 Glazz Campbell W RSC 8 Belfast *(British L. Heavyweight Title Defence)*

Career: 22 contests, won 18, lost 4.

Fidel Castro (Smith)

Sheffield. *Born* Nottingham, 17 April, 1963
British S. Middleweight Champion. Former Undefeated Central Area Middleweight Champion (11.13-12.0) ht. 5'9"
Manager B. Ingle

06.04.87 Ian Bayliss W RSC 5 Newcastle
28.04.87 Nick Gyaamie W RSC 2 Manchester
29.04.87 Leigh Wicks L PTS 6 Hastings
11.05.87 Steve Foster W PTS 8 Manchester
23.09.87 Ian Jackson W PTS 6 Stoke
11.11.87 Denys Cronin W PTS 8 Usk
24.02.88 Ian Bayliss W RSC 6 Sheffield *(Central Area Middleweight Title Challenge)*
09.05.88 Franki Moro W RSC 2 Nottingham
18.05.88 Chris Galloway W PTS 6 Gillingham
23.05.88 Sean Heron W RSC 4 Mayfair
08.07.88 Francesco dell Aquila L DIS 3 San Remo, Italy
19.11.88 Paul Tchoue W RSC 3 Chateau Thierry, France
23.01.89 Andre Mongalema L PTS 8 Paris, France
22.06.89 Denys Cronin W RSC 7 Stevenage
27.01.90 Thomas Covington W PTS 8 Sheffield
12.03.90 Darren McKenna W PTS 6 Hull

Fidel Castro Les Clark

20.05.90 Nigel Fairbairn W RSC 7 Sheffield
20.08.90 Elvis Parks W PTS 6 Helsinki, Finland
29.10.90 Dave Owens W PTS 6 Birmingham
24.11.90 Johnny Melfah W RSC 4 Benalmadena, Spain
24.09.91 Ian Strudwick W RSC 6 Basildon *(Vacant British S. Middleweight Title)*
01.10.91 Johnny Melfah W RSC 7 Sheffield
25.02.92 Lou Gent W PTS 12 Crystal Palace *(British S. Middleweight Title Defence)*

Career: 23 contests, won 20, lost 3.

Pat Clinton David Hayes

Pat Clinton

Croy. *Born* Croy, 4 April, 1964
WBO Flyweight Champion. Former Undefeated British & European Flyweight Champion. Former Undefeated Scottish Flyweight Champion (8.0-8.2¼) ht. 5'3½"
Manager T. Gilmour

10.10.85 Gordon Stobie W PTS 6 Alfreton
11.11.85 Tony Rahman W PTS 6 Glasgow
24.02.86 Tony Rahman W PTS 6 Glasgow
29.04.86 Des Gargano W PTS 6 Manchester
09.06.86 George Bailey W CO 2 Glasgow
20.10.86 Ginger Staples W RSC 2 Glasgow
17.11.86 Gypsy Johnny W RSC 5 Glasgow
19.01.87 Sean Casey W CO 6 Glasgow
16.02.87 Des Gargano W PTS 6 Glasgow
14.04.87 Jose Manuel Diaz W RSC 8 Cumbernauld
19.05.87 Miguel Pequeno W CO 4 Cumbernauld
22.09.87 Joe Kelly W RSC 2 Bethnal Green *(Final Elim. British Flyweight Title. Vacant Scottish Flyweight Title)*
09.03.88 Joe Kelly W PTS 12 Bethnal Green *(Vacant British Flyweight Title. Scottish Flyweight Title Defence)*
16.02.89 Eyup Can L PTS 12 Copenhagen, Denmark *(Vacant European Flyweight Title)*
24.10.89 Danny Porter W RSC 5 Watford *(British Flyweight Title Defence)*
19.12.89 David Afan-Jones W RSC 6 Gorleston *(British Flyweight Title Defence)*
03.08.90 Salvatore Fanni W PTS 12 Cagliari, Italy

(Vacant European Flyweight Title)
09.09.91 Armando Tapia W PTS 8 Glasgow
18.11.91 Alberto Cantu W PTS 8 Glasgow
18.03.92 Isidro Perez W PTS 12 Glasgow
(WBO Flyweight Title Challenge)

Career: 20 contests, won 19, lost 1.

Carl Crook

Chorley. *Born* Bolton, 10 November, 1963
British & Commonwealth Lightweight Champion. Former Central Area Lightweight Champion
(9.8-9.9) ht. 5'10"
Manager —

16.12.85 George Jones W PTS 6 Bradford
27.01.86 Russell Jones W RSC 4 Bradford
24.03.86 Doug Munro W CO 2 Bradford
17.04.86 Muhammad Lovelock W CO 6 Bradford
22.05.86 George Jones W RSC 1 Horwich
22.09.86 Sugar Gibiliru W PTS 6 Bradford
04.11.86 Brian Roche DREW 10 Oldham
(Vacant Central Area Lightweight Title)
15.12.86 Sugar Gibiliru W PTS 8 Bradford
27.01.87 Dean Marsden W RSC 1 Manchester
23.02.87 Muhammad Lovelock W PTS 10 Bradford
(Vacant Central Area Lightweight Title)
28.04.87 George Baigrie W PTS 8 Manchester
09.06.87 Tony Richards W PTS 8 Manchester
22.09.87 Joey Jacobs L PTS 10 Oldham
(Central Area Lightweight Title Defence)
07.10.87 Marvin P. Gray W PTS 8 Burnley
26.11.87 Marvin P. Gray W PTS 8 Horwich
26.04.88 Keith Parry W PTS 10 Bradford
(Elim. British Lightweight Title)
25.10.88 Patrick Kamy W PTS 8 Hartlepool
14.02.89 Steve Topliss W RTD 5 Manchester
14.04.89 Nedrie Simmons W RSC 8 Manchester
31.05.89 Steve Pollard W RSC 4 Manchester

Carl Crook Chris Bevan

13.10.89 Mohamed Ouhmad W PTS 8 Preston
24.01.90 Joel Dulys W RSC 3 Preston
21.03.90 Najib Daho W PTS 12 Preston
(Commonwealth Lightweight Title Challenge)
14.11.90 Tony Richards W PTS 12 Sheffield
(Vacant British Lightweight Title. Commonwealth Lightweight Title Defence)
19.12.90 Ian Honeywood W RSC 4 Preston
(British & Commonwealth Lightweight Title Defence)
24.04.91 Najib Daho W RSC 10 Preston
(British & Commonwealth Lightweight Title Defence)
22.06.91 Brian Roche W CO 10 Earls Court
(British & Commonwealth Lightweight Title Defence)
07.12.91 Antonio Renzo L RSC 6 Rossano Calabro, Italy
(European Lightweight Title Challenge)
05.05.92 Steve Boyle W RSC 7 Preston
(British & Commonwealth Lightweight Title Defence)

Career: 29 contests, won 26, drew 1, lost 2.

(Andrew) Drew Docherty

Croy. *Born* Glasgow, 29 November, 1965
Britistsh Bantamweight Champion (8.5¾-8.10) ht. 5'6"
Manager T. Gilmour

14.09.89 Gordon Shaw W PTS 6 Motherwell
23.11.89 Chris Clarkson W PTS 6 Motherwell
09.05.90 Rocy Lawlor DREW 8 Solihull
03.10.90 Steve Robinson W PTS 8 Solihull
21.11.90 Pete Buckley W PTS 8 Solihull
14.11.91 Stevie Woods W RSC 1 Edinburgh
27.01.92 Neil Parry W RSC 4 Glasgow
27.04.92 Pete Buckley W PTS 8 Glasgow
01.06.92 Joe Kelly W RSC 5 Glasgow
(British Bantamweight Title Challenge)

Career: 9 contests, won 8, drew 1.

Drew Docherty Sportapics Ltd

Chris Eubank

Brighton. *Born* Dulwich, 8 August, 1966
WBO S. Middleweight Champion. Former Undefeated WBO Middleweight Champion. Former Undefeated WBC International Middleweight Champion
(11.6-12.0) ht. 5'10"
Manager B. Hearn

03.10.85 Tim Brown W PTS 4 Atlantic City, USA
07.11.85 Kenny Cannida W PTS 4 Atlantic City, USA

Chris Eubank Les Clark

08.01.86 Mike Bragwell W PTS 4 Atlantic City, USA
25.02.86 Eric Holland W PTS 4 Atlantic City, USA
25.03.87 James Canty W PTS 4 Atlantic City, USA
15.02.88 Darren Parker W RSC 1 Copthorne
07.03.88 Winston Burnett W PTS 6 Hove
26.04.88 Michael Justin W RSC 5 Hove
04.05.88 Greg George W RSC 5 Wembley
18.05.88 Steve Aquilina W RSC 4 Portsmouth
31.01.89 Simon Collins W RSC 4 Bethnal Green
08.02.89 Anthony Logan W PTS 8 Kensington
01.03.89 Franki Moro W PTS 8 Bethnal Green
26.05.89 Randy Smith W PTS 10 Bethnal Green
28.06.89 Les Wisniewski W RSC 2 Brentwood
04.10.89 Ron Malek W RSC 5 Basildon
24.10.89 Jean-Noel Camara W RSC 2 Bethnal Green
05.11.89 Johnny Melfah W CO 4 Kensington
20.12.89 Jose da Silva W RTD 6 Kirkby
16.01.90 Denys Cronin W RSC 3 Cardiff
06.03.90 Hugo Corti W RSC 8 Bethnal Green
(WBC International Middleweight Title Challenge)
25.04.90 Eduardo Contreras W PTS 12 Brighton
(WBC International Middleweight Title Defence)
05.09.90 Kid Milo W RSC 8 Brighton
(WBC International Middleweight Title Defence)
22.09.90 Reginaldo Santos W CO 1 Kensington
18.11.90 Nigel Benn W RSC 9 Birmingham
(WBO Middleweight Title Challenge)
23.02.91 Dan Sherry W TD 10 Brighton
(WBO Middleweight Title Defence)
18.04.91 Gary Stretch W RSC 6 Earls Court
(WBO Middleweight Title Defence)
22.06.91 Michael Watson W PTS 12 Earls Court
(WBO Middleweight Title Defence)
21.09.91 Michael Watson W RSC 12 Tottenham
(Vacant WBO S. Middleweight Title)
01.02.92 Thulani Malinga W PTS 12 Birmingham
(WBO S. Middleweight Title Defence)
25.04.92 John Jarvis W CO 3 Manchester
(WBO S. Middleweight Title Defence)
27.06.92 Ronnie Essett W PTS 12 Quinta do Lago, Portugal
(WBO S. Middleweight Title Defence)

Career: 32 contests, won 32.

Herol Graham Derek Rowe (Photos) Ltd

Herol Graham

Sheffield. *Born* Nottingham, 13 September, 1959

British Middleweight Champion. Former European Middleweight Champion. Former Undefeated British, Commonwealth & European L. Middleweight Champion (11.5½-11.6) ht. 5'11"

Manager M. Duff

28.11.78 Vivian Waite W PTS 6 Sheffield
04.12.78 Curtis Marsh W RTD 1 Southend
22.01.79 Jimmy Roberts W RSC 2 Bradford
12.02.79 Dave Southwell W PTS 8 Reading
28.02.79 Dave Southwell W PTS 8 Burslem
27.03.79 George Walker W PTS 8 Southend
27.04.79 Mac Nicholson W PTS 8 Newcastle
16.05.79 Gordon George W PTS 8 Sheffield
26.09.79 Lloyd James W PTS 8 Sheffield
27.10.79 Billy Ahearne W RSC 3 Barnsley
27.11.79 Errol McKenzie W PTS 8 Sheffield
12.02.80 Glen McEwan W PTS 8 Sheffield
22.04.80 George Danahar W PTS 8 Sheffield
09.09.80 Joey Mack W PTS 8 Sheffield
30.10.80 Larry mayes W RSC 4 Liverpool
22.01.81 Lancelot Innes W PTS 10 Liverpool
24.03.81 Pat Thomas W PTS 15 Sheffield *(British L. Middleweight Title Challenge)*
17.06.81 Prince Rodney W RSC 1 Sheffield
25.11.81 Kenny Bristol W PTS 15 Sheffield *(Commonwealth L. Middleweight Title Challenge)*
24.02.82 Chris Christian W RSC 9 Sheffield *(British & Commonwealth L. Middleweight Title Defence)*
22.04.82 Fred Coranson W PTS 10 Liverpool
30.09.82 Hunter Clay W PTS 15 Lagos, Nigeria *(Commonwealth L. Middleweight Title Defence)*
15.03.83 Tony Nelson W RTD 5 Wembley
23.05.83 Clemente Tshinza W CO 2 Sheffield *(Vacant European L. Middleweight Title)*
11.10.83 Carlos Betancourt W CO 1 Kensington
09.12.83 Germain le Maitre W RSC 8 St Nazaire, France *(European L. Middleweight Title Defence)*
22.07.84 Lindell Holmes W RSC 5 Sheffield
25.09.84 Irwin Hines W CO 2 Wembley
16.10.84 Jose Seys W RSC 6 Kensington
26.11.84 Liam Coleman W RSC 3 Sheffield
06.03.85 Jose Rosemain W CO 5 Kensington
24.04.85 Jimmy Price W CO 1 Shoreditch *(Vacant British Middleweight Title)*
16.10.85 Roberto Ruiz W RSC 2 Kensington
03.12.85 Sanderline Williams W PTS 10 Belfast
05.02.86 Ayub Kalule W RSC 10 Sheffield *(European Middleweight Title Challenge)*
23.06.86 Ernie Rabotte W RSC 1 Las Vegas, USA
04.11.86 Mark Kaylor W RTD 8 Wembley *(European Middleweight Title Defence)*
17.01.87 Charlie Boston W RTD 7 Belfast
26.05.87 Sumbu Kalambay L PTS 12 Wembley *(European Middleweight Title Defence)*
05.12.87 Ricky Stackhouse W RSC 8 Doncaster
08.06.88 James Cook W RSC 5 Sheffield *(Vacant British Middleweight Title)*
23.11.88 Johnny Melfah W RSC 5 Bethnal Green *(British Middleweight Title Defence)*
10.05.89 Mike McCallum L PTS 12 Kensington *(Vacant WBA Middleweight Title)*
25.10.89 Rod Douglas W RSC 9 Wembley *(British Middleweight Title Defence)*
11.04.90 Ismael Negron W CO 3 Dewsbury
24.11.90 Julian Jackson L CO 4 Benalmadena, Spain *(Vacant WBC Middleweight Title)*
10.12.91 John Ashton W RSC 6 Sheffield *(British Middleweight Title Defence)*
12.03.92 Sumbu Kalambay L PTS 12 Pesaro, Italy *European Middleweight Title Challenge)*

Career: 48 contests, won 44, lost 4.

Paul Hodkinson

Paul Hodkinson

Liverpool. *Born* Liverpool, 14 September, 1965
WBC Featherweight Champion. Former Undefeated British & European Featherweight Champion (8-13¾) ht 5'4"
Manager B. Eastwood

19.07.86 Mark Champney W CO 2 Wembley
17.09.86 Phil Lashley W RSC 2 Kensington
29.09.86 Les Remikie W RTD 4 Mayfair
29.10.86 Craig Windsor W CO 2 Belfast
17.01.87 Steve Sammy Sims W CO 5 Belfast
26.02.87 Kamel Djadda W RSC 4 Bethnal Green
25.04.87 Russell Jones W RSC 6 Belfast
31.07.87 Tomas Arguelles DREW 8 Panama City, Panama
19.10.87 Tomas Arguelles W CO 6 Belfast
03.12.87 Marcus Smith W RSC 7 Belfast
27.01.88 Richie Foster W RSC 3 Belfast
18.05.88 Peter Harris W RSC 12 Aberavon
(British Featherweight Title Challenge)
14.12.88 Kevin Taylor W RSC 2 Kirkby
(British Featherweight Title Defence)
18.01.89 Johnny Carter W CO 1 Kensington
12.04.89 Raymond Armand W RSC 2 Belfast
(Vacant European Featherweight Title)
06.09.89 Peter Harris W RSC 9 Aberavon
(British & European Featherweight Title Defence)
13.12.89 Farid Benredjeb W RSC 8 Kirkby
(European Featherweight Title Defence)
28.03.90 Eduardo Montoya W RSC 3 Manchester
(Elim. IBF Featherweight Title)
02.06.90 Marcos Villasana L RSC 8 Manchester
(Vacant WBC Featherweight Title)
31.10.90 Guy Bellehigue W RSC 3 Wembley
(European Featherweight Title Defence)
13.11.91 Marcos Villasana W PTS 12 Belfast
(WBC Featherweight Title Challenge)
25.04.92 Steve Cruz W RSC 3 Belfast
(WBC Featherweight Title Defence)

Career: 22 contests, won 20, drew 1, lost 1.

Andy Holligan

Liverpool. *Born* Liverpool, 6 June, 1967
British & Commonwealth L. Welterweight Champion (9.13¼-11.3¼) ht. 5'5¼"
Manager M. Duff

19.10.87 Glyn Rhodes W PTS 6 Belfast
03.12.87 Jimmy Thornton W RTD 2 Belfast
27.01.88 Andrew Morgan W RSC 5 Belfast
26.03.88 Tony Richards W RSC 2 Belfast
08.06.88 David Maw W RSC 1 Sheffield
19.10.88 Lenny Gloster W PTS 8 Belfast
14.12.88 Sugar Gibiliru W PTS 8 Kirkby
16.03.89 Jeff Connors W RSC 5 Southwark

Andy Holligan

19.09.89 Billy Buchanan W RSC 5 Belfast
25.10.89 Tony Adams W RSC 3 Wembley
26.09.90 Mike Durvan W CO 1 Mayfair
31.10.90 Eric Carroyez W RTD 2 Wembley
17.04.91 Pat Ireland W RSC 2 Kensington

Gary Jacobs (left) on the attack against Mickey Hughes, before being knocked out in the eighth round of their 1990 battle
Les Clark

16.05.91 Simon Eubank W RSC 2 Liverpool
20.06.91 Tony Ekubia W PTS 12 Liverpool
(British & Commonwealth L. Welterweight Title Challenge)
28.11.91 Steve Larrimore W RSC 8 Liverpool
(Commonwealth L. Welterweight Title Defence)
27.02.92 Tony McKenzie W RSC 3 Liverpool
(British & Commonwealth L. Welterweight Title Defence)

Career: 17 contests, won 17.

Gary Jacobs

Glasgow. *Born* Glasgow, 10 December, 1965
British Welterweight Champion. Former WBC International & Commonwealth Welterweight Champion. Former Undefeated Scottish Welterweight Champion (10.6¼-10.9½) ht. 5'7½"
Manager M. Duff

20.05.85 John Conlan W PTS 6 Glasgow
03.06.85 Nigel Burke W PTS 6 Glasgow
12.08.85 Mike McKenzie W PTS 6 Glasgow
07.10.85 Albert Buchanan W PTS 6 Cumbuslang
11.11.85 Tyrell Wilson W CO 5 Glasgow
02.12.85 Dave Heaver W PTS 6 Glasgow
10.02.86 Courtney Phillips W RSC 5 Glasgow
10.03.86 Alistair Laurie W PTS 8 Glasgow
14.04.86 Billy Cairns W PTS 8 Glasgow
24.06.86 Dave Douglas L PTS 10 Glasgow
(Vacant Scottish Welterweight Title)
15.09.86 Jeff Connors W RSC 3 Glasgow
27.01.87 Dave Douglas W PTS 10 Glasgow
(Scottish Welterweight Title Challenge)
24.02.87 Gary Williams W CO 7 Glasgow
06.04.87 Robert Armstrong W RTD 5 Glasgow
19.05.87 Gary Williams W RSC 3 Cumbernauld
08.06.87 Tommy McCallum W RSC 5 Glasgow
(Scottish Welterweight Title Defence)
26.11.87 Jeff Connors W PTS 8 Fulham
24.02.88 Del Bryan W PTS 10 Glasgow
(Final Elim. British Welterweight Title)
19.04.88 Wilf Gentzen W PTS 12 Glasgow
(Commonwealth Welterweight Title Challenge)
06.06.88 Juan Alonzo Villa W RSC 5 Mayfair
16.09.88 Javier Suazo W CO 10 Las Vegas, USA
(Vacant WBC International Welterweight Title)
29.11.88 Richard Rova W CO 4 Kensington
(Commonwealth Welterweight Title Defence)
14.02.89 Rocky Kelly W RTD 7 Wandsworth
(Commonwealth & WBC International Welterweight Title Defence)
05.04.89 George Collins W PTS 12 Kensington
(Commonwealth & WBC International Welterweight Title Defence)
27.06.89 Rollin Williams W RSC 1 Kensington
27.08.89 James McGirt L PTS 10 New York, USA
23.11.89 Donovan Boucher L PTS 12 Motherwell
(Commonwealth Welterweight Title Defence)
26.04.90 Pascal Lorcy W RSC 2 Wandsworth
09.05.90 Mike Durvan W CO 1 Kensington
17.10.90 Mickey Hughes L CO 8 Bethnal Green
05.03.91 Kenny Louis W CO 2 Glasgow
20.11.91 Peter Eubank W PTS 8 Kensington
20.02.92 Del Bryan W PTS 12 Glasgow
(British Welterweight Title Challenge)
25.03.92 Tommy Small W RSC 2 Kensington
22.04.92 Cirillo Nino W PTS 10 Wembley

Career: 36 contests, won 32, lost 4.

Lennox Lewis

Crayford. *Born* London, 2 September, 1965
British, Commonwealth & European Heavyweight Champion (16.0-16.7) ht. 6'4¾"
Manager F. Maloney

27.06.89 Al Malcolm W CO 2 Kensington
21.07.89 Bruce Johnson W RSC 2 Atlantic City, USA
25.09.89 Andrew Gerrard W RSC 4 Crystal Palace
10.10.89 Steve Garber W CO 1 Hull
05.11.89 Melvin Epps W DIS 2 Kensington
18.12.89 Greg Gorrell W RSC 5 Kitchener, Canada
31.01.90 Noel Quarless W RSC 2 Bethnal Green
22.03.90 Calvin Jones W CO 1 Gateshead
14.04.90 Mike Simwelu W CO 1 Kensington
09.05.90 Jorge Dascola W CO 1 Kensington
20.05.90 Dan Murphy W RSC 6 Sheffield
27.06.90 Ossie Ocasio W PTS 8 Kensington
11.07.90 Mike Acey W RSC 2 Mississuaga, Canada
31.10.90 Jean Chanet W RSC 6 Crystal Palace
(European Heavyweight Title Challenge)
06.03.91 Gary Mason W RSC 7 Wembley
(British Heavyweight Title Challenge. European Heavyweight Title Defence)
12.07.91 Mike Weaver W CO 6 Lake Tahoe, USA
30.09.91 Glenn McCrory W CO 2 Kensington
(British & European Heavyweight Title Defence)
23.11.91 Tyrell Biggs W RSC 3 Atlanta, USA

Lennox Lewis Les Clark

01.02.92 Levi Billups W PTS 10 Las Vegas, USA
30.04.92 Derek Williams W RSC 3 Kensington
(British & European Heavyweight Title Defence. Commonwealth Heavyweight Title Challenge)

Career: 20 contests, won 20.

Colin McMillan

Barking. *Born* London, 12 February, 1966
WBO Featherweight Champion. Former Undefeated British & Commonwealth Featherweight Champion (8.12-9.3) ht. 5'5¼"
Manager —

Colin McMillan (left) outclassed and stopped Herbie Bivalacqua in three rounds at the begining of the 1991-92 season Les Clark

29.11.88 Mike Chapman W PTS 6 Battersea
10.12.88 Aldrich Johnson W PTS 6 Crystal Palace
31.01.89 Alan McKay L RSC 3 Bethnal Green
12.06.89 Miguel Matthews W RSC 3 Battersea
19.09.89 Graham O'Malley W PTS 8 Millwall
11.10.89 Marcel Herbert W PTS 6 Millwall
30.11.89 Sylvester Osuji W RSC 4 Barking
14.02.90 Vidal Tellez W RSC 2 Millwall
17.04.90 Jesus Muniz W PTS 8 Millwall
03.05.90 Steve Walker W PTS 6 Kensington
05.07.90 Tyrone Miller W CO 2 Greensville, USA
17.07.90 Malcolm Rougeaux W CO 1 Lake Charles, USA
25.09.90 Darren Weller W RSC 2 Millwall
10.10.90 Graham O'Malley W PTS 6 Millwall
12.11.90 Mark Holt W PTS 8 Norwich
05.03.91 Russell Davison W PTS 6 Millwall
26.04.91 Willie Richardson W PTS 8 Crystal Palace
22.05.91 Gary de Roux W RSC 7 Millwall
(British Featherweight Title Challenge)
03.07.91 Herbie Bivalacqua W RSC 3 Reading
04.09.91 Kevin Pritchard W RSC 7 Bethnal Green
(British Featherweight Title Defence)
29.10.91 Sean Murphy W PTS 12 Kensington
(British Featherweight Title Defence)
18.01.92 Percy Commey W PTS 12 Kensington
(Vacant Commonwealth Featherweight Title)
25.03.92 Tommy Valdez W CO 6 Dagenham
16.05.92 Maurizio Stecca W PTS 12 Muswell Hill
(WBO Featherweight Title Challenge)

Career: 24 contests, won 23, lost 1.

Chris Pyatt

Leicester. *Born* Islington, 3 July, 1963
Commonwealth L. Middleweight Champion. Former European L. Middleweight Champion. Former Undefeated British L. Middleweight Champion (10.12½-11.6) ht. 5'8½"
Manager —

01.03.83 Paul Murray W RTD 2 Kensington
05.04.83 Billy Waith W RSC 8 Kensington
28.04.83 Lee Hartshorn W RSC 3 Leicester
27.09.83 Darwin Brewster W PTS 8 Wembley
08.10.83 Tyrone Demby W RSC 2 Atlantic City, USA
22.11.83 Tony Britton W RSC 4 Wembley
22.02.84 Judas Clottey W PTS 8 Kensington
15.03.84 Pat Thomas W PTS 10 Leicester
09.05.84 Franki Moro W CO 4 Leicester
23.05.84 Alfonso Redondo W RSC 3 Mayfair
16.10.84 John Ridgman W RSC 1 Kensington
16.11.84 Brian Anderson W PTS 12 Leicester
(Final Elim. British L. Middleweight Title)
12.02.85 Helier Custos W RSC 5 Kensington

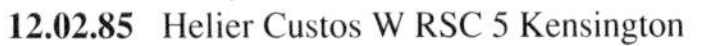

Chris Pyatt Les Clark

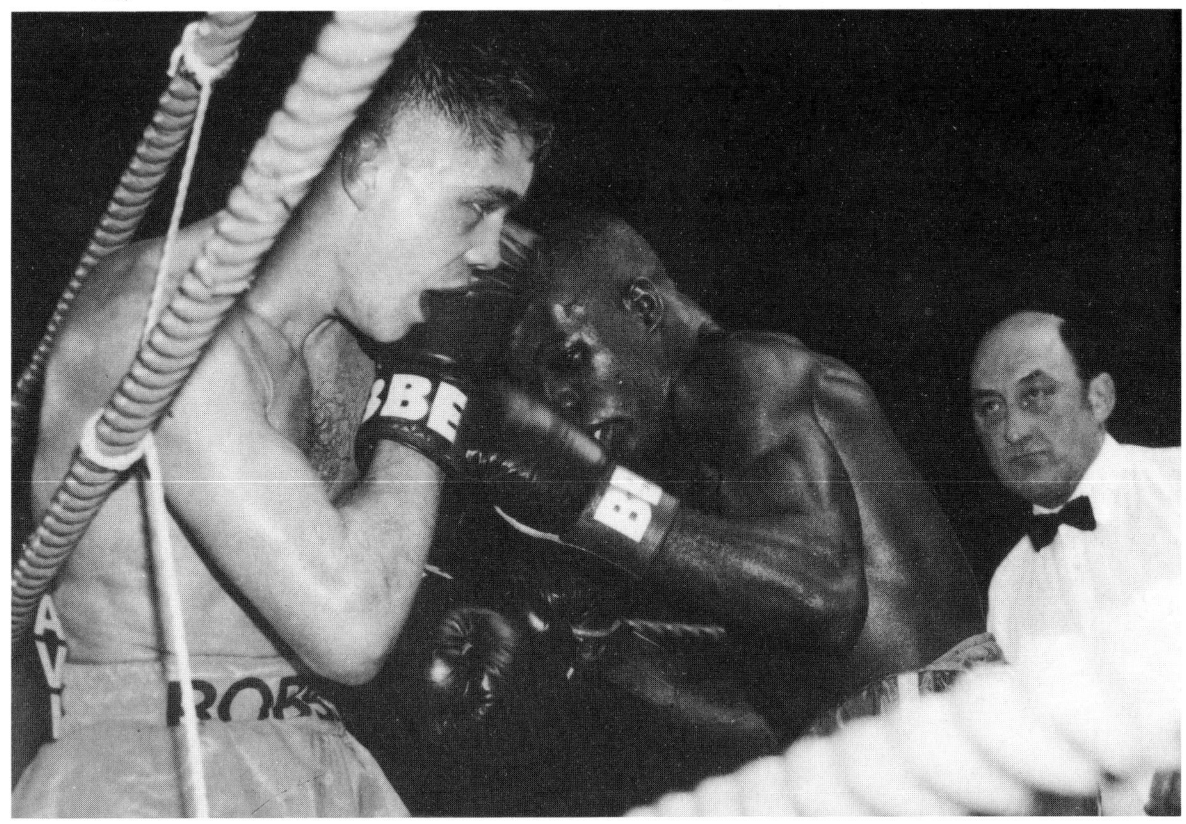

Robbie Regan (left) seen when winning the British flyweight title back from old adversary, Francis Ampofo Les Clark

Wally Swift, bruised, but not unbowed, at the end of his great win against Tony Collins Les Clark

Carl Thompson Chris Bevan

05.06.85 Graeme Ahmed W RSC 3 Kensington
01.07.85 Mosimo Maeleke W RSC 6 Mayfair
23.09.85 Sabiyala Diavilia L RSC 4 Mayfair
19.02.86 Prince Rodney W CO 9 Kensington *((British L. Middleweight Title Challenge)*
20.05.86 Thomas Smith W RSC 1 Wembley
17.09.86 John van Elteren W RSC 1 Kensington *(Vacant European L. Middleweight Title)*
25.10.86 Renaldo Hernandez W RSC 3 Paris, France
28.04.87 Gianfranco Rosi L PTS 12 Perugia, Italy *(European L. Middleweight Title Defence)*
18.04.87 Dennis Johnson W CO 2 Kensington
26.05.87 Sammy Floyd W RSC 2 Wembley
28.10.87 Gilbert Josamu W PTS 8 Wembley
28.05.88 Jose Duarte W RSC 4 Kensington
23.11.88 Eddie Hall W RSC 2 Bethnal Green
01.12.88 Knox Brown W RSC 2 Edmonton
14.12.88 Tyrone Moore W CO 1 Bethnal Green
15.02.89 Russell Mitchell W RSC 4 Bethnal Green
17.05.89 Daniel Dominguez W RSC 10 Millwall
11.10.89 Wayne Harris W RSC 3 Millwall
25.04.90 Daniel Sclarandi W RSC 2 Millwall
23.10.90 John David Jackson L PTS 12 Leicester *(WBO L. Middleweight Title Challenge)*
05.11.91 Craig Trotter W PTS 12 Leicester *(Vacant Commonwealth L. Middleweight Title)*
01.02.92 Ambrose Mlilo W RSC 3 Birmingham *(Commonwealth L. Middleweight Title Defence)*
31.03.92 Melvyn Wynn W CO 3 Norwich
28.04.92 James Tapisha W RSC 1 Wolverhampton *(Commonwealth L. Middleweight Title Defence)*
23.05.92 Ian Strudwick W PTS 10 Birmingham

Career: 38 contests, won 35, lost 3.

Robbie Regan

Cefn Forest. *Born* Caerphilly, 30 August, 1968
British Flyweight Champion. Former Undefeated Welsh Flyweight Champion (7.13-8.0¾) ht. 5'4"
Manager D. Gardiner

19.08.89 Eric George DREW 6 Cardiff
06.03.90 Francis Ampofo W PTS 6 Bethnal Green
26.04.90 Kevin Downer W RSC 4 Merthyr
20.06.90 Dave McNally DREW 6 Basildon
19.11.90 Ricky Beard W RSC 6 Cardiff
21.12.90 Michele Poddighe DREW 6 Sassari, Italy
12.02.91 Kevin Jenkins W PTS 10 Cardiff *(Vacant Welsh Flyweight Title)*
28.05.91 Joe Kelly W PTS 12 Cardiff *(Vacant British Flyweight Title)*
03.09.91 Francis Ampofo L RSC 11 Cardiff *(British Flyweight Title Defence)*
17.12.91 Francis Ampofo W PTS 12 Cardiff *(British Flyweight Title Challenge)*
11.02.92 Juan Bautista W CO 1 Cardiff
19.05.92 James Drummond W RSC 9 Cardiff *(British Flyweight Title Defence)*

Career: 12 contests, won 9, drew 3.

Wally Swift Jnr

Birmingham. *Born* Nottingham, 17 February, 1966
British L. Middleweight Champion. Former Undefeated Midlands Area L. Middleweight Champion (10.10-11.1) ht. 5'7"
Manager W. Swift

25.09.85 John Conlan W RTD 3 Stoke
11.11.85 Steve Craggs W RTD 4 Birmingham
09.12.85 Steve Tempro W RSC 4 Birmingham
22.01.86 Teddy Anderson W RSC 6 Solihull
03.02.86 Frankie Lake W PTS 8 Birmingham
24.03.86 Paul Cook W PTS 8 Mayfair
02.06.86 Gerry Beard W PTS 8 Mayfair
08.09.86 Steve Ellwood W PTS 8 Dulwich
13.10.86 Dean Barclay DREW 8 Dulwich
19.11.86 Franki Moro W PTS 8 Solihull
03.12.86 Ian Chantler W PTS 8 Stoke
22.01.87 Dave Dent L PTS 8 Bethnal Green
10.02.87 Granville Allen W RSC 4 Wolverhampton
24.02.87 Dave McCabe L PTS 8 Glasgow
30.03.87 John Ashton W PTS 8 Birmingham
20.10.87 John Ashton L PTS 8 Stoke
20.01.88 Tommy McCallum W PTS 8 Solihull
28.03.88 Ossie Maddix L PTS 8 Stoke
04.05.88 Chris Blake W PTS 8 Solihull
28.09.88 Terry Magee L PTS 8 Solihull

25.01.89 Kevin Hayde W PTS 8 Solihull
01.03.89 Andy Till L PTS 8 Bethnal Green
13.03.89 Tony Britton W PTS 8 Mayfair
08.04.89 Alfonso Redondo W PTS 8 Madrid, Spain
19.08.89 Suzuki Miranda W PTS 6 Benidorm, Spain
26.09.89 Ensley Bingham L PTS 10 Oldham *(Elim. British L. Middleweight Title)*
26.04.90 Shaun Cummins W PTS 10 Merthyr *(Vacant Midlands Area L. Middleweight Title & Elim. British L. Middleweight Title)*
18.09.90 Mark Holden W RSC 3 Stoke
21.11.90 Alan Richards W PTS 8 Solihull
23.01.91 Paul Wesley W PTS 10 Solihull *(Midlands Area L. Middleweight Title Defence)*
19.03.91 Ensley Bingham W RSC 4 Birmingham *(Vacant British L. Middlweight Title)*
03.07.91 Tony Collins W PTS 12 Reading *(British L. Middleweight Title Defence)*
08.01.92 Randy Williams W PTS 10 Burton
18.04.92 Jean-Claude Fontana L PTS 12 Hyeres, France *(European L. Middleweight Title Challenge)*

Career: 34 contests, won 25, drew 1, lost 8.

(Adrian) Carl Thompson

Manchester. *Born* Manchester, 26 May, 1964
British Cruiserweight Champion (13.0¾-13.7) ht. 6'0"
Manager N. Basso

06.06.88 Darren McKenna W RSC 2 Manchester
11.10.88 Paul Sheldon W PTS 6 Wolverhampton
13.02.89 Steve Osborne W PTS 6 Manchester
07.03.89 Sean O'Phoenix W RSC 4 Manchester
04.04.89 Keith Halliwell W RSC 1 Manchester
04.05.89 Tenko Ernie W CO 4 Mayfair
12.06.89 Steve Osborne W PTS 8 Manchester
11.07.89 Peter Brown W RSC 5 Batley
31.10.89 Crawford Ashley L RSC 6 Manchester *(Vacant Central Area L. Heavyweight Title)*
21.04.90 Francis Wanyama L PTS 6 St Amandsberg, Belgium
07.03.91 Terry Dixon W PTS 8 Basildon
01.04.91 Yawe Davis L RSC 2 Monaco, Monte Carlo
04.09.91 Nicky Piper W RSC 3 Bethnal Green
04.06.92 Steve Lewsam W RSC 8 Cleethorpes *(Vacant British Cruiserweight Title)*

Career: 14 contests, won 11, lost 3.

Henry Wharton

York. *Born* Leeds, 23 November, 1967
Commonwealth S. Middleweight Champion (11.13¾-12.4) ht. 5'10½"
Manager M. Duff

21.09.89 Dean Murray W RSC 1 Harrogate
25.10.89 Mike Aubrey W PTS 6 Wembley
05.12.89 Ron Malek W RSC 1 Dewsbury
11.01.90 Guillermo Chavez W CO 1 Dewsbury
03.03.90 Joe Potts W CO 4 Wembley
11.04.90 Juan Elizondo W RSC 3 Dewsbury
18.10.90 Chuck Edwards W RSC 1 Dewsbury
31.10.90 Dino Stewart W PTS 8 Wembley

Henry Wharton Les Clark

21.03.91 Francisco Lara W CO 1 Dewsbury
09.05.91 Frankie Minton W CO 7 Leeds
27.06.91 Rod Carr W PTS 12 Leeds *(Vacant Commonwealth S. Middleweight Title)*
30.10.91 Lou Gent DREW 12 Leeds *(Commonwealth S. Middleweight Title Defence)*
23.10.92 Nicky Walker W PTS 10 York
19.03.92 Kenny Schaefer W CO 1 York
08.04.92 Rod Carr W RSC 8 Leeds *(Commonwealth S. Middleweight Title Defence)*

Career: 15 contests, won 14, drew 1.

Richie Woodhall Les Clark

Richie Woodhall

Telford. *Born* Birmingham, 17 April, 1968
Commonwealth Middleweight Champion (11.1-11.4½) ht. 6'2"
Manager M. Duff

18.10.90 Kevin Hayde W RSC 3 Birmingham
30.11.90 Robbie Harron W RSC 2 Birmingham
16.01.91 Chris Haydon W RSC 3 Kensington
21.02.91 Shamus Casey W RSC 3 Walsall
30.05.91 Marty Duke W RSC 4 Birmingham
29.08.91 Nigel Moore W RSC 1 Oakengates
31.10.91 Colin Pitters W PTS 8 Oakengates
04.02.92 Graham Burton W RSC 2 Alfreton
26.03.92 Vito Gaudiosi W CO 1 Telford *(Vacant Commonwealth Middleweight Title)*

Career: 9 contests, won 9.

Active British-Based Boxers: Record Section

Shows the record since 1 January 1991 and a career summary for all British-based boxers, excluding current champions, who have been active between 1 July 1991 to 30 June 1992. Names in brackets are real names, where they differ from ring names. The first place name given is the boxer's domicile and his minimum/maximum weights for the 1991-92 season are shown in brackets alongside the weight division.

Ojay Abrahams

Watford. *Born* Lambeth, 17 December, 1964
Welterweight (10.7-10.10¼) ht. 5'8½"
Manager B. Hearn
Pro. Debut 21 September, 1991

21.09.91 Gordon Webster W RSC 3 Tottenham
26.10.91 Mick Reid W RSC 5 Brentwood
26.11.91 John Corcoran W PTS 6 Bethnal Green
21.01.92 Dave Andrews DREW 6 Norwich
31.03.92 Marty Duke W RSC 2 Norwich
19.05.92 Michael Smyth L PTS 6 Cardiff
16.06.92 Ricky Mabbett W PTS 6 Dagenham

Career: 7 contests, won 5, drew 1, lost 1.

Ojay Abrahams Les Clark

Dennis Adams

Billericay. *Born* Walthamstow, 18 March, 1967
S. Featherweight (9.2-9.4) ht. 5'8½"
Manager –
Pro. Debut 6 February, 1991

06.02.91 Neil Smith W PTS 6 Bethnal Green
26.03.91 Barrie Kelley L PTS 6 Bethnal Green
11.12.91 Tony Falcone L RTD 4 Basildon

Career: 3 contests, won 1, lost 2.

Kevin Adamson

Walthamstow. *Born* Hackney, 19 February, 1968
L. Middleweight (11.0-11.2) ht. 6'0½"
Manager B. Lynch
Pro. Debut 17 July, 1989

12.11.91 Danny Shinkwin W RSC 4 Milton Keynes
30.04.92 Wayne Appleton W RSC 2 Bayswater

Career: 4 contests, won 3, lost 1.

Dennis Afflick

Sheffield. *Born* Jamaica, 1 October, 1960
L. Heavyweight (12.6½-13.4½) ht. 5'10½"
Manager B. Ingle
Pro. Debut 6 February, 1991

06.02.91 Kevin Morton L PTS 6 Liverpool
25.04.91 Joey Peters L PTS 6 Basildon
03.06.91 Art Stacey L PTS 6 Glasgow
09.10.91 John Oxenham L DIS 4 Merton
17.10.91 Keith Inglis L RSC 4 Southwark

Career: 5 contests, lost 5.

Henry Akinwande

Lewisham. *Born* London, 12 October, 1965
Heavyweight (15.10-16.0) ht. 6'7"
Manager M. Duff
Pro. Debut 4 October, 1989

06.03.91 J. B. Williamson W RSC 2 Wembley
06.06.91 Ramon Voorn W PTS 8 Barking
28.06.91 Marshall Tillman W PTS 8 Nice, France
09.10.91 Gypsy John Fury W CO 3 Manchester *(Elim. British Heavyweight Title)*
06.12.91 Tim Bullock W CO 3 Dusseldorf, Germany
28.02.92 Young Joe Louis W RSC 3 Issy les Moulineaux, France
26.03.92 Tucker Richards W RSC 2 Telford
10.04.92 Lumbala Tshimba W PTS 8 Carquefou, France
05.06.92 Kimmuel Odum W DIS 6 Marseille, France

Career: 17 contests, won 17.

Korso Aleain (Boualem)

Leyton. *Born* Algeria, 18 October, 1962
L. Welterweight (9.13¾-10.3) ht. 5'5"
Manager I.Akay
Pro. Debut 5 March, 1992

05.03.92 Everald Williams L CO 6 Battersea
30.04.92 Erwin Edwards W PTS 6 Bayswater
17.05.92 Brian Coleman W RSC 5 Harringay

Career: 3 contests, won 2, lost 1.

Dean Allen

Swansea. *Born* Swansea, 3 August, 1967
L. Heavyweight (12.5-13.1) ht. 6'0"
Manager M. Copp
Pro. Debut 24 January, 1991

24.01.91 Max McCracken L PTS 6 Brierley Hill
24.04.91 Paul Hanlon W PTS 6 Aberavon
13.11.91 Terry Johnson W RSC 2 Liverpool

Career: 3 contests, won 2, lost 1.

Mark Allen (Hodgson)

Denaby. *Born* Mexborough, 11 January, 1970
L. Welterweight (10.2-10.2½) ht. 5'11"
Manager J. Rushton
Pro. Debut 24 March, 1992

24 03.92 Jamie Morris L PTS 6 Wolverhampton
04.06.92 Blue Butterworth L RSC 5 Burnley

Career: 2 contests, lost 2.

Trevor Ambrose

Leicester. *Born* Leicester, 8 September, 1963
Welterweight (10.7-10.10) ht. 5'11"
Manager W. Swift
Pro. Debut 19 February, 1990

14.02.91 Adrian Riley W CO 6 Southampton
28.03.91 Richard O'Brien W RSC 1 Alfreton
25.04.91 Gary Logan L PTS 8 Mayfair
03.07.91 Darren Dyer L PTS 6 Brentwood
24.09.91 Willie Beattie L PTS 8 Glasgow
11.03.92 John Davies L RSC 5 Cardiff
19.05.92 Paul Jones L PTS 6 Cardiff

Career: 15 contests, won 8, lost 7.

Derek Amory

Birmingham. *Born* Birmingham, 12 January, 1966
S. Featherweight (9.1½-9.8) ht. 5'5"
Manager –
Pro. Debut 25 September, 1986

29.01.91 Carl Roberts W PTS 4 Stockport
18.03.91 Joe Donohoe L PTS 8 Piccadilly
17.06.91 Kelton McKenzie L RSC 6 Edgbaston
07.10.91 Ervine Blake L PTS 6 Birmingham
22.01.92 J. T. Williams L PTS 6 Cardiff
11.02.92 Jimmy Clark L PTS 6 Barking
09.05.92 Luis Ramon Rolon L CO 7 Madrid, Spain

Career: 35 contests, won 14, drew 2, lost 19.

Francis Ampofo

Bethnal Green. *Born* Ghana, 5 June, 1967
Former British Flyweight Champion (7.13¼-8.3¾) ht. 5'1½"
Manager B. Hearn
Pro. Debut 31 January, 1990

26.03.91 Ricky Beard W PTS 8 Bethnal Green
22.06.91 Neil Johnston W RSC 2 Earls Court
03.09.91 Robbie Regan W RSC 11 Cardiff *(British Flyweight Title Challenge)*
17.12.91 Robbie Regan L PTS 12 Cardiff *(British Flyweight Title Defence)*
25.02.92 Ricky Beard W PTS 8 Crystal Palace
16.06.92 Shaun Norman W RSC 4 Dagenham

Career: 10 contests, won 8, lost 2.

Dave Anderson

Bellahouston. *Born* Glasgow, 23 December, 1966
Lightweight (9.5-9.12¾) ht. 5'8"
Manager A. Morrison
Pro. Debut 25 September, 1990

11.02.91 Steve Pollard W PTS 6 Glasgow
15.04.91 Tony Foster W PTS 8 Glasgow
24.09.91 Ian Honeywood W PTS 8 Glasgow
28.11.91 Pete Roberts W RSC 3 Glasgow

Career: 7 contests, won 7.

Shaun Anderson

Maybole. *Born* Girvan, 20 September, 1969
Bantamweight (8.7) ht. 5'5"
Manager A. Melrose
Pro. Debut 29 May, 1992

29.05.92 Tucker Thomas W RSC 1 Glasgow

Career: 1 contest, won 1.

(Alfie) Bullit Andrews

Birmingham. *Born* Birmingham, 29 April, 1964
L. Middleweight (10.9-11.2) ht. 5'10"
Manager –
Pro. Debut 11 October, 1988

15.04.91 Scott Newman L RSC 1 Wolverhampton
30.05.91 Darren Morris L RSC 3 Birmingham
21.05.92 Warren Stephens W PTS 6 Cradley Heath

Career: 13 contests, won 2, lost 11.

Dave Andrews

Trelewis. *Born* Merthyr, 27 July, 1968
Welterweight (10.10-10.11) ht. 5'10"
Manager D. Gardiner
Pro. Debut 12 September, 1988

05.03.91 Brian Cullen W RSC 1 Cardiff
12.04.91 Robert McCracken L RSC 4 Willenhall
19.11.91 Paul Dyer L PTS 6 Norwich
17.12.91 Mark Atkins W RSC 3 Cardiff
21.01.92 Ojay Abrahams DREW 6 Norwich
09.02.92 Paul Burke L PTS 6 Bradford
03.03.92 Howard Clarke L RSC 3 Cradley Heath

Career: 16 contests, won 6, drew 1, lost 9.

Dennis Andries

Hackney. *Born* Guyana, 5 November, 1953
Cruiserweight. Former WBC L. Heavyweight Champion. Former Undefeated WBC Continental L. Heavyweight Champion.Former Undefeated British & Southern Area L. Heavyweight Champion (12.6¾-13.9) ht. 5'11"
Manager M. Steward
Pro. Debut 16 May, 1978

19.01.91 Guy Waters W PTS 12 Adelaide, Australia *(WBC L. Heavyweight Title Defence)*
11.09.91 Jeff Harding L PTS 12 Hammersmith *(WBC L. Heavyweight Title Defence)*
15.11.91 Ed Neblett W RSC 4 Tampa, USA
11.12.91 Paul Madison W RTD 8 Duluth, USA
27.02.92 Akim Tafer L PTS 12 Beausoleil, France *(Vacant European Cruiserweight Title)*

Career: 53 contests, won 41, drew 2, lost 10.

Mark Antony (Brooks)

Doncaster. *Born* Worksop, 24 January, 1968
L. Welterweight (9.13-10.3) ht. 5'8"
Manager J. Rushton
Pro. Debut 16 November, 1987

05.03.91 Jim Moffat L PTS 6 Glasgow
12.03.91 Wayne Windle L CO 1 Mansfield
12.11.91 Shaun Cooper L CO 1 Wolverhampton
20.01.92 Jamie Morris W RSC 5 Coventry
11.02.92 Billy Robinson L RSC 5 Wolverhampton
11.03.92 Simon Hamblett W CO 1 Stoke
11.05.92 Pat Delargy L PTS 6 Coventry
04.06.92 Darren Powell W CO 2 Burnley

Career: 30 contests, won 11, lost 19.

Wayne Appleton

Pontefract. *Born* Hemsworth, 9 November, 1967
L. Middleweight (10.12½-11.3) ht. 5'10"
Manager T. Callighan
Pro. Debut 13 November, 1990

15.03.91 Andre Wharton L RSC 7 Willenhall
14.11.91 Dave Hindmarsh W RSC 8 Edinburgh
30.04.92 Kevin Adamson L RSC 2 Bayswater

Career: 6 contests, won 4, lost 2.

Lee Archer

Dudley. *Born* West Bromwich, 3 January, 1971
L. Heavyweight (12.5-12.8½) ht. 6'2"
Manager C. Flute
Pro. Debut 12 November, 1991

12.11.91 Paul Murray W PTS 6 Wolverhampton
24.03.92 Darryl Ritchie W PTS 6 Wolverhampton
28.04.92 Carl Smallwood L PTS 6 Wolverhampton
18.05.92 Marc Rowley W PTS 6 Bardon

Career: 4 contests, won 3, lost 1.

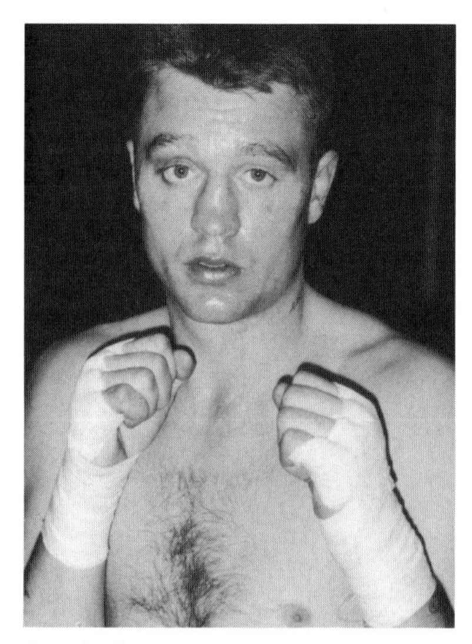

Lee Archer Les Clark

(Kevin) Henry Armstong (Morris)

Manchester. *Born* Manchester, 10 December, 1967
Featherweight (9.0-9.2) ht. 5'6"
Manager –
Pro. Debut 9 December, 1987

12.04.91 Ray Newby W PTS 8 Manchester
31.01.92 Steve Robinson W PTS 6 Manchester
02.03.92 Jyrki Vierela DREW 6 Helsinki, Finland

Career: 21 contests, won 15, drew 1, lost 5.

Neil Armstrong

Paisley. *Born* Glasgow, 19 June, 1970
Flyweight (8.1-8.2) ht. 5'5"
Manager A. Melrose
Pro. Debut 31 January, 1992

31.01.92 Mark Robertson W RSC 6 Glasgow
04.03.92 Des Gargano W PTS 6 Glasgow
12.03.92 Louis Veitch W PTS 6 Glasgow
10.04.92 Shaun Norman DREW 8 Glasgow

Career: 4 contests, won 3, drew 1.

Graham Arnold

Bury St. Edmunds. *Born* Fulford, 29 June, 1968

Heavyweight (14.7-14.12) ht. 6'3"
Manager G. Holmes
Pro. Debut 24 September, 1991

24.09.91 John Palmer W CO 2 Basildon
26.10.91 Gary Charlton L RSC 1 Brentwood
21.01.92 Steve Yorath L PTS 6 Norwich
31.03.92 Steve Yorath W PTS 6 Norwich

Career: 4 contests, won 2, lost 2.

John Ashton

Alfreton. *Born* Somercotes, 22 June, 1961
Former Undefeated Midlands Area Middleweight Champion. Former Undefeated Midlands Area L. Middleweight Champion (11.4¾-11.12) ht. 6'0¾"
Manager M. Shinfield
Pro. Debut 13 March, 1986

17.01.91 Graham Burton W PTS 10 Alfreton
28.03.91 Tony Burke W PTS 10 Alfreton *(Elim. British Middleweight Title)*
24.08.91 Sumbu Kalambay L RTD 6 Pesaro, Italy *(Vacant European Middleweight Title)*
10.12.91 Herol Graham L RSC 6 Sheffield *(British Middleweight Title Challenge)*
26.03.92 Marvin O'Brien W PTS 8 Telford

Career: 21 contests, won 12, drew 1, lost 8.

Abel Asinamali

Tooting. *Born* USA, 20 March, 1964
L. Heavyweight (12.1) ht. 5'10½"
Manager F. Maloney
Pro. Debut 8 January, 1990

23.04.92 Jason McNeil W CO 3 Eltham

Career: 8 contests, won 4, drew 2, lost 2.

Chris Aston

Leeds. *Born* Huddersfield, 7 August, 1961
L. Welterweight (9.12-10.4) ht. 5'7"
Manager K. Tate
Pro. Debut 7 October, 1991

Chris Aston Chris Bevan

07.10.91 Mick Holmes W RSC 2 Bradford
28.10.91 Charles Shepherd L PTS 6 Leicester
21.11.91 Dean Hiscox W PTS 6 Stafford
09.12.91 David Thompson W PTS 6 Bradford
21.01.92 Rob Stewart L RSC 4 Stockport
28.02.92 Mark Legg L RSC 5 Irvine
29.04.92 Richard Swallow L RSC 3 Solihull

Career: 7 contests, won 3, lost 4.

Mark Atkins

Cardiff. *Born* Cardiff, 3 January, 1964
L. Middleweight (11.0) ht. 5'5"
Manager –
Pro. Debut 28 September, 1989

17.12.91 Dave Andrews L RSC 3 Cardiff

Career: 2 contests, lost 2.

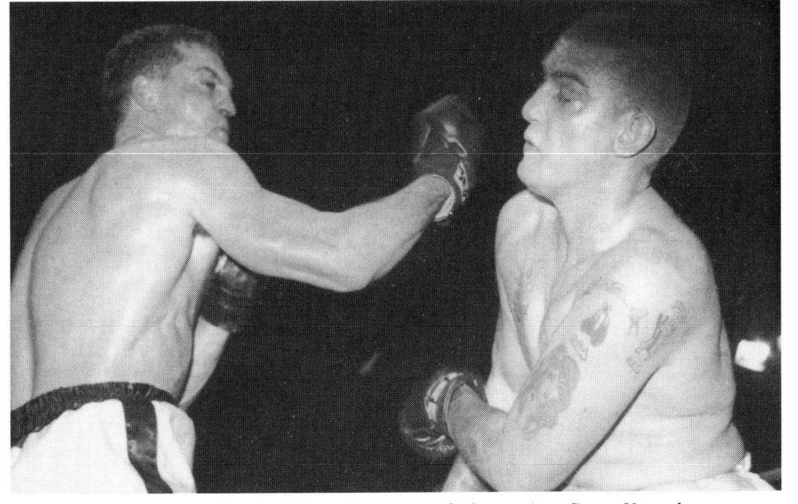

Graham Arnold (left) seen winning his return fight against Steve Yorath Les Clark

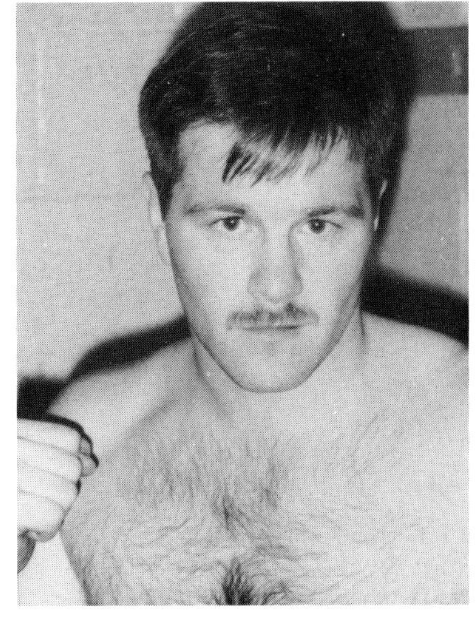

Mark Atkins Les Clark

Richard Atkinson

Dewsbury. *Born* Dewsbury, 25 February, 1973
L. Heavyweight (12.8) ht. 6'1"
Manager K. Tate
Pro. Debut 27 April, 1992

27.04.92 Greg Scott-Briggs W PTS 6 Bradford

Career: 1 contest, won 1.

Michael Ayers

Tooting. *Born* London, 26 January, 1965
Southern Area Lightweight Champion (9.7½-9.11) ht. 5'8"
Manager B. Hearn
Pro. Debut 16 May, 1989

04.06.91 Stuart Rimmer W CO 1 Bethnal Green
22.06.91 Wayne Weekes W RSC 6 Earls Court *(Vacant Southern Area Lightweight Title)*
21.09.91 Peter Till W RSC 5 Tottenham *(Elim. British Lightweight Title)*
28.01.92 Jorge Pompey W PTS 8 Hamburg, Germany
19.02.92 Rudy Valentino W RSC 7 Muswell Hill *(Southern Area Lightweight Title Defence. Elim. British Lightweight Title)*
27.06.92 Sugar Gibiliru W RSC 6 Quinta do Lago, Portugal

Career: 11 contests, won 11.

Mossa Azward

Hackney. *Born* Kings Cross, 11 August, 1962
Welterweight (11.4½) ht. 5'10½"
Manager H. Holland
Pro. Debut 17 May, 1992

17.05.92 Adrian Haughton L DIS 1 Harringay

Career: 1 contest, lost 1.

Tony Banks

Leeds. *Born* Leeds, 20 June, 1967
L. Welterweight (10.1) ht. 5'8"
Manager –
Pro. Debut 13 November, 1986

24.02.92 Rob Stewart DREW 6 Bradford

Career: 12 contests, won 5, drew 3, lost 4.

Nicky Bardle

Ealing. *Born* Ware, 30 January, 1972
Welterweight (9.11-10.6) ht. 5'9½"
Manager H. Holland
Pro. Debut 7 November, 1991

07.11.91 Michael Clynch W RSC 4 Peterborough
12.02.92 Steve Hearn W RSC 1 Watford
30.04.92 James Campbell L CO 1 Watford

Career: 3 contests, won 2, lost 1.

Nicky Bardle Les Clark

Jason Barker

Sheffield. *Born* Sheffield, 1 June, 1973
L. Welterweight (9.11-10.1) ht. 6'0"
Manager B. Ingle
Pro. Debut 30 January, 1992

30.01.92 Nicky Lucas W PTS 6 Southampton
12.02.92 Roger Hunte L RTD 4 Wembley
29.04.92 Dave Lovell L PTS 6 Stoke
03.06.92 John O'Johnson L PTS 6 Newcastle under Lyme

Career: 4 contests, won 1, lost 3.

Newton Barnett

Camberwell. *Born* Jamaica, 19 October, 1959
L. Middleweight (10.13-11.2½) ht. 6'0"
Manager –
Pro. Debut 3 October, 1983

Pat Barrett

06.02.91 Damien Denny L PTS 8 Bethnal Green
13.02.91 Derek Grainger L RSC 3 Wembley
13.07.91 Genaro Leon L CO 2 Forges les Eaux, France
07.09.91 Crisanto Espana L RTD 4 Belfast
31.10.91 Robert McCracken L DIS 2 Oakengates
30.04.92 Kevin Lueshing L PTS 6 Kensington
27.06.92 Carlo Colarusso L RTD 5 Quinta do Lago, Portugal

Career: 51 contests, won 11, drew 4, lost 36.

Mitchell Barney

Wolverhampton. *Born* Cheltenham, 26 October, 1965
L. Welterweight (9.12-10.0) ht. 5'7½"
Manager –
Pro. Debut 13 March, 1991

13.03.91 Alan Smith L PTS 6 Stoke
11.11.91 Jamie Morris DREW 6 Stratford on Avon

Career: 2 contests, drew 1, lost 1.

Pat Barrett

Manchester. *Born* Manchester, 22 July, 1967
Former Undefeated British and European L. Welterweight Champion. Former Undefeated Central Area L. Welterweight Champion (10.0-10.4½) ht. 5'9"
Manager M. Duff
Pro. Debut 1 May, 1987

16.01.91 Jimmy Harrison W RTD 1 Kensington
13.02.91 Salvatore Nardino W CO 6 Wembley *(European L. Welterweight Title Defence)*
17.04.91 Mark McCreath W RSC 6 Kensington *(European L. Welterweight Title Defence)*
09.10.91 Racheed Lawal W RSC 4 Manchester *(European L. Welterweight Title Defence)*
19.12.91 Mike Johnson W RSC 2 Oldham

Career: 34 contests, won 32, drew 1, lost 1.

(Garrett) Gary Barron

Peterborough. *Born* Peterborough, 21 December, 1964
L. Welterweight (9.12-10.10½) ht. 5'10"
Manager –
Pro. Debut 19 February, 1987

13.02.91 Robert McCracken L RTD 2 Wembley
19.04.91 Tony Swift DREW 8 Peterborough
14.11.91 Paul Charters L RSC 4 Gateshead
12.02.92 Carlos Chase L RSC 5 Watford
25.03.92 Donald Stokes L RSC 2 Dagenham
30.04.92 Mark McCreath L RSC 5 Mayfair
18.06.92 Marcel Herbert W PTS 6 Peterborough

Career: 20 contests, won 7, drew 3, lost 9, no contest 1.

Billy Barton

Blaengarw. *Born* Bridgend, 29 November, 1962
S. Featherweight (9.1½-9.2¼) ht. 5'2"
Manager –
Pro. Debut 19 May, 1984

18.07.91 J. T. Williams L PTS 6 Cardiff
15.10.91 Mark Holt L PTS 8 Dudley

Career: 21 contests, won 7, drew 3, lost 11.

Karl Barwise

Tooting. *Born* London, 19 September, 1965
S. Middleweight (11.11½-12.1¼) ht. 5'11"
Manager –
Pro. Debut 18 September, 1984

20.03.91 Lester Jacobs L PTS 6 Wandsworth
03.04.91 Ali Forbes L RTD 4 Bethnal Green
26.04.91 Benji Good L RSC 3 Crystal Palace
30.05.91 Ray Webb L PTS 8 Mayfair
16.10.91 Andrew Flute W RSC 8 Stoke
22.10.91 Tony McCarthy W PTS 6 Wandsworth
13.11.91 Sammy Storey L PTS 6 Belfast
07.12.91 Pietro Pellizzaro L PTS 6 Rossano Calabro, Italy
12.05.92 Roland Ericsson L PTS 6 Crystal Palace

Career: 31 contests, won 12, drew 3, lost 16.

Mark Bates

Stanford le Hope. *Born* Stanford le Hope, 22 January, 1967
S. Featherweight (9.2-9.7) ht. 5'7"
Manager –
Pro. Debut 15 December, 1986

23.01.91 Phil Lashley W RTD 3 Brentwood
01.05.91 Phil Lashley W PTS 6 Bethnal Green
24.09.91 Pete Buckley L RTD 5 Basildon
19.02.92 Lee Fox W PTS 6 Muswell Hill

Career: 12 contests, won 9, lost 3.

John Baxter

Leicester. *Born* Leicester, 21 January, 1964
L. Middleweight (11.0-11.2) ht. 5'11"
Manager –
Pro. Debut 18 March, 1991

18.03.91 Gerald Flood W RSC 2 Derby
15.04.91 Dave Hall L RSC 3 Leicester
25.11.91 Warren Bowers W RSC 3 Cleethorpes
05.12.91 Glen Payton L CO 3 Oakengates

Career: 4 contests, won 2, lost 2.

Ricky Beard

Dagenham. *Born* Hackney, 1 March, 1963
Flyweight (8.1-8.3) ht. 5'7½"
Manager B. Hearn
Pro. Debut 2 May, 1989

26.03.91 Francis Ampofo L PTS 8 Bethnal Green
30.09.91 Mickey Cantwell L PTS 8 Kensington
25.02.92 Francis Ampofo L PTS 8 Crystal Palace
14.04.92 Prince Nassem Hamed L CO 2 Mansfield

Career: 10 contests, won 2, drew 1, lost 7.

William Beaton (Beattie)

Glasgow. *Born* Glasgow, 3 October, 1962
Welterweight (10.10) ht. 5'8½"
Manager J. Murray
Pro. Debut 27 November, 1991

27.11.91 Ron Hopley L RSC 2 Marton

Career: 1 contest, lost 1.

Willie Beattie

Glasgow. *Born* Glasgow, 25 October, 1967
Scottish Welterweight Champion (10.6½-10.9) ht. 5'7½"
Manager –
Pro. Debut 13 December, 1988

11.02.91 Des Robinson W PTS 8 Glasgow
24.09.91 Trevor Ambrose W PTS 8 Glasgow
31.01.92 Gordon Blair W RSC 3 Glasgow *(Vacant Scottish Welterweight Title)*
10.04.92 Tony Swift L PTS 10 Glasgow *(Elim. British Welterweight Title)*

Career: 17 contests, won 14, lost 3.

Bobby Beckles

Manchester. *Born* Bolton, 19 June, 1967
S. Featherweight (9.4-9.7) ht. 5'8"
Manager P. Martin
Pro. Debut 13 March, 1991

13.03.91 Tony Doyle W PTS 6 Stoke
16.05.91 Barry Glanister W CO 1 Battersea
10.06.91 Trevor Royal W PTS 6 Manchester
09.10.91 Carl Tilley L RSC 4 Marton

Career: 4 contests, won 3, lost 1.

John Beckles

Tottenham. *Born* London, 1 January, 1963
L. Heavyweight (12.7) ht. 6'1"
Manager H. Holland
Pro. Debut 22 April, 1989

05.03.92 Tony Booth L RSC 6 Battersea

Career: 5 contests, won 2, drew 1, lost 2.

Tony Behan

Birmingham. *Born* Birmingham, 5 March, 1967
L. Heavyweight (12.4-12.9½) ht. 6'0"
Manager –
Pro. Debut 22 September, 1986

04.03.91 Paul Hanlon W PTS 6 Birmingham
13.05.91 Nigel Rafferty L DIS 7 Birmingham
23.05.91 Joey Peters L PTS 6 Southampton
02.12.91 Darryl Ritchie W RSC 1 Birmingham
20.01.92 Gil Lewis L PTS 8 Coventry

Career: 22 contests, won 6, drew 3, lost 13.

Nigel Benn

Ilford. *Born* Ilford, 22 January, 1964
S. Middleweight. Former WBO Middleweight Champion. Former Commonwealth Middleweight Champion (11.4½-12.0) ht. 5'9½"
Manager –
Pro. Debut 28 January, 1987

03.04.91 Robbie Sims W RSC 7 Bethnal Green
03.07.91 Kid Milo W RSC 4 Brentwood
26.10.91 Lenzie Morgan W PTS 10 Brentwood
07.12.91 Hector Lescano W CO 3 Manchester
19.02.92 Dan Sherry W RSC 3 Muswell Hill
23.05.92 Thulani Malinga W PTS 10 Birmingham

Career: 35 contests, won 33, lost 2.

Nigel Benn Les Clark

(Barry) B. K. Bennett

Aylesbury. *Born* Aylesbury, 13 March, 1963
L. Middleweight (10.12½-11.7) ht. 5'9"
Manager J. Barclay
Pro. Debut 20 February, 1987

28.11.91 Mick Mulcahy W PTS 6 Evesham
10.03.92 Warren Stowe L PTS 6 Bury

Career: 17 contests, won 7, lost 10.

Ady Benton Chris Bevan

Mervyn Bennett

Cardiff. *Born* Cardiff, 20 February, 1960
Lightweight (9.8½) ht. 5'6½"
Manager –
Pro. Debut 6 January, 1981

19.05.92 Edward Lloyd L RSC 5 Cardiff

Career: 16 contests, won 8, lost 8.

(Adrian) Ady Benton

Bradford. *Born* Dewsbury, 26 August, 1973
Bantamweight (8.10) ht. 5'6"
Manager K. Tate
Pro. Debut 27 April, 1992

27.04.92 Mark Hargreaves W PTS 6 Bradford

Career: 1 contest, won 1.

Ensley Bingham

Manchester. *Born* Manchester, 27 May, 1963
L. Middleweight (10.12½-11.4) ht. 5'8½"
Manager P. Martin
Pro. Debut 20 November, 1986

19.03.91 Wally Swift Jnr L RSC 4 Birmingham *(Vacant British L. Middleweight Title)*
29.11.91 Russell Washer W RSC 4 Manchester
29.05.92 Graham Jenner W CO 5 Manchester

Career: 13 contests, won 8, lost 5.

Dave Binsteed

Liverpool. *Born* Liverpool, 16 June, 1962
L. Middleweight (10.13-11.4) ht. 5'9½"
Manager –
Pro. Debut 28 April, 1986

13.05.91 Dave Hall W RSC 2 Birmingham
20.05.91 Darren McInulty DREW 6 Leicester
07.10.91 Willie Yeardsley L PTS 6 Liverpool
02.12.91 David Radford L RSC 6 Liverpool
31.01.92 Humphrey Harrison L CO 1 Manchester

Career: 8 contests, won 1, drew 1, lost 6.

Gordon Blair

Glasgow. *Born* Glasgow, 26 February, 1969
Welterweight (10.6¼-11.2) ht. 5'10"
Manager A. Morrison
Pro. Debut 21 November, 1989

25.01.91 Danny Quigg W PTS 6 Shotts
18.02.91 Gary Logan L CO 1 Mayfair
15.04.91 Rob Pitters L PTS 6 Glasgow
31.05.91 Paul King W PTS 8 Glasgow
20.06.91 Delroy Waul W CO 2 Liverpool
24.09.91 Bouzon Haule W RSC 8 Glasgow
19.11.91 Tony McKenzie L RSC 5 Norwich
31.01.92 Willie Beattie L RSC 3 Glasgow *(Vacant Scottish Welterweight Title)*
12.03.92 Mark Jay DREW 8 Glasgow
29.05.92 Ossie Maddix L PTS 6 Manchester

Career: 20 contests, won 12, drew 1, lost 7.

Chris Blake

Croydon. *Born* Croydon, 14 May, 1962
L. Middleweight. Former Undefeated Southern Area L. Welterweight Champion (10.12-11.0) ht. 5'8"
Manager –
Pro. Debut 16 October, 1985

19.04.91 Mauro Martelli L PTS 8 Marigane, France
22.05.91 Ludovic Proto L RSC 1 Paris, France
20.11.91 Derek Grainger DREW 8 Kensington
25.04.92 Oscar Checa L RSC 1 Belfast

Career: 29 contests, won 18, drew 1, lost 10.

Everton Blake (left) seen going down on points against Gypsy Carman in 1990 Les Clark

Ervine Blake
Worcester. *Born* Belfast, 17 February, 1966
S. Featherweight (9.4) ht. 5'7½"
Manager J. Gaynor
Pro. Debut 8 October, 1990

07.10.91 Derek Amory W PTS 6 Birmingham

Career: 3 contests, won 2, lost 1.

Everton Blake
Luton. *Born* Luton, 18 November, 1963
Southern Area Cruiserweight Champion (12.10-13.0½) ht. 6'3½"
Manager J. Barclay
Pro. Debut 6 April, 1989

22.02.91 Maurice Coore L RSC 8 Manchester
22.04.91 Terry Dixon W RSC 8 Mayfair
14.11.91 John Graham W PTS 10 Bayswater *(Southern Area Cruiserweight Title Challenge)*

Career: 11 contests, won 8, lost 3.

Andrew Bloomer
Ynysybwl. *Born* Pontypridd, 26 September, 1964
Bantamweight (8.7-8.11½) ht. 5'8½"
Manager D. Gardiner
Pro. Debut 30 June, 1991

30.06.91 Leigh Williams L PTS 6 Southwark
03.09.91 Alan Ley L PTS 6 Cardiff
02.10.91 Bradley Stone L PTS 6 Barking
17.10.91 Leigh Williams L PTS 6 Southwark
04.11.91 Ceri Farrell L PTS 6 Merthyr
20.11.91 Ceri Farrell L PTS 6 Cardiff
28.11.91 Chris Morris L PTS 6 Liverpool
24.02.92 Alex Docherty L PTS 6 Glasgow
08.04.92 Jacob Smith L PTS 6 Leeds
30.04.92 Tony Falcone L PTS 6 Mayfair
16.05.92 Bradley Stone L PTS 6 Muswell Hill
23.05.92 Prince Nassem Hamed L RSC 2 Birmingham

Career: 12 contests, lost 12.

Gary Booker
Midhurst. *Born* Haslemere, 24 July, 1968
Middleweight (11.6-11.9) ht. 5'11¼"
Manager H. Holland
Pro. Debut 26 September, 1990

06.02.91 Clayton Stewart W PTS 6 Battersea
01.06.91 Kenny Tyson W PTS 6 Bethnal Green
07.11.91 Stefan Wright L PTS 6 Peterborough

Career: 5 contests, won 4, lost 1.

Tony Booth
Sheffield. *Born* Hull, 30 January, 1970
L. Heavyweight (11.3½-12.0) ht. 5'11¼"
Manager B. Ingle
Pro. Debut 8 March, 1990

23.01.91 Darron Griffiths DREW 6 Stoke
06.02.91 Shaun McCrory L PTS 6 Liverpool
06.03.91 Billy Brough L PTS 6 Glasgow
18.03.91 Billy Brough W PTS 6 Glasgow
28.03.91 Neville Brown L PTS 6 Alfreton
17.05.91 Glenn Campbell L RSC 2 Bury *(Central Area S. Middleweight Title Challenge)*
25.07.91 Paul Murray W PTS 6 Dudley
01.08.91 Nick Manners DREW 8 Dewsbury
11.09.91 Jim Peters L PTS 8 Hammersmith
28.10.91 Eddie Smulders L RSC 6 Arnhem, Holland
09.12.91 Steve Lewsam L PTS 8 Cleethorpes
30.01.92 Serg Fame W PTS 6 Southampton
12.02.92 Tenko Ernie W RSC 4 Wembley
05.03.92 John Beckles W RSC 6 Battersea
26.03.92 Dave Owens W PTS 6 Hull
08.04.92 Michael Gale L PTS 8 Leeds
13.05.92 Phil Soundy W PTS 6 Kensington
02.06.92 Eddie Smulders L RSC 1 Rotterdam, Holland

Career: 25 contests, won 12, drew 2, lost 11.

Tony Borg
Cardiff. *Born* Cardiff, 17 December, 1964
L. Welterweight (9.10-9.12½) ht. 5'5"
Manager –
Pro. Debut 21 March, 1983

16.09.91 Peter Bradley L PTS 8 Mayfair
20.11.91 Felix Kelly W PTS 6 Cardiff
22.01.92 Ross Hale L PTS 6 Cardiff

Career: 24 contests, won 13, lost 11.

John Bosko (Waigo)
Mitcham. *Born* Uganda, 16 July, 1967
L. Middleweight (11.2½-11.2¾) ht. 5'8½"
Manager M. Duff
Pro. Debut 5 December, 1991

05.12.91 Tony Kosova W CO 2 Peterborough
17.02.92 Gilbert Jackson W PTS 6 Mayfair

Career: 2 contests, won 2.

Mark Bowen
Millwall. *Born* Redbridge, 23 July, 1966
Cruiserweight (13.4-13.8) ht. 6'1"
Manager J. Kramer
Pro. Debut 24 April, 1990

21.02.91 Denzil Browne L PTS 6 Walsall
25.04.91 Bruce Scott W PTS 6 Mayfair
27.06.91 Michael Gale L PTS 8 Leeds
25.03.92 Terry Dixon L RTD 1 Kensington

Career: 7 contests, won 3, lost 4.

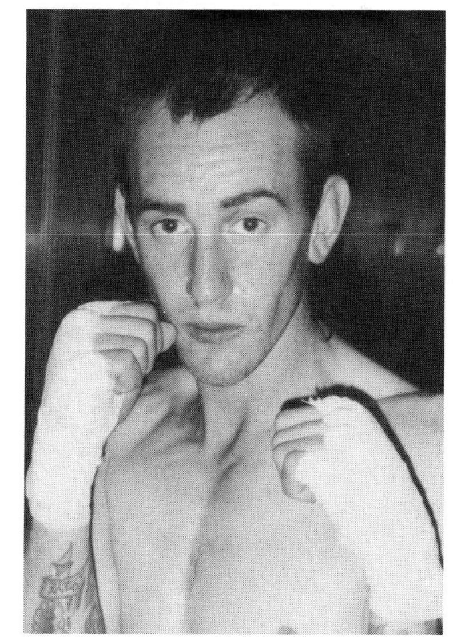

Andrew Bloomer Les Clark

Tony Booth (left) on his way to spoiling John Beckles' home debut with a sixth round stoppage at Battersea Les Clark

Mark Bowers

Lock Heath. *Born* Fareham, 19 October, 1970
Featherweight (9.0½) ht. 5'5"
Manager M. Duff
Pro. Debut 13 May, 1992

13.05.92 Hamid Moulay W CO 1 Kensington

Career: 1 contest, won 1.

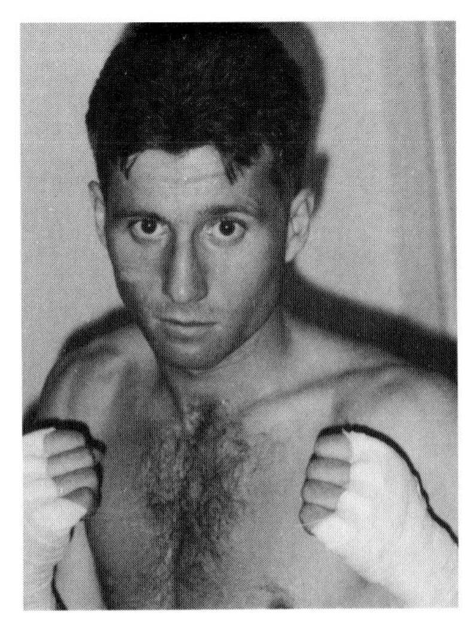

Mark Bowers Les Clark

Warren Bowers

Grimsby. *Born* Grimsby, 14 January, 1971
Welterweight (10.2-10.13½) ht. 5'7"
Manager L. Slater
Pro. Debut 8 May, 1989

02.03.91 Andy Kent L PTS 6 Cleethorpes
25.11.91 John Baxter L RSC 3 Cleethorpes
04.06.92 Peter Reid L RSC 2 Cleethorpes

Career: 6 contests, won 3, lost 3.

Steve Boyle

Glasgow. *Born* Glasgow, 28 November, 1962
Former Undefeated British, WBC International & Scottish Lightweight Champion (9.7¼-9.8¼) ht. 5'7"
Manager F. Warren
Pro. Debut 19 May, 1983

27.04.91 Antonio Renzo L RTD 7 Rossano Calabro, Italy
(Vacant European Lightweight Title)
05.05.92 Carl Crook L RSC 7 Preston
(British & Commonwealth Lightweight Title Challenge)

Career: 32 contests, won 24, drew 2, lost 6.

Robert Braddock

Bolton on Dearne. *Born* Mexborough, 14 January, 1971
Featherweight (8.10½-9.1½) ht. 5'7"
Manager –
Pro. Debut 3 April, 1989

10.06.91 Tony Smith DREW 6 Manchester
23.09.91 Al Garrett DREW 6 Glasgow
07.10.91 Glyn Shepherd DREW 6 Bradford
13.11.91 Chris Morris L RSC 5 Liverpool
16.12.91 Carl Roberts L PTS 6 Manchester
28.04.92 Chip O'Neill L PTS 6 Houghton le Spring
01.06.92 Alex Docherty L PTS 6 Glasgow

Career: 12 contests, won 1, drew 3, lost 8.

Nigel Bradley

Sheffield. *Born* Sheffield, 24 February, 1968
L. Welterweight (10.0-10.2¾) ht. 5'8"
Manager –
Pro. Debut 14 December, 1987

29.01.91 Sugar Gibiliru L PTS 8 Stockport
11.02.92 Dean Hollington L PTS 6 Barking
18.03.92 Kris McAdam W CO 2 Glasgow
14.04.92 Dave Whittle W CO 3 Mansfield

Career: 17 contests, won 10, drew 1, lost 5, no contest 1.

Peter Bradley

Glasgow. *Born* Glasgow, 14 November, 1963
L. Welterweight (9.8¼-10.1¼) ht. 5'8½"
Manager T. Gilmour
Pro. Debut 18 February, 1985

21.01.91 Paul Burke L PTS 10 Glasgow
(Elim. British Lightweight Title)
16.09.91 Tony Borg W PTS 8 Mayfair
30.03.92 Alan Peacock W PTS 8 Glasgow

Career: 27 contests, won 23, lost 4.

Dean Bramhald

Doncaster. *Born* Balby, 25 May, 1963
L. Welterweight (10.0-10.8) ht. 5'7½"
Manager J. Rushton
Pro. Debut 25 January, 1984

17.01.91 Richard Burton L RTD 1 Alfreton
05.03.91 Charlie Kane L RSC 6 Glasgow
10.04.91 Ronnie Campbell W PTS 6 Wolverhampton
24.04.91 Dave Jenkins L PTS 8 Aberavon
13.05.91 Andrew Robinson L RTD 1 Birmingham
17.06.91 Malcolm Melvin L PTS 6 Edgbaston
04.07.91 Shane Sheridan L PTS 6 Alfreton
10.09.91 Mark Elliot L CO 5 Wolverhampton
08.10.91 Colin Sinnott L PTS 8 Wolverhampton
21.10.91 Colin Sinnott W PTS 6 Cleethorpes
20.11.91 Rocky Feliciello L PTS 6 Solihull
04.12.91 Ron Shinkwin W PTS 8 Stoke
22.01.92 Ray Newby L PTS 8 Solihull
30.01.92 Ron Shinkwin L PTS 6 Southampton
11.02.92 Ray Newby L RSC 7 Wolverhampton
11.03.92 Andreas Panayi W PTS 8 Stoke
24.03.92 Richard Swallow L PTS 8 Wolverhampton
06.04.92 Richard Swallow L PTS 6 Northampton
28.04.92 Darren McInulty L PTS 6 Wolverhampton
11.05.92 Darren McInulty L PTS 6 Coventry
12.06.92 Carl Wright L PTS 6 Liverpool

Career: 124 contests, won 27, drew 13, lost 84.

Jason Brattley

Leeds. *Born* Leeds, 11 November, 1970
L. Welterweight (9.9½-10.3) ht. 5'5½"
Manager P. Duckworth
Pro. Debut 2 March, 1991

02.03.91 Barry North W PTS 6 Cleethorpes
25.03.91 James Clamp W RSC 3 Bradford
17.05.91 David Thompson DREW 6 Bury
07.10.91 Scott Doyle L PTS 6 Birmingham
30.03.92 David Thompson W PTS 6 Bradford
01.06.92 Mick Mulcahy W PTS 6 Manchester
08.06.92 Kevin McKenzie L RTD 3 Bradford

Career: 7 contests, won 4, drew 1, lost 2.

Steve Bricknell

Birmingham. *Born* Birmingham, 19 February, 1970
L. Welterweight (10.2-10.4) ht. 5'7"
Manager N. Nobbs
Pro. Debut 1 October, 1991

01.10.91 Billy Robinson L PTS 6 Bedworth
21.10.91 Rick North L PTS 6 Cleethorpes
26.11.91 Dean Carr L PTS 4 Wolverhampton
02.12.91 Dean Hiscox L PTS 6 Birmingham
28.01.92 Lee Soar L PTS 6 Piccadilly

Career: 5 contests, lost 5.

Tony Britland

Barmouth. *Born* Dolgellau, 26 November, 1960
Welterweight (10.6-10.13) ht. 5'7"
Manager –
Pro. Debut 12 January, 1987

21.02.91 Shaun Cogan L PTS 6 Walsall
06.03.91 Robert McCracken L RSC 2 Wembley
12.04.91 Darren Morris W PTS 6 Willenhall
14.05.91 Wayne Timmins L PTS 6 Dudley
03.10.91 John Corcoran W RSC 5 Burton
21.10.91 Leigh Wicks L RSC 3 Mayfair
02.12.91 Richard O'Brien L RSC 2 Birmingham

Career: 37 contests, won 6, drew 5, lost 26.

Mark Broome

Grimsby. *Born* Grimsby, 1 June, 1967
L. Welterweight (10.2-10.3) ht. 5'10½"
Manager L. Slater
Pro. Debut 30 September, 1985

25.11.91 Lee Soar L PTS 6 Cleethorpes
04.06.92 Darren Henderson W RSC 2 Cleethorpes

Career: 8 contests, won 3, lost 5.

Dave Brosnan
Eltham. *Born* Camberwell, 2 February, 1966
L. Middleweight (10-12¼) ht. 5'8¾"
Manager –
Pro. Debut 7 April, 1987

23.04.92 Bozon Haule L RSC 6 Eltham

Career: 6 contests, won 3, lost 3.

David Brown
Paddington. *Born* London, 1 January, 1965
L. Heavyweight (12.4) ht. 5'10¼"
Manager I. Akay
Pro. Debut 25 September, 1989

29.11.91 Bobbi Joe Edwards L RSC 4 Manchester

Career: 5 contests, drew 1, lost 4.

Neville Brown
Burton. *Born* Burton, 26 February, 1966
Middleweight (11.2-11.7) ht 5'10"
Manager –
Pro. Debut 8 November, 1989

17.01.91 Shamus Casey W RSC 4 Alfreton
13.02.91 Jimmy Thornton W RSC 1 Wembley
28.03.91 Tony Booth W PTS 6 Alfreton
12.04.91 Winston Wray W RSC 1 Willenhall
04.07.91 Paul Wesley L RSC 1 Alfreton
29.08.91 Paul Smith W RSC 3 Oakengates
03.10.91 Paul Wesley W PTS 8 Burton
21.11.91 Colin Pitters W RSC 3 Burton
26.03.92 Paul Murray W CO 3 Telford

Career: 16 contests, won 15, lost 1.

Denzil Browne
Leeds. *Born* Leeds, 21 January, 1969
Cruiserweight (13.6-13.13¾) ht. 6'2½"
Manager M. Duff
Pro. Debut 18 October, 1990

21.02.91 Mark Bowen W PTS 6 Walsall
21.03.91 R. F. McKenzie W PTS 6 Dewsbury
09.05.91 Darren McKenna W PTS 6 Leeds
27.06.91 Steve Yorath W PTS 6 Leeds
01.08.91 Tony Colclough W RSC 1 Dewsbury
09.10.91 R. F. McKenzie L PTS 6 Manchester
30.10.91 Gus Mendes W RSC 6 Leeds
23.01.92 Darren McKenna W PTS 6 York
19.03.92 Ian Bulloch W PTS 8 York

Career: 12 contests, won 10, lost 2.

Frank Bruno
Wandsworth. *Born* Hammersmith, 16 November, 1961
Former Undefeated European Heavyweight Champion (16.4¾-16.10) ht. 6'3½"
Manager –
Pro. Debut 17 March, 1982

20.11.91 John Emmen W CO 1 Kensington
22.04.92 Jose Ribalta W CO 2 Wembley

Career: 37 contests, won 34, lost 3.

Frank Bruno Peter Shaw

(Delroy) Del Bryan
Birmingham. *Born* Nottingham 16 April, 1967
Former British Welterweight Champion. Former Undefeated Midlands Area Welterweight Champion (10.4-10.8½) ht. 5'8"
Manager W. Swift
Pro. Debut 21 April, 1986

16.01.91 Kirkland Laing W PTS 12 Kensington *(British Welterweight Title Challenge)*
16.04.91 Anthony Ivory W PTS 10 Nottingham
26.11.91 Mickey Hughes W RSC 3 Bethnal Green *(British Welterweight Title Defence)*
20.02.92 Gary Jacobs L PTS 12 Glasgow *(British Welterweight Title Challenge)*
12.05.92 Darren Dyer W RSC 10 Crystal Palace

Career: 35 contests, won 24, drew 1, lost 10.

Denroy Bryan
Swindon. *Born* Birmingham, 15 November, 1959
Heavyweight (14.2-15.0) ht. 5'11¼"
Manager –
Pro. Debut 16 September, 1983

12.11.91 J. A. Bugner L PTS 4 Milton Keynes
11.12.91 Joe Egan W RSC 4 Dublin
31.01.92 Maurice Coore L RSC 1 Manchester

Career: 30 contests, won 6, drew 3, lost 21.

Wayne Buck
Nottingham. *Born* Nottingham, 31 August, 1966
Heavyweight (15.11¾) ht. 5'10¾"
Manager M. Shinfield
Pro. Debut 26 March, 1990

04.06.92 Gary Charlton W PTS 6 Cleethorpes

Career: 3 contests, won 2, lost 1.

Pete Buckley
Birmingham. *Born* Birmingham, 9 March, 1969
Midlands Area S. Featherweight Champion (8.9-9.4) ht. 5'8"
Manager N. Nobbs
Pro. Debut 4 October, 1989

10.01.91 Duke McKenzie L RSC 5 Wandsworth
18.02.91 Jamie McBride L PTS 8 Glasgow
04.03.91 Brian Robb W RSC 7 Birmingham
26.03.91 Neil Leitch DREW 8 Wolverhampton
01.05.91 Mark Geraghty W PTS 8 Solihull
05.06.91 Brian Robb W PTS 10 Wolverhampton *(Vacant Midlands Area S. Featherweight Title)*
09.09.91 Mike Deveney L PTS 8 Glasgow
24.09.91 Mark Bates W RTD 5 Basildon
29.10.91 John Armour L PTS 6 Kensington
14.11.91 Mike Deveney L PTS 6 Edinburgh
28.11.91 Craig Dermody L PTS 6 Liverpool
19.12.91 Craig Dermody L PTS 6 Oldham
18.01.92 Alan McKay DREW 8 Kensington
20.02.92 Brian Robb W RSC 10 Oakengates *(Midlands Area S. Featherweight Title Defence)*
27.04.92 Drew Docherty L PTS 8 Glasgow
15.05.92 Ruben Condori L PTS 10 Augsburg, Germany
29.05.92 Donnie Hood L PTS 8 Glasgow

Career: 40 contests, won 18, drew 5, lost 17.

(Joe) J. A. Bugner
St Ives. *Born* St Ives, 12 August, 1970
Heavyweight (15.13-16.4½) ht. 6'6"
Manager A. Smith
Pro. Debut 12 November,1991

12.11.91 Denroy Bryan W PTS 4 Milton Keynes
06.02.92 Gary Railton W CO 3 Peterborough
05.03.92 John Harewood W PTS 4 Battersea
22.04.92 Gary McCrory W PTS 4 Wembley

Career: 4 contests, won 4.

Ian Bulloch
Bolsover. *Born* Bolsover, 25 January, 1965
Cruiserweight (13.8-13.12) ht. 6'0"
Manager J. Gaynor
Pro. Debut 24 March, 1987

02.03.91 Roy Smith L PTS 10 Cleethorpes *(Midlands Area Cruiserweight Title Challenge)*
24.06.91 Pedro van Raamsdonk L PTS 8 Rotterdam, Holland
13.10.91 Przemyslaw Saleta L RSC 8 Warsaw, Poland
19.03.92 Denzil Browne L PTS 8 York
27.04.92 Terry Dixon L RSC 4 Mayfair

Career: 22 contests, won 10, drew 1, lost 11.

Nigel Burder
Gorseinon. *Born* Gorseinon, 7 September, 1963
Welterweight (9.13-10.6½) ht. 5'6"
Manager G. Davies
Pro. Debut 4 November, 1991

04.11.91 Chris Mylan L CO 3 Merthyr
02.03.92 Steve Edwards L RSC 1 Merthyr
11.05.92 Dewi Roberts L CO 3 Llanelli

Career: 3 contests, lost 3.

Paul Burke

Preston. *Born* Preston, 25 July, 1966
Lightweight (9.7½-10.3) ht. 5'10"
Manager P. Martin
Pro. Debut 21 January, 1987

21.01.91 Peter Bradley W PTS 10 Glasgow *(Elim. British Lightweight Title)*
31.05.91 Art Blackmore W RSC 3 Manchester
20.09.91 Tony Richards W PTS 8 Manchester
09.02.92 Dave Andrews W PTS 6 Bradford
28.04.92 Paul Charters W RSC 7 Houghton le Spring *(Final Elim. British Lightweight Title)*

Career: 23 contests, won 15, drew 2, lost 6.

Tony Burke

Croydon. *Born* Croydon, 7 April, 1963
Southern Area Middleweight Champion
(11.4½-11.12¾) ht. 5'10½"
Manager H. Holland
Pro. Debut 9 September, 1981

28.03.91 John Ashton L PTS 10 Alfreton *(Elim. British Middleweight Title)*
12.10.91 Vincenzo Nardiello L RSC 2 Monaco, Monte Carlo

Career: 33 contests, won 16, lost 17.

Graham Burton

Sheffield. *Born* Chesterfield, 16 June, 1964
S. Middleweight (11.8½-12.2) ht. 5'10"
Manager –
Pro. Debut 10 October, 1988

17.01.91 John Ashton L PTS 10 Alfreton
12.03.91 Peter Gorny W PTS 6 Mansfield
13.06.91 Michael Gale L CO 4 Hull
12.11.91 Paul Busby L RSC 3 Wolverhampton
04.02.92 Richie Woodhall L RSC 2 Alfreton
17.03.92 Andrew Flute L PTS 8 Wolverhampton

Career: 15 contests, won 10, lost 5.

Paul Burton

Sheffield. *Born* Chesterfield, 26 February, 1963
S. Middleweight (11.11-12.2) ht. 6'0½"
Manager –
Pro. Debut 11 February, 1986

18.02.91 Max McCracken L RTD 3 Birmingham
15.04.91 David Radford W RTD 1 Wolverhampton
23.04.91 Simon McDougall W PTS 8 Evesham
18.05.91 Cornelius Carr L RSC 3 Verbania, Italy
14.11.91 Paul Hitch L CO 2 Gateshead

Career: 21 contests, won 10, lost 11.

Richard Burton

Manchester. *Born* Jamaica, 7 November, 1970
Central Area L. Welterweight Champion
(9.13½-10.4) ht. 5'11"
Manager J. Doughty
Pro. Debut 18 September, 1989

17.01.91 Dean Bramhald W RTD 1 Alfreton
31.10.91 Mike Morrison W PTS 6 Bredbury
16.05.91 Chris Saunders W PTS 6 Liverpool
20.06.91 Jim Lawlor L PTS 6 Liverpool
21.11.91 John Smith W PTS 6 Burton
19.12.91 John Smith W PTS 6 Oldham
27.02.92 Chris Saunders W PTS 10 Liverpool *(Vacant Central Area L. Welterweight Title)*

Career: 12 contests, won 10, drew 1, lost 1.

(Wayne) Rocky Burton

Bedworth. *Born* Nuneaton, 28 October, 1958
Heavyweight (16.2) ht. 6'3"
Manager J. Griffin
Pro. Debut 18 October, 1977

24.02.92 David Jules L CO 1 Coventry

Career: 47 contests, won 22, drew 1, lost 24.

Paul Busby

Worcester. *Born* Worcester, 20 April, 1966
Middleweight (11.6¾-11.9) ht. 5'11½"
Manager B. Hearn
Pro. Debut 18 November, 1990

23.01.91 Tony Wellington W RSC 2 Brentwood
27.02.91 Paul Murray W PTS 6 Wolverhampton
19.03.91 Paul Smith W PTS 6 Leicester
10.09.91 Nigel Rafferty W RSC 2 Wolverhampton
12.11.91 Graham Burton W RSC 3 Wolverhampton
17.12.91 Paul Murray W CO 3 Cardiff
01.02.92 John Kaighin W PTS 4 Birmingham
23.05.92 Stinger Mason W RSC 2 Birmingham

Career: 10 contests, won 10.

Rick Bushell

Herne Bay. *Born* Bridge, 1 March, 1965
Lightweight (9.9½-10.0) ht. 5'8"
Manager P. Byrne
Pro. Debut 11 December, 1989

10.01.91 Mike Morrison W PTS 6 Wandsworth
07.02.91 B. F. Williams W RTD 2 Watford
18.02.91 Robert Smyth W PTS 6 Mayfair
28.02.91 Marvin P. Gray L PTS 6 Sunderland
10.04.91 Vaughan Carnegie W RSC 3 Newport
18.04.91 Felix Kelly L PTS 6 Earls Court
22.06.91 Felix Kelly W PTS 6 Earls Court
23.10.91 Mark Tibbs L RSC 4 Bethnal Green
11.12.91 Mark Tibbs L RSC 2 Basildon
02.03.92 Jose Tuominen DREW 4 Helsinki, Finland
14.03.92 Soren Sondergard L CO 3 Copenhagen, Denmark
16.05.92 Dean Hollington L RSC 2 Muswell Hill

Career: 18 contests, won 9, drew 1, lost 8.

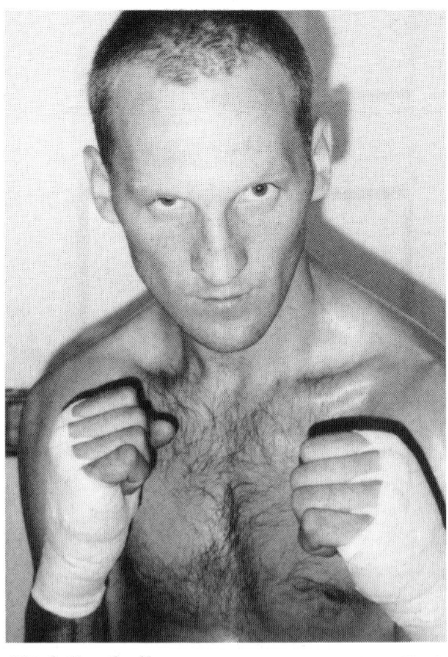

Rick Bushell Les Clark

Richard Bustin

Norwich. *Born* Norwich, 9 October, 1964
L. Heavyweight (12.6-12.11¼) ht. 5'9"
Manager G. Holmes
Pro. Debut 15 February, 1988

29.01.91 Simon Harris L RSC 3 Wisbech
18.04.91 John Foreman W PTS 8 Earls Court
11.06.91 Gary Ballard L PTS 8 Leicester
19.11.91 Glazz Campbell L CO 7 Norwich *(Vacant Southern Area L. Heavyweight Title)*
31.01.92 Bobbi Joe Edwards L PTS 6 Manchester
31.03.92 Gypsy Carman L PTS 6 Norwich
27.06.92 Darius Michaelezewski L RSC 4 Quinta do Lago, Portugal

Career: 19 contests, won 9, lost 10.

(Barrie) Blue Butterworth

Burnley. Born Lambeth, 5 October, 1970
L. Welterweight (10.1¼-10.3¼) ht. 5'8½"
Manager J. Doughty
Pro. Debut 31 March, 1992

31.03.92 Brian Coleman W PTS 6 Stockport
04.06.92 Mark Allen W RSC 5 Burnley

Career: 2 contests, won 2.

Dave Buxton

Redcar. *Born* Saltburn, 22 March, 1962
Featherweight (9.2) ht. 5'4¾"
Manager T. Miller
Pro. Debut 10 October, 1989

25.01.91 Donnie Hood L RSC 5 Shotts
10.04.91 J. T. Williams L PTS 8 Newport
01.08.91 Tony Silkstone L PTS 6 Dewsbury

Career: 13 contests, won 4, lost 9.

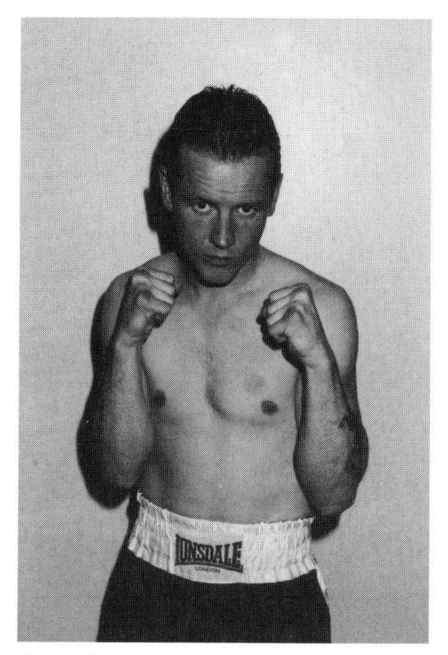

Dave Buxton Chris Bevan

Michael Byrne

Birmingham. *Born* Birmingham, 16 May, 1972
Welterweight (10.2-10.7) ht. 5'8"
Manager N. Nobbs
Pro Debut 16 September, 1991

16.09.91 Dean Carr L PTS 6 Cleethorpes
01.10.91 Jamie Morris DREW 4 Bedworth
16.10.91 Jamie Morris L PTS 6 Stoke
28.10.91 Kevin McKillan L PTS 6 Leicester
09.12.91 Rick North L RSC 2 Cleethorpes
04.04.92 Mick Mulcahy L RSC 4 Cleethorpes

Career: 6 contests, drew 1, lost 5.

Sean Byrne

Northampton. *Born* Manchester, 20 September, 1966
Middleweight (10.10-11.8) ht. 6'0"
Manager J. Cox
Pro. Debut 6 April, 1992

06.04.92 Mark Jolley W RSC 6 Northampton
28.04.92 John McKenzie W RSC 6 Corby

Career: 2 contests, won 2.

Damien Caesar

Stepney. *Born* Stepney, 2 October, 1965
Heavyweight (14.7¾-15.13) ht. 6'5"
Manager T. Lawless
Pro. Debut 22 April, 1991

22.04.91 Larry Peart W RSC 2 Mayfair
30.05.91 Tony Colclough W RSC 1 Mayfair
17.02.92 Steve Stewart W RSC 5 Mayfair
27.04.92 Gary Williams W RSC 4 Mayfair

Career: 4 contests, won 4.

Doug Calderwood

Sheffield. *Born* Scarborough, 28 April, 1964
S. Middleweight (12.1½-12.11) ht. 6'0½"
Manager P. Duckworth
Pro. Debut 6 December, 1985

13.05.91 Stinger Mason W CO 3 Manchester
30.09.91 Simon McDougall L RSC 4 Liverpool
12.12.91 Paul Hitch L PTS 6 Hartlepool
11.03.92 Chris Walker L PTS 6 Solihull

Career: 15 contests, won 6, drew 1, lost 8.

Mike Calderwood

Salford. *Born* Crumpsall, 17 September, 1964
L. Welterweight (10.1¾-10.5½) ht. 5'8½"
Manager –
Pro. Debut 14 February, 1983

10.06.91 Mick Mulcahy W PTS 6 Manchester
30.09.91 Kevin Toomey W RSC 2 Liverpool
21.10.91 Brian Cullen L PTS 6 Bury
02.12.91 John Smith DREW 8 Liverpool
09.03.92 Robert Lloyd W RSC 1 Manchester
31.03.92 Rob Stewart L PTS 4 Stockport

Career: 18 contests, won 4, drew 4, lost 10.

Dave Campbell

Middlesbrough. *Born* South Shields, 13 December, 1968
Bantamweight (8.6-8.7) ht. 5'4½"
Manager J. Spensley
Pro. Debut 11 September, 1991

11.09.91 Mark Hargreaves L RSC 4 Stoke
14.11.91 Dave Martin W PTS 6 Bayswater
27.11.91 Shaun Norman W PTS 6 Marton
18.05.92 Glyn Shepherd W RSC 1 Marton

Career: 4 contests, won 3, lost 1.

(Glasbourne) Glazz Campbell

Brockley. *Born* Sheffield, 9 August, 1962
Southern Area L. Heavyweight Champion (12.6-12.10½) ht. 6'0"
Manager P. Byrne
Pro. Debut 8 October, 1985

12.04.91 Maurice Coore L CO 2 Manchester
29.06.91 Christophe Girard L PTS 8 Le Touquet, France
24.08.91 Mwehu Beya L PTS 6 Pesaro, Italy
02.10.91 Tony Wilson W PTS 8 Solihull
19.11.91 Richard Bustin W CO 7 Norwich *(Vacant Southern Area L. Heavyweight Title)*
18.03.92 Tom Collins W PTS 10 Glasgow *(Final Elim. British L. Heavyweight Title)*
25.04.92 Crawford Ashley L RSC 8 Belfast *(British L. Heavyweight Title Challenge)*

Career: 24 contests, won 9, drew 2, lost 13.

Glenn Campbell

Bury. *Born* Bury, 22 April, 1970
Central Area S. Middleweight Champion (11.11¾-12.2) ht. 5'10"
Manager J. Doughty
Pro. Debut 19 April, 1990

28.02.91 Simon McDougall W PTS 10 Bury *(Central Area S. Middleweight Title Defence)*
17.05.91 Tony Booth W RSC 2 Bury *(Central Area S. Middleweight Title Defence)*
21.01.92 Nigel Rafferty W RSC 6 Stockport
10.03.92 Carlos Christie DREW 8 Bury
05.05.92 Ian Henry W RSC 1 Preston

Career: 12 contests, won 11, drew 1.

Glenn Campbell Chris Bevan

James Campbell

Birmingham. *Born* Birmingham, 2 July, 1967
Welterweight (10.6-10.9) ht. 5'10"
Manager N. Nobbs
Pro. Debut 21 October, 1991

21.10.91 Dean Carr W RSC 5 Cleethorpes
26.11.91 Julian Eavis L PTS 8 Wolverhampton
20.02.92 Peter Reid W PTS 6 Oakengates
30.04.92 Nicky Bardle W CO 1 Watford

Career: 4 contests, won 3, lost 1.

(Ray) Razza Campbell

Dudley. *Born* Dudley, 29 June, 1966
L. Welterweight (9.13) ht. 5'6½"
Manager R. Browne
Pro. Debut 26 November, 1991

26.11.91 Moses Sentamu L RSC 2 Wolverhampton
11.03.92 Jamie Morris W PTS 6 Stoke
30.03.92 Gavin Lane W PTS 6 Coventry

Career: 3 contests, won 2, lost 1.

Mickey Cantwell

Eltham. *Born* London, 23 November, 1964
Flyweight (7.10-8.3¼) ht. 5'2½"
Manager –
Pro. Debut 21 January, 1991

21.01.91 Eduardo Vallejo W RSC 4 Crystal Palace
26.03.91 Mario Alberto Cruz W PTS 6 Bethnal Green
30.09.91 Ricky Beard W PTS 8 Kensington
23.10.91 Carlos Manrigues W RSC 5 Bethnal Green
14.12.91 Shaun Norman W PTS 8 Bexleyheath
16.05.92 Louis Veitch W PTS 6 Muswell Hill

Career: 6 contests, won 6.

Mickey Cantwell Les Clark

(George) Gypsy Carman

Ipswich. *Born* Wisbech, 23 November, 1964
L. Heavyweight (12.9-13.4) ht. 6'0"
Manager W. Ball
Pro. Debut 30 January, 1984

22.10.91 Tenko Ernie W PTS 6 Wandsworth
21.01.92 Dave Lawrence W PTS 6 Norwich
31.03.92 Richard Bustin W PTS 6 Norwich

Career: 30 contests, won 12, drew 1, lost 17.

Ian Carmichael

Preston. *Born* Preston, 7 October, 1965
Cruiserweight (14.0) ht. 6'2"
Manager –
Pro. Debut 13 June, 1987

24.02.92 Dene Josham W PTS 6 Bradford

Career: 4 contests, won 3, lost 1.

(John) Cornelius Carr

Middlesbrough. *Born* Middlesbrough, 9 April, 1969
Middleweight (11.6-11.11) ht. 5'9½"
Manager –
Pro. Debut 22 September, 1987

16.02.91 Frank Eubanks W RSC 5 Thornaby
02.03.91 Carlo Colarusso W PTS 8 Darlington
18.05.91 Paul Burton W RSC 3 Verbania, Italy
06.09.91 Marvin O'Brien W RSC 7 Salemi, Italy

Career: 19 contests, won 18, lost 1.

Dean Carr

Doncaster. *Born* Doncaster, 29 June, 1967
Welterweight (10.3-10.8) ht. 5'10½"
Manager J. Rushton
Pro. Debut 29 April, 1991

29.04.91 Mick Reid L RSC 1 Cleethorpes
16.09.91 Michael Byrne W PTS 6 Cleethorpes
01.10.91 Darren McInulty L PTS 6 Bedworth
21.10.91 James Campbell L RSC 5 Cleethorpes
26.11.91 Steve Bricknell W PTS 4 Wolverhampton
04.12.91 Rob Stewart L RTD 5 Stoke

Career: 6 contests, won 2, lost 4.

Dean Carr Chris Bevan

Noel Carroll

Manchester. *Born* Dublin, 7 January, 1968
Featherweight (8.7¼-9.5½) ht. 5'2"
Manager J. Trickett
Pro. Debut 16 November, 1989

29.01.91 Neil Leitch W RSC 4 Stockport
21.02.91 Peter Judson L PTS 8 Leeds
18.03.91 Ian McGirr W PTS 6 Manchester
30.04.91 Colin Innes W PTS 4 Stockport
10.06.91 Mark Loftus W PTS 6 Manchester
19.09.91 Mike Deveney W PTS 6 Stockport
18.11.91 Graham O'Malley W PTS 6 Manchester
16.12.91 Chris Clarkson W PTS 6 Manchester
03.02.92 Barrie Kelley W PTS 8 Manchester
05.05.92 Kevin Jenkins W PTS 7 Preston

Career: 18 contests, won 15, lost 3.

Ronnie Carroll

Glasgow. *Born* Glasgow, 5 November, 1963
Bantamweight (8.6) ht. 5'5½"
Manager T. Gilmour
Pro. Debut 17 July, 1986

21.10.91 Joe Kelly DREW 12 Glasgow *(Vacant British Bantamweight Title)*
27.01.92 Joe Kelly L PTS 12 Glasgow *(Vacant British Bantamweight Title)*
29.05.92 John Green L PTS 10 Manchester *(Elim. British Bantamweight Title)*

Career: 21 contests, won 12, drew 2, lost 7.

Richard Carter

Wolverhampton. *Born* Wolverhampton, 3 September, 1970
Middleweight (11.6-11.10) ht. 5'10"
Manager R. Gray
Pro. Debut 22 September, 1988

15.03.91 Alan Pennington W CO 6 Willenhall
05.06.91 Colin Manners L CO 1 Wolverhampton
10.09.91 Paul Hanlon W RSC 3 Wolverhampton
05.12.91 Paul Murray W PTS 8 Cannock

Career: 11 contests, won 10, lost 1.

Shamus Casey (West)

Alfreton. *Born* Pinxton, 13 January, 1960
L. Middleweight (10.10¼-11.6) ht. 5'11"
Manager –
Pro. Debut 25 January, 1984

17.01.91 Neville Brown L RSC 4 Alfreton
21.02.91 Richie Woodhall L RSC 3 Walsall
28.03.91 Pete Bowman W PTS 6 Alfreton
12.04.91 Martin Rosamond W PTS 6 Willenhall
13.05.91 Paul King W PTS 6 Northampton
04.07.91 Dave Hall W PTS 6 Alfreton
11.09.91 Clay O'Shea L PTS 6 Hammersmith
10.10.91 Dave Johnson L PTS 6 Gateshead
17.10.91 Tyrone Eastmond L PTS 6 Mossley
14.11.91 Dave Johnson L PTS 6 Gateshead
28.11.91 Ian Vokes W PTS 6 Hull
07.12.91 Steve Foster L PTS 8 Manchester
17.03.92 Gary Osborne L RSC 5 Wolverhampton *(Vacant Midlands Area L. Middleweight Title)*
28.05.92 Mark Jay L PTS 8 Gosforth

Career: 108 contests, won 25, drew 5, lost 78.

Sean Cave

Leicester. *Born* Leicester, 4 May, 1967
Welterweight (10.9-10.12) ht. 5'8½"
Manager –
Pro. Debut 23 September, 1987

05.12.91 Dave Fallon L PTS 6 Peterborough
28.04.92 Kevin Mabbutt L PTS 6 Corby
18.06.92 George Wilson W PTS 6 Peterborough

Career: 4 contests, won 2, lost 2.

Ian Chantler (Ashton)

St Helens. *Born* St Helens, 13 June, 1960
Middleweight (11.0-11.6) ht. 6'0"
Manager –
Pro. Debut 24 June, 1982

23.01.91 Shaun Cummins L PTS 10 Brentwood
15.05.91 Silvio Branco L RSC 2 Montichiari, Italy
17.03.92 Stan King L CO 3 Mayfair
25.04.92 Ray Close L RSC 1 Belfast

Career: 60 contests, won 27, drew 1, lost 32.

Gary Charlton (Wilkes)

Leeds. *Born* Leeds, 6 April, 1968
Heavyweight (14.4-16.0) ht. 6'0"
Manager –
Pro. Debut 10 October, 1991

10.10.91 John Pierre L PTS 6 Gateshead
26.10.91 Graham Arnold W RSC 1 Brentwood
11.11.91 Gary Railton L PTS 6 Bradford
23.04.92 Wayne Llewelyn L RSC 4 Eltham
04.06.92 Wayne Buck L PTS 6 Cleethorpes

Career: 5 contests, won 1, lost 4.

Paul Charters

Newcastle. *Born* North Shields, 14 June, 1964
Northern Area Lightweight Champion (9.5-10.1½) ht. 5'7"
Manager T. Conroy
Pro. Debut 10 March, 1988

21.02.91 Peter Till W RSC 6 Walsall
10.05.91 Kevin Spratt W RSC 2 Gateshead
14.08.91 Antonio Renzo L CO 11 Alcamo, Italy *(European Lightweight Title Challenge)*
14.11.91 Gary Barron W RSC 4 Gateshead
03.03.92 John Smith W PTS 8 Houghton le Spring
28.04.92 Paul Burke L RSC 7 Houghton le Spring *(Final Elim. British Lightweight Title)*

Career: 29 contests, won 17, lost 12.

(Ivan) Carlos Chase

Bushey. *Born* Watford, 10 August, 1966
L. Welterweight (9.13-10.4) ht. 5'6¾"
Manager H. Holland
Pro. Debut 28 September, 1989

03.04.91 Seamus O'Sullivan W PTS 8 Bethnal Green
01.06.91 Marcel Herbert W PTS 6 Bethnal Green
12.11.91 Tony Swift L PTS 6 Milton Keynes
12.02.92 Gary Barron W RSC 5 Watford
30.04.92 Dave Pierre L RSC 7 Watford *(Southern Area L. Welterweight Title Challenge)*

Career: 9 contests, won 7, lost 2.

(Peter) Carlos Christie

Birmingham. *Born* Birmingham, 17 August, 1966
Midlands Area S. Middleweight Champion (11.13½-12.8) ht. 6'0"
Manager R. Gray
Pro. Debut 4 June, 1990

10.01.91 Ray Webb L PTS 6 Wandsworth
28.01.91 Gil Lewis W PTS 8 Birmingham
04.03.91 Nigel Rafferty W PTS 8 Birmingham
14.03.91 Michael Gale L PTS 8 Middleton
01.05.91 Peter Elliott W RSC 9 Solihull *(Vacant Midlands Area S. Middleweight Title)*
11.05.91 Ray Close L PTS 6 Belfast
07.09.91 Ray Close L PTS 6 Belfast
20.11.91 Nicky Piper L CO 6 Cardiff
10.03.92 Glenn Campbell DREW 8 Bury

Career: 16 contests, won 8, drew 1, lost 7.

Floyd Churchill

Kirkby. *Born* Liverpool, 19 January, 1969
Lightweight (9.8-9.12) ht. 5'4"
Manager C. Moorcroft
Pro. Debut 29 April, 1992

29.04.92 Terry Smith W RSC 2 Liverpool
14.05.92 Jamie Davidson W RSC 4 Liverpool
12.06.92 Kevin McKillan L PTS 6 Liverpool

Career: 3 contests, won 2, lost 1.

Cliff Churchward

Bournemouth. *Born* Weymouth, 7 June, 1966
Welterweight (10.3-11.1) ht. 5'11"
Manager K. Honniball
Pro. Debut 4 October, 1989

23.01.91 Ernie Loveridge L PTS 6 Solihull
04.02.91 Andreas Panayi L PTS 6 Leicester
08.05.91 Kevin Sheeran L PTS 6 Millwall
20.05.91 James McGee L PTS 6 Leicester
05.06.91 Ernie Loveridge L PTS 8 Wolverhampton
17.06.91 Eddie King L PTS 6 Edgbaston
12.02.92 B. F. Williams L PTS 6 Watford
30.04.92 Danny Shinkwin W PTS 6 Watford

Career: 16 contests, won 1, drew 1, lost 14.

Jimmy Clark

Chadwell Heath. *Born* Tilbury, 27 December, 1969
S. Featherweight (9.1-9.5) ht. 5'8½"
Manager J. Tibbs
Pro. Debut 21 September, 1988

02.10.91 Charlie Coke W PTS 6 Barking
11.12.91 Miguel Matthews W PTS 6 Basildon
11.02.92 Derek Amory W PTS 6 Barking
02.04.92 Chubby Martin W RSC 6 Basildon

Career: 15 contests, won 14, lost 1.

Howard Clarke

Warley. *Born* London, 23 September, 1967
Welterweight (10.3-10.9) ht. 5'10"
Manager –
Pro. Debut 15 October, 1991

15.10.91 Chris Mylan W PTS 4 Dudley
09.12.91 Claude Rossi W RSC 3 Brierley Hill
04.02.92 Julian Eavis W PTS 4 Alfreton
03.03.92 Dave Andrews W RSC 3 Cradley Heath
21.05.92 Richard O'Brien W CO 1 Cradley Heath

Career: 5 contests, won 5.

Carlos Chase (right) pounding Gary Barron to a fifth round defeat at Watford Town Hall
Les Clark

Chris Clarkson

Hull. *Born* Hull, 15 December, 1967
Central Area Bantamweight Champion. Former Undefeated Central Area Featherweight Champion (8.5½-9.0½) ht. 5'4"
Manager M. Toomey
Pro. Debut 18 March, 1985

02.03.91 Francesco Arroyo L RSC 4 Darlington *(Vacant IBF Intercontinental Bantamweight Title)*
04.04.91 Duke McKenzie L RSC 5 Watford
09.10.91 Mark Geraghty L PTS 6 Glasgow
21.10.91 Ian McGirr DREW 6 Glasgow
16.12.91 Noel Carroll L PTS 6 Manchester
03.03.92 Billy Hardy L RSC 5 Houghton le Spring

Career: 39 contests, won 17, drew 2, lost 20.

Kesem Clayton

Coventry. *Born* Coventry, 19 May, 1962
Middleweight (11.3½-11.12) ht. 5'9"
Manager P. Byrne
Pro. Debut 6 October, 1986

22.02.91 Steve Foster L CO 6 Manchester
02.12.91 Nigel Rafferty L PTS 8 Birmingham
31.03.92 Stan King L RSC 4 Norwich

Career: 28 contests, won 12, drew 2, lost 14.

Justin Clements

Birmingham. *Born* Birmingham, 25 September, 1971
Middleweight (11.9¼-11.11) ht. 5'11½"
Manager P. Cowdell
Pro. Debut 2 December, 1991

02.12.91 Adrian Wright W PTS 6 Birmingham
03.03.92 Andy Manning DREW 6 Cradley Heath

Career: 2 contests, won 1, drew 1.

Ray Close

Belfast. *Born* Belfast, 20 January, 1969
All-Ireland S. Middleweight Champion (11.10-12.1½) ht. 5'10"
Manager B. Eastwood
Pro. Debut 19 October, 1988

11.05.91 Carlos Christie W PTS 6 Belfast
07.09.91 Carlos Christie W PTS 6 Belfast
13.11.91 Simon Collins W PTS 6 Belfast
11.12.91 Terry Magee W RSC 7 Dublin *(All-Ireland S. Middleweight Title Defence)*
25.04.92 Ian Chantler W RSC 1 Belfast

Career: 18 contests, won 17, lost 1.

Michael Clynch

Peterborough. *Born* Ealing, 22 June, 1970
Lightweight (9.7-10.0) ht. 5'7½"
Manager K. Whitney
Pro. Debut 8 October, 1991

08.10.91 Gary Peynado W CO 2 Wolverhampton
07.11.91 Nicky Bardle L RSC 4 Peterborough
06.02.92 Brian Hickey W DIS 5 Peterborough
25.03.92 Paul Ryan L RSC 4 Dagenham
28.04.92 G. G. Goddard W RTD 4 Corby

Career: 5 contests, won 3, lost 2.

Shaun Cogan

Birmingham. *Born* Birmingham, 7 August, 1967
L. Welterweight (9.12-10.1½) ht. 5'8"
Manager –
Pro. Debut 25 September, 1989

21.02.91 Tony Britland W PTS 6 Walsall
19.03.91 Rocky Lawlor W RSC 2 Birmingham
25.07.91 David Thompson W CO 1 Dudley
05.12.91 Steve Pollard W PTS 6 Oakengates

Career: 10 contests, won 10.

Charlie Coke

Croydon. *Born* Jamaica, 23 January, 1959
S. Featherweight (9.3-9.5) ht. 5'5"
Manager –
Pro. Debut 27 April, 1983

12.03.91 Lee Fox L PTS 6 Mansfield
25.04.91 Nicky Lucas L PTS 6 Mayfair
20.06.91 Martin Evans W RTD 3 Liverpool
02.10.91 Jimmy Clark L PTS 6 Barking

Career: 12 contests, won 6, lost 6.

Carlo Colarusso

Llanelli. *Born* Swansea, 11 February, 1970
Welsh L. Middleweight Champion (10.12½-11.4½) ht. 5'7"
Manager –
Pro. Debut 14 September, 1989

24.01.91 Gary Pemberton W RSC 8 Gorseinon *(Vacant Welsh L. Middleweight Title)*
02.03.91 Cornelius Carr L PTS 8 Darlington
11.05.92 Russell Washer W RSC 5 Llanelli *(Welsh L. Middleweight Title Defence)*
27.06.92 Newton Barnett W RTD 5 Quinta do Lago, Portugal

Career: 14 contests, won 9, lost 5.

Tony Colclough

Birmingham. *Born* Birmingham, 9 May, 1960
L. Heavyweight (12.3½-14.7½) ht. 6'0"
Manager P. Cowdell
Pro. Debut 15 April, 1991

15.04.91 Steve Yorath L PTS 6 Wolverhampton
30.05.91 Damien Caesar L RSC 1 Mayfair
01.08.91 Denzil Browne L RSC 1 Dewsbury
07.10.91 Karl Guest DREW 6 Birmingham
15.10.91 Jason McNeill W PTS 6 Dudley
02.12.91 Carl Guest W RSC 2 Birmingham
03.03.92 Greg Scott-Briggs L RSC 2 Cradley Heath
21.05.92 Mark Hale DREW 6 Cradley Heath
01.06.92 Mark Hale W PTS 6 Solihull

Career: 9 contests, won 3, drew 2, lost 4.

Brian Coleman

Birmingham. *Born* Birmingham, 27 July, 1969
Welterweight (10.2-10.7) ht. 5'11"
Manager N. Nobbs
Pro. Debut 21 November, 1991

21.11.91 Jamie Morris DREW 6 Stafford
11.12.91 Craig Hartwell DREW 6 Leicester
22.01.92 John O'Johnson L PTS 6 Stoke
20.02.92 Davy Robb L PTS 6 Oakengates
31.03.92 Blue Butterworth L PTS 6 Stockport
17.05.92 Korso Aleain L RSC 5 Harringay

Career: 6 contests, drew 2, lost 4.

Benny Collins

Yateley. *Born* Camberley, 26 November, 1971
Welterweight (10.3-10.6) ht. 5'8"
Manager F. Warren
Pro. Debut 14 February, 1990

05.03.91 David Lake W RSC 4 Millwall
22.05.91 Clive Dixon L PTS 6 Millwall
03.07.91 Julian Eavis W PTS 6 Reading

Career: 6 contests, won 5, lost 1.

Simon Collins

Merthyr. *Born* Merthyr, 16 February, 1967
S. Middleweight (11.13-12.3¾) ht. 5'9"
Manager –
Pro. Debut 1 October, 1985

11.05.91 Noel Magee L PTS 8 Belfast
13.11.91 Ray Close L PTS 6 Belfast

Career: 24 contests, won 6, drew 3, lost 14, no contest 1.

(Elton) Tom Collins

Leeds. *Born* Curacao, ! July, 1955
Former Undefeated British & European L. Heavyweight Champion. Former Undefeated Central Area L. Heavyweight Champion (12.6½-12.7) ht. 5'11"
Manager T. Calllighan
Pro. Debut 17 January, 1977

09.05.91 Leonzer Barber L RTD 5 Leeds *(Vacant WBO L. Heavyweight Title)*
06.12.91 Henry Maske L RSC 8 Dusseldorf, Germany
18.03.92 Glazz Campbell L PTS 10 Glasgow *(Final Elim. British L. Heavyweight Title)*

Career: 48 contests, won 26, drew 1, lost 21.

Tom Collins

Tony Collins

Yateley. *Born* London, 11 May, 1970
Former Undefeated WBC International L. Middleweight Champion (10.12½-11.1) ht. 5'10"
Manager F. Warren
Pro. Debut 1 July, 1987

08.05.91 Ricardo Nunez W PTS 12 Millwall *(WBC International L. Middleweight Title Defence)*
03.07.91 Wally Swift Jnr L PTS 12 Reading *(British L. Middleweight Title Challenge)*
29.10.91 Paul Wesley DREW 8 Kensington
18.06.92 Russell Washer W RSC 2 Peterborough

Career: 29 contests, won 26, drew 1, lost 2.

Jim Conley

Bradford. *Born* Bradford, 13 November, 1967
L. Middleweight (10.12-11.0) ht. 5'10"
Manager K. Richardson
Pro. Debut 2 March, 1987

24.10.91 Allan Grainger L PTS 6 Glasgow
05.12.91 Charlie Moore L CO 2 Peterborough

Career: 17 contests, won 7, drew 1, lost 9.

Tony Connellan

Manchester. *Born* Rochdale, 30 May, 1968
Welterweight (10.8) ht. 5'7"
Manager –
Pro. Debut 24 November, 1986

21.10.91 Richard O'Brien W PTS 8 Bury

Career: 12 contests, won 9, drew 2, lost 1.

Danny Connelly

Glasgow. *Born* Glasgow, 14 May, 1971
S. Featherweight (9.4-9.5) ht. 5'4½"
Manager W. Connelly
Pro. Debut 10 December, 1990

31.05.91 Miguel Matthews W PTS 8 Glasgow
29.05.92 Lee Fox W PTS 6 Glasgow

Career: 3 contests, won 3.

Edward Cook

Larkhall. *Born* Lanark, 30 November, 1967
S. Featherweight (8.13-9.1) ht. 5'4¼"
Manager A. Morrison
Pro. Debut 17 May, 1989

02.03.91 Ian McGirr W PTS 6 Irvine
15.04.91 Darren Elsdon DREW 4 Glasgow
24.10.91 Des Gargano W RSC 5 Glasgow
31.01.92 Des Gargano W PTS 6 Glasgow
20.02.92 Miguel Matthews W PTS 6 Glasgow
08.04.92 Tony Silkstone L PTS 8 Leeds

Career: 16 contests, won 10, drew 1, lost 5.

James Cook

Peckham. *Born* Jamaica, 17 May, 1959
Former European S. Middleweight Champion. Former Undefeated British S. Middleweight Champion. Former Southern Area Middleweight Champion (11.12-12.0) ht. 6'2"
Manager M. Duff
Pro. Debut 20 October, 1982

10.03.91 Frank Winterstein W CO 12 Paris, France *(Vacant European S. Middleweight Title)*
01.06.91 Mark Kaylor W RTD 6 Bethnal Green *(European S. Middleweight Title Defence)*
22.10.91 Tarmo Uusiverta W RTD 7 Wandsworth *(European S. Middleweight Title Defence)*
03.04.92 Franck Nicotra L CO 1 Vitrolles, France *(European S. Middleweight Title Defence)*

Career: 27 contests, won 18, lost 9.

Danny Cooper

Southampton. *Born* Southampton, 11 July, 1967
L. Welterweight (10.4½) ht. 5'6½"
Manager –
Pro. Debut 12 April, 1986

16.12.91 Ron Shinkwin W PTS 6 Southampton

Career: 10 contests, won 8, lost 2.

Dean Cooper

Bristol. *Born* Southmead, 5 August, 1969
L. Middleweight (10.12-11.2) ht. 6'0"
Manager –
Pro. Debut 15 September, 1990

04.02.91 Mike Phillips W PTS 6 Leicester
18.02.91 Andre Wharton W PTS 8 Birmingham
22.10.91 Nick Meloscia W PTS 6 Wandsworth

Career: 8 contests, won 8.

Shaun Cooper

Dudley. *Born* Dudley, 9 February, 1968
L. Welterweight (9.11-9.12) ht. 5'8½"
Manager R. Browne
Pro. Debut 16 May, 1988

10.09.91 Stuart Rimmer W RSC 2 Wolverhampton
12.11.91 Mark Antony W CO 1 Wolverhampton
05.12.91 Eddie King W RSC 3 Cannock

Career: 16 contests, won 16.

Maurice Coore

Manchester. *Born* Manchester, 22 June, 1965
L. Heavyweight (12.8¾-12.13) ht. 6'5"
Manager P. Martin
Pro. Debut 15 January, 1990

22.02.91 Everton Blake W RSC 8 Manchester
12.04.91 Glazz Campbell W CO 2 Manchester
31.05.91 Rodney Brown W RSC 6 Manchester
29.11.91 Steve Osborne W PTS 6 Manchester
31.01.92 Denroy Bryan W RSC 1 Manchester
05.04.92 Willie Ball W RSC 3 Bradford

Career: 9 contests, won 8, drew 1.

John Corcoran

Alfreton. *Born* Chesterfield, 16 December, 1967
Welterweight (10.8-10.13) ht. 5'9¼"
Manager W. Swift
Pro. Debut 29 February, 1988

13.03.91 Ernie Loveridge L RSC 4 Stoke
03.10.91 Tony Britland L RSC 5 Burton
26.11.91 Ojay Abrahams L PTS 6 Bethnal Green
22.01.92 Dave Hall W PTS 8 Stoke
11.03.92 Dave Hall W PTS 8 Stoke
19.03.92 Charlie Moore L PTS 6 York
29.04.92 Steve Goodwin L PTS 8 Stoke

Career: 16 contests, won 8, drew 1, lost 7.

Chris Coughlan

Swansea. *Born* Swansea, 21 May, 1963
Cruiserweight (13.11-14.0) ht. 6'2½"
Manager C. Breen
Pro. Debut 3 October, 1989

16.01.91 Phil Soundy L PTS 6 Kensington
15.02.91 Neils K. H. Madsen L RSC 3 Randers, Denmark
04.11.91 Nick Howard W CO 3 Merthyr
11.12.91 Ray Kane L PTS 6 Dublin
18.01.92 Wayne Llewelyn L RSC 3 Kensington

Career: 13 contests, won 2, lost 11.

Lee Crocker

Swansea. *Born* Swansea, 9 May, 1969
Middleweight (11.0-11.11) ht. 6'0"
Manager M. Copp
Pro. Debut 31 January, 1991

31.01.91 Colin Manners L PTS 6 Bredbury
12.02.91 Paul Evans W RSC 2 Cardiff
04.04.91 Johnny Pinnock W RSC 5 Watford
30.06.91 Andrew Furlong DREW 6 Southwark
30.09.91 Fran Harding L RSC 3 Kensington
11.03.92 Russell Washer W PTS 6 Cardiff
30.04.92 Winston May W RSC 2 Bayswater

Career: 7 contests, won 4, drew 1, lost 2.

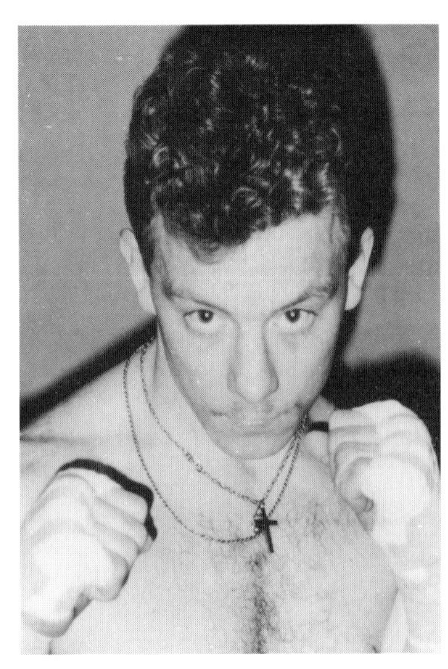

Lee Crocker Les Clark

Denys Cronin

Caerphilly. *Born* Caerphilly, 15 July, 1962
S. Middleweight. Former Undefeated Welsh Middleweight Champion (12.4) ht. 5'9¼"
Manager D. Gardiner
Pro. Debut 30 November, 1985

30.10.91 Michael Gale DREW 8 Leeds

Career: 21 contests, won 10, drew 1, lost 10.

Brian Cullen

Stoke. *Born* Dublin, 2 May, 1964
Welterweight (10.3-10.9) ht. 5'7"
Manager –
Pro. Debut 9 December, 1987

18.02.91 Michael Howell W PTS 6 Derby
05.03.91 Dave Andrews L RSC 1 Cardiff
21.10.91 Mike Calderwood W PTS 6 Bury
11.12.91 Jason Rowland L RSC 4 Basildon

Career: 25 contests, won 13, lost 12.

Phil Cullen

Swansea. *Born* Swansea, 4 February, 1972
Lightweight (9.8½) ht. 58"
Manager M. Copp
Pro. Debut 25 March, 1992

25.03.92 Roger Hunte L RSC 3 Kensington

Career: 1 contest, lost 1.

Shaun Cummins

Leicester. *Born* Leicester, 8 February, 1968
L. Middleweight (10.13¾-11.2) ht. 6'1"
Manager F. Warren
Pro. Debut 29 September, 1986

23.01.91 Ian Chantler W PTS 10 Brentwood
19.03.91 Martin Smith DREW 8 Leicester
07.11.91 Jason Rowe W RSC 2 Peterborough
05.12.91 Winston May W RSC 2 Peterborough
18.06.92 Leroy Owens W RSC 2 Peterborough

Career: 20 contests, won 16, drew 1, lost 3.

Derrick Daniel

Leyton. *Born* Bethnal Green, 3 April, 1963
L. Welterweight (10.0-10.1) ht. 5'9½"
Manager B. Hearn
Pro. Debut 6 March, 1990

26.03.91 Mick O'Donnell DREW 6 Bethnal Green
11.05.92 Carl Hook W PTS 6 Piccadilly
16.06.92 Carl Hook L RSC 2 Dagenham

Career: 6 contests, won 3, drew 1, lost 2.

Hughie Davey

Newcastle. *Born* Wallsend, 27 January, 1966
Welterweight (10.9-10.9½) ht. 5'8"
Manager: T. Conroy
Pro. Debut 30 March, 1992

30.03.92 Wayne Shepherd W PTS 6 Bradford
28.04.92 Benji Joseph W RSC 4 Houghton le Spring

Career: 2 contests, won 2.

(David) Jamie Davidson (Prescott)

Liverpool. *Born* Liverpool, 1 April, 1970
Lightweight (9.12-9.13½) ht. 6'0"
Manager M. Atkinson
Pro. Debut 18 November, 1991

18.11.91 Ty Zubair W PTS 6 Manchester
10.02.92 Kevin McKillan W PTS 6 Liverpool
11.03.92 Kevin McKillan DREW 6 Stoke
28.04.92 Micky Hall W PTS 6 Houghton le Spring
14.05.92 Floyd Churchill L RSC 4 Liverpool

Career: 5 contests, won 3, drew 1, lost 1.

John Davies

Ammanford. *Born* Swansea, 10 Sept. 1964
Welsh Welterweight Champion (10.12-10.13½) ht. 5'10"
Manager C. Breen
Pro. Debut 13 October, 1982

15.10.91 Andy Till L PTS 12 Dudley *(Vacant WBC International L. Middleweight Title)*
11.03.92 Trevor Ambrose W RSC 5 Cardiff

Career: 17 contests, won 14, drew 1, lost 2.

Derrick Daniel (left) sizes up Gavin Fitzpatrick before stopping him in the first round in May 1990 Les Clark

John Davison

Newcastle. *Born* Newcastle, 30 September, 1958
WBC International S. Bantamweight Champion. Former Undefeated WBC International Featherweight Champion (8.9¼-8.13¾) ht. 5'5"
Manager T. Conroy
Pro. Debut 22 September, 1988

25.05.91 Fabrice Benichou L PTS 12 Brest, France
(Vacant European Featherweight Title)
09.08.91 Richard Savage W RSC 6 Juan les Pins, France
22.10.91 Sakda Sorpakdee W PTS 12 Hartlepool
(WBC International S. Bantamweight Title Challenge)
29.05.92 Fabrice Benichou L PTS 12 Amneville les Thermes, France
(European Featherweight Title Challenge)

Career: 17 contests, won 14, lost 3.

Russell Davison

Salford. *Born* Salford, 2 October, 1961
Central Area Featherweight Champion (8.13-9.4) ht. 5'7"
Manager J. Trickett
Pro. Debut 22 May, 1986

29.01.91 Peter Judson W PTS 10 Stockport
(Vacant Central Area Featherweight Title)
05.03.91 Colin McMillan L PTS 6 Millwall
24.04.91 Steve Robinson L RTD 6 Preston
09.09.91 Jimmy Owens W PTS 10 Liverpool
(Central Area Featherweight Title Defence)
29.02.92 Moussa Sangaree L RSC 5 Gravelines, France

Career: 28 contests, won 11, drew 1, lost 16.

Mark Dawson

Burton. *Born* Burton, 26 February, 1971
Welterweight (10.5) ht. 5'8"
Manager W. Swift
Pro. Debut 3 June, 1992

03.06.92 Rick North W PTS 6 Newcastle under Lyme

Career: 1 contest, won 1.

Andy Deabreu

Cardiff. *Born* Cardiff, 28 September, 1964
Former Undefeated Welsh S. Featherweight Champion (9.4-9.5½) ht. 5'4"
Manager D. Gardiner
Pro. Debut 22 February, 1984

12.02.91 Mark Reefer L PTS 10 Cardiff
(Elim. British S. Featherweight Title)
17.12.91 Neil Haddock L RSC 3 Cardiff

Career: 20 contests, won 11, drew 2, lost 7.

Gary Delaney

West Ham. *Born* Newham, 12 August, 1970
L. Heavyweight (12.7-13.0) ht. 6'3"
Manager B. Hearn
Pro. Debut 2 October, 1991

02.10.91 Gus Mendes W RSC 1 Barking
23.10.91 Joe Frater W RSC 1 Bethnal Green
13.11.91 John Kaighin W PTS 6 Bethnal Green
11.12.91 Randy B. Powell W RSC 1 Basildon
11.02.92 Simon Harris DREW 8 Barking
12.05.92 John Williams W PTS 6 Crystal Palace
16.06.92 Nigel Rafferty W CO 5 Dagenham

Career: 7 contests, won 6, drew 1.

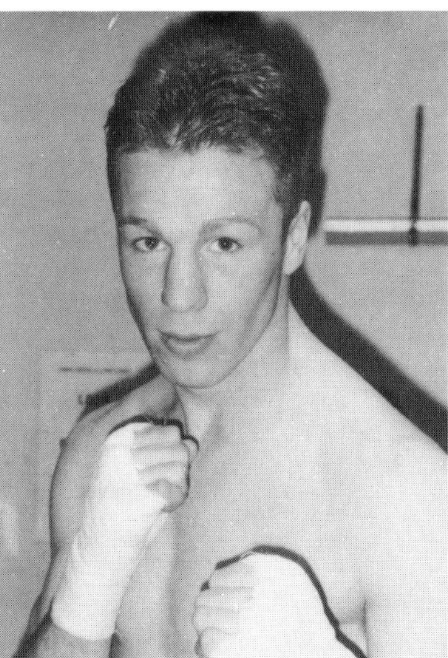

Gary Delaney Les Clark

Pat Delargy

Coventry. *Born* Hoddeston, 9 October, 1969
L. Welterweight (10.0-10.2) ht. 5'9"
Manager P. Byrne
Pro. Debut 14 February, 1989

24.09.91 Bernard Paul L RSC 5 Basildon
11.05.92 Mark Antony W PTS 6 Coventry

Career: 7 contests, won 3, lost 4.

Craig Dermody

Manchester. *Born* Manchester, 11 September, 1970
Bantamweight (8.7-8.12) ht. 5'6"
Manager J. Doughty
Pro. Debut 31 January, 1991

31.01.91 Karl Morling W RSC 5 Bredbury
14.03.91 Kelton McKenzie W RSC 3 Middleton
16.04.91 Miguel Matthews W PTS 6 Nottingham
16.05.91 Andrew Robinson W PTS 6 Liverpool
20.06.91 Gary Hickman W RSC 2 Liverpool
01.08.91 James Hunter W RSC 2 Dewsbury
21.11.91 Miguel Matthews W PTS 6 Burton
28.11.91 Pete Buckley W PTS 6 Liverpool
19.12.91 Pete Buckley W PTS 6 Oldham
27.02.92 Miguel Matthews W PTS 6 Liverpool

Career: 10 contests, won 10.

Craig Dermody Chris Bevan

Gary de Roux

Peterborough. *Born* Manchester, 4 November, 1962
Former British Featherweight Champion. Former Undefeated Southern Area Featherweight Champion (8.12½-9.0) ht. 5'6"
Manager –
Pro. Debut 25 September, 1986

05.03.91 Sean Murphy W CO 5 Millwall
(British Featherweight Title Challenge)
22.05.91 Colin McMillan L RSC 7 Millwall
(British Featherweight Title Defence)
13.11.91 Alan McKay L RSC 8 Bethnal Green
(Vacant Southern Area Featherweight Title)

Career: 20 contests, won 13, drew 1, lost 6.

Mike Deveney

Paisley. *Born* Elderslie, 14 December, 1965
S. Featherweight (8.12-9.8) ht. 5'5"
Manager N. Sweeney
Pro. Debut 18 February, 1991

18.02.91 John George W PTS 6 Glasgow
18.03.91 Frankie Ventura W PTS 6 Piccadilly
22.04.91 Neil Leitch W PTS 6 Glasgow
09.09.91 Pete Buckley W PTS 8 Glasgow
19.09.91 Noel Carroll L PTS 6 Stockport
14.11.91 Pete Buckley W PTS 6 Edinburgh
28.01.92 Graham O'Malley L RSC 1 Piccadilly
28.02.92 Gary Hickman W PTS 6 Irvine

Career: 8 contests, won 6, lost 2.

Eunan Devenney

Bushey. *Born* Donegal, 2 February, 1968
S. Featherweight (9.1-9.2) ht. 5'5"
Manager J. Barclay
Pro. Debut 4 September, 1991

04.09.91 Alan Smith W CO 1 Bethnal Green
26.09.91 Kevin Lowe L CO 2 Dunstable
28.11.91 Greg Upton L PTS 6 Evesham
30.03.92 David Ramsden L RSC 2 Bradford

Career: 4 contests, won 1, lost 3.

Norman Dhalie

Birmingham. *Born* Birmingham, 24 March, 1971
Featherweight (9.1-9.2¼) ht. 5'7"
Manager N. Nobbs
Pro. Debut 6 April, 1992

06.04.92 Karl Morling L PTS 6 Northampton
27.04.92 Wilson Docherty L RSC 2 Glasgow

Career: 2 contests, lost 2.

(Richard) Rick Dimmock

Wokingham. *Born* Feltham, 23 September, 1964
Lightweight (9.8-9.12) ht. 5'7"
Manager –
Pro. Debut 21 November, 1986

01.05.91 Steve Hearn L PTS 6 Bethnal Green
02.10.91 Chris Francis L PTS 6 Barking

Career: 17 contests, won 4, lost 13.

Clive Dixon

Dulwich. *Born* London, 11 May, 1965
L. Middleweight (10.4-11.4) ht. 5'6"
Manager B. Paget
Pro. Debut 22 May, 1991

22.05.91 Benny Collins W PTS 6 Millwall
04.09.91 Kevin Sheeran L RSC 4 Bethnal Green
22.02.92 Tracy Jocelyn L PTS 6 St. Leonards

Career: 3 contests, won 1, lost 2.

Terry Dixon

West Ham. *Born* London 29 July, 1966
Cruiserweight (12.11-13.7½) ht. 5'11"
Manager T. Lawless
Pro. Debut 21 September, 1989

07.03.91 Carl Thompson L PTS 8 Basildon
22.04.91 Everton Blake L RSC 8 Mayfair
25.03.92 Mark Bowen W RTD 1 Kensington
27.04.92 Ian Bulloch W RSC 4 Mayfair

Career: 9 contests, won 7, lost 2.

Alex Docherty

Craigneuk. *Born* Motherwell, 5 June, 1972
Bantamweight (8.8½) ht. 5'5"
Manager T. Gilmour
Pro. Debut 24 February, 1992

24.02.92 Andrew Bloomer W PTS 6 Glasgow
01.06.92 Robert Braddock W PTS 6 Glasgow

Career: 2 contests, won 2.

Wilson Docherty

Croy. *Born* Glasgow, 15 April, 1968
Featherweight (9.1) ht. 5'6"
Manager T. Gilmour
Pro. Debut 27 April, 1992

27.04.92 Norman Dhalie W RSC 2 Glasgow

Career: 1 contest, won 1.

(Pat) John Doherty

Bradford. *Born* Bradford, 17 July, 1962
Former British S. Featherweight Champion. Former Undefeated Central Area Featherweight Champion (9.2½-9.4) ht. 5'4½"
Manager –
Pro. Debut 26 May, 1982

22.04.91 Frankie Foster W PTS 10 Glasgow *(Elim. British S. Featherweight Title)*
19.09.91 Sugar Gibiliru W PTS 12 Stockport *(British S. Featherweight Title Challenge)*
25.04.92 Michael Armstrong L RSC 7 Manchester *(British S. Featherweight Title Defence)*

Career: 39 contests, won 28, drew 3, lost 8.

John Doherty Peter Shaw

Paul Donaghey

Islington. *Born* Londonderry, 22 August, 1969
S. Featherweight (9.0½-9.6) ht. 5'6"
Manager E. Secombe
Pro. Debut 4 June, 1991

04.06.91 Phil Lashley W CO 1 Bethnal Green
03.07.91 Paul Forrest L CO 2 Brentwood
11.02.92 Chris Francis W CO 2 Barking

Career: 3 contests, won 2, lost 1.

Scott Doyle

Birmingham. *Born* Birmingham, 14 June, 1968
L. Welterweight (9.12-10.4) ht. 5'8"
Manager –
Pro. Debut 15 March, 1991

15.03.91 Chris Cooper W RSC 1 Willenhall
12.04.91 Barry North W PTS 6 Willenhall
17.06.91 Tony Doyle W PTS 6 Edgbaston
07.10.91 Jason Brattley W PTS 6 Birmingham
21.11.91 Shane Sheridan W PTS 6 Ilkeston
09.12.91 Peter Till L CO 3 Brierley Hill
03.02.92 Ricky Sackfield L PTS 6 Manchester
03.03.92 Richard O'Brien W PTS 4 Cradley Heath
14.05.92 Joey Moffat L RSC 8 Liverpool

Career: 9 contests, won 6, lost 3.

Tony Doyle (Dodson)

Sheffield. *Born* Rotherham, 26 December, 1962
Lightweight (9.9-9.13) ht.5'10"
Manager A. Thompson
Pro. Debut 27 March, 1990

23.01.91 Richard Joyce L CO 6 Stoke
13.03.91 Bobby Beckles L PTS 6 Stoke
12.04.91 Roy Doyle DREW 6 Manchester
23.04.91 Barry North W PTS 6 Evesham
17.06.91 Scott Doyle L PTS 6 Edgbaston
17.10.91 Paul Hughes L PTS 6 Mossley
21.11.91 Brian Hickey W PTS 6 Ilkeston
05.12.91 Davy Robb L PTS 6 Oakengates
10.02.92 Joey Moffat L RSC 3 Liverpool
04.04.92 Andy Kent W RSC 5 Cleethorpes

Career: 17 contests, won 6, drew 1, lost 10.

Michael Driscoll

Portsmouth. *Born* Portsmouth, 18 May, 1969
L. Welterweight (9.12-10.0) ht. 5'10¼"
Manager M. Fawcett
Pro. Debut 16 June, 1988

02.05.91 Andrew Morgan W PTS 6 Kensington
22.06.91 Steve Foran W RSC 4 Earls Court
01.02.92 Peter Till W RSC 3 Birmingham
25.04.92 Alan Hall L PTS 6 Manchester

Career: 16 contests, won 11, drew 3, lost 2.

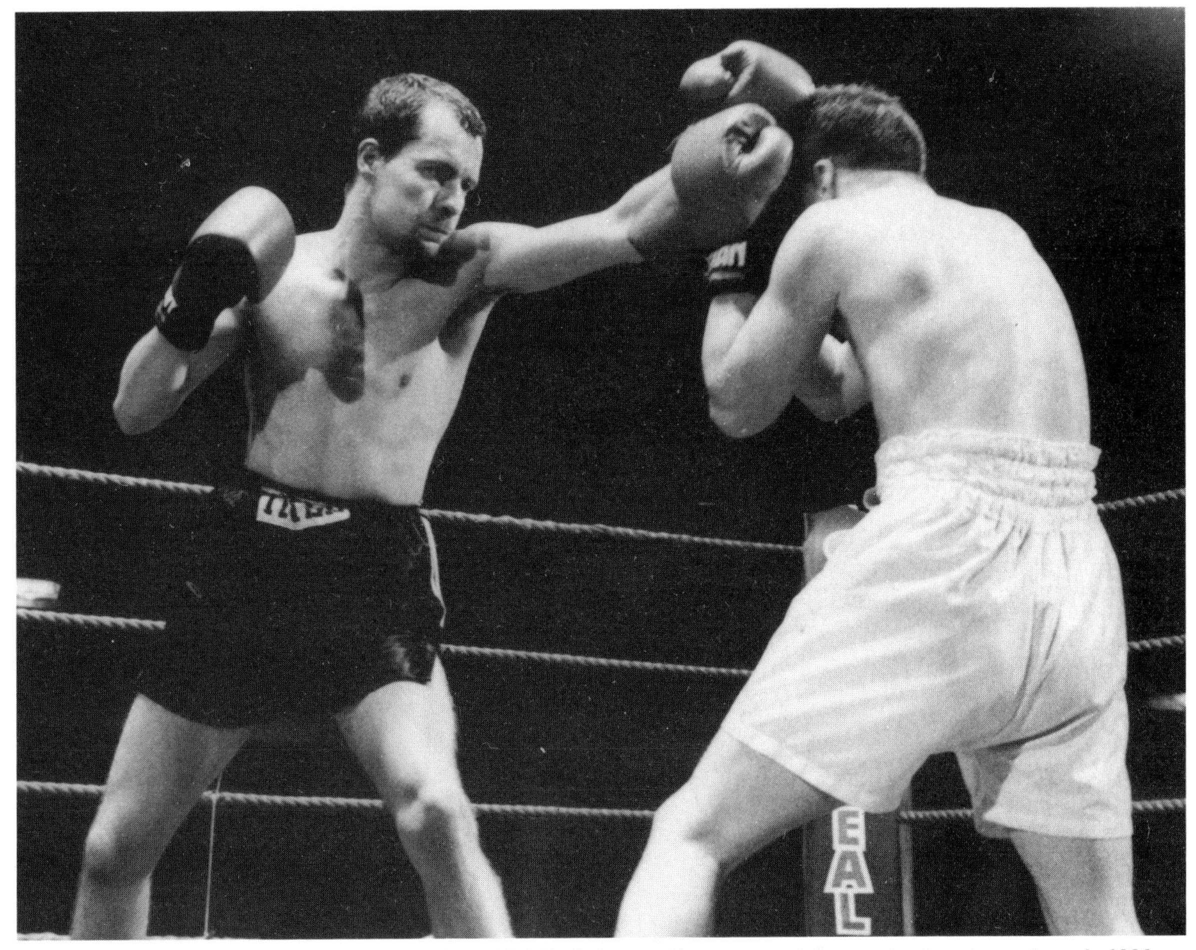

Tim Driscoll (left) jabs the left hand into Graham O'Malley's face on his way to a eight round points victory in early 1990
Les Clark

Tim Driscoll
Bermondsey. *Born* London, 15 May, 1964
Former Southern Area Featherweight Champion (8.13¼-9.2) ht. 5'7¼"
Manager B. Hearn
Pro. Debut 8 September, 1986

06.02.91 Des Gargano W PTS 6 Bethnal Green
18.04.91 Aldrich Johnson W PTS 8 Earls Court
22.06.91 Ruben Aguirre W PTS 8 Earls Court
09.11.91 Maurizio Stecca L RTD 9 Campione d'Italia, Italy
(WBO Featherweight Title Challenge)

Career: 20 contests, won 16, lost 4.

James Drummond
Kilmarnock. *Born* Kilmarnock, 11 February, 1969
Flyweight (7.13-8.6) ht. 5'6"
Manager T. Gilmour
Pro. Debut 18 September, 1989

18.03.91 Stewart Fishermac W RSC 8 Piccadilly
07.05.91 Des Gargano W PTS 8 Glasgow
01.06.91 Mercurio Ciaramitaro DREW 6 Ragusa, Italy
15.11.91 Salvatore Fanni L PTS 12 Omegna, Italy
(European Flyweight Title Challenge)
19.05.92 Robbie Regan L RSC 9 Cardiff
(British Flyweight Title Challenge)

Career: 12 contests, won 6, drew 1, lost 5.

John Duckworth
Burnley. *Born* Burnley, 25 May, 1971
L. Middleweight (11.0-11.1¼) ht. 6'2"
Manager N. Basso
Pro. Debut 4 April, 1992

04.04.92 Warren Stephens W RSC 5 Cleethorpes
13.04.92 Steve Goodwin L PTS 6 Manchester
04.06.92 Phil Foxon W RSC 4 Burnley

Career: 3 contests, won 2, lost 1.

Terry Duffus
Gloucester. *Born* Gloucester, 18 September, 1960
L. Heavyweight (12.7-13.9¼) ht. 5'11"
Manager –
Pro. Debut 29 February, 1988

31.01.91 Nick Manners L RSC 1 Bredbury
07.03.91 Phil Soundy L RSC 2 Basildon
12.09.91 Keith Inglis L CO 5 Wandsworth
25.03.92 Joey Peters L RSC 1 Kensington

Career: 16 contests, won 4, drew 1, lost 11.

Marty Duke
Yarmouth. *Born* Yarmouth, 19 June, 1967
L. Middleweight (10.6¼-11.3) ht. 5'9"
Manager –
Pro. Debut 16 May, 1988

29.01.91 Paul Smith L PTS 6 Wisbech
15.04.91 James McGee W PTS 6 Leicester
08.05.91 Martin Rosamond DREW 8 Millwall
16.05.91 Danny Shinkwin L PTS 6 Battersea

30.05.91 Richie Woodhall L RSC 4 Birmingham
04.07.91 Robert McCracken L RSC 1 Alfreton
03.09.91 Eamonn Loughran L PTS 6 Cardiff
26.09.91 Adrian Riley L PTS 6 Dunstable
05.11.91 Tony McKenzie L RSC 7 Leicester
31.03.92 Ojay Abrahams L RSC 2 Norwich

Career: 26 contests, won 7, drew 2, lost 17.

Mick Duncan

Newcastle. *Born* Newcastle, 24 August, 1969
L. Middleweight (10.8-11.4) ht. 5'11"
Manager G. McCrory
Pro. Debut 29 September, 1988

18.02.91 Tommy Milligan L PTS 6 Glasgow
06.03.91 Danny Quigg L PTS 6 Glasgow
18.03.91 Allan Grainger W PTS 6 Glasgow
10.05.91 Rob Pitters L RSC 2 Gateshead
23.09.91 Danny Quigg DREW 6 Glasgow
07.10.91 Tyrone Eastmond L RSC 5 Bradford
18.11.91 Allan Grainger W PTS 6 Glasgow
25.11.91 Willie Yeardsley W PTS 6 Liverpool
12.12.91 Dave Johnson L PTS 6 Hartlepool
20.01.92 Mark Jay L PTS 6 Bradford
20.02.92 Leigh Wicks W PTS 8 Glasgow
06.03.92 Oleg Chalajew W PTS 8 Berlin, Germany
13.05.92 Lloyd Honeyghan L RSC 2 Kensington
27.06.92 Reiner Gies L CO 7 Halle, Germany

Career: 27 contests, won 10, drew 2, lost 15.

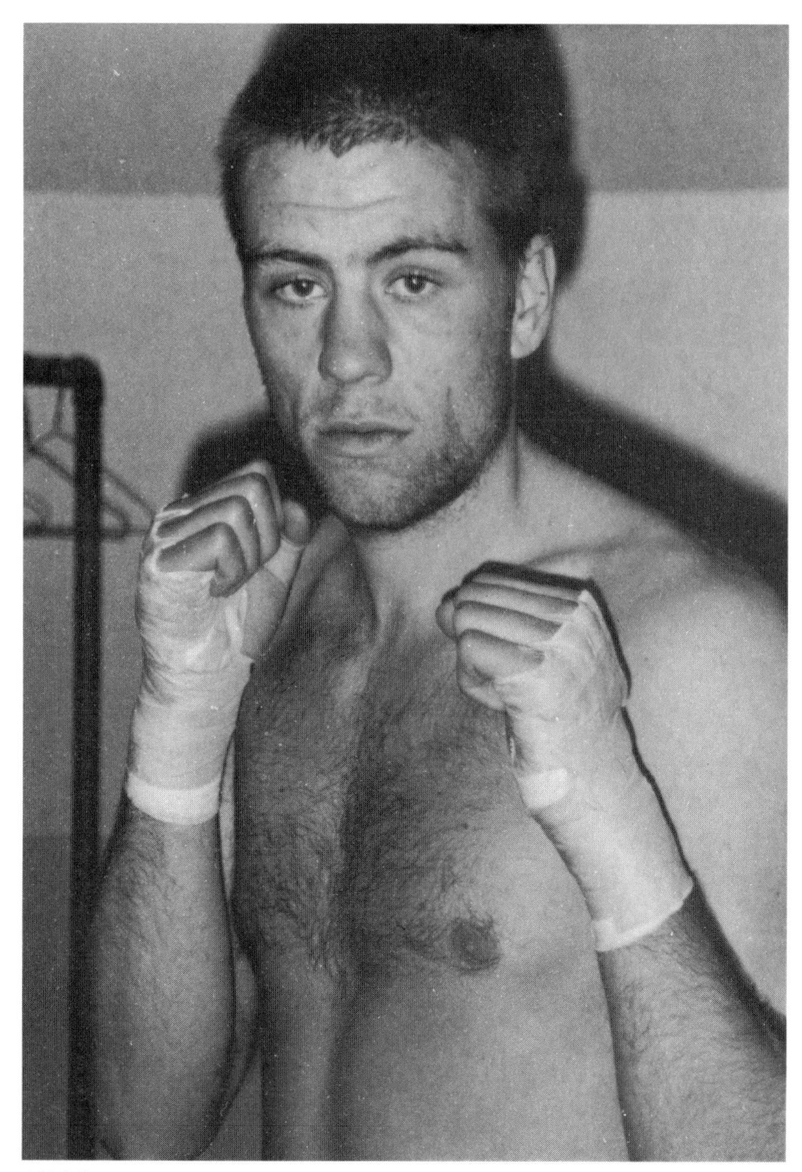

Mick Duncan Les Clark

Stuart Dunn

Leicester. *Born* Leicester, 19 January, 1970
L. Middleweight (10.13½-11.3½) ht. 5'10½"
Manager J. Baxter
Pro. Debut 15 October, 1991

15.10.91 Spencer McCracken DREW 6 Dudley
09.12.91 Wayne Panayiotiou W CO 4 Brierley Hill
23.01.92 Charlie Moore L RSC 3 York

Career: 3 contests, won 1, drew 1, lost 1.

Darren Dyer

Islington. *Born* London, 31 July, 1966
Welterweight (10.5¼-10.9) ht. 5'7½"
Manager –
Pro. Debut 20 November, 1986

03.07.91 Trevor Ambrose W PTS 6 Brentwood
26.10.91 Kelvin Mortimer W RSC 2 Brentwood
26.11.91 Robert Wright W RSC 3 Bethnal Green
19.02.92 Ian John-Lewis W RSC 2 Muswell Hill
12.05.92 Del Bryan W RSC 10 Crystal Palace

Career: 20 contests, won 17, lost 3.

Darren Dyer Les Clark

Paul Dyer

Portsmouth. *Born* Portsmouth, 11 July, 1970
Welterweight (10.4-10.7½) ht. 5'11½"
Manager B. Hearn
Pro. Debut 24 September, 1991

24.09.91 Mick Reid W PTS 6 Basildon
19.11.91 Dave Andrews W PTS 6 Norwich

Career: 2 contests, won 2.

Tyrone Eastmond

Oldham. *Born* Barbados, 26 September, 1960
L. Middleweight (10.13½-11.6) ht. 5'10"
Manager J. Doughty
Pro. Debut 25 March, 1991

25.03.91 Benji Joseph L PTS 6 Bradford
15.04.91 Jim Kirk W RSC 4 Glasgow
17.05.91 Tommy Warde W RSC 4 Bury
10.06.91 Dave Johnson L PTS 6 Manchester
07.10.91 Mick Duncan W RSC 5 Bradford
17.10.91 Shamus Casey W PTS 6 Mossley
11.11.91 Ian Midwood Tate W RSC 2 Bradford
16.12.91 Mark Jay W PTS 6 Manchester
09.03.92 David Radford DREW 6 Manchester

Career: 9 contests, won 6, drew 1, lost 2.

Julian Eavis

Yeovil. *Born* Bourton, 3 December, 1965
Welterweight (10.7-11.0) ht. 5'7¾"
Manager –
Pro. Debut 12 October, 1988

16.01.91 Gary Logan L RSC 5 Kensington
05.03.91 Eamonn Loughran L PTS 6 Cardiff
20.03.91 Kevin Plant L PTS 6 Solihull
10.04.91 Ernie Loveridge DREW 8 Wolverhampton
01.05.91 Humphrey Harrison L PTS 6 Solihull
28.05.91 Darren Liney L PTS 6 Cardiff
05.06.91 Wayne Timmins L PTS 6 Wolverhampton
11.06.91 James McGee L PTS 6 Leicester
03.07.91 Benny Collins L PTS 6 Reading
03.09.91 Michael Smyth L PTS 6 Cardiff
01.10.91 Lee Ferrie L PTS 6 Bedworth
23.10.91 Kevin Lueshing L RSC 2 Bethnal Green
26.11.91 James Campbell W PTS 8 Wolverhampton
04.12.91 Peter Reid W PTS 6 Stoke
11.12.91 James McGee DREW 6 Leicester
17.12.91 Michael Smyth L PTS 6 Cardiff
15.01.92 Robert Wright L PTS 8 Stoke
04.02.92 Howard Clarke L PTS 4 Alfreton
11.02.92 Jamie Robinson L PTS 6 Barking
24.02.92 Lee Ferrie L PTS 8 Coventry
11.03.92 Rob Pitters L PTS 6 Solihull
11.05.92 James McGee L RSC 3 Coventry

Career: 58 contests, won 12, drew 4, lost 42.

(Clive) Bobbie Joe Edwards

Manchester. *Born* Jamaica, 25 December, 1957
L. Heavyweight (12.8½-13.3½) ht. 5'10"
Manager P. Martin
Pro. Debut 9 October, 1990

22.02.91 Cordwell Hylton L RTD 6 Manchester
29.11.91 David Brown W RSC 4 Manchester
31.01.92 Richard Bustin W PTS 6 Manchester
29.05.92 John Foreman L RSC 4 Manchester

Career: 6 contests, won 4, lost 2.

Erwin Edwards

Clapham. *Born* Barbados, 31 October, 1966
L. Welterweight (10.0-10.0½) ht. 5'11"
Manager –
Pro. Debut 26 September, 1988

07.04.92 B. F. Williams L PTS 6 Southend
30.04.92 Korso Aleain L PTS 6 Bayswater

Career: 9 contests, won 2, lost 7.

Renny Edwards

Haverfordwest. *Born* Haverfordwest, 10 February, 1968
Featherweight (9.1-9.3) ht. 5'3½"
Manager D. Davies
Pro. Debut 7 December, 1988

29.08.91 Brian Robb L PTS 6 Oakengates
30.10.91 Tony Silkstone L PTS 6 Leeds

Career: 7 contests, won 4, lost 3.

Steve Edwards

Haverfordwest. *Born* Haverfordwest, 18 July, 1970
L. Welterweight (9.12½) ht. 5'4"
Manager D. Davies
Pro. Debut 2 March, 1992

02.03.92 Nigel Burder W RSC 1 Merthyr

Career: 1 contest, won 1.

Joe Egan

Dublin. *Born* London, 15 November, 1965
Heavyweight (14.8¾) ht. 6'1½"
Manager B. Eastwood
Pro. Debut 21 February, 1990

11.12.91 Denroy Bryan L RSC 4 Dublin

Career: 3 contests, won 2, lost 1.

Greg Egbuniwe

Hackney. *Born* Hackney, 12 October, 1964
Lightweight (9.9-10.0) ht. 5'7"
Manager E. Secombe
Pro. Debut 27 June, 1989

24.10.91 Ross Hale L RSC 4 Bayswater
12.02.92 Shaun Shinkwin W DIS 1 Watford
07.04.92 Alex Sterling W RSC 4 Southend
30.04.92 Carl Tilley W PTS 6 Kensington
16.05.92 Paul Ryan L RSC 4 Muswell Hill

Career: 11 contests, won 3, lost 8.

Tony Ekubia

Manchester. *Born* Nigeria, 6 March, 1960
Former British & Commonwealth L. Welterweight Champion. Former Undefeated Central Area Lighweight & Welterweight Champion (9.13¼-10.6½) ht. 5'8"
Manager J. Trickett
Pro. Debut 18 November, 1986

29.01.91 Juma Kutonda W RTD 6 Stockport *(Commonwealth L. Welterweight Title Defence)*
20.06.91 Andy Holligan L PTS 12 Liverpool *(British & Commonwealth L. Welterweight Title Defence)*
10.03.92 Eamonn Loughran W DIS 5 Bury *(Elim. British Welterweight Title)*
31.03.92 Verdell Smith W RSC 2 Stockport

Career: 21 contests, won 18, lost 3.

Greg Egbuniwe (left) shown in the first round against Shaun Shinkwin, before the latter was thrown out seconds later for fighting on after the bell had ended the round
Les Clark

Tony Ekubia Harry Goodwin

Mark Elliot

Telford. *Born* Telford, 2 February, 1966
L. Welterweight (10.2-10.3½) ht. 5'9"
Manager –
Pro. Debut 10 September, 1991

10.09.91 Dean Bramhald W CO 5 Wolverhampton
12.11.91 John Smith W PTS 6 Wolverhampton
05.12.91 Mick Mulcahy W RSC 2 Cannock
17.03.92 Andrew Morgan W PTS 6 Wolverhampton

Career: 4 contests, won 4.

Barry Ellis

Clapham. *Born* Islington, 25 October, 1957
Heavyweight (15.7) ht. 6'3"
Manager –
Pro. Debut 22 September, 1983

01.05.92 Mario Guedes L RSC 6 Aachen, Germany

Career: 33 contests, won 11, drew 2, lost 20.

Wayne Ellis

Cardiff. *Born* Cardiff, 18 July, 1968
Welsh Middleweight Champion (11.6-11.9) ht. 6'0"
Manager B. Hearn
Pro. Debut 25 June, 1988

05.03.91 Johnny Melfah W RSC 2 Cardiff
03.09.91 Colin Manners L RSC 1 Cardiff
11.02.92 Alan Richards W PTS 10 Cardiff *(Vacant Welsh Middleweight Title)*

Career: 13 contests, won 11, drew 1, lost 1.

Darren Elsdon

Hartlepool. *Born* Hartlepool, 16 February, 1971
Northern Area S. Featherweight Champion (9.2-9.5) ht. 5'5½"
Manager G. Robinson
Pro. Debut 13 November, 1990

06.04.91 Harry Escott W RSC 2 Darlington
15.04.91 Edward Cook DREW 4 Glasgow
22.10.91 Frankie Foster W RSC 7 Hartlepool *(Northern Area S. Featherweight Title Challenge)*
12.12.91 Ian McGirr W CO 4 Hartlepool
21.01.92 Michael Armstrong L RSC 1 Stockport *(Final Elim. British S. Featherweight Title)*

Career: 7 contests, won 5, drew 1, lost 1.

Darren Elsdon Chris Bevan

Phil Epton (Hampton)

Doncaster. *Born* Doncaster, 14 June, 1968
Welterweight (10.5¾-11.0) ht. 5'8"
Manager M. Duff
Pro. Debut 18 October, 1990

07.02.91 Pat Durkin W PTS 6 Watford
21.03.91 Paul King L PTS 6 Dewsbury
13.06.91 Willie Yeardsley W RSC 3 Hull
23.01.92 Carl Hook W PTS 6 York
19.03.92 Ricky Mabbett L RSC 3 York

Career: 7 contests, won 4, lost 3.

Roland Ericsson

Mayfair. *Born* Sweden, 15 February, 1962
S. Middleweight (11.12-12.4½) ht. 5'11"
Manager G. Steene
Pro. Debut 9 October, 1987

20.03.91 Mark Kaylor L RSC 4 Wandsworth
16.05.91 Johnny Melfah L RSC 4 Battersea
22.10.91 Frank Eubanks L RSC 3 Wandsworth
13.12.91 Marian Rudi W CO 3 Minden, Germany
25.02.92 Peter Vosper W RSC 6 Crystal Palace
04.04.92 Jan Franek W RSC 5 Minden, Germany
12.05.92 Karl Barwise W PTS 6 Crystal Palace

Career: 19 contests, won 16, lost 3.

Roland Ericsson (right) on the offensive, before suffering a fourth round stoppage at the hands of Johnny Melfah in May 1991 Les Clark

(Ernie) Tenko Ernie (Tenkorang)
Fulham. *Born* Fulham, 25 February, 1963
L. Heavyweight (12.4-12.12½) ht. 6'0"
Manager –
Pro. Debut 21 April, 1988

26.04.91 Dave Lawrence W RSC 3 Crystal Palace
22.10.91 Gypsy Carman L PTS 6 Wandsworth
12.02.92 Tony Booth L RSC 4 Wembley

Career: 10 contests, won 4, lost 6.

Harry Escott
Sunderland. *Born* West Germany, 17 October, 1969
S. Featherweight (9.3-9.6) ht. 5'8"
Manager T. Conroy
Pro. Debut 26 February, 1987

02.03.91 Steve Walker DREW 6 Darlington
06.04.91 Darren Elsdon L RSC 2 Darlington
06.07.91 Jackie Gunguluza L CO 6 Imperia, Italy
20.09.91 Steve Walker DREW 6 Manchester
04.02.92 Neil Smith W PTS 8 Alfreton
17.03.92 Floyd Havard L RSC 7 Mayfair
27.05.92 Wilson Rodriguez L PTS 10 Cologne, Germany

Career: 31 contests, won 20, drew 3, lost 8.

Peter Eubank
Brighton. *Born* Manchester, 23 March, 1962
Welterweight (10.8-10.9) ht. 5'6"
Manager –
Pro. Debut 20 October, 1980

02.10.91 Roy Rowland L PTS 8 Barking
20.11.91 Gary Jacobs L PTS 8 Kensington

Career: 35 contests, won 14, lost 21.

Simon Eubank
Brighton. *Born* Manchester, 23 March, 1962
Welterweight (10.8½-10.10½) ht. 5'7"
Manager P. Newman
Pro. Debut 29 November, 1984

29.01.91 Glyn Rhodes L RSC 3 Wisbech
16.05.91 Andy Holligan L RSC 2 Liverpool
01.10.91 Paul Jones L CO 6 Sheffield
18.01.92 Kevin Lueshing L CO 4 Kensington

Career: 27 contests, won 7, lost 20.

Frank Eubanks
Manchester. *Born* Manchester, 25 June, 1969
S. Middleweight (11.9¾-12.1) ht. 5'10½"
Manager –
Pro. Debut 26 September, 1989

16.02.91 Cornelius Carr L RSC 5 Thornaby
12.04.91 Peter Vosper W RSC 1 Manchester
24.06.91 Marvin O'Brien W PTS 6 Liverpool
22.10.91 Roland Ericsson W RSC 3 Wandsworth
22.01.92 Nicky Piper L PTS 10 Cardiff *(Elim. British S. Middleweight Title)*

Career: 15 contests, won 9, lost 6.

Jason Evans
Bargoed. *Born* Church Village, 10 June, 1972
S. Featherweight (9.3) ht. 5'7½"
Manager D. Gardiner
Pro. Debut 21 October, 1991

21.10.91 Johnny Patterson W PTS 6 Mayfair

Career: 1 contest, won 1.

Nigel Fairbairn
Peterborough. *Born* Peterborough, 16 August, 1962
Middleweight (10.13-11.5) ht. 5'10½"
Manager –
Pro. Debut 25 September, 1986

19.04.91 Jimmy McDonagh W RSC 1 Peterborough
07.11.91 W. O. Wilson L RSC 8 Peterborough *(Vacant Southern Area L. Middleweight Title)*

Career: 12 contests, won 7, drew 1, lost 4.

(Antonio) Tony Falcone
Chippenham. *Born* Chippenham, 15 October, 1966
Featherweight (8.12¾-9.3) ht. 5'6"
Manager D. Mancini
Pro. Debut 22 October, 1990

18.02.91 Barrie Kelley W PTS 6 Windsor
28.02.91 Paul Wynn W PTS 6 Sunderland
21.03.91 Tony Silkstone L PTS 6 Dewsbury
22.04.91 Alan Smith L RSC 5 Mayfair
30.05.91 Alan Smith W PTS 6 Mayfair
11.12.91 Dennis Adams W RTD 4 Basildon
30.04.92 Andrew Bloomer W PTS 6 Mayfair

Career: 9 contests, won 5, lost 4.

Dave Fallon
Watford. *Born* Watford, 22 June, 1967
Welterweight (10.5-10.9½) ht. 6'0"
Manager H. Holland
Pro. Debut 12 September, 1990

14.02.91 Richard Swallow L RSC 4 Southampton
12.11.91 Tim Harmey W PTS 6 Milton Keynes
05.12.91 Sean Cave W PTS 6 Peterborough

Career: 4 contests, won 2, lost 2.

Serg Fame (Theophane)
Paddington. *Born* London, 22 February, 1962
Former Southern Area L. Heavyweight Champion (12.6-12.7¼) ht. 6'1"
Manager –
Pro. Debut 1 March, 1985

14.02.91 Jim Peters L RSC 4 Southampton *(Southern Area L. Heavyweight Title Defence)*
30.01.92 Tony Booth L PTS 6 Southampton

Career: 23 contests, won 13, lost 10.

Ceri Farrell
Swansea. *Born* Swansea, 27 October, 1967
Bantamweight (8.3½-8.12) ht. 5'7"
Manager M. Copp
Pro. Debut 14 May, 1990

24.01.91 Kevin Jenkins L PTS 6 Gorseinon
07.02.91 Mark Tierney L PTS 6 Watford
06.03.91 Mark Tierney L PTS 6 Wembley
25.04.91 Mark Loftus L RSC 3 Basildon
04.11.91 Andrew Bloomer W PTS 6 Merthyr

20.11.91 Andrew Bloomer W PTS 6 Cardiff
29.11.91 John Green L RTD 4 Manchester
08.01.92 Miguel Matthews L PTS 6 Burton
22.01.92 Alan Ley L PTS 6 Cardiff
09.02.92 Peter Judson L PTS 6 Bradford

Career: 16 contests, won 3, drew 1, lost 12.

Lee Farrell

Pontypool. *Born* Pontypool, 3 July, 1967
L. Middleweight (10.10-11.0) ht. 6'0"
Manager –
Pro. Debut 23 November, 1988

28.01.91 Colin Pitters L PTS 6 Birmingham
12.02.91 Mike Betts L RSC 1 Wolverhampton
15.05.91 Mark Verikios L RSC 5 Swansea
02.03.92 Jerry Mortimer L PTS 6 Merthyr
16.05.92 Santo Serio L RSC 2 Muswell Hill

Career: 8 contests, lost 8.

(Raffaele) Rocky Feliciello

Rhyl. *Born* St Asaph, 11 January, 1963
Welterweight. Former Underfeated Welsh L. Middleweight Champion (10.5½-10.10) ht. 5'8"
Manager R. Gray
Pro. Debut 5 October, 1982

03.09.91 Kelvin Mortimer L RSC 2 Cardiff
16.10.91 Mick Reid L PTS 6 Stoke
20.11.91 Dean Bramhald W PTS 6 Solihull

Career: 32 contests, won 20, lost 12.

(Antonio) Tony Feliciello

Rhyl. *Born* Prestatyn, 15 February, 1968
S. Featherweight (9.4½-9.5¾) ht. 5'5"
Manager R. Gray
Pro. Debut 16 November, 1987

08.10.91 Ian McGirr W PTS 8 Wolverhampton
20.11.91 Mark Geraghty W RSC 4 Solihull

Career: 13 contests, won 10, drew 1, lost 1, no decision 1.

Antonio Fernandez (Golding)

Birmingham. *Born* Birmingham, 3 January, 1965
Midlands Area Middleweight Champion (11.5¾-11.10) ht. 5'11½"
Manager –
Pro. Debut 10 March, 1987

24.01.91 Franki Moro W PTS 6 Brierley Hill
07.10.91 Paul Murray W RSC 7 Birmingham
09.12.91 Paul McCarthy W PTS 8 Brierley Hill
03.03.92 Paul Wesley W PTS 10 Cradley Heath *(Vacant Midlands Area Middleweight Title)*

Career: 19 contests, won 15, lost 4.

Lee Ferrie

Coventry. *Born* Coventry, 10 July, 1964
L. Middleweight (10.13-11.5) ht. 5'11"
Manager J. Griffin
Pro. Debut 1 October, 1991

01.10.91 Julian Eavis W PTS 6 Bedworth
05.11.91 Trevor Meikle W PTS 6 Leicester
11.12.91 Noel Henry W RSC 5 Leicester
20.01.92 Martin Rosamond W RSC 2 Coventry
24.02.92 Julian Eavis W PTS 8 Coventry
25.03.92 Mick Reid W RSC 3 Hinckley

Career: 6 contests, won 6.

Crain Fisher

Rochdale. *Born* Littleborough, 28 February, 1966
L. Middleweight (10.11-10.12½) ht. 5'9"
Manager T. Hernon
Pro. Debut 22 October, 1990

28.02.91 Rob Pitters L RSC 6 Bury
21.10.91 James McGee W RSC 4 Bury
13.04.92 Trevor Meikle W PTS 6 Manchester
05.05.92 Frank Harrington W RSC 4 Preston

Career: 5 contests, won 4, lost 1.

Gary Flear

Birmingham. *Born* Birmingham, 28 May, 1965
L. Welterweight (9.11) ht. 5'8"
Manager W. Swift
Pro. Debut 20 September, 1984

03.10.91 Chris Saunders W PTS 6 Burton

Career: 27 contests, won 22, drew 1, lost 4.

Horace Fleary

Huddersfield. *Born* Huddersfield, 22 April, 1961
L. Middleweight. Former Undefeated German International L. Middleweight & S. Middleweight Champion (11.0-11.2) ht. 5'10½"
Manager O. Schroeder
Pro. Debut 4 July, 1987

20.03.91 Paul Wesley W RSC 5 Solihull
04.04.91 Juergen Broszeitt W CO 2 Bielfeld, Germany
22.06.91 Said Skouma L PTS 8 Paris, France
13.09.91 Nelson Alves L CO 7 Dusseldorf, Germany *(Vacant German International S. Middleweight Title)*
20.11.91 Kevin Sheeran L RSC 2 Cardiff
10.01.92 Teddy Jansen W CO 2 Aachen, Germany
28.02.92 Thomas Mateoi W RSC 2 Supplingen, Germany *(Vacant German International L. Middleweight Title)*
04.04.92 Jan Mazgut W RSC 4 Minden, Germany
01.05.92 Trpmir Jandrek W RSC 2 Aachen, Germany
12.05.92 Adrian Strachan L PTS 6 Crystal Palace

Career: 34 contests, won 13, drew 1, lost 20.

Stuart Fleet

Grimsby. *Born* Grimsby, 15 January, 1963
Cruiserweight (13.10½) ht. 6'0"
Manager R. Gray
Pro. Debut 9 December, 1991

09.12.91 Rocky Shelly L RSC 1 Cleethorpes

Career: 1 contest, lost 1.

Andrew Flute

Tipton. Born Wolverhampton, 5 March, 1970
Middleweight (11.7-11.12) ht. 6'1"
Manager –
Pro. Debut 24 May, 1989

13.03.91 Robert Peel W PTS 6 Stoke
10.04.91 Russell Washer W PTS 6 Wolverhampton
14.05.91 Alan Richards W PTS 8 Dudley
16.10.91 Karl Barwise L RSC 8 Stoke
05.12.91 Richard Okumu DREW 8 Cannock
17.03.92 Graham Burton W PTS 8 Wolverhampton
28.04.92 Paul Smith W RSC 5 Wolverhampton

Career: 14 contests, won 10, drew 1, lost 3.

Andy Flute Les Clark

Ali Forbes

Sydenham. *Born* London, 7 March, 1961
S. Middleweight (11.12-12.4½) ht. 5'9"
Manager H. Holland
Pro. Debut 16 February, 1989

06.02.91 Adrian Wright W PTS 6 Battersea
03.04.91 Karl Barwise W RTD 4 Bethnal Green
16.05.91 Quinn Paynter DREW 6 Battersea
01.06.91 Paul McCarthy W CO 2 Bethnal Green
11.03.92 Ian Strudwick L PTS 10 Solihull *(Southern Area S. Middleweight Title Challenge)*

Career: 8 contests, won 6, drew 1, lost 1.

Ali Forbes (right) seen earning a six round draw at Battersea against the dangerous Quinn Paynter in May 1991 Les Clark

Hugh Forde

Birmingham. *Born* Birmingham, 7 May, 1964
Former Commonwealth S. Featherweight Champion. Former British S. Featherweight Champion. Former Undefeated Midlands Area S. Featherweight Champion (9.4-9.11¼) ht. 5'9"
Manager M. Duff
Pro. Debut 13 May, 1986

27.02.91 Tony Pep L RSC 9 Wolverhampton
14.05.91 Richard Joyce W RTD 5 Dudley
10.09.91 Thunder Aryeh W PTS 12 Wolverhampton *(Commonwealth S. Featherweight Title Challenge)*
12.11.91 Paul Harvey L RSC 3 Wolverhampton *(Commonwealth S. Featherweight Title Defence)*

Career: 25 contests, won 22, lost 3.

John Foreman

Birmingham. *Born* Birmingham, 6 November, 1967
L. Heavyweight (12.6-13.2) ht. 6'0"
Manager –
Pro. Debut 26 October, 1987

18.04.91 Richard Bustin L PTS 8 Earls Court
22.06.91 Gil Lewis DREW 6 Earls Court
16.12.91 Steve McCarthy L PTS 8 Southampton
26.01.92 Fabrice Tiozzo L RSC 6 Saint-Ouen, France
29.05.92 Bobbi Joe Edwards W RSC 4 Manchester

Career: 18 contests, won 11, drew 1, lost 6.

Paul Forrest

Middlesbrough. *Born* Middlesbrough, 31 October, 1969
Featherweight (9.1-9.1½) ht. 5'5¾"
Manager –
Pro. Debut 19 November, 1990

03.07.91 Paul Donaghey W CO 2 Brentwood
01.10.91 Colin Lynch L PTS 6 Sheffield
10.12.91 Colin Lynch W PTS 6 Sheffield
28.01.92 John Lupu L RSC 4 Hamburg, Germany

Career: 6 contests, won 4, lost 2.

Frankie Foster

Newcastle. *Born* Newcastle, 25 May, 1968
Former Northern Area S. Featherweight Champion (9.2½-9.5¼) ht. 5'6"
Manager T. Conroy
Pro. Debut 22 September, 1988

22.04.91 John Doherty L PTS 10 Glasgow *(Elim. British S. Featherweight Title)*
14.08.91 Gianni di Napoli L PTS 8 Alcamo, Italy
22.10.91 Darren Elsdon L RSC 7 Hartlepool *(Northern Area S. Featherweight Title Defence)*
31.03.92 Sugar Gibiliru L PTS 8 Stockport

Career: 24 contests, won 10, drew 3, lost 11.

Steve Foster

Manchester. *Born* Salford, 28 December, 1960
L. Middleweight (11.2¼-11.3) ht. 5'8½"
Manager J. Trickett
Pro. Debut 9 February, 1981

22.02.91 Kesem Clayton W CO 6 Manchester
20.09.91 Colin Pitters W RTD 5 Manchester
07.12.91 Shamus Casey W PTS 8 Manchester
10.03.92 Mike Phillips W RSC 4 Bury
25.04.92 Mark Jay W RSC 7 Manchester

Career: 26 contests, won 14, drew 2, lost 10.

Tony Foster

Hull. *Born* Hull, 9 July, 1964
Lightweight (9.8-9.12) ht. 5'7"
Manager M. Toomey
Pro. Debut 4 September, 1987

15.02.91 Jimmy Bredahl L PTS 6 Randers, Denmark
05.03.91 Floyd Havard L PTS 8 Millwall
15.04.91 Dave Anderson L PTS 8 Glasgow
12.05.91 Alain Simoes W PTS 8 Voiron, France
11.09.91 Billy Schwer L PTS 8 Hammersmith
21.11.91 Giovanni Parisi L RSC 6 Perugia, Italy
31.01.92 Angel Mona L PTS 8 Esch, Luxembourg
30.03.92 Ian Honeywood L RSC 4 Eltham
13.06.92 Pierre Lorcy L PTS 8 Levallois Perret, France

Career: 41 contests, won 15, drew 2, lost 24.

Lee Fox

Chesterfield. *Born* Chesterfield, 20 January, 1970
S. Featherweight (9.4-9.8) ht. 5'3¼"
Manager B. Ingle
Pro. Debut 13 November, 1989

06.02.91 Bobby Guynan L PTS 6 Bethnal Green
12.03.91 Charlie Coke W PTS 6 Mansfield
26.03.91 Bobby Guynan W RTD 3 Bethnal Green
11.06.91 Neil Smith L PTS 6 Leicester
16.08.91 Felix Garcia Losada L CO 3 Marbella, Spain
21.01.92 Richard Woolgar L PTS 6 Norwich
19.02.92 Mark Bates L PTS 6 Muswell Hill
27.02.92 Wayne Rigby W PTS 6 Liverpool
14.04.92 Dean Lynch L PTS 6 Mansfield
29.04.92 Andrew Robinson W PTS 6 Stoke
29.05.92 Danny Connelly L PTS 6 Glasgow

Career: 20 contests, won 8, drew 1, lost 11.

Phil Foxon

Louth. *Born* Louth, 12 August, 1971
L. Middleweight (11.2-11.3) ht. 5'11"
Manager J. Gaynor
Pro. Debut 19 March, 1992

19.03.92 Tony Massey L RSC 1 York
04.06.92 John Duckworth L RSC 4 Burnley

Career: 2 contests, lost 2.

Chris Francis

Stepney. *Born* London, 23 October, 1968
S. Featherweight (9.5-9.7) ht. 5'6"
Manager M. Brennan
Pro. Debut 2 October, 1991

02.10.91 Rick Dimmock W PTS 6 Barking
11.02.92 Paul Donaghey L CO 2 Barking

Career: 2 contests, won 1, lost 1.

Joe Frater

Grimsby. *Born* Jamaica, 30 April, 1961
L. Heavyweight (12.8-12.13) ht. 6'1"
Manager L. Slater
Pro. Debut 6 February, 1980

02.03.91 Nick Vardy W RSC 1 Cleethorpes
23.04.91 Dave Owens L PTS 6 Evesham
23.10.91 Gary Delaney L RSC 1 Bethnal Green
04.06.92 Greg Scott-Briggs W PTS 6 Cleethorpes

Career: 35 contests, won 15, drew 2, lost 18.

Terry French

Newcastle. *Born* Newcastle, 15 January, 1967
Northern Area L. Heavyweight Champion (12.1-12.7) ht. 5'9½"
Manager T. Conroy
Pro. Debut 10 October, 1988

03.04.91 Sean O'Phoenix L PTS 8 Manchester
10.05.91 Eddie Collins W PTS 6 Gateshead
10.10.91 Simon McDougall W PTS 6 Gateshead
14.11.91 Quinn Paynter L CO 6 Gateshead
03.03.92 Dave Owens L CO 1 Houghton le Spring

Career: 26 contests, won 13, drew 1, lost 12.

Andrew Furlong

Hammersmith. *Born* Paddington, 29 July, 1967
L. Middleweight (10.13-11.2) ht. 5'9½"
Manager –
Pro. Debut 14 November, 1985

02.05.91 Delroy Waul L RSC 5 Northampton
30.06.91 Lee Crocker DREW 6 Southwark
12.02.92 Gary Pemberton W PTS 6 Wembley
25.03.92 Clay O'Shea DREW 6 Kensington
13.05.92 Clay O'Shea DREW 6 Kensington
16.06.92 Mickey Hughes L CO 1 Dagenham

Career: 32 contests, won 17, drew 5, lost 10.

Hugh Fury

Haslingden. *Born* Colchester, 23 May, 1964
Middleweight (11.7-11.9½) ht. 5'11"
Manager –
Pro. Debut 1 December, 1988

17.10.91 Wilf McGee DREW 6 Mossley
20.11.91 Matt Mowatt L PTS 6 Solihull
09.12.91 Matt Mowatt W RTD 5 Bradford
27.01.92 Willie Quinn L RSC 3 Glasgow

Career: 10 contests, won 3, drew 1, lost 6.

Gypsy John Fury

Haslingden. *Born* Leiston, 22 May, 1964
Heavyweight (15.4-15.11) ht. 6'3¼"
Manager T. Miller
Pro. Debut 28 April, 1987

16.02.91 Cesare di Benedetto W PTS 10 Thornaby
09.10.91 Henry Akinwande L CO 3 Manchester *(Elim. British Heavyweight Title)*

Career: 12 contests, won 8, drew 1, lost 3.

Carl Gaffney

Leeds. *Born* Leeds, 15 April, 1964
Heavyweight (16.3-16.4) ht. 6'5"
Manager T. Callighan
Pro. Debut 12 May, 1984

02.05.91 Sean Hunter W PTS 6 Kensington
19.09.91 Michael Murray L RSC 8 Stockport *(Vacant Central Area Heavyweight Title)*
09.02.92 Steve Garber W PTS 6 Bradford

Career: 16 contests, won 9, lost 7.

Michael Gale

Leeds. *Born* Cardiff, 28 October, 1967
L. Heavyweight (12.6-13.1) ht. 5'11"
Manager M. Duff
Pro. Debut 21 September, 1989

14.03.91 Carlos Christie W PTS 8 Middleton
21.03.91 David Haycock W RSC 2 Dewsbury
09.05.91 Steve Osborne W RSC 2 Leeds
13.06.91 Graham Burton W CO 4 Hull
27.06.91 Mark Bowen W PTS 8 Leeds
30.10.91 Denys Cronin DREW 8 Leeds
23.01.92 John Kaighin W PTS 8 York
08.04.92 Tony Booth W PTS 8 Leeds

Career: 17 contests, won 16, drew 1.

Steve Garber

Bradford. *Born* Bradford, 20 June, 1962
Heavyweight (15.8½-16.5½) ht. 6'6"
Manager P. Martin
Pro. Debut 22 April, 1985

19.03.91 Al Malcolm W RSC 5 Birmingham
30.04.91 Michael Murray L CO 1 Stockport
31.05.91 Axel Schulz L CO 5 Berlin, Germany
10.10.91 Paul Lister L PTS 8 Gateshead
09.02.92 Carl Gaffney L PTS 6 Bradford
05.04.92 David Jules W RSC 4 Bradford
08.05.92 Alexandra Miroshnichenko L RSC 1 Waregem, Belgium

Career: 36 contests, won 18, drew 1, lost 17.

Eddie Garbutt

Sunderland. *Born* Sunderland, 1 December, 1971
S. Featherweight (9.3) ht. 5'9"
Manager G. McCrory
Pro. Debut 25 November, 1991

25.11.91 Dave McHale L RSC 1 Liverpool

Career: 1 contest, lost 1.

Des Gargano (Southern)

Manchester. *Born* Brighton, 20 December, 1960
Featherweight (8.8-8.13) ht. 5'5"
Manager –
Pro. Debut 25 January, 1985

16.01.91 Tony Smith W PTS 6 Stoke
06.02.91 Tim Driscoll L PTS 6 Bethnal Green
28.02.91 Carl Roberts W PTS 6 Bury
07.05.91 James Drummond L PTS 8 Glasgow
16.05.91 Jimmy Owens L RSC 2 Liverpool
19.08.91 Petteri Rissanen L PTS 4 Helsinki, Finland
02.10.91 Eric George L PTS 6 Solihull
24.10.91 Edward Cook L RSC 5 Glasgow

Lou Gent (left) in action against Johnny Melfah last May

Les Clark

29.11.91 Harald Geier L DIS 8 Frohsdorf, Austria
31.01.92 Edward Cook L PTS 6 Glasgow
24.02.92 Colin Lynch L PTS 6 Coventry
04.03.92 Neil Armstrong L PTS 6 Glasgow
11.03.92 Dennis Oakes L PTS 6 Stoke
27.04.92 David Ramsden L PTS 6 Bradford
01.06.92 Mark Hargreaves L PTS 6 Manchester
08.06.92 David Ramsden L PTS 6 Bradford

Career: 87 contests, won 26, drew 2, lost 59.

Al Garrett (Garrity)

Glasgow. *Born* Glasgow, 21 December, 1966
Featherweight (9.2) ht. 5'5½"
Manager T. Gilmour
Pro. Debut 23 September, 1991

23.09.91 Robert Braddock DREW 6 Glasgow
09.12.91 Chris Jickells L RSC 2 Bradford

Career: 2 contests, drew 1, lost 1.

Steve Gee (Egege)

Birmingham. Born Bradford, 1 April, 1961
Heavyweight (15.4-16.6¼) ht. 6'2"
Manager E. Cashmore
Pro. Debut 15 April, 1980

23.01.91 Manny Burgo L PTS 6 Brentwood
13.03.91 Tucker Richards L PTS 6 Stoke
06.04.91 Corrie Sanders L RSC 4 Darlington
30.05.91 Al Malcolm L PTS 6 Birmingham
13.09.91 Axel Schulz L CO 2 Dusseldorf, Germany
15.11.91 Massimo Migliaccio L PTS 6 Omegna, Italy
07.12.91 Michael Murray L RSC 7 Manchester

Career: 50 contests, won 16, drew 2, lost 32.

Lou Gent

Streatham. *Born* London, 21 April, 1965
S. Middleweight. Former Undefeated Southern Area Cruiserweight Champion (11.11¾-12.3) ht. 5'10½"
Manager –
Pro. Debut 18 September, 1984

20.03.91 Derek Myers W RSC 7 Wandsworth *(Elim. British L. Heavyweight Title)*
16.05.91 Gus Mendes W CO 8 Battersea
30.10.91 Henry Wharton DREW 12 Leeds *(Commonwealth S. Middleweight Title Challenge)*
25.02.92 Fidel Castro L PTS 12 Crystal Palace *(British S. Middleweight Title Challenge)*
12.05.92 Johnny Melfah L RSC 3 Crystal Palace

Career: 29 contests, won 19, drew 2, lost 8.

Eric George

Swansea. *Born* Swansea, 19 August, 1968
Flyweight (8.4½-8.7) ht. 5'3"
Manager R. Gray
Pro. Debut 19 August, 1989

23.01.91 Tim Yeates L RSC 6 Brentwood
09.04.91 Neil Johnston DREW 6 Mayfair
02.10.91 Des Gargano W PTS 6 Solihull
07.12.91 Mercurio Ciaramitaro DREW 6 Rossano Calabro, Italy

Career: 9 contests, won 2, drew 3, lost 4.

Mark Geraghty

Glasgow. *Born* Paisley, 25 August, 1965
Scottish S. Featherweight Champion (9.1½-9.6½) ht. 5'6"
Manager T. Gilmour
Pro. Debut 14 November, 1988

06.03.91 Neil Leitch W PTS 10 Glasgow *(Vacant Scottish S. Featherweight Title)*
01.05.91 Pete Buckley L PTS 8 Solihull
03.06.91 Neil Leitch L PTS 8 Glasgow
23.09.91 Neil Leitch W PTS 10 Glasgow *(Scottish S. Featherweight Title Defence)*

09.10.91 Chris Clarkson W PTS 6 Glasgow
20.11.91 Tony Feliciello L RSC 4 Solihull
24.02.92 Colin Innes W PTS 8 Glasgow
18.03.92 Barrie Kelley W PTS 8 Glasgow

Career: 24 contests, won 14, lost 10.

Tony Gibbs

Barking. *Born* London, 20 January, 1964
Welterweight (10.4-10.12½) ht. 5'6¼"
Manager –
Pro. Debut 8 October, 1987

08.05.91 Robert McCracken L CO 1 Kensington
20.11.91 Robert Wright L RTD 2 Solihull
02.04.92 Dean Hollington L CO 1 Basildon

Career: 21 contests, won 5, drew 2, lost 14.

(Dramani) Sugar Gibiliru

Liverpool. *Born* Liverpool, 13 July, 1966
Former British S. Featherweight Champion. Former Undefeated Central Area S. Featherweight & Lightweight Champion (9.3¼-9.13) ht. 5'5½"
Manager J. Trickett
Pro. Debut 30 November, 1984

29.01.91 Nigel Bradley W PTS 8 Stockport
30.04.91 Robert Dickie W RSC 9 Stockport *(British S. Featherweight Title Challenge)*
19.09.91 John Doherty L PTS 12 Stockport *(British S. Featherweight Title Defence)*
07.12.91 Paul Harvey L PTS 12 Manchester *(Commonwealth S. Featherweight Title Challenge)*
31.03.92 Frankie Foster W PTS 8 Stockport
27.06.92 Michael Ayers L RSC 6 Quinta do Lago, Portugal

Career: 51 contests, won 14, drew 7, lost 30.

Barry Glanister

East Grinstead. *Born* Warrington, 27 April, 1964
Lightweight (9.10-10.0) ht. 5'7½"
Manager D. Bidwell
Pro. Debut 16 May, 1991

16.05.91 Bobby Beckles L RSC 1 Battersea
24.10.91 Moses Sentamu L PTS 6 Bayswater
13.11.91 Kevin McKillan L PTS 6 Liverpool
21.01.92 Danny Kett L RSC 1 Norwich

Career: 4 contests, lost 4.

(Godfrey) G. G. Goddard

Alfreton. *Born* Swaziland, 6 April, 1966
Lightweight (9.5-9.10) ht. 5'7"
Manager M. Shinfield
Pro. Debut 22 November, 1990

17.01.91 Paul Chedgzoy W RSC 3 Alfreton
13.05.91 Finn McCool L PTS 6 Northampton
20.05.91 Finn McCool W PTS 6 Bradford
23.10.91 Chubby Martin L PTS 8 Stoke
04.02.92 Kevin Toomey L PTS 6 Alfreton
11.03.92 Micky Hall DREW 6 Solihull
28.04.92 Michael Clynch L RTD 4 Corby

Career: 8 contests, won 3, drew 1, lost 4.

(Valentine) Val Golding

Croydon. *Born* Croydon, 9 May, 1964
Middleweight (11.7-11.8½) ht. 5'11"
Manager F. Warren
Pro. Debut 17 July, 1989

04.09.91 Russell Washer W RTD 5 Bethnal Green
29.10.91 Graham Jenner W RSC 3 Kensington
18.01.92 Quinn Paynter L RSC 7 Kensington

Career: 9 contests, won 6, lost 3.

(Benjamin) Benji Good

Brockley. *Born* Nottingham, 15 December, 1964
Middleweight (11.10-11.11) ht. 6'0"
Manager –
Pro. Debut 11 December, 1989

14.02.91 Jon Stocks L PTS 6 Southampton
06.03.91 Paul Smith W PTS 6 Croydon
26.04.91 Karl Barwise W RSC 3 Crystal Palace
08.05.91 John Kaighin L RSC 3 Kensington
24.10.91 Richard Okumu L CO 6 Bayswater

Career: 15 contests, won 5, lost 10.

Steve Goodwin

Sheffield. *Born* Derby, 17 February, 1966
Welterweight (10.10-11.2) ht. 5'11"
Manager B. Ingle
Pro. Debut 13 April, 1992

13.04.92 John Duckworth W PTS 6 Manchester
29.04.92 John Corcoran W PTS 8 Stoke

Career: 2 contests, won 2.

John Graham

Paddington. *Born* London, 12 April, 1962
Former Southern Area Cruiserweight Champion (13.7-13.7½) ht. 6'1"
Manager –
Pro. Debut 18 February, 1985

25.04.91 Mike Aubrey W PTS 10 Basildon *(Vacant Southern Area Cruiserweight Title)*
14.11.91 Everton Blake L PTS 10 Bayswater *(Southern Area Cruiserweight Title Defence)*

Career: 19 contests, won 15, drew 1, lost 3.

Allan Grainger

Glasgow. *Born* Glasgow, 28 May, 1968
L. Middleweight (10.11¼-11.1) ht. 6'2"
Manager R. Watt
Pro. Debut 18 March, 1991

18.03.91 Mick Duncan L PTS 6 Glasgow
09.09.91 Willie Yeardsley W PTS 6 Glasgow
24.10.91 Jim Conley W PTS 6 Glasgow
18.11.91 Mick Duncan L PTS 6 Glasgow
24.02.92 Calum Rattray W RTD 5 Glasgow
04.03.92 Steve Scott W PTS 6 Glasgow

Career: 6 contests, won 4, lost 2.

Derek Grainger

Bethnal Green. *Born* London, 15 May, 1967
L. Middleweight (10.10-10.11½) ht. 5'7¼"
Manager T. Lawless
Pro. Debut 28 January, 1988

13.02.91 Newton Barnett W RSC 3 Wembley
17.04.91 Humphrey Harrison L RSC 7 Kensington
20.11.91 Chris Blake DREW 8 Kensington

Career: 20 contests, won 18, drew 1, lost 1.

Frank Grant

Bradford. *Born* Bradford, 22 May, 1965
Middleweight (11.6-11.11½) ht. 5'11"
Manager P. Martin
Pro. Debut 20 October, 1986

12.04.91 Alan Richards W RSC 5 Manchester
31.05.91 Tim Dendy W PTS 8 Manchester
20.09.91 Conrad Oscar W CO 2 Manchester
29.11.91 Winston Wray W RSC 3 Manchester
09.02.92 Willie Ball W PTS 6 Bradford
05.04.92 Sammy Matos W CO 1 Bradford

Career: 22 contests, won 19, lost 3.

Marvin P. Gray

Stanley. *Born* Flint Hill, 14 December, 1965
L. Welterweight (10.1-10.2) ht. 5'9"
Manager –
Pro. Debut 27 March, 1985

Marvin P. Gray Les Clark

28.02.91 Rick Bushell W PTS 6 Sunderland
10.03.91 Alain Simoes L PTS 8 Paris, France
15.05.91 Giovanni Parisi L RSC 6 Montichiari, Italy
25.11.91 Andreas Panayi L PTS 8 Liverpool
06.02.92 Dave Pierre L RSC 7 Peterborough

Career: 44 contests, won 17, drew 2, lost 25.

John Green
Manchester. *Born* Manchester, 5 June, 1965
Former Undefeated Central Area Bantamweight Champion (8.5½-8.10½) ht. 5'5"
Manager P. Martin
Pro. Debut 31 March, 1987

22.02.91 Colin Lynch W PTS 6 Manchester
12.04.91 Sylvester Osuji W RSC 1 Manchester
31.05.91 Roland Gomez W CO 5 Manchester
20.09.91 Tony Rahman W RSC 3 Manchester
29.11.91 Ceri Farrell W RTD 4 Manchester
31.01.92 Miguel Matthews DREW 6 Manchester
09.02.92 Steve Young DREW 6 Bradford
29.05.92 Ronnie Carroll W PTS 10 Manchester *(Elim. British Bantamweight Title)*

Career: 17 contests, won 13, drew 2, lost 2.

Darron Griffiths
Cardiff. *Born* Pontypridd, 11 February, 1972
Middleweight (11.0½-11.10) ht. 6'0"
Manager B. Aird
Pro. Debut 26 November, 1990

23.01.91 Tony Booth DREW 6 Stoke
06.03.91 Barry Messam W PTS 6 Croydon
10.04.91 John Kaighin W PTS 6 Newport
25.04.91 Michael Graham W RSC 2 Mayfair
02.05.91 Carlton Myers W RTD 5 Kensington
21.10.91 John Ogiste W PTS 6 Mayfair
11.12.91 Adrian Wright W PTS 6 Stoke
22.01.92 Richard Okumu W PTS 8 Solihull
17.02.92 John Ogiste W RSC 5 Mayfair
29.04.92 Colin Manners DREW 8 Solihull

Career: 12 contests, won 9, drew 3.

Karl Guest
Preston. *Born* Preston, 10 July, 1966
L. Heavyweight (12.5-12.9½) ht. 6'2"
Manager –
Pro. Debut 12 November, 1990

11.02.91 Tony Lawrence L PTS 6 Manchester
07.10.91 Tony Colclough DREW 6 Birmingham
02.12.91 Tony Colclough L RSC 2 Birmingham

Career: 4 contests, won 1, drew 1, lost 2.

Neil Haddock
Llanelli. *Born* Newport, 22 June, 1964
Welsh S. Featherweight Champion (9.2½-9.5) ht. 5'6"
Manager G. Davies
Pro. Debut 16 February, 1987

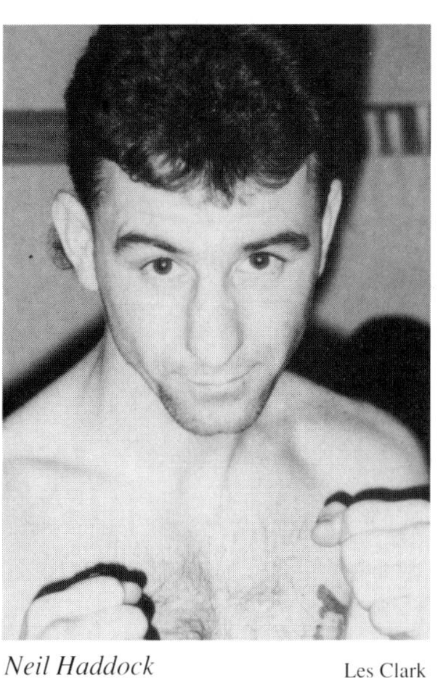

Neil Haddock Les Clark

20.11.91 Barrie Kelley W PTS 6 Cardiff
17.12.91 Andy Deabreu W RSC 3 Cardiff
11.05.92 Steve Robinson W PTS 10 Llanelli *(Vacant Welsh S. Featherweight Title)*

Career: 20 contests, won 10, drew 1, lost 9.

Mark Hale
Nuneaton. *Born* Nuneaton, 13 October, 1969
S. Middleweight (11.1-11.13) ht. 5'11
Manager J. Griffin
Pro. Debut 7 October, 1991

07.10.91 Andy Manning L PTS 6 Liverpool
07.11.91 Marc Rowley W PTS 6 Peterborough
15.01.92 Paul Murray W PTS 6 Stoke
25.03.92 Marc Rowley W PTS 6 Hinckley
11.05.92 Martin Jolley L PTS 6 Coventry
21.05.92 Tony Colclough DREW 6 Cradley Heath
01.06.92 Tony Colclough L PTS 6 Solihull

Career: 7 contests, won 3, drew 1, lost 3.

Ross Hale
Bristol. *Born* Bristol, 28 February, 1967
L. Welterweight (10.1½-10.3) ht. 5'9"
Manager C. Sanigar
Pro. Debut 16 November, 1989

24.10.91 Greg Egbuniwe W RSC 4 Bayswater
22.01.92 Tony Borg W PTS 6 Cardiff
30.04.92 Jason Matthews W RSC 3 Bayswater
12.05.92 John Smith W CO 1 Crystal Palace

Career: 12 contests, won 12.

Alan Hall
Darlington. *Born* Darlington, 16 November, 1969
L. Welterweight (9.12-10.2) ht. 5'8"
Manager F. Maloney
Pro. Debut 10 October, 1989

02.03.91 Steve Pollard W PTS 6 Darlington
06.04.91 Alan Peacock W PTS 6 Darlington
11.06.91 Abram Gumede W PTS 8 Leicester
25.04.92 Michael Driscoll W PTS 6 Manchester
25.06.92 Russell Mosley W PTS 6 San Diego, USA

Career: 13 contests, won 13.

Dave Hall
Birmingham. *Born* Birmingham, 25 July, 1964
L. Middleweight (11.0-11.9) ht. 5'9"
Manager –
Pro. Debut 15 April, 1991

15.04.91 John Baxter W RSC 3 Leicester
13.05.91 Dave Binsteed L RSC 2 Birmingham
04.07.91 Shamus Casey L PTS 6 Alfreton
16.09.91 Marc Rowley W PTS 6 Cleethorpes
08.10.91 Marc Rowley W PTS 6 Wolverhampton
29.10.91 Kevin Sheeran L RSC 1 Kensington
22.01.92 John Corcoran L PTS 8 Stoke
11.03.92 John Corcoran L PTS 8 Stoke
29.04.92 Matthew Jones L RSC 2 Solihull

Career: 9 contests, won 3, lost 6.

Micky Hall
Ludworth. *Born* Ludworth, 23 April, 1967
Lightweight (9.8-9.9½) ht. 5'8"
Manager T. Conroy
Pro. Debut 3 March, 1992

03.03.92 Mick Holmes W RSC 2 Houghton le Spring
11.03.92 G. G. Goddard DREW 6 Solihull
28.04.92 Jamie Davidson L PTS 6 Houghton le Spring

Career: 3 contests, won 1, drew 1, lost 1.

Simon Hamblett
Walsall. *Born* Walsall, 10 October, 1966
L. Welterweight (10.0) ht. 5'8"
Manager R. Gray
Pro. Debut 24 February, 1992

24.02.92 Jamie Morris DREW 6 Coventry
11.03.92 Mark Antony L CO 1 Stoke

Career: 2 contests, drew 1, lost 1.

Prince Nassem Hamed
Sheffield. *Born* Sheffield, 12 February, 1974
Flyweight (8.2) ht. 5'3"
Manager B. Ingle
Pro. Debut 14 April, 1992

14.04.92 Ricky Beard W CO 2 Mansfield
25.04.92 Shaun Norman W RSC 2 Manchester
23.05.92 Andrew Bloomer W RSC 2 Birmingham

Career: 3 contests, won 3.

Paul Hanlon

Birmingham. *Born* Birmingham, 25 May, 1962
L. Heavyweight (11.12-12.10) ht. 5'11"
Manager –
Pro. Debut 18 November, 1986

04.03.91 Tony Behan L PTS 6 Birmingham
18.03.91 Willy James W CO 1 Derby
10.04.91 Lee Prudden L PTS 6 Wolverhampton
24.04.91 Dean Allen L PTS 6 Aberavon
13.05.91 Lee Prudden L PTS 6 Birmingham
23.05.91 Lee Prudden W PTS 6 Southampton
10.06.91 Jason Frieze W RSC 2 Manchester
10.09.91 Richard Carter L RSC 3 Wolverhampton
22.01.92 Lee Prudden W RSC 4 Stoke
20.02.92 Glen Payton L PTS 6 Oakengates
27.04.92 Joey Peters L CO 2 Mayfair

Career: 16 contests, won 4, lost 12.

Dave Hardie

Glasgow. *Born* Glasgow, 10 February, 1971
Bantamweight (8.7½-8.9) ht. 5'5"
Manager A. Morrison
Pro. Debut 28 November, 1991

28.11.91 Miguel Matthews W PTS 6 Glasgow
20.02.92 Shaun Norman W PTS 6 Glasgow

Career: 2 contests, won 2.

Fran Harding

Liverpool. *Born* Liverpool, 5 September, 1966
Middleweight (11.7) ht. 6'0½"
Manager F. Maloney
Pro. Debut 27 July, 1987

30.09.91 Lee Crocker W RSC 3 Kensington

Career: 5 contests, won 5.

Keith Hardman

St. Helens. *Born* Preston, 20 February, 1963
L. Welterweight (10.1) ht. 5'7"
Manager –
Pro. Debut 12 September, 1990

11.12.91 Patrick Loughran L PTS 6 Stoke

Career: 2 contests, lost 2.

Steve Hardman

Liverpool. *Born* Chorley, 13 April, 1961
Welterweight (10.6-10.9) ht. 5'10"
Manager –
Pro. Debut 16 October, 1989

17.01.91 Richard O'Brien W PTS 6 Alfreton
28.01.91 Neil Porter W PTS 6 Bradford
11.02.91 Trevor Meikle W PTS 6 Manchester
25.03.91 Tommy Milligan L PTS 6 Bradford
30.09.91 Andreas Panayi L RSC 5 Liverpool

Career: 7 contests, won 4, drew 1, lost 2.

Billy Hardy

Billy Hardy

Sunderland. *Born* Sunderland, 15 September, 1964
Former Undefeated British Bantamweight Champion (8.6-8.12) ht. 5'6"
Manager D. Mancini
Pro. Debut 21 November, 1983

28.02.91 Francisco Ortiz W RSC 7 Sunderland
04.05.91 Orlando Canizales L RSC 8 Laredo, USA
(IBF Bantamweight Title Challenge)
03.03.92 Chris Clarkson W RSC 5 Houghton le Spring

Career: 33 contests, won 26, drew 1, lost 6.

John Harewood

Newcastle. *Born* Ipswich, 23 February, 1964
Heavyweight (17.4-17.12) ht. 6'3½"
Manager J. Spensley
Pro. Debut 29 November, 1990

06.04.91 Paddy Reilly L RSC 2 Darlington
01.08.91 Paddy Reilly L CO 1 Dewsbury
05.03.92 J. A. Bugner L PTS 4 Battersea
27.05.92 Freddy Soentgen L PTS 6 Cologne, Germany

Career: 5 contests, won 1, lost 4.

Mark Hargreaves

Burnley. *Born* Burnley, 13 September, 1970
Bantamweight (8.8-8.13) ht. 5'4"
Manager N. Basso
Pro. Debut 11 September, 1991

11.09.91 Dave Campbell W RSC 4 Stoke
23.10.91 Dave Martin W PTS 6 Stoke
10.02.92 Dennis Oakes L RSC 3 Liverpool
30.03.92 Ronnie Stephenson L PTS 6 Coventry
27.04.92 Ady Benton L PTS 6 Bradford
01.06.92 Des Gargano W PTS 6 Manchester

Career: 6 contests, won 3, lost 3.

Tim Harmey

Brighton. *Born* Croydon, 5 March, 1966
Welterweight (10.4-10.10) ht. 5'9"
Manager G. Nickels
Pro. Debut 25 April, 1990

23.02.91 Steve McGovern L PTS 6 Brighton
02.03.91 Jim Moffat L RSC 3 Irvine
06.06.91 Mark Verikios L CO 4 Barking
12.11.91 Dave Fallon L PTS 6 Milton Keynes

Career: 8 contests, won 2, drew 1, lost 5.

Carl Harney

Manchester. *Born* Manchester, 24 June, 1970
Middleweight (11.8-11.9) ht. 6'1"
Manager P. Martin
Pro. Debut 17 October, 1989

22.02.91 Mike Phillips L RSC 5 Manchester
31.05.91 Marvin O'Brien L RSC 5 Manchester
29.05.92 Matthew Jones W RSC 6 Manchester

Career: 5 contests, won 3, lost 2.

Frank Harrington

Lancaster. *Born* Glasgow, 1 October, 1961
L. Middleweight (10.9-10.13¾) ht. 5'7"
Manager –
Pro. Debut 21 April, 1986

23.04.91 Steve McGovern L PTS 6 Evesham
05.05.92 Crain Fisher L RSC 4 Preston

Career: 19 contests, won 10, lost 9.

Peter Harris

Swansea. *Born* Swansea, 23 August, 1962
Former British & Welsh Featherweight Champion (8.12¾-9.1) ht. 5'6½"
Manager C. Breen
Pro. Debut 28 February, 1983

24.04.91 Colin Lynch W PTS 8 Aberavon
18.07.91 Steve Robinson L PTS 10 Cardiff
(Welsh Featherweight Title Defence)
05.06.92 Stephane Haccoun L PTS 8 Marseille, France

Career: 25 contests, won 14, drew 2, lost 9.

Simon Harris

Hanwell. *Born* Isleworth, 26 December, 1961
L. Heavyweight (12.7½-12.9½) ht. 5'11"
Manager –
Pro. Debut 28 September, 1984

29.01.91 Richard Bustin W RSC 3 Wisbech
03.07.91 Nicky Piper L RSC 1 Reading
11.02.92 Gary Delaney DREW 8 Barking

Career: 15 contests, won 11, drew 1, lost 3.

Humphrey Harrison

Manchester. *Born* Jamaica, 25 September, 1958
Welterweight (10.7-10.10) ht. 5'8"
Manager N. Basso
Pro. Debut 5 October, 1987

17.04.91 Derek Grainger W RSC 7 Kensington
01.05.91 Julian Eavis W PTS 6 Solihull
31.01.92 Dave Binsteed W CO 1 Manchester
25.03.92 Roy Rowland L CO 7 Dagenham

Career: 15 contests, won 12, lost 3.

Oliver Harrison

Manchester. *Born* Jamaica, 17 October, 1960
L. Welterweight (9.13-10.0) ht. 5'7"
Manager N. Basso
Pro. Debut 15 June, 1987

11.02.91 Alan Peacock W RSC 6 Glasgow
19.04.91 Dave Pierre L PTS 8 Peterborough
07.09.91 Nigel Wenton L RTD 5 Belfast

Career: 10 contests, won 6, lost 4.

Paul Harvey (right) on the attack in his victorious Commonwealth super-featherweight title fight against Sugar Giliburu
Chris Bevan

Craig Hartwell

Rugby. *Born* Rugby, 24 August, 1968
Welterweight (10.7-10.8) ht. 5'9"
Manager J. Griffin
Pro. Debut 11 December, 1991

11.12.91 Brian Coleman DREW 6 Leicester
25.03.92 Benji Joseph L PTS 6 Hinckley
18.05.92 Dean Hiscox L PTS 6 Bardon

Career: 3 contests, drew 1, lost 2.

Paul Harvey

Ilford. *Born* Islington, 10 November, 1964
Former Commonwealth S. Featherweight Champion (9.1-9.4) ht. 5'8"
Manager B. Hearn
Pro. Debut 4 October, 1989

09.04.91 Alan McKay W RSC 4 Mayfair
24.04.91 Peter Gabbitus W RSC 5 Preston
26.10.91 Colin Lynch W RSC 1 Brentwood
12.11.91 Hugh Forde W RSC 3 Wolverhampton *(Commonwealth S. Featherweight Title Challenge)*
07.12.91 Sugar Gibiliru W PTS 12 Manchester *(Commonwealth S. Featherweight Title Defence)*
11.02.92 Tony Pep L PTS 12 Cardiff *(Commonwealth S. Featherweight Title Defence)*
02.06.92 Regilio Tuur L CO 5 Rotterdam, Holland

Career: 15 contests, won 12, drew 1, lost 2.

Adrian Haughton

Paddington. *Born* London, 16 October, 1965
L. Middleweight (11.2-11.3½) ht. 6'2"
Manager I. Akay
Pro. Debut 7 April, 1992

07.04.92 Nigel Kitching W RSC 5 Southend
17.05.92 Mossa Azward W DIS 1 Harringay

Career: 2 contests, won 2.

Bozon Haule

Woolwich. *Born* Tanzania, 4 January, 1961
L. Middleweight (10.8¾-10.12) ht. 5'7"
Manager G. Nickels
Pro. Debut 3 October, 1987

11.05.91 Oscar Checa L RSC 1 Belfast
24.09.91 Gordon Blair L RSC 8 Glasgow
23.04.92 Dave Brosnan W RSC 6 Eltham

Career: 16 contests, won 11, drew 1, lost 4.

Floyd Havard

Swansea. *Born* Swansea, 16 October, 1965
Former British S. Featherweight Champion (9.5½-9.8) ht. 5'8"
Manager C. Breen
Pro. Debut 30 November, 1985

05.03.91 Tony Foster W PTS 8 Millwall
29.10.91 Thunder Aryeh W RTD 6 Cardiff
17.12.91 Patrick Kamy W DIS 5 Cardiff
17.03.92 Harry Escott W RSC 7 Mayfair

Career: 26 contests, won 25, lost 1.

Steve Hearn

High Wycombe. *Born* Luton, 2 December, 1966
L. Welterweight (9.11-9.13½) ht. 5'8½"
Manager W. Ball
Pro. Debut 12 May, 1989

06.02.91 Trevor Royal DREW 6 Battersea
01.05.91 Rick Dimmock W PTS 6 Bethnal Green
26.11.91 Paul Knights L RSC 4 Bethnal Green
12.02.92 Nicky Bardle L RSC 1 Watford

Career: 7 contests, won 1, drew 1, lost 5.

Darren Henderson

Leeds. *Born* Leeds, 22 March, 1966
L. Welterweight (9.11) ht. 5'9"
Manager –
Pro. Debut 29 November, 1990

04.06.92 Mark Broome L RSC 2 Cleethorpes

Career: 2 contests, lost 2.

Ian Henry

Newcastle. *Born* Gateshead, 8 May, 1967
L. Heavyweight (11.13-12.7) ht. 6'1½"
Manager T. Conroy
Pro. Debut 26 April, 1990

21.01.91 Shaun McCrory W PTS 6 Glasgow
28.01.91 Simon McDougall L PTS 8 Bradford
18.03.91 Ian Vokes W RSC 2 Manchester
25.03.91 Dave Lawrence W PTS 6 Bradford
10.05.91 Simon McDougall W PTS 6 Gateshead
10.10.91 Chris Walker W PTS 6 Gateshead
14.11.91 Dave Owens W PTS 8 Gateshead
27.11.91 John Oxenham W PTS 6 Marton
11.03.92 Simon McDougall W PTS 8 Solihull
05.05.92 Glenn Campbell L RSC 1 Preston

Career: 15 contests, won 12, lost 3.

Noel Henry

Hinckley. *Born* Newham, 25 October, 1968
L. Middleweight (10.9½-11.0) ht. 5'5¼"
Manager J. Griffin
Pro. Debut 16 October, 1991

16.10.91 Eddie King W CO 2 Stoke
28.10.91 Wayne Shepherd L PTS 6 Leicester
11.12.91 Lee Ferrie L RSC 5 Leicester

Career: 3 contests, won 1, lost 2.

Marcel Herbert

Newport. *Born* Cardiff, 3 March, 1965
Lightweight (9.8¾-10.4¼) ht. 5'8½"
Manager S. Sims
Pro. Debut 19 August, 1989

10.04.91 Rudy Valentino L RSC 3 Newport *(Elim. British Lightweight Title)*
01.06.91 Carlos Chase L PTS 6 Bethnal Green
20.11.91 Billy Schwer L PTS 8 Kensington
18.06.92 Gary Barron L PTS 6 Peterborough

Career: 15 contests, won 7, drew 1, lost 7.

Brian Hickey

Sheffield. *Born* Sheffield, 24 January, 1973
L. Welterweight (10.3) ht. 5'9"
Manager B. Ingle
Pro. Debut 21 November, 1991

21.11.91 Tony Doyle L PTS 6 Ilkeston
06.02.92 Michael Clynch L DIS 5 Peterborough

Career: 2 contests, lost 2.

Gary Hickman

Sunderland. *Born* Easington, 9 April, 1970
Featherweight (8.10-8.12) ht. 5'6"
Manager T. Callighan
Pro. Debut 6 June, 1988

20.06.91 Craig Dermody L RSC 2 Liverpool
14.12.91 John Armour L RSC 6 Bexleyheath
28.02.92 Mike Deveney L PTS 6 Irvine

Career: 14 contests, won 4, drew 1, lost 9.

Herbie Hide

Norwich. *Born* Nigeria, 27 August, 1971
WBC International Heavyweight Champion (13.8-14.11½) ht. 6'1½"
Manager B. Hearn
Pro. Debut 24 October, 1989

29.01.91 Lennie Howard W RSC 1 Wisbech
09.04.91 David Jules W RSC 1 Mayfair
14.05.91 John Westgarth W RTD 4 Dudley
03.07.91 Tucker Richards W RSC 3 Brentwood
15.10.91 Eddie Gonzalez W CO 2 Hamburg, Germany

Herbie Hide Les Clark

29.10.91 Chris Jacobs W RSC 1 Cardiff
21.01.92 Conroy Nelson W RSC 2 Norwich *(Vacant WBC International Heavyweight Title)*
03.03.92 Percell Davis W CO 1 Amsterdam, Holland

Career: 16 contests, won 16.

Dave Hindmarsh

Newcastle. *Born* Newcastle, 2 July, 1964
L. Middleweight (11.3) ht. 5'9"
Manager –
Pro. Debut 16 October, 1987

14.11.91 Wayne Appleton L RSC 8 Edinburgh

Career: 17 contests, won 7, drew 1, lost 9.

Dean Hiscox

Dudley. *Born* Dudley, 15 January, 1969
Welterweight (10.3-10.7) ht. 5'8"
Manager C. Flute
Pro. Debut 6 October, 1988

14.05.91 Eddie King L PTS 6 Dudley
05.06.91 Eddie King L PTS 6 Wolverhampton
21.11.91 Chris Aston L PTS 6 Stafford
02.12.91 Steve Bricknell W PTS 6 Birmingham
17.03.92 Mark Legg L PTS 6 Wolverhampton
18.05.92 Craig Hartwell W PTS 6 Bardon

Career: 7 contests, won 3, lost 4.

Paul Hitch

Wingate. *Born* Hartlepool, 7 May, 1968
S. Middleweight (11.12-12.2) ht. 5'9½"
Manager T. Conroy
Pro. Debut 10 May, 1991

10.05.91 Tony Kosova W RTD 1 Gateshead
13.05.91 Terry Johnson W PTS 6 Marton
17.06.91 Max McCracken W PTS 6 Edgbaston
22.10.91 Chris Walker W PTS 6 Hartlepool
14.11.91 Paul Burton W CO 2 Gateshead
12.12.91 Doug Calderwood W PTS 6 Hartlepool
03.03.92 Simon McDougall W PTS 6 Houghton le Spring
28.04.92 Chris Walker L RSC 2 Houghton le Spring

Career: 8 contests, won 7, lost 1.

Dean Hollington

West Ham. *Born* Plaistow, 25 February, 1969
L. Welterweight (10.2-10.4) ht. 5'9"
Manager J. Tibbs
Pro. Debut 20 February, 1990

12.02.91 Andy Robins W RSC 4 Basildon
07.03.91 Dave Jenkins W PTS 6 Basildon
17.04.91 Jim Lawlor W PTS 6 Kensington
23.10.91 John Smith W PTS 6 Bethnal Green
13.11.91 Jim Lawlor W PTS 6 Bethnal Green
11.02.92 Nigel Bradley W PTS 6 Barking
02.04.92 Tony Gibbs W CO 1 Basildon
16.05.92 Rick Bushell W RSC 2 Muswell Hill

Career: 11 contests, won 11.

Dean Hollington (left) in winning action Les Clark

Mick Holmes

Barnsley. *Born* Burnley, 15 May, 1971
L. Welterweight (10.0-10.1) ht. 5'7"
Manager N. Basso
Pro. Debut 7 October, 1991

07.10.91 Chris Aston L RSC 2 Bradford
03.03.92 Micky Hall L RSC 2 Houghton le Spring

Career: 2 contests, lost 2.

Mark Holt

Birmingham. *Born* Birmingham, 7 March, 1967
Former Undefeated Midlands Area Featherweight Champion (9.2½-9.3) ht. 5'8"
Manager –
Pro. Debut 15 November, 1988

19.03.91 Steve Walker L PTS 8 Birmingham
15.10.91 Billy Barton W PTS 8 Dudley
07.12.91 Michael Armstrong L RSC 4 Manchester
28.02.92 Wilson Rodriguez L RSC 3 Madrid, Spain

Career: 15 contests, won 7, lost 8.

Lloyd Honeyghan

Bermondsey. *Born* Jamaica, 22 April, 1960
L. Middleweight. Former WBC Welterweight Champion. Former Undefeated British, Commonwealth, European & WBA/IBF Welterweight Champion. Former Undefeated Southern Area Welterweight Champion (11.1-11.10½) ht. 5'8½"
Manager M. Duff
Pro. Debut 8 December, 1980

10.01.91 Mario Olmedo W RSC 4 Wandsworth
12.02.91 John Welters W RSC 1 Basildon
08.05.91 Darryl Anthony W CO 2 Kensington
22.04.92 Alfredo Ramirez W PTS 8 Wembley
13.05.92 Mick Duncan W RSC 2 Kensington

Career: 42 contests, won 39, lost 3.

Ian Honeywood

Bexley. *Born* Newmarket, 20 July, 1964
Former Undefeated Southern Area Lightweight Champion (9.8½-9.13¾) ht. 5'7"
Manager –
Pro. Debut 22 October, 1986

10.03.91 Pierre Lorcy L CO 5 Paris, France
24.09.91 Dave Anderson L PTS 8 Glasgow
13.11.91 Steve Walker W PTS 6 Bethnal Green
18.01.92 Steve Pollard W PTS 6 Kensington
30.03.92 Tony Foster W RSC 4 Eltham
30.04.92 Sean Murphy L RSC 1 Kensington

Career: 33 contests, won 18, drew 1, lost 14.

Donnie Hood

Glasgow. *Born* Glasgow, 3 June, 1963
Scottish Bantamweight Champion. Former Undefeated WBC International Bantamweight Champion (8.6-8.10) ht 5'5"
Manager A. Morrison
Pro. Debut 22 September, 1986

25.01.91 Dave Buxton W RSC 5 Shotts
05.03.91 Virgilio Openio W PTS 12 Glasgow *(WBC International Bantamweight Title Defence)*
31.05.91 Willie Richardson W PTS 8 Glasgow
24.09.91 Rocky Commey W PTS 12 Glasgow *(WBC International Bantamweight Title Defence)*
24.10.91 Vinnie Ponzio W PTS 8 Glasgow

14.03.92 Johnny Bredahl L RSC 7 Copenhagen, Denmark
(Vacant European Bantamweight Title)
29.05.92 Pete Buckley W PTS 8 Glasgow

Career: 30 contests, won 23, drew 1, lost 6.

Carl Hook

Swansea. *Born* Swansea, 21 November, 1969
L. Welterweight (9.10-10.3¾) ht. 5'8"
Manager D. Davies
Pro. Debut 18 July, 1991

18.07.91 Jason Matthews L PTS 6 Cardiff
25.07.91 Wayne Taylor W PTS 6 Dudley
16.09.91 Nicky Lucas W PTS 6 Mayfair
26.09.91 Ron Shinkwin L PTS 8 Dunstable
24.10.91 John O'Johnson W PTS 6 Dunstable
31.10.91 Davy Robb L PTS 4 Oakengates
05.12.91 Mark Ramsey L RSC 4 Oakengates
23.01.92 Phil Epton L PTS 6 York
11.02.92 Jason Matthews L PTS 6 Cardiff
11.05.92 Derrick Daniel L PTS 6 Piccadilly
16.06.92 Derrick Daniel W RSC 2 Dagenham

Career: 11 contests, won 4, lost 7.

Ron Hopley

Ripon. *Born* Ripon, 3 April, 1969
Welterweight (10.7-10.10) ht. 5'8½"
Manager D. Mancini
Pro. Debut 27 November, 1991

27.11.91 William Beaton W RSC 2 Marton
23.01.92 Rick North W PTS 6 York
08.04.92 Steve Howden L PTS 6 Leeds

Career: 3 contests, won 2, lost 1.

Nick Howard

Bargoed. *Born* Bargoed, 13 June, 1966
Heavyweight (15.3) ht. 6'3½"
Manager. D Gardiner
Pro. Debut 4 November, 1991

04.11.91 Chris Coughlan L CO 3 Merthyr

Career: 1 contest, lost 1.

Steve Howden

Sheffield. *Born* Sheffield, 4 June, 1969
Lightweight (9.12-10.2) ht. 5'8¾"
Manager B. Ingle
Pro. Debut 8 April, 1992

08.04.92 Ron Hopley W PTS 6 Leeds
01.06.92 Kevin McKillan L RSC 2 Manchester

Career: 2 contests, won 1, lost 1.

Mickey Hughes

St. Pancras. *Born* London, 13 June, 1962
Welterweight (10.6-11.0½) ht. 5'9½"
Manager B. Hearn
Pro. Debut 1 October, 1985

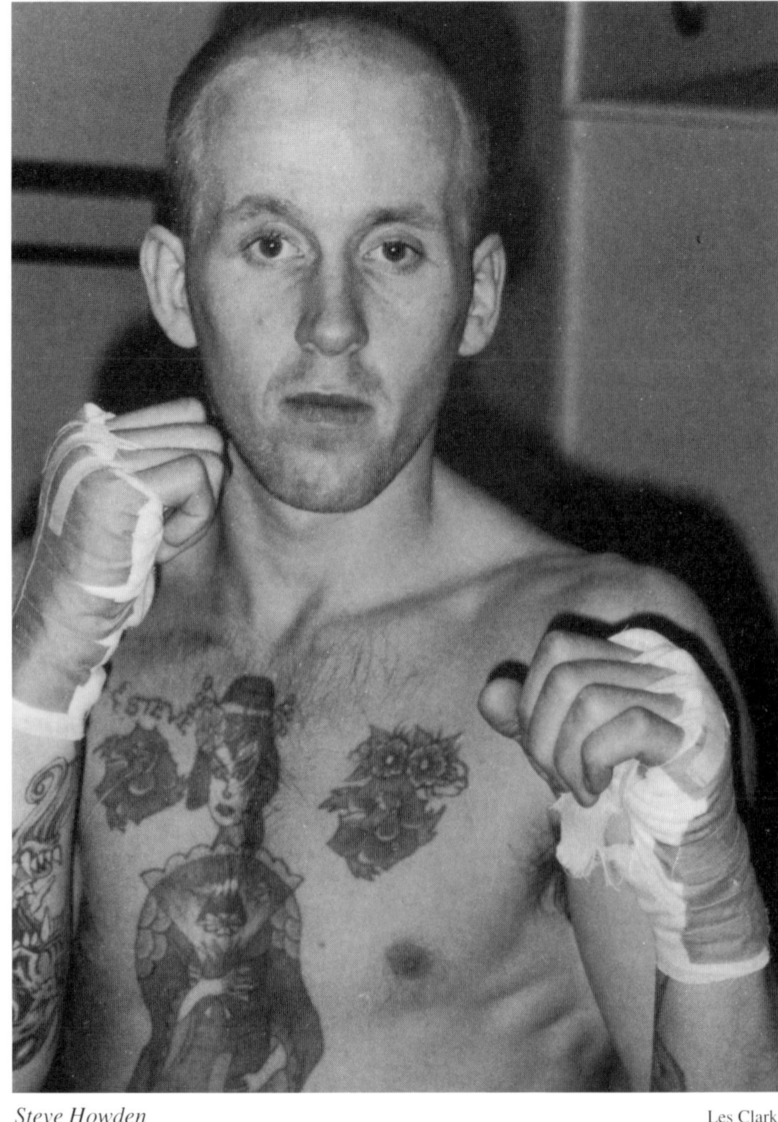

Steve Howden Les Clark

06.02.91 Ian John-Lewis W RSC 9 Bethnal Green
(Elim. British Welterweight Title)
04.06.91 Donovan Boucher L PTS 12 Bethnal Green
(Commonwealth Welterweight Title Challenge)
26.11.91 Del Bryan L RSC 3 Bethnal Green
(British Welterweight Title Challenge)
16.06.92 Andrew Furlong W CO 1 Dagenham

Career: 28 contests, won 23, lost 5.

Paul Hughes

Manchester. *Born* Manchester, 1 December, 1966
L. Welterweight (9.12-10.0) ht. 5'8½"
Manager N. Basso
Pro. Debut 9 October, 1991

09.10.91 Geoff Lawson W RSC 1 Marton
17.10.91 Tony Doyle W PTS 6 Mossley
13.11.91 Joey Moffat L RTD 4 Liverpool
01.06.92 Ty Zubair W PTS 6 Manchester

Career: 4 contests, won 3, lost 1.

Roger Hunte

Leyton. *Born* London, 28 October, 1971
Lightweight (9.8-9.9½) ht. 5'6"
Manager M. Duff
Pro. Debut 12 February, 1992

12.02.92 Jason Barker W RTD 4 Wembley
25.03.92 Phil Cullen W RSC 3 Kensington

Career: 2 contests, won 2.

James Hunter

Middlesbrough. *Born* Port Talbot, 12 May, 1969
Former Welsh S. Featherweight Champion (9.3-9.7) ht. 5'5"
Manager –
Pro. Debut 31 August, 1988

25.01.91 Rocky Ferrari L CO 1 Shotts
06.04.91 Doug Estaban DREW 6 Darlington
01.08.91 Craig Dermody L RSC 2 Dewsbury

Career: 19 contests, won 6, drew 2, lost 11.

Cordwell Hylton

Walsall. *Born* Jamaica, 20 September, 1958
Former Midlands Area Cruiserweight Champion (13.0-14.0) ht. 5'11"
Manager N. Basso
Pro. Debut 22 September, 1980

12.02.91 Steve Lewsam W RSC 8 Wolverhampton
22.02.91 Bobbi Joe Edwards W RTD 6 Manchester
20.03.91 Roy Smith W RSC 7 Solihull *(Midland Area Cruiserweight Title Challenge)*
17.05.91 Neils H. Madsen L RSC 2 Copenhagen, Denmark
22.06.91 Norbert Ekassi L CO 5 Paris, France
16.09.91 Steve Lewsam L PTS 10 Cleethorpes *(Midlands Area Cruiserweight Title Defence)*
26.11.91 Tony Wilson L PTS 8 Wolverhampton
21.02.92 Markus Bott L PTS 8 Hamburg, Germany
06.03.92 Yuri Razumov DREW 6 Berlin, Germany
27.03.92 Jean-Marie Emebe W RSC 3 Creil, France

Career: 58 contests, won 26, drew 1, lost 30, no contest 1.

Vance Idiens

Cannock. *Born* Walsall, 9 June, 1962
Heavyweight (15.7) ht. 6'4"
Manager R. Gray
Pro. Debut 24 October, 1989

05.12.91 David Jules W RSC 4 Cannock
06.03.92 Mario Scheisser L RSC 1 Berlin, Germany

Career: 11 contests, won 8, lost 3.

Keith Inglis

Tunbridge Wells. *Born* Tunbridge Wells, 3 November, 1964
L. Heavyweight (12.6-12.10¾) ht. 6'0"
Manager T. Lawless
Pro. Debut 26 November, 1990

23.05.91 Roger Silsby W CO 3 Southampton
12.09.91 Terry Duffus W CO 5 Wandsworth
17.10.91 Dennis Afflick W RSC 4 Southwark
20.11.91 John Kaighin L RSC 1 Kensington

Career: 5 contests, won 3, lost 2.

Keith Inglis Les Clark

Colin Innes

Newcastle. *Born* Newcastle, 24 July, 1964
S. Featherweight (9.1½-9.6) ht. 5'6"
Manager T. Conroy
Pro. Debut 10 September, 1990

11.02.91 Steve Armstrong W PTS 6 Manchester
18.02.91 Ian McGirr L PTS 6 Glasgow
02.03.91 Tony Smith W PTS 6 Darlington
28.03.91 Darryl Pettit W RTD 3 Alfreton
30.04.91 Noel Carroll L PTS 4 Stockport
19.09.91 Carl Roberts L PTS 4 Stockport
12.12.91 Tommy Smith L PTS 6 Hartlepool
24.02.92 Mark Geraghty L PTS 8 Glasgow
30.03.92 Chris Jickells L RSC 3 Bradford
28.05.92 Tommy Smith L PTS 6 Gosforth

Career: 15 contests, won 6, lost 9.

Billy Isaac

Hackney. *Born* Guildford, 14 August, 1968
Heavyweight (14.8½) ht. 6'4"
Manager G. Mason
Pro. Debut 19 December, 1991

19.12.91 Larry Peart W RSC 3 Oldham

Career: 1 contest, won 1.

Gilbert Jackson (Amponsan)

Battersea. *Born* Ghana, 21 August, 1970
Middleweight (11.1-11.5) ht. 5'10"
Manager M. Hill
Pro. Debut 17 February, 1992

17.02.92 John Bosko L PTS 6 Mayfair
05.03.92 Tony Wellington W CO 2 Battersea
22.04.92 Russell Washer W PTS 6 Wembley

Career: 3 contests, won 2, lost 1.

Chris Jacobs

Llanelli. *Born* Llanelli, 28 April, 1961
Welsh Heavyweight Champion (15.6) ht. 6'2"
Manager D. Davies
Pro. Debut 13 June, 1984

29.10.91 Herbie Hide L RSC 1 Cardiff

Career: 19 contests, w on 8, drew 1, lost 10.

Lester Jacobs

Peckham. *Born* London, 29 January, 1962
Middleweight (11.5½-11.12) ht. 5'7"
Manager H. Burgess
Pro. Debut 1 March, 1989

20.03.91 Karl Barwise W PTS 6 Wandsworth
16.05.91 Paul McCarthy W PTS 6 Battersea
11.09.91 John Kaighin W RSC 2 Hammersmith
05.03.92 John Kaighin W RSC 1 Battersea
17.05.92 Marvin O'Brien W PTS 6 Harringay

Career: 10 contests, won 10.

Mark Jay (Jackson)

Newcastle. *Born* Newcastle, 4 April, 1969
L. Middleweight (10.11-11.6) ht. 5'11"
Manager N. Fawcett
Pro. Debut 29 September, 1988

09.10.91 Willie Quinn W PTS 6 Glasgow
16.12.91 Tyrone Eastmond L PTS 6 Manchester
20.01.92 Mick Duncan W PTS 6 Bradford
24.02.92 David Radford W PTS 6 Bradford
03.03.92 Dave Johnson L PTS 6 Houghton le Spring
12.03.92 Gordon Blair DREW 8 Glasgow
02.04.92 Jamie Robinson L PTS 6 Basildon
25.04.92 Steve Foster L RSC 7 Manchester
28.05.92 Shamus Casey W PTS 8 Gosforth

Career: 21 contests, won 8, drew 3, lost 10.

Kevin Jenkins

Ammanford. *Born* Glanamman, 9 December, 1970
Bantamweight (7.13¾-8.7½) ht. 5'2½"
Manager D. Davies
Pro. Debut 21 December, 1989

24.01.91 Ceri Farrell W PTS 6 Gorseinon
12.02.91 Robbie Regan L PTS 10 Cardiff *(Vacant Welsh Flyweight Title)*
19.03.91 Danny Porter L RSC 7 Leicester
09.10.91 Stevie Woods DREW 8 Glasgow
19.11.91 Danny Porter L RSC 2 Norwich
18.03.92 Joe Kelly L PTS 8 Glasgow
05.05.92 Noel Carroll L PTS 7 Preston

Career: 15 contests, won 3, drew 2, lost 10.

Graham Jenner

Hastings. *Born* Hastings, 13 May, 1962
S. Middleweight (11.10-12.7) ht. 6'0"
Manager D. Harris
Pro. Debut 10 October, 1985

Lester Jacobs (right) seen outpointing Paul McCarthy in May 1991 Les Clark

29.10.91 Val Golding L RSC 3 Kensington
08.01.92 Paul McCarthy W PTS 6 Burton
29.02.92 Paul McCarthy W PTS 8 St Leonards
29.05.92 Ensley Bingham L CO 5 Manchester

Career: 12 contests, won 7, lost 5.

Chris Jickells

Brigg. *Born* Scunthorpe, 26 March, 1971
S. Featherweight (9.0-9.2) ht. 5'5"
Manager K. Tate
Pro. Debut 18 November, 1991

18.11.91 Tony Smith W RSC 4 Manchester
09.12.91 Al Garrett W RSC 2 Bradford
15.01.92 Ronnie Stephenson L PTS 6 Stoke
30.03.92 Colin Innes W RSC 3 Bradford
29.04.92 Kevin Middleton W RSC 6 Solihull
01.06.92 Dave McHale L RSC 4 Glasgow

Career: 6 contests, won 4, lost 2.

James Jiora (Iwenjiora)

Otley. *Born* Nigeria, 6 April, 1968
L. Welterweight (9.11-10.2¼) ht. 5'5"
Manager –
Pro. Debut 7 June, 1987

13.06.91 David Thompson DREW 6 Hull
01.08.91 Chris Saunders L PTS 6 Dewsbury
09.10.91 John O'Johnson L PTS 6 Manchester
21.10.91 Charlie Kane L PTS 6 Glasgow
02.03.92 Carl Tilley L PTS 6 Marton
12.03.92 Alan McDowall L CO 2 Glasgow

Career: 23 contests, won 8, drew 1, lost 14.

Tracy Jocelyn

Stafford. *Born* Stafford, 15 July, 1963
L. Middleweight (11.1¼-11.4) ht. 5'8¾"
Manager R. Gray
Pro. Debut 27 November, 1990

19.11.91 Adrian Strachan L PTS 6 Norwich
29.02.92 Clive Dixon W PTS 6 St Leonards
25.03.92 Kevin Lueshing L RSC 3 Dagenham
30.04.92 Kevin Sheeran L RSC 3 Kensington

Career: 6 contests, won 2, lost 4.

Ian John-Lewis

Gillingham. *Born* Gillingham, 28 November, 1962
Welterweight (10.5¾-10.6) ht. 5'10"
Manager –
Pro. Debut 4 March, 1987

06.02.91 Mickey Hughes L RSC 9 Bethnal Green
(Elim. British Welterweight Title)
19.02.92 Darren Dyer L RSC 2 Muswell Hill

Career: 21 contests, won 13, lost 8.

Dave Johnson

Sunderland. *Born* Boldon, 10 August, 1972
Middleweight (11.4-11.10½) ht. 5'10"
Manager T. Conroy
Pro. Debut 13 May, 1991

13.05.91 Rocky Tyrrell W PTS 6 Manchester
20.05.91 Kenny Tyson W PTS 6 Bradford
10.06.91 Tyrone Eastmond W PTS 6 Manchester
10.10.91 Shamus Casey W PTS 6 Gateshead
14.11.91 Shamus Casey W PTS 6 Gateshead
25.11.91 Mike Phillips L PTS 6 Liverpool
12.12.91 Mick Duncan W PTS 6 Hartlepool
03.03.92 Mark Jay W PTS 6 Houghton le Spring
28.04.92 Shaun McCrory DREW 6 Houghton le Spring

Career: 9 contests, won 7, drew 1, lost 1.

Julian Johnson

Swansea. *Born* Swansea, 4 October, 1967
L. Heavyweight (12.1-12.10) ht. 5'10½"
Manager C. Breen
Pro. Debut 20 November, 1991

20.11.91 Nigel Rafferty DREW 6 Cardiff
22.01.92 Paul McCarthy DREW 6 Cardiff
29.02.92 Johnny Uphill W CO 3 St Leonards
11.03.92 Nicky Wadman L PTS 6 Cardiff
11.05.92 Andy Manning L PTS 6 Llanelli

Career: 5 contests, won 1, drew 2, lost 2.

Terry Johnson

Liverpool. *Born* Liverpool, 4 October, 1964
S. Middleweight (12.0-12.3) ht. 5'10"
Manager T. Miller
Pro. Debut 1 May, 1991

01.05.91 Mark Spencer W RSC 2 Liverpool
13.05.91 Paul Hitch L PTS 6 Marton
09.09.91 John Kaighin L RTD 2 Liverpool
13.11.91 Dean Allen L RSC 2 Liverpool

Career: 4 contests, won 1, lost 3.

Neil Johnston

Middlesbrough. *Born* Middlesbrough, 12 October, 1967
Flyweight (8.1½-8.2) ht. 5'4"
Manager –
Pro. Debut 3 October, 1990

09.04.91 Eric George DREW 6 Mayfair
22.06.91 Francis Ampofo L RSC 2 Earls Court
21.10.91 Neil Parry W PTS 8 Glasgow

Career: 5 contests, won 1, drew 2, lost 2.

Martin Jolley

Alfreton. *Born* Chesterfield, 22 November, 1967
S. Middleweight (12.0-12.3) ht. 5'11½"
Manager M. Shinfield
Pro. Debut 10 March, 1992

10.03.92 Gypsy Johnny Price W RSC 3 Bury
06.04.92 Sean Byrne L RSC 6 Northampton
11.05.92 Mark Hale W PTS 6 Coventry

Career: 3 contests, won 2, lost 1.

Matthew Jones

Dudley. *Born* Bloxwich, 20 January, 1968
Middleweight (11.4-11.6) ht. 5'11"
Manager R. Browne
Pro. Debut 6 October, 1988

29.04.92 Dave Hall W RSC 2 Solihull
29.05.92 Carl Harney L RSC 6 Manchester

Career: 9 contests, won 7, lost 2.

Paul Jones

Sheffield. *Born* Sheffield, 19 November, 1966
Central Area L. Middleweight Champion (10.7½-11.2) ht. 6'0"
Manager B. Hearn
Pro. Debut 8 December, 1986

12.03.91 Tony Velinor W PTS 8 Mansfield
16.08.91 Hugo Marinangelli L CO 2 Marbella, Spain
01.10.91 Simon Eubank W CO 6 Sheffield
14.04.92 Paul Lynch W RSC 3 Mansfield
19.05.92 Trevor Ambrose W PTS 6 Cardiff
02.06.92 Patrick Vungbo W PTS 10 Rotterdam, Holland

Career: 26 contests, won 18, drew 1, lost 7.

Seth Jones

Dyffryn. *Born* St Asaph, 9 February, 1968
L. Welterweight (10.1¼-10.3¾) ht. 5'8¼"
Manager D. Davies
Pro. Debut 29 August, 1991

29.08.91 John O'Johnson L DIS 1 Oakengates
19.09.91 Ricky Sackfield L RSC 1 Stockport
20.11.91 Jess Rundan W CO 4 Cardiff
09.12.91 Spencer McCracken L RSC 2 Brierley Hill
19.02.92 Paul Knights L RSC 5 Muswell Hill
31.03.92 Danny Kett W CO 1 Norwich
16.06.92 Paul Knights L PTS 6 Dagenham

Career: 7 contests, won 2, lost 5.

Benji Joseph

Warrington. *Born* Ipswich, 28 March, 1969
L. Middleweight (10.8-11.4) ht. 5'9½"
Manager R. Jones
Pro. Debut 4 February, 1991

04.02.91 Richard Okumu L PTS 6 Leicester
05.03.91 Tommy Warde L PTS 6 Leicester
25.03.91 Tyrone Eastmond W PTS 6 Bradford
24.06.91 Dave Maj L RSC 4 Liverpool
07.10.91 Wayne Shepherd L PTS 6 Bradford
18.11.91 Mick Mulcahy W PTS 6 Manchester
20.01.92 Willie Yeardsley L PTS 6 Bradford
06.02.92 Willie Yeardsley L RSC 4 Peterborough
25.03.92 Craig Hartwell W PTS 6 Hinckley
28.04.92 Hughie Davey L RSC 4 Houghton le Spring

Career: 10 contests, won 3, lost 7.

Dene Josham

Louth. *Born* Louth, 3 July, 1971
Heavyweight (14.8) ht. 6'3"
Manager J. Gaynor
Pro. Debut 24 February, 1992

24.02.92 Ian Carmichael L PTS 6 Bradford

Career: 1 contest, lost 1.

Richard Joyce

Burton. *Born* Burton, 2 August, 1966
Lightweight (9.8-9.13) ht. 5'8"
Manager –
Pro. Debut 28 March, 1988

23.01.91 Tony Doyle W CO 6 Stoke
06.03.91 Nigel Senior W PTS 8 Croydon
24.04.91 Brendan Ryan W PTS 8 Stoke
14.05.91 Hugh Forde L RTD 5 Dudley
11.12.91 Mark O'Callaghan W RSC 3 Stoke

Career: 13 contests, won 11, lost 2.

Peter Judson

Keighley. *Born* Keighley, 14 January, 1970
Featherweight (8.12-9.5) ht. 5'7"
Manager P. Martin
Pro. Debut 24 April, 1989

29.01.91 Russell Davison L PTS 10 Stockport *(Vacant Central Area Featherweight Title)*
21.02.91 Noel Carroll W PTS 8 Leeds
20.03.91 Colin Lynch W RTD 5 Solihull
01.05.91 Jimmy Owens L PTS 6 Liverpool
28.05.91 Scott Durham W PTS 6 Cardiff
24.09.91 Ian McGirr L PTS 6 Glasgow
11.11.91 Miguel Matthews W PTS 6 Stratford on Avon
18.11.91 Jamie McBride DREW 6 Glasgow
09.02.92 Ceri Farrell W PTS 6 Bradford
05.04.92 Barrie Kelley W PTS 6 Bradford

Career: 27 contests, won 15, drew 2, lost 10.

David Jules

Doncaster. *Born* Doncaster, 11 July, 1965
Heavyweight (15.7-15.12) ht. 6'2"
Manager J. Rushton
Pro. Debut 12 June, 1987

09.04.91 Herbie Hide L RSC 1 Mayfair
05.12.91 Vance Idiens L RSC 4 Cannock
24.02.92 Rocky Burton W CO 1 Coventry
05.04.92 Steve Garber L RSC 4 Bradford

Career: 19 contests, won 6, drew 1, lost 12.

John Kaighin

Swansea. *Born* Brecknock, 26 August, 1967
S. Middleweight (11.3-12.8) ht. 5'11¼"
Manager M. Copp
Pro. Debut 17 September, 1990

24.01.91 Robert Peel L PTS 6 Gorseinon
12.02.91 Robert Peel W PTS 6 Cardiff
15.03.91 Max McCracken DREW 6 Willenhall
10.04.91 Darron Griffiths L PTS 6 Newport
24.04.91 Paul Murray W PTS 6 Aberavon
08.05.91 Benji Good W RSC 3 Kensington
15.05.91 Robert Peel L PTS 8 Swansea
06.06.91 Peter Vosper DREW 6 Barking
30.06.91 John Ogiste L PTS 6 Southwark
29.08.91 Adrian Wright W PTS 6 Oakengates
09.09.91 Terry Johnson W RTD 2 Liverpool
11.09.91 Lester Jacobs L RSC 2 Hammersmith
22.10.91 Andy Wright DREW 6 Wandsworth
13.11.91 Gary Delaney L PTS 6 Bethnal Green
20.11.91 Keith Inglis W RSC 1 Kensington
23.01.92 Michael Gale L PTS 8 York
01.02.92 Paul Busby L PTS 4 Birmingham
25.02.92 Andy Wright L PTS 6 Crystal Palace
05.03.92 Lester Jacobs L RSC 1 Battersea
27.04.92 Bruce Scott L CO 4 Mayfair

Career: 26 contests, won 7, drew 3, lost 16.

Patrick Kamy (Kamya)

Tottenham. *Born* Uganda, 3 April, 1965
Lightweight (9.7-9.11) ht. 5'6¼"
Manager R. Colson
Pro. Debut 6 October, 1987

23.02.91 Antonio Rivera L CO 5 Cagliari, Italy
24.10.91 Billy Schwer L CO 1 Dunstable
17.12.91 Floyd Havard L DIS 5 Cardiff

Career: 17 contests, won 7, lost 10.

Charlie Kane

Clydebank. *Born* Glasgow, 2 July, 1968
L. Welterweight (10.2-10.3) ht. 5'10½"
Manager J. Cresswell
Pro. Debut 5 March, 1991

05.03.91 Dean Bramhald W RSC 6 Glasgow
21.10.91 James Jiora W PTS 6 Glasgow
24.02.92 Karl Taylor W PTS 8 Glasgow

Career: 3 contests, won 3.

Ray Kane

Belfast. *Born* Dublin, 4 June, 1968
Cruiserweight (13.9½-13.10¼) ht. 6'0"
Manager B. Eastwood
Pro. Debut 7 September, 1991

07.09.91 R. F. McKenzie W PTS 4 Belfast
11.12.91 Chris Coughlan W PTS 6 Dublin

Career: 2 contests, won 2.

Barrie Kelley

Llanelli. *Born* Llanelli, 14 February, 1972
S. Featherweight (9.2-9.5½) ht. 5'6"
Manager D. Davies
Pro. Debut 16 October, 1990

24.01.91 Martin Evans W PTS 6 Gorseinon
18.02.91 Tony Falcone L RSC 6 Mayfair
26.03.91 Dennis Adams W PTS 6 Bethnal Green
18.07.91 Robert Smyth DREW 6 Cardiff
16.09.91 Dominic McGuigan DREW 6 Mayfair
14.10.91 Michael Armstrong L CO 4 Manchester
20.11.91 Neil Haddock L PTS 6 Cardiff
03.02.92 Noel Carroll L PTS 8 Manchester
18.03.92 Mark Geraghty L PTS 8 Glasgow
05.04.92 Peter Judson L PTS 6 Bradford

Career: 13 contests, won 5, drew 2, lost 6.

Felix Kelly

Paddington. *Born* Sligo, 6 June, 1965
Lightweight (9.7-9.11) ht. 5'7"
Manager I. Akay
Pro. Debut 18 October, 1990

06.02.91 Wayne Windle W PTS 6 Bethnal Green
18.02.91 Trevor Royal W RSC 4 Windsor
26.03.91 Chris Saunders W PTS 6 Bethnal Green
18.04.91 Rick Bushell W PTS 6 Earls Court
22.06.91 Rick Bushell L PTS 6 Earls Court
26.09.91 Billy Schwer L RSC 2 Dunstable
20.11.91 Tony Borg L PTS 6 Cardiff
25.03.92 Mark Tibbs DREW 8 Dagenham

Career: 11 contests, won 6, drew 2, lost 3.

Joe Kelly

Glasgow. *Born* Glasgow, 18 May, 1964
Former British Bantamweight Champion. Former Undefeated IBF Intercontinental Flyweight Champion (7.13¼-8.8¼) ht. 5'1½"
Manager P. Byrne
Pro. Debut 28 January, 1985

Barrie Kelley Les Clark

23.02.91 Salvatore Fanni L RSC 2 Cagliari, Italy *(Vacant European Flyweight Title)*
28.05.91 Robbie Regan L PTS 12 Cardiff *(Vacant British Flyweight Title)*
21.10.91 Ronnie Carroll DREW 12 Glasgow *(Vacant British Bantamweight Title)*
27.01.92 Ronnie Carroll W PTS 12 Glasgow *(Vacant British Bantamweight Title)*
18.03.92 Kevin Jenkins W PTS 8 Glasgow
01.06.92 Drew Docherty L RSC 5 Glasgow *(British Bantamweight Title Defence)*

Career: 27 contests, won 18, drew 2, lost 7.

Mark Kelly

Doncaster. *Born* Denaby, 15 July, 1968
Welterweight (10.5-10.11) ht. 5'7"
Manager –
Pro. Debut 19 October, 1987

06.06.91 Roy Rowland L RSC 4 Barking
25.11.91 Trevor Meikle L PTS 8 Cleethorpes
11.12.91 Andreas Panayi DREW 8 Stoke
21.05.92 Malcolm Melvin L PTS 8 Cradley Heath
01.06.92 Darren Morris L PTS 8 Solihull

Career: 28 contests, won 12, drew 3, lost 13.

Paul Kelly (Nettleship)

Doncaster. *Born* Mexborough, 18 May, 1968
Bantamweight (8.11) ht. 5'7"
Manager J. Rushton
Pro. Debut 21 May, 1992

21.05.92 Graham McGrath L RSC 2 Cradley Heath

Career: 1 contest, lost 1.

Andy Kent

Northampton. *Born* Scunthorpe, 10 February, 1963
S. Featherweight (9.4-9.10½) ht. 5'7"
Manager L. Slater
Pro. Debut 6 March, 1989

18.02.91 Kevin Toomey W RSC 5 Derby
02.03.91 Warren Bowers W PTS 6 Cleethorpes
02.05.91 Peter Campbell W PTS 6 Northampton
04.04.92 Tony Doyle L RSC 5 Cleethorpes

Career: 10 contests, won 5, drew 1, lost 4.

Danny Kett

Norwich. *Born* Norwich, 8 October, 1970
L. Welterweight (9.11-10.2½) ht. 5'8"
Manager G. Holmes
Pro. Debut 21 January, 1992

21.01.92 Barry Glanister W RSC 1 Norwich
31.03.92 Seth Jones L CO 1 Norwich

Career: 2 contests, won 1, lost 1.

Joe Kilshaw

Preston. *Born* Preston, 27 June, 1963
Middleweight (11.7-11.8) ht. 5'10½"
Manager –
Pro. Debut 22 October, 1990

22.04.91 Ian Vokes DREW 6 Bradford
30.09.91 Matt Mowatt DREW 6 Liverpool

Career: 3 contests, drew 2, lost 1.

Eddie King

Doncaster. *Born* Doncaser, 21 February, 1966
Welterweight (10.2-10.8) ht. 5'9¾"
Manager J. Rushton
Pro. Debut 15 March, 1986

16.01.91 Gerald Flood W RSC 3 Stoke
29.01.91 Gordon Webster W PTS 6 Wisbech
12.02.91 Andreas Panayi L CO 2 Wolverhampton
29.04.91 Gerald Flood W RSC 4 Cleethorpes
14.05.91 Dean Hiscox W PTS 6 Dudley
05.06.91 Dean Hiscox W PTS 6 Wolverhampton
17.06.91 Cliff Churchward W PTS 6 Edgbaston
16.09.91 Rick North L RSC 5 Cleethorpes
16.10.91 Noel Henry L CO 2 Stoke
05.12.91 Shaun Cooper L RSC 3 Cannock
11.02.92 Chris Saunders L RSC 4 Wolverhampton
11.03.92 Darren McInulty L RSC 1 Stoke

Career: 29 contests, won 12, lost 17.

Paul King

Newcastle. *Born* Newcastle, 3 June, 1965
Welterweight (10.8-10.13) ht. 5'8½"
Manager –
Pro. Debut 4 September, 1987

28.02.91 Dave Kettlewell W RSC 1 Sunderland
21.03.91 Phil Epton W PTS 6 Dewsbury
13.05.91 Shamus Casey L PTS 6 Northampton
31.05.91 Gordon Blair L PTS 8 Glasgow
09.10.91 Delroy Waul L RSC 6 Manchester

Career: 12 contests, won 7, lost 5.

Stan King (Hibbert)

Forest Hill. *Born* Jamaica, 25 April, 1964
Middleweight (11.4½-11.9) ht. 5'10½"
Manager –
Pro. Debut 5 November, 1987

03.04.91 Ian Strudwick L RSC 8 Bethnal Green
24.06.91 Gilbert Hallie L PTS 8 Rotterdam, Holland
17.03.92 Ian Chantler W CO 3 Mayfair
31.03.92 Kesem Clayton W RSC 4 Norwich
11.05.92 Tony Velinor W RSC 3 Piccadilly

Career: 22 contests, won 9, drew 2, lost 11.

Nigel Kitching

Bethnal Green. *Born* Tidworth, 23 December, 1965
L. Middleweight (11.1½) ht. 5'11"
Manager M. Brennan
Pro. Debut 7 April, 1992

07.04.92 Adrian Haughton L RSC 5 Southend

Career: 1 contest, lost 1.

Paul Knights

Redhill. *Born* Redhill, 5 February, 1971
L. Welterweight (9.13-10.2) ht. 5'10"
Manager –
Pro. Debut 26 November, 1991

26.11.91 Steve Hearn W RSC 4 Bethnal Green
19.02.92 Seth Jones W RSC 5 Muswell Hill
16.06.92 Seth Jones W PTS 6 Dagenham

Career: 3 contests, won 3.

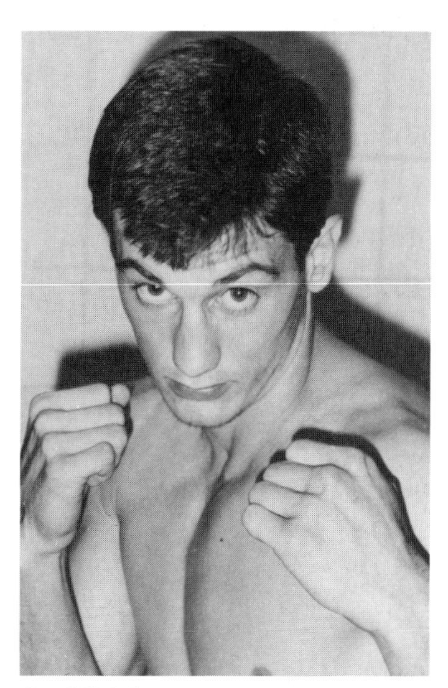

Paul Knights Les Clark

(Isenovic) Tony Kosova (Nedjmedin)

Nottingham. *Born* Yugoslavia, 12 December, 1964
Middleweight (11.4-11.8) ht. 5'10"
Manager –
Pro. Debut 26 September, 1990

16.01.91 David Radford L PTS 6 Stoke
10.05.91 Paul Hitch L RTD 1 Gateshead
05.12.91 John Bosko L CO 2 Peterborough

Career: 6 contests, lost 6.

Gavin Lane (Keeble)

Paignton. *Born* Rainham, 14 July, 1971
L. Welterweight (9.12½-10.0) ht. 5'11¼"
Manager J. Gaynor
Pro. Debut 28 November, 1991

28.11.91 Dewi Roberts W PTS 6 Evesham
30.03.92 Razza Campbell L PTS 6 Coventry

Career: 2 contests, won 1, lost 1.

Phil Lashley

Birmingham. *Born* Birmingham, 1 May, 1965
S. Featherweight (8.13-9.4) ht. 5'5"
Manager –
Pro. Debut 27 April, 1986

23.01.91 Mark Bates L RTD 3 Brentwood
04.03.91 Dave Annis W CO 2 Birmingham
01.05.91 Mark Bates L PTS 6 Bethnal Green
04.06.91 Paul Donaghey L CO 1 Bethnal Green
21.10.91 Ronnie Stephenson L PTS 6 Cleethorpes
21.11.91 Ronnie Stephenson L PTS 6 Stafford
30.03.92 Jamie McBride L RSC 1 Glasgow

Career: 47 contests, won 9, drew 1, lost 37.

Jim Lawlor

Birmingham. *Born* Birmingham, 1 March, 1961
Welterweight (10.2-10.10) ht. 5'9"
Manager –
Pro. Debut 17 June, 1988

05.03.91 Mark Pearce W PTS 6 Cardiff
17.04.91 Dean Hollington L PTS 6 Kensington
20.06.91 Richard Burton W PTS 6 Liverpool
07.09.91 Abram Gumede L PTS 6 Belfast
13.11.91 Dean Hollington L PTS 6 Bethnal Green
05.12.91 Ernie Loveridge L PTS 8 Cannock
20.02.92 Wayne Timmins L PTS 6 Oakengates

Career: 16 contests, won 5, drew 4, lost 7.

Dave Lawrence

Norwich. *Born* Thetford, 14 October, 1963
L. Heavyweight (12.6-13.1½) ht. 5'11"
Manager –
Pro. Debut 21 March, 1988

25.03.91 Ian Henry L PTS 6 Bradford

19.04.91 Eddie Collins W PTS 6 Peterborough
26.04.91 Tenko Ernie L RSC 3 Crystal Palace
19.11.91 Paul McCarthy DREW 6 Norwich
21.01.92 Gypsy Carman L PTS 6 Norwich

Career: 24 contests, won 6, drew 3, lost 15.

Geoff Lawson

Washington. *Born* Sunderland, 2 June, 1968
L. Welterweight (9.13½-10.1) ht. 5'6"
Manager J. Spensley
Pro. Debut 9 October, 1991

09.10.91 Paul Hughes L RSC 1 Marton
09.12.91 Tony Robinson L RSC 1 Bradford

Career: 2 contests, lost 2.

Mark Legg

Newcastle. *Born* South Shields, 25 March, 1970
L. Welterweight (9.11-10.1) ht. 5'9½"
Manager A. Walker
Pro. Debut 28 February, 1992

28.02.92 Chris Aston W RSC 5 Irvine
17.03.92 Dean Hiscox W PTS 6 Wolverhampton
18.05.92 Charles Shepherd L PTS 6 Marton

Career: 3 contests, won 2, lost 1.

Neil Leitch

Scunthorpe. *Born* Scunthorpe, 24 March, 1966
S. Featherweight (9.2-9.6) ht. 5'7"
Manager –
Pro. Debut 3 April, 1989

29.01.91 Noel Carroll L RSC 4 Stockport
06.03.91 Mark Geraghty L PTS 10 Glasgow *(Vacant Scottish S. Featherweight Title)*
26.03.91 Pete Buckley DREW 8 Wolverhampton
03.04.91 Carl Roberts W RSC 6 Manchester
22.04.91 Mike Deveney L PTS 6 Glasgow
01.05.91 Elvis Parsley L CO 2 Solihull
03.06.91 Mark Geraghty W PTS 8 Glasgow
23.09.91 Mark Geraghty L PTS 10 Glasgow *(Scottish S. Featherweight Title Challenge)*
05.11.91 Neil Smith L RSC 1 Leicester
05.12.91 Brian Robb L CO 2 Oakengates

Career: 33 contests, won 14, drew 3, lost 16.

Jason Lepre

Portsmouth. *Born* Portsmouth, 11 July, 1969
S. Featherweight (9.5¼-9.8½) ht. 5'10"
Manager –
Pro. Debut 26 April, 1989

23.05.91 Miguel Matthews W PTS 6 Southampton
16.12.91 Mark Loftus W PTS 6 Southampton
22.01.92 Kevin Simons W PTS 6 Cardiff

Career: 7 contests, won 5, lost 2.

Mickey Lerwill

Telford. *Born* Telford, 6 April, 1965
Welterweight (10.7-10.10) ht. 5'5"
Manager G. Hayward
Pro. Debut 23 June, 1983

10.04.91 Gary Osborne L PTS 10 Wolverhampton *(Vacant Midlands Area Welterweight Title)*
29.08.91 John McGlynn L PTS 6 Oakengates
12.11.91 Ernie Loveridge L PTS 6 Wolverhampton
05.12.91 Trevor Meikle W PTS 6 Oakengates

Career: 26 contests, won 9, drew 4, lost 13.

Alan Levene

Liverpool. *Born* Liverpool, 26 February, 1968
Lightweight (9.8) ht. 5'7½"
Manager B. Hearn
Pro. Debut 13 October, 1989

05.05.92 Steve Winstanley W RSC 2 Preston

Career: 5 contests, won 3, drew 2.

(Gilbert) Gil Lewis

Willenhall. *Born* Coventry, 29 July, 1965
L. Heavyweight (12.4-12.11) ht. 5'10½"
Manager R. Gray
Pro. Debut 22 November, 1989

28.01.91 Carlos Christie L PTS 8 Birmingham
27.02.91 Alan Baptiste W RSC 1 Wolverhampton
22.06.91 John Foreman DREW 6 Earls Court
01.10.91 Lee Prudden DREW 8 Bedworth
21.11.91 Art Stacey W RSC 4 Stafford
20.01.92 Tony Behan W PTS 8 Coventry
01.02.92 Ginger Tshabalala L RSC 4 Birmingham

Career: 13 contests, won 9, drew 2, lost 2.

Steve Lewsam Chris Bevan

Steve Lewsam

Grimsby. *Born* Cleethorpes, 8 September, 1960
Midlands Area Cruiserweight Champion (13.2-13.8) ht. 6'2"
Manager –
Pro. Debut 22 November, 1982

12.02.91 Cordwell Hylton L RSC 8 Wolverhampton
29.04.91 Dave Muhammed L PTS 8 Cleethorpes
16.09.91 Cordwell Hylton W PTS 10 Cleethorpes *(Midlands Area Cruiserweight Title Challenge)*
09.12.91 Tony Booth W PTS 8 Cleethorpes
04.06.92 Carl Thompson L RSC 8 Cleethorpes *(Vacant British Cruiserweight Title)*

Career: 19 contests, won 11, drew 2, lost 6.

Alan Ley

Newport. *Born* Newport, 29 December, 1968
Bantamweight (8.3½-8.6) ht. 5'6"
Manager S. Sims
Pro. Debut 3 September, 1991

03.09.91 Andrew Bloomer W PTS 6 Cardiff
22.01.92 Ceri Farrell W PTS 6 Cardiff
17.02.92 Leigh Williams W PTS 6 Mayfair

Career: 3 contests, won 3.

Paul Lister

Newcastle. *Born* Newcastle, 20 December, 1959
Northern Area Heavyweight Champion (15.5) ht. 6'3½"
Manager J. Spensley
Pro. Debut 22 October, 1984

10.10.91 Steve Garber W PTS 8 Gateshead

Career: 19 contests, won 14, lost 5.

Wayne Llewelyn

Deptford. *Born* Greenwich, 20 April, 1970
Heavyweight (14.2-14.10¾) ht. 6'3½"
Manager B. Paget
Pro. Debut 18 January, 1992

18.01.92 Chris Coughlan W RSC 3 Kensington
30.03.92 Steve Stewart W RSC 4 Eltham
23.04.92 Gary Charlton W RSC 4 Eltham

Career: 3 contests, won 3.

Edward Lloyd

Rhyl. *Born* St Asaph, 23 April, 1963
Lightweight (9.6¾-9.7) ht. 5'7½"
Manager –
Pro. Debut 7 February, 1983

11.02.92 Dewi Roberts W RSC 1 Cardiff
19.05.92 Mervyn Bennett W RSC 5 Cardiff

Career: 29 contests, won 13, drew 2, lost 14.

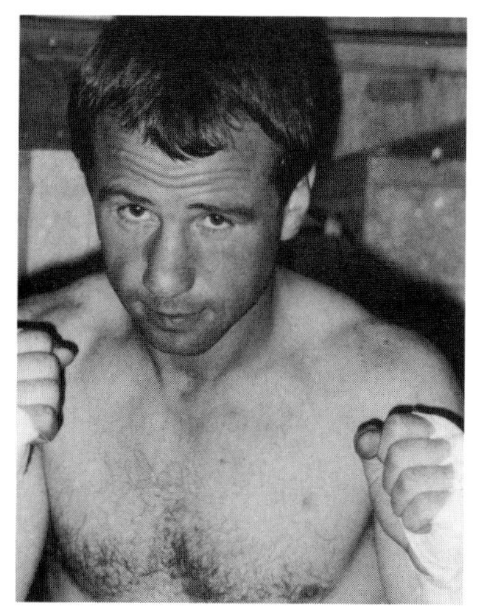

Edward Lloyd Les Clark

Robert Lloyd

Rhyl. *Born* Prestatyn, 4 August, 1960
L. Welterweight (10.2½) ht. 5'9"
Manager N. Basso
Pro. Debut 17 February, 1983

09.03.92 Mike Calderwood L RSC 1 Manchester

Career: 13 contests, won 5, drew 2, lost 6.

Mark Loftus

Luton. *Born* Newmarket, 5 August, 1960
Featherweight (8.8-9.1½) ht. 5'4½"
Manager J. Barclay
Pro. Debut 22 April, 1991

22.04.91 Akash D. Paul W CO 1 Mayfair
25.05.91 Ceri Farrell W RSC 3 Basildon
10.06.91 Noel Carroll L PTS 6 Manchester
09.10.91 Miguel Matthews DREW 6 Manchester
12.11.91 Conn McMullen L PTS 6 Milton Keynes
16.12.91 Jason Lepre L PTS 6 Southampton

Career: 6 contests, won 2, drew 1, lost 3.

Gary Logan

Brixton. *Born* Lambeth, 10 October, 1968
Welterweight (10.8-10.10½) ht. 5'8¾"
Manager M. Duff
Pro. Debut 5 October, 1988

16.01.91 Julian Eavis W RSC 5 Kensington
18.02.91 Gordon Blair W CO 1 Mayfair
25.04.91 Trevor Ambrose W PTS 8 Mayfair
17.10.91 Des Robinson W PTS 8 Southwark

Career: 20 contests, won 19, lost 1.

Eamonn Loughran

Ballymena. *Born* Ballymena, 5 June, 1970
Welterweight (10.6½-10.12) ht. 5'9"
Manager B. Hearn
Pro. Debut 3 December, 1987

12.02.91 Nick Meloscia W CO 1 Cardiff
05.03.91 Julian Eavis W PTS 6 Cardiff
26.03.91 Stan Cunningham W RSC 2 Bethnal Green
24.04.91 Kevin Plant W RTD 1 Preston
28.05.91 Terry Morrill W CO 1 Cardiff
03.09.91 Marty Duke W PTS 6 Cardiff
21.09.91 Glyn Rhodes W PTS 8 Tottenham
15.10.91 Juan Carlos Ortiz W PTS 8 Hamburg, Germany
10.03.92 Tony Ekubia L DIS 5 Bury *(Elim. British Welterweight Title)*
19.05.92 Kelvin Mortimer W RSC 1 Cardiff

Career: 19 contests, won 17, drew 1, lost 1.

Patrick Loughran

Ballymena. *Born* Ballymena, 15 September, 1972
L. Welterweight (9.9-10.3) ht. 5'6"
Manager P. Brogan
Pro. Debut 11 September, 1991

11.09.91 Kevin Lowe W PTS 6 Stoke
11.12.91 Keith Hardman W PTS 6 Stoke
11.03.92 Rick North W PTS 6 Stoke

Career: 3 contests, won 3.

Gary Logan (left) shown winning on points against Des Robinson last October Les Clark

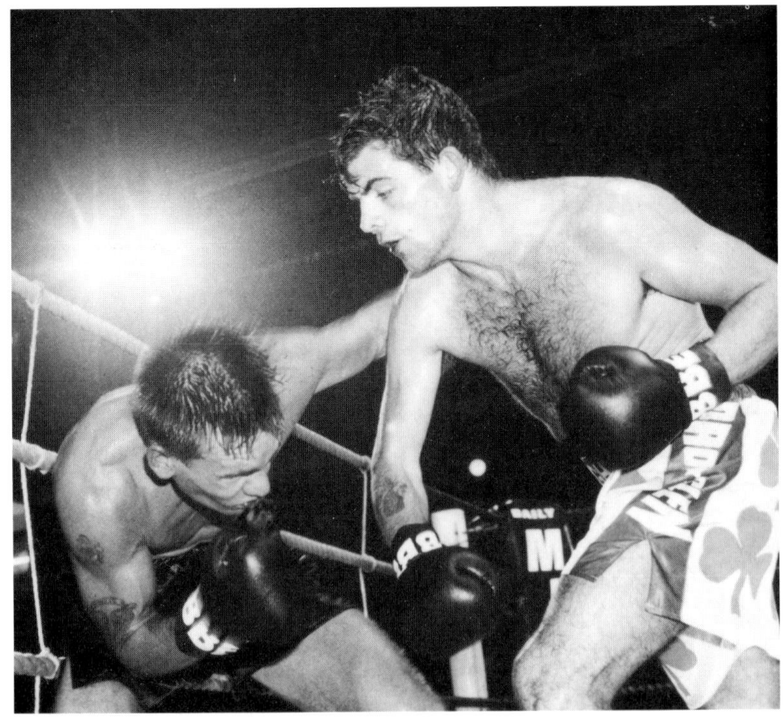

Eamonn Loughran (right) cruised to an easy points win over the game Marty Duke at Cardiff in September 1991 Les Clark

Dave Lovell

Birmingham. *Born* Birmingham, 15 April, 1962
L. Welterweight (10.2-10.3) ht. 5'7½"
Manager E. Cashmore
Pro. Debut 25 March, 1992

25.03.92 Billy Robinson L PTS 6 Hinckley
29.04.92 Jason Barker W PTS 6 Stoke

Career: 2 contests, won 1, lost 1.

Ernie Loveridge

Ernie Loveridge

Wolverhampton. *Born* Bromsgrove, 7 July, 1970
Midlands Area Welterweight Champion (10.7-11.0½) ht. 5'10"
Manager –
Pro. Debut 6 February, 1989

23.01.91 Cliff Churchward W PTS 6 Solihull
27.02.91 Ronnie Campbell W PTS 8 Wolverhampton
13.03.91 John Corcoran W RSC 4 Stoke
10.04.91 Julian Eavis DREW 8 Wolverhampton
14.05.91 Paul Murray W PTS 8 Dudley
05.06.91 Cliff Churchward W PTS 8 Wolverhampton
10.09.91 Gary Osborne W RSC 1 Wolverhampton *(Midlands Area Welterweight Title Challenge)*
12.11.91 Mickey Lerwill W PTS 6 Wolverhampton
05.12.91 Jim Lawlor W PTS 8 Cannock
01.02.92 Michael Oliver W PTS 8 Birmingham

Career: 26 contests, won 18, drew 3, lost 5.

Kevin Lowe

Sheffield. *Born* Sheffield, 24 August, 1964
Lightweight (9.2-9.10) ht. 5'6"
Manager –
Pro. Debut 11 September, 1991

11.09.91 Patrick Loughran L PTS 6 Stoke
26.09.91 Eunan Devenney W CO 2 Dunstable
14.10.91 Carl Roberts L PTS 6 Manchester
22.10.91 Tommy Smith L RSC 4 Hartlepool
28.11.91 Joey Moffat L PTS 6 Liverpool
10.12.91 Richard Woolgar L PTS 6 Sheffield
27.02.92 Joey Moffat L PTS 6 Liverpool
30.03.92 Dave McHale L RSC 5 Glasgow
30.04.92 Dominic McGuigan L RSC 6 Mayfair

Career: 9 contests, won 1, lost 8.

Nicky Lucas

Waltham Abbey. *Born* Epping, 17 February, 1969
L. Welterweight (9.3-10.1) ht. 5'7¼"
Manager –
Pro. Debut 11 May, 1988

25.04.91 Charlie Coke W PTS 6 Mayfair
08.05.91 Frankie Ventura DREW 6 Kensington
06.06.91 Martin Evans W PTS 6 Barking
30.06.91 David Thompson L PTS 6 Southwark
16.09.91 Carl Hook L PTS 6 Mayfair
24.10.91 Mark O'Callaghan L PTS 6 Dunstable
30.01.92 Jason Barker L PTS 6 Southampton

Career: 19 contests, won 8, drew 2, lost 9.

Kevin Lueshing

Beckenham. *Born* Beckenham, 17 April, 1968
Welterweight (10.9½-10.10¾) ht. 5'11"
Manager F. Maloney
Pro. Debut 30 September, 1991

30.09.91 John McGlynn W RSC 2 Kensington
23.10.91 Julian Eavis W RSC 2 Bethnal Green
14.12.91 Trevor Meikle W CO 3 Bexleyheath
18.01.92 Simon Eubank W CO 4 Kensington
25.03.92 Tracy Jocelyn W RSC 3 Dagenham
30.04.92 Newton Barnett W PTS 6 Kensington

Career: 6 contests, won 6.

Kevin Lueshing Les Clark

Colin Lynch

Coventry. *Born* Coventry, 9 November, 1961
Former Midlands Area Featherweight Champion (9.0½-9.3) ht. 5'6"
Manager P. Byrne
Pro. Debut 26 January, 1987

22.02.91 John Green L PTS 6 Manchester
20.03.91 Peter Judson L RTD 5 Solihull
24.04.91 Peter Harris L PTS 8 Aberavon
28.05.91 Steve Robinson L RSC 6 Cardiff
01.10.91 Paul Forrest W PTS 6 Sheffield
26.10.91 Paul Harvey L RSC 1 Brentwood
10.12.91 Paul Forrest L PTS 6 Sheffield
22.01.92 Kelton McKenzie L RSC 5 Solihull
24.02.92 Des Gargano W PTS 6 Coventry
02.04.92 Bradley Stone L RSC 3 Basildon

Career: 27 contests, won 9, lost 18.

Dean Lynch

Swansea. *Born* Swansea, 21 November, 1964
S. Featherweight (9.2½) ht. 5'6"
Manager –
Pro. Debut 18 September, 1986

14.04.92 Lee Fox W PTS 6 Mansfield

Career: 15 contests, won 5, lost 10.

Paul Lynch

Swansea. *Born* Swansea, 27 December, 1966
L. Middleweight (10.12-11.0) ht. 5'11"
Manager C. Breen
Pro. Debut 23 October, 1989

12.02.91 Roy Rowland W RTD 4 Basildon
01.10.91 Peter Manfredo L PTS 8 Providence, USA
12.02.92 Robert McCracken L RSC 4 Wembley
14.04.92 Paul Jones L RSC 3 Mansfield

Career: 10 contests, won 7, lost 3.

Chris Lyons

Birmingham. *Born* Birmingham, 2 September, 1972
Featherweight (8.9-9.1) ht. 5'9"
Manager N. Nobbs
Pro. Debut 2 December, 1991

02.12.91 Ronnie Stephenson L PTS 6 Birmingham
09.12.91 Ronnie Stephenson L PTS 6 Cleethorpes
22.01.92 Dennis Oakes L RSC 3 Stoke
17.05.92 Dave Martin DREW 6 Harringay

Career: 4 contests, drew 1, lost 3.

Kris McAdam

Glasgow. *Born* Glasgow, 1 January, 1964
Scottish Lightweight Champion (9.8½-10.0½) ht. 5'9½"
Manager T. Gilmour
Pro. Debut 15 October, 1984

21.01.91 John Smith W PTS 6 Glasgow
22.04.91 Brian Roche L RSC 2 Glasgow
(Elim. British Lightweight Title)
18.11.91 Colin Sinnott W PTS 6 Glasgow
27.01.92 Pete Roberts W CO 2 Glasgow
18.03.92 Nigel Bradley L CO 2 Glasgow

Career: 17 contests, won 9, drew 1, lost 7.

Dave Boy McAuley

Larne. *Born* Larne, 15 June, 1961
Former IBF Flyweight Champion. Former Undefeated British Flyweight Champion (8.0) ht. 5'7½"
Manager B. Eastwood
Pro. Debut 5 October, 1983

11.05.91 Pedro Feliciano W PTS 12 Belfast
(IBF Flyweight Title Defence)
07.09.91 Jacob Matlala W CO 10 Belfast
(IBF Flyweight Title Defence)
11.06.92 Rodolfo Blanco L PTS 12 Bilbao, Spain
(IBF Flyweight Title Defence)

Career: 23 contests, won 18, drew 2, lost 3.

Dave Boy McAuley

Mark McBiane

Skegness. *Born* Leamington Spa, 6 April, 1970
L. Heavyweight (12.2-12.10) ht. 5'11"
Manager J. Gaynor
Pro. Debut 28 November, 1991

28.11.91 Jason McNeill L PTS 6 Evesham
04.02.92 Greg Scott-Briggs L PTS 6 Alfreton
23.04.92 Nicky Wadman L RSC 1 Eltham
08.06.92 Simon McDougall L PTS 6 Bradford

Career: 4 contests, lost 4.

Jamie McBride

Glasgow. *Born* Glasgow, 21 October, 1963
Scottish Featherweight Champion (9.0½-9.4) ht. 5'6"
Manager T. Gilmour
Pro. Debut 16 September, 1985

18.02.91 Pete Buckley W PTS 8 Glasgow
18.11.91 Peter Judson DREW 6 Glasgow
30.03.92 Phil Lashley W RSC 1 Glasgow

Career: 22 contests, won 11, drew 2, lost 9.

Paul McCarthy

Southampton. *Born* London, 24 March, 1961
Former Southern Area S. Middleweight Champion (12.0-13.0) ht. 6'0"
Manager J. Bishop
Pro. Debut 29 January, 1987

08.02.91 Fabrice Tiozzo L CO 2 Villeurbanne, France
20.03.91 Andy Wright L CO 5 Wandsworth
(Southern Area S. Middleweight Title Defence)
16.05.91 Lester Jacobs L PTS 6 Battersea
01.06.91 Ali Forbes L CO 2 Bethnal Green
19.11.91 Dave Lawrence DREW 6 Norwich
09.12.91 Antonio Fernandez L PTS 8 Brierley Hill
16.12.91 Peter Vosper W PTS 6 Southampton
08.01.92 Graham Jenner L PTS 6 Burton
22.01.92 Julian Johnson DREW 6 Cardiff
29.02.92 Graham Jenner L PTS 8 St Leonards
11.03.92 Jason McNeill L PTS 6 Cardiff
30.04.92 Hussain Shah L RTD 4 Kensington

Career: 37 contests, won 17, drew 3, lost 17.

Steve McCarthy

Southampton. *Born* East Ham, 30 July, 1962
Former Undefeated British L. Heavyweight Champion. Former Undefeated Southern Area L. Heavyweight Champion (12.7-12.7¼) ht. 5'11½"
Manager J. Bishop
Pro. Debut 5 February, 1987

16.12.91 John Foreman W PTS 8 Southampton
04.04.92 Henry Maske L DIS 9 Dusseldorf, Germany

Career: 14 contests, won 11, drew 1, lost 2.

Tony McCarthy

Crayford. *Born* Barnhurst, 10 April, 1968
Middleweight (11.4½-11.6) ht. 5'10"
Manager G. Steene
Pro. Debut 16 September, 1991

16.09.91 Erich Ecker W RSC 2 Hamburg, Germany
22.10.91 Karl Barwise L PTS 6 Wandsworth
29.11.91 Jan Franek L CO 3 Frohsdorf, Austria
25.02.92 Mike Russell W PTS 6 Crystal Palace
04.04.92 Tritmar Jandrek W PTS 6 Minden, Germany

Career: 5 contests, won 3, lost 2.

Joe McCluskey

Croy. *Born* Glasgow, 13 March, 1970
L. Heavyweight (12.7½) ht. 6'0"
Manager T. Gilmour
Pro. Debut 27 April, 1992

27.04.92 John Oxenham W PTS 4 Glasgow

Career: 1 contest, won 1.

Robert McCracken

Birmingham. *Born* Birmingham, 31 May, 1968
L. Middleweight (10.7-11.2¾) ht. 6'0"
Manager M. Duff
Pro. Debut 24 January, 1991

24.01.91 Mick Mulcahy W RSC 1 Brierley Hill
13.02.91 Gary Barron W RTD 2 Wembley
06.03.91 Tony Britland W RSC 2 Wembley
12.04.91 Dave Andrews W RSC 4 Willenhall
08.05.91 Tony Gibbs W CO 1 Kensington
30.05.91 Paul Murray W RSC 2 Birmingham
04.07.91 Marty Duke W RSC 1 Alfreton
25.07.91 John Smith W RTD 1 Dudley
31.10.91 Newton Barnett W DIS 2 Oakengates
28.11.91 Michael Oliver W RSC 3 Liverpool
12.02.91 Paul Lynch W RSC 4 Wembley

Career: 11 contests, won 11.

Spencer McCracken

Birmingham. *Born* Birmingham, 8 August, 1969
Welterweight (10.6-11.0) ht. 5'9"
Manager P. Cowdell
Pro. Debut 15 October, 1991

15.10.91 Stuart Dunn DREW 6 Dudley
09.12.91 Seth Jones W RSC 2 Brierley Hill

Career: 2 contests, won 1, drew 1.

Mark McCreath

Lincoln. *Born* Bradford, 30 May, 1964
L. Welterweight. Former Undefeated Benelux Welterweight Champion (10.3½) ht. 5'8½"
Manager M. Duff
Pro. Debut 10 May, 1989

17.04.91 Pat Barrett L RSC 6 Kensington *(European L. Welterweight Title Defence)*
21.06.91 Freddy Demeulenaere W RSC 5 Waregem, Belgium *(Vacant Benelux Welterweight Title)*
30.04.92 Gary Barron W RSC 5 Mayfair

Career: 13 contests, won 11, lost 2.

Gary McCrory

Annfield Plain. *Born* Blackhill, 20 October, 1960
Heavyweight (14.0½-15.2) ht. 6'2"
Manager –
Pro. Debut 29 September, 1988

18.02.91 Pedro van Raamsdonk L PTS 8 Valkenswaard, Holland
05.04.91 Markus Bott L PTS 8 Hamburg, Germany
06.03.92 Axel Schulz L RSC 2 Berlin, Germany
22.04.92 J. A. Bugner L PTS 4 Wembley

Career: 13 contests, won 5, lost 8.

Glenn McCrory

Annfield Plain. *Born* Stanley, 23 September, 1964
Heavyweight. Former IBF Cruiserweight Champion. Former Undefeated British & Commonwealth Cruiserweight Champion (15.11-17.7½) ht. 6'4"
Manager –
Pro. Debut 6 February, 1984

16.02.91 Terry Armstrong W CO 2 Thornaby
30.09.91 Lennox Lewis L CO 2 Kensington *(British & European Heavyweight Title Challenge)*

Career: 35 contests, won 28, lost 7.

Shaun McCrory

Stanley. *Born* Shotley Bridge, 13 June, 1969
S. Middleweight (11.10-12.4) ht. 6'2"
Manager –
Pro. Debut 3 June, 1989

21.01.91 Ian Henry L PTS 6 Glasgow
06.02.91 Tony Booth L PTS 6 Liverpool
13.05.91 John Oxenham W PTS 6 Marton
03.08.91 Ron Collins L PTS 8 Selvino, Italy
13.04.92 Paul Wright L PTS 6 Manchester
28.04.92 Dave Johnson DREW 6 Houghton le Spring

Career: 16 contests, won 7, drew 1, lost 8.

Errol McDonald

Nottingham. *Born* Nottingham, 11 March, 1964
Welterweight (10.7¼-10.8½) ht. 5'10"
Manager B. Hearn
Pro. Debut 21 October, 1985

23.02.91 Juan Rondon W RSC 7 Brighton
08.06.91 Patrizio Oliva L DIS 12 La Spezia, Italy *(European Welterweight Title Challenge)*
10.12.91 Jose Luis Saldivia W PTS 8 Sheffield
10.03.92 Robert Wright L CO 3 Bury

Career: 28 contests, won 25, drew 1, lost 2.

Simon McDougall

Blackpool. *Born* Manchester, 11 July, 1968
L. Heavyweight (11.12¼-12.11) ht. 5'10½"
Manager –
Pro. Debut 14 November, 1988

28.01.91 Ian Henry W PTS 8 Bradford
28.02.91 Glenn Campbell L PTS 10 Bury *(Central Area S. Middleweight Title Challenge)*
23.04.91 Paul Burton L PTS 8 Evesham
10.05.91 Ian Henry L PTS 6 Gateshead
30.09.91 Doug Calderwood W RSC 4 Liverpool
10.10.91 Terry French L PTS 6 Gateshead
19.10.91 Andrea Magi L RSC 5 Terni, Italy
03.03.92 Paul Hitch L PTS 6 Houghton le Spring
11.03.92 Ian Henry L PTS 8 Solihull
30.03.92 Nigel Rafferty L PTS 8 Coventry
08.06.91 Mark McBiane W PTS 6 Bradford

Career: 24 contests, won 9, lost 15.

Alan McDowall

Renfrew. *Born* Renfrew, 29 September, 1967
Lightweight (9.6½-9.12) ht. 5'10"
Manager A. Morrison
Pro. Debut 24 September, 1991

24.09.91 Johnny Patterson W PTS 4 Glasgow
28.11.91 Johnny Patterson W PTS 6 Glasgow
31.01.92 Charles Shepherd W RSC 3 Glasgow
20.02.92 Mark O'Callaghan W PTS 6 Glasgow
12.03.92 James Jiora W CO 2 Glasgow
29.05.92 Karl Taylor W PTS 6 Glasgow

Career: 6 contests, won 6.

James McGee

Bedworth. *Born* Nuneaton, 9 May, 1968
L. Middleweight (10.12-11.4) ht. 6'1"
Manager J. Griffin
Pro. Debut 19 March, 1991

19.03.91 Adrian Din W PTS 6 Leicester
15.04.91 Marty Duke L PTS 6 Leicester
20.05.91 Cliff Churchward W PTS 6 Leicester
11.06.91 Julian Eavis W PTS 6 Leicester
01.10.91 Trevor Meikle L PTS 6 Bedworth
21.10.91 Crain Fisher L RSC 4 Bury
11.12.91 Julian Eavis DREW 6 Leicester
11.02.92 Chris Mulcahy W PTS 6 Wolverhampton
25.03.92 Darren Morris DREW 6 Hinckley
11.05.92 Julian Eavis W RSC 3 Coventry

Career: 10 contests, won 5, drew 2, lost 3.

(William) Wilf McGee

Bedworth. *Born* Nuneaton, 2 April, 1967
Middleweight (11.8-11.10) ht. 6'0"
Manager J. Griffin
Pro. Debut 17 October, 1991

17.10.91 Hugh Fury DREW 6 Mossley
31.10.91 Glen Payton L RSC 6 Oakengates

Career: 2 contests, drew 1, lost 1.

Ian McGirr

Clydebank. *Born* Clydebank, 14 April, 1968
S. Featherweight (9.2-9.6) ht. 5'6¼"
Manager –
Pro. Debut 23 November, 1989

18.02.91 Colin Innes W PTS 6 Glasgow
22.03.91 Edward Cook L PTS 6 Irvine

Steve McGovern (right) on the attack against Mark Dinnadge, who he outpointed in January 1991 Les Clark

18.03.91 Noel Carroll L PTS 6 Manchester
24.09.91 Pete Judson W PTS 6 Glasgow
08.10.91 Tony Feliciello L PTS 8 Wolverhampton
21.10.91 Chris Clarkson DREW 6 Glasgow
12.12.91 Darren Elsdon L CO 4 Hartlepool

Career: 13 contests, won 5, drew 1, lost 7.

Brian McGloin

Doncaster. *Born* Glasgow, 20 March, 1964
S. Middleweight (11.7-12.0) ht. 5'7½"
Manager J. Rushton
Pro. Debut 11 December, 1991

11.12.91 Marc Rowley W PTS 6 Leicester
18.05.92 Chad Strong DREW 6 Bardon

Career: 2 contests, won 1, drew 1.

John McGlynn

Swansea. *Born* Swansea, 3 October, 1962
Welterweight (10.9½-10.10) ht. 5'8"
Manager –
Pro. Debut 7 June, 1982

29.08.91 Mickey Lerwill W PTS 6 Oakengates
30.09.91 Kevin Lueshing L RSC 2 Kensington

Career: 19 contests, won 12, lost 7.

Steve McGovern

Bembridge. *Born* Newport IOW, 17 April, 1969
Welterweight (10.6-10.9) ht. 5'9"
Manager J. Bishop
Pro. Debut 21 September, 1989

21.01.91 Mark Dinnadge W PTS 6 Crystal Palace
23.02.91 Tim Harmey W PTS 6 Brighton
23.04.91 Frank Harrington W PTS 6 Evesham
08.05.91 A. M. Milton W PTS 6 Millwall
16.12.91 Chris Mylan W PTS 8 Southampton
03.03.92 Tony Swift L RSC 4 Cradley Heath

Career: 8 contests, won 7, lost 1.

Graham McGrath

Warley. *Born* West Bromwich, 31 July, 1962
Bantamweight (8.7-8.10) ht. 5'4"
Manager P. Cowdell
Pro. Debut 21 May, 1992

21.05.92 Paul Kelly W RSC 2 Cradley Heath
01.06.92 Greg Upton L PTS 6 Solihull

Career: 2 contests, won 1, lost 1.

Dominic McGuigan

Newcastle. *Born* Hexham, 13 June, 1963
S. Featherweight (9.4-9.8) ht. 5'6"
Manager D. Mancini
Pro. Debut 10 October, 1989

16.09.91 Barrie Kelley DREW 6 Mayfair
28.11.91 John Milne L RTD 3 Glasgow
30.04.92 Kevin Lowe W RSC 6 Mayfair
15.05.92 Rene Weller L PTS 8 Augsburg, Germany

Career: 9 contests, won 3, drew 3, lost 3.

Dave McHale

Glasgow. *Born* Glasgow, 29 April, 1967
S. Featherweight (9.2½-9.8¼) ht. 5'7"
Manager T. Gilmour
Pro. Debut 8 October, 1990

25.11.91 Eddie Garbutt W RSC 1 Liverpool
30.03.92 Kevin Lowe W RSC 5 Glasgow
01.06.92 Chris Jickells W RSC 4 Glasgow

Career: 4 contests, won 4.

Darren McInulty

Nuneaton. *Born* Coventry, 10 November, 1970

Welterweight(10.3-11.0) ht. 5'11"
Manager J. Griffin
Pro. Debut 20 May, 1991

20.05.91 Derek Binsteed DREW 6 Leicester
01.10.91 Dean Carr W PTS 6 Bedworth
11.11.91 Rick North W PTS 6 Stratford on Avon
20.01.92 Chris Mulcahy W PTS 6 Coventry
04.02.92 Richard O'Brien L PTS 4 Alfreton
11.03.92 Eddie King W RSC 1 Stoke
25.03.92 Robert Riley L PTS 6 Hinckley
28.04.92 Dean Bramhald W PTS 6 Wolverhampton
11.05.92 Dean Bramhald W PTS 6 Coventry

Career: 9 contests, won 6, drew 1, lost 2.

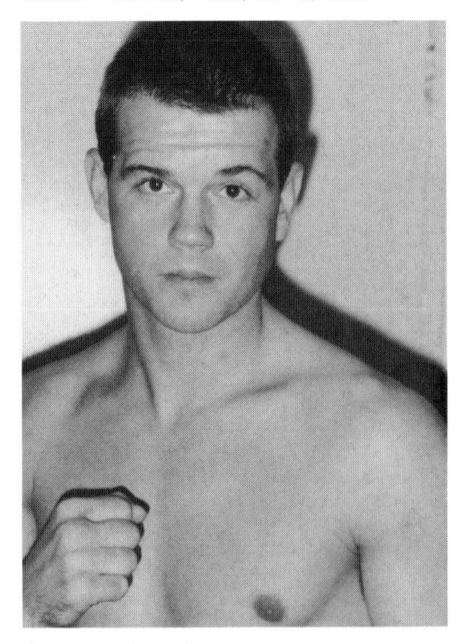

Darren McInulty Les Clark

Alan McKay

Willesden. *Born* Watford, 1 June, 1967
Southern Area Featherweight Champion (9.0-9.2) ht. 5'6"
Manager –
Pro. Debut 19 September, 1988

09.04.91 Paul Harvey L RSC 4 Mayfair
13.11.91 Gary de Roux W RSC 8 Bethnal Green *(Vacant Southern Area Featherweight Title)*
18.01.92 Pete Buckley DREW 8 Kensington

Career: 16 contests, won 10, drew 3, lost 3.

Darren McKenna

Alfreton. *Born* Sheffield, 21 December, 1962
L. Heavyweight (12.0-13.4) ht. 5'11"
Manager B. Ingle
Pro. Debut 19 November, 1987

09.05.91 Denzil Browne L PTS 6 Leeds
24.06.91 Johnny Held L PTS 8 Rotterdam, Holland
23.01.92 Denzil Browne L PTS 6 York
03.06.92 Morris Thomas W RSC 2 Newcastle under Lyme

Career: 26 contests, won 6, drew 1, lost 19.

Duke McKenzie

Croydon. *Born* Croydon, 5 May, 1963
Former WBO Bantamweight Champion. Former IBF Flyweight Champion. Former Undefeated British & European Flyweight Champion (8.5½-8.9) ht. 5'7"
Manager M. Duff
Pro. Debut 23 November, 1982

10.01.91 Pete Buckley W RSC 5 Wandsworth
07.02.91 Julio Blanco W RSC 7 Watford
04.04.91 Chris Clarkson W RSC 5 Watford
30.06.91 Gaby Canizales W PTS 12 Southwark *(WBO Bantamweight Title Challenge)*
12.09.91 Cesar Soto W PTS 12 Wandsworth *(WBO Bantamweight Title Defence)*
25.03.92 Wilfredo Vargas W RSC 8 Kensington *(WBO Bantamweight Title Defence)*
13.05.92 Rafael del Valle L CO 1 Kensington *(WBO Bantamweight Title Defence)*

Career: 34 contests, won 31, lost 3.

John McKenzie

Corby. *Born* Paisley, 8 February, 1972
Middleweight (11.7½-11.10) ht. 5'11"
Manager K. Whitney
Pro. Debut 5 December, 1991

05.12.91 Tony Wellington W PTS 6 Peterborough
06.02.92 Paul Murray W PTS 6 Peterborough
30.03.92 Willie Quinn L RSC 4 Glasgow
28.04.92 Sean Byrne L RSC 6 Corby

Career: 4 contests, won 2, lost 2.

Kelton McKenzie

Nottingham. *Born* Leicester, 18 September, 1968
Midlands Area Featherweight Champion (8.11-9.4) ht. 5'7"
Manager K. Squires
Pro. Debut 18 October, 1990

21.01.91 J. T. Williams DREW 6 Crystal Palace
14.03.91 Craig Dermody L RSC 3 Middleton
01.05.91 Tim Yeates W PTS 6 Bethnal Green
17.06.91 Derek Amory W RSC 6 Edgbaston
05.11.91 Richard Woolgar W RSC 5 Leicester
22.01.92 Colin Lynch W RSC 5 Solihull
26.03.92 Brian Robb W RSC 4 Telford
29.04.92 Elvis Parsley W RSC 5 Solihull *(Vacant Midlands Area Featherweight Title)*

Career: 11 contests, won 7, drew 2, lost 2.

Kevin McKenzie

Hartlepool. *Born* Hartlepool, 18 October, 1968
L. Welterweight (10.1) ht. 5'7½"
Manager G. Robinson
Pro. Debut 8 June, 1992

08.06.92 Jason Brattley W RTD 3 Bradford

Career: 1 contest, won 1.

Kevin McKenzie Chris Bevan

(Roger) R. F. McKenzie

Croydon. *Born* Croydon, 3 October, 1965
Cruiserweight (13.1-14.0½) ht. 6'2"
Manager –
Pro. Debut 31 January, 1989

12.02.91 Noel Magee L PTS 6 Belfast
21.03.91 Denzil Browne L PTS 6 Dewsbury
28.05.91 Steve Yorath L PTS 6 Cardiff
07.09.91 Ray Kane L PTS 4 Belfast
09.10.91 Denzil Browne W PTS 6 Manchester
28.10.91 Pedro van Raamsdonk W CO 7 Arnhem, Holland
12.12.91 Norbert Ekassi L RSC 3 Massy,
14.03.92 Neils H. Madsen L PTS 6 Copenhagen, Denmark
25.04.92 Noel Magee L PTS 8 Belfast

Career: 12 contests, won 4, lost 8.

Tony McKenzie

Leicester. *Born* Leicester, 4 March, 1963
Former British L. Welterweight champion (9.13½-10.4½) ht. 5'9"
Manager B. Hearn
Pro. Debut 22 November, 1983

19.03.91 King Zaka W RSC 1 Leicester
11.06.91 Alberto Machong W CO 3 Leicester *(Elim. Commonwealth L. Welterweight Title)*
05.11.91 Marty Duke W RSC 7 Leicester
19.11.91 Gordon Blair W RSC 5 Norwich
27.02.92 Andy Holligan L RSC 3 Liverpool *(British & Commonwealth L. Welterweight Title Challenge)*

Career: 32 contests, won 25, drew 1, lost 6.

Kevin McKillan

Manchester. *Born* Belfast, 1 March, 1969
Lightweight (9.10-10.1) ht. 5'8"
Manager N. Basso
Pro. Debut 28 October, 1991

28.10.91 Michael Byrne W PTS 6 Leicester

13.11.91 Barry Glanister W PTS 6 Liverpool
22.01.92 Sugar Boy Wright W PTS 6 Solihull
10.02.92 Jamie Davidson L PTS 6 Liverpool
11.03.92 Jamie Davidson DREW 6 Stoke
01.06.92 Steve Howden W RSC 2 Manchester
12.06.92 Floyd Churchill W PTS 6 Liverpool

Career: 7 contests, won 5, drew 1, lost 1.

Conn McMullen

Acton. *Born* Larne, 21 June, 1967
Featherweight (9.0) ht. 5'6"
Manager H. Holland
Pro. Debut 6 June, 1990

12.11.91 Mark Loftus W PTS 6 Milton Keynes

Career: 3 contests, won 3.

Conn McMullen Les Clark

Jason McNeill

Swansea. *Born* Bristol, 12 August, 1971
S. Middleweight (12.1¼-12.5) ht. 6'1"
Manager D. Davies
Pro. Debut 3 October, 1991

03.10.91 Mark Pain L PTS 6 Burton
15.10.91 Tony Colclough L PTS 6 Dudley
28.11.91 Mark McBiane W PTS 6 Evesham
21.01.92 Gypsy Johnny Price L PTS 4 Stockport
11.03.92 Paul McCarthy W PTS 6 Cardiff
23.04.92 Abel Asinamali L CO 3 Eltham

Career: 6 contests, won 2, lost 4.

Steve McNess

Bethnal Green. *Born* Bow, 17 November, 1969
Welterweight (10.10½-10.12) ht. 5'10½"
Manager M. Duff
Pro. Debut 22 April, 1992

22.04.92 Rick North W PTS 6 Wembley
13.05.92 Mark Verikios L RSC 5 Kensington

Career: 2 contests, won 1, lost 1.

Ricky Mabbett

Leicester. *Born* Leicester, 27 November, 1971
Welterweight (10.2½-10.9) ht. 5'9"
Manager K. Squires
Pro. Debut 19 March, 1992

19.03.92 Phil Epton W RSC 3 York
16.06.92 Ojay Abrahams L PTS 6 Dagenham

Career: 2 contests, won 1, lost 1.

Kevin Mabbutt

Northampton. *Born* Northampton, 23 February, 1969
Welterweight (10.13) ht. 5'8¾"
Manager J. Cox
Pro. Debut 6 April, 1992

06.04.92 Peter Reid L PTS 6 Northampton
28.04.92 Sean Cave W PTS 6 Corby

Career: 2 contests, won 1, lost 1.

Ossie Maddix

Manchester. *Born* London, 10 September, 1964
Central Area Welterweight Champion (10.8-10.13) ht. 5'9"
Manager P. Martin
Pro. Debut 31 March, 1987

22.02.91 Judas Clottey W PTS 8 Manchester
29.11.91 Kelvin Mortimer W PTS 6 Manchester
09.02.92 Michael Oliver W RTD 3 Bradford
29.05.92 Gordon Blair W PTS 6 Manchester

Career: 17 contests, won 15, lost 2.

Noel Magee

Belfast. *Born* Belfast, 16 Decmeber, 1965
L. Heavyweight (12.6-12.9¼) ht. 6'1"
Manager B. Eastwood
Pro. Debut 22 May,1985

12.02.91 R. F. McKenzie W PTS 6 Belfast
11.05.91 Simon Collins W PTS 8 Belfast
13.11.91 Frankie Minton W RSC 3 Belfast
11.12.91 Tony Wilson W RSC 3 Dublin
25.04.92 R. F. McKenzie W PTS 8 Belfast

Career: 28 contests, won 23, drew 2, lost 3.

Terry Magee

Ammanford. *Born* Belfast, 1 November, 1964
S. Middleweight. Former Undefeated All-Ireland L. Middleweight Champion (11.2¼-11.11¼) ht. 5'10½"
Manager –
Pro. Debut 29 November, 1982

01.06.91 Andy Till L RSC 4 Bethnal Green
11.12.91 Ray Close L RSC 7 Dublin *(All-Ireland S. Middleweight Title Challenge)*

Career: 28 contests, won 20, drew 1, lost 7.

Pat Maher

Hackney. *Born* Sunderland, 24 November, 1964
Bantamweight (8.9-8.13) ht. 5'5½"
Manager –
Pro. Debut 7 May, 1987

30.09.91 John Armour L CO 1 Kensington
07.04.92 Kevin Middleton L CO 4 Southend

Career: 4 contests, won 1, lost 3.

Dave Maj (Majekodunmi)

Liverpool. *Born* Liverpool, 21 November, 1964
Welterweight (10.5-10.9¾) ht. 5'10¼"
Manager J. Trickett
Pro. Debut 24 June, 1991

24.06.91 Benji Joseph W RSC 4 Liverpool
09.09.91 Mark Verikios L PTS 6 Liverpool
14.10.91 David Maw L PTS 6 Manchester
16.12.91 Wayne Shepherd DREW 6 Manchester
03.02.92 Wayne Shepherd W PTS 6 Manchester
09.03.92 Willie Yeardsley W RSC 1 Manchester
13.04.92 Peter Reid W CO 1 Manchester
14.05.92 Andreas Panayi L CO 6 Liverpool

Career: 8 contests, won 4, drew 1, lost 3.

Al Malcolm

Birmingham. *Born* Birmingham, 10 April,1958
Former Midlands Area Heavyweight Champion (15.5½-15.11) ht. 6'3"
Manager –
Pro. Debut 30 September, 1983

19.03.91 Steve Garber L RSC 5 Birmingham
16.05.91 Haken Brock L PTS 6 Battersea
30.05.91 Steve Gee W PTS 6 Birmingham
14.08.91 Salvatore Inserra W RSC 1 Alcamo, Italy

Career: 33 contests, won 13, drew 1, lost 19.

Colin Manners

Leeds. *Born* Leeds 4 July, 1962
Middleweight (11.2¾-11.7½) ht. 5'10"
Manager J. Rushton
Pro. Debut 26 April, 1990

31.01.91 Lee Crocker W PTS 6 Bredbury
18.02.91 John Ogiste L PTS 6 Mayfair
01.05.91 Darren Parker W CO 2 Solihull
05.06.91 Richard Carter W CO 1 Wolverhampton
03.09.91 Wayne Ellis W RSC 1 Cardiff
29.04.92 Darron Griffiths DREW 8 Solihull

Career: 11 contests, won 6, drew 1, lost 4.

Nick Manners

Leeds. *Born* Leeds, 23 November, 1966
S. Middleweight (11.13-12.4) ht. 6'2"
Manager M. Duff
Pro. Debut 18 October, 1990

31.01.91 Terry Duffus W RSC 1 Bredbury
21.03.91 Marvin O'Brien W CO 2 Dewsbury
09.05.91 Peter Gorny W RSC 1 Leeds
27.06.91 Peter Vosper W RSC 1 Leeds
01.08.91 Tony Booth DREW 8 Dewsbury
30.10.91 Kevin Morton L PTS 8 Leeds

Career: 8 contests, won 6, drew 1, lost 1.

Andy Manning

Warrington. *Born* Sheffield, 1 June, 1970
L. Heavyweight (11.8-12.9¾) ht. 5'7½"
Manager R. Jones
Pro. Debut 7 October, 1991

07.10.91 Mark Hale W PTS 6 Liverpool
04.11.91 Steve Thomas L PTS 6 Merthyr
02.12.91 Marc Rowley W PTS 6 Liverpool
03.03.92 Justin Clements DREW 6 Cradley Heath
18.03.92 Willie Quinn L PTS 6 Glasgow
29.04.92 Adrian Wright W PTS 6 Stoke
11.05.92 Julian Johnson W PTS 6 Llanelli
18.05.92 John Oxenham L PTS 6 Marton

Career: 8 contests, won 4, drew 1, lost 3.

(Raphael) Chubby Martin

Islington. *Born* Cardiff, 8 June, 1964
Lightweight (9.3¾-9.9½) ht. 5'10"
Manager –
Pro. Debut 4 December, 1984

06.03.91 Billy Schwer L RSC 3 Wembley
23.10.91 G. G. Goddard W PTS 8 Stoke
14.11.91 Alex Sterling W RSC 5 Bayswater
02.04.92 Jimmy Clark L RSC 6 Basildon

Career: 27 contests, won 10, drew 4, lost 13.

Dave Martin

Cardiff. *Born* Cardiff, 11 May, 1967
Bantamweight (8.7¾-8.8½) ht. 5'9"
Manager H. Burgess
Pro. Debut 23 October, 1991

23.10.91 Mark Hargreaves L PTS 6 Stoke
14.11.91 Dave Campbell L PTS 6 Bayswater
17.05.92 Chris Lyons DREW 6 Harringay

Career: 3 contests, drew 1, lost 2.

Stinger Mason *Chris Bevan*

(Paul) Stinger Mason

Sheffield. *Born* Sheffield, 27 February, 1964
Middleweight (11.8-12.1) ht. 5'8"
Manager –
Pro. Debut 19 April, 1989

13.03.91 Mike Phillips DREW 6 Stoke
13.05.91 Doug Calderwood L CO 3 Manchester
23.10.91 Roger Wilson DREW 6 Stoke
11.11.91 Russell Washer W PTS 4 Stratford on Avon
23.05.92 Paul Busby L RSC 2 Birmingham

Career: 13 contests, won 5, drew 3, lost 5.

Tony Massey

Leeds. *Born* Leeds, 24 January, 1968
L. Middleweight (11.3) ht. 5'10"
Manager D. Mancini
Pro. Debut 19 March, 1992

19.03.92 Phil Foxon W RSC 1 York

Career: 1 contest, won 1.

Delroy Matthews

Lewisham. *Born* Dulwich, 28 May, 1965
L. Middleweight (11.1-11.2) ht. 5'11¼"
Manager –
Pro. Debut 25 September, 1989

30.09.91 Winston Tomlinson W RSC 4 Kensington
14.12.91 David Radford W CO 1 Bexleyheath

Career: 5 contests, won 4, lost 1.

Jason Matthews

Bargoed. *Born* Caerphilly, 26 June, 1969
L. Welterweight (9.11¾-10.3½) ht. 5'9"
Manager D. Gardiner
Pro. Debut 18 July, 1991

18.07.91 Carl Hook W PTS 6 Cardiff
29.10.91 Robert Peel W RSC 6 Cardiff
21.11.91 Chris Saunders W RSC 4 Burton
11.02.92 Carl Hook W PTS 6 Cardiff
30.04.92 Ross Hale L RSC 3 Bayswater

Career: 5 contests, won 4, lost 1.

(Nicholas) Miguel Matthews

Ystalfera. *Born* Glanamman, 22 December, 1965
Featherweight (8.6-9.4) ht. 5'7"
Manager –
Pro. Debut 21 September, 1988

07.03.91 Bradley Stone L RSC 4 Basildon
04.04.91 Mark Tierney L PTS 6 Watford
16.04.91 Craig Dermody L PTS 6 Nottingham
25.04.91 Bradley Stone L PTS 6 Basildon
23.05.91 Jason Lepre L PTS 6 Southampton
31.05.91 Danny Connelly L PTS 8 Glasgow
13.06.91 Tony Silkstone L PTS 6 Hull
24.06.91 Jimmy Owens L PTS 6 Liverpool
09.09.91 Moussa Sangare L RSC 5 Forges les Eux, France
09.10.91 Mark Loftus DREW 6 Manchester
24.10.91 Kevin Middleton L PTS 6 Dunstable
31.10.91 Brian Robb DREW 6 Oakengates
11.11.91 Peter Judson L PTS 6 Stratford on Avon
21.11.91 Craig Dermody L PTS 6 Burton
28.11.91 Dave Hardie L PTS 6 Glasgow
11.12.91 Jimmy Clark L PTS 6 Basildon
08.01.92 Ceri Farrell W PTS 6 Burton
31.01.92 John Green DREW 6 Manchester
20.02.92 Edward Cook L PTS 6 Glasgow
27.02.92 Craig Dermody L PTS 6 Liverpool
25.03.92 John Armour L PTS 6 Dagenham
01.06.92 Danny Porter L PTS 6 Glasgow

Career: 50 contests, won 6, drew 8, lost 36.

David Maw

Sunderland. *Born* Sunderland, 14 January, 1967
Welterweight (10.9) ht. 5'9½"
Manager G. Robinson
Pro. Debut 22 May, 1987

14.10.91 Dave Maj W PTS 6 Manchester

Career: 10 contests, won 5, drew 1, lost 4.

Winston May

West Ham. *Born* London, 21 November, 1962
L. Middleweight (11.0) ht. 5'10½"
Manager –
Pro. Debut 29 November, 1988

05.12.91 Shaun Cummins L RSC 2 Peterborough
30.04.92 Lee Crocker L RSC 2 Bayswater

Career: 13 contests, won 6, drew 2, lost 5.

Trevor Meikle

Scunthorpe. *Born* Scunthorpe, 29 January, 1967
Welterweight (10.3½-10.13) ht. 5'9"
Manager –
Pro. Debut 16 May, 1989

11.02.91 Steve Hardman L PTS 6 Manchester
21.02.91 Colin Sinnott W PTS 6 Leeds
27.02.91 Andreas Panayi W PTS 6 Wolverhampton
03.04.91 Mick Mulcahy W PTS 6 Manchester
10.04.91 Wayne Timmins L PTS 6 Wolverhampton
22.04.91 Nick Cope W RSC 2 Glasgow
01.05.91 Tommy Milligan L PTS 6 Liverpool
09.05.91 Tod Riggs L PTS 6 Leeds
03.06.91 Tommy Milligan L PTS 6 Glasgow
10.06.91 Chris Mulcahy DREW 6 Manchester
14.08.91 Efren Calamati L RSC 4 Alcamo, Italy
23.09.91 Alan Peacock W PTS 6 Glasgow
01.10.91 James McGee W PTS 6 Bedworth
05.11.91 Lee Ferrie L PTS 6 Leicester
25.11.91 Mark Kelly W PTS 8 Cleethorpes
05.12.91 Mickey Lerwill L PTS 6 Oakengates
14.12.91 Kevin Lueshing L CO 3 Bexleyheath
28.01.92 Alan Peacock L PTS 8 Piccadilly
29.02.92 Andre Kimbu L RTD 5 Gravelines, France
13.04.92 Crain Fisher L PTS 6 Manchester
30.04.92 B. F. Williams L PTS 6 Watford

Career: 48 contests, won 15, drew 6, lost 27.

Johnny Melfah

Gloucester. *Born* Gloucester, 14 December, 1960
S. Middleweight (11.10½-12.2) ht. 5'9½"
Manager –
Pro. Debut 8 September, 1986

23.02.91 Sean Heron W PTS 8 Brighton
05.03.91 Wayne Ellis L RSC 2 Cardiff
16.05.91 Roland Ericsson W RSC 4 Battersea
07.09.91 Sammy Storey L PTS 8 Belfast
01.10.91 Fidel Castro L RSC 7 Sheffield
12.05.92 Lou Gent W RSC 3 Crystal Palace

Career: 22 contests, won 13, lost 9.

Nick Meloscia

Gloucester. *Born* Gloucester, 15 February, 1965
Welterweight (10.0½-10.9) ht. 5'8"
Manager –
Pro. Debut 10 April, 1986

12.02.91 Eamonn Loughran L CO 1 Cardiff
22.10.91 Dean Cooper L PTS 6 Wandsworth
29.10.91 Mark Pearce L RTD 2 Cardiff

Career: 18 contests, won 8, lost 10.

Malcolm Melvin

Birmingham. *Born* Birmingham, 5 February, 1967
Midlands Area L. Welterweight Champion (10.3-10.8) ht. 5'7"
Manager –
Pro. Debut 29 November, 1985

18.03.91 Carl Brasier W PTS 6 Piccadilly
17.06.91 Dean Bramhald W PTS 6 Edgbaston
21.05.92 Mark Kelly W PTS 8 Cradley Heath

Career: 19 contests, won 12, drew 1, lost 6.

(Robert) Gus Mendes

Birmingham. *Born* London, 9 August, 1963
Cruiserweight (13.0-13.7½) ht. 6'0½"
Manager –
Pro. Debut 1 October, 1986

12.02.91 Phil Soundy L RSC 3 Basildon
16.05.91 Lou Gent L CO 8 Battersea
11.09.91 Phil Soundy W RSC 3 Hammersmith
02.10.91 Gary Delaney L RSC 1 Barking
30.10.91 Denzil Browne L RSC 6 Leeds

Career: 17 contests, won 3, lost 14.

Barry Messam

Nottingham. *Born* Nottingham, 19 August, 1965
L. Middleweight (10.4-11.2) ht. 5'8½"
Manager. M Shinfield
Pro. Debut 9 March, 1987

10.01.91 Leigh Wicks L PTS 6 Wandsworth
17.01.91 Marvin O'Brien W PTS 6 Alfreton
04.02.91 Colin Pitters L PTS 6 Leicester
06.03.91 Darron Griffiths L PTS 6 Croydon
23.04.91 Martin Rosamond W PTS 6 Evesham
13.05.91 Dave Whittle W PTS 6 Marton
04.07.91 Darren Morris W PTS 6 Alfreton

Career: 35 contests, won 17, lost 18.

Kevin Middleton

Downham. *Born* Deptford, 5 July, 1968
S. Featherweight (9.0-9.3½) ht. 5'7"
Manager B. Aird
Pro. Debut 24 October, 1991

24.10.91 Miguel Matthews W PTS 6 Dunstable
07.04.92 Pat Maher W CO 4 Southend
29.04.92 Chris Jickells L RSC 6 Solihull

Career: 3 contests, won 2, lost 1.

Ian Midwood-Tate

Bradford. *Born* Huddersfield, 9 December, 1968
L. Middleweight (11.4) ht. 5'7½"
Manager –
Pro. Debut 12 January, 1987

11.11.91 Tyrone Eastmond L RSC 2 Bradford

Career: 9 contests, won 4, lost 5.

John Milne

Dundee. *Born* Dundee, 24 May, 1969
S. Featherweight (9.7) ht. 5'6"
Manager A. Morrison
Pro. Debut 18 December, 1989

28.11.91 Dominic McGuigan L RTD 3 Glasgow

Career: 5 contests, won 1, drew 3, lost 1.

(Winston) Kid Milo (Walters)

Birmingham. *Born* Birmingham, 15 February, 1964
Former Undefeated WBC International Middleweight Champion (11.2¼-11.8) ht. 5'9"
Manager M. Barrett
Pro. Debut 22 April, 1985

23.01.91 Lou Cafaro W CO 10 Solihull *(Vacant WBC International Middleweight Title)*
03.07.91 Nigel Benn L RSC 4 Brentwood

Career: 20 contests, won 14, drew 1, lost 5.

(Alkis) A. M. Milton (Alkiviadov)

Streatham. *Born* London, 5 May, 1965
Welterweight (10.7½-10.9½) ht. 5'3¼"
Manager –
Pro. Debut 24 October, 1984

08.05.91 Steve McGovern L PTS 6 Millwall
08.01.92 Darren Morris L PTS 6 Burton

Career: 14 contests, won 5, drew 1, lost 8.

Dave Mitchell

Croydon. *Born* Wandsworth, 25 December, 1963
Featherweight (9.3½) ht. 5'6"
Manager G. Mason
Pro. Debut 12 September, 1991

12.09.91 Akash D. Paul W RSC 5 Wandsworth

Career: 1 contests, won 1.

Joey Moffat

Liverpool. *Born* Liverpool, 14 February, 1964
Lightweight (9.9-9.12) ht. 5'8"
Manager C. Moorcroft
Pro. Debut 10 March, 1990

13.11.91 Paul Hughes W RTD 4 Liverpool
28.11.91 Kevin Lowe W PTS 6 Liverpool
10.02.92 Tony Doyle W RSC 3 Liverpool
27.02.92 Kevin Lowe W PTS 6 Liverpool
29.04.92 Pete Roberts W RSC 3 Liverpool
14.05.92 Scott Doyle W RSC 8 Liverpool

Career: 7 contests, won 6, lost 1.

Charlie Moore

Darlington. *Born* Darlington, 20 November, 1971
L. Middleweight (10.10-10.13½) ht. 5'7½"
Manager M. Duff
Pro. Debut 5 December, 1991

05.12.91 Jim Conley W CO 2 Peterborough
19.12.91 Robert Riley W PTS 6 Oldham
23.01.92 Stuart Dunn W RSC 3 York
19.03.92 John Corcoran W PTS 6 York
08.04.92 Steve Thomas W RSC 3 Leeds

Career: 5 contests, won 5.

Charlie Moore Chris Bevan

Nigel Moore

Thamesmead. *Born* Lewisham, 5 April, 1966
L. Middleweight (10.12) ht. 5'10¼"
Manager –
Pro. Debut 16 October, 1986

29.08.91 Richie Woodhall L RSC 1 Oakengates

Career: 7 contests, won 3, drew 1, lost 3.

Andrew Morgan

Merthyr. *Born* Neath, 20 February, 1963
L. Welterweight (9.12-10.4) ht. 5'6"
Manager –
Pro. Debut 22 June, 1987

12.02.91 Stuart Rimmer W PTS 8 Wolverhampton
26.03.91 John Smith W RSC 4 Wolverhampton
24.04.91 John Smith W PTS 6 Aberavon
02.05.91 Michael Driscoll L PTS 6 Kensington
17.03.92 Mark Elliot L PTS 6 Wolverhampton

Career: 17 contests, won 9, drew 1, lost 7.

Karl Morling

Northampton. *Born* Douglas, IOM, 26 December, 1970
Featherweight (8.10½-9.0) ht. 5'4"
Manager J. Cox
Pro. Debut 15 October, 1990

31.01.91 Craig Dermody L RSC 5 Bredbury
02.05.91 Sol Francis W RSC 3 Northampton
13.05.91 Paul Wynn W RSC 2 Northampton
06.04.92 Norman Dhalie W PTS 6 Northampton

Career: 6 contests, won 5, lost 1.

(Moro) Franki Moro (Tahiru)

Liverpool. *Born* Ghana, 4 February, 1957
S. Middleweight (11.10-12.1½) ht. 6'0½"
Manager T. Miller
Pro. Debut 20 February, 1984

24.01.91 Antonio Fernandez L PTS 6 Brierley Hill
29.10.91 Nicky Piper L RSC 4 Kensington

Career: 52 contests, won 13, drew 2, lost 37.

Chris Morris

Liverpool. *Born* Liverpool, 28 December, 1970
Featherweight (9.0½-9.2) ht. 5'6½"
Manager C. Moorcroft
Pro. Debut 13 November, 1991

13.11.91 Robert Braddock W RSC 5 Liverpool
28.11.91 Andrew Bloomer W PTS 6 Liverpool
10.02.92 Hamid Moulay W CO 1 Liverpool
29.04.92 Greg Upton L RSC 2 Liverpool

Career: 4 contests, won 3, lost 1.

Darren Morris

Birmingham. *Born* Birmingham, 26 May, 1966
Welterweight (10.6-11.2) ht. 5'6½"
Manager –
Pro. Debut 3 September, 1990

21.02.91 Richard O'Brien L PTS 6 Walsall
05.03.91 Mick Mulcahy W PTS 6 Leicester
12.04.91 Tony Britland L PTS 6 Willenhall
24.04.91 Andreas Panayi DREW 6 Stoke
30.05.91 Bullit Andrews W RSC 3 Birmingham
04.07.91 Barry Messam L PTS 6 Alfreton
23.10.91 Andreas Panayi L PTS 6 Stoke
31.10.91 John O'Johnson L PTS 6 Oakengates
02.12.91 Chris Mylan L PTS 8 Birmingham
08.01.92 A. M. Milton W PTS 6 Burton
17.03.92 Wayne Timmins DREW 6 Wolverhampton
25.03.92 James McGee DREW 6 Hinckley
30.04.92 Leigh Wicks DREW 6 Mayfair
01.06.92 Mark Kelly W PTS 8 Solihull

Career: 21 contests, won 6, drew 5, lost 10.

Jamie Morris

Nuneaton. *Born* Nuneaton, 15 February, 1970
L. Welterweight (9.12-10.3) ht. 5'9"
Manager J. Griffin
Pro. Debut 28 June, 1989

01.10.91 Michael Byrne DREW 4 Bedworth
16.10.91 Michael Byrne W PTS 6 Stoke
11.11.91 Mitchell Barney DREW 6 Stratford on Avon
21.11.91 Brian Coleman DREW 6 Stafford
04.12.91 Sugar Boy Wright L PTS 6 Stoke
20.01.92 Mark Antony L RSC 5 Coventry
24.02.92 Simon Hamblett DREW 6 Coventry
11.03.92 Razza Campbell L PTS 6 Stoke
24.03.92 Mark Allen W PTS 6 Wolverhampton

Career: 21 contests, won 6, drew 4, lost 11.

Mike Morrison

Pembroke. *Born* Prestatyn, 24 February, 1963
Welterweight (9.8½-10.5) ht. 5'7"
Manager D. Davies
Pro. Debut 14 September, 1989

10.01.91 Rick Bushell L PTS 6 Wandsworth
24.01.91 Andy Williams L PTS 8 Gorseinon
31.01.91 Richard Burton L PTS 6 Bredbury
06.03.91 Mark Tibbs L RSC 4 Wembley
02.05.91 Richard Swallow L PTS 6 Northampton
23.05.91 Martin Rosamond L PTS 6 Southampton
18.07.91 Michael Smyth L RSC 2 Cardiff

Career: 29 contests, won 1, lost 28.

Jerry Mortimer

Clapham. *Born* Mauritius, 22 June, 1962
Middleweight (11.5-11.9) ht. 5'9"
Manager B. Aird
Pro. Debut 21 October, 1991

21.10.91 Steve Thomas L PTS 6 Mayfair
12.02.92 Darren Murphy W PTS 6 Watford
02.03.92 Lee Farrell W PTS 6 Merthyr
28.04.92 Stefan Wright L RSC 4 Corby

Career: 4 contests, won 2, lost 2.

Kelvin Mortimer

Trebanog. *Born* Rhondda, 20 May, 1966
Welterweight (10.7-10.8) ht. 5'6"
Manager –
Pro. Debut 30 July, 1986

03.09.91 Rocky Feliciello W RSC 2 Cardiff
26.10.91 Darren Dyer L RSC 2 Brentwood
29.11.91 Ossie Maddix L PTS 6 Manchester
22.01.91 Lindon Scarlett L RSC 1 Solihull
19.05.92 Eamonn Loughran L RSC 1 Cardiff

Career: 32 contests, won 9, drew 1, lost 22.

Kevin Morton

Leicester. *Born* Leicester, 17 April, 1969
L. Heavyweight (12.0-12.5) ht. 6'0"
Manager W. Swift
Pro. Debut 6 February, 1991

06.02.91 Dennis Afflick W PTS 6 Liverpool
28.02.91 Stevie R. Davies W RSC 3 Bury
04.04.91 Johnny Uphill W CO 1 Watford
02.05.91 Alan Baptiste W RSC 2 Northampton
30.10.91 Nick Manners W PTS 8 Leeds
03.06.92 Mark Pain W PTS 6 Newcastle under Lyme

Career: 6 contests, won 6.

Hamid Moulay (Boutaoua)

Leeds. *Born* Algiers, 27 November, 1962
Featherweight (9.1-9.2) ht. 5'7"
Manager T. Miller
Pro. Debut 10 February, 1992

10.02.92 Chris Morris L CO 1 Liverpool
13.05.92 Mark Bowers L CO 1 Kensington

Career: 2 contests, lost 2.

Matt Mowatt

Sheffield. *Born* Sheffield, 8 March, 1967
Middleweight (11.4-11.8) ht. 5'10"
Manager R. Jones
Pro. Debut 22 October, 1990

23.01.91 Mike Phillips L RSC 6 Stoke
30.09.91 Joe Kilshaw DREW 6 Liverpool
21.10.91 Warren Stowe L RSC 3 Bury
20.11.91 Hugh Fury W PTS 6 Solihull
28.11.91 Rob Stevenson W PTS 6 Hull
09.12.91 Hugh Fury L RTD 5 Bradford
24.02.92 Willie Yeardsley L PTS 6 Bradford

Career: 11 contests, won 2, drew 1, lost 8.

(Dawuda) Dave Muhammed

Eastbourne. *Born* Ghana, 2 March, 1960
Cruiserweight (13.8) ht. 5'9¾"
Manager T. Miller
Pro. Debut 13 September, 1988

29.04.91 Steve Lewsam W PTS 8 Cleethorpes
12.10.91 Axel Schulz L PTS 8 Halle, Germany
27.03.92 Norbert Ekassi L RSC 3 Creil, France

Career: 10 contests, won 5, lost 5.

Kelvin Mortimer (right) on his way to stopping Rocky Feliciello in the second round at Cardiff last September Les Clark

Chris Mulcahy

Manchester. *Born* Rochdale, 18 June, 1963
L. Middleweight (10.9-11.1) ht. 6'0"
Manager N. Basso
Pro. Debut 11 October, 1988

05.03.91 Pat Durkin W PTS 6 Leicester
03.04.91 Willie Yeardsley L PTS 6 Manchester
10.06.91 Trevor Meikle DREW 6 Manchester
02.10.91 Robert Wright L RSC 1 Solihull
21.11.91 Richard O'Brien L RSC 2 Ilkeston
20.01.92 Darren McInulty L PTS 6 Coventry
11.02.92 James McGee L PTS 6 Wolverhampton
04.04.92 Rob Stevenson W PTS 8 Cleethorpes
01.06.92 Rob Stevenson W PTS 6 Manchester

Career: 25 contests, won 13, drew 1, lost 11.

Mick Mulcahy

Manchester. *Born* Rochdale, 9 May, 1966
L. Welterweight (9.12-10.10) ht. 5'8"
Manager N. Basso
Pro. Debut 6 June, 1988

24.01.91 Robert McCracken L RSC 1 Brierley Hill
05.03.91 Darren Morris L PTS 6 Leicester
03.04.91 Trevor Meikle L PTS 6 Manchester
15.04.91 Andreas Panayi L RSC 2 Leicester
10.06.91 Mike Calderwood L PTS 6 Manchester
18.11.91 Benji Joseph L PTS 6 Manchester
28.11.91 B. K. Bennett L PTS 6 Evesham
05.12.91 Mark Elliot L RSC 2 Cannock
17.03.92 Bernard Paul L PTS 6 Mayfair
04.04.92 Michael Byrne W RSC 4 Cleethorpes
01.06.92 Jason Brattley L PTS 6 Manchester

Career: 39 contests, won 9, drew 2, lost 28.

Darren Murphy

Burnt Oak. *Born* Edgware, 9 May, 1970
Middleweight (11.2-11.3¼) ht. 5'9"
Manager H. Holland
Pro. Debut 25 October, 1990

06.02.91 Ian Brough W RSC 1 Battersea
18.02.91 Clayon Stewart W PTS 6 Windsor
01.06.91 Johnny Pinnock W PTS 6 Bethnal Green
12.02.92 Jerry Mortimer L PTS 6 Watford

Career: 6 contests, won 4, lost 2.

Sean Murphy

St Albans. *Born* St Albans, 1 December, 1964
S. Featherweight. Former British Featherweight Champion (8.12¾-9.8¾) ht. 5'6"
Manager –
Pro. Debut 20 September, 1986

05.03.91 Gary de Roux L CO 5 Millwall *(British Featherweight Title Defence)*
22.05.91 Ines Alvarado W PTS 8 Millwall
29.10.91 Colin McMillan L PTS 12 Kensington *(British Featherweight Title Challenge)*
30.04.92 Ian Honeywood W RSC 1 Kensington

Career: 24 contests, won 21, lost 3.

Sean Murphy Derek Rowe

Craig Murray

Rochdale. *Born* Rochdale, 23 January, 1971
S. Featherweight (9.6½) ht. 5'7¼"
Manager N. Basso
Pro. Debut 1 June, 1992

01.06.92 Tony Smith W RSC 2 Manchester

Career: 1 contest, won 1.

Michael Murray

Manchester. *Born* Preston, 3 September, 1964
Central Area Heavyweight Champion (16.0-17.1) ht. 6'1"
Manager J. Trickett
Pro. Debut 23 February, 1988

30.04.91 Steve Garber W CO 1 Stockport
19.09.91 Carl Gaffney W RSC 8 Stockport *(Vacant Central Area Heavyweight Title)*
15.10.91 Markus Bott W RSC 7 Hamburg, Germany
07.12.91 Steve Gee W RSC 7 Manchester
14.04.92 Paddy Reilly L RSC 8 Mansfield

Career: 14 contests, won 10, lost 4.

Paul Murray

Birmingham. *Born* Birmingham, 8 January, 1961
Middleweight (11.2-12.6) ht. 5'9"
Manager P. Byrne
Pro. Debut 4 September, 1980

28.01.91 Lee Prudden L PTS 6 Birmingham
06.02.91 Paul Walters DREW 6 Liverpool
27.02.91 Paul Busby L PTS 6 Wolverhampton
13.03.91 Lee Prudden DREW 6 Stoke
24.04.91 John Kaighin L PTS 6 Aberavon
14.05.91 Ernie Loveridge L PTS 8 Dudley
30.05.91 Robert McCracken L RSC 2 Birmingham
25.07.91 Tony Booth L PTS 6 Dudley
07.10.91 Antonio Fernandez L RSC 7 Birmingham
12.11.91 Lee Archer L PTS 6 Wolverhampton
05.12.91 Richard Carter L PTS 8 Cannock
17.12.91 Paul Busby L CO 3 Cardiff
15.01.92 Mark Hale L PTS 6 Stoke
06.02.92 John McKenzie L PTS 6 Peterborough
19.02.92 James F. Woolley W CO 4 Muswell Hill
26.03.92 Neville Brown L CO 3 Telford

Career: 88 contests, won 15, drew 11, lost 61, no contest 1.

Chris Mylan

Swansea. *Born* Swansea, 6 November, 1972
Welterweight (9.13-10.6½) ht. 5'9"
Manager D. Davies
Pro. Debut 26 September, 1991

26.09.91 Paul Ryan L PTS 6 Dunstable
03.10.91 Mark O'Callaghan DREW 6 Burton
15.10.91 Howard Clarke L PTS 4 Dudley
04.11.91 Nigel Burder W CO 3 Merthyr
02.12.91 Darren Morris W PTS 8 Birmingham
16.12.91 Steve McGovern L PTS 8 Southampton

Career: 6 contests, won 2, drew 1, lost 3.

Johnny Nelson

Sheffield. *Born* Sheffield, 4 January, 1967
Former Undefeated European & British Cruiserweight Champion. Former Undefeated Central Area Cruiserweight Champion (13.7-13.7¼) ht. 6'2"
Manager B. Ingle
Pro. Debut 18 March, 1986

12.03.91 Yves Monsieur W RTD 8 Mansfield *(European Cruiserweight Title Defence)*
16.05.92 James Warring L PTS 12 Fredricksburg, USA *(IBF Cruiserweight Title Challenge)*

Career: 28 contests, won 21, drew 1, lost 6.

Ray Newby

Nottingham. *Born* Sunderland, 16 December, 1963
Former Midlands Area Lightweight Champion (9.8-10.5½) ht. 5'7"
Manager J. Griffin
Pro. Debut 20 September, 1984

12.04.91 Henry Armstrong L PTS 8 Manchester
22.01.92 Dean Bramhald W PTS 8 Solihull
11.02.92 Dean Bramhald W RSC 7 Wolverhampton
24.03.92 Ron Shinkwin W PTS 8 Wolverhampton
18.05.92 Ron Shinkwin W RSC 5 Bardon

Career: 45 contests, won 25, drew 2, lost 18.

Shaun Norman

Leicester. *Born* Leicester, 1 April, 1970

Flyweight (8.2-8.5) ht. 5'3"
Manager W. Swift
Pro. Debut 11 November, 1991

11.11.91 Louis Veitch W RSC 5 Bradford
27.11.91 Dave Campbell L PTS 6 Marton
14.12.91 Mickey Cantwell L PTS 8 Bexleyheath
20.02.91 Dave Hardie L PTS 6 Glasgow
10.04.92 Neil Armstrong DREW 8 Glasgow
25.04.92 Prince Nassem Hamed L RSC 2 Manchester
16.06.92 Francis Ampofo L RSC 4 Dagenham

Career: 7 contests, won 1, drew 1, lost 5.

Rick North

Grimsby. *Born* Grimsby, 2 February, 1968
Welterweight (10.2-10.8) ht. 5'8½"
Manager B. Ingle
Pro. Debut 28 May, 1991

28.05.91 Michael Smyth L RSC 1 Cardiff
16.09.91 Eddie King W RSC 5 Cleethorpes
21.10.91 Steve Bricknell W PTS 6 Cleethorpes
11.11.91 Darren McInulty L PTS 6 Stratford on Avon
09.12.91 Michael Byrne W RSC 2 Cleethorpes
23.01.92 Ron Hopley L PTS 6 York
19.02.92 Bernard Paul L PTS 6 Muswell Hill
11.03.92 Patrick Loughran L PTS 6 Stoke
22.04.92 Steve McNess L PTS 6 Wembley
03.06.92 Mark Dawson L PTS 6 Newcastle under Lyme

Career: 10 contests, won 3, lost 7.

Dennis Oakes

Liverpool. *Born* Prescot, 16 June, 1966
Bantamweight (8.10) ht. 5'6"
Manager M. Atkinson
Pro. Debut 22 January, 1992

22.01.92 Chris Lyons W RSC 3 Stoke
10.02.92 Mark Hargreaves W RSC 3 Liverpool
11.03.92 Des Gargano W PTS 6 Stoke

Career: 3 contests, won 3.

(David) Marvin O'Brien (Powell)

Leeds. *Born* Leeds, 3 September, 1966
S. Middleweight (11.12-12.7) ht. 5'11"
Manager T. Miller
Pro. Debut 31 January, 1990

17.01.91 Barry Messam L PTS 6 Alfreton
21.02.91 Russell Washer DREW 6 Walsall
02.03.91 Quinn Paynter DREW 6 Irvine
21.03.91 Nick Manners L CO 2 Dewsbury
31.05.91 Carl Harney W RSC 5 Manchester
24.06.91 Frank Eubanks L PTS 6 Liverpool
06.09.91 Cornelius Carr L RSC 7 Salemi, Italy
02.03.92 John Oxenham L PTS 6 Marton
26.03.92 John Ashton L PTS 8 Telford
05.04.92 Quinn Paynter L PTS 6 Bradford
17.05.92 Lester Jacobs L PTS 6 Harringay

Career: 15 contests, won 2, drew 2, lost 11.

Marvin O'Brien Chris Bevan

Richard O'Brien

Alfreton. *Born* Chesterfield, 29 October, 1971
Welterweight (10.5-10.11½) ht. 5'10"
Manager –
Pro. Debut 14 May, 1990

17.01.91 Steve Hardman L PTS 6 Alfreton
11.02.91 Neil Porter W RSC 4 Manchester
21.02.91 Darren Morris W PTS 6 Walsall
28.03.91 Trevor Ambrose L RSC 1 Alfreton
21.10.91 Tony Connellan L PTS 8 Bury
21.11.91 Chris Mulcahy W RSC 2 Ilkeston
02.12.91 Tony Britland W RSC 2 Birmingham
04.02.92 Darren McInulty W PTS 4 Alfreton
03.03.92 Scott Doyle L PTS 4 Cradley Heath
21.05.92 Howard Clarke L CO 1 Cradley Heath

Career: 16 contests, won 8, drew 1, lost 7.

Mark O'Callaghan

Tunbridge Wells. *Born* Tunbridge Wells, 17 January, 1969
Lightweight (9.9-9.13) ht. 5'7"
Manager B. Aird
Pro. Debut 3 October, 1991

03.10.91 Chris Mylan DREW 6 Burton
24.10.91 Nicky Lucas W PTS 6 Dunstable
11.12.91 Richard Joyce L RSC 3 Stoke
20.02.92 Alan McDowall L PTS 6 Glasgow

Career: 4 contests, won 1, drew 1, lost 2.

John Ogiste

Islington. *Born* London, 16 July, 1965
Middleweight (11.3-11.8¼) ht. 5'9"
Manager D. Mancini
Pro. Debut 7 December, 1988

18.02.91 Colin Manners W PTS 6 Mayfair
30.06.91 John Kaighin W PTS 6 Southwark
21.10.91 Darron Griffiths L PTS 6 Mayfair
17.02.92 Darron Griffiths L RSC 5 Mayfair
18.05.92 William Krijnen L PTS 8 Valkenswaard, Holland

Career: 11 contests, won 4, drew 2, lost 5.

(Paul) John O'Johnson (Johnson)

Nottingham. *Born* Nottingham, 2 November, 1969
L. Welterweight (9.13-10.5) ht. 5'5"
Manager W. Swift
Pro. Debut 29 August, 1991

29.08.91 Seth Jones W DIS 1 Oakengates
09.10.91 James Jiora W PTS 6 Manchester
24.10.91 Carl Hook L PTS 6 Dunstable
31.10.91 Darren Morris W PTS 6 Oakengates
26.11.91 Bernard Paul L PTS 6 Bethnal Green
22.01.92 Brian Coleman W PTS 6 Stoke
30.01.92 Chris Saunders W PTS 6 Southampton
20.02.92 Alan Peacock W PTS 6 Glasgow
09.03.92 Ricky Sackfield W PTS 6 Manchester
26.03.92 Davy Robb L PTS 6 Telford
03.06.92 Jason Barker W PTS 6 Newcastle under Lyme

Career: 11 contests, won 8, lost 3.

Richard Okumu

Bristol. *Born* Uganda, 18 December, 1970
L. Middleweight (10.10½-11.10) ht. 6'0"
Manager M. Barrett
Pro. Debut 4 February, 1991

04.02.91 Benji Joseph W PTS 6 Leicester
18.02.91 Colin Pitters L PTS 6 Birmingham
05.03.91 Kevin Sheeran W RSC 2 Millwall
24.10.91 Benji Good W CO 6 Bayswater
05.12.91 Andrew Flute DREW 8 Cannock
22.01.92 Darron Griffiths L PTS 8 Solihull

Career: 6 contests, won 3, drew 1, lost 2.

Michael Oliver

Cefn Hengoed. *Born* Caerphilly, 1 December, 1969
Welterweight (10.7-10.13) ht. 6'0"
Manager D. Gardiner
Pro. Debut 6 June, 1988

24.10.91 Adrian Riley L PTS 6 Dunstable
13.11.91 Jamie Robinson L PTS 6 Bethnal Green
28.11.91 Robert McCracken L RSC 3 Liverpool
01.02.92 Ernie Loveridge L PTS 8 Birmingham
09.02.92 Ossie Maddix L RTD 3 Bradford

Career: 19 contests, won 7, drew 1, lost 11.

Graham O'Malley

Middlesbrough. Born Middlesbrough, 9 January, 1963
S. Featherweight (9.2-9.5) ht. 5'3"
Manager T. Calligan
Pro. Debut 23 April, 1987

26.04.91 Daniel Londas L PTS 10 Reims, France

05.07.91 Mehdi Labdouni L PTS 6 Autun, France
18.11.91 Noel Carroll L PTS 6 Manchester
28.01.92 Mike Deveney W RSC 1 Piccadilly
10.03.92 Carl Roberts W PTS 6 Bury
31.03.92 Richie Wenton L PTS 6 Stockport
14.05.92 Jimmy Owens L PTS 6 Liverpool

Career: 31 contests, won 8, drew 1, lost 22.

(Mike) Chip O'Neill

Sunderland. *Born* Sunderland, 10 December, 1963
Featherweight (9.2) ht. 5'6½"
Manager T. Conroy
Pro. Debut 28 June, 1982

28.04.92 Robert Braddock W PTS 6 Houghton le Spring

Career: 4 contests, won 1, lost 3.

Gary Osborne

Walsall. *Born* Bloxwich, 24 August, 1963
Midlands Area L Middleweight Champion. Former Midlands Area Welterweight Champion (10.6-11.2) ht. 5'10"

Manager R. Gray
Pro. Debut 8 May, 1989

10.04.91 Mickey Lerwill W PTS 10 Wolverhampton *(Vacant Midlands Area Welterweight Title)*
10.09.91 Ernie Loveridge L RSC 1 Wolverhampton *(Midlands Area Welterweight Title Defence)*
17.03.92 Shamus Casey W RSC 5 Wolverhampton *(Vacant Midlands Area L Middleweight Title)*
28.04.92 Gary Pemberton W CO 3 Wolverhampton

Career: 11 contests, won 10, lost 1.

Gary Osborne Les Clark

Steve Osborne

Nottingham. *Born* Nottingham, 27 June, 1965
Cruiserweight (12.10½-13.6) ht. 5'9"
Manager W. Swift
Pro. Debut 28 May, 1987

16.04.91 Art Stacey DREW 6 Nottingham
09.05.91 Michael Gale L RSC 2 Leeds
11.11.91 Art Stacey L PTS 6 Bradford
21.11.91 Bruce Scott L PTS 6 Burton
29.11.91 Maurice Coore L PTS 6 Manchester
12.02.92 Phil Soundy L PTS 6 Wembley

Career: 26 contests, won 7, drew 1, lost 18.

Conrad Oscar

Paddington. *Born* Dominica, 25 April, 1960
Middleweight (11.6¾) ht. 5'11"
Manager G. Steene
Pro. Debut 16 February, 1982

20.09.91 Frank Grant L CO 2 Manchester

Career: 18 contests, won 9, drew 1, lost 8.

Clay O'Shea

Islington. *Born* London, 3 November,1966
L. Middleweight (10.13-11.2¼) ht. 6'0"
Manager D. Mancini
Pro. Debut 20 February, 1990

04.04.91 Robert Peel W PTS 6 Watford
11.09.91 Shamus Casey W PTS 6 Hammersmith
26.09.91 Tony Wellington W CO 1 Dunstable
25.03.92 Andrew Furlong DREW 6 Kensington
13.05.92 Andrew Furlong DREW 6 Kensington

Career: 9 contests, won 7, drew 2.

Dave Owens

Castleford. *Born* Castleford, 11 December, 1954
L. Heavyweight. Former Undefeated Central Area Middleweight Champion (11.12-12.8) ht. 6'1"
Manager –
Pro. Debut 12 May, 1986

17.02.91 Anton Josipovic L PTS 8 Prijedor, Yugoslavia
24.03.91 Christophe Girard L RSC 7 Vichy, France
23.04.91 Joe Frater W PTS 6 Evesham
27.05.91 Eddie Smulders L RSC 1 Rotterdam, Holland
14.11.91 Ian Henry L PTS 8 Gateshead
03.03.92 Terry French W CO 1 Houghton le Spring
26.03.92 Tony Booth L PTS 6 Hull
14.04.92 Martin Smith L PTS 6 Mansfield

Career: 51 contests, won 20, drew 4, lost 27.

Jimmy Owens

Liverpool. *Born* Liverpool, 15 February, 1966
Featherweight (8.13-9.5½) ht. 5'6½"
Manager C. Moorcroft
Pro. Debut 29 January, 1990

01.05.91 Peter Judson W PTS 6 Liverpool
16.05.91 Des Gargano W RSC 2 Liverpool
24.06.91 Miguel Matthews W PTS 6 Liverpool
09.09.91 Russell Davison L PTS 10 Liverpool *(Central Area Featherweight Title Challenge)*
14.05.92 Graham O'Malley W PTS 6 Liverpool

Career: 11 contests, won 10, lost 1.

John Oxenham

Doncaster. *Born* Doncaster, 11 June, 1968
L. Heavyweight (12.4-12.10) ht. 6'0½"
Manager F. Maloney
Pro. Debut 4 September, 1990

13.05.91 Shaun McCrory L PTS 6 Marton
09.10.91 Dennis Afflick W DIS 4 Marton
24.10.91 Morris Thomas W RSC 6 Glasgow
27.11.91 Ian Henry L PTS 6 Marton
02.03.92 Marvin O'Brien W PTS 6 Marton
27.04.92 Joe McCluskey L PTS 4 Glasgow
18.05.92 Andy Manning W PTS 6 Marton

Career: 8 contests, won 5, lost 3.

John Oxenham Chris Bevan

Gary Pagden

Boston. *Born* Boston, 12 August, 1963
L. Welterweight (10.0½) ht. 5'10"
Manager J. Gaynor
Pro. Debut 14 October, 1991

14.10.91 Rob Stewart L PTS 6 Manchester

Career: 1 contest, lost 1.

Mark Pain (Leslie)

Wolverhampton. *Born* Wolverhampton, 7 April, 1972
L. Heavyweight (12.7-13.0) ht. 5'9½"
Manager B. Crooks
Pro. Debut 3 October, 1991

03.10.91 Jason McNeill W PTS 6 Burton
12.02.92 Vic Wright W RSC 1 Watford
03.06.92 Kevin Morton L PTS 6 Newcastle under Lyme

Career: 3 contests, won 2, lost 1.

John Palmer

Leicester. *Born* Leicester, 11 June, 1969
Heavyweight (14.13) ht. 6'3½"
Manager J. Griffin
Pro. Debut 24 September, 1991

24.09.91 Graham Arnold L CO 2 Basildon

Career: 1 contest, lost 1.

Andreas Panayi

St Helens. *Born* Cyprus, 14 July, 1969
Welterweight (10.6-10.8) ht.
Manager R. Gray
Pro. Debut 21 November, 1990

04.02.91 Cliff Churchward W PTS 6 Leicester
12.02.91 Eddie King W CO 2 Wolverhampton
27.02.91 Trevor Meikle L PTS 6 Wolverhampton
15.04.91 Mick Mulcahy W RSC 2 Leicester
24.04.91 Darren Morris DREW 6 Stoke
11.09.91 Robert Riley W PTS 6 Stoke
30.09.91 Steve Hardman W RSC 5 Liverpool
23.10.91 Darren Morris W PTS 6 Stoke
25.11.91 Marvin P. Gray W PTS 8 Liverpool
11.12.91 Mark Kelly DREW 8 Stoke
11.03.92 Dean Bramhald L PTS 8 Stoke
14.05.92 Dave Maj W CO 6 Liverpool

Career: 13 contests, won 8, drew 2, lost 3.

Wayne Panayiotiou

Llanelli. *Born* Llanelli, 19 October, 1965
L. Middleweight (11.0-11.11) ht. 5'11"
Manager D. Davies
Pro. Debut 16 October, 1990

24.01.91 Russell Washer L RSC 4 Gorseinon
09.12.91 Stuart Dunn L CO 4 Brierley Hill

Career: 3 contests, lost 3.

Neil Parry

Middlesbrough. *Born* Middlesbrough, 21 June, 1969
Bantamweight (8.3-8.11) ht. 5'5"
Manager –
Pro. Debut 12 June, 1989

21.01.91 Stevie Woods L PTS 8 Glasgow
06.02.91 Paul Dever W PTS 6 Liverpool
05.03.91 Tony Smith DREW 6 Leicester
24.04.91 Paul Dever DREW 6 Stoke
17.05.91 Gary White L PTS 6 Bury
03.06.91 Stevie Woods W RSC 2 Glasgow
20.06.91 Tony Smith W PTS 6 Liverpool
12.09.91 Mark Tierney L PTS 6 Wandsworth
21.10.91 Neil Johnston L PTS 8 Glasgow
27.01.92 Drew Docherty L RSC 4 Glasgow
28.02.92 Stevie Woods W PTS 6 Irvine
11.05.92 Tim Yeates L PTS 6 Piccadilly

Career: 19 contests, won 6, drew 2, lost 11.

Bernard Paul (right) in a tit-for-tat against John O'Johnson. The unbeaten Paul won on points over six rounds Les Clark

Elvis Parsley

Bloxwich. *Born* Walsall, 6 December, 1962
Featherweight (8.12-9.7) ht. 5'7½"
Manager –
Pro. Debut 4 June, 1990

18.02.91 Peter Campbell W RSC 3 Derby
01.05.91 Neil Leitch W CO 2 Solihull
20.05.91 Neil Smith L RSC 5 Leicester
02.10.91 Muhammad Shaffique W CO 1 Solihull
29.04.92 Kelton McKenzie L RSC 5 Solihull *(Vacant Midlands Area Featherweight Title)*

Career: 9 contests, won 6, lost 3.

Johnny Patterson

Newcastle. *Born* Newcastle, 30 March, 1972
Lightweight (9.5-9.8½) ht. 5'7½"
Manager N. Fawcett
Pro. Debut 29 November, 1990

16.02.91 Tommy Smith L PTS 6 Thornaby
24.09.91 Alan McDowall L PTS 4 Glasgow
21.10.91 Jason Evans L PTS 6 Mayfair
28.11.91 Alan McDowall L PTS 6 Glasgow

Career: 5 contests, won 1, lost 4.

Steve Patton

Wembley. *Born* Ballyshannon, 3 August, 1970
S. Featherweight (9.4) ht. 6'0"
Manager H. Holland
Pro. Debut 12 February, 1992

12.02.92 Jas Dip Singh W RSC 1 Watford

Career: 1 contest, won 1.

Akash D. Paul (Saroye)

Paddington. *Born* India, 6 May, 1963
Featherweight (9.1¼-9.3) ht. 5'5"
Manager A. Kasler
Pro. Debut 24 September, 1990

22.04.91 Mark Loftus L CO 1 Mayfair
12.09.91 Dave Mitchell L RSC 5 Wandsworth

Career: 3 contests, lost 3.

Bernard Paul

Tottenham. *Born* Mauritius, 22 October, 1965
L. Welterweight (9.13½-10.2) ht. 5'7½"
Manager B. Hearn
Pro. Debut 1 May, 1991

01.05.91 Trevor Royal W CO 1 Bethnal Green
04.06.91 Dave Jenkins W RSC 1 Bethnal Green
24.09.91 Pat Delargy W RSC 5 Basildon
26.10.91 Gordon Webster W RSC 4 Brentwood
26.11.91 John O'Johnson W PTS 6 Bethnal Green
19.02.92 Rick North W PTS 6 Muswell Hill
17.03.92 Mick Mulcahy W PTS 6 Mayfair
16.06.92 Brendan Ryan W CO 6 Dagenham

Career: 8 contests, won 8.

Quinn Paynter

Manchester. *Born* Bermuda, 19 August, 1965
Middleweight (11.2-12.1) ht. 5'9"
Manager P. Martin
Pro. Debut 12 October, 1989

21.01.91 W. O. Wilson W PTS 8 Crystal Palace
02.03.91 Marvin O'Brien DREW 6 Irvine
16.05.91 Ali Forbes DREW 6 Battersea
14.11.91 Terry French W CO 6 Gateshead
18.01.92 Val Golding W RSC 7 Kensington
05.04.92 Marvin O'Brien W PTS 6 Bradford

Career: 16 contests, won 10, drew 2, lost 4.

Glen Payton (Kennedy)

Telford. *Born* Gateshead, 15 May, 1964
Middleweight (11.4-11.8) ht. 5'11"
Manager D. Gill
Pro. Debut 31 October, 1991

31.10.91 Wilf McGee W RSC 6 Oakengates
05.12.91 John Baxter W CO 3 Oakengates
20.02.92 Paul Hanlon W PTS 6 Oakengates
26.03.92 Chris Richards L PTS 6 Telford

Career: 4 contests, won 3, lost 1.

Alan Peacock

Cumbernauld. *Born* Glasgow, 17 February, 1969
L. Welterweight (9.11½-10.5) ht. 5'7"
Manager T. Gilmour
Pro. Debut 23 February, 1990

11.02.91 Oliver Harrison L RSC 6 Glasgow
18.03.91 Darren Mount W PTS 8 Glasgow
27.03.91 Giovanni Parisi L PTS 6 Mestre, Italy
06.04.91 Alan Hall L PTS 6 Darlington
25.05.91 Giorgio Campanella L CO 1 Trezzano, Italy
23.09.91 Trevor Meikle L PTS 6 Glasgow
27.11.91 Dave Whittle L PTS 6 Marton
28.01.92 Trevor Meikle W PTS 8 Piccadilly
20.02.92 John O'Johnson L PTS 6 Glasgow
04.03.92 Rob Stewart DREW 8 Glasgow
12.03.92 Dave Whittle DREW 8 Glasgow
30.03.92 Peter Bradley L PTS 8 Glasgow

Career: 19 contests, won 8, drew 2, lost 9.

Mark Pearce

Cardiff. *Born* Cardiff, 29 June, 1963
Welterweight (10.3-10.6¾) ht. 5'7"
Manager C. Breen
Pro. Debut 16 May, 1983

05.03.91 Jim Lawlor L PTS 6 Cardiff
29.10.91 Mick Meloscia W RTD 2 Cardiff

Career: 33 contests, won 8, drew 4, lost 21.

(Laurieston) Larry Peart

Wolverhampton. *Born* Telford, 26 February, 1962
Heavyweight (15.2) ht. 5'11¼"
Manager D. Nelson
Pro. Debut 22 April, 1991

22.04.91 Damien Caesar L RSC 2 Mayfair
19.12.91 Billy Isaac L RSC 3 Oldham

Career: 2 contests, lost 2.

Robert Peel

Llandovery. *Born* Birmingham, 11 January, 1969
Middleweight (10.13-11.7) ht. 5'10"
Manager D. Davies
Pro. Debut 24 January, 1991

24.01.91 John Kaighin W PTS 6 Gorseinon
12.02.91 John Kaighin L PTS 6 Cardiff
13.03.91 Andrew Flute L PTS 6 Stoke
04.04.91 Clay O'Shea L PTS 6 Watford
12.04.91 Adrian Wright L RSC 6 Willenhall
15.05.91 John Kaighin L PTS 8 Swansea
29.10.91 Jason Matthews L RSC 6 Cardiff
03.02.92 Warren Stowe L PTS 6 Manchester
02.03.92 Steve Thomas DREW 6 Merthyr
11.05.92 Steve Thomas L PTS 6 Llanelli
04.06.92 Darren Pilling L PTS 6 Burnley

Career: 11 contests, won 1, drew 1, lost 9.

Gary Pemberton

Cardiff. *Born* Cardiff, 15 May, 1960
L. Middleweight (10.13½-11.4¾) ht. 5'10"
Manager –
Pro. Debut 10 September, 1986

24.01.91 Carlo Colarusso L RSC 8 Gorseinon *(Vacant Welsh L Middleweight Title)*
10.04.91 Colin Pitters L RSC 3 Newport
01.10.91 Adrian Strachan L RSC 2 Sheffield
12.02.92 Andrew Furlong L PTS 6 Wembley
28.04.92 Gary Osborne L CO 3 Wolverhampton

Career: 33 contests, won 11, drew 1, lost 21.

Jim Peters

Southampton. *Born* Southampton, 24 October, 1964
Former Undefeated Southern Area L. Heavyweight Champion (12.4½-12.12½) ht. 6'0½"
Manager T. Lawless
Pro. Debut 6 April, 1987

14.02.91 Serg Fame W RSC 4 Southampton *(Southern Area L. Heavyweight Title Challenge)*
23.05.91 Dino Stewart W RSC 6 Southampton
11.09.91 Tony Booth W PTS 8 Hammersmith
30.01.92 Crawford Ashley L RSC 1 Southampton *(British L. Heavyweight Title Challenge)*

Career: 20 contests, won 18, lost 2.

Joey Peters

Southampton. *Born* Southampton, 10 December, 1971
L. Heavyweight (12.8-12.10½) ht. 5'9½"
Manager T. Lawless
Pro. Debut 25 April, 1991

25.04.91 Dennis Afflick W PTS 6 Basildon
23.05.91 Tony Behan W PTS 6 Southampton
04.07.91 Randy B. Powell W PTS 6 Alfreton
17.10.91 Lee Prudden W PTS 6 Southwark
25.03.92 Terry Duffus W RSC 1 Kensington
27.04.92 Paul Hanlon W CO 2 Mayfair

Career: 6 contests, won 6.

Joey Peters Les Clark

Gary Peynado

Birmingham. *Born* Birmingham, 1 September, 1966
L. Welterweight (10.1) ht. 5'2½"
Manager –
Pro. Debut 13 February, 1986

08.10.91 Michael Clynch L CO 2 Wolverhampton

Career: 12 contests, won 8, lost 4.

Mike Phillips

Warrington. *Born* Wells, 15 July,1964
L. Middleweight (11.3-11.7½) ht. 5'9¼"
Manager R. Jones
Pro. Debut 7 September, 1990

23.01.91 Matt Mowatt W RSC 6 Stoke
04.02.91 Dean Cooper L PTS 6 Leicester
22.02.91 Carl Harney W RSC 5 Manchester
13.03.91 Stinger Mason DREW 6 Stoke
30.04.91 Rocky McGran W RSC 2 Stockport
17.05.91 Rob Pitters W PTS 8 Bury
01.10.91 Martin Smith L PTS 6 Sheffield
22.10.91 Rob Pitters L PTS 4 Hartlepool
25.11.91 Dave Johnson W PTS 6 Liverpool
10.03.92 Steve Foster L RSC 4 Bury

Career: 19 contests, won 11, drew 2, lost 6.

Dave Pierre

Peterborough. *Born* Peterborough, 10 September, 1964
Southern Area L. Welterweight Champion (10.0-10.2) ht. 5'7½"
Manager K. Whitney
Pro. Debut 28 November, 1986

19.04.91 Oliver Harrison W PTS 8 Peterborough
06.02.92 Marvin P. Gray W RSC 7 Peterborough
30.04.92 Carlos Chase W RSC 7 Watford *(Southern Area L. Welterweight Title Defence)*

Career: 19 contests, won 14, lost 5.

(Warren) John Pierre

Newcastle. *Born* Newcastle, 22 April, 1966
Cruiserweight (13.9-14.10½) ht. 6'0"
Manager G. McCrory
Pro. Debut 10 October, 1991

10.10.91 Gary Charlton W PTS 6 Gateshead
20.01.92 Art Stacey L PTS 6 Bradford
Career: 2 contests, won 2.

Darren Pilling

Burnley. *Born* Burnley, 18 January, 1967
Middleweight (11.1½) ht. 5'8½"
Manager J. Doughty
Pro. Debut 3 September, 1988

04.06.92 Robert Peel W PTS 6 Burnley

Career: 10 contests, won 6, lost 4.

Nicky Piper

Cardiff. *Born* Cardiff, 5 May, 1966
S. Middleweight (12.0-12.10) ht. 6'3"
Manager F. Warren
Pro. Debut 6 September, 1989

05.03.91 Johnny Held W RSC 3 Millwall
08.05.91 Serge Bolivard W RSC 1 Millwall
22.05.91 Martin Lopez W CO 1 Millwall
03.07.91 Simon Harris W RSC 1 Reading
04.09.91 Carl Thompson L RSC 3 Bethnal Green
29.10.91 Franki Moro W RSC 4 Kensington
20.11.91 Carlos Christie W CO 6 Cardiff
22.01.92 Frank Eubanks W PTS 10 Cardiff *(Elim. British S. Middleweight Title)*
11.03.92 Ron Amundsen W PTS 10 Cardiff
16.05.92 Larry Prather W PTS 8 Muswell Hill

Career: 17 contests, won 15, drew 1, lost 1.

Nicky Piper Les Clark

Colin Pitters

Birmingham. *Born* Birmingham, 1 October, 1956
L. Middleweight (11.0-11.3½) ht. 6'3"
Manager E. Cashmore
Pro. Debut 3 December, 1989

28.01.91 Lee Farrell W PTS 6 Birmingham
04.02.91 Barry Messam W PTS 6 Leicester
18.02.91 Richard Okumu W PTS 6 Birmingham
10.04.91 Gary Pemberton W RSC 3 Newport
24.04.91 Chris Richards W RSC 6 Stoke
20.09.91 Steve Foster L RTD 5 Manchester
31.10.91 Richie Woodhall L PTS 8 Oakengates
21.11.91 Neville Brown L RSC 3 Burton

Career: 13 contests, won 6, lost 7.

Rob Pitters

Gateshead. *Born* Birmingham, 28 May, 1960
L. Middleweight (10.9¾-11.1½) ht. 6'1"
Manager T. Conroy
Pro. Debut 26 September, 1990

21.02.91 Martin Rosamond W RSC 2 Walsall
28.02.91 Crain Fisher W RSC 6 Bury
15.04.91 Gordon Blair W PTS 6 Glasgow
10.05.91 Mick Duncan W RSC 2 Gateshead
17.05.91 Mike Phillips L PTS 8 Bury
22.10.91 Mike Phillips W PTS 4 Hartlepool
11.03.92 Julian Eavis W PTS 6 Solihull
04.06.92 Warren Stowe L PTS 8 Burnley

Career: 13 contests, won 9, drew 2, lost 2.

Steve Pollard

Hull. *Born* Hull, 18 December, 1957
Lightweight. Former Central Area Featherweight Champion (9.7-10.2½) ht. 5'7"
Manager –
Pro. Debut 28 April, 1980

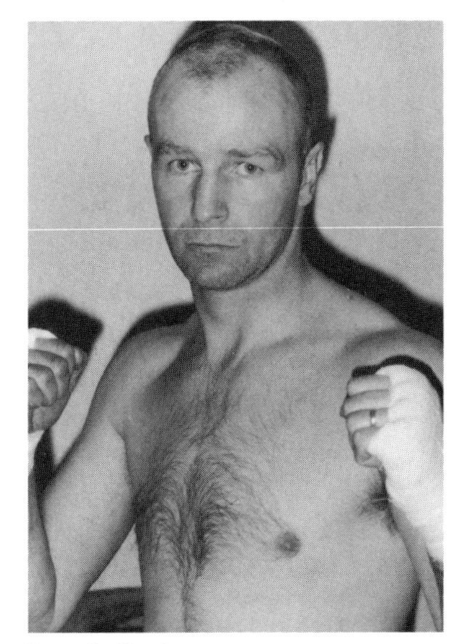

Steve Pollard Les Clark

11.02.91 Dave Anderson L PTS 6 Glasgow
02.03.91 Alan Hall L PTS 6 Darlington
05.12.91 Shaun Cogan L PTS 6 Oakengates
18.01.92 Ian Honeywood L PTS 6 Kensington
30.03.92 J. T. Williams W PTS 6 Eltham
30.04.92 Jason Rowland L RSC 2 Kensington

Career: 60 contests, won 19, drew 4, lost 37.

Danny Porter

Hitchin. *Born* Biggleswade, 27 April, 1964
Flyweight (7.1¾-8.5) ht. 5'3"
Manager B. Hearn
Pro. Debut 9 November, 1986

19.03.91 Kevin Jenkins W RSC 7 Leicester
12.06.91 Salvatore Fanni L RSC 9 Sassari, Italy *(European Flyweight Title Challenge)*
19.11.91 Kevin Jenkins W RSC 2 Norwich
12.02.92 Salvatore Fanni DREW 12 Sarno, Italy *(European Flyweight Title Challenge)*
01.06.92 Miguel Matthews W PTS 6 Glasgow

Career: 20 contests, won 12, drew 1, lost 7.

Darren Powell

Manchester. *Born* Manchester, 13 June, 1969
L. Welterweight (10.2) ht. 5'11"
Manager J. Doughty
Pro. Debut 4 June, 1992

04.06.92 Mark Antony L CO 2 Burnley

Career: 1 contest, lost 1.

(Andrew) Randy B. Powell

Brockley. *Born* London, 9 October, 1962
Cruiserweight (12.11½-13.8) ht. 5'9½"
Manager –
Pro. Debut 15 September, 1987

04.07.91 Joey Peters L PTS 6 Alfreton
16.09.91 Bruce Scott L RSC 5 Mayfair
12.11.91 Vic Wright L RTD 4 Milton Keynes
11.12.91 Gary Delaney L RSC 1 Basildon

Career: 12 contests, won 2, drew 1, lost 9.

Gypsy Johnny Price

Bolton. *Born* Wigan, 10 April, 1973
S. Middleweight (12.0-12.2) ht. 5'10"
Manager J. Doughty
Pro. Debut 21 October, 1991

21.10.91 Graham Wassell W RSC 5 Bury
21.01.92 Jason McNeill W PTS 4 Stockport
10.03.92 Mark Jolley L RSC 3 Bury

Career: 3 contests, won 2, lost 1.

Kevin Pritchard

Liverpool. *Born* Ipswich, 26 September, 1961
Former British S. Featherweight Champion (8.13¼-9.3) ht. 5'5"
Manager J. McMillan
Pro. Debut 21 December, 1981

05.03.91 Robert Dickie L RSC 8 Cardiff *(British S. Featherweight Title Defence)*

17.05.91 Jimmy Bredahl L RSC 3 Copenhagen, Denmark
04.09.91 Colin McMillan L RSC 7 Bethnal Green
(British Featherweight Title Challenge)

Career: 48 contests, won 23, drew 3, lost 22.

Lee Prudden

Redditch. *Born* Birmingham, 3 December, 1968
L. Heavyweight (11.3-13.5) ht. 6'0"
Manager –
Pro. Debut 28 January, 1991

28.01.91 Paul Murray W PTS 6 Birmingham
27.02.91 Barry Downes W PTS 6 Wolverhampton
13.03.91 Paul Murray DREW 6 Stoke
26.03.91 Nigel Rafferty L PTS 6 Wolverhampton
10.04.91 Paul Hanlon W PTS 6 Wolverhampton
13.05.91 Paul Hanlon W PTS 6 Birmingham
23.05.91 Paul Hanlon L PTS 6 Southampton
05.06.91 Nigel Rafferty L PTS 6 Wolverhampton
03.07.91 James F. Woolley W PTS 6 Brentwood
21.09.91 James F. Woolley W PTS 6 Tottenham
01.10.91 Gil Lewis DREW 8 Bedworth
17.10.91 Joey Peters L PTS 6 Southwark
22.01.92 Paul Hanlon L RSC 4 Stoke
22.04.92 Phil Soundy L RSC 5 Wembley

Career: 14 contests, won 6, drew 2, lost 6.

Danny Quigg

Paisley. *Born* Glasgow, 12 February, 1960
L. Middleweight (10.11½-11.3½) ht. 5'11"
Manager N. Sweeney
Pro. Debut 1 February, 1985

25.01.91 Gordon Blair L PTS 6 Shotts
06.03.91 Mick Duncan W PTS 6 Glasgow
07.05.91 Martin Smith L PTS 6 Glasgow
23.09.91 Mick Duncan DREW 6 Glasgow

Career: 12 contests, won 7, drew 1, lost 4.

Willie Quinn

Haddington. *Born* Edinburgh, 17 February, 1972
Middleweight (11.3-11.8¾) ht. 5'11½"
Manager T. Gilmour
Pro. Debut 9 October, 1991

09.10.91 Mark Jay L PTS 6 Glasgow
27.01.92 Hugh Fury W RSC 3 Glasgow
18.03.92 Andy Manning W PTS 6 Glasgow
30.03.92 John McKenzie W RSC 4 Glasgow

Career: 4 contests, won 3, lost 1.

David Radford

Hemsworth. *Born* Hemsworth, 30 May, 1969
L. Middleweight (11.2-11.8) ht. 6'0"
Manager K. Tate
Pro. Debut 27 March, 1990

16.01.91 Tony Kosova W PTS 6 Stoke
21.02.91 Kenny Tyson L PTS 6 Leeds
15.04.91 Paul Burton L RTD 1 Wolverhampton
13.05.91 Pete Bowman W CO 2 Manchester
02.12.91 Dave Binsteed W RSC 6 Liverpool
14.12.91 Delroy Matthews L CO 1 Bexleyheath
24.02.92 Mark Jay L PTS 6 Bradford
09.03.92 Tyrone Eastmond DREW 6 Manchester
25.04.92 Warren Stowe L RSC 3 Manchester

Career: 14 contests, won 6, drew 1, lost 7.

Nigel Rafferty

Wolverhampton. *Born* Wolverhampton, 29 December, 1967
L. Heavyweight (11.10-13.0) ht. 5'11"
Manager –
Pro. Debut 5 June, 1989

28.01.91 Alan Richards DREW 8 Birmingham
04.03.91 Carlos Christie L PTS 8 Birmingham
26.03.91 Lee Prudden W PTS 6 Wolverhampton
13.05.91 Tony Behan W DIS 7 Birmingham
05.06.91 Lee Prudden W PTS 6 Wolverhampton
10.09.91 Paul Busby L RSC 2 Wolverhampton
20.11.91 Julian Johnson DREW 6 Cardiff
02.12.91 Kesem Clayton W PTS 8 Birmingham
21.01.92 Glenn Campbell L RSC 6 Stockport
30.03.92 Simon McDougall W PTS 8 Coventry
25.04.92 Sammy Storey L RSC 3 Belfast
16.06.92 Gary Delaney L CO 5 Dagenham

Career: 32 contests, won 14, drew 4, lost 14.

Tony Rahman

Newport. *Born* London, 26 March, 1960
Bantamweight (8.8-8.8¾) ht. 5'5¼"
Manager –
Pro. Debut 8 November, 1983

12.09.91 Leigh Williams L PTS 6 Wandsworth
20.09.91 John Green L RSC 3 Manchester

Career: 15 contests, won 2, lost 13.

Gary Railton

Burnopfield. *Born* Consett, 15 July, 1966
Heavyweight (15.2-15.7) ht. 6'2"
Manager G. McCrory
Pro. Debut 30 April, 1987

11.11.91 Gary Charlton W PTS 6 Bradford
06.02.92 J. A. Bugner L CO 3 Peterborough

Career: 8 contests, won 4, lost 4.

David Ramsden

Bradford. *Born* Bradford, 22 January, 1970
Featherweight (8.10-8.13) ht. 5'4"
Manager J. Celebanski
Pro. Debut 20 January, 1992

20.01.92 Glyn Shepherd W RSC 1 Bradford
30.03.92 Eunan Devenney W RSC 2 Bradford
27.04.92 Des Gargano W PTS 6 Bradford
08.06.92 Des Gargano W PTS 6 Bradford

Career: 4 contests, won 4.

Mark Ramsey

Small Heath. *Born* Birmingham, 24 January, 1968
L. Welterweight (9.13-10.2) ht. 5'7½"
Manager –
Pro. Debut 15 November, 1989

30.05.91 Colin Sinnott W PTS 6 Birmingham
05.12.91 Carl Hook W RSC 5 Oakengates

Career: 8 contests, won 6, lost 2.

Calum Rattray

Aberdeen. *Born* Aberdeen, 30 March, 1963
L. Middleweight (10.11½) ht. 5'10"
Manager –
Pro. Debut 6 March, 1989

24.02.92 Allan Grainger L RTD 5 Glasgow

Career: 9 contests, lost 9.

Mark Reefer (Thompson)

Bethnal Green. *Born* Hackney, 16 March, 1964
Lightweight. Former Commonwealth S. Featherweight Champion. Former Undefeated Southern Area Lightweight Champion (9.3-9.10) ht. 5'5"
Manager –
Pro. Debut 4 October, 1983

12.02.91 Andy Deabreu W PTS 10 Cardiff
(Elim. British S. Featherweight Title)
18.04.91 Thunder Aryeh L RSC 2 Earls Court
(Commonwealth S. Featherweight Title Defence)
17.03.92 Peter Till L RSC 3 Mayfair

Career: 32 contests, won 23, drew 1, lost 8.

Mick Reid

Rugby. *Born* Rugby, 27 November, 1968
Welterweight (10.7-10.13) ht. 5'7"
Manager P. Byrne
Pro. Debut 29 April, 1991

29.04.91 Dean Carr W RSC 1 Cleethorpes
20.05.91 Chad Strong L PTS 6 Leicester
24.09.91 Paul Dyer L PTS 6 Basildon
16.10.91 Rocky Feliciello W PTS 6 Stoke
26.10.91 Ojay Abrahams L RSC 5 Brentwood
25.03.92 Lee Ferrie L RSC 3 Hinckley

Career: 6 contests, won 2, lost 4.

Peter Reid

Alfreton. *Born* Derby, 19 February, 1966
Welterweight (10.4-10.12) ht. 5'10½"
Manager M. Shinfield
Pro. Debut 1 September, 1986

21.11.91 Robert Riley W PTS 6 Ilkeston
04.12.91 Julian Eavis L PTS 6 Stoke
20.02.92 James Campbell L PTS 6 Oakengates
06.04.92 Kevin Mabbutt W PTS 6 Northampton
13.04.92 Dave Maj L CO 1 Manchester
04.06.92 Warren Bowers W RSC 2 Cleethorpes

Career: 21 contests, won 8, lost 13.

Peter Reid Chris Bevan

(Clifton) Paddy Reilly (Mitchell)
Sheffield. *Born* Derby, 29 October, 1965
Heavyweight (16.7-17.7) ht. 6'2½"
Manager B. Ingle
Pro. Debut 6 April, 1991

06.04.91 John Harewood W RSC 2 Darlington
01.08.91 John Harewood W CO 1 Dewsbury
03.10.91 Tucker Richards W PTS 6 Burton
21.11.91 Tucker Richards W RSC 6 Burton
14.04.92 Michael Murray W RSC 8 Mansfield

Career: 5 contests, won 5.

Paddy Reilly Chris Bevan

Glyn Rhodes
Sheffield. *Born* Sheffield, 22 October, 1959
Welterweight. Former Central Area Lightweight Champion (10.6-10.11½) ht. 5'11"
Manager –
Pro. Debut 15 November, 1979

29.01.91 Simon Eubank W RSC 3 Wisbech
23.02.91 Neil Foran W RSC 2 Brighton
18.05.91 Itoro Mkpanam L RSC 5 Verbania, Italy
29.06.91 Antoine Fernandez L CO 2 Le Touquet, France
21.09.91 Eamonn Loughran L PTS 8 Tottenham
26.12.91 Jean-Charles Meuret L CO 2 Berne, Switzerland

Career: 60 contests, won 30, drew 5, lost 25.

Alan Richards
Barry. *Born* Cardiff, 9 April, 1965
Middleweight (11.5¾-12.0) ht. 5'9"
Manager –
Pro. Debut 22 May, 1989

28.01.91 Nigel Rafferty DREW 8 Birmingham
06.02.91 Andy Till L PTS 8 Battersea
12.04.91 Frank Grant L RSC 5 Manchester
14.05.91 Andrew Flute L PTS 8 Dudley
20.11.91 Russell Washer W PTS 6 Cardiff
11.02.92 Wayne Ellis L PTS 10 Cardiff *(Vacant Welsh Middleweight Title)*

Career: 21 contests, won 9, drew 1, lost 11.

Chris Richards
Nottingham. *Born* Nottingham, 4 April, 1964
Middleweight (11.2-11.8) ht. 5'5¼"
Manager W. Swift
Pro. Debut 7 September, 1987

Chris Richards Les Clark

13.02.91 Delroy Waul L PTS 6 Wembley
16.04.91 Paul Smith DREW 6 Nottingham
24.04.91 Colin Pitters L RSC 6 Stoke
26.11.91 Adrian Strachan L PTS 6 Bethnal Green
26.03.92 Glen Payton W PTS 6 Telford
18.06.92 Stefan Wright L PTS 6 Peterborough

Career: 30 contests, won 9, drew 1, lost 20.

Tony Richards
Nottingham. *Born* Nottingham, 24 September, 1962
Lightweight (9.11-9.13) ht. 5'3½"
Manager –
Pro. Debut 10 October, 1985

15.02.91 Racheed Lawal L PTS 8 Randers, Denmark
20.09.91 Paul Burke L PTS 8 Manchester
13.11.91 Nigel Wenton L RSC 5 Belfast

Career: 30 contests, won 14, drew 1, lost 15.

(Michael) Tucker Richards
Wolverhampton. *Born* Wolverhampton, 3 June, 1967. *Died* May 1992
Former Undefeated Midlands Area Heavyweight Champion (16.3-17.4) ht. 6'3"
Manager –
Pro. Debut 29 January, 1990

13.03.91 Steve Gee W PTS 6 Stoke
03.07.91 Herbie Hide L RSC 3 Brentwood
03.10.91 Paddy Reilly L PTS 6 Burton
21.11.91 Paddy Reilly L RSC 6 Burton
26.03.92 Henry Akinwande L RSC 2 Telford

Career: 10 contests, won 5, lost 5.

Warren Richards
Eltham. *Born* London, 10 July, 1964
Heavyweight (15.5-16.8) ht. 6'3"
Manager –
Pro. Debut 24 April, 1990

21.03.91 Joe Adams W CO 4 Meridan, USA
12.04.91 Johnny Wright W CO 2 Greenville, USA
30.03.92 John Westgarth DREW 6 Eltham
23.04.92 Newbirth Mukosi W CO 1 Eltham

Career: 7 contests, won 5, drew 1, lost 1.

Wayne Rigby
Manchester. *Born* Manchester, 19 July, 1973
S. Featherweight (9.3½-9.4) ht. 5'6"
Manager J. Doughty
Pro. Debut 27 February, 1992

27.02.92 Lee Fox L PTS 6 Liverpool
08.06.92 Leo Turner W PTS 6 Bradford

Career: 2 contests, won 1, lost 1.

Wayne Rigby Chris Bevan

Adrian Riley
Christchurch. *Born* Salford, 29 July, 1968
Welterweight (10.7½-10.10½) ht. 5'9"
Manager –
Pro. Debut 6 November, 1987

14.02.91 Trevor Ambrose L CO 6 Southampton
26.09.91 Marty Duke W PTS 6 Dunstable
24.10.91 Michael Oliver W PTS 6 Dunstable
09.11.91 Piero Severini L RSC 1 Campione d'Italia, Italy

Career: 19 contests, won 15, lost 4.

Robert Riley
Sheffield. *Born* Sheffield, 22 June, 1965
Welterweight (10.10-11.0) ht. 5'11¼"
Manager –
Pro. Debut 4 February, 1985

11.09.91 Andreas Panayi L PTS 6 Stoke
21.11.91 Peter Reid L PTS 6 Ilkeston
19.12.91 Charlie Moore L PTS 6 Oldham
25.03.92 Darren McInulty W PTS 6 Hinckley

Career: 8 contests, won 4, lost 4.

Stuart Rimmer
St Helens. *Born* St Helens, 22 April, 1971
L. Welterweight (9.9-9.13) ht. 5'6"
Manager R. Gray
Pro. Debut 13 February, 1990

12.02.91 Andrew Morgan L PTS 8 Wolverhampton
24.04.91 Steve Winstanley L PTS 6 Preston
04.06.91 Michael Ayers L CO 1 Bethnal Green
10.09.91 Shaun Cooper L RSC 2 Wolverhampton

Career: 15 contests, won 5, lost 10.

Darryl Ritchie (Jones)
Rhyl. *Born* Rhyl, 26 April, 1963
L. Heavyweight (12.6-12.7) ht. 6'0½"
Manager R. Gray
Pro. Debut 8 April, 1986

02.12.91 Tony Behan L RSC 1 Birmingham
24.03.92 Lee Archer L PTS 6 Wolverhampton

Career: 13 contests, won 6, drew 1, lost 6.

Brian Robb
Telford. *Born* Liverpool, 5 April, 1967
S. Featherweight (9.1-9.5) ht. 5'6"
Manager D. Gill
Pro. Debut 14 February, 1989

23.01.91 Jason Primera L RSC 7 Solihull
04.03.91 Pete Buckley L RSC 7 Birmingham
05.06.91 Pete Buckley L PTS 10 Wolverhampton *(Vacant Midlands Area S. Featherweight Title)*
29.08.91 Renny Edwards W PTS 6 Oakengates
31.10.91 Miguel Matthews DREW 6 Oakengates
05.12.91 Neil Leitch W CO 2 Oakengates
20.02.92 Pete Buckley L RSC 10 Oakengates *(Midlands Area S. Featherweight Title Challenge)*
26.03.92 Kelton McKenzie L RSC 4 Telford

Career: 15 contests, won 5, drew 1, lost 9.

Davy Robb
Telford. *Born* Liverpool, 14 August, 1964
L. Welterweight (9.13-10.2¼) ht. 5'10"
Manager D. Gill
Pro. Debut 9 November, 1987

31.10.91 Carl Hook W PTS 4 Oakengates
05.12.91 Tony Doyle W PTS 6 Oakengates
20.02.92 Brian Coleman W PTS 6 Oakengates
26.03.92 John O'Johnson W PTS 6 Telford

Career: 15 contests, won 10, lost 5.

Carl Roberts
Blackburn. *Born* Blackburn, 19 March, 1970
S. Featherweight (8.13½-9.3¼) ht. 5'7"
Manager J. Trickett
Pro. Debut 26 September, 1990

29.01.91 Derek Amory L PTS 4 Stockport
28.02.91 Des Gargano L PTS 6 Bury
03.04.91 Neil Leitch L RSC 6 Manchester
19.09.91 Colin Innes W PTS 4 Stockport
14.10.91 Kevin Lowe W PTS 6 Manchester
16.12.91 Robert Braddock W PTS 6 Manchester
10.03.92 Graham O'Malley L PTS 6 Bury

Career: 11 contests, won 6, lost 5.

Dewi Roberts
Dolgellau. *Born* Bangor, 11 September, 1968
Welterweight (9.13-10.7½) ht. 5'10"
Manager D. Davies
Pro. Debut 28 November, 1991

28.11.91 Gavin Lane L PTS 6 Evesham
11.02.92 Edward Lloyd L RSC 1 Cardiff
11.05.92 Nigel Burder W CO 3 Llanelli

Career: 3 contests, won 1, lost 2.

Pete Roberts
Hull. *Born* Liverpool, 15 July, 1967
L. Welterweight (9.7¼-10.2) ht. 5'4"
Manager M. Toomey
Pro. Debut 25 October, 1988

25.02.91 Peter Crook W RSC 6 Bradford
13.06.91 Wayne Windle L RSC 7 Hull *(Vacant Central Area Lightweight Title)*
07.10.91 John Smith W PTS 8 Liverpool
28.11.91 Dave Anderson L RSC 3 Glasgow
27.01.92 Kris McAdam L CO 2 Glasgow
29.04.92 Joey Moffat L RSC 3 Liverpool

Career: 14 contests, won 5, lost 9.

Mark Robertson
Kilwinning. *Born* Johnston, 30 April, 1965
Flyweight (8.2-8.3) ht. 5'3¼"
Manager J. Murray
Pro. Debut 21 September, 1987

31.01.92 Neil Armstrong L RSC 6 Glasgow
10.04.92 Louis Veitch W PTS 6 Glasgow

Career: 7 contests, won 2, drew 1, lost 4.

Andrew Robinson (White)
Birmingham. *Born* Birmingham, 6 November, 1965
Lightweight (9.1½-9.9) ht. 5'6"
Manager –
Pro. Debut 14 June, 1988

15.04.91 Finn McCool DREW 6 Leicester
13.05.91 Dean Bramhald W RTD 1 Birmingham
16.05.91 Craig Dermody L PTS 6 Liverpool
29.04.92 Lee Fox L PTS 6 Stoke

Career: 21 contests, won 6, drew 2, lost 13.

Billy Robinson
Hinckley. *Born* Desford, 3 October, 1963
L. Welterweight (10.2-10.4) ht. 5'8½"
Manager J. Griffin
Pro. Debut 1 October, 1991

01.10.91 Steve Bricknell W PTS 6 Bedworth
11.02.92 Mark Antony W RSC 5 Wolverhampton
25.03.92 Dave Lovell W PTS 6 Hinckley

Career: 3 contests, won 3.

Des Robinson
Manchester. *Born* Manchester, 5 January, 1969
Welterweight (10.7¼-10.10½) ht. 5'9"
Manager P. Martin
Pro. Debut 26 September, 1989

11.02.91 Willie Beattie L PTS 8 Glasgow
19.03.91 Lindon Scarlett L RSC 4 Birmingham
17.10.91 Gary Logan L PTS 8 Southwark

Career: 16 contests, won 10, drew 1, lost 5.

Jamie Robinson

West Ham. *Born* London, 12 September, 1968
L. Middleweight (10.13-11.4) ht. 5'9"
Manager J. Tibbs
Pro. Debut 17 August, 1990

23.10.91 Dave Whittle W RSC 4 Bethnal Green
13.11.91 Michael Oliver W PTS 6 Bethnal Green
11.02.92 Julian Eavis W PTS 6 Barking
02.04.92 Mark Jay W PTS 6 Basildon

Career: 6 contests, won 5, lost 1.

Jamie Robinson Les Clark

Steve Robinson

Cardiff. *Born* Cardiff, 13 December, 1968
Welsh Featherweight Champion (8.13-9.1) ht. 5'8"
Manager –
Pro. Debut 1 March, 1989

24.04.91 Russell Davison W RTD 6 Preston
28.05.91 Colin Lynch W RSC 6 Cardiff
18.07.91 Peter Harris W PTS 10 Cardiff *(Welsh Featherweight Title Challenge)*
31.01.92 Henry Armstrong L PTS 6 Manchester
11.05.92 Neil Haddock L PTS 10 Llanelli *(Vacant Welsh S. Featherweight Title)*

Career: 18 contests, won 9, drew 1, lost 8.

Tony Robinson

Blyth. *Born* Blyth, 22 March, 1967
Lightweight (9.10) ht. 5'6"
Manager T. Conroy
Pro. Debut 9 December, 1991

09.12.91 Geoff Lawson W RSC 1 Bradford

Career: 1 contest, won 1.

Martin Rosamond

Southampton. *Born* Cyprus, 10 March, 1969
L. Middleweight (10.10-11.7) ht. 5'10"
Manager –
Pro. Debut 2 March, 1989

21.02.91 Rob Pitters L RSC 2 Walsall
12.04.91 Shamus Casey L PTS 6 Willenhall
23.04.91 Barry Messam L PTS 6 Evesham
08.05.91 Marty Duke DREW 8 Millwall
23.05.91 Mike Morrison W PTS 6 Southampton
04.06.91 Adrian Strachan L PTS 6 Bethnal Green
03.07.91 Kevin Sheeran L CO 1 Reading
24.09.91 Adrian Strachan L PTS 6 Basildon
20.01.92 Lee Ferrie L RSC 2 Coventry

Career: 21 contests, won 7, drew 1, lost 13.

(Clive) Claude Rossi (Fearon)

Derby. *Born* London, 3 April, 1962
Welterweight (10.7¾) ht. 5'8"
Manager –
Pro. Debut 16 May, 1983

09.12.91 Howard Clarke L RSC 3 Brierley Hill

Career: 27 contests, won 8, drew 3, lost 16.

Jason Rowe

Leeds. *Born* Huddersfield, 5 May, 1967
Former Central Area L. Middleweight Champion (10.9-11.2) ht. 5'8"
Manager T. Callighan
Pro. Debut 26 September, 1987

09.04.91 Damien Denny W CO 7 Mayfair
03.07.91 Tony Velinor L RSC 1 Brentwood
07.11.91 Shaun Cummins L RSC 2 Peterborough
19.12.91 Delroy Waul L RSC 4 Oldham

Career: 14 contests, won 7, lost 7.

Jason Rowland

West Ham. *Born* London, 6 August, 1970
L. Welterweight (10.1-10.3½) ht. 5'9¼"
Manager J. Tibbs
Pro. Debut 19 September, 1989

12.02.91 Vaughan Carnegie W PTS 6 Basildon
07.03.91 Vaughan Carnegie W CO 2 Basildon
11.12.91 Brian Cullen W RSC 4 Basildon
30.04.92 Steve Pollard W RSC 2 Kensington

Career: 9 contests, won 9.

Roy Rowland

West Ham. *Born* London, 19 May, 1967
Welterweight (10.7½-10.10) ht. 5'10"
Manager J. Tibbs
Pro. Debut 29 October, 1986

12.02.91 Paul Lynch L RTD 4 Basildon
06.06.91 Mark Kelly W RSC 4 Barking
02.10.91 Peter Eubank W PTS 8 Barking
25.03.92 Humphrey Harrison W CO 7 Dagenham

Career: 21 contests, won 19, lost 2.

Marc Rowley

Nuneaton. *Born* Chatham, 3 October, 1972
S. Middleweight (11.7-12.8) ht. 5'11½"
Manager J. Griffin
Pro. Debut 16 September, 1991

16.09.91 Dave Hall L PTS 6 Cleethorpes
08.10.91 Dave Hall L PTS 6 Wolverhampton
07.11.91 Mark Hale L PTS 6 Peterborough
02.12.91 Andy Manning L PTS 6 Liverpool
11.12.91 Brian McGloin L PTS 6 Leicester
15.01.92 Danny Walker W CO 5 Stoke
25.03.92 Mark Hale L PTS 6 Hinckley
18.05.92 Lee Archer L PTS 6 Bardon

Career: 8 contests, won 1, lost 7.

Jess Rundan

Plymouth. *Born* Redruth, 17 October, 1961
L. Welterweight (9.13-10.2½) ht. 5'8"
Manager N. Christian
Pro. Debut 10 October, 1984

20.11.91 Seth Jones L CO 4 Cardiff
30.04.92 Ron Shinkwin L RSC 1 Watford

Career: 14 contests, won 2, drew 1, lost 11.

Mike Russell

Plymouth. *Born* Plymouth, 12 July, 1967
L. Middleweight (11.0-11.7) ht. 5'7½"
Manager N. Christian
Pro. Debut 19 May, 1986

20.11.91 Michael Smyth L RSC 3 Cardiff
12.02.92 Danny Shinkwin L PTS 6 Watford
25.02.92 Tony McCarthy L PTS 6 Crystal Palace
02.04.92 Kevin Sheeran L RSC 2 Basildon

Career: 38 contests, won 6, drew 1, lost 30, no contest 1.

Brendan Ryan

Nottingham. *Born* Nottingham, 2 November, 1970
L. Welterweight (10.3-10.4) ht. 5'9¼"
Manager J. Griffin
Pro. Debut 6 March, 1989

24.04.91 Richard Joyce L PTS 8 Stoke
14.05.92 Carl Wright L PTS 4 Liverpool
16.06.92 Bernard Paul L CO 6 Dagenham

Career: 25 contests, won 11, drew 4, lost 10.

Paul Ryan

Hackney. *Born* South Ockenham, 2 February, 1965
Lightweight (9.10-9.13½) ht. 5'8"
Manager T. Haynes
Pro. Debut 26 September, 1991

26.09.91 Chris Mylan W PTS 6 Dunstable
18.01.92 Alex Sterling W RSC 4 Kensington
25.03.92 Michael Clynch W RSC 4 Dagenham
16.05.92 Greg Egbuniwe W RSC 4 Muswell Hill

Career: 4 contests, won 4.

Ricky Sackfield

Salford. *Born* Birmingham, 11 April, 1967
L. Welterweight (10.1-10.7) ht. 5'7"
Manager J. Trickett
Pro. Debut 30 April, 1991

30.04.91 Willie Yeardsley W PTS 4 Stockport
19.09.91 Seth Jones W RSC 1 Stockport
21.10.91 Rob Stewart L PTS 6 Bury
21.01.92 David Thompson W CO 1 Stockport
03.02.92 Scott Doyle W PTS 6 Manchester
09.03.92 John O'Johnson L PTS 6 Manchester
31.03.92 Carl Wright L RSC 1 Stockport

Career: 7 contests, won 4, lost 3.

Chris Saunders

Barnsley. *Born* Barnsley, 15 August, 1969
L. Welterweight (9.10-10.7) ht. 5'8"
Manager B. Ingle
Pro. Debut 22 February, 1990

05.03.91 Rocky Ferrari L PTS 4 Glasgow
19.03.91 Richard Woolgar W RSC 3 Leicester
26.03.91 Felix Kelly L PTS 6 Bethnal Green
17.04.91 Billy Schwer L RSC 1 Kensington
16.05.91 Richard Burton L PTS 6 Liverpool
06.06.91 Mark Tibbs W RSC 6 Barking
30.06.91 Billy Schwer L RSC 3 Southwark
01.08.91 James Jiora W PTS 6 Dewsbury
03.10.91 Gary Flear L PTS 6 Burton
24.10.91 Ron Shinkwin W PTS 6 Dunstable
21.11.91 Jason Matthews L RSC 4 Burton
30.01.92 John O'Johnson L PTS 6 Southampton
11.02.92 Eddie King W RSC 4 Wolverhampton
27.02.92 Richard Burton L PTS 10 Liverpool *(Vacant Central Area L. Welterweight Title)*

Career: 18 contests, won 8, lost 10.

Lindon Scarlett

Dudley. *Born* Dudley, 11 January, 1967
Welterweight (10.6½-10.9½) ht. 5'10"
Manager R. Browne
Pro. Debut 22 April, 1987

19.03.91 Des Robinson W RSC 4 Birmingham
24.10.91 Razor Addo W PTS 8 Bayswater
22.01.92 Kelvin Mortimer W RSC 1 Solihull
08.02.92 Javier Castillejos L PTS 8 Madrid, Spain
23.05.92 Chris Peters DREW 8 Birmingham

Career: 18 contests, won 10, drew 2, lost 6.

Billy Schwer

Luton. *Born* Luton, 12 April, 1969
Lightweight (9.7¾-9.9¾) ht. 5'8½"
Manager M. Duff
Pro. Debut 4 October, 1990

16.01.91 Dave Jenkins W PTS 6 Kensington
07.02.91 John Smith W RSC 2 Watford
06.03.91 Chubby Martin W RSC 3 Wembley
04.04.91 Andy Robins W RSC 2 Watford
17.04.91 Chris Saunders W RSC 1 Kensington
02.05.91 Karl Taylor W RSC 2 Northampton
30.06.91 Chris Saunders W RSC 3 Southwark
11.09.91 Tony Foster W PTS 8 Hammersmith
26.09.91 Felix Kelly W RSC 2 Dunstable
24.10.91 Patrick Kamy W CO 1 Dunstable
20.11.91 Marcel Herbert W PTS 8 Kensington
12.02.92 Tomas Quinones W CO 8 Wembley
25.03.92 Bobby Brewer W RSC 4 Kensington

Career: 16 contests, won 16.

Bruce Scott

Hackney. *Born* Jamaica, 16 August, 1969
Cruiserweight (12.11½-13.11) ht. 5'9½"
Manager M. Duff
Pro. Debut 25 April, 1991

25.04.91 Mark Bowen L PTS 6 Mayfair
16.09.91 Randy B. Powell W RSC 5 Mayfair
21.11.91 Steve Osborne W PTS 6 Burton
27.04.92 John Kaighin W CO 4 Mayfair

Career: 4 contests, won 3, lost 1.

Steve Scott

Chorley. *Born* Fulwood, 20 January, 1966
L. Middleweight (10.8-10.11) ht. 5'11"
Manager J. McMillan
Pro. Debut 4 March, 1992

04.03.92 Allan Grainger L PTS 6 Glasgow
26.03.92 Rob Stevenson L PTS 6 Hull

Career: 2 contests, lost 2.

Greg Scott-Briggs

Chesterfield. *Born* Swaziland, 6 February, 1966
L. Heavyweight (12.2-12.10) ht. 6'1"
Manager M. Shinfield
Pro. Debut 4 February, 1992

04.02.92 Mark McBiane W PTS 6 Alfreton
03.03.92 Tony Colclough W RSC 2 Cradley Heath
30.03.92 Carl Smallwood L PTS 6 Coventry
27.04.92 Richard Atkinson L PTS 6 Bradford
28.05.92 Steve Walton W PTS 6 Gosforth
04.06.92 Joe Frater L PTS 6 Cleethorpes

Career: 6 contests, won 3, lost 3.

Moses Sentamu

Tooting. *Born* Uganda, 6 December, 1971
Lightweight (9.8½-9.10) ht. 5'8"
Manager M. Barrett
Pro. Debut 24 October, 1991

24.10.91 Barry Glanister W PTS 6 Bayswater
26.11.91 Razza Campbell W RSC 2 Wolverhampton

Career: 2 contests, won 2.

Muhammad Shaffique

Huddersfield. *Born* Huddersfield, 19 February, 1969
S. Featherweight (9.4½) ht. 5'9"
Manager T. Callighan
Pro. Debut 7 February, 1989

02.10.91 Elvis Parsley L CO 1 Solihull

Career: 7 contests, won 4, lost 3.

Kevin Sheeran

Crawley. *Born* Redhill, 10 August, 1971
L. Middleweight (10.13½-11.5) ht. 6'0"
Manager F. Warren
Pro. Debut 5 March, 1991

05.03.91 Richard Okumu L RSC 2 Millwall
08.05.91 Cliff Churchward W PTS 6 Millwall
22.05.91 Stuart Good W PTS 6 Millwall
03.07.91 Martin Rosamond W CO 1 Reading
04.09.91 Clive Dixon W RSC 4 Bethnal Green
29.10.91 Dave Hall W RSC 1 Kensington
20.11.91 Horace Fleary W RSC 2 Cardiff
02.04.92 Mike Russell W RSC 2 Basildon
30.04.92 Tracy Jocelyn W RSC 3 Kensington

Career: 9 contests, won 8, lost 1.

Kevin Sheeran Les Clark

(Rufus) Rocky Shelly (Davies)

Mansfield. *Born* Oldham, 18 August, 1970
Cruiserweight (13.3) ht. 5'10½"
Manager B. Ingle
Pro. Debut 9 December, 1991

09.12.91 Stuart Fleet W RSC 1 Cleethorpes
26.12.91 Stefan Angehrn L CO 2 Berne, Switzerland
05.03.92 Des Vaughan L RSC 5 Battersea

Career: 3 contests, won 1, lost 2.

Charles Shepherd

Carlisle. *Born* Burnley, 28 June, 1970
Lightweight (9.9) ht. 5'4"
Manager N. Basso
Pro. Debut 28 October, 1991

28.10.91 Chris Aston W PTS 6 Leicester
31.01.92 Alan McDowall L RSC 3 Glasgow
18.05.92 Mark Legg W PTS 6 Marton

Career: 3 contests, won 2, lost 1.

Glyn Shepherd

Carlisle. *Born* Whiston, 30 May, 1963
Bantamweight (8.7-8.12) ht. 5'4"
Manager N. Basso
Pro. Debut 7 October, 1991

07.10.91 Robert Braddock DREW 6 Bradford
28.10.91 Tony Smith W PTS 6 Leicester
20.01.92 David Ramsden L RSC 1 Bradford
18.05.92 Dave Campbell L RSC 1 Marton

Career: 4 contests, won 1, drew 1, lost 2.

Wayne Shepherd

Carlisle. *Born* Whiston, 3 June, 1959
Welterweight (10.7½-10.10) ht. 5'6"
Manager N. Basso
Pro. Debut 7 October, 1991

07.10.91 Benji Joseph W PTS 6 Bradford
28.10.91 Noel Henry W PTS 6 Leicester
16.12.91 Dave Maj DREW 6 Manchester
03.02.92 Dave Maj L PTS 6 Manchester
30.03.92 Hughie Davey L PTS 6 Bradford
18.05.92 Dave Whittle W PTS 6 Marton

Career: 6 contests, won 3, drew 1, lost 2.

Shane Sheridan

Derby. *Born* Reading, 5 November, 1968
L. Welterweight (10.1-10.3) ht. 5'9"
Manager M. Shinfield
Pro. Debut 28 March, 1991

28.03.91 David Thompson W CO 5 Alfreton
04.07.91 Dean Bramhald W PTS 6 Alfreton
21.11.91 Scott Doyle L PTS 6 Ilkeston

Career: 3 contests, won 2, lost 1.

Danny Shinkwin

Boreham Wood. *Born* Watford, 25 November, 1961
Welterweight (10.8-11.1½) ht. 5'9¼"
Manager J. Barclay
Pro. Debut 1 April, 1982

16.05.91 Marty Duke W PTS 6 Battersea
12.11.91 Kevin Adamson L RSC 4 Milton Keynes
12.02.92 Mike Russell W PTS 6 Watford
30.04.92 Cliff Churchward L PTS 6 Watford

Career: 16 contests, won 6, lost 10.

Ron Shinkwin

Boreham Wood. *Born* Watford, 27 November, 1964
L. Welterweight (9.13-10.4¾) ht. 5'11"
Manager J. Barclay
Pro. Debut 6 May, 1982

26.09.91 Carl Hook W PTS 8 Dunstable
24.10.91 Chris Saunders L PTS 6 Dunstable
04.12.91 Dean Bramhald L PTS 8 Stoke
16.12.91 Danny Cooper L PTS 6 Southampton
30.01.92 Dean Bramhald W PTS 6 Southampton
24.03.92 Ray Newby L PTS 8 Wolverhampton
30.04.92 Jess Rundan W RSC 1 Watford
18.05.92 Ray Newby L RSC 5 Bardon

Career: 37 contests, won 15, drew 3, lost 19.

Shaun Shinkwin

Boreham Wood. *Born* Watford 30 November, 1962
Lightweight (9.9) ht. 5'9½"
Manager J. Barclay
Pro. Debut 1 April, 1982

12.02.92 Greg Egbuniwe L DIS 1 Watford

Career: 16 contests, won 8, drew 1, lost 7.

Tony Silkstone

Leeds. *Born* Leeds, 2 March, 1968
Featherweight (8.13¾-9.3) ht. 5'5"
Manager M. Duff
Pro. Debut 11 April, 1990

21.03.91 Tony Falcone W PTS 6 Dewsbury
09.05.91 Alan Smith W PTS 6 Leeds
13.06.91 Miguel Matthews W PTS 6 Hull
01.08.91 Dave Buxton W PTS 6 Dewsbury
30.10.91 Renny Edwards W PTS 6 Leeds
08.04.92 Edward Cook W PTS 8 Leeds

Career: 11 contests, won 11.

Kevin Simons

Swansea. *Born* Swansea, 8 November, 1968
S. Featherweight (9.5) ht. 5'6"
Manager C. Breen
Pro. Debut 22 January, 1992

22.01.92 Jason Lepre L PTS 6 Cardiff

Career: 1 contest, lost 1.

Jas Dip Singh

West Ham. *Born* Romford, 12 June, 1965
S. Featherweight (9.4) ht. 5'5"
Manager B. Lynch
Pro. Debut 12 February, 1992

12.02.92 Steve Patton L RSC 1 Watford

Career: 1 contest, lost 1.

Colin Sinnott

Preston. *Born* Preston, 10 September, 1965
L. Welterweight (9.13½-10.4) ht. 5'8"
Manager –
Pro. Debut 26 March, 1990

28.01.91 Dave Kettlewell W RSC 3 Bradford
21.02.91 Trevor Meikle L PTS 6 Leeds
22.04.91 J. B. Chadwick W CO 3 Bradford
30.05.91 Mark Ramsey L PTS 6 Birmingham
08.10.91 Dean Bramhald W PTS 8 Wolverhampton
21.10.91 Dean Bramhald L PTS 6 Cleethorpes
18.11.91 Kris McAdam L PTS 6 Glasgow

Career: 12 contests, won 6, lost 6.

Roy Skeldon

Tipton. *Born* Tipton, 15 December, 1952
Midlands Area L. Heavyweight Champion (12.7) ht. 5'9½"
Manager –
Pro. Debut 20 September, 1972

25.07.91 Crawford Ashley L RSC 7 Dudley
(Vacant British L. Heavyweight Title)

Career: 38 contests, won 19, drew 2, lost 17.

Carl Smallwood

Atherstone. *Born* Nuneaton, 15 April, 1973
L. Heavyweight (12.7-12.8) ht. 6'1¼"
Manager R. Gray
Pro. Debut 30 March, 1992

30.03.92 Greg Scott-Briggs W PTS 6 Coventry
28.04.92 Lee Archer W PTS 6 Wolverhampton

Career: 2 contests, won 2.

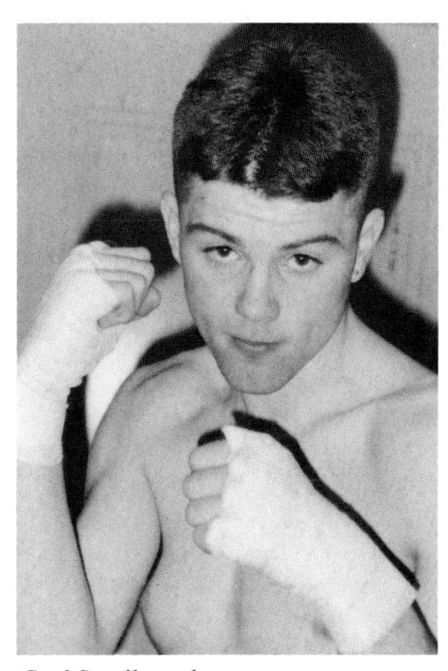

Carl Smallwood Les Clark

Alan Smith

Swansea. *Born* Pembroke Dock, 15 September, 1964
Featherweight (8.11-9.6) ht. 5'7"
Manager D. Davies
Pro. Debut 13 March, 1991

13.03.91 Mitchell Barney W PTS 6 Stoke
22.04.91 Tony Falcone W RSC 5 Mayfair
09.05.91 Tony Silkstone L PTS 6 Leeds
30.05.91 Tony Falcone L PTS 6 Mayfair
04.09.91 Eunan Devenney L CO 1 Bethnal Green
27.02.92 John White L RSC 1 Liverpool

Career: 6 contests, won 2, lost 4.

Jacob Smith

Darlington. *Born* Darlington, 30 January, 1974
Bantamweight (8.7) ht. 5'6¼"
Manager M. Duff
Pro. Debut 8 April, 1992

08.04.92 Andrew Bloomer W PTS 6 Leeds

Career: 1 contest, won 1.

John Smith

Liverpool. *Born* Liverpool, 13 October, 1959
L. Welterweight (9.12½-10.6) ht. 5'9"
Manager –
Pro. Debut 26 June, 1986

21.01.91 Kris McAdam L PTS 6 Glasgow
07.02.91 Billy Schwer L RSC 2 Watford
26.03.91 Andrew Morgan L RSC 4 Wolverhampton
24.04.91 Andrew Morgan L PTS 6 Aberavon
16.05.91 Kevin Toomey L PTS 6 Liverpool
13.06.91 Kevin Toomey L PTS 6 Hull
25.07.91 Robert McCracken L RTD 1 Dudley
07.10.91 Pete Roberts L PTS 8 Liverpool
23.10.91 Dean Hollington L PTS 6 Bethnal Green
12.11.91 Mark Elliot L PTS 6 Wolverhampton
21.11.91 Richard Burton L PTS 6 Burton
02.12.91 Mike Calderwood DREW 8 Liverpool
19.12.91 Richard Burton L PTS 6 Oldham
01.02.92 George Scott L RSC 3 Birmingham
03.03.92 Paul Charters L PTS 8 Houghton le Spring
12.05.92 Ross Hale L CO 1 Crystal Palace

Career: 47 contests, won 8, drew 3, lost 36.

Martin Smith

Tottenham. *Born* London, 16 August, 1967
L. Middleweight (10.13½-11.4) ht. 6'0"
Manager B. Ingle
Pro. Debut 24 September, 1987

12.02.91 Rex Kortram W PTS 6 Rotterdam, Holland
19.03.91 Shaun Cummins DREW 8 Leicester
07.05.91 Danny Quigg W PTS 6 Glasgow
01.10.91 Mike Phillips W PTS 6 Sheffield
28.10.91 Gilbert Hallie DREW 8 Arnhem, Holland
10.01.92 Said Skouma W PTS 8 Vitrolles, France
14.04.92 Dave Owens W PTS 6 Mansfield
08.05.92 Freddie Demeulenaere DREW 8 Waregem, Belgium

Career: 23 contests, won 14, drew 5, lost 3, no contest 1.

Neil Smith

Leicester. *Born* Leicester, 15 January, 1972
S. Featherweight (9.2-9.6½) ht. 6'1½"
Manager K. Squires
Pro. Debut 13 December, 1990

06.02.91 Dennis Adams L PTS 6 Bethnal Green
14.03.91 John Naylor W RSC 6 Middleton
20.05.91 Elvis Parsley W RSC 5 Leicester
11.06.91 Lee Fox W PTS 6 Leicester
05.11.91 Neil Leitch W RSC 1 Leicester
04.02.92 Harry Escott L PTS 8 Alfreton

Career: 7 contests, won 4, lost 3.

Paul Smith

Sheffield. *Born* Sheffield, 14 July, 1960
Middleweight (11.6-11.10) ht. 5'10"
Manager –
Pro. Debut 3 October, 1983

29.01.91 Marty Duke W PTS 6 Wisbech
06.03.91 Benji Good L PTS 6 Croydon
19.03.91 Paul Busby L PTS 6 Leicester
16.04.91 Chris Richards DREW 6 Nottingham
29.08.91 Neville Brown L RSC 3 Oakengates
28.04.92 Andrew Flute L RSC 5 Wolverhampton

Career: 33 contests, won 12, drew 3, lost 18.

Terry Smith

Kettering. *Born* Poplar, 6 November, 1964
Lightweight (9.8) ht. 5'7"
Manager C. Hall
Pro. Debut 29 April, 1992

29.04.92 Floyd Churchill L RSC 2 Liverpool

Career: 1 contest, lost 1.

Tommy Smith

Darlington. *Born* Darlington, 18 December, 1970
S. Featherweight (9.2½-9.8½) ht. 5'7"
Manager G. Bowes
Pro. Debut 10 December, 1990

16.02.91 Johnny Patterson W PTS 6 Thornaby
06.04.91 Paul Wynn W PTS 6 Darlington
22.10.91 Kevin Lowe W RSC 4 Hartlepool
12.12.91 Colin Innes W PTS 6 Hartlepool
28.05.92 Colin Innes W PTS 6 Gosforth

Career: 6 contests, won 5, lost 1.

Tony Smith

Burnley. *Born* Burnley, 4 May, 1969
Bantamweight (8.8-9.6) ht. 5'5"
Manager N. Basso
Pro. Debut 18 May, 1987

16.01.91 Des Gargano L PTS 6 Stoke
02.03.91 Colin Innes L PTS 6 Darlington
05.03.91 Neil Parry DREW 6 Leicester
18.03.91 Gary White L PTS 6 Manchester
07.05.91 Stevie Woods L RTD 2 Glasgow
10.06.91 Robert Braddock DREW 6 Manchester
20.06.91 Neil Parry L PTS 6 Liverpool
28.10.91 Glyn Shepherd L PTS 6 Leicester
18.11.91 Chris Jickells L RSC 4 Manchester
01.06.92 Craig Murray L RSC 2 Manchester

Career: 38 contests, won 9, drew 4, lost 25.

Michael Smyth

Barry. *Born* Caerphilly, 22 February, 1970
Welterweight (10.0-10.9¼) ht. 5'9¾"
Manager D. Gardiner
Pro. Debut 2 May, 1991

02.05.91 Carl Brasier W RSC 2 Kensington
28.05.91 Rick North W RSC 1 Cardiff
18.07.91 Mike Morrison W RSC 2 Cardiff
03.09.91 Julian Eavis W PTS 6 Cardiff
20.11.91 Mike Russell W RSC 3 Cardiff
17.12.91 Julian Eavis W PTS 6 Cardiff
19.05.92 Ojay Abrahams W PTS 6 Cardiff

Career: 7 contests, won 7.

Michael Smyth Les Clark

Robert Smyth

Newport. *Born* Newport, 11 January, 1966
S. Featherweight (9.5-9.9¼) ht. 5'7"
Manager –
Pro. Debut 10 February, 1987

18.02.91 Rick Bushell L PTS 6 Mayfair
10.04.91 Trevor Royal W PTS 6 Newport
18.07.91 Barrie Kelley DREW 6 Cardiff

Career: 10 contests, won 5, drew 1, lost 4.

Lee Soar

Barnsley. *Born* Barnsley, 12 October, 1970
L. Welterweight (10.8-11.3) ht. 5'10"
Manager K. Tate
Pro. Debut 25 November, 1991

25.11.91 Mark Broome W PTS 6 Cleethorpes
28.01.92 Steve Bricknell W PTS 6 Piccadilly

Career: 2 contests, won 2.

Phil Soundy

Benfleet. *Born* Benfleet, 24 October, 1966
Cruiserweight (13.1-13.6½) ht. 5'11½"
Manager T. Lawless
Pro. Debut 4 October, 1989

16.01.91 Chris Coughlan W PTS 6 Kensington
12.02.91 Gus Mendes W RSC 3 Basildon
07.03.91 Terry Duffus W RSC 2 Basildon
24.04.91 Steve Yorath L PTS 6 Basildon
11.09.91 Gus Mendes L RSC 3 Hammersmith
12.02.92 Steve Osborne W PTS 6 Wembley
22.04.92 Lee Prudden W RSC 5 Wembley
13.05.92 Tony Booth L PTS 6 Kensington

Career: 17 contests, won 14, lost 3.

(Mick) Art Stacey

Leeds. *Born* Leeds, 26 September, 1964
Cruiserweight (12.11-13.7) ht. 6'0½"
Manager K. Tate
Pro. Debut 9 October, 1990

21.02.91 Tony Lawrence W PTS 6 Leeds
18.03.91 Paul Gearon W RSC 1 Derby
16.04.91 Steve Osborne DREW 6 Nottingham
03.06.91 Dennis Afflick W PTS 6 Glasgow
11.11.91 Steve Osborne W PTS 6 Bradford
21.11.91 Gil Lewis L RSC 4 Stafford
20.01.92 John Pierre W PTS 8 Bradford

Career: 10 contests, won 7, drew 2, lost 1.

Art Stacey Chris Bevan

Warren Stephens

Birmingham. *Born* Birmingham, 18 May, 1970
L. Middleweight (11.0-11.2) ht. 6'0"
Manager N. Nobbs
Pro. Debut 4 April, 1992

04.04.92 John Duckworth L RSC 5 Cleethorpes
21.05.92 Bullit Andrews L PTS 6 Cradley Heath

Career: 2 contests, lost 2.

Ronnie Stephenson

Doncaster. *Born* Doncaster, 18 November, 1960
Featherweight (9.0-9.2) ht. 5'8"
Manager –
Pro. Debut 22 January, 1986

21.10.91 Phil Lashley W PTS 6 Cleethorpes
21.11.91 Phil Lashley W PTS 6 Stafford
02.12.91 Chris Lyons W PTS 6 Birmingham
09.12.91 Chris Lyons W PTS 6 Cleethorpes
15.01.92 Chris Jickells W PTS 6 Stoke
30.03.92 Mark Hargreaves W PTS 6 Coventry

Career: 47 contests, won 20, drew 4, lost 23.

Alex Sterling

Tottenham. *Born* London, 21 December, 1969
Lightweight (9.11-9.12¾) ht. 5'7½"
Manager –
Pro. Debut 13 March, 1989

14.11.91 Chubby Martin L RSC 5 Bayswater
18.01.92 Paul Ryan L RSC 4 Kensington
07.04.92 Greg Egbuniwe L RSC 4 Southend

Career: 7 contests, won 1, lost 6.

Rob Stevenson

Hull. *Born* Hull, 16 March, 1971
L. Middleweight (10.10-11.2) ht. 5'9"
Manager M. Toomey
Pro. Debut 28 November, 1991

28.11.91 Matt Mowatt L PTS 6 Hull
26.03.92 Steve Scott W PTS 6 Hull
04.04.92 Chris Mulcahy L PTS 8 Cleethorpes
29.04.92 Alan Williams W PTS 6 Liverpool
01.06.92 Chris Mulcahy L PTS 6 Manchester

Career: 5 contests, won 2, lost 3.

Rob Stewart

Darwen. *Born* Blackburn, 17 January, 1965
L. Welterweight (10.0-10.2½) ht. 5'8¼"
Manager J. McMillan
Pro. Debut 14 October, 1991

14.10.91 Gary Pagden W PTS 6 Manchester
21.10.91 Ricky Sackfield W PTS 6 Bury
04.12.91 Dean Carr W RTD 5 Stoke
21.01.92 Chris Aston W RSC 4 Stockport
24.02.92 Tony Banks DREW 6 Bradford
04.03.92 Alan Peacock DREW 8 Glasgow
31.03.92 Mike Calderwood W PTS 4 Stockport

Career: 7 contests, won 5, drew 2.

Steve Stewart

Clapham. *Born* Luton, 10 August, 1967
Heavyweight (16.7) ht. 6'5"
Manager M. Hill
Pro. Debut 17 February, 1992

17.02.92 Damien Caesar L RSC 5 Mayfair
30.03.92 Wayne Llewelyn L RSC 4 Eltham

Career: 2 contests, lost 2.

Bradley Stone

Canning Town. *Born* Mile End, 27 May, 1970
Featherweight (8.12½-9.2) ht. 5'5¼"
Manager J. Tibbs
Pro. Debut 6 March, 1990

12.02.91 Stewart Fishermac W PTS 6 Basildon
07.03.91 Miguel Matthews W RSC 4 Basildon
25.04.91 Miguel Matthews W PTS 6 Basildon
02.10.91 Andrew Bloomer W PTS 6 Barking
02.04.92 Colin Lynch W RSC 3 Basildon
16.05.92 Andrew Bloomer W PTS 6 Muswell Hill

Career: 12 contests, won 11, drew 1.

Sammy Storey

Belfast. *Born* Belfast, 9 August, 1963
Former British S. Middleweight Champion (11.13½-12.2¾) ht. 6'0"
Manager –
Pro. Debut 3 December, 1985

31.05.91 Saldi Ali L PTS 8 Berlin, Germany
07.09.91 Johnny Melfah W PTS 8 Belfast
13.11.91 Karl Barwise W PTS 6 Belfast
25.04.92 Nigel Rafferty W RSC 3 Belfast

Career: 21 contests, won 18, lost 3.

Warren Stowe

Burnley. *Born* Burnley, 30 January, 1965
L. Middleweight (11.0¼-11.8) ht. 5'8"
Manager J. Doughty
Pro. Debut 21 October, 1991

21.10.91 Matt Mowatt W RSC 3 Bury
07.12.91 Kenny Tyson W RSC 6 Manchester
03.02.92 Robert Peel W PTS 6 Manchester
10.03.92 B. K. Bennett W PTS 6 Bury
25.04.92 David Radford W RSC 3 Manchester
04.06.92 Rob Pitters W PTS 8 Burnley

Career: 6 contests, won 6.

Warren Stowe Chris Bevan

Adrian Strachan

Richmond. *Born* Bromley, 8 April, 1966
L. Middleweight (10.12¾-11.3) ht. 5'10"
Manager B. Hearn
Pro. Debut 4 June, 1991

04.06.91 Martin Rosamond W PTS 6 Bethnal Green
24.09.91 Martin Rosamond W PTS 6 Basildon
01.10.91 Gary Pemberton W RSC 2 Sheffield
19.11.91 Tracy Jocelyn W PTS 6 Norwich
26.11.91 Chris Richards W PTS 6 Bethnal Green
12.05.92 Horace Fleary W PTS 6 Crystal Palace

Career: 6 contests, won 6.

Chad Strong

Leicester. *Born* Leicester, 26 September, 1970
Middleweight (11.0-11.5) ht. 5'11½"
Manager –
Pro. Debut 20 May, 1991

20.05.91 Mick Reid W PTS 6 Leicester
05.11.91 Kenny Tyson L PTS 6 Leicester
18.05.92 Brian McGloin DREW 6 Bardon

Career: 3 contests, won 1, drew 1, lost 1.

Ian Strudwick

Hockley. *Born* Orsett, 1 April, 1964
Southern Area S. Middleweight Champion (11.7½-12.0) ht. 5'10½"
Manager –
Pro. Debut 26 October, 1988

03.04.91 Stan King W RSC 8 Bethnal Green
24.09.91 Fidel Castro L RSC 6 Basildon *(Vacant British S. Middleweight Title)*
11.12.91 Ray Webb W CO 8 Basildon *(Vacant Southern Area S. Middleweight Title)*
11.03.92 Ali Forbes W PTS 10 Solihull *(Southern Area S. Middleweight Title Defence)*
23.05.92 Chris Pyatt L PTS 10 Birmingham

Career: 18 contests, won 14, lost 4.

Richard Swallow

Northampton. *Born* Northampton, 10 February, 1970
L. Welterweight (10.1-10.4) ht. 5'8"
Manager R. Gray
Pro. Debut 15 October, 1990

14.02.91 Dave Fallon W RSC 4 Southampton
06.03.91 Carl Brasier W PTS 6 Croydon
02.05.91 Mike Morrison W PTS 6 Northampton
24.03.92 Dean Bramhald W PTS 8 Wolverhampton
06.04.92 Dean Bramhald W PTS 6 Northampton
29.04.92 Chris Aston W RSC 3 Solihull

Career: 7 contests, won 6, lost 1.

Tony Swift

Birmingham. *Born* Solihull, 29 June, 1968
Welterweight (9.13-10.5½) ht. 5'10½"
Manager W. Swift
Pro. Debut 25 September, 1986

19.04.91 Gary Barron DREW 8 Peterborough
12.11.91 Carlos Chase W PTS 6 Milton Keynes
03.03.92 Steve McGovern W RSC 4 Cradley Heath
10.04.92 Willie Beattie W PTS 10 Glasgow *(Elim. British Welterweight Title)*

Career: 26 contests, won 20, drew 3, lost 3.

Karl Taylor

Birmingham. *Born* Birmingham, 5 January, 1966
Lightweight (9.7-10.3) ht. 5'5"
Manager –
Pro. Debut 18 March, 1987

16.01.91 Wayne Windle W PTS 8 Stoke
02.05.91 Billy Schwer L RSC 2 Northampton
25.07.91 Peter Till L RSC 4 Dudley *(Midlands Area Lightweight Title Challenge)*
24.02.92 Charlie Kane L PTS 8 Glasgow
28.04.92 Richard Woolgar W PTS 6 Wolverhampton
29.05.92 Alan McDowall L PTS 6 Glasgow

Career: 18 contests, won 6, drew 1, lost 11.

Wayne Taylor

Birmingham. *Born* Birmingham, 12 July, 1968
L. Welterweight (9.11½) ht. 5'8"
Manager E. Cashmore
Pro. Debut 6 December, 1989

30.05.91 Barry North W RSC 2 Birmingham
25.07.91 Carl Hook L PTS 6 Dudley

Career: 5 contests, won 2, lost 3.

Morris Thomas

Bradford. *Born* Bradford, 11 September, 1968
L. Heavyweight (12.5-12.9) ht. 5'11"
Manager K. Richardson
Pro. Debut 23 March, 1987

24.10.91 John Oxenham L RSC 6 Glasgow
03.06.92 Darren McKenna L RSC 2 Newcastle under Lyme

Career: 13 contests, won 6, drew 1, lost 6.

Steve Thomas

Merthyr. *Born* Merthyr, 13 June, 1970
Middleweight (11.0-11.7) ht. 6'0"
Manager D. Gardiner
Pro. Debut 21 October, 1991

21.10.91 Jerry Mortimer W PTS 6 Mayfair
04.11.91 Andy Manning W PTS 6 Merthyr
02.03.92 Robert Peel DREW 6 Merthyr
08.04.92 Charlie Moore L RSC 3 Leeds
11.05.92 Robert Peel W PTS 6 Llanelli

Career: 5 contests, won 3, drew 1, lost 1.

(Jason) Tucker Thomas (Lee)

Leeds. *Born* Leeds, 21 June, 1972
Bantamweight (8.8-8.11) ht. 5'8"
Manager T. Miller
Pro. Debut 9 October, 1991

09.10.91 Louis Veitch L RSC 4 Marton
29.05.92 Shaun Anderson L RSC 1 Glasgow

Career: 2 contests, lost 2.

Adrian Strachan (left) bores in on Horace Fleary, en-rout to a six rounds points victory last May Les Clark

David Thompson

Hull. *Born* Hull, 14 March, 1969
L. Welterweight (9.9-10.4) ht. 5'8"
Manager M. Toomey
Pro. Debut 26 March, 1990

18.02.91 Barry North W PTS 6 Birmingham
25.02.91 Steve Winstanley W RTD 4 Bradford
28.03.91 Shane Sheridan L CO 5 Alfreton
17.05.91 Jason Brattley DREW 6 Bury
13.06.91 James Jiora DREW 6 Hull
30.06.91 Nicky Lucas W PTS 6 Southwark
25.07.91 Shaun Cogan L CO 1 Dudley
13.11.91 Mark Tibbs L PTS 6 Bethnal Green
28.11.91 Kevin Toomey L PTS 6 Hull
09.12.91 Chris Aston L PTS 6 Bradford
21.01.92 Ricky Sackfield L CO 1 Stockport
30.03.92 Jason Brattley L PTS 6 Bradford

Career: 19 contests, won 6, drew 3, lost 10.

Jimmy Thornton

Sheffield. *Born* Sheffield, 22 September, 1964
L. Middleweight (10.12-11.3) ht. 5'8"
Manager H. Carnall
Pro. Debut 25 November, 1982

13.02.91 Neville Brown L RSC 1 Wembley
02.03.92 Dave Whittle W PTS 6 Marton

Career: 40 contests, won 17, lost 23.

Mark Tibbs

West Ham. *Born* London, 7 May, 1969
Lightweight (9.10-9.12) ht. 5'10"
Manager J. Tibbs
Pro. Debut 15 November,1988

06.03.91 Mike Morrison W RSC 4 Wembley
06.06.91 Chris Saunders L RSC 6 Barking
23.10.91 Rick Bushell W RSC 4 Bethnal Green
13.11.91 David Thompson W PTS 6 Bethnal Green
11.12.91 Rick Bushell W RSC 2 Basildon
25.03.92 Felix Kelly DREW 8 Dagenham

Career: 18 contests, won 16, drew 1, lost 1.

Mark Tierney (Smith)

Watford. *Born* Watford, 22 May, 1966
Bantamweight (8.2-8.6) ht. 5'5¾"
Manager M. Duff
Pro. Debut 13 September, 1990

07.02.91 Ceri Farrell W PTS 6 Watford
06.03.91 Ceri Farrell W PTS 6 Wembley
04.04.91 Miguel Matthews W PTS 6 Watford
12.09.91 Neil Parry W PTS 6 Wandsworth

Career: 6 contests, won 6.

Andy Till

Northolt. *Born* Perivale, 22 August, 1963
WBC International L. Middleweight Champion. Former Undefeated Southern Area L. Middleweight Champion (10.12-11.1) ht. 5'9"
Manager H. Holland
Pro. Debut 1 September, 1986

06.02.91 Alan Richards W PTS 8 Battersea
01.06.91 Terry Magee W RSC 4 Bethnal Green
15.10.91 John Davies W PTS 12 Dudley *(Vacant WBC International L. Middleweight Title)*

Career: 18 contests, won 16, lost 2.

Peter Till

Walsall. *Born* Walsall, 19 August, 1963
Midlands Area Lightweight Champion (9.8-9.12) ht. 5'6"
Manager –
Pro. Debut 25 April, 1985

21.02.91 Paul Charters L RSC 6 Walsall
31.05.91 Valery Kayumba L RSC 3 Grenoble, France
25.07.91 Karl Taylor W RSC 4 Dudley *(Midlands Area Lightweight Title Defence)*
21.09.91 Michael Ayers L RSC 5 Tottenham *(Elim. British Lightweight Title)*
09.12.91 Scott Doyle W CO 3 Brierley Hill
01.02.92 Michael Driscoll L RSC 3 Birmingham
17.03.92 Mark Reefer W RSC 3 Mayfair
04.06.92 Racheed Lawal L RSC 1 Randers, Denmark

Career: 35 contests, won 25, drew 1, lost 9.

Carl Tilley

Doncaster. *Born* Doncaster, 4 October, 1967
Lightweight (9.9-9.12) ht. 5'6½"
Manager F. Maloney
Pro. Debut 4 September, 1990

13.05.91 Steve Winstanley W RTD 4 Marton
09.10.91 Bobby Beckles W RSC 4 Marton
02.03.92 James Jiora W PTS 6 Marton
30.04.92 Greg Egbuniwe L PTS 6 Kensington

Career: 6 contests, won 5, lost 1.

Wayne Timmins

Wolverhampton. *Born* Dudley, 18 March, 1966
Welterweight (10.8½-10.10) ht. 5'9½"
Manager –
Pro. Debut 16 May, 1988

10.04.91 Trevor Meikle W PTS 6 Wolverhampton
14.05.91 Tony Britland W PTS 6 Dudley
05.06.91 Julian Eavis W PTS 6 Wolverhampton
20.02.92 Jim Lawlor W PTS 6 Oakengates
17.03.92 Darren Morris DREW 6 Wolverhampton

Career: 19 contests, won 14, drew 2, lost 3.

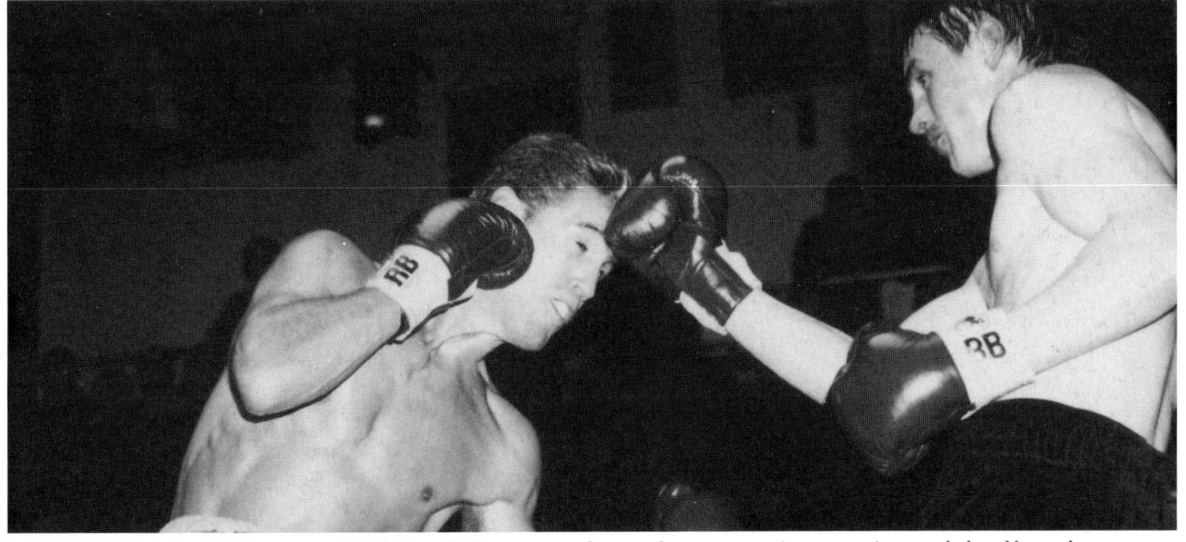

Mark Tibbs (left) moves in against Hull's David Thompson, who was beaten on points over six rounds last November
Les Clark

Winston Tomlinson

Leicester. *Born* Hastings, 12 January, 1966
L. Middleweight (11.2) ht. 5'7"
Manager W. Swift
Pro. Debut 30 September, 1991

30.09.91 Delroy Matthews L RSC 4 Kensington

Career: 1 contest, lost 1.

Kevin Toomey

Hull. *Born* Hull, 19 September, 1967
Central Area Lightweight Champion (9.8-10.5¼) ht. 5'9"
Manager M. Toomey
Pro. Debut 24 April, 1989

24.01.91 Barry North W PTS 6 Brierley Hill
18.02.91 Andy Kent L RSC 5 Derby
22.04.91 Trevor Royal W PTS 6 Bradford
16.05.91 John Smith W PTS 6 Liverpool
13.06.91 John Smith W PTS 6 Hull
30.09.91 Mike Calderwood L RSC 2 Liverpool
28.11.91 David Thompson W PTS 6 Hull
10.12.91 Wayne Windle L PTS 6 Sheffield
04.02.92 G. G. Goddard W PTS 6 Alfreton
26.03.92 Wayne Windle W DIS 8 Hull
(Central Area Lightweight Title Challenge)

Career: 15 contests, won 9, drew 1, lost 5.

Leo Turner

Bradford. *Born* Bradford, 17 September, 1970
S. Featherweight (9.5) ht. 5'9"
Manager J. Celebanski
Pro. Debut 8 June, 1992

08.06.92 Wayne Rigby L PTS 6 Bradford

Career: 1 contest, lost 1.

Kenny Tyson (Griffin)

Leeds. *Born* Leeds, 26 July, 1970
Middleweight (11.5-11.10¼) ht. 6'0"
Manager T. Miller
Pro. Debut 21 January, 1991

21.01.91 David Radford W PTS 6 Leeds
28.02.91 Jon Stocks L PTS 6 Sunderland
20.05.91 Dave Johnson L PTS 6 Bradford
01.06.91 Gary Booker L PTS 6 Bethnal Green
05.11.91 Chad Strong W PTS 6 Leicester
07.12.91 Warren Stowe L RSC 6 Manchester

Career: 6 contests, won 2, lost 4.

Johnny Uphill

Hastings. *Born* Welling, 27 January, 1967
L. Heavyweight (12.3-12.9) ht. 6'2"
Manager D. Harris
Pro. Debut 7 March, 1988

04.04.91 Kevin Morton L CO 1 Watford
29.02.92 Julian Johnson L CO 3 St Leonards

Career: 5 contests, won 2, lost 3.

Greg Upton

Teignmouth. *Born* Canada, 11 June, 1971
Featherweight (9.0-9.2) ht. 5'5½"
Manager J. Gaynor
Pro. Debut 28 November, 1991

28.11.91 Eunan Devenney W PTS 6 Evesham
29.04.92 Chris Morris W RSC 2 Liverpool
01.06.92 Graham McGrath W PTS 6 Solihull

Career: 3 contests, won 3.

Rudy Valentino (Isaacs)

Plumstead. *Born* London, 6 July, 1964
Lightweight (9.6½-9.11½) ht. 5'6¼"
Manager P. Byrne
Pro. Debut 22 October, 1986

10.04.91 Marcel Herbert W RSC 3 Newport
(Elim. British Lightweight Title)
17.07.91 Giovanni Parisi L PTS 8 Abbiategrasso, Italy
13.09.91 Giorgio Campanella L PTS 8 Gaggiano, Italy

Andy Till (left) slugs it out with Alan Richards, before settling for a points win at Battersea in February 1991 Les Clark

19.02.92 Michael Ayers L RSC 7 Muswell Hill *(Southern Area Lightweight Title Challenge. Elim. British Lightweight Title)*

Career: 26 contests, won 12, drew 1, lost 13.

Des Vaughan

Sydenham. *Born* Lewisham, 3 January, 1965
Cruiserweight (13.8-13.9) ht. 6'4"
Manager H. Holland
Pro. Debut 25 October, 1990

18.02.91 Rob Albon L PTS 6 Windsor
05.03.92 Rocky Shelly W RSC 5 Battersea

Career: 3 contests, won 2, lost 1.

Louis Veitch

Glasgow. *Born* Glasgow, 9 March, 1963
Flyweight (8.0-8.3) ht. 5'2"
Manager J. McMillen
Pro. Debut 9 October, 1991

09.10.91 Tucker Thomas W RSC 4 Marton
11.11.91 Shaun Norman L RSC 5 Bradford
12.03.92 Neil Armstrong L PTS 6 Glasgow
10.04.92 Mark Robertson L PTS 6 Glasgow
16.05.92 Mickey Cantwell L PTS 6 Muswell Hill

Career: 5 contests, won 1, lost 4.

Tony Velinor

Stratford. *Born* London, 21 December,1964
L. Middleweight (11.2-11.4) ht. 5'8"
Manager B. Hearn
Pro. Debut 28 October, 1988

12.03.91 Paul Jones L PTS 8 Mansfield
03.07.91 Jason Rowe W RSC 1 Brentwood
11.05.92 Stan King L RSC 3 Piccadilly

Career: 13 contests, won 8, lost 5.

Mark Verikios

Swansea. *Born* Swansea, 31 October, 1965
Welterweight (10.8-10.10) ht. 5'10"
Manager M. Copp
Pro. Debut 15 May, 1991

15.05.91 Lee Farrell W RSC 5 Swansea
06.06.91 Tim Harmey W CO 4 Barking
09.09.91 Dave Maj W PTS 6 Liverpool
13.05.92 Steve McNess W RSC 5 Kensington

Career: 4 contests, won 4.

Ian Vokes

Hull. *Born* Hull, 27 March, 1966
L. Heavyweight (12.2-12.10) ht. 6'0"
Manager –
Pro. Debut 13 March, 1989

18.02.91 Barry Downes W PTS 6 Derby
18.03.91 Ian Henry L RSC 2 Manchester
22.04.91 Joe Kilshaw DREW 6 Bradford
13.05.91 Steve Truepenny L CO 2 Manchester
28.11.91 Shamus Casey L PTS 6 Hull

Career: 21 contests, won 4, drew 1, lost 16.

Peter Vosper

Plymouth. *Born* Plymouth, 6 October,1966
S. Middleweight (11.10¾-12.2¾) ht. 5'10"
Manager –
Pro. Debut 15 February, 1989

12.04.91 Frank Eubanks L RSC 1 Manchester
30.05.91 Russell Washer W PTS 6 Mayfair
06.06.91 John Kaighin DREW 6 Barking
27.06.91 Nick Manners L RSC 1 Leeds
16.12.91 Paul McCarthy L PTS 6 Southampton
25.02.92 Roland Ericsson L RSC 6 Crystal Palace

Career: 17 contests, won 5, drew 2, lost 10.

Nicky Wadman

Brighton. *Born* Brighton, 8 August, 1965
L. Heavyweight (12.9-12.10) ht. 6'1"
Manager B. Paget
Pro. Debut 11 March, 1992

11.03.92 Julian Johnson W PTS 6 Cardiff
23.04.92 Mark McBiane W RSC 1 Eltham

Career: 2 contests, won 2.

Chris Walker (Bonnick)

Nottingham. *Born* Trowbridge, 25 December, 1961
S. Middleweight (11.11-12.2) ht. 5'8"
Manager J. Griffin
Pro. Debut 22 January, 1987

13.03.91 Adrian Wright W PTS 4 Stoke
10.10.91 Ian Henry L PTS 6 Gateshead
22.10.91 Paul Hitch L PTS 6 Hartlepool
11.03.92 Doug Calderwood W PTS 6 Solihull
28.04.92 Paul Hitch W RSC 2 Houghton le Spring
14.05.92 Paul Wright L PTS 6 Liverpool

Career: 21 contests, won 12, lost 9.

Danny Walker

Port Talbot. *Born* Neath, 19 January, 1967
S. Middleweight (11.9-11.12) ht. 6'4"
Manager P. Boyce
Pro. Debut 27 November, 1990

15.03.91 Alan Gandy W PTS 6 Willenhall
15.01.92 Marc Rowley L CO 5 Stoke

Career: 4 contests, won 2, lost 2.

Steve Walker

Manchester. *Born* Manchester, 25 June, 1963
S. Featherweight (9.3½-9.11½) ht. 5'7"
Manager P. Martin
Pro. Debut 14 September, 1989

24.01.91 Richie Foster W PTS 8 Brierley Hill
02.03.91 Harry Escott DREW 6 Darlington
19.03.91 Mark Holt W PTS 8 Birmingham
20.09.91 Harry Escott DREW 6 Manchester
13.11.91 Ian Honeywood L PTS 6 Bethnal Green

Career: 20 contests, won 10, drew 7, lost 3.

Steve Walton

Whitley Bay. *Born* Wallsend, 3 December, 1972
L. Heavyweight (12.7) ht. 6'2"
Manager N. Fawcett
Pro. Debut 28 May, 1992

28.05.92 Greg Scott-Briggs L PTS 6 Gosforth

Career: 1 contest, lost 1.

Russell Washer

Swansea. *Born* Swansea, 21 January, 1962
Middleweight (10.9¼-12.0) ht. 5'10"
Manager M. Copp
Pro. Debut 15 September, 1990

24.01.91 Wayne Panayiotiou W RSC 4 Gorseinon
21.02.91 Marvin O'Brien DREW 6 Walsall
19.03.91 Tony Meszaros L PTS 6 Birmingham
10.04.91 Andrew Flute L PTS 6 Wolverhampton
30.05.91 Peter Vosper L PTS 6 Mayfair
04.09.91 Val Golding L RTD 5 Bethnal Green
11.11.91 Stinger Mason L PTS 4 Stratford on Avon
20.11.91 Alan Richards L PTS 6 Cardiff
29.11.91 Ensley Bingham L RSC 4 Manchester
11.03.92 Lee Crocker L PTS 6 Cardiff
22.04.92 Gilbert Jackson L PTS 6 Wembley
11.05.92 Carlo Colarusso L RSC 5 Llanelli *(Welsh L. Middleweight Title Challenge)*
18.06.92 Tony Collins L RSC 2 Peterborough

Career: 18 contests, won 4, drew 1, lost 13.

Graham Wassell

Pontefract. *Born* Wakefield, 29 December, 1966
S. Middleweight (12.0) ht. 6'4"
Manager T. Callighan
Pro. Debut 13 November, 1990

21.10.91 Gypsy Johnny Price L RSC 5 Bury

Career: 2 contests, drew 1, lost 1.

Michael Watson

Islington. *Born* London, 15 March, 1965
Former Undefeated Commonwealth Middleweight Champion (11.6-11.12) ht. 5'11"
Manager –
Pro. Debut 16 October, 1984

23.01.91 Craig Trotter W RTD 6 Basildon *(Commonwealth Middleweight Title Defence)*

01.05.91 Anthony Brown W CO 1 Bethnal Green
22.06.91 Chris Eubank L PTS 12 Earls Court *(WBO Middleweight Title Challenge)*
21.09.91 Chris Eubank L RSC 12 Tottenham *(Vacant WBO S. Middleweight Title)*

Career: 30 contests, won 25, drew 1, lost 4.

Delroy Waul

Manchester. *Born* Manchester, 3 May, 1970
Welterweight (10.7-11.1) ht. 6'1"
Manager J. Doughty
Pro. Debut 29 May, 1989

31.01.91 Kevin Hayde W RSC 6 Bredbury
13.02.91 Chris Richards W PTS 6 Wembley
14.03.91 Terry Morrill DREW 8 Middleton
02.05.91 Andrew Furlong W RSC 5 Northampton
16.05.91 Paul Wesley W RSC 7 Liverpool
20.06.91 Gordon Blair L CO 2 Liverpool
09.10.91 Paul King W RSC 6 Manchester
19.12.91 Jason Rowe W RSC 4 Oldham
31.01.92 Patrick Vungbo L DIS 8 Waregem, Belgium

Career: 18 contests, won 15, drew 1, lost 2.

Ray Webb

Stepney. *Born* Hackney, 10 March, 1966
S. Middleweight (11.12-12.1¼") ht. 5'11½"
Manager –
Pro. Debut 2 November, 1988

10.01.91 Carlos Christie W PTS 6 Wandsworth
27.03.91 Silvio Branco L PTS 8 Mestre, Italy
30.05.91 Karl Barwise W PTS 8 Mayfair
11.12.91 Ian Strudwick L CO 8 Basildon *(Vacant Southern Area S. Midleweight Title)*
06.03.92 Oleg Volkov L PTS 8 Berlin, Germany

Career: 12 contests, won 6, lost 6.

Gordon Webster

Norwich. *Born* Peterborough, 7 March, 1965
Welterweight (10.2½-10.5) ht. 5'7½"
Manager –
Pro. Debut 16 February, 1989

29.01.91 Eddie King L PTS 6 Wisbech
21.09.91 Ojay Abrahams L RSC 3 Tottenham
26.10.91 Bernard Paul L RSC 4 Brentwood

Career: 5 contests, lost 5.

Paul Weir

Irvine. *Born* Glasgow, 16 September, 1967
Flyweight (7.11) ht. 5'3"
Manager T. Gilmour
Pro. Debut 27 April, 1992

27.04.92 Eddie Vallejo W CO 2 Glasgow

Career: 1 contest, won 1.

Richie Wenton Chris Bevan

Tony Wellington

Deptford. *Born* Nottingham, 23 April, 1965
Middleweight (11.5½-11.8) ht. 6'1"
Manager G. White
Pro. Debut 26 September, 1990

23.01.91 Paul Busby L RSC 2 Brentwood
26.09.91 Clay O'Shea L CO 1 Dunstable
05.12.91 John McKenzie L PTS 6 Peterborough
05.03.92 Gilbert Jackson L CO 2 Battersea

Career: 10 contests, won 2, lost 8.

Nigel Wenton

Liverpool. *Born* Liverpool, 5 April, 1969
Lightweight (9.10¼-9.12) ht. 5'7"
Manager B. Eastwood
Pro. Debut 8 June, 1988

07.09.91 Oliver Harrison W RTD 5 Belfast
13.11.91 Tony Richards W RSC 5 Belfast
11.12.91 Jeff Roberts W CO 2 Dublin
25.04.92 Ed Pollard W RTD 6 Belfast

Career: 25 contests, won 22, drew 1, lost 2.

Richie Wenton

Liverpool. *Born* Liverpool, 28 October, 1967
Bantamweight (8.13½) ht. 5'8"
Manager F. Warren
Pro. Debut 14 December, 1988

12.02.91 Sean Casey W PTS 4 Belfast
31.03.92 Graham O'Malley W PTS 6 Stockport

Career: 13 contests, won 13.

Paul Wesley

Birmingham. *Born* Birmingham, 2 May, 1962
Middleweight (11.0-11.10) ht. 5'9"
Manager N. Nobbs
Pro. Debut 20 February, 1987

23.01.91 Wally Swift Jnr L PTS 10 Solihull *(Midlands Area L. Middleweight Title Challenge)*
20.03.91 Horace Fleary L RSC 5 Solihull
16.05.91 Delroy Waul L RSC 7 Liverpool
04.07.91 Neville Brown W RSC 1 Alfreton
31.07.91 Francesco dell'Aquila L PTS 8 Casella, Italy
03.10.91 Neville Brown L PTS 8 Burton
29.10.91 Tony Collins DREW 8 Kensington
03.03.92 Antonio Fernandez L PTS 10 Cradley Heath *(Vacant Midlands Area Middleweight Title)*
10.04.92 Jean-Charles Meuret L PTS 8 Geneva, Switzerland
03.06.92 Sumbu Kalambay L PTS 10 Salice Terme, Italy

Career: 35 contests, won 12, drew 4, lost 19.

John Westgarth

Newcastle. *Born* Malta, 23 December, 1959
Heavyweight (16.6-17.1) ht. 6'5"
Manager M. Barrett
Pro. Debut 29 November, 1982

14.05.91 Herbie Hide L RTD 4 Dudley
30.03.92 Warren Richards DREW 6 Eltham

Career: 29 contests, won 11, drew 3, lost 15.

John White

Salford. *Born* Manchester, 6 November, 1970
Featherweight (8.13) ht. 5'6"
Manager J. Doughty
Pro. Debut 27 February, 1992

27.02.92 Alan Smith W RSC 1 Liverpool

Career: 1 contests, won 1.

Dave Whittle

Newcastle. *Born* North Shields, 19 May, 1966
Welterweight (10.6-11.6) ht. 5'9"
Manager –
Pro. Debut 22 November, 1988

13.05.91 Barry Messam L PTS 6 Marton
23.10.91 Jamie Robinson L RSC 4 Bethnal Green
27.11.91 Alan Peacock W PTS 6 Marton
02.03.92 Jimmy Thornton L PTS 6 Marton
12.03.92 Alan Peacock DREW 8 Glasgow
14.04.92 Nigel Bradley L CO 3 Mansfield
18.05.92 Wayne Shepherd L PTS 6 Marton

Career: 16 contests, won 7, drew 2, lost 7.

Leigh Wicks

Brighton. *Born* Worthing, 29 July,1965
Welterweight (10.8-10.10¾) ht. 5'9¼"
Manager T. Lawless
Pro. Debut 29 April, 1987

10.01.91 Barry Messam W PTS 6 Wandsworth
14.02.91 Kevin Thompson W PTS 8 Southampton
21.10.91 Tony Britland W RSC 3 Mayfair
20.02.92 Mick Duncan L PTS 8 Glasgow
30.04.92 Darren Morris DREW 6 Mayfair

Career: 20 contests, won 13, drew 4, lost 3.

Alan Williams

Liverpool. *Born* Liverpool, 2 August, 1962
Welterweight (10.7-11.9) ht. 5'10½"
Manager C. Moorcroft
Pro. Debut 11 June, 1984

18.03.91 Stephen Welford L CO 1 Derby
29.04.92 Rob Stevenson L PTS 6 Liverpool

Career: 7 contests, won 1, lost 6.

(Robert) B. F. Williams

Watford. *Born* Park Royal, 14 December, 1965
Welterweight (10.0-10.6) ht. 5'11"
Manager R. Colson
Pro. Debut 28 May, 1986

07.02.91 Rick Bushell L RTD 2 Watford
12.02.92 Cliff Churchward W PTS 6 Watford
07.04.92 Erwin Edwards W PTS 6 Southend
30.04.92 Trevor Meikle W PTS 6 Watford

Career: 27 contests, won 16, drew 1, lost 10.

Derek Williams

Battersea. *Born* Stockwell, 11 March, 1965
Former Commonwealth & European Heavyweight Champion (16.9-17.5) ht. 6'5"
Manager –
Pro. Debut 24 October, 1984

01.05.91 Jimmy Thunder W RSC 2 Bethnal Green *(Commonwealth Heavyweight Title Defence)*
30.09.91 David Bey W RTD 6 Kensington
18.01.92 Tim Anderson W RSC 1 Kensington
30.04.92 Lennox Lewis L RSC 3 Kensington *(Commonwealth Heavyweight Title Defence. British & European Heavyweight Title Challenge)*

Career: 24 contests, won 19, lost 5.

Derek Williams Derek Rowe

Everald Williams

Hornsey. *Born* Jamaica, 10 June, 1969
L. Welterweight (10.0½) ht. 5'9"
Manager J. Ryan
Pro. Debut 5 March,1992

05.03.92 Korso Aleain W CO 6 Battersea

Career: 1 contest, won 1.

Gary Williams

Nottingham. *Born* Nottingham, 25 September, 1965
Heavyweight (14.4) ht. 5'11½"
Manager W. Swift
Pro. Debut 27 April, 1992

27.04.92 Damien Caesar L RSC 4 Mayfair

Career: 1 contest, lost 1.

(Kirk) John Williams (Gibbon)

Birmingham. *Born* Birmingham, 26 October, 1963
Cruiserweight (13.3) ht. 6'2½"
Manager G. Steene
Pro. Debut 12 February, 1985

12.05.92 Gary Delaney L PTS 6 Crystal Palace

Career: 18 contests, won 5, drew 1, lost 12.

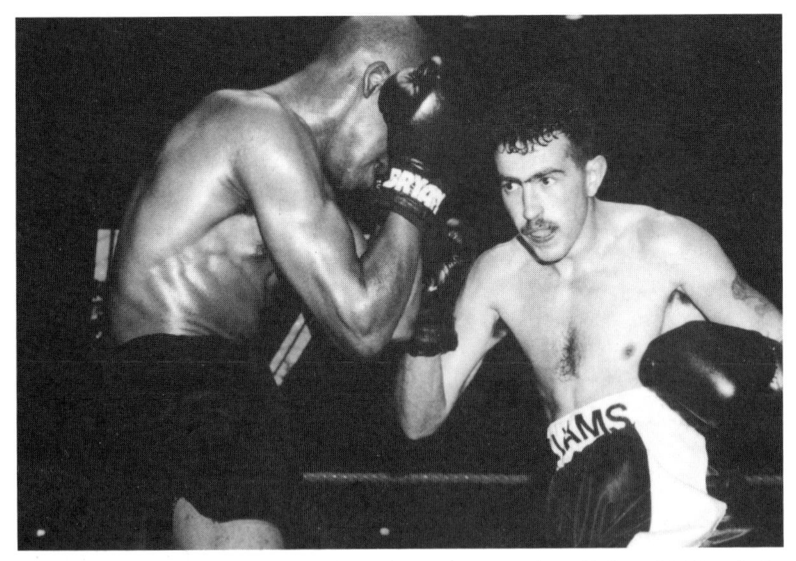

J. T. Williams (right) battled away for a draw against Kelton McKenzie in January 1991 Les Clark

(John) J. T. Williams
Cwmbran. *Born* Pontylottyn, 22 May, 1970
S. Featherweight (9.0½-9.6) ht. 5'6¾"
Manager F. Maloney
Pro. Debut 21 January, 1991

21.01.91 Kelton McKenzie DREW 6 Crystal Palace
10.04.91 Dave Buxton W PTS 8 Newport
28.05.91 Frankie Ventura W PTS 6 Cardiff
18.07.91 Billy Barton W PTS 6 Cardiff
22.01.92 Derek Amory W PTS 6 Cardiff
30.03.92 Steve Pollard L PTS 6 Eltham

Career: 6 contests, won 4, drew 1, lost 1.

Leigh Williams
Chelsea. *Born* London, 23 July, 1967
Bantamweight (8.6¾-8.9½) ht. 5'4"
Manager D. Mancini
Pro. Debut 30 June, 1991

30.06.91 Andrew Bloomer W PTS 6 Southwark
12.09.91 Tony Rahman W PTS 6 Wandsworth
17.10.91 Andrew Bloomer W PTS 6 Southwark
17.02.92 Alan Ley L PTS 6 Mayfair

Career: 4 contests, won 3, lost 1.

George Wilson
Camberwell. *Born* London, 7 April, 1966
Welterweight (10.7) ht. 5'10"
Manager G. Steene
Pro. Debut 18 June, 1992

18.06.92 Sean Cave L PTS 6 Peterborough

Career: 1 contest, lost 1.

Roger Wilson
Newport. *Born* Newport, 30 October,1966
S. Middleweight (11.12) ht. 6'1"
Manager N. Trigg
Pro. Debut 4 June, 1990

23.10.91 Stinger Mason DREW 6 Stoke

Career: 4 contests, won 1, drew 1, lost 2.

Stuart Wilson
Rochdale. *Born* Derby, 11 April, 1969
L. Middleweight (11.2) ht. 6'3"
Manager J. Doughty
Pro. Debut 4 June, 1992

04.06.92 Willie Yeardsley L PTS 6 Burnley

Career: 1 contest, lost 1.

Tony Wilson
Wolverhampton. *Born* Wolverhampton, 25 April, 1964

Former British L. Heavyweight champion (12.7-12.13) ht. 5'11"
Manager –
Pro. Debut 12 February, 1985

02.10.91 Glazz Campbell L PTS 8 Solihull
26.11.91 Cordwell Hylton W PTS 8 Wolverhampton
11.12.91 Noel Magee L RSC 3 Dublin
21.03.92 Fabrice Tiozzo L PTS 8 Saint Denis, France
23.05.92 Ginger Tshabalala L RSC 3 Birmingham

Career: 27 contests, won 20, lost 7.

(Winston) W. O. Wilson
Wandsworth. *Born* Coventry, 9 March, 1965
Southern Area L. Middleweight Champion (10.13-11.4) ht. 6'3"
Manager H. Holland
Pro. Debut 25 March, 1986

21.01.91 Quinn Paynter L PTS 8 Crystal Palace
07.11.91 Nigel Fairbairn W RSC 8 Peterborough *(Vacant Southern Area L. Middleweight Title)*

Career: 16 contests, won 12, lost 4.

W. O. Wilson (facing camera) failed to beat Quinn Paynter, prior to winning the Southern Area light-middleweight title Les Clark

Wayne Windle

Sheffield. *Born* Sheffield, 18 October, 1968
Former Central Area Lightweight Champion (9.9-10.2) ht. 5'8"
Manager –
Pro. Debut 25 October, 1988

16.01.91 Karl Taylor L PTS 8 Stoke
06.02.91 Felix Kelly L PTS 6 Bethnal Green
12.03.91 Mark Antony W CO 1 Mansfield
24.04.91 Steve Foran L CO 3 Preston
13.06.91 Pete Roberts W RSC 7 Hull *(Vacant Central Area Lightweight Title)*
16.08.91 Aukunun L PTS 6 Marbella, Spain
21.09.91 George Scott L CO 2 Tottenham
10.12.91 Kevin Toomey W PTS 6 Sheffield
26.03.92 Kevin Toomey L DIS 8 Hull *(Central Area Lightweight Title Defence)*

Career: 29 contests, won 12, drew 3, lost 14.

Steve Winstanley

Chorley. *Born* Blackburn, 19 August, 1965
Lightweight (9.6-9.9) ht. 5'7½"
Manager –
Pro. Debut 26 February, 1987

25.02.91 David Thompson L RTD 4 Bradford
24.04.91 Stuart Rimmer W PTS 6 Preston
13.05.91 Carl Tilley L RTD 4 Marton
05.05.92 Alan Levene L RSC 2 Preston

Career: 18 contests, won 9, drew 2, lost 7.

Stevie Woods

Kirkcaldy. *Born* Manchester, 3 September, 1967
Bantamweight (8.3½-8.7¾) ht. 5'6"
Manager –
Pro. Debut 18 September,1989

21.01.91 Neil Parry W PTS 8 Glasgow
28.02.91 Gary White L PTS 6 Bury
07.05.91 Tony Smith W RTD 2 Glasgow
03.06.91 Neil Parry L RSC 2 Glasgow
09.10.91 Kevin Jenkins DREW 8 Glasgow
14.11.91 Drew Docherty L RSC 1 Edinburgh
28.02.92 Neil Parry L PTS 6 Irvine

Career: 16 contests, won 6, drew 1, lost 9.

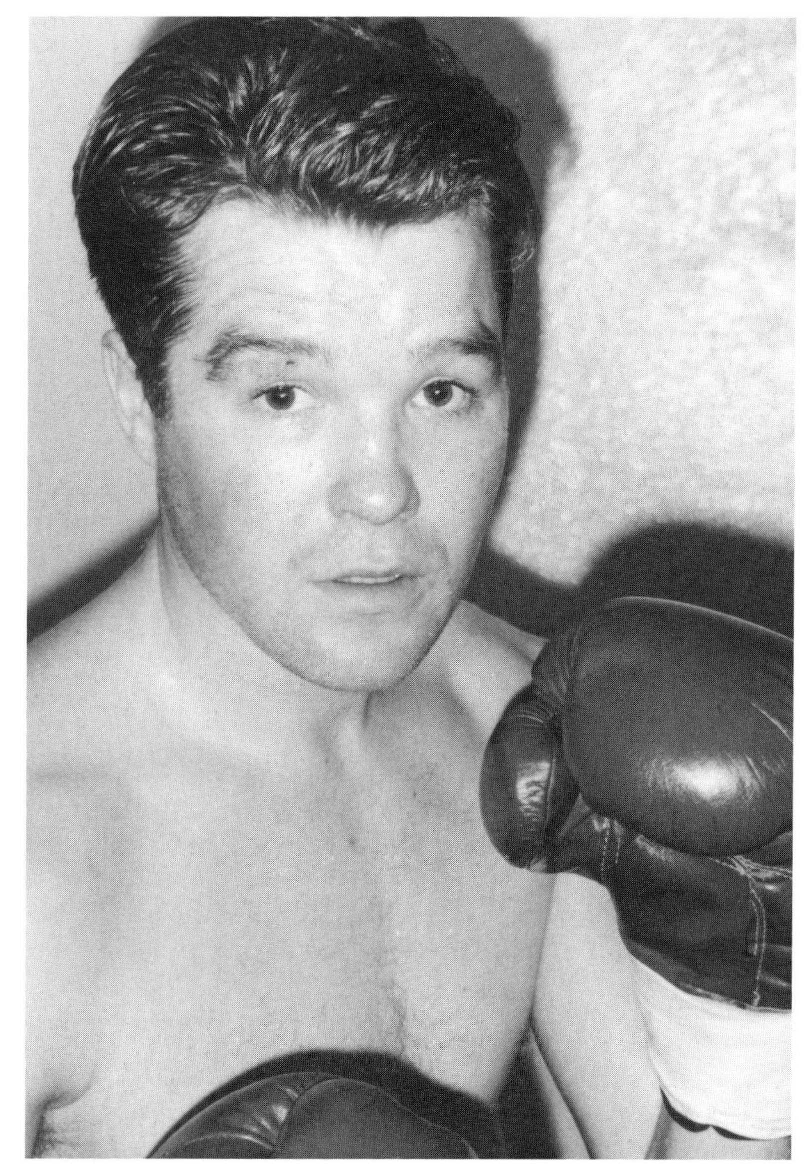

Richard Woolgar Les Clark

Richard Woolgar

Northampton. *Born* Newport Pagnell, 29 September,1967
Lightweight (9.4-9.11) ht. 5'5½"
Manager B. Hearn
Pro. Debut 24 October, 1990

19.03.91 Chris Saunders L RSC 3 Leicester
05.11.91 Kelton McKenzie L RSC 5 Leicester
10.12.91 Kevin Lowe W PTS 6 Shefffield
21.01.92 Lee Fox W PTS 6 Norwich
28.04.92 Karl Taylor L PTS 6 Wolverhampton

Career: 7 contests, won 4, lost 3.

James F. Woolley

Camden Town. *Born* Epping, 29 August, 1964
S. Midleweight (12.2-12.5) ht. 5'9¾"
Manager B. Hearn
Pro. Debut 24 September, 1990

04.06.91 Mark Spencer W RSC 1 Bethnal Green
03.07.91 Lee Prudden L PTS 6 Brentwood
21.09.91 Lee Prudden L PTS 6 Tottenham
19.02.92 Paul Murray L CO 4 Muswell Hill

Career: 7 contests, won 4, lost 3.

Winston Wray

Bolton. *Born* Jamaica, 30 October, 1960
L. Middleweight (11.2) ht. 6'0"
Manager –
Pro. Debut 22 November, 1982

12.04.91 Neville Brown L RSC 1 Willenhall
29.11.91 Frank Grant L RSC 3 Manchester

Career: 31 contests, won 13, drew 1, lost 17.

Adrian Wright

Wolverhampton. *Born* Wolverhampton, 8 November, 1967
Middleweight (11.9-12.2¾) ht. 5'9½"
Manager B. Crooks
Pro. Debut 5 September, 1990

06.02.91 Ali Forbes L PTS 6 Battersea
13.03.91 Chris Walker L PTS 4 Stoke
12.04.91 Robert Peel W RSC 6 Willenhall
29.08.91 John Kaighin L PTS 6 Oakengates
02.12.91 Justin Clements L PTS 6 Birmingham
11.12.91 Darron Griffiths L PTS 6 Stoke
29.04.92 Andy Manning L PTS 6 Stoke

Career: 11 contests, won 4, lost 7.

Andy Wright

Tooting. *Born* Aldershot, 20 December, 1963
Former Undefeated Southern Area S. Middleweight Champion (11.13½-12.4) ht. 5'11½"
Manager G. Steene
Pro. Debut 20 March, 1986

20.03.91 Paul McCarthy W CO 5 Wandsworth *(Southern Area S. Middleweight Title Challenge)*
22.10.91 John Kaighin DREW 6 Wandsworth
25.02.92 John Kaighin W PTS 6 Crystal Palace

Career: 17 contests, won 9, drew 2, lost 6.

Carl Wright

Liverpool. *Born* Liverpoool, 19 February, 1969
L. Welterweight (10.1-10.1½) ht. 5'7"
Manager C. Moorcroft
Pro. Debut 13 October, 1989

31.03.92 Ricky Sackfield W RSC 1 Stockport
14.05.92 Brendan Ryan W PTS 4 Liverpool
12.06.92 Dean Bramhald W PTS 6 Liverpool

Career: 7 contests, won 7.

Paul Wright

Liverpool. *Born* Liverpool, 24 June, 1966
S. Middleweight (11.13-12.1¾) ht. 5'9¾"
Manager C. Moorcroft
Pro. Debut 13 October, 1989

13.04.92 Shaun McCrory W PTS 6 Manchester
14.05.92 Chris Walker W PTS 6 Liverpool

Career: 5 contests, won 4, drew 1.

Robert Wright

Dudley. *Born* Dudley, 25 August, 1966
Welterweight (10.5¾-10.10) ht. 5'11"
Manager R. Browne
Pro. Debut 16 May, 1988

02.10.91 Chris Mulcahy W RSC 1 Solihull
20.11.91 Tony Gibbs W RTD 2 Solihull
26.11.91 Darren Dyer L RSC 3 Bethnal Green
15.01.92 Julian Eavis W PTS 8 Stoke
10.03.92 Errol McDonald W CO 3 Bury
17.03.92 Donovan Boucher L RSC 11 Mayfair *(Commonwealth Welterweight Title Challenge)*

Career: 15 contests, won 12, lost 3.

Stefan Wright

Peterborough. *Born* Peterborough, 23 May, 1970
Middleweight (11.2¾-11.10) ht. 5'10"
Manager –
Pro. Debut 22 October, 1990

24.01.91 Andre Wharton L RSC 5 Brierley Hill
07.11.91 Gary Booker W PTS 6 Peterborough
28.04.92 Jerry Mortimer W RSC 4 Corby
18.06.92 Chris Richards W PTS 6 Peterborough

Career: 6 contests, won 5, lost 1.

(Andrew) Sugar Boy Wright

Dudley. *Born* Dudley, 13 December, 1969
Lightweight (9.9-9.11) ht. 5'7"
Manager R. Browne
Pro. Debut 4 December, 1991

04.12.91 Jamie Morris W PTS 6 Stoke
22.01.92 Kevin McKillan L PTS 6 Solihull

Career: 2 contests, won 1, lost 1.

Vic Wright

Milton Keynes. *Born* Bethnal Green, 8 July, 1966
Cruiserweight (13.0-13.6) ht. 6'1"
Manager H. Holland
Pro. Debut 12 November, 1991

12.11.91 Randy B. Powell W RTD 4 Milton Keynes
12.02.92 Mark Pain L RSC 1 Watford

Career: 2 contests, won 1, lost 1.

Vic Wright Les Clark

Willie Yeardsley

Isle of Man. *Born* Isle of Man, 1 May, 1962
L. Middleweight (10.9-11.2½) ht. 5'10"
Manager M. Toomey
Pro. Debut 25 February, 1991

25.02.91 Pat Durkin W PTS 6 Bradford
03.04.91 Chris Mulcahy W PTS 6 Manchester
30.04.91 Ricky Sackfield L PTS 4 Stockport
13.06.91 Phil Epton L RSC 3 Hull
09.09.91 Allan Grainger L PTS 6 Glasgow
07.10.91 Dave Binsteed W PTS 6 Liverpool
25.11.91 Mick Duncan L PTS 6 Liverpool
20.01.92 Benji Joseph W PTS 6 Bradford
06.02.92 Benji Joseph W RSC 4 Peterborough
24.02.92 Matt Mowatt W PTS 6 Bradford
09.03.92 Dave Maj L RSC 1 Manchester
04.06.92 Stuart Wilson W PTS 6 Burnley

Career: 12 contests, won 7, lost 5.

Tim Yeates

Stanford le Hope. *Born* Worcester, 19 August, 1966
Featherweight (8.10-9.0) ht. 5'7"
Manager B. Hearn
Pro. Debut 3 October, 1990

23.01.91 Eric George W RSC 6 Brentwood
01.05.91 Kelton McKenzie L PTS 6 Bethnal Green
11.05.92 Neil Parry W PTS 6 Piccadilly

Career: 6 contests, won 5, lost 1.

Steve Yorath

Cardiff. *Born* Cardiff, 8 August, 1965
Cruiserweight (13.9-14.7) ht. 6'2"
Manager D. Gardiner
Pro. Debut 8 May, 1990

15.04.91 Tony Colclough W PTS 6 Wolverhampton
24.04.91 Phil Soundy W PTS 6 Basildon
28.05.91 R. F. McKenzie W PTS 6 Cardiff
27.06.91 Denzil Browne L PTS 6 Leeds
21.01.92 Graham Arnold W PTS 6 Norwich
31.03.92 Graham Arnold L PTS 6 Norwich
18.05.92 Maro van Spaendonck L PTS 4 Valkenswaard, Holland

Career: 15 contests, won 5, lost 10.

(Tahir) Ty Zubair

Nelson. *Born* Pakistan, 22 July, 1969
L. Welterweight (9.11-9.12) ht. 5'8½"
Manager J. Doughty
Pro. Debut 24 November, 1986

18.11.91 Jamie Davidson L PTS 6 Manchester
01.06.92 Paul Hughes L PTS 6 Manchester

Career: 4 contests, lost 4.

British Title Bouts, 1991-92

3 July, 1991 Wally Swift Jnr 10.10 (England) W PTS 12 Tony Collins 10.13 (England), Reading. Light-Middleweight Title Defence.

Making a measured start, both fighters felt each other out for the first round and a half. Then the action became more hectic as a cut that suddenly appeared at the side of Swift's right eye in the second, only served to galvanise him into action and he stunned Collins twice with solid right-handers. First one and then the other would appear to be in the driving seat, but with Swift consistently countering Collins' left-jab with a right over the top, you got the sure feeling that the champion wasn't going to let go of his title in a hurry. The eighth saw Collins pile in to the attack after inflicting a bad vertical gash on the champion's upper lip, but it was noticeable even then that Swift was taking his best punches unflinchingly. Then, with Collins still pressuring, Swift nailed him with the best punch of the night, a cracking right-hand to the head. The ninth through to the final bell, saw the action still see-sawing and it took a brave referee, Mickey Vann, to decide that Collins had lost by a point in front of his own fans. *Referees Scorecard:* 118-117.

25 July, 1991 Crawford Ashley 12.5 (England) W RSC 7 Roy Skeldon 12.7 (England), Dudley. Vacant Light-Heavyweight Title.

Soaking up the best that Ashley could offer over the first three rounds was Skeldon's tactical answer, but unfortunately for him a right-uppercut, which badly cut his left eye early in the first, affected his plan of campaign. Skeldon's chin yet again proved to be sound as he had to sustain a steady battery of heavy punches, but it was the nagging left-jab of the Yorkshireman, which constantly beat a tatoo on the damaged eye, that was ultimately his undoing. In the fifth, the Midlander began to throw caution to the wind as he literally hurled himself into the fray and on occasion had a fair bit of success, but luckily for Ashley many of the punches thrown didn't hit the target bang on. But after 69 seconds of the seventh had elapsed, Skeldon's eye let him down completely and as the blood flowed, Adrian Morgan had no alternative than to bring matters to a halt.

British light-middles champion, Wally Swift (right), looks to open up the defences of the challenger, Tony Collins

Les Clark

3 September, 1991 Francis Ampofo 7.13¼ (England) W RSC 11 Robbie Regan 7.13 (Wales), Cardiff. Flyweight Title Challenge.

Despite being by far the better boxer of the two, Regan could not stop the onward march of the teak-tough little challenger and eventually it led to his undoing. Round after round, Ampofo, as tireless as ever, kept looking to land solid blows on the skilful Welshman and while many were either blocked, whistled over the champion's shoulder, or were simply out of range, others got home to good effect. This was the pattern of the contest right up to the eleventh round, with Regan out in front, but never able to relax as Ampofo continued to look dangerous. Then, in the eleventh, an accidential clash of heads as the two men came to grips with each other turned Regan's face into a bloody mask. Mickey Vann immediately stopped the action to inspect the damaged left eye, which later needed 30 stitches and called it off with 44 seconds of the round remaining.

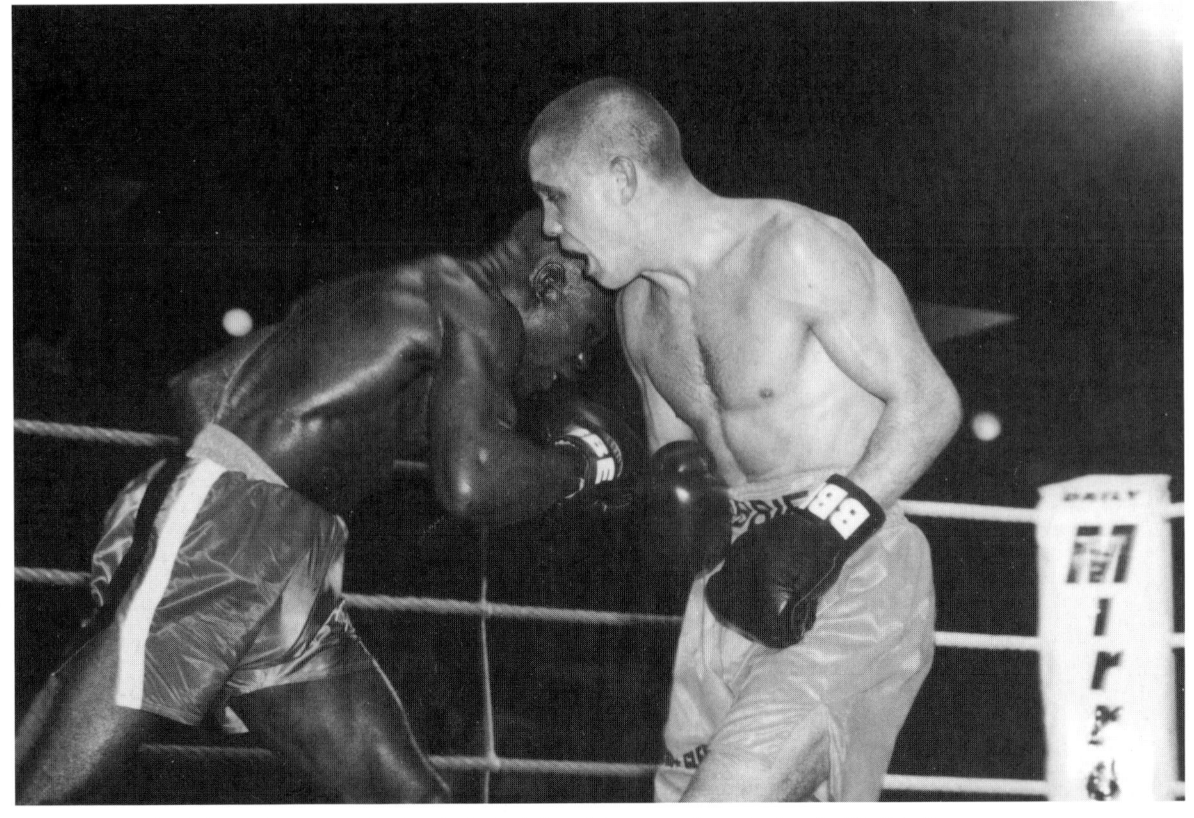

Francis Ampofo (left) on his way to winning the British flyweight crown from the head of Robbie Regan Les Clark

4 September, 1991 Colin McMillan 9.0 (England) W RSC 7 Kevin Pritchard 8.13¼ (England), London. Featherweight Title Defence.

The former super-featherweight champion, Pritchard, immediately took the fight to McMillan, pressing forward in an effort to catch his man cold and neutralise the champion's greater variety of skills. But he was too sluggish and McMillan either danced away, or slipped the oncoming blows and returned them with interest. In the third round, a left-hook opened up a cut over Pritchard's right eye, which spurred McMillan into action, but through to round five, the champion allowed the pace to drop as he probed for further weaknesses. By now McMillan had decided to work the body and in the fifth this paid dividends as Pritchard was downed for counts of eight and seven, respectively. The champion now looked to finish it in the sixth and a series of blows to the head had Pritchard on the deck for a further count of seven. Round seven turned out to be the last for Pritchard as he was floored for two more counts of eight from solid body shots and on getting up from the latter, he was humanely rescued by the referee, John Coyle, with a minute on the clock left.

19 September, 1991 John Doherty 9.4 (England) W PTS 12 Sugar Gibiliru 9.4 (England), Stockport. Super-Featherweight Title Challenge.

For the eleventh consecutive time, the super-featherweight division saw the title change hands as a defending champion made his first defence a losing one. By dint of his victory, the former two-time title-holder, John Doherty, won a Lonsdale Belt outright and immediately declared himself the man to break the hoodoo surrounding his weight class. Making a fairly measured start, Doherty was content to move around the ring for the first three rounds in order to find his feet and fathom out the champion's style. Every now and again their heads came too close for comfort, but from the fourth round onwards, the challenger began to find the range for his jab. At around the middle stage he started to gain the ascendancy, as Gibiliru's work became more ragged and although he was cut over the left eye in the ninth from another clash of heads, it merely steeled his resolve. Keeping his composure, jabbing and moving well, Doherty just about remained in front to receive Roy Francis' close, but just verdict. *Referees Scorecard:* 118-117.

24 September, 1991 Fidel Castro 12.0 (England) W RSC 6 Ian Strudwick 11.12 (England), Basildon. Vacant Super-Middleweight Title.

Following a cautious start, the action livened up somewhat in the second when Strudwick emerged from a fiery exchange with a cut by the side of his right eye. This inspired Castro to launch a salvo of hooks and uppercuts, which although Strudwick took well, drove him back to the ropes and saw him under fire as the round ended. By the fourth, Castro had got himself firmly in the driving seat and started to vary his tactics. Instead of being content to box only at distance, he decided that as Strudwick hadn't the power to take him out, he would move to close quarters in an effort to find the punches to finish the job summarily. Strudwick, as game as a pebble, nearly always returned the fire, but it was noticeable that he was making little impression on his rival and was marking up rapidly. In the sixth the inevitable happened. Strudwick, after making a good start was badly cut, this time over the right eye and while fighting back well, on inspecting the cut, Paul Thomas brought matters to an immediate halt with just 18 seconds of the round remaining.

30 September, 1991 Lennox Lewis 16.7 (England) W CO 2 Glenn McCrory 15.11 (England), London. Heavyweight Title Defence.

When former IBF cruiserweight champion, Glenn McCrory, challenged Lennox Lewis for his British and European heavyweight titles, those most knowledgeable in boxing felt that the likeable Geordie would lack the power required to do the job. They reasoned that his skills could make it tough for Lewis, but that he wouldn't be able to keep the champion at bay indefinitely. But right from the opening bell, Lewis surprised McCrory with his speed, as he came out fast with both hands, winging punches in from all angles. McCrory, whose only answer was to clutch and hold, was put under constant pressure throughout the first and appeared lucky to survive the round out. Lewis continued the second where he had left off and it wasn't long before a big right-uppercut had the challenger down. Getting up at nine, McCrory, apart from a brief flurry, was on a hiding to nothing as Lewis measured him with three heavy left-jabs, followed by a right, which once again deposited him on the deck. This time John Coyle counted McCrory out, while in the act of rising, with one minute, 50 seconds of the round remaining.

21 October, 1991 Joe Kelly 8.4 (Scotland) DREW 12 Ronnie Carroll 8.6 (Scotland), Glasgow. Vacant Bantamweight Title.

At the end of this absorbing little battle when Dave Parris raised both fighters' hands aloft and announced a draw, the first in a British title fight for some 57 years, the crowd errupted. A vast majority of onlookers and thousands of television viewers couldn't believe that the diminutive Kelly hadn't done enough to win handsomely. That certainly appeared to be the case, other than for the more discerning, who might just have noticed that many of Kelly's blows didn't land with the full knuckle part of the glove. But even for sheer volume, Kelly still seemed to have done enough. However, had Carroll stuck with his better boxing skills, getting behind the jab and relying on his ability to counter-punch when the occasion presented itself, then the result could possibly have been different. As it was he generally got himself involved at close quarters, often unnecessarily with the superbly conditioned Kelly giving him no respite whatsoever. *Referees Scorecard:* 117½-117½.

29 October, 1991 Colin McMillan 8.13 (England) W PTS 12 Sean Murphy 8.12¾ (England), London. Featherweight Title Defence.

The former champion, Sean Murphy, was reckoned to be a solid test for the current champion, but he eventually went the way of all, bar one, of McMillan's previous opponents. The referee gave only one round to Murphy, the eighth, but he was far from disgraced and was never on the floor. From the fourth round onwards, however, it had become apparent that the champion was well on his way to victory after making an excellent start, popping the jab in and out of Murphy's features and getting away before his rival could react. Round after round saw McMillan dominating, without being able to bring the contest to an early conclusion and although Murphy was hurt on several occasions, he was always trying to fight back. McMillan never appeared to be in danger and at times almost treated the bout as a sparring session, but for all that and for all the beautiful moves, slippery footwork and pure quality, he will still need the added ingredient of punching power once he steps up into world class. When Larry O'Connell automatically reached for his arm at the final bell, McMillan had also won a Lonsdale Belt in the record time of 160 days. *Referees Scorecard:* 119½-114½.

26 November, 1991 Del Bryan 10.5 (England) W RSC 3 Mickey Hughes 10.7 (England), London. Welterweight Title Defence.

In looking for a repeat win over the challenger, Bryan

made a very fast start, catching his man with a good left-hook inside the first fifteen seconds. Rights and lefts continued to smack into Hughes' face, which was already showing signs of damage to the nose, as the champion continued to unload without reply. The second round saw the pattern continuing with Hughes coming forward, but running on to punches without being able to get to grips with the elusive Bryan. Then, just as the unfortunate Hughes finally stepped up a gear during the third, he suffered a bad cut by the corner of his right eye, following an accidental clash of heads. Adrian Morgan allowed the action to continue temporarily in order to give Hughes every chance of victory, but following two inspections and with the blood still flowing, he was forced to bring matters to a halt after two minutes, 36 seconds of the round.

Looking to capture the British welterweight title from Del Bryan, Mickey Hughes (left) bores in on the champion. Hughes was stopped in the third round, following a clash of heads Les Clark

10 December, 1991 Herol Graham 11.6 (England) W RSC 6 John Ashton 11.6 (England), Sheffield. Middleweight Title Defence.

After over twelve months out of the ring following that dreadful knockout at the hands of big-hitting Julian Jackson for the vacant WBC title, Herol Graham came back to defend his British crown against a man of lesser ability, but one who was undaunted by the champion's reputation. In his previous contest, Ashton had performed magnificently when going down to the European champion, Sumbu Kalambay and was well prepared for this one. A mauling start saw Graham suffer a cut over the left eye in the second, but by the fourth he had settled down into a rhythm, beginning to shake off the ring-rust and dominating with the southpaw jab. Ashton, who had also picked up a cut left eye from a collision in the second, suddenly found himself all over the place in the fifth as the champion went to work with a wide repertoire of punches, but manfully struggled through to the bell. Coming out for the sixth, with the air of a champion ready to finish the job, Graham continued to pour in the punches without return until Larry O'Connell stepped in to rescue the brave challenger after two minutes and 34 seconds of the round had elapsed.

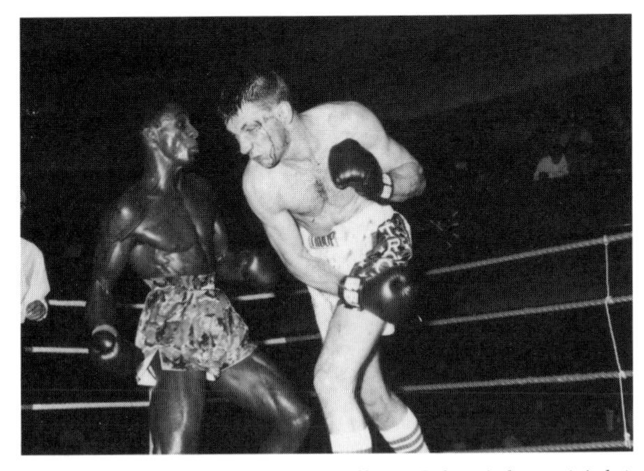

In a last ditch sixth round effort, John Ashton (right) steams into British middles king, Herol Graham. Moments later, he was stopped Chris Bevan

17 December, 1991 Robbie Regan 8.0 (Wales) W PTS 12 Francis Ampofo 7.13½ (England), Cardiff. Flyweight Title Challenge.

In a return match, another fierce battle ensued, with Regan regaining the title he had lost to the tough little non-stop battler the previous September. This time round, however, there were no knockdowns or cut eyes to spoil the action and both men again proved themselves a credit to British boxing. Once the opening round got underway, Regan immediately settled into a pattern that was to last all evening, keeping at distance and using his longer reach to perfection and protecting himself on the inside at all times. Ampofo fought the only way he knew in coming forward and desperately trying to get close quarters where he could work away and inflict the utmost damage. But it wasn't to be his night as the elusive Regan would not allow himself to be drawn into any mauls and carried on picking up points with an immaculate left-lead. Despite a strong finish by the champion, there wasn't one person in the hall who doubted that the title hadn't returned to Wales at the final bell. Referee for the contest was Mickey Vann. *Referees Scorecard:* 118-116.

27 January, 1992 Joe Kelly 8.6 (Scotland) W PTS 12 Ronnie Carroll 8.6 (Scotland), Glasgow. Vacant Bantamweight Title.

This was yet another return contest, their previous one having been the first drawn British title fight since 1934 and the fans north of the border eagerly awaited its outcome. For the first three rounds, Carroll controlled the contest at distance, making full use of Kelly's slow start, but in the fourth that all changed when the smaller man mounted a vicious attack which ended with both men battling toe-to-toe on the ropes. From that moment on, Kelly crowded his rival at every given opportunity, cutting down the ring and forcing Carroll to stand his ground and trade. In the ninth, however, Carroll's fortunes began to change as he started to use the ring to his advantage and began drawing Kelly on to some heavy counters. The final round saw a grandstand finish by both men as first one and then the other landed telling punches. When Kelly's hand was held up as the winner and new champion, there was much controversy following the announcement that Carroll had only won two rounds on Larry O'Connell's scorecard. *Referees Scorecard:* 119-116½.

30 January, 1992 Crawford Ashley 12.4½ (England) W RSC 1 Jim Peters 12.5¾ (England), Southampton. Light-Heavyweight Title Defence.

By destroying Jim Peters in just 55 seconds, Crawford Ashley came within spitting distance of beating the record for the quickest British title victory held by Dave Charnley, following his 40 second demolition job on Darkie Hughes back in 1961. The fight itself, or what passed for one, saw Ashley make a very fast start with solid jabs paving the way for his heavy combinations. Peters was both bemused and shaken by the pace of such an early attack and sought immediate refuge on the ropes. But instead of rushing in wildly, Ashley showed remarkable calm as he continued to pick his punches with great accuracy, while at the same time not giving the challenger any chance to recover. With Peters beginning to sway side-to-side on the ropes and not fighting back, Ashley mounted his final attack. Fierce rights and lefts to head and body were driven in and although Peters remained in an upright position, Roy Francis was left with no alternative other than to bring the proceedings to a halt.

20 February, 1992 Gary Jacobs 10.6¼ (Scotland) W PTS 12 Del Bryan 10.5½ (England), Glasgow. Welterweight Title Challenge.

Who would have thought, following the shocking knockout defeat at the hands of Mickey Hughes, that within three fights, Jacobs would have lifted the British title. In hindsight, it was probably less than remarkable, considering the fact that he had already beaten Bryan over ten rounds, some four years earlier. Unfortunately for the fans, southpaws rarely make good viewing when matched against each other and this was one of those occasions. Bryan should have used those long arms of his to keep at distance more often, while Jacobs was at his most effective when getting to work inside and taking the champion out of his stride. But in allowing his rival to get to close quarters so often, it was painfully noticeable to see how many punches Bryan wasted on thin air when short counters would have been more productive in curtailing Jacobs' progress. Although both Jacobs and Bryan picked up cuts over their right eyes during the latter stages, neither were in serious difficulty, but Mickey Vann, who was kept busy throughout, issuing several warnings, was probably every bit as pleased as the fighters to hear the final bell. *Referees Scorecard:* 118½-117.

Lou Gent (right) put up a brave challenge, but to no avail, against the British super-middleweight champion, Fidel Castro

Les Clark

25 February, 1991 Fidel Castro 11.13¾ (England) W PTS 12 Lou Gent 12.0 (England), London. Super-Middleweight Title Defence.

Gent followed up his cracking Commonwealth title challenge against Henry Wharton, by taking Castro close for his British title and again gave full value as an honest to goodness battler who never knows when he is beaten. After making a fair start, picking his punches sparingly, but accurately, Castro partly lost his way during the middle rounds as Gent came on strong. But the challenger's busier workrate was not always translated into quality, with many of his blows being taken on the champion's arms, gloves or even plain falling short. The heavier punching generally came from Castro, but he couldn't sustain any real bouts of pressure, allowing Gent to come right back into it. The last round saw Castro landing heavy uppercuts which shook Gent up, but instead of backing off, the challenger just gritted his teeth and forced his rival to hang on until the final bell came as a welcome respite. Adrian Morgan had no hesitation in naming Castro as the winner, much to the chagrin of the crowd. *Referees Scorecard:* 118-117.

27 February, 1992 Andy Holligan 10.0 (England) W RSC 3 Tony McKenzie 9.13½ (England), Liverpool. Light-Welterweight Title Defence.

The first round saw Holligan stalking McKenzie, forcing him to box off the back foot. And while the former champion seemed content to slip the punches that came his way and occasionally crack in a few blows of his own, the writing was on the wall once he had sampled a Holligan left-hook special towards the end of the session. At the beginning of the second, it was clear that Holligan had decided to go for broke as he immediately crashed in a tremendous left-hook to McKenzie's jaw. Just how the challenger stood up to that and how he remained on his feet until the bell to end the round was a sure sign of his durability. He had been punched from pillar to post, cut over the right eye and generally beaten up. Amazingly, McKenzie came out for the third full of fight, but again his best shots merely bounced off Holligan, who then got down to business. A devastating barrage of blows without reply, left McKenzie lurching drunkenly along the ropes and with 16 seconds of the round remaining, Dave Parris leapt in between the two men and rescued the almost too brave for his own good challenger.

25 April, 1992 Crawford Ashley 12.6½ (England) W RSC 8 Glazz Campbell 12.6 (England), Belfast. Light-Heavyweight Title Defence.

The champion, Crawford Ashley, made a hesitant start, probably due to the fact that Campbell had beaten him at an earlier stage of his career and he didn't want to take any undue risks. For a championship contest, however, it fell well below the normal standards expected, with neither man able to exploit any weaknesses over the first six rounds and with the contest merely petering along. Suddenly, out of the blue, towards the end of the seventh, Ashley burst into action with a solid left to the head and a long right to the body which sent Campbell crashing for a nine count. He got up and answered the bell for the eighth, but was constantly stalked by a champion who now knew that he had the punch to finish the job. After two thirds of the round had elapsed, another long right crashed against Campbell's jaw and the fight was as good as over. Getting up at nine, the challenger was subjected to a steady bombardment of punches which had him slumping to the floor yet again and the referee, Adrian Morgan, called it off with 22 seconds of the round remaining.

25 April, 1992 Michael Armstrong 9.2½ (England) W RSC 7 John Doherty 9.2½ (England), Manchester. Super-Featherweight Title Challenge.

After both men had scaled well within the title weight limit, Armstrong made a good start, taking the first four rounds handily as he banged in good punches with both hands, almost without return. To his credit, Doherty, as ever, as game as a pebble, strived hard to get his jab working and had a better round in the fifth, while the challenger appeared to take a breather. But once the sixth round was underway, it became apparent that Doherty had little left as he continued to get clobbered by the left-hook, although defiantly fighting back on occasion. In the final moments of the seventh, Doherty crashed face first to the canvas, having being caught solidly by a right-cross, left-hook and the referee, Billy Rafferty, called a halt after the champion had risen at the count of nine, but was in an unfit state to continue. Doherty thus became the fourteenth super-featherweight champion to lose the title in his first defence.

30 April, 1992 Lennox Lewis 16.6½ (England) W RSC 3 Derek Williams 16.9 (England), London. Heavyweight Title Defence.

With three titles on the line for the first time at the weight since Joe Bugner beat Richard Dunn in October 1976, there was much at stake. And by jabbing and moving, Williams made Lewis look positively ordinary for the first two rounds as the latter threw wild overarm rights at his opponent. But to be fair, the double champion, Lewis, obviously felt that Williams could not harm him and was prepared to walk through the latter's defences to let his punches go. Keeping up the offensive in the third round, Lewis forced Williams to the ropes where he finally landed some solid rights, but the opportunity to finish the fight there and then appeared lost as the Commonwealth champion fiddled his way out of apparent trouble. Suddenly, Lewis finally found the world class punches he had been looking for, a left-jab, a right-uppercut and a left-uppercut, to finish the job and although Williams was on his feet at nine, Larry O'Connell waved it off with 30 seconds of the round remaining.

5 May, 1992 Carl Crook 9.8½ (England) W RSC 7 Steve Boyle 9.8¼ (Scotland), Preston. Lightweight Title Defence.

Looking to equal Maurice Cullen's record of three successful British lightweight title defences, Carl Crook put his British and Commonwealth crowns up for grabs against the Scot, Steve Boyle. Making a good start, Crook boxed his way into a clear lead by the end of the third round but, unfortunately, the mood of the contest changed in the fourth. During that round, Boyle was warned for taunting and then in the fifth, he picked up a bad cut by the side of his left eye, which he claimed was caused by a butt. After falling well behind on points, the challenger came back strongly in the sixth when his southpaw stance had the champion slightly perplexed and Crook collected a few blows he really should have avoided. However, in the seventh, the champion once again took control of the fight and a couple of decent punches re-opened Boyle's cut eye and referee John Coyle felt that he had no alternative other than to call it off after two minutes and 58 seconds of the round.

19 May, 1992 Robbie Regan 7.12½ (Wales) W RSC 9 James Drummond 7.13 (Scotland), Cardiff. Flyweight Title Defence.

Getting quickly down to business, Regan shaded the first with good body work, but in the following two rounds he was kept at bay by Drummond's left-hand. After coming back well in the fourth, the champion really took over in the fifth, forcing the taller Scot to the ropes with hooks and uppercuts. By the eighth round, Regan's body punches were beginning to pay dividends and early in the ninth, Drummond sank to the canvas, claiming that he had been hit with kidney punches. Paul Thomas, the referee, continued the count and although the challenger was up at nine he was unable to defend himself and the contest was stopped after 25 seconds of the round had elapsed.

1 June, 1992 Drew Docherty 8.5¾ (Scotland) W RSC 5 Joe Kelly 8.5¾ (Scotland), Glasgow. Bantamweight Title Challenge.

Both men got down to work on the bell, with Kelly making the body his target, while the challenger cleverly sidestepped the attacks and hit back with good punches of his own from both hands. By the second round, Docherty's longer reach was already paving the way home as he speared the oncoming Kelly with jabs and in the third he measured the champion with a good left-hook to send him sprawling for a count of five. On rising, Kelly was subjected to a further battery of jabs and hooks, but gamely made it through the next round, although beginning to look very battleworn. Charging into Docherty in the fifth, Kelly failed to take advantage of a good right to the head and was

Robbie Regan (left) steams into his British flyweight title challenger, James "Bulldog" Drummond. The game Scot was beaten in the ninth round Les Clark

floored himself by a heavy right to the jaw. Up at nine, Kelly walked straight into another bombardment of two-fisted blows and after being battered from pillar to post, he was put down for a further count. Scrambling up at nine, his legs betrayed him, leaving him wobbling around the ring and with two minutes, four seconds of the round gone he was rescued by the referee, John Coyle.

4 June, 1992 Carl Thompson 13.7 (England) W RSC 8 Steve Lewsam 13.2 (England), Cleethorpes. Vacant Cruiserweight Title.

With Britain's top two cruiserweights both unavailable, the number three rated fighter Carl Thompson was chosen to box the Midlands Area champion, Steve Lewsam, for the vacant title. The first four rounds were closely contested, with Thompson working the body and countering to the head, while Lewsam took the fight to his opponent at every opportunity. However, in the fifth, as Lewsam tired from his exertions, The Mancunian began to take control and it was amazing that the former was able to stay on his feet for so long. Showing great courage and fortitude, Lewsam somehow survived a steady beating from head to body throughout rounds five and seven, but the end was just around the corner. In the eighth, two heavy rights, a cross and an uppercut, deposited Lewsam on the canvas and although he somehow managed to be in a standing position at the count of ten, Dave Parris had seen enough and called a halt to the proceedings with one minute, nine seconds of the round gone.

Lord Lonsdale Challenge Belts: Outright Winners

The original belts were donated to the National Sporting Club by Lord Lonsdale and did not bear his name, the inscription reading "The National Sporting Club's Challenge Belt." It was not until the British Boxing Board of Control was formed that the emblems were reintroduced and the belts became known as the Lord Lonsdale Challenge Belts. The first contest involving the BBBoC belt was Benny Lynch versus Pat Palmer for the flyweight title on 16 September 1936. To win a belt outright a champion must score three title match victories at the same weight, not necessarily consecutively.

Outright Winners of the National Sporting Club's Challenge Belt, 1909-1935 (20)

FLYWEIGHT	Jimmy Wilde; Jackie Brown
BANTAMWEIGHT	Digger Stanley; Joe Fox; Jim Higgins; Johnny Brown; Johnny King
FEATHERWEIGHT	Jim Driscoll; Tancy Lee; Johnny Cuthbert; Nel Tarleton
LIGHTWEIGHT	Freddie Welsh
WELTERWEIGHT	Johnny Basham; Jack Hood
MIDDLEWEIGHT	Pat O'Keefe; Len Harvey; Jock McAvoy
L. HEAVYWEIGHT	Dick Smith
HEAVYWEIGHT	Bombardier Billy Wells; Jack Petersen

Outright Winners of the BBBoC Lord Lonsdale Challenge Belts, 1936-1992 (78)

FLYWEIGHT	Jackie Paterson; Terry Allen; Walter McGowan; John McCluskey; Hugh Russell; Charlie Magri; Pat Clinton; Robbie Regan
BANTAMWEIGHT	Johnny King; Peter Keenan (2); Freddie Gilroy; Alan Rudkin; Johnny Owen; Billy Hardy
FEATHERWEIGHT	Nel Tarleton; Ronnie Clayton (2); Charlie Hill; Howard Winstone (2); Evan Armstrong; Pat Cowdell; Robert Dickie; Paul Hodkinson; Colin McMillan
S. FEATHERWEIGHT	Jimmy Anderson; John Doherty
LIGHTWEIGHT	Eric Boon; Billy Thompson; Joe Lucy; Dave Charnley; Maurice Cullen; Ken Buchanan; Jim Watt; George Feeney; Tony Willis; Carl Crook
L. WELTERWEIGHT	Joey Singleton; Colin Power; Clinton McKenzie (2); Lloyd Christie
WELTERWEIGHT	Ernie Roderick; Wally Thom; Brian Curvis (2); Ralph Charles; Colin Jones; Lloyd Honeyghan; Kirkland Laing
L. MIDDLEWEIGHT	Maurice Hope; Jimmy Batten; Pat Thomas; Prince Rodney
MIDDLEWEIGHT	Pat McAteer; Terry Downes; Johnny Pritchett; Bunny Sterling; Alan Minter; Kevin Finnegan; Roy Gumbs; Tony Sibson; Herol Graham
L. HEAVYWEIGHT	Randy Turpin; Chic Calderwood; Chris Finnegan; Bunny Johnson; Tom Collins; Dennis Andries; Tony Wilson; Crawford Ashley
CRUISERWEIGHT	Johnny Nelson
HEAVYWEIGHT	Henry Cooper (3); Horace Notice; Lennox Lewis

NOTES: Jim Driscoll was thefirst champion to win an NSC belt outright, whilst Eric Boon later became the first champion to put three notches on a BBBoC belt.
Nel Tarleton and Johnny King are the only champions to have won both belts outright.
Freddie Welsh, with just two notches on an NSC belt, along with Johnny King, who had two notches on a BBBoC belt and Walter McGowan and Charlie Magri, both with just one notch on a BBBoC belt, were all allowed to keep their awards under the three years/no available challengers ruling.
Henry Cooper holds the record number of belts won by a single fighter, three in all.
Chris and Kevin Finnegan are the only brothers to have won belts outright.
Jim Higgins holds the record for winning an NSC belt outright in the shortest time, 279 days, whilst Colin McMillan won a BBBoC belt in just 160 days.

British Champions, 1891-1992

Shows the tenure of each British champion at each weight from 1891, when the National Sporting Club was founded and championship bouts were contested under Marquess of Queensberry Rules, using gloves.

Between 1891 and 1929, the year that the BBBoC was formed, men who held general recognition are shown **in bold,** as champions, while the others are seen purely as claimants.

Champions born outside Britain, who won open titles in this country, are not shown at the risk of confusing the issue further.

Also, it must be stated that many of the champions and claimants listed below, prior to 1909, were no more than English titleholders, having fought for the "Championship of England", but for our purposes they carry the "British" label.

Prior to 1909, the year that the Lord Lonsdale Challenge Belt was introduced and weight classes subsequently standardised, poundages within divisions could vary quite substantially, thus enabling men fighting at different weights to claim the same "title" at the same time. A brief history of the weight fluctuations between 1891 and 1909, shows:

Bantamweight Billy Plimmer was recognised as the British titleholder in 1891 at 110 lbs and became accepted as world champion when George Dixon, the number one in America's eyes, gradually increased his weight. In 1895 Pedlar Palmer took the British title at 112 lbs, but by 1900 he had developed into a 114 pounder. Between 1902 and 1904, Joe Bowker defended regularly at 116 lbs and in 1909 the NSC standardised the weight at 118 lbs, even though the USA continued for a short while to accept only 116 lbs.

Featherweight Between 1891 and 1895, one of the most prestigious championship belts in this country was fought for at 126 lbs and although George Dixon was recognised in the USA as world featherweight champion, gradually moving from 114 to 120 lbs, no major contests took place in Britain during the above period at his weight. It was only in 1895 when Fred Johnson took the British title at 120 lbs, losing it to Ben Jordan two years later, that we came into line with the USA. Ben Jordan became an outstanding champion, who, between 1898 and 1899, was seen by the NSC as world champion at 120 lbs. However, first Harry Greenfield, then Jabez White and Will Curley continued to claim the 126 lbs version of the British title and it was only in 1900 when Jack Roberts beat Curley, that the weight limit was finally standardised at nine stone.

Lightweight Outstanding champions often carried their weights as they grew in size. A perfect example of this was Dick Burge, the British lightweight champion from 1891-1901, who gradually increased from 134 to 144 lbs, while still maintaining his right to the title. It was not until 1902 that Jabez White brought the division into line with the USA. Later, both White and then Goldswain carried their weight up to 140 lbs and it was left to Johnny Summers to set the current limit of 135 lbs.

Welterweight The presence of Dick Burge fighting from 134 to 144 lbs plus up until 1900, explains quite adequately why the welterweight division, although very popular in the USA, did not take off in this country until 1902. The championship was contested between 142 and 146 lbs in those days and was not really supported by the NSC, but by 1909 with their backing it finally became established at 147 lbs.

Note that the Lonsdale Belt notches (title bout wins) relate to NSC, 1909-1935, and BBBoC, 1936-1990.
Champions in **bold** are accorded national recognition.
*Undefeated champions.

Former British, Commonwealth, European and World wealterweight champion, Lloyd Honeyghan (left), now on the comeback trail at light-middleweight Les Clark

Flyweight (112 lbs)

Title Holder	Lonsdale Belt Notches	Tenure
Sid Smith		1911
Sid Smith	1	1911-1913
Bill Ladbury		1913-1914
Percy Jones*	1	1914
Tancy Lee	1	1915
Joe Symonds	1	1915-1916
Jimmy Wilde*	3	1916-1923
Elky Clark*	2	1924-1927
Johnny Hill*	1	1927-1929
Jackie Brown		1929-1930
Bert Kirby	1	1930-1931
Jackie Brown	3	1931-1935
Benny Lynch*	2	1935-1938
Jackie Paterson	4	1939-1948
Rinty Monaghan*	1	1948-1950
Terry Allen	1	1951-1952
Teddy Gardner*	1	1952
Terry Allen*	2	1952-1954
Dai Dower*	1	1955-1957
Frankie Jones	2	1957-1960
Johnny Caldwell*	1	1960-1961
Jackie Brown	1	1962-1963
Walter McGowan*	1	1963-1966
John McCluskey*	3	1967-1977
Charlie Magri*	1	1977-1981
Kelvin Smart	1	1982-1984
Hugh Russell*	3	1984-1985
Duke McKenzie*	2	1985-1986
Dave Boy McAuley*	1	1986-1988
Pat Clinton*	3	1988-1991
Robbie Regan	1	1991
Francis Ampofo	1	1991
Robbie Regan	2	1991-

Bantamweight (118 lbs)

Title Holder	Lonsdale Belt Notches	Tenure
Billy Plimmer		1891-1895
Tom Gardner		1892
Willie Smith		1892-1896
Nunc Wallace		1893-1895
George Corfield		1893-1895
Pedlar Palmer		1895-1900
George Corfield		1895-1896
Billy Plimmer		1896-1898
Harry Ware		1899-1900
Harry Ware		1900-1902
Andrew Tokell		1901-1902
Jim Williams		1902
Andrew Tokell		1902
Harry Ware		1902
Joe Bowker		1902-1910
Owen Moran		1905-1907
Digger Stanley		1906-1910
Digger Stanley	2	1910-1913
Bill Beynon	1	1913
Digger Stanley	1	1913-1914
Curley Walker*	1	1914-1915
Joe Fox*	3	1915-1917
Tommy Noble	1	1918-1919
Walter Ross*	1	1919-1920
Jim Higgins	3	1920-1922
Tommy Harrison		1922-1923
Bugler Harry Lake	1	1923
Johnny Brown*	3	1923-1928
Alf Pattenden	2	1928-1929
Johnny Brown		1928
Teddy Baldock		1928-1929
Teddy Baldock*	1	1929-1931
Dick Corbett	1	1931-1932
Johnny King	1	1932-1934
Dick Corbett*	1	1934
Johnny King	1+2	1935-1947
Jackie Paterson	2	1947-1949
Stan Rowan*	1	1949
Danny O'Sullivan	1	1949-1951
Peter Keenan	3	1951-1953
John Kelly	1	1953-1954
Peter Keenan	3	1954-1959
Freddie Gilroy*	4	1959-1963
Johnny Caldwell	1	1964-1965
Alan Rudkin	1	1965-1966
Walter McGowan	1	1966-1968
Alan Rudkin*	4	1968-1972
Johnny Clark*	1	1973-1974
Dave Needham	1	1974-1975
Paddy Maguire	1	1975-1977
Johnny Owen*	4	1977-1980
John Feeney	1	1981-1983
Hugh Russell	1	1983
Davy Larmour	1	1983
John Feeney	1	1983-1985
Ray Gilbody	2	1985-1987
Billy Hardy*	5	1987-1991
Joe Kelly	1	1992
Drew Docherty	1	1992-

Robbie Regan (left) with his arm around the winner and new British flyweight champion, Francis Ampofo Les Clark

Featherweight (126 lbs)

Title Holder	Lonsdale Belt Notches	Tenure
Fred Johnson		1890-1895
Billy Reader		1891
Billy Reader		1891-1892
Harry Spurden		1892-1895
Fred Johnson		1895-1897
Harry Greenfield		1896-1899
Ben Jordan*		1897-1900
Jabez White		1899-1900
Will Curley		1900-1901
Jack Roberts		1901-1902
Will Curley		1902-1903
Ben Jordan*		1902-1905
Joe Bowker*		1905
Johnny Summers		1906
Joe Bowker		1905-1906
Jim Driscoll		1906-1907
Spike Robson*		1906-1907
Jim Driscoll*	3	1907-1913
Spike Robson		1907-1910
Ted Kid Lewis*	1	1913-1914
Llew Edwards*	1	1915-1917
Charlie Hardcastle	1	1917
Tancy Lee*	3	1917-1919
Mike Honeyman	2	1920-1921
Joe Fox*	1	1921-1922
George McKenzie	2	1924-1925
Johnny Curley	2	1925-1927
Johnny Cuthbert	1	1927-1928
Harry Corbett	1	1928-1929
Johnny Cuthbert	2	1929-1931
Nel Tarleton	1	1931-1932
Seaman Tommy Watson	2	1932-1934
Nel Tarleton	2	1934-1936
Johnny McGrory*	1	1936-1938
Jim Spider Kelly	1	1938-1939
Johnny Cusick	1	1939-1940
Nel Tarleton*	3	1940-1947
Ronnie Clayton	6	1947-1954
Sammy McCarthy	1	1954-1955
Billy Spider Kelly	1	1955-1956
Charlie Hill	3	1956-1959
Bobby Neill	1	1959-1960
Terry Spinks	2	1960-1961
Howard Winstone*	7	1961-1969
Jimmy Revie	2	1969-1971
Evan Armstrong	2	1971-1972
Tommy Glencross	1	1972-1973
Evan Armstrong*	2	1973-1975
Vernon Sollas	1	1975-1977
Alan Richardson	2	1977-1978
Dave Needham	2	1978-1979
Pat Cowdell*	3	1979-1982

Title Holder	Lonsdale Belt Notches	Tenure
Steve Sims*	1	1982-1983
Barry McGuigan*	2	1983-1986
Robert Dickie	3	1986-1988
Peter Harris	1	1988
Paul Hodkinson*	3	1988-1990
Sean Murphy	2	1990-1991
Gary de Roux	1	1991
Colin McMillan*	3	1991-1992

S. Featherweight (130 lbs)

Title Holder	Lonsdale Belt Notches	Tenure
Jimmy Anderson*	3	1968-1970
John Doherty	1	1986
Pat Cowdell	1	1986
Najib Daho	1	1986-1987
Pat Cowdell	1	1987-1988
Floyd Havard	1	1988-1989
John Doherty	1	1989-1990
Joey Jacobs	1	1990
Hugh Forde	1	1990
Kevin Pritchard	1	1990-1991
Robert Dickie	1	1991
Sugar Gibiliru	1	1991
John Doherty	1	1991-1992
Michael Armstrong	1	1992-

Lightweight (135 lbs)

Title Holder	Lonsdale Belt Notches	Tenure
Dick Burge		1891-1897
Harry Nickless		1891-1894
Tom Causer		1894-1897
Tom Causer		1897
Dick Burge*		1897-1901
Jabez White		1902-1906
Jack Goldswain		1906-1908
Johnny Summers		1908-1909
Freddie Welsh	1	1909-1911
Matt Wells	1	1911-1912
Freddie Welsh*	1	1912-1919
Bob Marriott*	1	1919-1920
Ernie Rice	1	1921-1922
Seaman Nobby Hall		1922-1923
Harry Mason*		1923-1924
Ernie Izzard	2	1924-1925
Harry Mason		1924-1925
Harry Mason*	1	1925-1928
Sam Steward		1928-1929
Fred Webster		1929-1930
Al Foreman*	1	1930-1932
Johnny Cuthbert		1932-1934
Harry Mizler		1934
Jackie Kid Berg		1934-1936
Jimmy Walsh	1	1936-1938
Dave Crowley	1	1938
Eric Boon	3	1938-1944
Ronnie James*	1	1944-1947
Billy Thompson	3	1947-1951
Tommy McGovern	1	1951-1952
Frank Johnson*	1	1952-1953
Joe Lucy	1	1953-1955
Frank Johnson	1	1955-1956
Joe Lucy	2	1956-1957
Dave Charnley*	3	1957-1965
Maurice Cullen*	4	1965-1968
Ken Buchanan*	2	1968-1971
Willie Reilly*	1	1972
Jim Watt	1	1972-1973
Ken Buchanan*	1	1973-1974
Jim Watt*	2	1975-1977
Charlie Nash*	1	1978-1979
Ray Cattouse	2	1980-1982
George Feeney*	3	1982-1985
Tony Willis	3	1985-1987
Alex Dickson	1	1987-1988
Steve Boyle*	2	1988-1990
Carl Crook	5	1990-

L. Welterweight (140 lbs)

Title Holder	Lonsdale Belt Notches	Tenure
Des Rea	1	1968-1969
Vic Andreetti*	2	1969-1970
Des Morrison	1	1973-1974
Pat McCormack	1	1974
Joey Singleton	3	1974-1976
Dave Boy Green*	1	1976-1977
Colin Power*	2	1977-1978
Clinton McKenzie	1	1978-1979
Colin Power	1	1979
Clinton McKenzie	5	1979-1984
Terry Marsh*	1	1984-1986
Tony Laing*	1	1986
Tony McKenzie	2	1986-1987
Lloyd Christie	3	1987-1989
Clinton McKenzie*	1	1989
Pat Barrett*	2	1989-1990
Tony Ekubia	1	1990-1991
Andy Holligan	2	1991-

Welterweight (147 lbs)

Title Holder	Lonsdale Belt Notches	Tenure
Charlie Allum		1903-1904
Charlie Knock		1904-1906
Curly Watson*		1906-1910
Young Joseph		1908-1910
Young Joseph	1	1910-1911
Arthur Evernden		1911-1912
Johnny Summers		1912
Johnny Summers	2	1912-1914
Tom McCormick		1914
Matt Wells*		1914
Johnny Basham	3	1914-1920
Matt Wells		1914-1919
Ted Kid Lewis		1920-1924
Tommy Milligan*		1924-1925
Hamilton Johnny Brown		1925
Harry Mason		1925-1926
Jack Hood*	3	1926-1934
Harry Mason		1934
Pat Butler*		1934-1936
Dave McCleave		1936
Jake Kilrain	1	1936-1939
Ernie Roderick	5	1939-1948
Henry Hall	1	1948-1949
Eddie Thomas	2	1949-1951
Wally Thom	1	1951-1952
Cliff Curvis*	1	1952-1953
Wally Thom	2	1953-1956
Peter Waterman*	2	1956-1958
Tommy Molloy	2	1958-1960
Wally Swift	1	1960
Brian Curvis*	7	1960-1966
Johnny Cooke	2	1967-1968
Ralph Charles*	3	1968-1972
Bobby Arthur	1	1972-1973
John H. Stracey*	1	1973-1975
Pat Thomas	2	1975-1976
Henry Rhiney	2	1976-1979
Kirkland Laing	1	1979-1980
Colin Jones*	3	1980-1982
Lloyd Honeyghan*	2	1983-1985
Kostas Petrou	1	1985
Sylvester Mittee	1	1985
Lloyd Honeyghan*	1	1985-1986
Kirkland Laing	4	1987-1991
Del Bryan	2	1991-1992
Gary Jacobs	1	1992-

L. Middleweight (154 lbs)

Title Holder	Lonsdale Belt Notches	Tenure
Larry Paul	2	1973-1974
Maurice Hope*	3	1974-1977
Jimmy Batten	3	1977-1979
Pat Thomas	3	1979-1981
Herol Graham*	2	1981-1983
Prince Rodney*	1	1983-1984
Jimmy Cable	2	1984-1985
Prince Rodney	2	1985-1986
Chris Pyatt*	1	1986
Lloyd Hibbert*	1	1987
Gary Cooper	1	1988
Gary Stretch*	2	1988-1990
Wally Swift Jnr	2	1991-

Middleweight (160 lbs)

Title Holder	Lonsdale Belt Notches	Tenure
Ted Pritchard*		1891-1892
Ted White		1893-1896
Ted Pritchard		1894
Anthony Diamond		1898
Dido Plumb		1900
Jack Palmer		1902-1903
Charlie Allum		1905-1906
Pat O'Keefe		1906
Pat O'Keefe		1906
Tom Thomas	1	1906-1910
Jim Sullivan*	1	1910-1912
Jack Harrison*	1	1912-1913
Pat O'Keefe	2	1914-1916
Bandsman Jack Blake	1	1916-1918
Pat O'Keefe*	1	1918-1919
Ted Kid Lewis		1920-1921
Tom Gummer	1	1920-1921
Gus Platts		1921
Johnny Basham*		1921
Ted Kid Lewis	2	1921-1923
Johnny Basham		1921
Roland Todd*		1923-1925
Roland Todd		1925-1927
Tommy Milligan	1	1926-1928
Frank Moody		1927-1928
Alex Ireland		1928-1929
Len Harvey	5	1929-1933
Jock McAvoy*	3+2	1933-1944
Ernie Roderick	1	1945-1946
Vince Hawkins	1	1946-1948
Dick Turpin	2	1948-1950
Albert Finch	1	1950
Randy Turpin*	1	1950-1954
Johnny Sullivan	1	1954-1955
Pat McAteer*	3	1955-1958
Terry Downes	1	1958-1959
John Cowboy McCormack	1	1959
Terry Downes*	2	1959-1962
George Aldridge	1	1962-1963
Mick Leahy	1	1963-1964
Wally Swift	1	1964-1965
Johnny Pritchett*	4	1965-1969
Les McAteer	1	1969-1970
Mark Rowe	1	1970
Bunny Sterling	4	1970-1974
Kevin Finnegan*	1	1974
Bunny Sterling*	1	1975
Alan Minter*	3	1975-1977

Title Holder	Lonsdale Belt Notches	Tenure
Kevin Finnegan	1	1977
Alan Minter*	1	1977-1978
Tony Sibson	1	1979
Kevin Finnegan*	1	1979-1980
Roy Gumbs	3	1981-1983
Mark Kaylor	1	1983-1984
Tony Sibson*	1	1984
Herol Graham*	1	1985-1986
Brian Anderson	1	1986-1987
Tony Sibson*	1	1987-1988
Herol Graham	4	1988-

S. Middleweight (168 lbs)

Title Holder	Lonsdale Belt Notches	Tenure
Sammy Storey	2	1989-1990
James Cook*	1	1990-1991
Fidel Castro	2	1991-

L. Heavyweight

Title Holder	Lonsdale Belt Notches	Tenure
Dennis Haugh		1913-1914
Dick Smith	2	1914-1916
Harry Reeve*	1	1916-1917
Dick Smith*	1	1918-1919
Boy McCormick*	1	1919-1921
Jack Bloomfield*	1	1922-1924
Tom Berry	1	1925-1927
Gipsy Daniels*	1	1927
Frank Moody	1	1927-1929
Harry Crossley	1	1929-1932
Jack Petersen*	1	1932
Len Harvey*	1	1933-1934
Eddie Phillips		1935-1937
Jock McAvoy	1	1937-1938
Len Harvey	2	1938-1942
Freddie Mills*	1	1942-1950
Don Cockell	2	1950-1952
Randy Turpin*	1	1952
Dennis Powell	1	1953
Alex Buxton	2	1953-1955
Randy Turpin	1	1955
Ron Barton*	1	1956
Randy Turpin*	2	1956-1958
Chic Calderwood*	4	1960-1966
Young John McCormack	2	1967-1969
Eddie Avoth	2	1969-1971
Chris Finnegan	2	1971-1973
John Conteh*	2	1973-1974
Johnny Frankham	1	1975
Chris Finnegan*	1	1975-1976
Tim Wood	1	1976-1977
Bunny Johnson*	3	1977-1981
Tom Collins	3	1982-1984
Dennis Andries*	5	1984-1986
Tom Collins*	1	1987
Tony Wilson	3	1987-1989
Tom Collins*	1	1989-1990
Steve McCarthy*	1	1990-1991
Crawford Ashley	3	1991-

Cruiserweight (190 lbs)

Title Holder	Lonsdale Belt Notches	Tenure
Sam Reeson*	1	1985-1986
Andy Straughn	1	1986-1987
Roy Smith	1	1987
Tee Jay	1	1987-1988
Glenn McCrory*	2	1988
Andy Straughn	1	1988-1989
Johnny Nelson*	3	1989-1991
Derek Angol*	2	1991-1992
Carl Thompson	1	1992-

Heavyweight (190 lbs +)

Title Holder	Lonsdale Belt Notches	Tenure
Charlie Mitchell*		1882-1894
Ted Pritchard		1891-1895
Jem Smith*		1895-1896
George Chrisp		1901
Jack Scales		1901-1902
Jack Palmer		1903-1906
Gunner Moir		1906-1909
Iron Hague		1909-1910
P.O. Curran		1910-1911
Iron Hague		1910-1911
Bombardier Billy Wells	3	1911-1919
Joe Beckett*		1919
Frank Goddard	1	1919
Joe Beckett		1919
Joe Beckett*	1	1919-1923
Frank Goddard		1923-1926
Phil Scott*		1926-1931
Reggie Meen		1931-1932
Jack Petersen	3	1932-1933
Len Harvey		1933-1934
Jack Petersen		1934-1936
Ben Foord		1936-1937
Tommy Farr*	1	1937-1938
Len Harvey*	1	1938-1942
Jack London	1	1944-1945
Bruce Woodcock	2	1945-1950
Jack Gardner	1	1950-1952
Johnny Williams	1	1952-1953
Don Cockell*	1	1953-1956
Joe Erskine	2	1956-1958
Brian London	1	1958-1959
Henry Cooper*	9	1959-1969
Jack Bodell	1	1969-1970
Henry Cooper	1	1970-1971
Joe Bugner	1	1971
Jack Bodell	1	1971-1972
Danny McAlinden	1	1972-1975
Bunny Johnson	1	1975
Richard Dunn	2	1975-1976
Joe Bugner*	1	1976-1977
John L. Gardner*	2	1978-1980
Gordon Ferris	1	1981
Neville Meade	1	1981-1983
David Pearce*	1	1983-1985
Hughroy Currie	1	1985-1986
Horace Notice*	4	1986-1988
Gary Mason	2	1989-1991
Lennox Lewis	3	1991-

The current holder of the British light-heavyweight title is Crawford Ashley (seen here on the left) Les Clark

British Area Title Bouts, 1991-92

Central Area

Titleholders at 30 June 1992

Fly: *vacant.* **Bantam:** Chris Clarkson. **Feather:** Russell Davison. **S. Feather:** *vacant.* **Light:** Kevin Toomey. **L. Welter:** Richard Burton. **Welter:** Ossie Maddix. **L. Middle:** *vacant.* **Middle:** *vacant.* **L. Heavy:** *vacant.* **Cruiser:** *vacant:* **Heavy:** Michael Murray.

Title Bouts (1 July 1991 - 30 June 1992)

9 September 1991 Russell Davison w pts 10 Jimmy Owens, Liverpool (Featherweight Defence)
19 September 1991 Michael Murray w rsc 8 Carl Gaffney, Stockport (Vacant Heavyweight)
27 February 1992 Richard Burton w pts 10 Chris Saunders, Liverpool (Vacant L. Welterweight)
26 March 1992 Kevin Toomey w dis 8 Wayne Windle, Hull (Lightweight Challenge)
During the above period, Kevin Spratt (L. Welter), Fidel Castro (Middle), Crawford Ashley (Cruiser) and Neil Malpass (Heavy), all relinquished their titles.

Midlands Area

Titleholders at 30 June 1992

Fly: *vacant.* **Bantam:** *vacant.* **Feather:** Kelton McKenzie. **S. Feather:** Pete Buckley. **Light:** Peter Till. **L. Welter:** Malcolm Melvin. **Welter:** Ernie Loveridge. **L. Middle:** Gary Osborne. **Middle:** Antonio Fernandez. **L. Heavy:** Roy Skeldon. **Cruiser:** Steve Lewsam. **Heavy:** *vacant.*

Title Bouts (1 July 1991 - 30 June 1992)

25 July 1991 Peter Till w rsc 4 Karl Taylor, Dudley (Lightweight Defence)
10 September 1991 Ernie Loveridge w rsc 1 Gary Osborne, Wolverhampton (Welterweight Challenge)
16 September 1991 Steve Lewsam w pts 10 Cordwell Hylton, Cleethorpes (Cruiserweight Challenge)
20 February 1992 Pete Buckley w rsc 10 Brian Robb, Telford (S. Featherweight Defence)
3 March 1992 Antonio Fernandez w pts 10 Paul Wesley, Cradley Heath (Vacant Middleweight)
17 March 1992 Gary Osborne w rsc 5 Shamus Casey, Wolverhampton (Vacant L. Middleweight)
29 April 1992 Kelton McKenzie w rsc 5 Elvis Parsley, Solihull (Vacant Featherweight)
During the above period, Rocky Lawlor (Bantam), Mark Holt (Feather) and John Ashton (Middle), all relinquished their titles. Tucker Richards (Heavy) - deceased.

Northern Area

Titleholders at 30 June 1992

Fly: *vacant.* **Bantam:** *vacant.* **Feather:** *vacant.* **S. Feather:** Darren Elsdon. **Light:** Paul Charters. **L. Welter:** *vacant.* **Welter:** *vacant.* **L. Middle:** *vacant.* **Middle:** *vacant.* **S. Middle:** *vacant.* **L. Heavy:** Terry French. **Heavy:** Paul Lister.

Title Bouts (1 July 1991 - 30 June 1992)

22 October 1991 Darren Elsdon w rsc 7 Frankie Foster, Hartlepool (S. Featherweight Challenge)

Northern Ireland Area

Titleholders at 30 June 1992 - None.

Scottish Area

Titleholders at 30 June 1992

Fly: *vacant.* **Bantam:** Donnie Hood. **Feather:** Jamie McBride. **S. Feather:** Mark Geraghty. **Light:** Kris McAdam. **L. Welter:** Robert Harkin. **Welter:** Willie Beattie. **L. Middle:** *vacant.* **Middle:** *vacant.* **S. Middle:** *vacant.* **L. Heavy:** *vacant.* **Cruiser:** *vacant.* **Heavy:** *vacant.*

Title Bouts (1 July 1991 - 30 June 1992)

23 September 1991 Mark Geraghty w pts 10 Neil Leitch, Glasgow (S. Featherweight Defence)
31 January 1992 Willie Beattie w rsc 3 Gordon Blair, Glasgow (Vacant Welterweight)

Southern Area

Titleholders at 30 June 1992

Fly: *vacant.* **Bantam:** *vacant.* **Feather:** Alan McKay. **S. Feather:** *vacant.* **Light:** Michael Ayers. **L. Welter:** Dave Pierre. **Welter:** *vacant.* **L. Middle:** W. O. Wilson. **Middle:** Tony Burke. **S. Middle:** Ian Strudwick. **L. Heavy:** Glazz Campbell. **Cruiser:** Everton Blake. **Heavy:** *vacant.*

Title Bouts (1 July 1991 - 30 June 1992)

7 November 1991 W. O. Wilson w rsc 8 Nigel Fairbairn, Peterborough (Vacant L. Middleweight)
13 November 1991 Alan McKay w rsc 8 Gary de Roux, Bethnal Green (Vacant Featherweight)
14 November 1991 Everton Blake w pts 10 John Graham, Bayswater (Cruiserweight Challenge)
19 November 1991 Glazz Campbell w co 7 Richard Bustin, Norwich (Vacant L. Heavy)
11 December 1991 Ian Strudwick w co 8 Ray Webb, Basildon (Vacant S. Middleweight)
19 February 1992 Michael Ayers w rsc 7 Rudy Valentino, Muswell Hill (Lightweight Defence)
11 March 1992 Ian Strudwick w pts 10 Ali Forbes, Solihull (S. Middleweight Defence)
30 April 1992 Dave Pierre w rsc 7 Carlos Chase, Watford (L. Welterweight Defence)
During the above period, Trevor Smith (Welter), Andy Wright (S. Middle) and Jim Peters (L. Heavy), all relinquished their titles.

Welsh Area

Titleholders at 30 June 1992

Fly: *vacant.* **Bantam:** *vacant.* **Feather:** Steve Robinson. **S. Feather:** Neil Haddock. **Light:** *vacant.* **L. Welter:** *vacant.* **Welter:** John Davies. **L. Middle:** Carlo Colarusso. **Middle:** Wayne Ellis. **S. Middle:** *vacant.* **L. Heavy:** *vacant.* **Cruiser:** *vacant.* **Heavy:** Chris Jacobs.

Title Bouts (1 July 1991 - 30 June 1992)

18 July 1991 Steve Robinson w pts 10 Peter Harris, Cardiff (Featherweight Challenge)
11 February 1992 Wayne Ellis w pts 10 Alan Richards, Cardiff (Vacant Middleweight)
11 May 1992 Neil Haddock w pts 10 Steve Robinson, Llanelli (Vacant S. Featherweight)
11 May 1992 Carlo Colarusso w rsc 5 Russell Washer, Llanelli (L. Middleweight Defence)

Western Area

Titleholders at 30 June 1992 - None.

During the above period, Mark Purcell (Welter) - retired.

Commonwealth Title Bouts, 1991-92

10 September, 1991 Hugh Forde 9.4 (England) W PTS 12 Thunder Aryeh 9.4 (Ghana), Wolverhampton, England. Super-Featherweight Title Challenge.

In what turned out to be a very undistinguished contest, the defending champion, Aryeh, found Forde too awkward to handle and eventually became increasingly frustrated by his own inability to fathom his opponent's style. Forde, for his part, did very little work, being merely content to produce just enough to win and basically relying on the champion's inactivity. When he did produce any movement, Aryeh threw flapping, flailing punches, from way out of range, which Forde had no difficulty in avoiding. To be fair to Forde, he had recently suffered two bad back-to-back defeats against Pritchard and Pep and was obviously not going to take any undue risks. The only real action came in the last two minutes of the final round when Aryeh was cut over the right eye and stormed forward only to find the Englishman showboating around the ring out of harm's way on his way to John Coyle's decision. *Referees Scorecard*: 119½-114½.

13 September, 1991 Guy Waters 12.4¾ (Australia) W PTS 12 Leslie Stewart 12.4¾ (Trinidad), Melbourne, Australia. Light-Heavyweight Title Defence.

Former WBA champion, Leslie Stewart, who learnt his boxing at the Repton club in London, has now possibly reached the end of the road, at least, as far as championships are concerned. Over twelve non-eventful rounds, the champion, Waters, made a fair start when picking up points in the early rounds with a prodding left-jab, but, as in recent contests, he had retreated into his shell by the mid-way point. With the champion's workrate diminishing fast, Stewart was able to get himself back into the fight, using his straight-left to good effect, before going down on a split decision. *Judges Scorecards*: 118-112, 115-113, 113-115.

Ghana's Thunder Aryeh (left) found Hugh Forde too awkward a customer to handle and lost his Commonwealth super-featherweight title in his second defence Chris Bevan

17 October, 1991 Derek Angol 13.8 (England) W RSC 4 Dave Russell 13.7 (Australia), London England. Cruiserweight Title Defence.

The long-armed champion quickly assumed control, picking the British-born Russell off with lefts and rights and by the end of the first round had opened a cut over his rival's left eye. Upping the pace in the second, Angol soon had the challenger holding, following some heavy attacks and it became apparent that they were having the desired effect when Russell began to blow hard by the end of the round. In the third, Angol got totally on top, fighting on both the inside and at distance and Russell's only response seemed to be to hold and frustrate. As the fourth got underway, it was clear that Angol was looking for the finish and as a right-cross forced Russell to give ground, a left-hook sent him sprawling on his left side. Although getting to his feet without a count, he had nothing left and under renewed pressure, Mickey Vann called it off with two minutes, fourteen seconds of the round remaining.

17 October, 1991 Donovan Boucher 10.4½ (Canada) W RSC 6 Stan Cunningham 10.6½ (Canada), Winnipeg, Canada. Welterweight Title Defence.

Cunningham, although beaten in two rounds by Eamonn Loughran in London last March, had been extremely well prepared for the fight and came out buzzing. Using speedy tactics he was able to keep out of Boucher's way and while not posing too much of a threat, he still forced the champion to look hard for an opening. Once the challenger showed signs of tiring, however, Boucher was in for the kill. He finally cornered Cunningham in the sixth with a blistering body attack and floored his rival three times before the third man stepped in at two minutes, 19 seconds of the round, following the third knockdown which incurred an automatic stoppage.

30 October, 1991 Henry Wharton 11.13¾ (England) DREW 12 Lou Gent 11.11¾ (England), Leeds, England. Super-Middleweight Title Defence.

For anyone fortunate enough to witness this wonderful battle, none would have been surprised if it was ultimately voted "Fight of the Year". As a contest it had everything and as an advertisement for the noble art, it excelled itself. For the first four rounds, Gent surpassed himself as he took an early lead with darting two-handed flurries, leaving Wharton flustered and hitting at thin air. However, in the fifth, sixth and seventh, Wharton finally got his body punching on target, inflicting two counts of eight and one of seven, respectively. It was a tribute to Gent's conditioning that he survived those attacks, but survive them he did, by getting on his bike, keeping out of trouble and scoring with light blows. Yet again in the ninth, Gent was the recipient of a damaging body blow, this time a low one that decked him, but he kept his cool, battling back quite magnificently in the tenth when driving Wharton around the ring. Unfortunately, for him, Gent was now totally exhausted and how he managed it to the final bell and the draw he so richly deserved, speaks volumes. The contest was refereed by Roy Francis. *Referees Scorecard:* 118-118.

5 November, 1991 Chris Pyatt 10.12½ (England) W PTS 12 Craig Trotter 11.0 (Australia), Leicester, England. Vacant Light-Middleweight Title.

Pyatt made a terrific start, putting the Aussie down for a count of seven in the first round, following a left-hook counter smack on the button. From that point onwards, Trotter decided that it was unwise to mix it and began to use hit and run tactics most effectively. Moving well, he was always a difficult target for Pyatt to make contact with and all the time he was scoring with accurate nagging punches. Eventually in the middle stages, Pyatt settled down, countering the jab with hooks and crosses and using his greater power to better advantage. The last two or three rounds saw Pyatt's greater strength become the deciding factor, with both men by now very tired and although the scoring indicates how close it was, Adrian Morgan had no hesitation in raising the Englishman's arm aloft at the final bell. *Referees Scorecard:* 118-117.

12 November, 1991 Paul Harvey 9.3 (England) W RSC 3 Hugh Forde 9.4 (England), Wolverhampton, England. Super-Featherweight Title Challenge.

The fact that the champion came to the scales two and a half pounds overweight and then had to weaken himself to get inside the limit was always going to make him extremely vulnerable at the hands of a young ambitious hard-hitting fighter like Harvey. And so it proved to be, as Forde, looking most apprehensive, made a tentative start over the first two rounds. In the third, with Harvey looking to wind up some big punches, a tremendous left-hook, followed by an ensuing right-uppercut to the head had Forde stretched out on the deck. On rising, when the count had reached four, Forde, on unsteady legs, grimly tried to hang on, but to no avail. Another big left-hook to the jaw left him taut against the ropes and as Harvey slammed in a further volley of blows, Paul Thomas pulled him off to stop the fight as Forde crashed face downwards on the canvas.

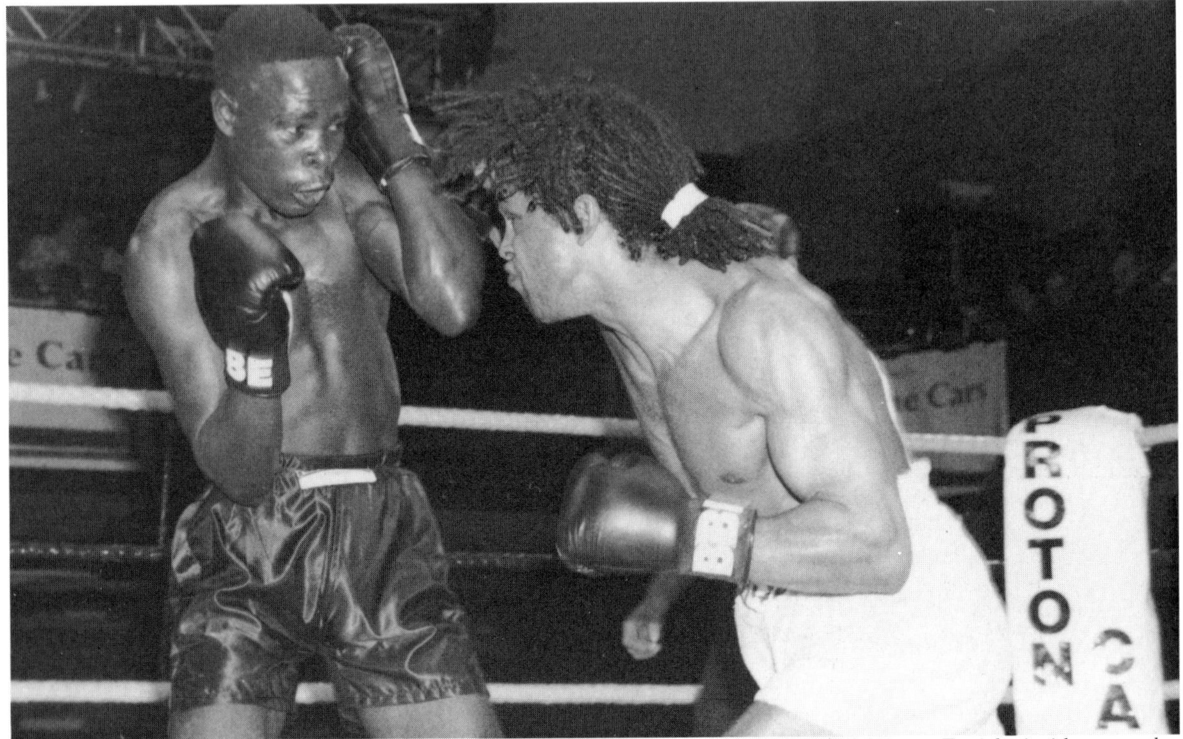

Chris Pyatt (right), the Commonwealth light-middleweight champion, finished off the woeful James Tapisha inside a round
Les Clark

28 November, 1991 Andy Holligan 9.13¾ (England) W RSC 8 Steve Larrimore 9.12¾ (Bahamas), Liverpool, England. Light-Welterweight Title Defence.

Larrimore made a blistering start. Using his height and reach advantages to great effect and working from top to bottom, he met Holligan head on. The pattern continued through the fourth, with the challenger working well with both hands, while Holligan had yet to find any real rhythm and was still looking for the openings. In the fifth, Holligan dramatically found a couple of big punches and battered Larrimore from pillar to post, but was unable to put his man away. How the Bahamian not only stayed upright, but managed to come back strongly in the next two sessions, only he knew. But by now, Larrimore's punches were having very little effect on the champion and at the beginning of the eighth, Holligan badly hurt him. Cutting down the ring space, Holligan gave his rival no chance to recover and when a battery of heavy blows to the head sent Larrimore staggering around crazily, the referee, Paul Thomas, stepped in with just fourteen seconds of the round remaining.

7 December, 1991 Paul Harvey 9.3¼ (England) W PTS 12 Sugar Gibiliru 9.2½ (England), Manchester, England. Super-Featherweight Title Defence.

The challenger proved just how durable he was, while Harvey showed he also had stamina as he went twelve rounds for the first time. Round after round, Harvey's long left-lead would stab into Gibiliru's features, but the Liverpudlian showed all his wiles as he effectively avoided the majority of heavy rights that came his way. He even put Harvey down for a short count in the fourth round when the champion, in missing with a right, walked on to one himself. This probably set the pattern for the rest of the bout as the inexperienced titleholder, being much the taller man, decided from that point on it was in his best interests to keep Gibiliru at distance where his inside work would carry no advantage. Even when Harvey hurt Gibiliru, the challenger would just soak it up and though there were cries of "stop it ref", Paul Thomas felt obliged to give both fighters every chance right through to the final bell. *Referees Scorecard:* 119-117.

18 January, 1992 Colin McMillan 9.0 (England) W PTS 12 Percy Commey 8.11½ (Ghana), London, England. Vacant Featherweight Title.

Commey, a Ghanaian beanpole of a fighter at 5'9" and extremely unorthodox with it, made McMillan's life a misery for most of the contest. A long left-lead that unerringly found its way through the champion's defences was bad enough, but in having to get inside Commey's guard, McMillan was also exposed to being roughed up. And it was while getting involved in close quarter exchanges in the last minute of the fourth round, that McMillan emerged with a nasty looking cut over the left eye. From then on, by constantly switching to confuse his opponent, the champion sought to nullify Commey's reach advantage. These were proved better tactics as he began to move in and out with crisp scoring punches from both hands, often without reply. When the bell rang for the final round, Commey needed a big effort, but it didn't come, with both men desperately tired and at the finish the referee, Roy Francis, had no hesitation naming McMillan the winner. *Referees Scorecard:* 118½-116½.

1 February, 1992 Chris Pyatt 11.0 (England) W RSC 3 Ambrose Mlilo 10.11½ (Zimbabwe), Birmingham, England. Light-Middleweight Title Defence.

This time round, another unheard of African found himself badly matched and although unbeaten in nine fights, he never stood a real chance from the moment the bell rang to open proceedings. Mlilo came out with his hands held high, while Pyatt probed for openings and even when the chmpion landed, there was no response forthcoming. In the second, while Pyatt had upped his workrate and was beginning to get fired up, there was still no positive action stemming from the challenger, who seemed content to hold his ground without fighting back. Pyatt obviously sensed that he could be in for a early night and in the third began to concentrate on uppercuts to bring Mlilo's guard down. This had the desired effect when a heavy right to the head forced the challenger backwards, before he fell to the canvas for a count of seven. On rising he looked positively shaken and following another burst of punches from Pyatt, Paul Thomas rescued the African with one and a half minutes of the round still remaining.

11 February, 1992 Tony Pep 9.3½ (Canada) W PTS 12 Paul Harvey 9.3 (England), Cardiff, Wales. Super-Featherweight Title Challenge.

We all thought that Harvey at 5'8" was tall for a super-feather, but compared to the experienced 6'1" Canadian, he seemed relatively small. Pep, with those long arms of his was mainly content to keep the champion on the end of an endless supply of stiff, punishing jabs, but you always had the feeling that if the going got tough, he had a bit more to offer than merely a trombone left-hand. It didn't take Harvey long to recognise that his best line of attack was to get inside and work the body, but when he did get through, Pep made sure he paid for the indiscretion. In the eleventh, the challenger was warned by Paul Thomas for a low blow, which, unfortunately for Harvey, slowed his major effort down, somewhat. And even while Harvey continued his desperate rally into the final round, it was noticeable that although Pep kept the fight at distance, he continued to look like a man who had plenty left in the tank and at the finish there was only likely to be one winner. *Referees Scorecard:* 119-116½.

27 February, 1992 Andy Holligan 10.0 (England) W RSC 3 Tony McKenzie 9.13½ (England), Liverpool, England. Light-Welterweight Title Defence.

For a report, see under British Title Bouts, 1991-92.

17 March, 1992 Donovan Boucher 10.6½ (Canada) W RSC 11 Robert Wright 10.5¾ (England), London, England. Welterweight Title Defence.

Although the contest was arranged at short notice, both men seemed well prepared and while Boucher took time to warm up, the challenger was certainly not intimidated by any step up in class. But once it had become apparent that Wright's punches didn't have the desired effect, the forever stalking Boucher always looked likely to finish the job quickly. By the fifth, Wright was beginning to tire and was trying to hold the champion at bay with long left-leads. From then on, every round looked to be the last, but the Englishman showed great character in stubbornly trying to stem the tide and occasionally surprised Boucher with sudden bursts of punches just when it seemed likely that he was ready to fold. In the tenth, it was noticeable that Wright was now suffering from severe cramp in the left leg and at one stage he actually fell over. The penultimate round of the contest turned out to be the last, as a left-hook sent the brave challenger to his knees. On rising and being subjected to a further fierce battery of blows, the referee, John Coyle, waved it off with 37 seconds of the eleventh remaining.

26 March, 1992 Richie Woodhall 11.4½ (England) W CO 1 Vito Gaudiosi 11.2 (Australia), Telford, England. Vacant Middleweight Title.

Fighting on home ground, the former Olympic bronze medallist, Richie Woodhall, was elevated to championship standard after only eight pro fights, but proved he was good enough with a 61 second knockout victory over the Australian, Vito Gaudiosi. As a 6'2" light-middleweight, Woodhall had only recently started to fill out and it took good matchmaking to get him a shot at the title left vacant by the unfortunate Michael Watson, after so few contests and none at the 160 lbs limit. From the opening bell, the much shorter Gaudiosi moved in, hands held high, while Woodhall circled around with the left-jab, making openings for a smart right-cross. It was this tactic that brought the fight to its dramatic summary conclusion as Woodhall feinted with the jab and shot a right over what appeared to glance off the Australian's temple. The effect was instant as Gaudiosi crashed to the canvas for the first time in his career, looked to get up, but then collapsed onto his back to be counted out by the referee, Paul Thomas.

8 April, 1992 Henry Wharton 12.0 (England) W RSC 8 Rod Carr 11.13 (Australia), Leeds, England. Super-Middleweight Title Defence.

Once again, hard-hitting champion, Henry Wharton, rescued a contest that was in danger of slipping away from him, this time in the eighth round of a re-match against the Australian, Rod Carr. For seven rounds the action had been fast and furious and there was little to choose between either man and although Carr was cut by the right eye as early as the second round it did not appear to hinder him too much. It was obvious that the challenger had come to the ring well prepared as he stood up well under Wharton's blows and at the same time hit back, especially with long stiff left-jabs. But in the seventh, the champion went up a gear, leaving Carr with a cut over the left eye and a damaged nose. With Carr now really beginning to feel the pace, Wharton cut loose in the eighth and downed his man for an eight count and although the challenger got up and tried to fight back, the contest was halted by Dave Parris after two minutes and seven seconds to save a game fighter from suffering further punishment.

28 April, 1992 Chris Pyatt 10.13¾ (England) W RSC 1 James Tapisha 10.10½ (Zambia), Wolverhampton, England. Light-Middleweight Title Defence.

A farcical mis-match saw the Zambian challenger quickly despatched inside two minutes, 17 seconds of the first round and prove at the same time that untested fighters, even though champions of their own country, should be more carefully vetted in future, prior to being given a shot at the title. Pyatt spent less than a minute sizing his opponent up, before cracking in a right over the top that had Tapisha down for a short count. Up at three, another short burst of punches had him over again and after rising quickly, the Zambian was all over the place, going down for the third time, until he was rescued by Mickey Vann.

30 April, 1992 Lennox Lewis 16.6½ (England) W RSC 3 Derek Williams 16.9 (England), London, England. Heavyweight Title Challenge.

For a report, see under British Title Bouts, 1991-92.

30 April, 1992 John Armour 8.3¼ (England) W RSC 12 Ndaba Dube 8.3¾ (Zimbabwe), London, England. Vacant Bantamweight Title.

Until being overtaken by fatigue towards the end of a long hard contest, the African proved himself a more than useful opponent for Armour and appeared to have a good lead coming into the twelfth round. Dube's good boxing skills had put him ahead of the Englishman throughout and it was only Armour's tenacity and resilience that kept him in contention for so long. It was noticeable early on that Armour's best chance lay in getting to work on the inside, but showing great speed of hand and foot, Dube was nearly always one move ahead. Coming into the twelfth, after rocking his man in the penultimate round, Armour finally caught up with Dube, pinning him against the ropes for over a minute, before the referee, Dave Parris, rescued the defenceless African with just eleven seconds of the bout remaining.

7 May, 1992 Carl Crook 9.8½ (England) W RSC 7 Steve Boyle 9.8¼ (Scotland), Preston, England. Lightweight Title Defence.

For a report, see under British Title Bouts, 1991-92.

Commonwealth Champions, 1908-1992

Prior to 1970, the championship was contested as for the British Empire title. Shows the tenure of each Commonwealth champion at each weight.

COMMONWEALTH COUNTRY CODE
A = Australia; BAH = Bahamas; BAR = Barbados; BER = Bermuda; C = Canada; E = England; F = Fiji; GH = Ghana; GU = Guyana; I = Ireland; J = Jamaica; K = Kenya; N = Nigeria; NZ = New Zealand; NI = Northern Ireland; PNG = Papua New Guinea; SA = South Africa; SAM = Samoa; S = Scotland; T = Tonga; TR = Trinidad; U = Uganda; W = Wales; ZA = Zambia; ZI = Zimbabwe.

*Undefeated champions

Flyweight (112 lbs)

Title Holder	Country	Tenure
Elky Clark*	S	1924-1927
Jackie Paterson	S	1940-1948
Rinty Monaghan*	NI	1948-1950
Teddy Gardner	E	1952
Jake Tuli	SA	1952-1954
Dai Dower*	W	1954-1957
Frankie Jones	S	1957
Dennis Adams*	SA	1957-1962
Jackie Brown	S	1962-1963
Walter McGowan*	S	1963-1969
John McCluskey	S	1970-1971
Henry Nissen	A	1971-1974
Big Jim West*	A	1974-1975
Patrick Mambwe	ZA	1976-1979
Ray Amoo	N	1980
Steve Muchoki	K	1980-1983
Keith Wallace*	E	1983-1984
Richard Clarke*	J	1986-1987
Nana Yaw Konadu*	GH	1987-1989
Alfred Kotei	GH	1989-

Bantamweight (118 lbs)

Title Holder	Country	Tenure
Jim Higgins	S	1920-1922
Tommy Harrison	E	1922-1923
Bugler Harry Lake	E	1923
Johnny Brown	E	1923-1928
Teddy Baldock*	E	1928-1930
Dick Corbett	E	1930-1932
Johnny King	E	1932-1934
Dick Corbett*	E	1934
Jim Brady	S	1941-1945
Jackie Paterson	S	1945-1949
Stan Rowan	E	1949
Vic Toweel	SA	1949-1952
Jimmy Carruthers*	A	1952-1954
Peter Keenan	S	1955-1959
Freddie Gilroy*	NI	1959-1963
Johnny Caldwell	NI	1964-1965
Alan Rudkin	E	1965-1966
Walter McGowan	S	1966-1968
Alan Rudkin	E	1968-1969
Lionel Rose*	A	1969
Alan Rudkin*	E	1970-1972
Paul Ferreri	A	1972-1977
Sulley Shittu*	GH	1977-1978
Johnny Owen*	W	1978-1980
Paul Ferreri	A	1981-1986
Ray Minus*	BAH	1986-1991
John Armour	E	1992-

Featherweight (126 lbs)

Title Holder	Country	Tenure
Jim Driscoll*	W	1908-1913
Llew Edwards*	W	1915-1917
Johnny McGory*	S	1936-1938
Jim Spider Kelly	NI	1938-1939
Johnny Cusick	E	1939-1940
Nel Tarleton*	E	1940-1947
Tiger Al Phillips	E	1947
Ronnie Clayton	E	1947-1951
Roy Ankrah	GH	1951-1954
Billy Spider Kelly	NI	1954-1955
Hogan Kid Bassey*	N	1955-1957
Percy Lewis	TR	1957-1960
Floyd Robertson	GH	1960-1967
John O'Brien	S	1967
Johnny Famechon*	A	1967-1969
Toro George	NZ	1970-1972
Bobby Dunne	A	1972-1974
Evan Armstrong	S	1974
David Kotey*	GH	1974-1975
Eddie Ndukwu	N	1977-1980
Pat Ford*	GU	1980-1981
Azumah Nelson*	GH	1981-1985
Tyrone Downes*	BAR	1986-1988
Thunder Aryeh	GH	1988-1989
Oblitey Commey	GH	1989-1990
Modest Napunyi	K	1990-1991
Barrington Francis*	C	1991
Colin McMillan*	E	1992

S. Featherweight (130 lbs)

Title Holder	Country	Tenure
Billy Moeller	A	1975-1977
Johnny Aba*	PNG	1977-1982
Langton Tinago	ZI	1983-1984
John Sichula	ZA	1984
Lester Ellis*	A	1984-1985
John Sichula	ZA	1985-1986
Sam Akromah	GH	1986-1987
John Sichula	ZA	1987-1989
Mark Reefer*	E	1989-1990
Thunder Aryeh	GH	1990-1991
Hugh Forde	E	1991
Paul Harvey	E	1991-1992
Tony Pep	C	1992-

Lightweight (135 lbs)

Title Holder	Country	Tenure
Freddie Welsh*	W	1912-1914
Al Foreman	E	1930-1933
Jimmy Kelso	A	1933
Al Foreman*	E	1933-1934
Laurie Stevens*	SA	1936
Arthur King	C	1948-1951
Frank Johnson	E	1953
Pat Ford	A	1953-1954
Ivor Germain	BAR	1954
Pat Ford*	A	1954-1955
Johnny van Rensburg	SA	1955-1956
Willie Toweel	SA	1956-1959
Dave Charnley	E	1959-1962
Bunny Grant	J	1962-1967
Manny Santos*	NZ	1967
Love Allotey	GH	1967-1968
Percy Hayles*	J	1968-1975
Jonathan Dele	N	1975-1977
Lennox Blackmore	GU	1977-1978
Hogan Jimoh	N	1978-1980
Langton Tinago	ZI	1980-1981
Barry Michael	A	1981-1982
Claude Noel	T	1982-1984
Graeme Brooke	A	1984-1985
Barry Michael	A	1985-1986
Langton Tinago	ZI	1986-1987
Mo Hussein	E	1987-1989
Pat Doherty	E	1989
Najib Daho	E	1989-1990
Carl Crook	E	1990-

L. Welterweight (140 lbs)

Title Holder	Country	Tenure
Joe Tetteh	GH	1972-1973
Hector Thompson	A	1973-1977
Baby Cassius Austin	A	1977-1978
Jeff Malcolm	A	1978-1979
Obisia Nwankpa	N	1979-1983
Billy Famous*	N	1983-1986
Tony Laing	E	1987-1988
Lester Ellis	A	1988-1989
Steve Larrimore	BAH	1989
Tony Ekubia	E	1989-1991
Andy Holligan	E	1991-

Welterweight (147 lbs)

Title Holder	Country	Tenure
Johnny Summers	E	1912-1914
Tom McCormick	I	1914
Matt Wells	E	1914-1919
Johnny Basham	W	1919-1920
Ted Kid Lewis	E	1920-1924
Tommy Milligan*	S	1924-1925
Eddie Thomas	W	1951
Wally Thom	E	1951-1952
Cliff Curvis	W	1952
Gerald Dreyer	SA	1952-1954
Barry Brown	NZ	1954
George Barnes	A	1954-1956
Darby Brown	A	1956
George Barnes	A	1956-1958
Johnny van Rensburg	SA	1958
George Barnes	A	1958-1960
Brian Curvis*	W	1960-1966
Johnny Cooke	E	1967-1968
Ralph Charles*	E	1968-1972
Clyde Gray	C	1973-1979

COMMONWEALTH CHAMPIONS, 1908-1992

Title Holder	Country	Tenure
Chris Clarke	C	1979
Clyde Gray*	C	1979-1980
Colin Jones*	W	1981-1984
Sylvester Mittee	E	1984-1985
Lloyd Honeyghan*	E	1985-1986
Brian Janssen	A	1987
Wilf Gentzen	A	1987-1988
Gary Jacobs	S	1988-1989
Donovan Boucher	C	1989-

L. Middleweight (154 lbs)

Title Holder	Country	Tenure
Charkey Ramon*	A	1972-1975
Maurice Hope*	E	1976-1979
Kenny Bristol	GU	1979-1981
Herol Graham*	E	1981-1984
Ken Salisbury	A	1984-1985
Nick Wilshire	E	1985-1987
Lloyd Hibbert	E	1987
Troy Waters*	A	1987-1991
Chris Pyatt	E	1991-

Middleweight (160 lbs)

Title Holder	Country	Tenure
Ted Kid Lewis	E	1922-1923
Roland Todd*	E	1923-1925
Len Johnson*	E	1926
Tommy Milligan	S	1926-1928
Alex Ireland	S	1928-1929
Len Harvey	E	1929-1933
Jock McAvoy*	E	1933-1939
Ron Richards*	A	1940-1941
Bos Murphy	NZ	1948
Dick Turpin	E	1948-1949
Dave Sands*	A	1949-1952
Randy Turpin*	E	1952-1954
Johnny Sullivan	E	1954-1955
Pat McAteer	E	1955-1958
Dick Tiger	N	1958-1960
Wilf Greaves	C	1960
Dick Tiger*	N	1960-1962
Gomeo Brennan	BAH	1963-1964
Tuna Scanlon*	NZ	1964
Gomeo Brennan	BAH	1964-1966
Blair Richardson*	C	1966-1967
Milo Calhoun	J	1967
Johnny Pritchett*	E	1967-1969
Les McAteer	E	1969-1970
Mark Rowe	E	1970
Bunny Sterling	E	1970-1972
Tony Mundine*	A	1972-1975
Monty Betham	NZ	1975-1978
Al Korovou	A	1978
Ayub Kalule*	U	1978-1980
Tony Sibson*	E	1980-1983
Roy Gumbs	E	1983
Mark Kaylor	E	1983-1984
Tony Sibson*	E	1984-1988
Nigel Benn	E	1988-1989
Michael Watson*	E	1989-1991
Richie Woodhall	E	1992-

S. Middleweight (168 lbs)

Title Holder	Country	Tenure
Rod Carr	A	1989-1990
Lou Cafaro*	A	1990-1991
Henry Wharton	E	1991-

L. Heavyweight (175 lbs)

Title Holder	Country	Tenure
Jack Bloomfield*	E	1923-1924
Tom Berry	E	1927
Gipsy Daniels*	W	1927
Len Harvey	E	1939-1942
Freddie Mills*	E	1942-1950
Randy Turpin*	E	1952-1955
Gordon Wallace	C	1956-1957
Yvon Durelle*	C	1957-1959
Chic Calderwood*	S	1960-1966
Bob Dunlop*	A	1968-1970
Eddie Avoth	W	1970-1971
Chris Finnegan	E	1971-1973
John Conteh*	E	1973-1974
Steve Aczel	A	1975
Tony Mundine	A	1975-1978
Gary Summerhays	C	1978-1979
Lottie Mwale	ZA	1979-1985
Leslie Stewart*	TR	1985-1987
Willie Featherstone	C	1987-1989
Guy Waters	A	1989-

Cruiserweight (190 lbs)

Title Holder	Country	Tenure
Stewart Lithgo	E	1984
Chisanda Mutti	ZA	1984-1987
Glenn McCrory*	E	1987-1989
Apollo Sweet	A	1989
Derek Angol	E	1989-

Heavyweight (190 lbs +)

Title Holder	Country	Tenure
Tommy Burns	C	1910
P.O. Curran	I	1911
Dan Flynn	I	1911
Bombardier Billy Wells	E	1911-1919
Joe Beckett*	E	1919-1923
Phil Scott	E	1926-1931
Larry Gains	C	1931-1934
Len Harvey	E	1934
Jack Petersen	W	1934-1936
Ben Foord	SA	1936-1937
Tommy Farr*	W	1937-1938
Len Harvey*	E	1939-1942
Jack London	E	1944-1945
Bruce Woodcock	E	1945-1950
Jack Gardner	E	1950-1952
Johnny Williams	W	1952-1953
Don Cockell*	E	1953-1956
Joe Bygraves	J	1956-1957
Joe Erskine	W	1957-1958
Brian London	E	1958-1959
Henry Cooper	E	1959-1971
Joe Bugner	E	1971
Jack Bodell	E	1971-1972
Danny McAlinden	NI	1972-1975
Bunny Johnson	E	1975
Richard Dunn	E	1975-1976
Joe Bugner*	E	1976-1977
John L. Gardner*	E	1978-1981
Trevor Berbick*	C	1981-1986
Horace Notice*	E	1986-1988
Derek Williams	E	1988-1992
Lennox Lewis	E	1992-

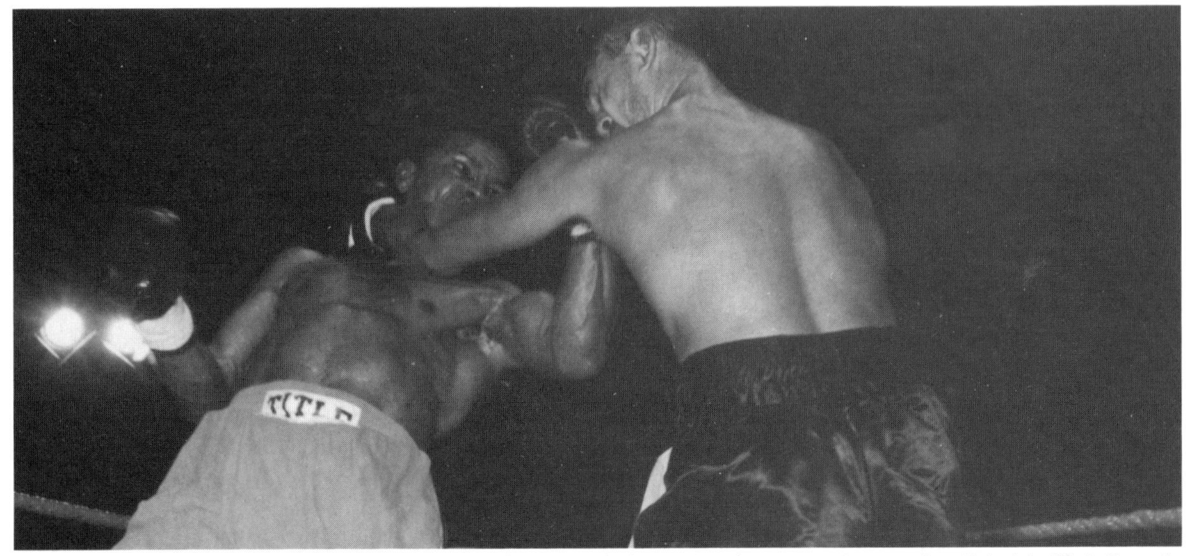

Australia's Craig Trotter (right) put up a titanic performance, before going down on points, against Britain's Chris Pyatt in a battle for the vacant Commonwealth light-middleweight title last November Chris Bevan

European Title Bouts, 1991-92

9 August, 1991 Fabrice Benichou 8.13½ (France) W CO 8 Salvatore Bottiglieri 8.13½ (Italy), Juan les Pins, France. Featherweight Title Defence.

Both men traded blows for the first six rounds with neither really looking to get on top. The Italian, with his well organised defences made it difficult for Benichou to land solidly, while at the same time he was prepared to mix it, often with some success. The seventh saw a shift in honours. The champion finally got his act together and a combination of heavy hooks floored Bottiglieri for a count of eight. Although getting up and fighting back quite stongly, the next round proved to be his last. Benichou sensing the fight was now his for the taking, leapt into action with some solid hooks, paving the way for a wild crunching punch which exploded on the challenger's head, sending him spinning to the canvas. Although Bottiglieri was on his feet, the referee completed the count out, considering him to be in no fit state to continue.

14 August, 1991 Jean-Claude Fontana 10.11¾ (France) W RTD 4 Mourad Louati 10.13¼ (Holland), La Seyne Sur Mer, France. Light-Middleweight Title Challenge.

Louati, the Tunisian-born Dutchman, made a powerful start when he caught the challenger with a tremendous right. Somehow, Fontana remained errect and hammered back, walking into Louati and backing him up. Louati is nothing if not a big puncher and it was obviously dangerous for the Frenchman to trade, but he was having a fair amount of success, especially in slipping punches. In the fourth, as both men exchanged left-hooks, it was noticeable that Fontana was getting the best of it. Suddenly, a terrific left-uppercut sent Louati crashing to the deck. On rising, the champion walked back to his corner and retired himself, complaining that he had broken his nose and was unable to carry on.

14 August, 1991 Antonio Renzo 9.6½ (Italy) W CO 11 Paul Charters 9.7 (GB), Alcamo, Italy. Lightweight Title Defence.

Taking the fight to the champion, Charters made a great start, but on getting too casual in the second round, he was made to pay when floored by a left over the top. Getting up straight away he was soon trading punches again. From that point through to the sixth, the challenger went ahead, keeping Renzo on the back foot and not letting him get set. However, the humid conditions finally caught up with Charters in the eleventh and he was put down by a left and although rising he had very little left, being pushed over in a heap where he remained, while the referee counted him out.

Lennox Lewis (left) sets up Glenn McCrory for a second round kayo in defence of his European heavyweight title

Action Images

24 August, 1991 Sumbu Kalambay 11.4¾ (Italy) W RTD 6 John Ashton 11.5½ (GB), Pesaro, Italy. Middleweight Title Defence.

Within 30 seconds of the opening bell, massive underdog, Ashton, floored the champion with a heavy right-hand counter. On receiving the mandatory eight count, Kalambay still looked shaky, but the challenger did not rush in, being content to bide his time and strike with long range punches when the opportunities presented themselves. Towards the end of the second, Kalambay suffered a deep gash over his right eye and it was only good cornerwork that kept him in the fight. Although Ashton was still boxing well above himself, the champion had begun to pick up the pace and near the end of the fourth, he floored his man with a solid body shot. Ashton continued to box well, but was now suffering from bad cuts as well as impaired vision and on getting up from another body shot, this time in the sixth, his corner wisely retired him at the end of that round on his stool.

13 September, 1991 Graciano Rocchigiani 12.4 (Germany) W RSC 9 Alex Blanchard 12.5 (Holland), Dusseldorf, Germany. Light-Heavyweight Title Defence.

In a bruising war of attrition, Blanchard's long left-leads had opened up a bad cut over the champion's right eye as early as the second round and by the third the eye was very nearly closed tight. But fighting back aggressively in the fourth, Rocchigiani cut the challenger's right eye and began to get on top. Neither man was decked, but Rocchigiani's strength was now telling as he continuously bulled his way in. Trailing behind on points, with his damaged eye worsening, the referee, Larry O'Connell, called the contest off with just two minutes, four seconds of the ninth gone and led Blanchard back to his corner.

30 September, 1991 Lennox Lewis 16.7 (GB) W CO 2 Glenn McCrory 15.11 (GB), London, England. Heavyweight Title Defence.

for a report, see under British Title Bouts, 1991-92.

6 October, 1991 Thierry Jacob 8.4¾ (France) W RTD 4 Antonio Picardi 8.5½ (Italy), Calais, France. Bantamweight Title Defence.

The Italian gave it his best shot for the first two rounds until Jacob went into overdrive. Putting together clusters of punches, the champion drove Picardi round the ring and in the fourth, a further barrage opened a bad cut over the Italian's right eye. Immediately, following on from that, a series of blows to the head and body sent Picardi to his knees and although he made it to the bell, his seconds wisely called the referee over, declaring their man unfit to come out for the fifth.

9 October, 1991 Pat Barrett 10.0 (GB) W RSC 4 Racheed Lawal 9.12½ (Denmark), Manchester, England. Light-Welterweight Title Defence.

Dazed by a long looping right-hand in the first round, Barrett was forced to pay for a sloppy start and it wasn't until the second that he began to find his composure. Even then, Lawal kept the punches coming, but by now the champion's sheer power was having its effect. In the third round, Lawal was still absorbing heavy punches and one wondered how long it would be before he wilted. Then came the breakthrough, as Barrett got through with a left-uppercut to the jaw and a right to the head. Lawal went down heavily on his back, but managed to haul himself up at seven, only to be smashed around the ring by a welter of leather. Although he managed to last the round out, the challenger was again in difficulty in the fourth when a succession of heavy blows forced him to be giving a standing count. On reaching the count of eight, the referee saw that Lawal's legs were betraying him and waved it over with just fifteen seconds of the round remaining.

22 October, 1991 James Cook 11.12 (GB) W RTD 7 Tarmo Uusiverta 11.12¾ (Finland), London, England. Super-Middleweight Title Defence.

Both men seemed intent on blasting each other out, with Uusiverta seeming to be the more powerful of the two, although Cook's punches carried more snap, especially the right-uppercut. If Cook had only stuck to his boxing, rather than trying to match the Finn punch for punch, he would probably have had more success early on. But as the fight progressed, it became apparent that Cook was trying his utmost to discourage his challenger by matching him punch-for-punch. However, Uusiverta still looked strong in the seventh, but it was becoming apparent that the champion had a fair bit in hand. And with only 58 seconds of the round gone, Uusiverta decided he had had enough, raising his hands in surrender, before walking back to his corner.

14 November, 1991 Sumbu Kalambay 11.4½ (Italy) W RSC 4 Miodrag Perunovic 11.4¾ (Yugoslavia), Ancona, Italy. Middleweight Title Defence.

Both fighters made a positive start, jabbing well and looking for openings, but once he had found his ring legs, Kalambay began to move out in front. Although Perunovic continuously trundled forward, he was having to absorb more than the odd right-uppercut from as early as the second round as the champion began to show his class. Coming out for the third, Perunovic immediately walked on to a solid right, but while he stayed calm under pressure, he was still having to absorb a lot as Kalambay started to let the punches go. The fourth was extremely one sided as Kalambay rained in jabs and hooks on his by now outclassed challenger and with just one second remaining of the round, the referee, Roy Francis, decided he had seen enough, bringing the unequal contest to a halt.

15 November, 1991 Fabrice Benichou 8.13½ (France) W CO 10 Vincenzo Limatola 8.13 (Italy), Nimes, France. Featherweight Title Defence.

Taking his time to get into the fight, Benichou, although trained to box a southpaw, had some difficulty fathoming

Steaming in for the finish, Pat Barrett (left), the European light-welterweight titleholder, hammers Racheed Lawal to the mid-section
Chris Bevan

the awkard style of portsider, Limatola. Meanwhile, the Italian began to gain in confidence, moving to the champion's right and generally messing him about. By the fifth round, however, Benichou was beginning to find some answers, landing heavy rights and lefts during surging attacks. By the seventh, Limatola was bleeding badly over the left eye and looked to be fighting mainly for survival at this stage. Come the tenth and Benichou was looking to do the job. A series of punches had Limatola slumping to the floor, but although he got up early and listened intently to the count, he then decided to go back to his corner in the act of quitting, leaving the referee no alternative other than to continue to ten and out.

15 November, 1991 Salvatore Fanni 7.9¾ (Italy) W PTS 12 James Drummond 7.13 (GB), Omegna, Italy. Flyweight Title Defence.

Dominating virtually throughout, massive underdog, James "Bulldog" Drummond, became the latest in a long line of victims at the hands of judging on Italian soil. Holding the centre of the ring from the start, the challenger used his longer reach to great advantage, often following up with stinging blows from both hands. In the fourth round, Drummond nailed Fanni with a great right-cross and while the champion was up almost instantly, he still had to take the eight count. This led to hectic activity and during the fifth, Fanni's headwork finally had some effect when he cut the challenger's left eye. However, Drummond continued to box with composure and although Fanni was doing a lot of work, it appeared wild and ineffective. The champion put in a grandstand finish in the latter stages, but Drummond was still more correct with his punching and had more than a legitimate beef when the decision was announced. *Judges Scorecards:* 116-115, 118-117, 117-116.

7 December, 1991 Antonio Renzo 9.9 (Italy) W RSC 6 Carl Crook 9.9 (GB), Rossano Calabro, Italy. Lightweight Title Defence.

Crook could not have hoped for a better start when he unbalanced the champion and sent him down for the mandatory eight count. But it soon became apparent that the British champion did not have the power to really hurt Renzo and instead of moving and using his far greater skills, he eventually got drawn into close quarters, where the Italian proved far too strong for him. By the fourth, Renzo was ignoring the jab and just piling in and soon a nasty looking cut appeared over Crook's right eye. Almost inevitably, due to the continuing pressure, Crook walked on to a heavy left-uppercut at the end of the fifth and while clambering up on legs that betrayed him, somehow made it to the bell. The next round turned out to be the last as Crook, still fighting gamely, was pounded by heavy uppercuts until rescued on his feet at two minutes, one second of the sixth.

12 February, 1992 Salvatore Fanni 7.13¼ (Italy) DREW 12 Danny Porter 7.13¾ (GB), Sarno, Italy. Flyweight Title Defence.

This time it was the turn of another British unfortunate, Danny Porter, to be on the wrong end of a dodgy Italian decision, yet again, while in opposition to the European champion, Fanni. Although he did not floor his rival in this return bout, the challenger's far more accurate, crisper punching, should have assured him taking the crown. The champion fought in his usual fashion, gloves held high and skittering around the ring, before tearing in, head dangerously down, with clusters of blows, which generally appeared to lack power. Still seemingly in control, Porter finished the eleventh with a cut on the corner of his left eye, but Fanni then had his best round to-date in the twelfth. Even then it was hardly enough to warrant the drawn verdict. *Judges Scorecards:* 117-116, 116-116, 116-117.

19 February, 1992 Patrizio Oliva 10.6 (Italy) W PTS 12 Antoine Fernandez 10.6½ (France), San Pellegrino, Italy. Welterweight Title Defence.

Oliva soon got to work on his French challenger, cutting his right eye in the first round and picking up valuable points with long rangy jabs. However, in the third round he received a nasty shock when the southpaw Fernandez caught him with a good left-hook which dumped him on the seat of his pants for a short count. On getting up, Oliva used all his experience and cunning to avoid any immediate trouble, by boxing effectively on the outside and keeping well out of range from his rival's southpaw hooks. Having got well on top, the champion received a cut on the left eye himself in the tenth, but by dint of more clever work, including delaying and clutching tactics, he stayed clear of any further trouble to coast to a comprehensive points victory, on paper at least. Adrian Morgan was the referee. *Judges Scorecards:* 118-112, 118-112, 118-114.

27 February, 1992 Akim Tafer 13.6½ (France) W PTS 12 Dennis Andries 13.7¾ (England), Beausoleil, France. Vacant Cruiserweight Title.

Unfortunately, when age finally appeared to catch up with the mercurial Andries and the fact he did not carry the superfluous weight well enough to impose himself upon his opponent, the task in hand became just too great for him to overcome. But, because he never ceased trying, Tafer was never able to relax and was simply not good enough to stop him. The 6' 2¾" Frenchman was at his best jabbing and moving, but on occasion he followed up with an effective uppercut and although Andries took them unflinchingly, they were good scoring punches. It was only when Tafer took a breather that the older man came back into the fight by his sheer persistence and when the final bell rang, the former world light-heavyweight champion almost certainly knew that not only was it not going to be his night, but it was not going to be his weight division either. *Judges Scorecards:* 116-113, 116-115, 116-116.

7 March, 1992 Jimmy Bredahl 9.3½ (Denmark) W RSC 11 Pierre Lorcy 9.3½ (France), Paris, France. Vacant Super-Featherweight Title.

Boxing delightfully, Bredahl immediately got down to business, controlling the fight with his left-jab and bringing the Frenchman up short when he attempted to move inside. Apart from a brief spell in the fourth round when Lorcy met with some success, Bredahl had moved into a commanding points lead by the end of the seventh. At the beginning of the eighth, however, Lorcy must have realised that any thoughts he may have harboured about winning the title were fast evaporating, because he leapt from his stool at the bell determined to turn things around. From that point through to the eleventh, Lorcy was at last able to get to work on the body for a concerted period, while Bredahl, although tiring, tucked himself up nicely and appeared to be taking a breather until the storm blew over. At the start of the eleventh, Lorcy again tore across the ring only to be met this time by a solid left-lead as Bredahl started to dictate matters again. Not to be outdone, the Frenchman persisted in trying to get inside until an unfortunate crack of heads left him badly cut over the right eye and when Bredahl quickly followed up with a barrage of punches to worsen the injury, the referee stepped in and rescued Lorcy, virtually on the bell to end the round.

12 March, 1992 Sumbu Kalambay 11.4 (Italy) W PTS 12 Herol Graham 11.4¾ (GB), Pesaro, Italy. Middleweight Title Defence.

Having to travel to Italy in order to win a title is always a calculated risk that the boxer involved has to weigh up very carefully. It has to be said, in this instance, that Herol Graham, while boxing well and on my card possibly one or two rounds ahead at the final bell, did not influence the judges enough to win on Italian soil, especially after receiving two public cautions for spinning his opponent around. Although having Kalambay down twice in the second round from southpaw counters, after outboxing his man in the first, Graham continuously left himself wide open to punches through the middle. He also picked up a cut over the left eye as early as the second and finished the contest looking more the worst for wear than he has done previously. Every time Graham stopped boxing behind the jab and began to mix it, Kalambay had his successes, often hurting the challenger with heavy right-hand punches which rocked him right down to his boots. There was, of course, the normal fiasco when the decision was announced, the referee holding up Graham's hand, but on reflection, Herol probably knew beforehand that in order to win it would have to be by the short route. *Judges Scorecards:* 116-111, 115-114, 115-112.

14 March, 1992 Johnny Bredahl 8.5 (Denmark) W RSC 7 Donnie Hood 8.2¾ (GB), Copenhagen, Denmark. Vacant Bantamweight Title.

Using a traditional English left-jab to perfection, Bredahl skated the first two rounds as Hood vainly tried to block, rather than slip, the punches coming his way. Hood, however, kept trying to come forward, mainly by way of long left-hooks that more often than not were off target. But in the third he struck lucky when a cracking left-hook to the jaw dramatically put the Dane on the seat of his pants. Although stunned, Bredahl clambered to his feet at the count of three and while forced to take a standing eight, he soon got back into the successful routine of jab and move. It was obvious to most that the Scot's only hope was the left-hook, but as much as he tried, Bredahl was nearly always one move ahead. Early in the sixth, Hood was beaten to the punch as he tried with another wide hook and was dropped for two. By now he was fast running out of ways and means to combat the quicksilver Dane and on resumption, was pounded incessantly. In the seventh, following a series of combination punches, he was downed again, this time for a count of four and judging him to be so far behind on points, the referee humanely called a halt to proceedings.

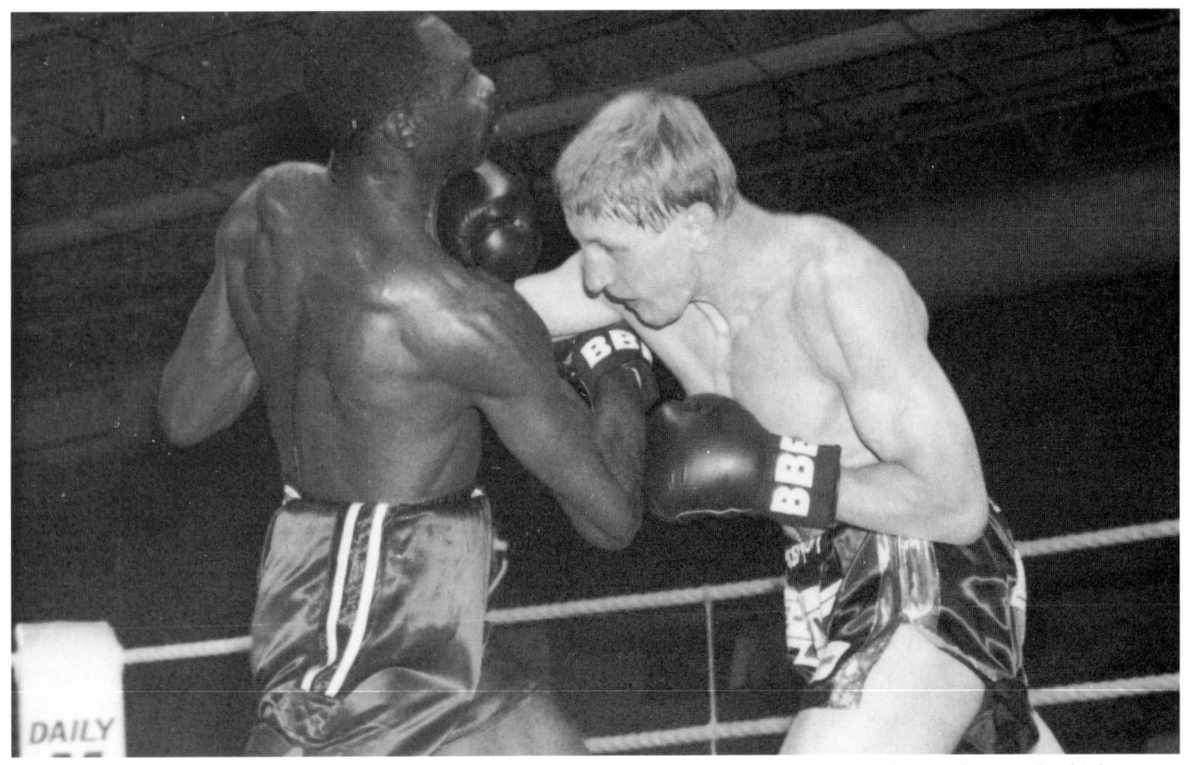

The European super-middleweight champion, James Cook (left), uppercuts Tarmo Uusiverta. It was this punch which eventually brought Cook victory in the seventh round Les Clark

27 March, 1992 Jean-Baptiste Mendy 9.6¾ (France) W RSC 9 Antonio Renzo 9.8½ (Italy), Creil, France. Lightweight Title Challenge.

Somewhat surprisingly, the champion, Renzo, decided to risk a defence on foreign soil, albeit against a 32-year-old veteran of the ring. It turned into a disastrous night for him and as early as the second round a dreadful cut was opened up on his right eyelid. Nervous of being stopped, Renzo tore into his fellow southpaw opponent, who cleverly used his height and reach advantages to weather the storm. While steadily taking charge, Mendy was nevertheless constantly subjected to rushing, crouching attacks as Renzo desperately strove to get inside where he could expect to exact the most damage. But the Frenchman stood up to all of that and despite carrying a noticeable swelling over his right eye, he began to treat Renzo to a whole range of hooks, uppercuts and left-crosses. The game Italian still continued to press forward, having the occasional success, although it became apparent during the eighth that he was fast running out of ideas when he was jolted by several right-hooks. At the beginning of round nine a wide arcing left opened up another cut over Renzo's right eye and on the doctor's advice, the referee led the demoralised ex-champion back to his corner.

3 April, 1992 Franck Nicotra 12.0 (France) W CO 1 James Cook 12.0 (GB), Vitrolles, France. Super-Middleweight Title Challenge.

Making his third defence of the title, Cook was subjected to a shocking 63 second defeat in his opponent's back yard. Earlier, he had been caught cold by a heavy right and from that moment never had a chance to compose himself.

Nicotra followed up with another right-hander and he and Cook exchanged punches, but it was already noticeable that the champion was coming apart at the seams. Then, to the joy of the locals, Nicotra slipped inside Cook's guard and found the range for a further right-hand, followed by a chopping blow to the back of the head as the champion crashed to the floor to be counted out.

18 April, 1992 Jean-Claude Fontana 10.12 (France) W PTS 12 Wally Swift Jnr 10.8¼ (GB), Hyeres, France. Light-Middleweight Title Defence.

The British challenger came into the ring almost four pounds lighter than Fontana and was made to pay as the champion bulled forward, not giving his rival an opportunity to use his excellent countering skills. This became the pattern of the fight, round after round, with Fontana's physical advantages dominating the action. At the end of the fourth, Swift's left eye had become noticeably swollen and within a round or so he also began to tire as the Frenchman came on incessantly. Fontana continued to force the fight, with Swift unable to come forward to take the play away, but bravely accepting what came his way, unflinchingly. To win the title away from home, the challenger lacked the power required to force Fontana onto his back foot and thus be able to dominate and at the final bell there was only one winner. *Judges Scorecards:* 120-112, 119-113, 118-111.

30 April, 1992 Lennox Lewis 16.6½ (GB) W RSC 3 Derek Williams 16.9 (GB), London, England. Heavyweight Title Defence.

For a report, see under British Title Bouts, 1991-92.

30 April, 1992 Salvatore Fanni 7.11¾ (Italy) W PTS 12 Michele Poddighe 7.11¾ (Italy), Cagliari, Italy. Flyweight Title Defence.

For once, Fanni retained his title in uncontroversial circumstances as he easily outpointed his fellow-Italian challenger. Although much taller, the negative Poddighe, a late substitute for the injured Francis Ampofo, was comprehensively beaten in a non-action affair. There were no knockdowns or cut eyes as the contest drearily went the full course, with neither man able to bring the proceedings to an early conclusion. It was the first time that Fanni had defended his title against a non-British opponent and yet again the bout showed up his limitations, which will almost certainly be capitalised on if he ever defends abroad. *Judges Scorecards:* 119-112, 115-113, 117-116.

28 May, 1992 Jean-Baptiste Mendy 9.8 (France) W RTD 3 Stefano Cassi 9.8 (Italy), Creil, France. Lightweight Title Defence.

Coming into the ring, the challenger, Stefano Cassi from Italy, had lost three of his last four bouts, hardly the right credentials to sustain a successful challenge for the title. And so it proved, as the challenger was systematically outboxed and outpunched by the much taller southpaw, Mendy. The bout was deemed to be over when Cassi was unable to answer the bell at the start of the fourth, having bravely fought from the second round onwards with a broken jaw.

29 May, 1992 Fabrice Benichou 8.13½ (France) W PTS 12 John Davison 8.12¼ (GB), Amneville les Thermes, France. Featherweight Title Defence.

In a rematch, Davison made a great start when jabbing to head and body and appeared to take three of the first four rounds, with one even. The next three rounds were also even, as first one fighter and then the other tried to take the initiative. Benichou finally came out of his shell in the eighth and produced a non-stop barrage of punches, only to find Davison returning the compliment with interest in the ninth. The bell ended the eleventh with Davison ramming in heavy blows to the body after a couple of fairly even rounds. Both men gave everything that they had in the final round and although one judge declared a draw, the other two decided that the champion had retained his crown. It was just another body blow for Davison, who had seemingly done enough in the eyes of most neutrals to have justified the verdict. *Judges Scorecards:* 116-113, 118-115, 117-117.

12 June, 1992 Akim Tafer 13.6 (France) W RTD 6 Fernando Aiello 13.6½ (Italy), Alencon, France. Cruiserweight Title Defence.

With the first punch of the fight, Tafer made a cracking start when he floored his rival with a solid right to the head. Unfortunately, for some reason he held back and when Aiello arose at the count of six, he chose to stay behind a long left-lead, rather than take the initiative in an effort to finish it there and then. In the second round, Aiello was cut, but it wasn't until the fourth that Tafer upped the pace with his jab rarely out of the Italian's face. With the contest rapidly becoming more one-sided as the challenger showed neither the technical ability, nor the inclination, his manager pulled him out before round seven got underway. Mickey Vann of Great Britain refereed the contest.

13 June, 1992 Valery Kayumba 9.13½ (Italy) W CO 1 Bruno Vottero 9.13½ (Italy), Levallois, France. Vacant Light-Welterweight Title.

With the injured Pat Barrett stripped of the crown, the EBU sanctioned a bout between the two Italians as for the vacant title. Unfortunately, Vottero was not up to championship standard and was quickly under pressure. The apprehensive Vottero was soon on the canvas, following a right to the head and on continuing, after taking a standing count, he was immediately back in the firing line. Kayumba, who was extremely well conditioned, having prepared for a tough fight against Barrett, began to open up and soon put his rival down again after a series of lefts and rights got through. This time, the bewildered Vottero stayed down and was counted out by the referee just as the bell rang to end the first round.

European Champions, 1909-1992

Shows the tenure of each European champion at each weight.

EUROPEAN COUNTRY CODE
AU = Austria; BEL = Belgium; CZ = Czechoslovakia; DEN = Denmark; FIN = Finland; FR = France; GB = Great Britain; GER = Germany; GRE = Greece; HOL = Holland; HUN = Hungary; ITA = Italy; LUX = Luxembourg; NOR = Norway; POR = Portugal; ROM = Romania; SP = Spain; SWE = Sweden; SWI = Switzerland; TU = Turkey; YUG = Yugoslavia.

*Undefeated champions

Flyweight (112 lbs)

Title Holder	Country	Tenure
Sid Smith	GB	1913
Bill Ladbury	GB	1913-1914
Percy Jones*	GB	1914
Tancy Lee	GB	1915-1916
Jimmy Wilde*	GB	1916-1923
Michel Montreuil	BEL	1923-1925
Elky Clark	GB	1925-1927
Emile Pladner	FR	1928
Johnny Hill	GB	1928-1929
Emile Pladner	FR	1929
Eugene Huat*	FR	1929
Kid Oliva	FR	1930
Lucien Popescu	ROM	1930-1931
Jackie Brown*	GB	1931-1932
Praxile Gyde	FR	1932-1935
Kid David*	BEL	1935-1936
Ernst Weiss	AU	1936
Valentin Angelmann*	FR	1936-1938
Enrico Urbinati*	ITA	1938-1943
Raoul Degryse	BEL	1946-1947
Maurice Sandeyron	FR	1947-1949
Rinty Monaghan*	GB	1949-1950
Terry Allen	GB	1950
Jean Sneyers*	BEL	1950-1951
Teddy Gardner*	GB	1952
Louis Skena*	FR	1953-1954
Nazzareno Giannelli	ITA	1954-1955
Dai Dower	GB	1955
Young Martin	SP	1955-1959
Risto Luukkonen	FIN	1959-1961
Salvatore Burruni*	ITA	1961-1965
Rene Libeer*	FR	1965-1966
Fernando Atzori	ITA	1967-1972
Fritz Chervet*	SWI	1972-1973
Fernando Atzori	ITA	1973
Fritz Chervet*	SWI	1973-1974
Franco Udella	ITA	1974-1979
Charlie Magri*	GB	1979-1983
Antoine Montero*	FR	1983-1984
Charlie Magri*	GB	1984-1985
Franco Cherchi	ITA	1985
Charlie Magri	GB	1985-1986
Duke McKenzie*	GB	1986-1988
Eyup Can*	TU	1989-1990
Pat Clinton*	GB	1990-1991
Salvatore Fanni	ITA	1991-

Bantamweight (118 lbs)

Title Holder	Country	Tenure
Joe Bowker	GB	1910
Digger Stanley	GB	1910-1912
Charles Ledoux	FR	1912-1921
Tommy Harrison	GB	1921-1922
Charles Ledoux	FR	1922-1923
Bugler Harry Lake	GB	1923
Johnny Brown*	GB	1923-1924
Henry Scillie*	BEL	1925-1928
Domenico Bernasconi	ITA	1929
Carlos Flix	SP	1929-1931
Lucien Popescu	ROM	1931-1932
Domenico Bernasconi*	ITA	1932
Nicholas Biquet	BEL	1932-1935
Maurice Dubois	SWI	1935-1936
Joseph Decico	FR	1936
Aurel Toma*	ROM	1936-1937
Nicholas Biquet*	BEL	1937-1938
Aurel Toma	ROM	1938-1939
Ernst Weiss	AU	1939
Gino Cattaneo	ITA	1939-1941
Gino Bondavilli*	ITA	1941-1943
Jackie Paterson	GB	1946
Theo Medina	FR	1946-1947
Peter Kane	GB	1947-1948
Guido Ferracin	ITA	1948-1949
Luis Romero	SP	1949-1951
Peter Keenan	GB	1951-1952
Jean Sneyers*	BEL	1952-1953
Peter Keenan	GB	1953
John Kelly	GB	1953-1954
Robert Cohen*	FR	1954-1955
Mario D'Agata	ITA	1955-1958
Piero Rollo	ITA	1958-1959
Freddie Gilroy	GB	1959-1960
Pierre Cossemyns	BEL	1961-1962
Piero Rollo	ITA	1962
Alphonse Halimi	FR	1962
Piero Rollo	ITA	1962-1963
Mimoun Ben Ali	SP	1963
Risto Luukkonen*	FIN	1963-1964
Mimoun Ben Ali	SP	1965
Tommaso Galli	ITA	1965-1966
Mimoun Ben Ali	SP	1966-1968
Salvatore Burruni*	ITA	1968-1969
Franco Zurlo	ITA	1969-1971
Alan Rudkin	GB	1971
Agustin Senin*	SP	1971-1973
Johnny Clark*	GB	1973-1974
Bob Allotey	SP	1974-1975
Daniel Trioulaire	FR	1975-1976
Salvatore Fabrizio	ITA	1976-1977
Franco Zurlo	ITA	1977-1978
Juan Francisco Rodriguez	SP	1978-1980
Johnny Owen*	GB	1980
Valerio Nati	ITA	1980-1982
Giuseppe Fossati	ITA	1982-1983
Walter Giorgetti*	ITA	1983-1984
Ciro de Leva*	ITA	1984-1986
Antoine Montero	FR	1986-1987
Louis Gomis*	FR	1987-1988
Fabrice Benichou	FR	1988
Vincenzo Belcastro*	ITA	1988-1990
Thierry Jacob*	FR	1990-1992
Johnny Bredahl	DEN	1992-

Featherweight (126 lbs)

Title Holder	Country	Tenure
Young Joey Smith	GB	1911
Jean Poesy	FR	1911-1912
Jim Driscoll*	GB	1912-1913
Ted Kid Lewis*	GB	1913-1914
Louis de Ponthieu*	FR	1919-1920
Arthur Wyns	BEL	1920-1922
Eugene Criqui*	FR	1922-1923
Edouard Mascart	FR	1923-1924
Charles Ledoux	FR	1924
Henri Hebrans	BEL	1924-1925
Antonio Ruiz	SP	1925-1928
Luigi Quadrini	ITA	1928-1929
Knud Larsen	DEN	1929
Jose Girones*	SP	1929-1934
Maurice Holtzer*	FR	1935-1938
Phil Dolhem	BEL	1938-1939
Lucien Popescu	ROM	1939-1941
Ernst Weiss	AU	1941
Gino Bondavilli	ITA	1941-1945
Ermanno Bonetti*	ITA	1945-1946
Tiger Al Phillips	GB	1947
Ronnie Clayton	GB	1947-1948
Ray Famechon	FR	1948-1953
Jean Sneyers	BEL	1953-1954
Ray Famechon	FR	1954-1955
Fred Galiana*	SP	1955-1956
Cherif Hamia*	FR	1957-1958
Sergio Caprari	ITA	1958-1959
Gracieux Lamperti	FR	1959-1962
Alberto Serti	ITA	1962-1963
Howard Winstone*	GB	1963-1967
Jose Legra*	SP	1967-1968
Manuel Calvo	SP	1968-1969
Tommaso Galli	ITA	1969-1970
Jose Legra*	SP	1970-1972
Gitano Jiminez	SP	1973-1975
Elio Cotena	ITA	1975-1976
Nino Jimenez	SP	1976-1977
Manuel Masso	SP	1977
Roberto Castanon*	SP	1977-1981
Salvatore Melluzzo	ITA	1981-1982
Pat Cowdell*	GB	1982-1983
Loris Stecca*	ITA	1983
Barry McGuigan*	GB	1983-1985
Jim McDonnell*	GB	1985-1987
Valerio Nati*	ITA	1987
Jean-Marc Renard*	BEL	1988-1989
Paul Hodkinson*	GB	1989-1991
Fabrice Benichou	FR	1991-

S. Featherweight (130 lbs)

Title Holder	Country	Tenure
Tommaso Galli	ITA	1971-1972

Title Holder	Country	Tenure
Domenico Chiloiro	ITA	1972
Lothar Abend	GER	1972-1974
Sven-Erik Paulsen*	NOR	1974-1976
Roland Cazeaux	FR	1976
Natale Vezzoli	ITA	1976-1979
Carlos Hernandez	SP	1979
Rodolfo Sanchez	SP	1979
Carlos Hernandez	SP	1979-1982
Cornelius Boza-Edwards*	GB	1982
Roberto Castanon	SP	1982-1983
Alfredo Raininger	ITA	1983-1984
Jean-Marc Renard	BEL	1984
Pat Cowdell*	GB	1984-1985
Jean-Marc Renard*	BEL	1986-1987
Salvatore Curcetti	ITA	1987-1988
Piero Morello	ITA	1988
Lars Lund Jensen	DEN	1988
Racheed Lawal	DEN	1988-1989
Daniel Londas*	FR	1989-1991
Jimmy Bredahl	DEN	1992-

Lightweight (135 lbs)

Title Holder	Country	Tenure
Freddie Welsh	GB	1909-1911
Matt Wells	GB	1911-1912
Freddie Welsh*	GB	1912-1914
Bob Marriott	GB	1919-1920
Georges Papin	FR	1920-1921
Ernie Rice	GB	1921-1922
Seaman Nobby Hall	GB	1922-1923
Harry Mason*	GB	1923
Fred Bretonnel	FR	1924
Lucien Vinez	FR	1924-1927
Luis Rayo*	SP	1927-1928
Aime Raphael	FR	1928-1929
Francois Sybille	BEL	1929-1930
Alf Howard	GB	1930
Francois Sybille	BEL	1930-1931
Bep van Klaveren	HOL	1931-1932
Cleto Locatelli	ITA	1932
Francois Sybille	BEL	1932-1933
Cleto Locatelli*	ITA	1933
Francois Sybille	BEL	1934
Carlo Orlandi*	ITA	1934-1935
Enrico Venturi*	ITA	1935-1936
Vittorio Tamagnini	ITA	1936-1937
Maurice Arnault	FR	1937
Gustave Humery*	FR	1937-1938
Aldo Spoldi*	ITA	1938-1939
Karl Blaho	AU	1940-1941
Bruno Bisterzo	ITA	1941
Ascenzo Botta	ITA	1941
Bruno Bisterzo	ITA	1941-1942
Ascenzo Botta	ITA	1942
Roberto Proietti	ITA	1942-1943
Bruno Bisterzo	ITA	1943-1946
Roberto Proietti*	ITA	1946
Emile Dicristo	FR	1946-1947
Kid Dussart	BEL	1947
Roberto Proietti	ITA	1947-1948
Billy Thompson	GB	1948-1949
Kid Dussart	BEL	1949
Roberto Proietti*	ITA	1949-1950
Pierre Montane	FR	1951
Elis Ask	FIN	1951-1952
Jorgen Johansen	DEN	1952-1954
Duilio Loi*	ITA	1954-1959
Mario Vecchiatto	ITA	1959-1960
Dave Charnley*	GB	1960-1963
Conny Rudhof*	GER	1963-1964
Willi Quatuor	GER	1964-1965

Title Holder	Country	Tenure
Franco Brondi	ITA	1965
Maurice Tavant	FR	1965-1966
Borge Krogh	DEN	1966-1967
Pedro Carrasco*	SP	1967-1969
Miguel Velazquez	SP	1970-1971
Antonio Puddu	ITA	1971-1974
Ken Buchanan*	GB	1974-1975
Fernand Roelandts	BEL	1976
Perico Fernandez*	SP	1976-1977
Jim Watt*	GB	1977-1979
Charlie Nash*	GB	1979-1980
Francisco Leon	SP	1980
Charlie Nash	GB	1980-1981
Joey Gibilisco	ITA	1981-1983
Lucio Cusma	ITA	1983-1984
Rene Weller	GER	1984-1986
Gert Bo Jacobsen*	DEN	1986-1988
Rene Weller*	GER	1988
Policarpo Diaz*	SP	1988-1990
Antonio Renzo	ITA	1991-1992
Jean-Baptiste Mendy	FR	1992-

L. Welterweight (140 lbs)

Title Holder	Country	Tenure
Olli Maki*	FIN	1964-1965
Juan Sombrita-Albornoz	SP	1965
Willi Quatuor*	GER	1965-1966
Conny Rudhof	GER	1967
Johann Orsolics	AU	1967-1968
Bruno Arcari*	ITA	1968-1970
Rene Roque	FR	1970-1971
Pedro Carrasco*	SP	1971-1972
Roger Zami	FR	1972
Cemal Kamaci	TU	1972-1973
Toni Ortiz	SP	1973-1974
Perico Fernandez*	SP	1974
Jose Ramon Gomez-Fouz	SP	1975
Cemal Kamaci*	TU	1975-1976
Dave Boy Green*	GB	1976-1977
Primo Bandini	ITA	1977
Jean-Baptiste Piedvache	FR	1977-1978
Colin Power	GB	1978
Fernando Sanchez	SP	1978-1979
Jose Luis Heredia	SP	1979
Jo Kimpuani*	FR	1979-1980
Giuseppe Martinese	ITA	1980
Antonio Guinaldo	SP	1980-1981
Clinton McKenzie	GB	1981-1982
Robert Gambini	FR	1982-1983
Patrizio Oliva*	ITA	1983-1985
Terry Marsh*	GB	1985-1986
Tusikoleta Nkalankete	FR	1987-1989
Efren Calamati	ITA	1989-1990
Pat Barrett*	GB	1990-1992
Valery Kayumba	ITA	1992-

Welterweight (147 lbs)

Title Holder	Country	Tenure
Young Joseph	GB	1910-1911
Georges Carpentier*	FR	1911-1912
Albert Badoud*	SWI	1915-1919
Johnny Basham	GB	1919-1920
Ted Kid Lewis*	GB	1920
Piet Hobin*	BEL	1921-1925
Mario Bosisio*	ITA	1925-1928
Alf Genon	BEL	1928-1929
Gustave Roth	BEL	1929-1932
Adrien Aneet	BEL	1932-1933
Jack Hood*	GB	1933
Gustav Eder*	GER	1934-1936
Felix Wouters	BEL	1936-1938
Saverio Turiello	ITA	1938-1939
Marcel Cerdan*	FR	1939-1942

Title Holder	Country	Tenure
Ernie Roderick	GB	1946-1947
Robert Villemain*	FR	1947-1948
Livio Minelli	ITA	1949-1950
Michele Palermo	ITA	1950-1951
Eddie Thomas	GB	1951
Charles Humez*	FR	1951-1952
Gilbert Lavoine	FR	1953-1954
Wally Thom	GB	1954-1955
Idrissa Dione	FR	1955-1956
Emilio Marconi	ITA	1956-1958
Peter Waterman*	GB	1958
Emilio Marconi	ITA	1958-1959
Duilio Loi*	ITA	1959-1963
Fortunato Manca*	ITA	1964-1965
Jean Josselin	FR	1966-1967
Carmelo Bossi	ITA	1967-1968
Fighting Mack	HOL	1968-1969
Silvano Bertini	ITA	1969
Jean Josselin	FR	1969
Johann Orsolics	AU	1969-1970
Ralph Charles	GB	1970-1971
Roger Menetrey	FR	1971-1974
John H. Stracey*	GB	1974-1975
Marco Scano	ITA	1976-1977
Jorgen Hansen	DEN	1977
Jorg Eipel	GER	1977
Alain Marion	FR	1977-1978
Jorgen Hansen	DEN	1978
Josef Pachler	AU	1978
Henry Rhiney	GB	1978-1979
Dave Boy Green	GB	1979
Jorgen Hansen*	DEN	1979-1981
Hans-Henrik Palm	DEN	1982
Colin Jones*	GB	1982-1983
Gilles Elbilia*	FR	1983-1984
Gianfranco Rosi	ITA	1984-1985
Lloyd Honeyghan*	GB	1985-1986
Jose Varela	GER	1986-1987
Alfonso Redondo	SP	1987
Mauro Martelli*	SWI	1987-1988
Nino la Rocca	ITA	1989
Antoine Fernandez	FR	1989-1990
Kirkland Laing	GB	1990
Patrizio Oliva*	ITA	1990-1992

L. Middleweight (154 lbs)

Title Holder	Country	Tenure
Bruno Visintin	ITA	1964-1966
Bo Hogberg	SWE	1966
Yolande Leveque	FR	1966
Sandro Mazzinghi*	ITA	1966-1968
Remo Golfarini	ITA	1968-1969
Gerhard Piaskowy	GER	1969-1970
Jose Hernandez	SP	1970-1972
Juan Carlos Duran	ITA	1972-1973
Jacques Kechichian	FR	1973-1974
Jose Duran	SP	1974-1975
Eckhard Dagge	GER	1975-1976
Vito Antuofermo	ITA	1976
Maurice Hope*	GB	1976-1978
Gilbert Cohen	FR	1978-1979
Marijan Benes	YUG	1979-1981
Louis Acaries	FR	1981
Luigi Minchillo*	ITA	1981-1983
Herol Graham*	GB	1983-1984
Jimmy Cable	GB	1984
Georg Steinherr*	GER	1984-1985
Said Skouma*	FR	1985-1986
Chris Pyatt	GB	1986-1987
Gianfranco Rosi*	ITA	1987
Rene Jacquot*	FR	1988-1989
Edip Secovic	AU	1989

Title Holder	Country	Tenure
Giuseppe Leto	ITA	1989
Gilbert Dele*	FR	1989-1990
Said Skouma	FR	1991
Mourad Louati	HOL	1991
Jean-Claude Fontana	FR	1991-

Middleweight (160 lbs)

Title Holder	Country	Tenure
Georges Carpentier*	FR	1912-1918
Ercole Balzac	FR	1920-1921
Gus Platts	GB	1921
Johnny Basham	GB	1921
Ted Kid Lewis	GB	1921-1923
Roland Todd	GB	1923-1924
Bruno Frattini	ITA	1924-1925
Tommy Milligan*	GB	1925
Rene Devos*	BEL	1926-1927
Mario Bosisio	ITA	1928
Leone Jacovacci	ITA	1928-1929
Marcel Thil	FR	1929-1930
Mario Bosisio	ITA	1930-1931
Poldi Steinbach	AU	1931
Hein Domgoergen*	GER	1931-1932
Ignacio Ara*	SP	1932-1933
Gustave Roth	BEL	1933-1934
Marcel Thil	FR	1934-1938
Edouard Tenet	FR	1938
Bep van Klaveren	HOL	1938
Anton Christoforidis	GRE	1938-1939
Edouard Tenet*	FR	1939
Josef Besselmann*	GER	1942-1943
Marcel Cerdan	FR	1947-1948
Cyrille Delannoit	BEL	1948
Marcel Cerdan*	FR	1948
Cyrille Delannoit	BEL	1948-1949
Tiberio Mitri*	ITA	1949-1950
Randy Turpin	GB	1951-1954
Tiberio Mitri	ITA	1954
Charles Humez	FR	1954-1958
Gustav Scholz*	GER	1958-1961
John Cowboy McCormack	GB	1961-1962
Chris Christensen	DEN	1962
Laszlo Papp*	HUN	1962-1965
Nino Benvenuti*	ITA	1965-1967
Juan Carlos Duran	ITA	1967-1969
Tom Bogs	DEN	1969-1970
Juan Carlos Duran	ITA	1970-1971
Jean-Claude Bouttier*	FR	1971-1972
Tom Bogs*	DEN	1973
Elio Calcabrini	ITA	1973-1974
Jean-Claude Bouttier	FR	1974
Kevin Finnegan	GB	1974-1975
Gratien Tonna*	FR	1975
Bunny Sterling	GB	1976
Angelo Jacopucci	ITA	1976
Germano Valsecchi	ITA	1976-1977
Alan Minter	GB	1977
Gratien Tonna*	FR	1977-1978
Alan Minter*	GB	1978-1979
Kevin Finnegan	GB	1980
Matteo Salvemini	ITA	1980
Tony Sibson*	GB	1980-1982
Louis Acaries	FR	1982-1984
Tony Sibson*	GB	1984-1985
Ayub Kalule	DEN	1985-1986
Herol Graham	GB	1986-1987
Sumbu Kalambay*	ITA	1987
Pierre Joly	FR	1987-1988
Christophe Tiozzo*	FR	1988-1989
Francesco dell' Aquila	ITA	1989-1990
Sumbu Kalambay	ITA	1990-

S. Middleweight (168 lbs)

Title Holder	Country	Tenure
Mauro Galvano	ITA	1990-1991
James Cook	GB	1991-1992
Franck Nicotra	FR	1992-

L. Heavyweight (175 lbs)

Title Holder	Country	Tenure
Georges Carpentier	FR	1913-1922
Battling Siki	FR	1922-1923
Emile Morelle	FR	1923
Raymond Bonnel	FR	1923-1924
Louis Clement	SWI	1924-1926
Herman van T'Hof	HOL	1926
Fernand Delarge	BEL	1926-1927
Max Schmeling*	GER	1927-1928
Michele Bonaglia*	ITA	1929-1930
Ernst Pistulla*	GER	1931-1932
Adolf Heuser*	GER	1932
John Andersson*	SWE	1933
Martinez de Alfara	SP	1934
Marcel Thil*	FR	1934-1935
Merlo Preciso	ITA	1935
Hein Lazek	AU	1935-1936
Gustave Roth	BEL	1936-1938
Adolf Heuser*	GER	1938-1939
Luigi Musina*	ITA	1942-1943
Freddie Mills*	GB	1947-1950
Albert Yvel	FR	1950-1951
Don Cockell*	GB	1951-1952
Conny Rux*	GER	1952
Jacques Hairabedian	FR	1953-1954
Gerhard Hecht	GER	1954-1955
Willi Hoepner	GER	1955
Gerhard Hecht	GER	1955-1957
Artemio Calzavara	ITA	1957-1958
Willi Hoepner	GER	1958
Erich Schoeppner*	GER	1958-1962
Giulio Rinaldi	ITA	1962-1964
Gustav Scholz*	GER	1964-1965
Giulio Rinaldi	ITA	1965-1966
Piero del Papa	ITA	1966-1967
Lothar Stengel	GER	1967-1968
Tom Bogs*	DEN	1968-1969
Yvan Prebeg	YUG	1969-1970
Piero del Papa	ITA	1970-1971
Conny Velensek	GER	1971-1972
Chris Finnegan	GB	1972
Rudiger Schmidtke	GER	1972-1973
John Conteh*	GB	1973-1974
Domenico Adinolfi	ITA	1974-1976
Mate Parlov*	YUG	1976-1977
Aldo Traversaro	ITA	1977-1979
Rudi Koopmans	HOL	1979-1984
Richard Caramonolis	FR	1984
Alex Blanchard	HOL	1984-1987
Tom Collins	GB	1987-1988
Pedro van Raamsdonk	HOL	1988
Jan Lefeber	HOL	1988-1989
Eric Nicoletta	FR	1989-1990
Tom Collins*	GB	1990-1991
Graciano Rocchigiani*	GER	1991-1992

Cruiserweight (190 lbs)

Title Holder	Country	Tenure
Sam Reeson*	GB	1987-1988
Angelo Rottoli	ITA	1989
Anaclet Wamba*	FR	1989-1990
Johnny Nelson*	GB	1990-1992
Akim Tafer	FR	1992-

Heavyweight (190 lbs +)

Title Holder	Country	Tenure
Georges Carpentier	FR	1913-1922
Battling Siki*	FR	1922-1923
Erminio Spalla	ITA	1923-1926
Paolino Uzcudun*	SP	1926-1928
Pierre Charles	BEL	1929-1931
Hein Muller	GER	1931-1932
Pierre Charles	BEL	1932-1933
Paolino Uzcudun	SP	1933
Primo Carnera*	ITA	1933-1935
Pierre Charles	BEL	1935-1937
Arno Kolblin	GER	1937-1938
Hein Lazek	AU	1938-1939
Adolf Heuser	GER	1939
Max Schmeling*	GER	1939-1941
Olle Tandberg	SWE	1943
Karel Sys*	BEL	1943-1946
Bruce Woodcock*	GB	1946-1949
Joe Weidin	AU	1950-1951
Jack Gardner	GB	1951
Hein Ten Hoff	GER	1951-1952
Karel Sys	BEL	1952
Heinz Neuhaus	GER	1952-1955
Franco Cavicchi	ITA	1955-1956
Ingemar Johansson*	SWE	1956-1959
Dick Richardson	GB	1960-1962
Ingemar Johansson*	SWE	1962-1963
Henry Cooper*	GB	1964
Karl Mildenberger	GER	1964-1968
Henry Cooper*	GB	1968-1969
Peter Weiland	GER	1969-1970
Jose Urtain	SP	1970
Henry Cooper	GB	1970-1971
Joe Bugner	GB	1971
Jack Bodell	GB	1971
Jose Urtain	SP	1971-1972
Jurgen Blin	GER	1972
Joe Bugner*	GB	1972-1975
Richard Dunn	GB	1976
Joe Bugner*	GB	1976-1977
Jean-Pierre Coopman	BEL	1977
Lucien Rodriguez	FR	1977
Alfredo Evangelista	SP	1977-1979
Lorenzo Zanon*	SP	1979-1980
John L. Gardner*	GB	1980-1981
Lucien Rodriguez	FR	1981-1984
Steffen Tangstad	NOR	1984-1985
Anders Eklund	SWE	1985
Frank Bruno*	GB	1985-1986
Steffen Tangstad*	NOR	1986
Alfredo Evangelista	SP	1987
Anders Eklund	SWE	1987
Francesco Damiani*	ITA	1987-1989
Derek Williams	GB	1989-1990
Jean Chanet	FR	1990
Lennox Lewis	GB	1990-

A-Z of the World's Leading Fighters

by Eric Armit

Shows the record since 1 July, 1991 and a career summary for over 200 of the world's leading fighters. The author has also produced a synopsis of the fighter's career and has shown all nicknames where applicable. The place name given is the boxer's domicile, not necessarily his birthplace.

Terrence (Halley) Alli

Atlantic City, USA. *Born* Georgetown, Guyana, 29 July, 1960

NABF and USBA L. Welterweight Champion. Former Undefeated USBA Lightweight Champion

Real name is Terrence Halley. Born in Guyana, he turned professional there in December 1979. Lost to Walter Smith in only his second fight in March 1980. Moved his base to Trinidad later in 1980 and from there eventually to Canada and Atlantic City. Beat good opponents such as Primo Ramos, Jerome Artis and Melvin Paul, before losing to Harry Arroyo on an eleventh round stoppage for the IBF lightweight title in January 1985. Drew with Cornelius Boza-Edwards in March 1986 and then won the USBA lightweight title by outpointing Miguel Santana. Lost to Jose Luis Ramirez for the WBC lightweight title in July 1987 and moved up to light-welterweight. Won the NABF title in January 1991 with a points victory over John Meekins and defended it by decisioning Charles Murray in May 1991. Has scored wins over Jerry Page, Santos Cardona and African David Thio, who tragically died after the bout. A classy, tough fighter, but losses to Rodolfo Aguilar and Roger Mayweather at crucial times have prevented him landing a third shot at a world title.

14.01.92	Alfredo Rojas W RTD 4 Atlantic City
01.05.92	Primo Ramos W PTS 8 Sete
13.06.92	Steve Larrimore W CO 5 Georgetown

Career: 59 contests, won 50, drew 2, lost 7.

Elvis Alvarez

Medellin, Colombia. *Born* 2 February, 1965

Former WBA Flyweight Champion. Former Undefeated WBO, Colombian & Latin American Flyweight Champion

The Medellin southpaw turned professional in July 1983 after winning 54 of his 62 amateur fights. Lost on points to Rodolfo Blanco in his sixth fight, but won the Colombian super-flyweight title in May 1986 by outpointing Toribio Riasco. Outpointed the future WBA world bantamweight champion Israel Contrerras in February 1987, but was beaten by the world rated Panamanian Edgar Monserrat in July 1987. Won the Latin American Flyweight Crown in his next fight and made three successful defences of the title. Won the vacant WBO flyweight title in March 1989 by outpointing Miguel Mercedes, but relinquished the title in 1990 without making a defence, so that he could challenge for the WBA version. Won the WBA title in March 1991 by beating Leopard Tamakuma in Tokyo, but lost the title in his first defence to Yong-Kang Kim in June and announced his retirement. The retirement lasted only three months, but he lost his comeback fight to Guillermo Salcedo. Has scored four stoppage wins since then. Good boxer and sharp puncher.

17.08.91	Jose Benitez W RSC 4 Apartado
14.09.91	Guillermo Salcedo L PTS 10 San Andres
28.09.91	Emiliano Tamarillo W CO 4 Araquiel
20.12.91	Manuel Ariza W RSC 8 Barranquilla
11.04.92	Alvaro Vega W PTS 10 Bogota
22.05.92	Jose Luis Bueno L PTS 12 Mexico City *(WBC Con Am S. Flyweight Title Challenge)*

Career: 35 contests, won 29, drew 1, lost 5.

Yuri Arbachakov

Russia. *Born* 22 October, 1966

WBC Flyweight Champion. Former Undefeated Japanese Flyweight Champion

Former Amateur star who won gold medals at the 1989 World championships and the 1989 European championships. Won 165 of his 186 amateur fights. Was immediately scouted by a Japanese promoter and had his first professional fight in Tokyo in February 1990. Won the vacant Japanese flyweight title by knocking out Takahiro

Yuri Arbachakov

Mizumi in one round in July 1991, but relinquished the title in November due to the lack of challengers. Became the first citizen of the CIS to win a world title when he climbed off the floor to knock out Thai, Muangchai Kitikasem, to collect the WBC flyweight title. With his cool style and hard punching he could be champion for quite a while. Holds stoppage wins over useful Mexican Justo Zuniga and the former IBF champion Rolando Bohol. Has stopped all but one of his opponents.

15.07.91	Takahiro Mizumi W CO 1 Tokyo *(Vacant Japanese Flyweight Title)*
30.09.91	Byung-Kap Kim W CO 5 Tokyo
25.11.91	Shun Hazama W RSC 5 Tokyo
16.03.92	Smanchai Chalermsri W PTS 10 Tokyo
20.04.92	Smanchai Chalermsri W RSC 3 Tokyo
23.06.92	Muangchai Kitikasem W CO 8 Tokyo *(WBC Flyweight Title Challenge)*

Career: 13 contests, won 13.

Paul Banke

Pomona, USA. *Born* 1 March, 1964
Former WBC S. Bantamweight Champion

Tough face-first southpaw battler. Turned professional in August 1985 and fought with only modest success. Was stopped by Jesus Poll in August 1987, but then won six fights in a row to earn a shot at Daniel Zaragoza for the WBC super-bantamweight title in June 1989. Paul had Zaragoza badly cut and on the floor, but lost a split decision. In April 1990 he challenged Zaragoza again and this time won the title by halting the champion in the ninth round. Defended his title against Ki-Jun Lee in Inchon in August 1990 and was on the verge of defeat until Lee folded and was halted in the last round. Paul surprisingly lost his title in November 1990 when he was outclassed and stopped in four rounds by Pedro Decima. He returned after eleven months out of the ring and after one contest challenged Zaragoza again for the WBC title, losing clearly on points. In March this year he retired in the sixth round of a USBA title fight against Kennedy McKinney and may be at the end of his career.

26.10.91	Antonio Vazquez W PTS 10 Indio
09.12.91	Daniel Zaragoza L PTS 12 Los Angeles *(WBC S. Bantamweight Title Challenge)*
20.03.92	Kennedy McKinney L RTD 6 Las Vegas *(USBA S. Bantamweight Title Challenge)*

Career: 28 contests, won 21, lost 7.

Leonzer Barber

Detroit, USA. *Born* 18 February, 1966
WBO L. Heavyweight Champion. Former Undefeated WBC Con AM Champion

Member of the famous Kronk Team in Detroit. 6'3" tall, strong and a hard right hand puncher. Turned professional in December 1986, but had only one fight in 1987 and was inactive throughout 1988. Returned to the ring in August 1989 and lost his first fight for 30 months when he was outpointed by James Flowers. Was unbeaten in 1990 with seven wins, including victories over Elvis Parks and Jim McDonald. In February 1991 he won the Vacant WBC Continental Americas light-heavyweight title by stopping Robert Johnson. Won the vacant WBO title in Leeds in May 1991, forcing Tom Collins to retire at

Leonzer Barber

the end of the sixth round. Won non-title fights against Tony Willis and Ron Martin at the end of 1991 and then retained his WBO title with a controversial split decision over Anthony Hembrick. A knockdown in the eleventh round being the margin of Leonzer's victory. Has stopped ten opponents.

09.10.91	Tony Willis W CO 5 Detroit
11.12.91	Ron Martin W RSC 3 Duluth
07.01.92	Anthony Hembrick W PTS 12 Detroit *(WBO L. Heavyweight Title Defence)*

Career: 16 contests, won 15, lost 1.

Iran (The Blade) Barkley

New York, USA. *Born* 9 May, 1960
IBF S. Middleweight Champion. Former Undefeated WBA L. Heavyweight Champion. Former WBC Middleweight Champion. Former Undefeated WBC Con Am Middleweight Champion

Tall, aggressive puncher who is always dangerous. Won a bronze medal in the 1982 World Amateur championships and turned professional in December 1982. Lost to Osley Silas on points in his fifth fight and was stopped by Robbie Sims in 1984. Won the WBC Continental Americas middleweight title in 1985 with a split decision over Mike Tinley and beat James Kinchen in 1986 to earn a shot at Sumbu Kalambay for the vacant WBA title. Iran lost clearly on points, but bounced back in March 1986 to halt Michael Olajide. In June 1988 a bloodied and battered Iran won a dramatic victory and the WBC middleweight title by stopping Thomas Hearns with one punch in the third round. Iran lost his title in his first defence in February 1989 when he was outpointed by Roberto Duran on a split decision and in August he lost a majority decision to Michael Nunn for the IBF title. He was inactive for one year and then was stopped by Nigel Benn in one round in a challenge for the WBO title in August 1990. Iran then retired. He returned in 1991 as a light-heavyweight, but in January 1992 moved down to super-middleweight to win the IBF crown by halting Darrin van Horn in two rounds. In March, Iran moved up to light-heavyweight again and beat Thomas Hearns for the second time to win the WBA title, but he relinquished the title a month later. Has stopped 17 opponents.

16.08.91	Juan Hernandez W PTS 10 Las Vegas
03.10.91	Jesus Castaneda W TD 8 Great Falls
10.01.92	Darrin van Horn W RSC 2 New York *(IBF S. Middleweight Title Challenge)*
20.03.92	Thomas Hearns W PTS 12 Las Vegas *(WBA L. Heavyweight Title Challenge)*

Career: 36 contests, won 29, lost 7.

Jesse Benavides

Corpus Christi, USA. *Born* 3 November, 1963
WBO S. Bantamweight Champion. Former Undefeated USBA S. Bantamweight Champion

Southpaw 5'4" tall. Member of the Kronk Team. As an amateur won five National titles at light-flyweight, flyweight and bantamweight, but failed to make the United States team for the 1984 Olympic Games and turned professional in September 1984. Won the USBA super-bantamweight title in November 1987 with a split points victory over Greg Richardson. Retained his title in May 1988 by halting James Pipps, but suffered his first defeat in July, being floored twice and stopped in three rounds by Pedro Decima. Retained his USBA title in April 1989 by halting Danny Garcia and in March 1990 won a majority decision over the former WBA super-bantamweight champion Jesus Salud. Retained the USBA title again in May 1990 with a first round stoppage of the former IBF bantamweight champion Kelvin Seabrooks. Won the WBO super-bantamweight title in May 1991 with a unanimous points decision over Orlando Fernandez. Defended it in August by stopping Fernando Ramos in five rounds. His bout with Efrain Pintor was ruled a technical draw after Jesse was cut. Stopped 23 victims.

31.08.91 Fernando Ramos W RSC 5 Corpus Christi (WBO S. Bantamweight Title Defence)
21.03.92 Efrain Pintor TEC DRAW 2 Waco
Career: 36 contests, won 34, drew 1, lost l.

Fabrice Benichou

France. *Born* Madrid, 5 April, 1965
European Featherweight Champion. Former IBF S. Bantamweight Champion. Former European Bantamweight Champion

Comes from a circus family. His mother danced at the Moscow State Circus and his father was a magician. Fabrice worked as a trapeze artist and a contortionist and was Israeli amateur champion. Turned professional in Italy in July 1984 and then fought in Venezuela, Panama and the United States before basing himself in France in 1986. Won the European bantamweight title by knocking out Thierry Jacob in nine rounds in January 1988, but lost it three months later, being stopped by Vincenzo Belcastro. Fabrice challenged for the IBF super-bantamweight title in September 1988 against Jose Sanabria and was ahead on points until his left eye closed and the fight was halted in the tenth round. He seemed to have slipped badly when he lost his next fight to Ray Armand, but in March 1989 he challenged Sanabria again and won the IBF title on a points decision. He made two defences of the title beating Fransie Badenhorst and Ramon Cruz, but lost the crown to Welcome Ncita on a points decision in March 1990. Challenged for the WBA super-bantamweight title in October 1990, but lost on points to Luis Mendoza. Fabrice moved up to featherweight and won the vacant European title by outpointing John Davison in May 1991. In March this year he lost in another world title attempt, being outpointed by the IBF featherweight champion Manuel Medina, but retained his European title with another victory over Davison. Halted 18 opponents.

09.08.91 Salvatore Bottiglieri W CO 8 Juan Les Pins *(European Featherweight Title Defence)*
15.11.91 Vincenzo Limatola W CO 10 Nimes *(European Featherweight Title Defence)*
14.03.92 Manuel Medina L PTS 12 Antibes *(IBF Featherweight Title Challenge)*
29.05.92 John Davison W PTS 12 Amneville les Thermes *(European Featherweight Title Defence)*
Career: 44 contests, won 33, lost 11.

Rodolfo Blanco

San Onofre, Colombia. *Born* 14 June, 1966.
IBF Flyweight Champion. Former Undefeated Colombian L. Flyweight Champion

Turned professional in March 1982. Lost three of his first four fights. Challenged Agustin Garcia for the Colombian light-flyweight title in July 1984, but lost on points. Turned in an excellent win in March 1985 by outpointing former world champion Elvis Alvarez, but was held to a draw in December by Panamanian Benedicto Murillo. Challenged Garcia again in January 1986 and this time won the Colombian light-flyweight crown. Beat useful fighters Hermogenes Murillo and Rafael Julio later in the year. In September 1987 he challenged Myung-Woo Yuh for the WBA light-flyweight title, but was knocked out in the eighth round Won his next eight fights and then had his second shot at a world title, facing Dave McAuley in Belfast. Rodolfo floored McAuley four times, but lost a unanimous decision. Had only one fight in 1991, and was then inactive until June 1992 when he won a close decision to end Dave McAuley's reign. Has stopped 17 opponents.

11.06.92 Dave McAuley W PTS 12 Bilbao *(IBF Flyweight Title Challenge)*
Career: 33 contests, won 26, drew 1, lost 6.

Maurice (Thin Man) Blocker

Washington DC, USA. *Born* 15 May, 1963
IBF Welterweight Champion. Former WBC Welterweight Champion. Former Undefeated NABF Welterweight Champion

Tall 6'1", converted southpaw, smooth boxer, but not a big puncher. Claimed 56 wins in 59 amateur fights before turning professional in February 1982. Won the vacant NABF welterweight title in July 1985 with a unanimous points verdict over Pedro Vilella. Was stripped of the NABF title in 1986. Came to London in 1987 to challenge Lloyd Honeyghan for the WBC and IBF titles and lost on points in a very close, but dull fight. Beat old pro Saoul Mamby in February 1990 and then won the WBC title with a majority decision over Marlon Starling in August 1990. Lost the title in his first defence in March 1991 when he was stopped in two rounds by his former stablemate Simon Brown. Won the vacant IBF title in October with a split decision over Glenwood Brown. His career has been badly affected in its early stages by contract disputes. Also has wins over Danny Paul, Jerome Artis and Adam George. Has stopped 18 opponents.

04.10.91 Glenwood Brown W PTS 12 Atlantic City *(Vacant IBF Welterweight Title)*
Career: 35 contests, won 33, lost 2.

Kamel Bou Ali

Somrane, Tunisia. *Born* 6 December, 1958
Former WBO S. Featherweight Champion. Former Undefeated WBC International S. Featherweight Champion

Tunisian, but based in Italy. Had his first professional fight in December 1977, but was inactive in 1978. Fought only once in 1979, did not fight in 1980 and had only two bouts in 1981. With more regular action, he quickly climbed the ratings and in January 1985 challenged Rocky Lockridge for the WBA super-featherweight title, but was halted in seven rounds. Scored fifteen consecutive victories and then in August 1988 stopped Robert Dickie in six rounds to win the WBC International title. Retained the title with a victory against Manuel Billalba in April 1989. In December sprang an upset by stopping Antonio Rivera in nine rounds to collect the vacant WBO title. His first defence ended in a no contest against Pedro Villegas due to a cut and he knocked out Joey Jacobs in June 1991 in his second defence. Lost the title to veteran Daniel Londas on a close decision last March. Good box puncher who has stopped 30 opponents.

21.11.91	Benito Martinez W PTS 8 Perugia
21.03.92	Daniel Londas L PTS 12 San Rufo *(WBO S. Featherweight Title Defence)*
17.06.92	Jorge Pompe W PTS 6 Salice Terme

Career: 48 contests, won 43, drew 2, lost 2, no contest 1.

Donovan Boucher

Toronto Canada. *Born* Jamaica, 1962
Commonwealth & Canadian Welterweight Champion

Turned professional in August 1985 and won his first ten fights before losing on points to Chris Clarke in November 1986. Won the Vacant Canadian welterweight title in July 1987 by knocking out Danny Winters in seven rounds. Defended it in November by halting Wayne Gordon in eleven rounds and then scored a big win in March, 1988 by flooring and stopping former amateur star Shawn O' Sullivan in two rounds in another title defence. Suffered two defeats in 1989, losing on points to J. J. Watters and being stopped in seven rounds by Glenwood Brown. Won the Commonwealth title in November 1989 by outpointing Gary Jacobs and has defended his title five times beating Brad Jeffries, Kirkland Laing, Mickey Hughes, Stan Cunningham and Robert Wright and was voted Commonwealth Champion of the Year in January. Has stopped 16 of his opponents.

17.10.91	Stan Cunningham W RSC 6 Winnipeg *(Commonwealth & Canadian Welterweight Title Defence)*
17.03.92	Robert Wright W RSC 11 London *(Commonwealth Welterweight Title Defence)*

Career: 31 contests, won 28, lost 3.

Riddick Bowe

New York, USA. *Born* 10 August, 1967
WBC Con Am Heavyweight Champion

Born in Brooklyn. Former world junior champion and silver medal winner in the 1988 Olympic Games, losing to Lennox Lewis on a stoppage in the final. Won 205 Out of 213 amateur fights. 6'5" tall. Turned professional in March 1989. In 1990 he knocked out Pinklon Thomas in eight rounds and Bert Cooper in two rounds. Won the vacant WBC Continental Americas title when Elijah Tillery was disqualified in the first round for kicking him. Also holds wins over Art Tucker, Rodolfo Marin, Tyrell Biggs and Tony Tubbs. Good boxer with fast hands and a hard punch, but doubts remain over his heart. Has stopped 26 opponents.

23.07.91	Phil Brown W RSC 3 Atlantic City
09.08.91	Bruce Seldon W CO 1 Atlantic City
29.10.91	Elijah Tillery W DIS 1 Washington *(Vacant WBC Con Am Heavyweight Title)*
13.12.91	Elijah Tillery W RSC 4 Atlantic City
07.04.92	Conroy Nelson W RSC 1 Atlantic City
08.05.92	Everett Martin W RSC 5 Las Vegas

Career: 30 contests, won 30.

Jimmy Bredahl

Copenhagen, Denmark. *Born* 26 August, 1967
European S. Featherweight Champion

Stylish southpaw. Excellent jab and can only improve with experience.

Riddick Bowe (left) tangles with Elijah Tillery, before the latter was thrown out by the referee for kicking Tom Casino

His younger brother Johnny is European bantamweight champion. Won Danish national titles in 1985, 86, 87 and 89 and competed in the 1987 European championships. Became a professional in March 1989 with a points win over Des Gargano. Knocked out Rocky Lawlor with a body punch in one round in December 1989. Halted Kevin Pritchard in three rounds in May 1991 and French champion Areski Bakir in three rounds in December. Although considered an outsider, he outboxed and stopped Pierre Lorcy to win the vacant European title last March. Has five quick wins.

06.12.91	Areski Bakir W RSC 3 Copenhagen
07.03.92	Pierre Lorcy W RSC 11 Paris *(Vacant European S. Featherweight Title)*

Career: 11 contests, won 11.

Glenwood (The Real Beast) Brown

Plainfield, USA. *Born* 25 July, 1967
Former Undefeated USBA & WBA Americas Welterweight Champion

Former New York Golden Gloves champion and won 82 of his 93 amateur fights. Turned professional in June 1986 under the management of the late Mike Jones. Won his first 18 fights before losing on points in June 1988 to the former WBC light-welterweight champion Saoul Mamby. Beat Mamby in a return bout in February 1989 for the vacant WBA Americas welterweight title and kept it in 1989 by outpointing Young Dick Tiger and stopping Donovan Boucher. Defended in February 1990 and won the vacant USBA title in the same fight by halting Luis Santana. Lost on points to Maurice Blocker in October 1991 for the vacant IBF title. Had Meldrick Taylor on the floor twice, but lost the decision in a challenge for the WBA title last January. An aggressive fighter who hits hard with both hands, but against Taylor he also showed he can box. Holds win over Orlando Orozco, Tyrone Moore and Joe Alexander. Has stopped 25 opponents.

23.07.91	Artie Bright W RSC 2 Monticello
04.10.91	Maurice Blocker L PTS 12 Atlantic City *(Vacant IBF Welterweight Title)*
18.01.92	Meldrick Taylor L PTS 12 Philadelphia *(WBA Welterweight Title Challenge)*
27.03.92	Miguel Santana W PTS 10 Catskills
04.06.92	Roque Montoya W RSC 2 Atlantic City

Career: 39 contests, won 36, lost 3.

Simon (Mantequilla) Brown

Washington DC, USA. *Born* Jamaica, 15 August, 1963
Former WBC Welterweight Champion. Former Undefeated IBF Welterweight Champion

Claims 54 wins in 56 amateur fights. His brother Freddie Brown fought as a professional. Simon turned professional in February 1982. Won his first 21 fights, but then lost on points to Marlon Starling in November 1985 for the USBA welterweight title. In June 1986 he outclassed and halted the Canadian hope Shawn O'Sullivan in three rounds. A contract dispute kept him out of the ring for over a year and he managed only one fight in a 22 month period. In April 1988 he climbed off the canvas to floor Tyrone Trice four times and stopped him in the fourteenth round to win the vacant IBF welterweight title. He defended the title twice in 1988, stopping Jorge Vaca and outpointing Mauro Martelli. Made four defences in 1989, halting Jorge Maysonet, Al Long and Bobby Joe Young and decisioning Luis Santana. Faced Trice again in a title defence in April 1990 and stopped him in ten rounds. Simon relinquished the IBF title and in March 1991 won the WBC title by outpointing his former stablemate Maurice Blocker. Lost the title in his first defence, being floored and easily outpointed by James McGirt. Has now moved up a division to fight at light-middleweight. Smooth, classy boxer and great puncher with either hand.

29.11.91	James McGirt L PTS 12 Las Vegas *(WBC Welterweight Title Defence)*
26.06.92	Melvin Wynn W CO 2 Cleveland

Career: 37 contests, won 35, lost 2.

Jose Luis Bueno

Mexico City, Mexico. *Born* 8 December, 1969
WBC Con Am S. Flyweight Champion

Turned professional in March 1985, but lost on a stoppage to Miguel Banda in only his second fight. Stopped his next eight opponents before being halted in eight rounds in April 1989 by world rated bantamweight Javier Leon. Won the WBC Continental Americas super-flyweight title in September 1991 by halting top rated Armando Salazar in four rounds. Jose Luis had Salazar down twice and badly cut when the fight was stopped. Defended his title in November with a points win over Jose Luis Vegagil, but his prestige was dented when he could only draw in Japan with unrated Aljoe Jaro in February. Scored a big win in May 1992 when he retained his title with a points win over the former double world champion Elvis Alvarez. Has stopped 17 opponents.

28.09.91	Armando Salazar W RSC 4 Mexico City *(WBC Con Am S. Flyweight Title Challenge)*
11.11.91	Jose Luis Vegagil W PTS 12 Mexico City *(WBC Con Am S. Flyweight Title Defence)*
01.02.92	Aljoe Jaro DREW 10 Tokyo
22.05.92	Elvis Alvarez W PTS 12 Mexico City *(WBC Con Am S. Flyweight Title Defence)*

Career: 24 contests, won 21, drew 1, lost 2.

Luis Ramon (Yori Boy) Campas

Navojoa, Mexico. *Born* 5 August, 1971
NABF & Mexican Welterweight Champion

Turned professional in October 1987 and stopped his first twelve opponents. Won the Mexican welterweight title in May 1991 by knocking out Jesus Cardenas in seven rounds. Has defended his title twice, stoping Jose Luis Bedolla and Julian Benitez. Failed the controversial Californian neurological test in 1991, but the test is not recognised by other States so "Yori Boy" can still box throughout the USA and Mexico. Won the NABF title with a close decision over his first world class opponent, Roger Turner, who also came into the ring undefeated. Has stopped 38 of his victims. Holds wins over Luis Mora, Martin Quiroz and Cassius Clay Horne.

08.07.91	Cassius Clay Horne W RSC 2 Tijuana
09.08.91	Jose Luis Bedolla W RSC 3 Navojoa *(Mexican Welterweight Title Defence)*
05.10.91	Frankie Davis W RSC 4 Reno
11.11.91	Greg Dickson W RSC 2 Tijuana
02.03.92	Julian Benitez W CO 1 Tijuana *(Mexican Welterweight Title Defence)*
04.04.92	Ultiminio Martinez W CO 3 Navojoa
02.05.92	Samuel Martinez W RSC 5 Reno
19.06.92	Roger Turner W PTS 12 Las Vegas *(NABF Welterweight Title Challenge)*

Career: 41 contests, won 41.

Orlando Canizales

Laredo, USA. *Born* 25 November, 1965

IBF Bantamweight Champion. Former Undefeated USBA S. Flyweight Champion. Former Undefeated NABF Flyweight Champion

Turned professional in August 1984, following his brother Gaby in to the paid ranks. Was held to a draw by Rogelio Leanos in his second fight in March 1985. Challenged Paul Gonzalez for the NABF flyweight title in July 1986 and had Gonzales on the floor, but lost on points. Won the vacant NABF flyweight title in November 1987 by stopping Armando Velasco in four rounds and defended it in April 1988, halting Louis Curtis in two rounds. Collected the IBF bantamweight title in July 1988 with a fifteenth round stoppage of Kelvin Seabrooks again, this time in eleven rounds. Made three title defences in 1990, scoring a close points win over Billy Hardy, stopping Eddie Rangel and reversing his only defeat by halting Paul Gonzales in two rounds. Crushed brave Hardy in eight rounds in a return fight in May 1991 and made two other title defences when outpointing Fernie Morales and halting Ray Minus in eleven rounds. Strong, hard puncher. Also holds wins over Armando Castro, Prudencio Cardona, Javier Lucas and Alonzo Gonzales. Has stopped 24 opponents.

Orlando Canizales

22.09.91	Fernie Morales W PTS 12 Indio *(IBF Bantamweight Title Defence)*
21.12.91	Ray Minus W RSC 11 Laredo *(IBF Bantamweight Title Defence)*
23.04.92	Francisco Alvarez W PTS 12 Paris *(IBF Bantamweight Title Defence)*

Career: 33 contests, won 31, drew 1, lost 1.

Michael (Little Hands Of Stone) Carbajal

Phoenix, USA. *Born* 17 September, 1967

IBF L. Flyweight Champion. Former Undefeated NABF L. Flyweight Champion

Won silver medals in both the Olympic Games and Pan American championships. Lost only eight of over 100 amateur fights. Turned professional in February 1989. Became the NABF light-flyweight champion in his twelfth fight by outpointing Tony de Luca and defended the title in June by stopping Fernando Martinez. Won the IBF light-flyweight title in July 1990 by halting Thai, Muangchai Kitikasem, in seven rounds. Retained the title with a fourth round stoppage of Leon Salazar in December 1990. Defended his title three times in 1991, knocking out Macario Santos and outpointing Hector Patri and Marcos Pacheco. Looked a very good fighter in his title victory over Kitikasem, but

Michael Carbajal

has not been so impressive in his most recent defences and the lack of big money matches may force him to move up to flyweight. 5'5" tall. Holds wins over Pedro Feliciano, Luis Monzote and Jesus Chong. Has stopped thirteen opponents.

18.10.91	Jesus Chong W PTS 10 Atlantic City
15.02.92	Marcos Pacheco W PTS 12 Phoenix *(IBF L. Flyweight Title Defence)*
30.04.92	Jose Luis Velarde W PTS 10 Albuquerque

Career: 24 contests, won 24.

Santos Cardona

Toa Bajo, Puerto Rico. *Born* 12 November, 1965

IBC Welterweight Champion. Former Undefeated WBC Con Am & Fecarbox L. Welterweight Champion. Former NABF L. Welterweight Champion

Turned professional in New York in July 1984. Won the WBC Continental Americas Lightweight title in December 1985 with a points victory over Angel Garcia in Puerto Rico. In July 1988, won the Central American and Caribbean light-welterweight crown by halting Abraham Mieses. Competed in the Inglewood Forum competition, but was stopped in two rounds by Sammy Fuentes in January 1989. Lost on points to Terrence Alli in January 1990, but in February won the NABF light-welterweight title by outpointing Livingstone Bramble. Dropped his title in his first defence in June 1990 to John Meekins on a points decision and moved up to welter-weight. Knocked out Kevin Pompey in eight rounds in April 1991 to take the vacant IBC title. Holds wins over Manuel De Leon, Miguel Santana and Tim Rabon and has stopped fourteen opponents.

23.09.91	Tim Rabon W RTD 5 Metairie
06.12.91	David Taylor W PTS 10 Bayamon
01.05.92	Martin Quiroz W PTS 10 Miami

Career: 27 contests, won 24, lost 3.

Oba Carr

Detroit, USA. *Born* 11 May, 1972
L. Welterweight

Brilliant young member of the Kronk team. Won USA Junior Olympics title and turned professional in December 1989 at the age of 16. Beat experienced Anthony Fletcher in three rounds in August 1990 and outpointed veteran Martin Quiroz in October. Scored good wins in 1991 over Ramon Zavala and Bernard Gray, but almost came unstuck against the former WBA lightweight champion Livingstone Bramble in October. Carr was floored twice in the first round and almost knocked out. He did well to recover and win on a split decision, but it has left question marks over his chin and also against the stamina of the classy youngster. Has beaten Manuel Rojas and David Taylor, and stopped fifteen of his opponents.

13.08.91	Ramon Zavala W PTS 10 Tampa
17.09.91	Bernard Gray W RSC 5 Orlando
09.10.91	Livingstone Bramble W PTS 10 Detroit
12.11.91	Alberto Alcaraz W PTS 10 Jacksonville
07.01.92	Erskine Wade W RTD 4 Detroit
17.03.92	Roland Commings W PTS 10 Detroit

Career: 24 contests, won 24.

Armando (Monstruo) Castro

Mexico City, Mexico. Born 13 February, 1963
Mexican S. Flyweight Champion

Heavy punching young fighter who has overcome an indifferent start to his career to become a top contender. Turned professional in February 1984 and lost on points to Orlando Canizales in December 1985. Further losses to Fernando Varguez and Francisco Gonzalez hurt his career and in October 1987 he was halted in one round by Victor Rabanales. Bounced back in December that year to stop Jimmy Fernandez to win the Mexican super-fly-weight title. Defended his title in 1988 with wins over Jose Montiel and Sergio Cornejo, but dropped the title to Montiel in July and was beaten by Montiel in a title challenge in October. Lost again, this time to Paul Gonzalez for the WBA Americas title in 1989, and in 1990 was outpointed by Cesar Soto. Turned his career around in September 1990 by stopping the former WBC flyweight champion, Gabriel Bernal, to take the vacant Mexican super-flyweight title once more. Defended his title against Montiel, Javier Lucas Juan Jose Xool, Francisco Gonzalez and Jose Quirino, but failed in a challenge to Kaosai Galaxy for the WBA title in December 1991., Won the Inglewood Forum super-flyweight competition by halting Esteban Ayala. Has stopped 33 oppo-nents.

30.09.91	Jose Quirino W RSC 9 Tijuana *(Mexican S. Flyweight Title Defence)*
21.10.91	Steve Mwema W RTD 5 Los Angeles
22.12.91	Khosai Galaxy L PTS 12 Bangkok *(WBA S. Flyweight Title Challenge)*
10.02.92	Antonio Ramirez W RSC 10 Los Angeles
30.03.92	Esteban Ayala W RSC 4 Los Angeles
05.06.92	Valente Flores W RSC 4 Actopan

Career: 52 contests, won 38, drew 2, lost 12.

Jorge Fernando (Locomotora) Castro

Puerto Deseado, Argentina. *Born* 18 August, 1967
South American L. Middleweight Champion. Former Undefeated Argentinian L. Middleweight Champion

Unorthodox and undisciplined fighter with plenty of natural ability. Lost only two of 55 amateur fights and beat the world champion, Carlos Garcia. Turned professional in February 1987 and was unbeaten in his first 39 fights with 37 wins and two draws. Captured the Argentinian light-middleweight title in 1989 by knocking out Hugo Marinangeli, but relinquished the title later in the year. Won the South American title in October 1990, again with a stoppage of Marinangeli. Defended the title in March 1991 by knocking out danger-ous Miguel Arroyo in one round and forcing Mario Gaston to retire in eight. Lost on points to Terry Norris in a challenge for the WBC title last December. Holds wins over Lorenzo Garcia, Judas Clottey, Hector Vilte and Daniel Dominguez. Lost his Argentinian title when he failed to make the weight for his fight with Ernesto Sena. One of the most active fighters in the world. Has stopped 51 opponents. Only fighter to have taken Roy Jones the distance.

27.07.91	Mario Sanchez W CO 1 Buenos Aires
17.08.91	Juan Italo Meza W PTS 10 Buenos Aires
06.09.91	Edmundo Diaz W RSC 5 Caleta Olivia
13.09.91	Julio A. Gonzalez W PTS 10 Posadas
24.10.91	Joe Hernandez W RSC 1 Paris
13.12.91	Terry Norris L PTS 12 Paris *(WBC L. Middleweight Title Challenge)*
11.04.92	Ernesto Sena W CO 6 Buenos Aires
09.05.92	Anibal Miranda W PTS 10 Buenos Aires
12.06.92	Eduardo Contreras W CO 7 Junin
30.06.92	Roy Jones L PTS 10 Pensacola

Career: 77 contests, won 71, drew 2, lost 4.

Ricardo Cepeda

Santurce, Puerto Rico. *Born* 25 March, 1966
Former Undefeated WBC Con Am Featherweight Champion

Three times amateur champion of Puerto Rico and cousin of famed baseball star Orlando Cepeda. Moved to New York in March 1987 to fight under the Madison Square Gardens banner and had his first fight in April.

He was held to a draw in his second fight by Juan Martinez, but it was then wins all the way until 1991. Won the WBC Continental Americas featherweight title in March 1990 by outpointing Roberto Rivera and defended it in November with a decision over Ray Medel. Relinquished the title and challenged Marcos Villasana for the WBC crown in August 1991, losing on points. His hopes of a second title shot were dented when he was hurt by the first punch of the fight and floored twice and stopped by Jose Vidal in three rounds. Holds wins over Albert Rendon, Tony Duran and Nelson Rodriguez. Has scored 17 stoppage victories.

06.07.91	Nelson Rodriguez W PTS 10 Greenville
16.08.91	Marcos Villasana L PTS 12 Marbella *(WBC Featherweight Title Challenge)*
12.11.91	Gerardo Sanchez W RTD 4 Las Vegas
11.03.92	Jose Vidal L RSC 3 New York

Career: 26 contests, won 23, drew 1, lost 2.

Nam Hoon-Cha

South Korea. *Born* 16 November, 1970
OPBF L. Flyweight Champion.
Former Undefeated South Korean L. Flyweight Champion

Tall for a light-flyweight, Cha is a fast, talented fighter and one of South Korea's big hopes for a world title. Turned professional in April 1988. Lost on a cuts stoppage in his second fight, but is unbeaten since then. Won the vacant national light-flyweight title in November 1989 by outpointing Keum-Soo Yuh. Climbed off the floor to win the vacant OPBF crown in June 1990 with a split decision over the unbeaten Filipino, Bert Rengifo. Has defended the title four times with victories against Little Baguio, Anhar Azadin, Fernando Baja and Leo Ramirez.

03.08.91	Fernando Baja W CO 3 Changhowon *(OPBF L. Flyweight Title Defence)*
14.12.91	Leo Ramirez W RSC 11 Kwangju *(OPBF L. Flyweight Title Defence)*

Career: 21 contests, won 19, drew 1, lost 1.

Julio Cesar Chavez

Ciudad Obregon, Mexico. *Born* 12 July, 1962
WBC L. Welterweight Champion. Former Undefeated IBF L. Welterweight Champion. Former Undefeated WBC & WBA Lightweight Champion. Former Undefeated WBC S. Featherweight Champion

Arguably the best fighter pound for pound in the world today. A craftsman at cutting down the ring and forcing his opponents to fight his fight. Turned professional in February 1980. There has been some controversy over a fight with Miguel Ruiz when Chavez was originally disqualified, but the local commision later declared Julio the winner on a knockout. Won the WBC super-featherweight title in September 1984 by stopping Mario Martinez and made nine defences before moving up and halting Edwin Rosario in November 1987 to take the WBA lightweight title. Collected the WBC lightweight title in October 1988 with a technical decision over Jose Luis Ramirez. In May 1989 he moved up again and won the WBC light-welterweight title by forcing Roger Mayweather to retire in the tenth round. Added the IBF title in March 1990 with a dramatic last round victory over Meldrick Taylor. Chavez was well behind on points, but halted Taylor with only two seconds remaining in the fight. Relinquished the IBF title, but continues to rule as WBC champion. Is unbeaten in 21 world title fights, with 80 consecutive victories and 66 stoppages. Has also beaten Rocky Lockridge, Juan Laporte, Sammy Fuentes, Rodolfo Aguilar and Lonnie Smith.

Julio Cesar Chavez

14.09.91	Lonnie Smith W PTS 12 Las Vegas *(WBC L. Welterweight Title Defence)*
11.11.91	Jorge Melian W CO 4 Mexico City
13.12.91	Ignacio Perdomo W RTD 4 Hermosillo
13.03.92	Juan Soberanes W CO 4 La Paz
10.04.92	Angel Hernandez W RSC 5 Mexico City *(WBC L. Welterweight Title Defence)*

Career: 80 contests, won 80.

Yun-Un Chin

Chunnam, South Korea. *Born* 11 July, 1967
Flyweight

Turned professional in June 1985. Not a typical South Korean in-fighter, Chin is a lanky box-puncher who has tried to become more aggressive to attract the crowds. Had a close shave in January 1988 when he had to climb off the floor four times to outpoint Filipino Romeo Opriasa and was lucky to take a points win over the future WBA flyweight champion Jesus Rojas in March 1989. Has shown good punching power by halting 18 inside the distance.

28.07.91	Sergio Pepito W PTS 10 Seoul
14.12.91	Mario Parcon W RSC 3 Kwangju

Career: 26 contests, won 26.

Sot Chitalada

Chonburi, Thailand. *Born* 24 May, 1962
Former WBC Flyweight Champion

Former kickboxer. Turned professional in March 1982 and was given a world rating on the basis of a falsified record to cover his lack of fights. Despite this, in March 1984, after only four contests, he lost a close decision to Jung-Koo Chang for the WBC light-flyweight title. Seven months later, in his eighth fight, he outpointed Gabriel Bernal to win the WBC flyweight title. Sot came to London for his first title defence in February 1985 and beat Charlie Magri in four rounds, and then drew with Bernal in June 1985. Made two defences in 1986, beating Freddie Castillo and Bernal and also beat Rae-Ki Ahn and Hideaki Kamishiro to

Sot Chitalada

retain his title before losing on points to Yong-Kang Kim in July 1988. Regained the title by beating Kim in June 1989 and made four more defences, including a victory over Jung-Koo Chang, before being stopped in six rounds by Muangchai Kitikasem in February 1991. Lost in nine rounds in a return with Kitikasem in February 1992. Throughout his career he has had a battle against weight as well as his opponents and is one of the greatest flyweights of all time. Halted 16 opponents.

06.07.91 Chong-Pil Park W RSC 5 Bangkok
28.08.91 Jerry Tarona W PTS 10 Bangkok
28.02.92 Muangchai Kitikasem L RSC 9 Samut Prakan
(WBC Flyweight Title Challenge)

Career: 30 contests, won 25, drew 1, lost 4.

Hi-Yon Choi

Pusan, South Korea. *Born* 13 September, 1965
WBA M. Flyweight Champion. Former Undefeated OPBF M. Flyweight Champion

Former outstanding amateur who turned professional in July 1987. Won the vacant OPBF mini-flyweight title in only his fourth fight and defended twice. Took the WBA crown in February 1991 by outpointing Bong-Jun Kim in a fight in which both fighters were on the floor. The decision was so controversial that the WBA ordered a rematch. Choi made two defences in the year, decisioning Filipino, Sugar Ray Mike and Kim in their return match. Choi is a slim, fast boxer, but not a big puncher. Holds wins over In-Kyu Hwang, Sam-Jong Lee and Kom Sorthanikul. Has stopped seven opponents.

26.10.91 Bong-Jun Kim W PTS 12 Seoul
(WBA M. Flyweight Title Defence)
22.02.92 Ruichi Hosono W RSC 10 Seoul
(WBA M. Flyweight Title Defence)
14.06.92 Rommel Lawas W CO 3 Inchon
(WBA M. Flyweight Title Defence)

Career: 14 contests, won 14.

Chil-Sung Chun

Sinan, South Korea. *Born* 7 July, 1961
Lightweight

Won a silver medal in the World championships and lost to Pernell Whitaker in the 1984 Olympic Games, losing only two of 125 amateur fights. Turned professional in March 1986 and overcame a standing count to outbox the top American Darryl Tyson in June 1987 in only his seventh fight. Met disaster in a trip to Los Angeles in October 1987, when he was beaten in four rounds by club fighter Rico Velasquez. Continued his activity back in Korea, outpointing the former WBC super-featherweight champion Rafael Limon in 1989. Had only one fight in 1990 and one in 1991. This lack of activity counted against him in his fight with Joey Gamache for the vacant WBA title last June. Has halted ten opponents.

12.06.92 Joey Gamache L RSC 8 Portland
(Vacant WBA Lightweight Title)

Career: 19 contests, won 17, lost 2.

Melchor (Baby) Cob Castro

Campeche, Mexico. *Born* 18 April, 1968
Former WBC L. Flyweight Champion. Former Undefeated WBC Con Am L. Flyweight Champion

Tough little southpaw. Turned professional in January 1985, drawing and losing to fellow prospect Alfredo Xeque in a couple of early fights. Ran up fourteen consecutive wins, but then lost a controversial decision to Jose Lagos in Argentina for the vacant WBC

Melchor Cob Castro (right) seen losing his WBC light-flyweight title to Humberto Gonzalez in June 1991 Chris Farina

International light-flyweight title. Became the WBC Continental Americas champion in February 1990 by knocking out Julio Cardona in five rounds and defended the title with victories over Lalo Ramirez and Javier Varguez. Won the WBC crown in March 1991 by battering Rolando Pascua to defeat in ten rounds with body punches. Lost the title in his first defence in June 1991 to the former champion Humberto Gonzalez , but looked to be worth at least a draw. Holds wins over Rafael Alonso and Marcos Pacheco. Has stopped 16 opponents.

03.08.91	Jorge Rivera W CO 7 Campeche
25.10.91	Wilfredo Urbina W PTS 10 Campeche
14.12.91	Santiago Mendez W PTS 10 Merida
14.03.92	Jose Juarez W DIS 3 Merida
12.06.92	Justo Zuniga W PTS 10 Campeche

Career: 42 contests , won 35, drew 4, lost 3.

Pierre Coezter

South Africa. *Born* 12 June, 1961
Heavyweight

Won many amateur titles, scoring 41 of his 45 victories inside the distance, before turning professional in February 1983 as a cruiserweight. Quickly moved up to heavyweight and won nine fights before being outpointed by the former WBC cruiserweight champion Bernard Benton in July 1984. Won a further thirteen fights, including a first round knockout of Benton, which saw Pierre cut but fire back with one left-hook to put Benton out cold. Suffered a bout of hepatitus and in his first bout back in March 1988, he again lost to a former WBC cruiserweight champion, Osvaldo Ocasio, on points. Has won 16 fights in a row since then, beating Ocasio and fighting in South Africa, Puerto Rico, England, America and Italy. Has beaten Mike White, James Pritchard, Michael Greer, Johnny Du Plooy and Jose Ribalta. Good left-jab and heavy right hand puncher, but has been cut in a few fights Stopped 27 victims.

27.07.91	Jerry Halstead W PTS 10 Sun City
19.10.91	Dan Murphy W RSC 3 Williamsburg
16.05.92	Carlton West W RSC 1 Bealton

Career: 41 contests, won 39, lost 2.

Juan Martin (Latigo) Coggi

Santa Fe, Argentina. *Born* 19 December, 1961
Former WBA L. Welterweight Champion. Former Undefeated Argentinian L. Welterweight Champion

Southpaw. Nickname means "The Whip". Lost only two of 37 amateur fights. Cool stylish fighter. Turned professional in April 1982 and won his first 22 fights, before losing on points to veteran Adolfo Arce Rossi in March 1985, the only time he has lost to an Argentinian. Won the Argentinian light-welterweight title in October 1986 by knocking out Hugo Hernandez. In July 1987, he outpointed Patrizio Oliva in Italy to lift the WBA title. It was Oliva' s first loss after 48 consecutive wins. Defended his crown twice in 1988 by knocking out Sang-Ho Lee and decisioning Harold Brazier. In April 1989, he outpointed the current WBA champion Akinobu Hiranaka. Coggi was down twice, but won a unanimous decision. Defeated the former WBC lightweight champion Jose Luis Ramirez in a title defence in March 1990, but then lost his title to Loreto Garza on a majority decision in August 1990. Juan has scored eleven victories since then, but has not been impressive. Has accounted for 31 opponents inside the distance.

27.07.91	Fernando Segura W CO 7 Buenos Aires
06.09.91	Juan A. Contreras W CO 10 Buenos Aires
17.11.91	Joe Alexander W PTS 10 Carpenteras
03.04.92	Julian Rodriguez W CO 3 La Plata
02.05.92	Francisco Bobadilla W PTS 10 Buenos Aires

Career: 60 contests, won 56 , drew 2, lost 2.

Alfred (Ice) Cole

Spring Valley, USA. *Born* 21 April, 1964
USBA Cruiserweight Champion

6'4" tall. Won the US Olympic trials for the 1988 Games, but lost to Andy Maynard in a box-off. Member of the Triple Threat Boxing team, along with Ray Mercer and Charles Murray. Turned professional in March 1989. Won his eight bouts in 1989, beating Aundrey Nelson, John Beckles and Drake Thadzi. Scored a further seven wins in 1990 and then in December lost his unbeaten record when outpointed on a split decision by Leon Taylor. Cole revenged the defeat in March 1991 and also collected the vacant USBA cruiserweight title with a unanimous points verdict over Taylor. Has defended the title twice with wins over Nate Miller and Frankie Swindell. Steady boxer, but not a hard puncher. Has halted eleven opponents.

25.07.91	Frankie Swindell W RSC 11 Atlantic City *(USBA Cruiserweight Title Defence)*
25.09.91	Mike de Vito W RSC 3 Stanhope
12.12.91	Governer Chavers W RSC 6 Atlantic City

Career: 21 contests, won 20, lost l.

Steve Collins

Dublin, Ireland. *Born* 21 July, 1964
Irish Middleweight Champion. Former Undefeated USBA Middleweight Champion

Former Irish international. Turned professional in America in October 1986 with the Petronelli brothers, who managed Marvin Hagler. Won the Irish middleweight title in March 1988 by outpointing Sammy Storey in Boston. In May 1989, he collected the USBA title, being floored by a body punch, but winning easily on points against Kevin Watts. Steve retained the title in July by outpointing Tony Thornton. He was cut over both eyes, but won easily, despite the majority decision. Challenged Mike McCallum for the WBA title in February 1990 in Boston, but was well beaten, losing a unanimous decision and being cut again. Had a second shot at the WBA crown in April 1992, but this time lost a majority decision to Reggie Johnson for the vacant title. Is now based in Belfast and boxing for Barney Eastwood. Tough brave fighter with a good jab, but not a puncher. Has stopped ten opponents.

11.12.91	Danny Morgan W RSC 3 Dublin
22.04.92	Reggie Johnson L PTS 12 East Rutherford *(Vacant WBA Middleweight Title)*

Career: 23 contests , won 21, lost 2.

Israel Contrerras

Guiria, Venezuela. *Born* 27 December, 1960

Former WBA Bantamweight Champion. Former Undefeated WBO Bantamweight Champion

Turned professional in August 1981 as a flyweight. Undefeated with only one draw in his first 24 fights. Suffered his first set back in November 1986 when he was knocked out in five rounds by Kaosai Galaxy in a challenge for the WBA super-flyweight title. In his next fight, in February 1987, he lost on points to Elvis Alvarez in Colombia. Won the vacant Venezuelan bantamweight title in September 1987 by outpointing Ali Camacho and in February 1989 took the vacant WBO crown by knocking out Maurizio Lupino in the first round. Defended the title in 1990 by knocking out Pascual Polanco and stopping Ray Minus, but then relinquished the title. Won the WBA crown in October by knocking out Luisito Espinosa in a fight that featured five knockdowns, with Contrerras down twice in the third round and storming back to floor the former three times in the fifth. A major surprise saw Contrerras lose his title in his first defence when he was knocked out in five rounds by Eddie Cook. Holds wins over Francisco Iluiroz, Oscar Bolivar and a first round knockout of the current WBA super-bantamweight champion, Wilfredo Vasquez. Has stopped 25 opponents.

19.10.91 Luisito Espinosa W CO 5 Manila *(WBA Bantamweight Title Challenge)*
15.03.92 Eddie Cook L CO 5 Las Vegas *(WBA Bantamweight Title Defence)*

Career: 39 contests, won 35, drew 1, lost 3.

Eddie Cook, the WBA bantamweight champion, shown halting fellow southpaw, Johnny Vasquez in June 1991 Chris Farina

Eddie Cook

Las Vegas, USA. *Born* 21 December, 1966

WBA Bantamweight Champion. Former Undefeated USBA Bantamweight Champion

5'3" tall, muscular southpaw, member of the Las Vegas Gloves team and promoted by the Top Rank outfit. As an amateur, he won the North American title and National Sports Festival championship. Lost 20 out of 150 fights. Turned professional in March 1990 and stopped his first twelve opponents, all within four rounds. Was floored by Jose Vasquez and Steve Mwema, but got up to halt both of them. Won the Vacant USBA bantamweight title in April 1991 by outpointing veteran Diego Avila, despite two bad cuts and losing a point for low blows. In June he retained the title by halting fellow southpaw, Johnny Vasquez, although again losing a point for a low punch. Eddie suffered a bad defeat in September when he was floored five times and cut badly before being halted in four rounds by the dangerous Filipino, Dio Andujar. Despite the loss, Cook landed a shot at the WBA champion, Israel Contrerras and dominated the fight all the way, before knocking out the champion in the fifth round. Excellent offensive boxer and a hard puncher with either hand, but his own chin is questionable and he can be cut easily. Stopped fifteen opponents.

27.09.91 Dio Andujar L RSC 4 Scottsdale
26.12.91 Lee Cargle W RSC 3 Las Vegas
15.03.92 Israel Contrerras W CO 5 Las Vegas *(WBA Bantamweight Title Challenge)*

Career: 18 contests, won 17, lost 1.

Bert (Smokin) Cooper

Sharon Hill, USA. *Born* 10 January, 1966

Former Undefeated NABF Heavyweight Champion. Former NABF Cruiserweight Champion

Turned professional in September 1984, being trained by Joe Frazier and getting his nickname from his resemblance in style to Joe. Started as cruiserweight and has shifted between cruiserweight and heavyweight throughout his career. Won the NABF cruiserweight title in June 1986 by outpointing Henry Tillman and defended it twice in that year when beating Tyrone Booze and Spencer Chavis. Moved up to heavyweight in February 1987 and halted the Canadian hope Willie DeWit in two rounds. Was stopped in seven rounds by Carl Williams for the USBA heavyweight title in June 1987 and then moved down to cruiserweight again, to defend his NABF title, with wins over Andre McCall, Tony Fulilangi and Tony Morrison. Lost the NABF crown in February 1989, being stopped by Nate Miller. In June 1989, Bert collapsed in two rounds against George Foreman, but then won the NABF heavyweight title by stopping Orlin Norris in two rounds. Defeated by Ray Mercer for the title in August, he was knocked out in two rounds by Riddick Bowe. Bounced back with a stoppage win over Joe Hipp in October 1990 and then stepped in as a late substitute against Evander Holyfield. Bert had the champion badly hurt before being stopped in the seventh round. Also had Michael Moorer on the canvas in their fight for the vacant WBO title. Has stopped 23 opponents, but has also been halted six times.

08.08.91	Anthony Wade W RSC 8 Atlantic City
18.10.91	Joe Hipp W RSC 5 Atlantic City
23.11.91	Evander Holyfield L RSC 7 Atlanta *(IBF, WBC & WBA Heavyweight Title Challenge)*
15.02.92	Cecil Coffee W RSC 2 Las Vegas
15.05.92	Michael Moorer L RSC 5 Atlantic City *(Vacant WBO Heavyweight Title)*

Career: 36 contests, won 27, lost 9.

Victor Cordoba

Punta Alegre, Panama. *Born* 15 March, 1963
WBA S. Middleweight Champion. Former Undefeated Panamanian & Latin American Middleweight Champion

6'1" tall, southpaw. Turned professional in May 1981 and lost two and drew two of his first four fights. Won the Panamanian and Latin American middleweight titles in August 1985 by knocking out Nestor Flores in three rounds. Was inactive from December 1987 until he moved to Belfast and stopped Anthony Logan in one round in March 1989. Lost on a disqualification for a low blow against Abner Blackstock in September 1989. Became the WBA super-middleweight champion in April 1991, by scoring an upset win over Christophe Tiozzo in Marseille, halting the French hero in the ninth round. Victor was less impressive in a defence in December against Vincenzo Nardiello in an all southpaw battle. He had Nardiello down in the second round, but the fight was very close when the referee halted the bout in the eleventh round. A big strong fighter, Cordoba has stopped fourteen opponents.

13.12.91	Vincenzo Nardiello W RSC 11 Paris *(WBA S. Middleweight Title Defence)*

Career: 23 contests, won 18, drew 2, lost 3.

Freddy Cruz

Dominican Republic. *Born* 14 April, 1962
Featherweight

Born in the Dominican Republic, he turned professional in Italy in January 1986 and has been based there throughout his career. Made a bad start with four losses and three draws in his first ten fights, but then went 39 fights before losing again. A fair boxer but not a puncher, he has stopped only twelve opponents. Holds wins over Alberto Mercado, Azael Moran and Farid Benredjeb and drawn with Miguel Francia. Gave Wilfredo Vasquez a tough fight for the WBA title, despite losing a unanimous decision and could come again as he has the backing.

20.07.91	Cirilo Figueredo W PTS 8 Palermo
05.09.91	Ramon Astorga W PTS 8 San Pellegrino
05.10.91	Farid Benredjeb W PTS 8 Laigueglia
16.11.91	Ruben Aguirre W RSC 2 Omegna
04.12.91	Raul Gomez W PTS 8 San Pellegrino
12.02.92	Pedro Davila W RSC 4 Sarno
18.03.92	Jose de Jesus Trinidad W CO 2 San Pellegrino
01.04.92	Willie Richardson W RSC 4 San Pellegrino
27.06.92	Wilfredo Vasquez L PTS 12 Gorle *(WBA S. Bantamweight Title Challenge)*

Career: 46 contests, won 37, drew 4, lost 5.

Robinson Cuestas

Darien, Panama. *Born* 9 May, 1969
L. Flyweight

Turned professional in August 1989 and is still unbeaten. Gained a world rating after beating Santos Becerra in February 1991. Fine boxer with a hard punch, but has yet to fight outside Panama, or to meet top ten opposition, so is still an unknown quantity. Holds wins over Leonardo Paredes, Allan de Leon and Roy Thompson and has halted 16 opponents.

27.07.91	Roger Guevara W RSC 2 Panama City
31.08.91	Roy Thompson W CO 9 Panama City
15.02.92	Carlos Orobio W CO 4 Colon

Career: 22 contests, won 22.

Bobby Czyz

Wanaque, USA. *Born* 10 February, 1962
WBA Cruiserweight Champion. Former IBF L. Heavyweight Champion

5'10" tall with a 69" reach. Was an amateur international. Selected to represent the USA against Poland, but failed to make the trip and as a result avoided the tragic air crash that killed a number of members of the team. Turned professional in April 1980 as a middleweight and won his first 20 fights, before losing on points to Mustafa Hamsho in November 1982. Took the IBF light-heavyweight title in September 1986 by halting Slobodan Kacar. Defended the title three times, but was then beaten in nine rounds by Charles Williams in October 1987. Lost to Dennis Andries in May 1988. Attempting to take the WBA light-heavyweight title, he was outpointed by Virgil Hill in March 1989. Halted in ten rounds by Charles Williams in June 1989 when he tried to regain his IBF crown and announced his retirement. Returned as a cruiserweight in March 1990, beating Uriah Grant and in March 1991 won the WBA title by decisioning Robert Daniels. Defended the title with an easy points win over Bash Ali in August 1991 and then showed too much ability and power for Don Lalonde in a defence in May 1992. Has beaten Elisha Obed, Robbie Sims, Murray Sutherland, Leslie Stewart and Andy Maynard. Stopped 26 opponents.

09.08.91	Bash Ali W PTS 12 Atlantic City *(WBA Cruiserweight Title Defence)*
08.05.92	Don Lalonde W PTS 12 Las Vegas *(WBA Cruiserweight Title Defence)*

Career: 45 contests, won 40, lost 5.

Francesco Damiani

Bagnocanallo, Italy. *Born* 4 October, 1958
Former WBO Heavyweight Champion. Former Undefeated Italian Heavyweight Champion. Former Undefeated WBC J. Heavyweight Champion

6'4" tall. Outstanding amateur who won gold medals at the European championships and the World Cup and a silver medal at the 1984 Olympic Games. Beat Teofillo Stevenson in the

World Cup. Had his first paid fight in January 1985. Won the WBC Junior-heavyweight title, now their International crown, in February 1987, by halting Eddie Gregg in the first round. Added the European title in October 1987 with a sixth round stoppage of Anders Eklund and defended it with third round wins over John Emmen and Manfred Jassmann. Relinquished the title and became WBO champion with a third round knock out of Johnny DuPlooy to lift the vacant crown in May 1989. Retained the crown by stopping Daniel Netto in two rounds in December. Lost the title to Ray Mercer in January 1991. Francesco was streets ahead until caught in the ninth round and put down for the count. Was inactive for fourteen months, but has returned with victories over Frankie Swindell and Michael Greer. Good boxer, fast for a big man. Also has wins over James Broad and Tyrell Biggs, with 24 victims halted.

Francesco Damiani

07.03.92	Frankie Swindell W PTS 10 Fano
22.04.92	Michael Greer W CO 1 East Rutherford

Career: 30 contests, won 29, lost 1.

Carl (The Squirrel) Daniels

St Louis, USA. *Born* 26 August, 1970
L. Middleweight

Southpaw. As an amateur, he was National Golden Gloves and World Junior champion at flyweight in 1987. Won the US championship in 1988 as a featherweight. Turned professional just after his 18th birthday in November 1988 as a light-welterweight. Moved up to welterweight and then light-middleweight. Challenged Terry Norris for the WBC title. Boxed very well and gave Norris a good fight until he tired and was knocked out in the ninth round. A slick boxer with a good jab and fast hands. Still only 21-years-old, so he can come again. Holds victories over Jake Torrance, Oscar Ponce and Anthony Williams Has stopped 17 of his opponents.

02.07.91	Kenneth Kidd W RSC 3 Providence
12.10.91	Anthony Ivory W PTS 8 Monte Carlo
22.02.92	Terry Norris L RSC 9 San Diego *(WBC L. Middleweight Title Challenge)*
23.04.92	Curtis Summitt W PTS 8 Paris

Career: 28 contests, won 27, lost 1.

Aaron (Superman) Davis

New York, USA. *Born* 7 April, 1967
Former WBA Welterweight Champion. Former Undefeated WBC Con Am & NABF Welterweight Champion

5'9" tall. Son of a former professional, Larry "Tumbler" Davis. Won the 1986 New York Golden Gloves title and turned professional in May of the same year. Was unbeaten in his first 32 fights, appearing seven times in France and winning all of his fights there. Took the vacant WBC Continental Americas welterweight title in April 1989 by outpointing Luis Santana. Added the NABF crown by knocking out Russell Mitchell in six rounds in November 1989. Won the WBA title in July 1990 when he came back from almost being stopped, due to a closed right eye, to knock out Mark Breland with a right hand in the ninth round. After a couple of non-title fights, Aaron lost his crown in January 1991 when he was clearly outpointed by Meldrick Taylor. Was inactive for over a year and has now moved up to light-middleweight. Holds wins over Judas Clottey, Horace Shufford, Gene Hatcher and Jorge Maysonet. Has stopped 19 opponents.

28.02.92	Cirilo Nino W PTS 10 Charleston

Career: 34 contests, won 33, lost 1.

Pedro Decima

Tucuman, Argentina. *Born* 10 March, 1964
Former WBC S. Bantamweight Champion. Former Undefeated Argentinian & South American S. Bantamweight Champion

Former golf caddy. Outstanding amateur who lost to Dale Waters in the quarter-finals of the 1984 Olympics and suffered only three defeats in his 50 fights. Turned professional in November 1984 and won his first 14 fights, before losing to the experienced Ramon Soria in November 1986. Became the Argentinian super-bantamweight champion in January 1987 by stopping Ramon Dominguez in three rounds and was proclaimed the South American champion later in the year. Moved to Las Vegas in May 1988 and in July ruined the unbeaten record of Jesse Benavides by stopping him in three rounds. In his next fight, in September 1988, Pedro was floored three times and halted in eight rounds by Louie Espinoza. Scored five wins, although almost coming a cropper when he was floored twice by Pedro Villegas and then challenged Paul Banke for the WBC super-bantamweight title in November 1990. Pedro outclassed Banke, flooring him three times and stopping him in three rounds. Lost his title in his first defence when he was weakened by weight making and halted in eight rounds by Kiyoshi Hatanaka in February 1991. Was inactive until December 1991. Came back with some wins in Argentina, but had his hopes dashed when he was battered to defeat by Rudy Zavala last June. Holds victories over Miguel Francia, Ramon Soria, Robert Shannon, Joe Orewa and Julian Solis. Has halted 20 opponents

21.12.91	Humberto Escudero W CO 3 Buenos Aires
31.01.92	Cirilo Figueredo W DIS 4 Lanus
23.05.92	Roberto Schonning W RSC 4 Buenos Aires
19.06.92	Rudy Zavala L RSC 6 Las Vegas

Career: 33 contests, won 29, lost 4.

Gilbert Dele

Guadalupe, France. *Born* 1 January, 1964
Former WBA L. Middleweight Champion. Former Undefeated European & French L. Middleweight Champion

French amateur champion in 1985. Turned professional in October 1986 and was held to a draw in his second fight by Romeo Kensmil. Won the vacant French light-middleweight title in April 1988 by stopping Jean-Paul Roux in two rounds. Defended his title three times and then acquired the European title with a first round knockout of Giuseppe Leto in December 1989. Retained the crown in 1990 with victories over Terry Magee and Giovanni de Marco. Won the vacant WBA title in February 1991 by breaking the jaw of his opponent Carlos Elliott and stopping him in seven rounds. Defended the title in May 1991 with an easy points win over South Korean Jun-Sok Hwan. Dropped his title to Vinnie Pazienza in an upset. Gilbert was well behind on points in the last round when he turned his back on Pazienza, forcing the referee to stop the fight. Holds wins over Marc Ruocco, Lorenzo Garcia and Martin Camara. Has 21 wins by the short route.

14.08.91	Shannon Landberg W RSC 6 La Seyne
03.10.91	Vinnie Pazienza L RSC 12 Providence *(WBA L. Middleweight Title Defence)*
13.12.91	Rocky Berg W RSC 1 Paris
09.02.92	Lamark Davis W PTS 8 Le Mans
23.02.92	Alfredo Ramirez W RSC 8 Levallois
04.04.92	Johnny Gutierrez W RSC 10 Levallois
21.05.92	Eric Rhineart W CO 4 Paris

Career: 36 contests, won 34, drew 1, lost 1.

Rafael Del Valle

Puerto Rico
WBO Bantamweight Champion

Won a bronze medal in the 1987 Pan American Games. Had his initial paid fight in May 1989 and halted his first five opponents. Scored six wins in 1990, including two points victories over useful Hector Medina. Made a big move when he decisioned the former WBC super-flyweight champion Juan Carazo in June 1991. Had never fought outside of Puerto Rico as a professional when he came in as a late substitute against Duke McKenzie and it was a major surprise when he put Duke out cold in the first round. Has stopped nine of his twelve victims, but is really untested at the top level and has yet to prove that his destruction of McKenzie was not a flash in the pan.

Raphael del Valle Les Clark

04.11.91	Luis Yampier W PTS 8 San Juan
13.05.92	Duke McKenzie W CO 1 London *(WBO Bantamweight Title Challenge)*

Career: 13 contests, won 13.

Troy Dorsey

Mansfield, USA. *Born* 19 November, 1962
Former IBF Featherweight Champion. Former Undefeated NABF Featherweight Champion

Tough Texan who came into boxing through karate and kickboxing and occasionally returned to the martial arts during his early career, winning a world title at karate. Never actually boxed as an amateur and had his first professional fight in April 1985. Won only two of his first five bouts. Came to prominence with an upset victory in February 1989 over previously unbeaten Anthony Boyle. Took the NABF featherweight title in August 1989 with another upset as he halted Harold Rhodes in ten rounds. When challenging Jorge Paez in February 1990 for the IBF crown, Troy climbed off the floor to pressure the champion for the whole fight and lost a controversial split decision. Faced Paez again for the title in July 1990 and this fight ended in a draw. Retained his NABF crown in November 1990 with a draw against Tom Johnson. Won the vacant IBF featherweight title in June 1991 by knocking out Alfred Rangel in the first round. Dropped the crown in his first defence, being outpointed by Manuel Medina. Troy had Medina down twice, but the Mexican won a clear decision. Lost a controversial points verdict to Kevin Kelley for the WBC Continental Americas title in February 1992. Strong, aggressive pressure fighter, who is never in a bad contest. Not a one shot hitter, with only eleven quick wins.

12.08.91	Manuel Medina L PTS 12 Los Angeles *(IBF Featherweight Title Defence)*
18.02.92	Kevin Kelley L PTS 12 New York *(WBC Con Am Featherweight Title Challenge)*
02.05.92	Juan Valenzuela W RSC 4 Fort Worth

Career: 22 contests, won 13, drew 4, lost 5.

Massimiliano Duran

Ferrara, Italy. *Born* 3 November, 1963
Former WBC Cruiserweight Champion. Former Undefeated Italian Cruiserweight Champion

Comes from a fighting family. His father, Argentinian born Carlo, was European middleweight champion, and his brother Alessandro is the current Italian welterweight champion. Former University Student. Turned professional in May 1986, but lost two of his first five bouts. Became Italian cruiserweight champion in November 1989 by halting Alfredo Cacciatore and won the WBC crown in July 1990 when the champion Carlos De Leon was disqualified for hitting Duran after the bell to end the eleventh round. Massimiliano was ahead on points at the time. Retained his title in December 1990 in another controversial ending when challenger Anaclet Wamba was thrown out in the last round for butting. Wamba had already had five points deducted for the same offence during the fight. In a return in July 1991, Duran tired and cut, was stopped in the eleventh round. He challenged Wamba for the title in December 1991, but was halted in the eleventh round again. 6'2" tall with a very awkward style and an ability to frustrate his opponents. Not a big puncher, with only six opponents stopped.

20.07.91	Anaclet Wamba L RSC 11 Palermo *(WBC Cruiserweight Title Defence)*
09.11.91	Rick Enis W PTS 8 Campione D'Italia
13.12.91	Anaclet Wamba L RSC 11 Paris *(WBC Cruiserweight Title Challenge)*
25.06.92	Tim Knight W PTS 6 Naples

Career: 21 contests, won 17, lost 4.

Cristano Espana

Venezuela. *Born* 25 October, 1964
Former Undefeated WBC International Welterweight Champion

His elder brother Ernesto Espana was WBA lightweight champion in 1979. Cristano won a gold medal for Venezuela in the 1981 South American championships and competed in the 1991 World Cup. Turned professional in Venezuela in March 1984. Had three fights that year, fought once in 1985 and once in Panama in 1987. Was then inactive until he joined the Barney Eastwood stable in October 1988. Beat Dave Pierre, Judas Clottey, Del Bryan, Lloyd Christie and Luis Santana to win the vacant WBC International title. Cristano made one defence, halting tough Hugo Vilte in seven rounds in November 1991, but was later stripped of the title for failing to defend against Donovan Boucher. Excellent boxer and devastating puncher, who would have a chance against any of the world champions. Has halted 22 of his opponents.

07.09.91	Newton Barnett W RSC 4 Belfast
13.11.92	Hector Hugo Vilte W RSC 7 Belfast *(WBC International Welterweight Title Defence)*
11.06.92	Kevin Wahley-El W RSC 1 Bilbao

Career: 26 contests, Won 26.

Cecilio Espino

Tijuana, Mexico. *Born* 6 September, 1970
NABF Bantamweight Champion

5'2" tall. Turned professional at the age of 17 in April 1988 as a flyweight. Halted 16 of his first 17 opponents. Was involved in a tragedy in May 1989 when his opponent Hector Ruiz died after being knocked out in six rounds. Had six fights in California at the end of 1990 and won them all. Lost his unbeaten record in August 1991, being halted in seven rounds by fellow prospect Makito Martinez. Was beaten again in October 1991, but moved up to bantamweight and collected the vacant NABF title by stopping Luigi Camputaro in eleven rounds. Retained the crown by halting Antonio Ramirez and decisioning Jose(Pepillo)Valdez. Both fighters were on the floor in the Valdez bout, but a badly cut Cecilio came through with a split verdict. Has also defeated Jose Montiel and Steve Mwema. His record shows 19 wins inside the distance.

01.07.91	Jose F. Montiel W CO 3 Los Angeles
05.08.91	Makito Martinez L RSC 7 Tijuana
07.10.91	Abner Barajas L PTS 10 Los Angeles
09.12.91	Steve Mwema W PTS 10 Los Angeles
26.01.92	Luigi Camputaro W RSC 11 Indianapolis *(Vacant NABF Bantamweight Title)*
20.04.92	Antonio Ramirez W RTD 5 Los Angeles *(NABF Bantamweight Title Defence)*
15.06.92	Jose "Pepillo" Valdez W PTS 12 Los Angeles *(NABF Bantamweight Title Defence)*

Career: 25 contests, won 23, lost 2.

Louie Espinosa

Globe, USA. *Born* 12 May, 1962
USBA Featherweight Champion. Former WBA S. Bantamweight Champion. Former NABF S. Bantamweight Champion. Former WBO Featherweight Champion

Won 44 out of 48 amateur fights before turning professional in November 1982. Lost a points decision to Dana Roston in October 1983 but then stopped eleven of his next thirteen opponents to earn a shot at the vacant WBA super-bantamweight title. Collected the crown in January 1987 by halting Tommy Valoy in four rounds. Made three defences in five months in 1987, stopping Manuel Vilchez, knocking out Mike Ayala, but then dropping his title to Julio Gervacio in November. Came back to win the Vacant NABF title in April 1988 with a fifth round victory over Jerome Coffee, but was beaten in his first defence in May by Jesus Poll. Drew with Jorge Paez for the IBF featherweight crown in May 1989 and then took the WBO title from Maurizio Stecca with a seventh round victory in November 1989. Stecca was floored

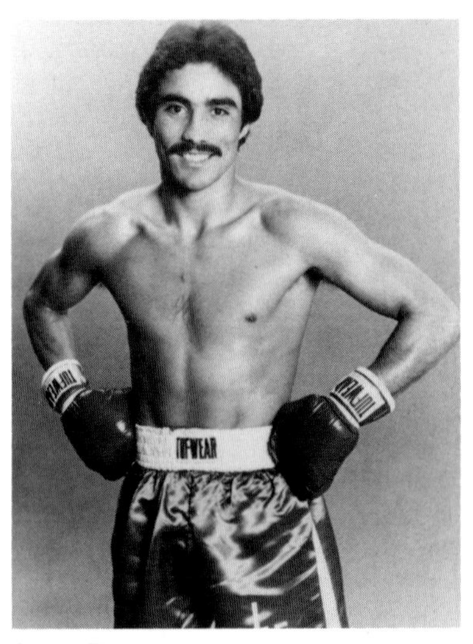

Louie Espinosa

by a body punch and when he made it back to his feet he refused to fight on. Louie challenged for the IBF title and defended his WBO title in a fight with Jorge Paez in April 1990, but lost a split decision. It looked as though Louie was slipping when he was knocked out in eight rounds by Jose Luis Martinez for the vacant NABF featherweight title in August 1991, but he bounced back again by outclassing Lupe Gutierrez to win the USBA crown. Also has wins over Refugio Rojas, Pedro Decima and Jose Sanabria. Stopped 38 opponents.

12.08.91	Jose L. Martinez L CO 8 Los Angeles *(Vacant NABF Featherweight Title)*
29.11.91	Rafael Ortega W RSC 3 Phoenix
23.02.92	Lupe Gutierrez W RSC 3 San Francisco *(USBA Featherweight Title Challenge)*
30.04.92	Freddie Santos W RSC 2 Albuquerque

Career: 51 contests, won 44, drew 2, lost 5.

Luisito (Golden Boy) Espinosa

Manila, Philippines. *Born* 26 June, 1967
Former WBA Bantamweight Champion

Nephew of former top Filipino boxer, Leo Espinosa. Turned professional in May 1984 when only 16 years of age. Lost early fights to more experienced Jun Resma and dangerous Dadoy Andujar, whilst growing from a flyweight to a bantamweight. Challenged Juan Jose Estrada for the WBC International title in Mexico in March 1988, but was stopped in ten rounds. Moved his base to California and won the vacant Californian bantamweight title in July 1988 by knocking out Mauro Diaz. Lost a very disputed decision to Yung-Chun Min in Korea in December 1988. Luisito looked the clear winner and his hand was raised, but later it was declared that there had been an error in the scorecards and Min was given the verdict. Won the WBA bantamweight crown in sensational style in October 1989 by halting Kaokor Galaxy in one round. Defended his title twice in 1990, defeating Hurley Snead in eight rounds and outpointing Thalerngsak Sitbobay. Increasing weight problems weakened him for his title defence against Israel Contrreras in October 1991 and after flooring Contrreras twice, Luisito was decked three times himself and knocked out in the fifth round. He has now moved up to featherweight and has thirteen inside the distance wins.

19.10.91	Israel Contrreras L CO 5 Manila *(WBA Bantamweight Title Defence)*
14.03.92	Rudy Cabiles W PTS 10 Manila

Career: 32 contests, won 26, lost 6.

Ronnie (The Dragon) Essett

Indianapolis, USA. *Born* 19 February, 1963
Former Undefeated NABF Middleweight Champion

Comes from the same boxing club that produced Marvin Johnson and J. B. Williamson. Won both National Golden Gloves and USA championships as an amateur, but lost to Frank Tate in the US Olympic trials. Turned professional in October 1984. Lost disappointing decisions in 1986 to Dale Jackson and Charles Campbell, but outpointed Dave Tiberi in 1987 and drew with Doug de Witt in January 1988. Became NABF middleweight champion in October 1988, winning the title with a points victory over Sanderline Williams. Challenged for the WBA super-middleweight crown a year later, but was knocked out in the eleventh round by In-Chul Baek in South Korea. Ran up five victories, including a win over Robbie Sims and then challenged Mauro Galvano for the WBC title. A dull fight saw Galvano retain the title on a unanimous decision. Put himself back in the picture by decisioning Frank Winterstein in March. Fought Chris Eubank for the WBO title last June, but lost a unanimous decision in a boring fight. Clever fighter, but too defensive and seems to lack motivation. Has stopped fifteen opponents, but is not a big puncher.

27.07.91	Mauro Galvano L PTS 12 Capo d'Orlando *(WBC S. Middleweight Title Challenge)*
07.03.92	Frank Winterstein W PTS 8 Paris
27.06.92	Chris Eubank L PTS 12 Quinta do Lago *(WBO S. Middleweight Title Challenge)*

Career: 32 contests, won 25, drew 2, lost 5.

Jeff Fenech

Marrickville, Australia. *Born* 28 May, 1964
Former Undefeated IBF & Australian Bantamweight Champion. Former Undefeated WBC S. Bantamweight Champion. Former Undefeated WBC & Australian Featherweight Champion

A product of the Sydney street gangs, Jeff did not pull on a glove until he was 17. Won a bronze medal in the 1983 Commonwealth Fereration Games and competed in the 1984 Olympics. Had his first professional fight in October 1984 and won the Australian super-flyweight title six weeks later. In only his seventh fight in August 1985 he halted Satoshi Shingaki to become the IBF bantamweight champion. Defended the title with victories over Shingaki, Jerome Coffee and Steve McCrory and then relinquished the title due to weight problems. Collected his second world title when he knocked out Samart Payakaroon in two rounds in May 1987 for the WBC super-bantamweight title. Retained his crown with wins over Greg Richardson and Carlos Zarate, and then moved up again to become the WBC featherweight champion with a seventh round stoppage of Victor Callejas in March 1988. Defeated Tyrone Downes and George Navarro in title bouts in 1988 and decisioned Marcos Villasana in April 1989. Relinquished the crown in May 1990 and in May 1991 fought a disputed draw with Azumah Nelson in a challenge for the WBC super-featherweight title. A return bout in March 1992 saw Nelson prove his greatness by flooring and halting Jeff in eight rounds. Jeff has suffered from brittle hands throughout his career and has been close to retirement on a couple of occasions due to the pain. He is a pressure fighter with a relentless style and has held titles from super-flyweight through to featherweight. Has stopped 19 opponents

13.09.91	Miguel Francia W PTS 10 Melbourne
01.03.92	Azumah Nelson L RSC 8 Melbourne *(WBC S. Featherweight Title Challenge)*

Career: 28 contests, won 26, drew 1, lost 1.

Jean-Claude (Monzon du Var) Fontana

La Seyne, France. *Born* 16 March, 1960
European L. Middleweight Champion. Former Undefeated French L. Middleweight Champion

Turned professional October 1981 and lost his first fight. It was ten years before he lost again. Won his next fourteen fights through to October 1983 and was then inactive for four years. Returned in December 1987, but from the end of 1988 was out of action for another 18 months. Collected the vacant French light-middleweight title in May 1990 with an eighth round stoppage of Mario Lavouiray. Met Said Skoma for the vacant European title in February 1991. Fontana was knocked out by a butt in the second round. Justice was served in August as he forced new champion Mourad Louati to retire in the fourth round to take the title. Defended the crown with a points win over Wally Swift in April 1992. Tough under rated fighter, who has been held back by his life style and bad luck. His career has been interupted by a motor accident and a prison sentence, but he now seems to have settled down. Holds victories over Helier Custos and Hugo Vilte. Scored 20 wins inside the distance.

14.08.91 Mourad Louati W RTD 4 La Seyne Sur Mer *(European L. Middleweight Title Challenge)*
03.11.91 Hector Guzman W CO 2 Carpenteras
18.04.92 Wally Swift W PTS 12 Hyeres *(European L. Middleweight Title Defence)*

Career: 30 contests, won 28, lost 2.

George Foreman

Houston, USA. *Born* 22 January, 1949
Former World Heavyweight Champion

Came out of the Job Corps to win a gold medal in the 1968 Olympics and turned professional in June 1969. Crushed all of his opposition on the way to the world title. George Chuvalo and Boone Kirkman fell in three and two rounds respectively, in 1970 and Greg Peralta in ten rounds in 1971, as George stopped 21 opponents in a row. Challenged Joe Frazier for the world title in Jamaica in January 1973 and destroyed Joe in just three brutal rounds. Defended the title in a mis-match in September when he knocked out Joe Roman in one round in Tokyo. Started to look unbeatable when he crushed Ken Norton in two rounds in Caracas in March 1974, but in October 1974 in Zaire, he lost his title on a sensational ninth round knockout to Muhammad Ali in the famous "Rumble in the Jungle". Big George still looked a force when he returned to the ring in 1976 as he knocked out Ron Lyle, Joe Frazier, Scott Le Doux and Pedro Agosta and stopped John Dennis but, in March 1977, he was floored and lost a unanimous decision to Jimmy Young and retired. George came back in March 1987 after a break of ten years and won 24 fights in a row, including victories over Dwight Muhammad Qawi, Bert Cooper and Gerry Cooney. Had his title chance against Evander Holyfield in April 1991, but lost a points decision. Is still looking for a second shot at the world title. His sheer strength still makes George a formidable opponent, but time is marching on and he struggled against Alex Stewart. Has stopped 66 of his victims.

07.12.91 Jimmy Ellis W RSC 3 Reno
11.04.92 Alex Stewart W PTS 10 Las Vegas

Career: 74 contests, won 71, lost 3.

Manning (The Spoiler) Galloway

Columbus, USA. *Born* 27 April, 1960
WBO Welterweight Champion.
Former Undefeated USBA Welterweight Champion

Improved from travelling journeyman into a respected holder of a version of the world welterweight title. Made his professional debut in December 1978 and was an in-and-out performer, beat-

The former world heavyweight champion, George Foreman (right), still campaigning at the age of 43, roars into Alex Stewart
Chris Farina

ing Darnell Knox and Jerome Kinney and drawing with Roy Gumbs, but losing to Danny Paul, Charlie Weir and Nino la Rocca. Won the Inglewood Forum tournament in 1985 and took the USBA welterweight crown in July 1988 with a points victory over Rollin Williams. Retained the title with a decision over Eric Heranandez in March 1989. Became WBO champion by decisioning Al Hamza UFO for the vacant crown in December 1989. Took his title on the road with defences against Kika Khumalo in 1990 and Gert Bo Jacobsen, Racheed Lawal, Jeff Malcolm and Khumalo again in 1991, stopping Jacobsen and Lawal. Clever experienced southpaw, who has fought all over the world. Light puncher, but expert at frustrating the opposition. Also has beaten Diomedes Colome and Said Skouma.

15.09.91	Jeff Malcolm W PTS 12 Broadbeach *(WBO Welterweight Title Defence)*
14.12.91	Kika Khumalo W PTS 12 Cape Town *(WBO Welterweight Title Defence)*

Career: 61 contests, won 49, drew 1, lost 11.

Mauro Galvano

Fiumicino, Italy. *Born* 30 March, 1964
WBC S. Middleweight Champion. Former Undefeated European S. Middleweight Champion.

As an amateur he was Italian champion at middleweight in 1984 and at light-heavyweight in 1985. Turned professional in February 1986 as a light-heavyweight and in November 1988 drew with Mwehu Beya for the Italian title. Challenged Beya again in June 1989 and lost on points. Moved down to super-middleweight and decisioned Mark Kaylor in March 1990 in a disappointing fight to win the vacant European crown. In December 1990, he won the vacant WBC title by decisioning Argentinian Dario Matteoni. Made his first defence in July 1991 with a dull points win over Ronnie Essett and his second in February when he won the verdict over Paraguyan Juan Carlos Gimenez. One of the least impressive champions, Galvano is a crafty boxer, a light puncher and a roughhouse type, but his tactics have proved effective. Has stopped only four opponents.

27.07.91	Ronnie Essett W PTS 12 Capo d'Orlando *(WBC S. Middleweight Title Defence)*
23.11.91	Ramon Ramos W PTS 10 Castiglione
06.02.92	Juan Carlos Gimenez W PTS 12 Marino *(WBC S. Middleweight Title Defence)*
25.04.92	Eladio Cinturion W PTS 10 Grosseto

Career: 23 contests, won 20, drew 2, lost 1.

Joey Gamache

Lewiston, USA. *Born* 20 May, 1966
WBA Lightweight Champion. Former Undefeated WBA S. Featherweight Champion. Former Undefeated IBF Inter Cont S. Featherweight Champion

Cocky but talented young fighter, 5'6" tall. Claims 84 wins in 96 amateur bouts. Had his first professional fight in May 1987 under the management of well known agent Johnny Bos. Built up a tremendous following in Lewiston as he stopped eight of his first twelve opponents. Won the IBF Intercontinental super-featherweight title in January 1990 by halting experienced Irving Mitchell in four rounds. Retained his title by outpointing Nelson Rodriguez and Jeff Franklin in defences in 1990. When the WBA crown became vacant, Joey defeated South African Jerry Ngobeni, flooring him twice for a tenth round stoppage to become the new champion. It had been a struggle to make the weight as Joey had been eleven pounds over the super-featherweight limit in a fight only two months before. He never defended the title, relinquishing it in October to move up to lightweight. Collected the vacant WBA title in June by outclassing the South Korean Chil-Sung Chun to become a world champion for the second time. Classy fighter, good tactician and sharp puncher. Has also beaten Jackie Beard and John Kalbhenn and stopped 18 opponents.

Joey Gamache

22.11.91	Tim Tipton W CO 2 Epernay
24.01.92	Rick Souce W RSC 3 Paris
27.03.92	Tommy Hanks W PTS 10 Portland
12.06.92	Chil-Sung Chun W RSC 8 Portland *(Vacant WBA Lightweight Title)*

Career: 29 contests, won 29.

Luis Gabriel Garcia

Caracas, Venezuela. *Born* 22 December, 1963
Former Undefeated WBC International & Latin American Welterweight Champion

Just failed to reach the heights as an amateur, winning a silver medal in the Latin American championships and bronze medals in the Pan American Games and the World Cup. Entered the paid ranks in April 1985, fighting in Guyana, the Dominican Republic and Panama, as well as Venezuela. Halted Erik Perea in September 1988 to win the Latin American welterweight title and in April 1990 beat Nino la Rocca on a disqualification in Italy to collect the vacant WBC International crown. Was defeated in a challenge to Meldrick Taylor for the WBA crown in June 1991. Gave Taylor a good fight and the decision was split, with one judge voting for Garcia. Sinewy, 5'10" tall. Good boxer in the Alexis Arguello mould and a good puncher who has halted 20 of his victims. Has also beaten Wayne Harris and Barry Cambridge.

19.10.91	Carlos Zambrano W RSC 9 Caracas
27.02.92	Cruz Ramos W CO 4 Beausoliel

Career: 25 contests, won 24, lost 1.

Loreto Garza

Sacramento, USA. *Born* 23 May, 1962
Former WBA L. Welterweight Champion. Former Undefeated USBA & WBC Con Am L. Welterweight Champion

5'10½" tall, stylish boxer and a good counterpuncher. Claims 38 wins against four losses as an amateur. Turned professional in February 1983 and stopped his first five opponents, before being halted in four rounds by Brazilian Francisco Tomas Cruz. Came through in 1988 as he beat two former IBF lightweight champions in successive fights. In February he stopped Charlie Brown in four rounds and in April floored Harry Arroyo twice and halted him in just over two minutes. Confirmed his promise in 1989 as he knocked out the former IBF light-welterweight champion Joe Manley in seven rounds and gained revenge by halting Tomas Cruz in May and won the USBA light-welterweight crown with a points win against Frankie Warren in August. It was a good win as Loreto fought from the sixth round with his right eye closed. Came in as a late substitute to challenge the WBA champion Juan Coggi in Nice in August 1990. Loreto looked a clear winner, but only took the title on a split decision. Defended his title in December 1990 with a victory when Vinny Pazienza was disqualified for rough tactics in the eleventh round of a fight that Loreto was winning with ease. Lost his crown in June 1991, being floored by Edwin Rosario in the first ten seconds of the fight and halted in the third round. He has stopped 24 opponents and has the talent to come back to championship level.

15.11.91	Armando Castro W CO 7 Sacramento
Career: 32 contests, won 29, drew 1, lost 2.	

Carlos (Bolillo) Gonzalez

Xochimilo, Mexico. *Born* 17 June, 1972
WBO L. Welterweight Champion

Comes from a fighting family following in the footsteps of his brother Reyes Gonzalez, who was a sharp-punching featherweight. Lost only two of 85 amateur bouts. In his first professional fight in September 1988 he stopped his opponent in the opening round and went on to halt his next 16 victims, before being taken the distance for a points win over Oscar Lopez in September 1990. Crushed the former WBO title contender, Colombian Amancio Castro, in one round in March 1991 and did the same to the WBC International light-welterweight champion Memo Cruz in December. Disappointed in his first

Carlos Gonzalez

fight outside Mexico when only decisioning Tim Brooks, he showed his power in destroying veteran Jimmy Paul for the vacant WBO title. A 5'8" tall fearsome puncher, but still green and his defence needs tightening. Sixteen of his victims have failed to last beyond the first round and only Lopez and Brooks have heard the final bell.

28.09.91	Jose Mendez W RSC 6 Mexico City
19.10.91	Fernando Rodriguez W RSC 1 Mexico City
30.11.91	Alberto Llanes W RSC 1 Mexico
20.12.91	Memo Cruz W RSC 1 Mexico City
05.02.92	Daniel Hernandez W RSC 5 Mexico City
16.03.92	Cesar Flores W CO 1 Mexico City
11.05.92	Tim Brooks W PTS 10 Los Angeles
30.06.92	Jimmy Paul W RSC 2 Los Angeles *(Vacant WBO L. Welterweight Title)*
Career: 32 contests, won 32.	

David Gonzales

Tampa, USA. *Born* 16 September, 1968
Former Undefeated NABF Welterweight Champion

A fighter who seems dogged by bad luck. Was seriously injured by a gunshot wound on one occasion and on another, accidently killed a friend in an incident with a gun. Has also been prone to injury and involved in a ring tragedy. Won National Junior Olympic and Texas Golden Gloves titles and turned professional in June 1985 when still only 16-years-old. Lost in only his fifth fight, being knocked out by Ed Parker in September 1985, but has not been defeated since. Beat Parker on points in May 1986 and then moved from Texas to California. Drew with Ernie Landeros in April 1987. Tragedy struck in August 1988 when Ricardo Velasquez died after being stopped by David in eight rounds. Stopped Cassius Clay Horne in March 1991 and won the vacant NABF title with a points win over former amateur star Louis Howard in July. Born in San Antonio, he is now based in Tampa. Strong boxer-puncher who is still developing. Holds wins over Martin Quiroz, Dwayne Swift and Henry Anaya and has 20 stoppages. Unbeaten in his last 24 fights.

26.07.91	Louis Howard W PTS 12 Tampa *(Vacant NABF Welterweight Title)*
28.02.92	Juan Rondon W RSC 6 Tampa
21.05.92	David Taylor W PTS 10 Erie
Career: 31 contests, won 29, drew 1, lost 1.	

Humberto (Chiquita) Gonzalez

Mexico City, Mexico. *Born* 25 March, 1966
WBC L. Flyweight Champion. Former Undefeated Mexican L. Flyweight Champion

Tough little Battler, 5'1" tall, with a heavy punch and described as the Pipino Cuevas of the light-flyweight division. Turned professional in September 1984 as a stablemate of Cuevas and showed his power immediately with three first round stoppages in his first four fights. Won the Mexican light-flyweight title in September 1987 by outpointing clever Jorge Cano and in defences in 1988, he knocked out Jose Zepeda and halted Javier Varguez. Travelled to Korea in June 1989 and decisioned Yul-Woo Lee to become the WBC champion. Returned to Korea in December to outpoint the great Jung-Koo Chang in his first defence. Looked unbeatable as he knocked out Francisco Tejedor, halted Luis Monzote and stopped Jung-Keung Lim in 1990, but in December he lost his title in a big upset, being knocked out in six rounds by Rolando Pascua. Humberto was cut badly and seemed to lose heart. Regained the title in June 1991 with a disputed points win over the new champion Melchor Cob Castro. Outpointed Dominican Domingo Sosa last January, but again looked a shadow of the fighter he was in 1989 and 1990. Had a desperate battle with new South Korean star Kwang-Sun Kim, but pulled out a dramatic win with a last round stoppage. Has halted 25 victims.

27.01.92 Domingo Sosa W PTS 12 Los Angeles
(WBC L. Flyweight Title Defence)
07.06.92 Kwang-Sun Kim W RSC 12 Seoul
(WBC L. Flyweight Title Defence)
Career: 34 contests, won 33, lost 1.

Miguel Angel Gonzalez

Ensenada, Mexico. *Born* 15 November, 1970
WBC International Lightweight Champion

An outstanding amateur who started boxing at the age of fifteen and had over 60 amateur fights and competed for Mexico in the 1988 Olympic Games. Had his first professional fight in January 1989 and is still unbeaten. Was taken to Japan to gain experience and scored three quick wins there, including one over former world title challenger Tae-Jin Moon and used the Japanese ring name of Santa Tokyo. Won the WBC International title in March 1992 with a fifth round victory over world rated Ramon Marchena. Compared in style to Julio Cesar Chavez, having a tight defence, a cool approach and some beautiful counterpunching. May need to increase his punching power, but is a real title threat. Has also beaten Paquito Openeo and Juan Soberanes and disposed of 23 victims inside the distance.

23.07.91 Il-Koo Chi W CO 5 Hakata
19.08.91 William Magahin W RSC 4 Tokyo
28.09.91 Filipe Fuentes W RSC 2 Mexico City
08.11.91 Juan Soberanes W RSC 6 Mexico City
05.02.92 Jose Mendez W RSC 8 Mexico City
16.03.92 Ramon Marchena W RSC 5 Mexico City
(WBC International Lightweight Title Challenge)
22.05.92 Francisco Tomas da Cruz W RSC 3 Mexico City
Career: 25 contests, won 25.

Dave Griman

Caracas, Venezuela.
Former Undefeated Venezuelan S. Flyweight Champion

Formerly one of Venezuela's top amateurs, winning silver medals in both the World championships and the Pan American Games, before turning professional in March 1989. Won the Venezuelan super-flyweight title in December 1989 and in February 1990 moved to Tokyo where he halted Ebo Danquah in the eighth round. Took his winning score to thirteen fights in Japan, and then in July 1991 challenged Kaosai Galaxy for the WBA crown at a crocodile farm near Bangkok. Boxed well, but found the Thai too strong and was stopped in the fifth round. 5'7" tall, David is a fast skillful boxer who may have a chance at winning the title now that Galaxy has retired. Halted nine opponents.

20.07.91 Kaosai Galaxy L RSC 5 Bangkok
(WBA S. Flyweight Title Challenge)
06.12.91 Oscar Bolivar W PTS 10 Turmero
Career: 15 contests, won 14, lost 1.

Calvin (Silky) Grove

Pottstown, USA. *Born* 5 August, 1962
Former IBF Featherweight Champion. Former Undefeated USBA Featherweight Champion. Former USBA S. Featherweight Champion

Joined the Houston Boxing Club and turned professional with them in June 1982. Won his first 34 fights. Lifted the USBA featherweight title in June 1985 with a points verdict against Irving Mitchell and made successful defences against Dana Roston and Billy White. Became IBF champion in January 1988 by climbing off the floor to drop the title holder Antonio Rivera twice, stopping him in four rounds in France. Four months later, decisioned Myron Taylor in his first defence. Dropped the title in sensational fashion in August 1988 as he was well ahead on points against Jorge Paez in March 1989, but was floored three times and stopped in the eleventh round. Moved up to super-featherweight and collected the USBA crown with a points victory over Anthony English in August 1989. Lost the title in February 1990 when in front on two cards, but put down twice and halted by Bernard Taylor in the eleventh round. Seemed to be on the slide when he lost on a third round knockout to Bryant Paden, but came back in style with a points victory over Regilio Tuur in March 1992. Not a big puncher, with only 16 victories inside the distance.

01.07.91 Felipe Orozco W RSC 3 Cheyney
22.10.91 Bryant Paden L CO 3 Philadelphia
27.03.92 Regilio Tuur W PTS 10 Catskills
Career: 45 contests, won 41, lost 4.

Jeff (Hitman) Harding

Sydney, Australia. *Born* 5 February, 1965
WBC L. Heavyweight Champion. Former Undefeated Australian L. Heavyweight Champion

Tough, relentless pressure fighter, who trades on his stamina and chin. Had his first fight in the professional ranks in November 1986. Forced Doug Sam to retire in the fifth round of their bout in Sydney in April 1988 to become the OPBF light-heavyweight champion. It was only Jeff's eighth fight. Won the WBC crown in a desperate battle against Dennis Andries in Atlantic City in June 1989. Jeff had been floored and badly cut, but in a dramatic last round he overpowered Dennis to collect the title. Retained the title in a disappointing fight against Tom Collins in October when Tom retired after the second round claiming a throat injury. Made another defence in March 1990, halting

Argentinian Nestor Giovannini in six rounds. Jeff's iron chin let him down in a return with Dennis Andries in July in Melbourne when Andries came from behind to knock him out in the seventh round to regain the title. These two met again in September 1991 and in another total war Jeff took back the title with a majority decision. Retained the title with an impressive win over Christophe Tiozzo. Has stopped 17 opponents. Makes news due to his beach bum life style, but his fitness and strength are his big assets.

11.09.91 Dennis Andries W PTS 12 London *(WBC L. Heavyweight Title Challenge)*
05.06.92 Christophe Tiozzo W RSC 8 Marseille *(WBC L. Heavyweight Title Defence)*
Career: 23 contests, won 22, lost 1.

Greg (The Mutt) Haugen

Auburn, USA. *Born* 31 August, 1960
NABF L. Welterweight Champion. Former WBO L. Welterweight Champion. Former IBF Lightweight Champion. Former Undefeated NABF Lightweight Champion

Part Sioux Indian and former tough-men tournament competitor who turned professional in Alaska in November 1982, winning the Alaskan lightweight title in his second fight. Won the vacant NABF lightweight title in May 1986 with a unanimous decision over Edwin Curet. Later that year, in December, he scored a major upset as he took a majority verdict over Jimmy Paul to lift the IBF title. Dropped the title in a bitter battle with Vinny Pazienza, losing on points in Pazienza's home town in June 1987. An equally acrimonious return in February 1988, saw Greg regain the title with a points victory. He made two more defences in 1988, beating Miguel Santana on a technical decision in a very controversial ending. Greg was badly cut and after stopping the fight in the eleventh round the referee lifted Santana's hand as the winner without checking the scorecards. When the cards were checked later it turned out that Greg was ahead and the decision was reversed. His second defence saw him halt Gert Bo Jacobsen in ten rounds. Lost his title in February 1989 on a unanimous decision to Pernell Whitaker. In August 1990 he lost a decision to Pazienza, but in February won the WBO light-welterweight title with a close decision over Hector Camacho. However, Greg failed a post fight drug test and was stripped of the title. Faced Camacho for the vacant crown in May 1991, but lost on a split decision. In April this year he halted Ray Mancini to win the vacant NABF title. Tough, gritty fighter with a sharp jab, but not a big puncher. Stopped fifteen opponents.

29.10.91 Alfonso Perez W RSC 8 Reseda
03.04.92 Ray Mancini W RSC 7 Reno (Vacant NABF L. Welterweight Title)
Career: 35 contests, won 30, drew 1, lost 4.

Magne Havnaa

Oslo, Norway. *Born* 16 September, 1963
Former Undefeated WBO Cruiserweight Champion

Won 68 out of 84 amateur fights. Competed in the Olympic Games in 1984 and the World championships in 1986. Started as a professional in Denmark in October 1986 with a points win over Johnny Nelson in his first fight. Defeated Stewart Lithgo and Andy Gerrard in 1987 and Alfonzo Ratliff, Roy Smith and John Westgarth in 1988. Fought Angelo Rottoli for the vacant European cruiserweight title in Italy in May 1989. Magne climbed off the floor to take the lead on points, but was badly cut and stopped in the fourth round. In his next bout, in December 1989, he met Boone Pultz for the vacant WBO title, but was defeated on a split decision. In a return contest, in May 1990, Magne became Norway's first ever world champion as he floored Pultz twice and halted him in five rounds. Retained the title with points verdicts against Daniel Netto in December 1990 and Tyrone Booze in February 1991, but relinquished the crown due to weight problems and has moved up to heavyweight. Halted ten opponents.

06.12.91 Greg Gorrell W RSC 1 Copenhagen
14.03.92 David Jaco W CO 4 Copenhagen
Career: 21 contests, won 19, lost 2.

Thomas (Hit Man) Hearns

Detroit, USA. *Born* 18 October, 1958
Former WBA L. Heavyweight Champion. Former Undefeated WBO S. Middleweight Champion. Former WBC Middleweight Champion. Former Undefeated WBC L. Heavyweight Champion. Former Undefeated WBC L. Middleweight Champion. Former WBA Welterweight Champion. Former Undefeated USBA Welterweight Champion. Former Undefeated NABF Middleweight Champion

A great fighter nearing the end of a great career. Turned professional with the Kronk team in November 1977 after winning National AAU and Golden Gloves titles. Stopped his first 17 opponents. The first of his many titles was the USBA welterweight crown which he collected by halting Angel Espada in four rounds in March 1980. Crushed the feared Mexican Pipino Cuevas in just two rounds in August 1980 to become the WBA champion. Stopped Luis Primera, Randy Shields and Pablo Baez in title defences, but then lost his crown to Sugar Ray Leonard, who came from behind to halt Tommy in the fourteenth round. Moved up to light-middleweight and won his second world title with a majority decision over Wilfred Benitez for the WBC crown in December 1982. Made three defences, including a devastating second round dismissal of Roberto Duran in June 1984 and then challenged Marvin Hagler for the world middleweight crown in April 1985. Three of the most exciting rounds seen in boxing ended with Hagler the convincing victor on a stoppage. Tommy then won the NABF middleweight title by knocking out prospect James Shuler in one round in March 1986. Defended his WBC light-middleweight crown by stopping Mark Medal in June and relinquished the title in September. Won the WBC light-heavyweight title by outclassing a game Dennis Andries and halting him in ten rounds in March 1987, only to relinquish and move down to kayo Juan Roldan in four rounds in October to become WBC middleweight champion. A big upset saw Tommy halted in three rounds in his first title defence in June 1988 by Iran Barkley, but he bounced back only five months later to win a split decision over James Kinchen for the vacant WBO and NABF super-middleweight titles. Looked to have gained revenge in a title challenge against Sugar Ray Leonard in June 1989 for the WBC super-middleweight title, but had to settle for a draw. Made one defence of his WBO crown against Michael Olajide in 1990 and then relinquished the title and in June 1991 became a world champion for the sixth time by outpointing Virgil Hill for the WBA light-heavyweight crown. Lost the title last March on a split decision to Iran Barkley. Has stopped 40 opponents.

20.03.92 Iran Barkley L PTS 12 Las Vegas (WBA L. Heavyweight Title Defence)
Career: 55 contests, won 50, drew 1, lost 4.

Anthony Hembrick

Detroit, USA. *Born* 22 February, 1966
Cruiserweight

Made as much news by missing the bus at the 1988 Olympic Games as others did by winning medals. A 6'2" tall former soldier, he won 132 of 145 amateur fights. First professional bout in April 1989. Had a busy 1989 with ten victories in six months. Suffered shock defeat in June 1990 when Booker T. Word floored him three times and stopped him in the first round for the vacant USBA light-heavyweight crown. Came back five months later with a points win over Leslie Stewart. Suffered a minor set back when he was held to a disputed draw by Mike Sedillo in May 1991, even though a judge had Anthony a mile ahead. Challenged Leonzer Barber for the WBO title in January, but lost a loudly booed split decision after coming off the floor in the eleventh round. Moved up to cruiserweight but, despite having Angelo Dundee in his corner, lost to Orlin Norris for the NABF title, being floored three times before being stopped in the eighth. Good boxer with a strong jab, but a questionable chin.

17.09.91 James Williamson W RSC 3 Detroit
15.11.91 Robert Johnson W CO 1 Roanoke
17.12.91 Joe McKnight W RSC 1 Honolulu
07.01.92 Leonzer Barber L PTS 12 Detroit *(WBO L. Heavyweight Title Challenge)*
25.03.92 Orlin Norris L RSC 8 San Diego *(NABF Cruiserweight Title Challenge)*
Career: 27 contests, won 23, drew 1, lost 3.

Angel (Pelayito) Hernandez

Rio Pedras, Puerto Rico. *Born* 21 February, 1962
Former Undefeated WBC Con Am L. Welterweight Champion

A 5'10" tall switch hitter with a difficult style, but not a big puncher. Entered the paid ranks in October 1979 and was then unbeaten for almost twelve years. Kept busy but did not make the headlines as most of his bouts were in Puerto Rico with only an occasional trip to Florida where the opposition was modest. Won the vacant WBC Continental Americas lightweight title in September 1987 by stopping Juan Minaya in five rounds. Outpointed Timmy Burgess in April 1988 and halted Chris Calvin in November 1989. In 1990, beat former world super-featherweight champion Rafael Limon in three rounds and in June 1991 halted Steve Larrimore in six rounds. Challenged Julio Cesar Chavez for the WBC light-welterweight crown and posed Julio a few problems for a while, but was ground down and halted in the fifth round. Despite his lack of a big punch he has registered 22 stoppages.

07.08.91 Alberto Alcaraz W PTS 10 San Juan
10.04.92 Julio Cesar Chavez L RSC 5 Mexico City *(WBC L. Welterweight Title Challenge)*
Career: 39 contests, won 36, drew 2, lost l.

Genaro (Chicanito) Hernandez

Los Angeles, USA. *Born* 10 May, 1966
WBA S. Featherweight Champion

Followed his brother Rudy into the professional ranks after reputedly winning 80 of his 90 amateur fights. Had his initial paid fight in September 1984. Made his first big impression in November 1988 when he floored veteran Refugio Rojas twice and knocked him out in six rounds to win the Californian super-featherweight title. Entered the Inglewood Forum tournament in 1989, beating Ed Pollard and Felipe Orozco. In May 1990, he travelled to Tokyo and knocked out Filipino Leon Collins in three rounds. Impressive stoppage wins over Benny Lopez and Rodolfo Gomez in 1990 saw him gain a high rating, but he had to wait until November 1991 for a shot at the world title. Won the vacant WBA crown as he outclassed the French veteran Daniel Londas, decking him three times and forcing an end in the ninth round. Was less impressive in his first defence in February 1992 when he outpointed Venezuelan Omar Catari. His height and strength make him a tough fighter at this weight and allied with his punching power, seem to indicate that only weight problems could rob him of his title.

22.11.91 Daniel Londas W RTD 9 Epernay *(Vacant WBA S. Featherweight Title)*
24.02.92 Omar Catari W PTS 12 Los Angeles *(WBA S. Featherweight Title Defence)*
Career: 25 contests, won 25.

Virgil Hill

Williston, USA. *Born* 18 January, 1964
WBC International L. Heavyweight Champion. Former WBA L. Heavyweight Champion. Former Undefeated WBC Con Am L. Heavyweight Champion

A converted southpaw, he won a silver medal in the 1984 Olympic Games and a bronze medal in the World Cup in 1983. Reportedly won 250 of his 261 amateur fights. Turned professional in November 1984, but initially made slow progress as his style was not considered commercial enough. Outpointed Clarence Osby in December 1986 to become WBC Con Am light-heavyweight champion.

Virgil Hill (left) in action, losing his WBA light-heavyweight title to Thomas Hearns in June 1991 Tom Casino

Was considered an outsider when he challenged Leslie Stewart for the WBA title in September 1987, but outclassed the Trinidadian, flooring him twice and knocking him out in the fourth round. Retained his title in November with a points victory over Rufino Angulo. Made three defences in 1988, halting Jean-Marie Emebe and Willie Featherstone and decisioning Ramzi Hassan. Continued the pattern in 1989 by beating Bobby Czyz, Joe Lasisi and James Kinchen, and in 1990, by outpointing Dave Vedder and Tyrone Frazier. Made his tenth successful defence in January 1991 with a points win over Mike Peak, but then lost the title to Thomas Hearns in June. After nine months, he returned to action with a win over Aundrey Nelson and in April 1992 won the WBC International crown by destroying veteran Lottie Mwale. Trained by Eddie Futch, he has stopped 22 victims.

01.03.92 Aundrey Nelson W PTS 10 Melbourne
11.04.92 Lottie Mwale W RSC 4 Bismark *(WBC International L. Heavyweight Title Challenge)*
Career: 33 contests, won 32, lost 1.

Jemal Hinton

District Heights, USA. *Born* 26 November, 1969
Former Undefeated WBC Con Am S. Bantamweight Champion

Member of the Kronk team. Is trained by his father Junius Hinton who was a sparring partner to Emile Griffith. Jemal was born in the same Brooklyn hospital as Michael Moorer. Had a 98-14 record as an amateur, but lost to Kennedy McKinney in the Olympic trials. Knocked out Juan Lopez in two rounds in Phoenix in October 1988 in his first professional match and made rapid progress. In his eleventh fight, in November 1989, he won the WBC Continental Americas title by flooring experienced Robert Shannon twice, before stopping him on a cut in the eleventh round. Retained his title in 1990 by stopping Hector Diaz, Fred Hernandez and Rafael Ortega. In his fourth defence in January 1991 he outpointed the tough Mexican Diego Avila, but relinquished the title later in the year. Good stylish fighter who will get better with more experience. Sharp punching has accounted for 17 opponents inside the distance.

13.08.91 Juan Bisono W RSC 4 Detroit
21.09.91 Mario Lozano W CO 2 Washington
18.01.92 Lucilo Nolasco W PTS 10 Detroit
Career: 22 contests, won 22.

Akinobu Hiranaka

Japan. *Born* 14 November, 1963
WBA L. Welterweight Champion.
Former Undefeated Japanese L. Welterweight Champion

Born in Okinawa. As an amateur he won a gold medal in the Asian Games and represented Japan in the 1984 Olympics. Scored 43 victories in 52 bouts before entering the paid ranks in March 1985. Blasted his way to the Japanese title in only his fourth fight in January 1986. He made three defences in the year, stopping all of his challengers. Swept his way through three more title fights, all victories, in 1987, and four in 1988. Relinquished the title in late 1988 and in April 1989, he challenged for the WBA title. He had the champion, Juan Coggi, down twice, but faded in the late rounds and lost on points, being hospitalised after the fight due to exhaustion. Stopped Boy Masuay in November 1989, but was then inactive until January 1991 when he halted Kwon-Shik Kim. Did not fight again until April 1992 when in a major upset he overwhelmed Edwin Rosario and stopped him in the first round to take the WBA crown. his explosive punching has accounted for 18 quick wins.

Akinobu Hiranaka

10.04.92 Edwin Rosario W RSC 1 Mexico City *(WBA L. Welterweight Title Challenge)*
Career: 21 contests, won 20, lost 1.

Larry (Easton Assassin) Holmes

Easton, USA. *Born* 3 November, 1949
Former IBF & WBC Heavyweight Champion

Former truck driver who has established his claim to being one of the great heavyweight champions. Turned professional in March 1973 and won the WBC title in June 1978 by decisioning Ken Norton. Made 17 defences of his title, beating fighters such as Mike Weaver, Earnie Shavers, Muhammad Ali, Trevor Berbick, Leon Spinks, Gerry Cooney and Tim Witherspoon, before relinquishing it in 1983 when the WBC insisted he make a defence against Greg Page for a small purse. Was recognised as champion by the IBF and made the first defence of that title against James "Bonecrusher" Smith in November 1984. Defended the IBF title twice, but then lost it to Mike Spinks in September 1985. Failed in an attempt to regain the crown against Spinks in 1986 and retired. Came out of retirement in January 1988 to challenge Mike Tyson, but suffered a brutal knockout defeat in four rounds and retired again. Returned to the ring in April 1991 and after five easy wins, re-established himself as a title contender with a points win over Ray Mercer. Lost clearly to Evander Holyfield, but lasted the distance with dignity. Stopped 37 opponents.

13.08.91	Eddie Gonzalez W PTS 10 Tampa
24.08.91	Mike Greer W CO 4 Honolulu
17.09.91	Art Card W PTS 10 Orlando
12.11.91	Jaime Howe W RSC 1 Jacksonville
07.02.92	Ray Mercer W PTS 12 Atlantic City
19.06.92	Evander Holyfield L PTS 12 Las Vegas *(WBC, WBA & IBF Heavyweight Title Challenge)*

Career: 57 contests, won 53, lost 4.

Evander (The Real Deal) Holyfield

Atlanta, USA. *Born* 19 October, 1962
IBF, WBA & WBC Heavyweight Champion. Former Undefeated WBC, WBA & IBF Cruiserweight Champion. Former Undefeated WBC Con Am Heavyweight Champion

Born in Atmore, Alabama. 6'2½" tall with a 77½" reach, he was robbed of an Olympic gold medal when he was disqualified in the semi-finals at light-heavyweight. Signed up with the Main Events team and had his first professional fight in November 1984, weighing 12st 9½lb. Won the WBA cruiserweight title in July 1986 with a split decision over Dwight Muhammad Qawi. Retained the title in February 1987 by halting Henry Tillman and then won the IBF title in May 1987, knocking out Rickey Parkey. Stopped Osvaldo Ocasio and Qawi in title defences and in April 1988 halted Carlos DeLeon to win the WBC title to become undisputed champion. He never again fought at cruiser-

Evander Holyfield

weight, moving up to heavyweight and forcing James Tillis to retire in the fifth round of their fight in July 1988. Wins over former champions, Pinklon Thomas and Michael Dokes and leading contenders, Adilson Rodrigues and Alex Stewart, earned Evander a shot at the heavyweight title. Won the title in October 1990 with a third round knockout of James Douglas and retained the title in 1991 with a points win over George Foreman and a stoppage of Bert Cooper, but looked vulnerable when badly hurt by Cooper. Outpointed Larry Holmes, but fought without conviction and has a long way to go to establish himself. Halted 22 victims.

23.11.91	Bert Cooper W RSC 7 Atlanta *(IBF, WBC & WBA Heavyweight Title Defence)*
19.06.92	Larry Holmes W PTS 12 Las Vegas *(WBC, WBA & IBF Heavyweight Title Defence)*

Career: 28 contests, won 28.

Bernard (The Executioner) Hopkins

Philadelphia, USA. *Born* 15 January, 1965
Middleweight

Born in the tough north Philadelphia district that has spawned many good fighters. His uncle Art McCloud was a professional. Started boxing in his teens, but walked away from the game after failing to make the United States team for the 1984 Olympics. Lost a decision to Clinton Mitchell in his first professional fight when he returned to boxing in October 1988. Retired until February 1990 when, under new management, he came back and recorded eight wins in the year. Scored another seven victories in 1991, halting six of his victims, four in the first round. Showed what a dangerous fighter he was by stopping clever Dennis Milton in four rounds in January, but was then taken the distance by Randy Smith and Anibal Miranda. A 6'0" tall, exciting fighter with a hard punch, he is co-promoted by Ring Warriors and Top Rank. Now has 18 wins in a row with 13 stoppages, nine in the first round. Has beaten Percy Harris and Ralph Moncrief.

09.07.91	Danny Mitchell W RSC 1 Philadelphia
23.09.91	Ralph Moncrief W RSC 1 Philadelphia
26.11.91	David McCluskey W RSC 7 Philadelphia
13.12.91	Willie Kemp W PTS 10 Atlantic City
31.01.92	Dennis Milton W RSC 4 Philadelphia
03.04.92	Randy Smith W PTS 10 Atlantic City
21.05.92	Anibal Miranda W PTS 10 Paris

Career: 19 contests, won 18, lost 1.

Hiroki Ioka

Sakai City, Japan. *Born* 8 January, 1969
WBA L. Flyweight Champion. Former WBC M. Flyweight Champion

Baby-faced battler who turned professional in January 1986 without any amateur experience. Became the youngest ever Japanese national champion when winning the mini-flyweight title from Kenji Ono in July 1987. In his next fight, only his ninth, he won a unanimous decision over Thailand's Thonburifarm to become the first WBC mini-flyweight champion. Halted the tough South Korean Kyung-Yun Lee in January 1988 to defend his crown, despite the tragedy of having his trainer Ed Townsend die at the fight. Looked to have benefited from some hometown influence when getting a draw against Napa Kiatwanchai in a title defence in June 1988. Hiroki's luck ran out against Kiatwanchai in a return in November as he lost a majority decision. Moved up to light-flyweight and ended the long reign of Myung-Woo Yuh with a points victory in December 1991 to lift the WBA title. He then defended it against Filipino Noel Tunacao with a points win in March 1992. Had a tough defence against former WBA mini-flyweight champion Bong-Jun Kim, but came out on top with a points win.

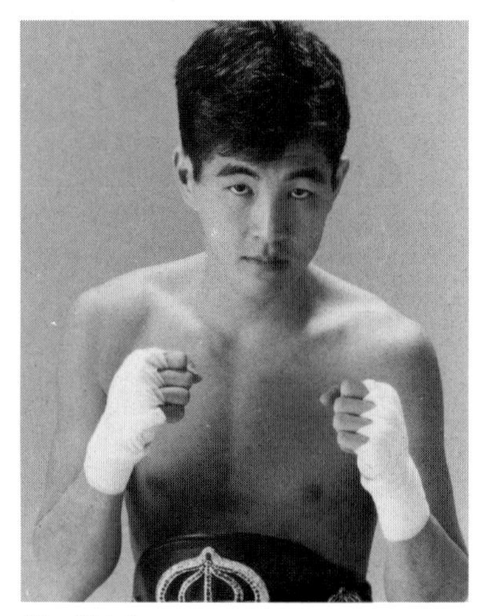

Hiroki Ioka

5'7½" tall, 68" reach. Good stick and move boxer. has stopped nine opponents. Also holds wins over John Ireng, Max Forrosuelo and Katsumi Komiyama.

17.12.91	Myung-Woo Yuh W PTS 12 Osaka *(WBA L. Flyweight Title Challenge)*
31.03.92	Noel Tunacao W PTS 12 Osaka *(WBA L. Flyweight Title Defence)*
15.06.92	Bong-Jun Kim W PTS 12 Osaka *(WBA L. Flyweight Title Defence)*

Career: 24 contests, won 21, drew 1, lost 2.

John David Jackson

Seattle, USA. *Born* 17 May, 1963
WBO L. Middleweight Champion

Born Denver. Slick boxing southpaw, but has changed management and promoters often and is almost the forgotten champion. Had over 200 amateur fights before handing in his vest in March 1984. Did not really make his mark until July 1987 when he upset the former WBA light-middleweight champion Davey Moore with a unanimous points verdict. That victory earned him a fight with Lupe Aquino for the vacant WBO title and John easily defeated the favoured Mexican, forcing him to retire in the eighth round. Made only one defence in 1989, stopping Steve Little in eight rounds in April. In February 1990 was very lucky to retain his title in controversial circumstances against Martin Camara in France. John was hurt and almost knocked out when the crowd invaded the ring thinking that the fight had been stopped. It had not and after proving impossible to restart the fight, it was ruled a no contest. In October John comprehensively outpointed Chris Pyatt in a title fight. His first title fight in 1991 saw him decision Tyrone Trice. In June 1992 he easily defeated Pat Lawlor to retain the crown. Has stopped fourteen opponents.

20.07.91	Tyrone Trice W PTS 12 McKee City *(WBO L. Middleweight Title Defence)*
09.06.92	Pat Lawlor W RTD 9 San Francisco *(WBO L. Middleweight Title Defence)*

Career: 26 contests, won 25, no contest 1.

Julian Jackson

St Thomas, Virgin Islands. *Born* 12 September, 1960
WBC Middleweight Champion. Former Undefeated WBA L. Middleweight Champion. Former Undefeated WBC Con Am L. Middleweight Champion

Comes from St Thomas, the same island as Emile Griffith. 5'1" tall. Probably the hardest one shot hitter in boxing today. Career was almost ended by retina problems and there are still some States and countries where he will not be able to fight. Had only 17 amateur fights. Turned professional in February 1981 and was carefully protected in his early days. Won the WBC Continental Americas light-middleweight title in June 1984 by beating Ronnie Warrior. Challenged Mike McCallum for the WBA title in August 1986 and after having the Jamaican hurt in the first round, was knocked out in round two. Won the vacant WBA crown in November 1987 by halting In-Chul Baek in three rounds. Stopped Buster Drayton in three rounds in a defence in 1988 and in 1989 knocked out Francisco de Jesus and beat Terry Norris in two rounds. His eye problems then required surgery and he relinquished the WBA title. He returned in 1990 as a middleweight and came from behind to knock out Herol Graham to win the vacant WBC title in November. Destroyed Dennis Milton and Ismael Negron in title defences, but had a harder task before stopping Ron Collins in Mexico City last April. Has stopped 42 opponents.

14.09.91	Dennis Milton W CO 1 Las Vegas *(WBC Middleweight Title Defence)*
15.02.92	Ismael Negron W CO 1 Las Vegas *(WBC Middleweight Title Defence)*
10.04.92	Ron Collins W RSC 5 Mexico City *(WBC Middleweight Title Defence)*

Career: 45 contests, won 44, lost 1.

Phil Jackson

Miami, USA. *Born* 11 May, 1964
Former Undefeated IBC Cruiserweight Champion

Started boxing in the Police Athletic League in Miami and won Florida Golden Gloves titles in 1984, 85 and 86. Reached the US Olympic trials for the 1988 team, but finished as runner-up and turned professional in December that year. Fought as a cruiserweight and in December 1990 flattened Olian Alexander in one round to win the vacant IBC title. Moved up to heavyweight without defending the title and in April 1991 halted Jeff Sims in five rounds. 6'1" tall with a 70" reach, he was put in his place in his clash with Razor Ruddock, being overwhelmed in four rounds. Has stopped 22 opponents and holds wins over Jesse Shelby, Alvino Manson and Tony Willis, but lacks mobility.

14.09.91	Carl Williams W RSC 5 Las Vegas
13.12.91	Melvin Epps W RTD 4 Tampa
25.04.92	Everett Mayo W RSC 3 Miami
26.02.92	Razor Ruddock L RSC 4 Cleveland

Career: 25 contests, won 24, lost 1.

Thierry Jacob

Calais, France. *Born* 8 March, 1965
Former WBC S. Bantamweight Champion. Former Undefeated European Bantamweight Champion. Former Undefeated French Bantamweight Champion

Comes from a fighting family with his brother Herve being one of the leading featherweights in Europe. Southpaw. Former leading amateur who won French titles at light-fly and flyweight and a silver medal in the World championships. Turned professional in October 1984 and won the French bantamweight title in January 1987 by stopping Alain Limarola. Challenged Kelvin Seabrooks for the IBF crown in July 1987. Thierry had Seabrooks down three times but was cut. His father would not let him out for the tenth round thinking that the IBF rules would make his son the winner on a technical decision. But as the cut was not from an intentional butt, the bout was called a no contest and the IBF much later ruled Seabrooks the winner on a knockout. Thierry challenged Fabrice Benichou for the European bantamweight title in January 1988, but was knocked out in the ninth round. Had a second shot at an IBF title in November 1988, but was stopped on a cut by the super-bantamweight champion, Jose Sanabria. Won the vacant European bantamweight title in September 1990 with a points victory against Duke McKenzie and finally became a world champion as he decisioned Daniel Zaragoza for the WBC super-bantamweight crown. Reigned for only three months and was then relieved of the crown by Tracy Patterson. Has 19 stoppage victories.

06.10.91 Antonio Picardi W RTD 4 Calais
(EBU Bantamweight Title Defence)
18.01.92 Francisco Gomez W CO 2 Calais
20.03.92 Daniel Zaragoza W PTS 12 Calais
(WBC S. Bantamweight Title Challenge)
23.06.92 Tracy Harris Patterson L RSC 2 Albany
(WBC S. Bantamweight Title Defence)

Career: 42 contests, won 38, lost 4.

Alberto (Raton) Jimenez

Mexico City, Mexico. *Born* 8 April, 1969
Former Undefeated Mexican Flyweight Champion

The "Little Mouse" hails from the tough Tepito district of Mexico City, which has spawned many great fighters. Guided by his uncle Hilario Jimenez, who was also a professional boxer, he had his first paid fight in June 1988. Lost to Mauricio Aceves on a disqualification in July 1989 when Aceves was cut by a clash of heads. Alberto then halted his next eleven opponents. Won the Mexican fly-weight title in June 1991 by stopping Gonzalo Villalobos in four rounds. Challenged Muangchai Kitikasem for the WBC title in Bangkok in October and almost won the title. He dropped Kitikasem for a nine count in the third round and one judge scored the fight a draw, but the other two voted for the champion. Alberto has relinquished the Mexican title. Has stopped 17 opponents and holds wins over Willy Salazar and Edgar Decenas.

25.10.91 Muangchai Kitikasem L PTS 12 Bangkok
(WBC Flyweight Title Challenge)
22.02.92 Eduardo Ramirez W RSC 7 Merida
01.04.92 Edgar Decenas W RSC 4 Mexico City

Career: 23 contests, won 20, drew 1, lost 2.

Reggie (Sweet) Johnson

Houston, USA. Born 28 August, 1966
WBA Middleweight Champion. Former Undefeated USBA & WBA Intercontinental Middleweight Champion

Southpaw. Lost to Frank Tate in the 1984 US Olympic Trials and turned professional immediately afterwards. Travelled to South Africa in November 1988 and stopped Charles Oosthuizen, but forfeited his WBC ranking as a result. Won the vacant WBA Intercontinental title in September 1989 with a points victory against Israel Cole and defended it by knocking out Spaniard Victor Fernandez in Leon in October. Collected the vacant USBA crown in February 1990 with an eleventh round stoppage of Ismael Negron and beat Sanderline Williams, Greg Dickson and Eddie Hall in defences. Challenged James Toney for the IBF title in June 1991. He put Toney on the floor in the second round and lost on a split decision. Won the vacant WBA title in April 1992 with a majority verdict over Steve Collins. Skilful boxer and a good puncher. Has halted 20 victims.

17.12.91 Melvin Wynn W CO 2 Pensacola
22.04.92 Steve Collins W PTS 12 East Rutherford
(Vacant WBA Middleweight Title)

Career: 34 contests, won 31, drew 1, lost 2.

In a fight that went to a split decision, Reggie Johnson (right) acquitted himself well against the IBF middleweight champion, James Toney Chris Farina

Tom Johnson

Tom (Boom Boom) Johnson
Detroit, USA. *Born* 15 July, 1964
Former Undefeated WBA Americas Featherweight Champion

Born Evansville, Indiana. Promoted by the Madison Square Gardens boxing team. Turned professional in October 1986 and scored a good early victory when he outpointed Troy Dorsey in only his eighth bout. Became A Americas Champion at featherweight in November 1988 when outpointing the useful Gilbert Contreras. His careful build up was thrown off the rails in July 1990 when he lost a split decision to little Harold Warren. In November 1990 he met Troy Dorsey in a return, this time for the vacant NABF crown. After a hard fight, one judge voted for Johnson, but the other two saw it as a draw. Challenged Manuel Medina for the IBF title in November 1991. Johnson started well, but was being outfought when the fight was stopped due to Medina being cut and the technical decision went to the champion. Johnson is being well protected in preparation for another title shot, but much of his recent opposition has been very poor. He has halted 21 victims.

03.08.91	Arturo Padilla W CO 4 Columbus
04.10.91	Gerardo Sanchez W RSC 2 Atlantic City
18.11.91	Manuel Medina L TD 9 Los Angeles *(IBF Featherweight Title Challenge)*
21.01.92	Rafael Ortega W TD 5 Las Vegas
04.04.92	Mario Lozano W CO 1 El Dorado
11.06.92	Kelvin Seabrooks W RTD 7 New York

Career: 32 contests, won 29, drew 1, lost 2.

Anthony (Baby Face) Jones
Detroit, USA. *Born* 10 May, 1966
Former Undefeated IBC Lightweight Champion. Former Undefeated WBC Con Am Lightweight Champion

Was once known as "Mad Anthony", but has quietened down since then. Claims wins as an amateur over Mike Spinks and Sammy Nesmith. Had his first professional fight in February 1985 and was unbeaten until April 1988 when he was stopped in an upset by veteran Martin Quiroz. Wins over Primo Ramos and Irleis Perez put him high in the ratings and he was matched with Edwin Rosario for the vacant WBA lightweight title in July 1989. Anthony was ahead in the fight until nailed and halted in the sixth round. Won the vacant IBC lightweight title in May 1990 and the vacant WBC Con Am title 18 days later against mediocre opposition. Challenged Pernell Whitaker for the world title in February 1991, but was easily outpointed. Has now moved up to light-welterweight. Stopped 20 opponents. Has wins over Shelton LeBlanc and Ramon Zavala.

17.09.91	Octavio Montero W RSC 2 Detroit
12.11.91	Terry Ford W RSC 2 Detroit
20.02.92	Leonardo Macias W RSC 4 Winnipeg

Career: 34 contests, won 30, drew 1, lost 3.

Junior (Poison) Ivey Jones
New York, USA. *Born* 19 December, 1970
USBA Bantamweight Champion

5'8" tall. Lost to Kennedy McKinney in the US Olympic Trials. Won 150 of his 159 amateur bouts. Great natural talent who could soon outgrow the bantamweight division. Halted George Young in one round in his professional debut in June 1989 and is still unbeaten. Beat the former WBC super-flyweight champion Juan Carazo on points in March 1991. Collected his second scalp of a former world champion in October 1991 with a win over Rolando Bohol. Followed that with a brilliant ninth round victory to collect the vacant USBA bantamweight title, stopping Filipino Dio Andujar. Halted the durable Mexican veteran Diego Avila in five rounds in March 1992. Has beaten 17 victims inside the distance. Holds wins over Felix Marti, Jose Vegagil and Alejandro Sanabria.

15.08.91	Ramon Solis W RTD 2 Atlantic City
24.10.91	Rolando Bohol W PTS 10 Worcester
12.12.91	Dio Andujar W RSC 9 Atlantic City *(USBA Bantamweight Title Challenge)*
06.03.92	Diego Avila W RSC 5 New York
23.06.92	Arturo Nava W CO 1 Albany

Career: 24 contests, won 24.

Roy Jones
Pensacola, USA. *Born* 16 January, 1969
Middleweight

Gained a great deal of world-wide sympathy when he was robbed of a gold medal in the 1988 Olympics by some strange judging. 5'11" tall. Spent two years fighting in his hometown against mediocre opposition under his father's direction, or he could have been a world champion by now. Turned professional as a light-middleweight in May 1989 and beat Steve Johnson and Roy Amundsen in two early fights. Went backwards for a while after that as far as opposition was concerned. Knocked out Reggie Miller in November 1990 and put away Ricky Stackhouse in one round in January 1991. Moved up to middleweight and faced his first world rated opponent in Mexico Jorge Vaca last February, destroying him in the first round. Did the same to Art Serwano in April. Was taken the distance for the first time in June by Argentinian Jorge Castro, but it was a good learning fight. Talented fighter with great potential who could be a world champion in 1993. In 18 fights, only Castro has lasted the distance.

03.08.91	Kevin Daigle W RSC 2 Pensacola
31.08.91	Lester Yarbrough W CO 9 Pensacola
10.01.92	Jorge Vaca W RSC 1 New York
03.04.92	Art Serwano W CO 1 Reno
30.06.92	Jorge Castro W PTS 10 Pensacola

Career: 18 contests, won 18.

Jose Eliecer Julio

El Reten, Colombia. *Born* 26 April, 1969

Bantamweight

Won an Olympic bronze medal in 1988 at the age of 19. Turned professional in March 1989 with a first round kayo of Luis Salcedo. Illustrated his potential in May 1990 when he stopped Venezuelan Abraham Torres in six rounds. Torres went on to draw with the future WBC champion Joichiro Tatsuyoshi in Japan. Beat the experienced Eduo Bermudez on a fourth round retirement in August 1990 and the useful Argentinian Roberto Schonning in the tenth round in December. In February 1991, he knocked out seasoned campaigner Jesus Flores in five and scored two more quick victories before winning on points against Manuel Ariza to end a run of 19 stoppages at the start of his career, a Colombian record. Excellent boxer and a sharp puncher. 5'5½" tall, but prone to cuts. Considered the outstanding prospect in Colombia. Has halted 21 victims. Also holds wins over Wilson Sarabia and Humberto Beleno.

02.08.91	Robinson Mosquera W RSC 5 Santa Fe
15.11.91	Manuel Ariza W PTS 10 Barranquilla
28.02.92	Luis Malave W PTS 10 Cartagena
11.04.92	William Solano W CO 4 Bogota

Career: 22 contests, won 22.

Sumbu Kalambay

Pesaro, Italy. *Born* Zaire 10 April, 1956

European Middleweight Champion. Former WBA Middleweight Champion. Former Undefeated Italian Middleweight Champion

Born Lubumbasi, Zaire, but is now an Italian citizen and has adopted an Italian name and lives in Pesaro. A professional since October 1980. Lost on points to Aldo Buzzetti in his third fight in December 1980, but did not lose again for five years. Beat Buster Drayton in 1982, but lost on points to Duane Thomas in April 1985 in Atlantic City. Won the Italian middleweight title by defeating Giovanni de Marco in September 1985, but lost a close decision to Ayub Kalule for the European crown in December. Ruined Herol Graham's world title plans in May 1987 with a points win which earned him the European title. Became WBA champion with a points victory over Iran Barkley in October 1987 and beat Mike McCallum, Robbie Sims and Doug DeWitt in title defences, before suffering a shock first round knockout loss to Michael Nunn in March 1989. Regained the European title with a victory over Francesco Dell'Aquila in January 1990. Failed in a challenge for the WBA title in April 1991, losing on points to McCallum, but has successfully defended his European title against Frederic Seiller, John Ashton, Miodrag Perunovic and Graham again. Showing some signs of age, but still a good campaigner. Halted 32 opponents.

24.08.91	John Ashton W RTD 6 Pesaro *(Vacant EBU Middleweight Title)*
14.11.91	Miodrag Perunovic W RSC 4 Ancona
12.03.92	Herol Graham W PTS 12 Pesaro *(EBU Middleweight Title Defence)*
03.06.92	Paul Wesley W PTS 10 Salice Terme

Career: 61 contests, won 55, drew 1, lost 5.

Sumbu Kalambay

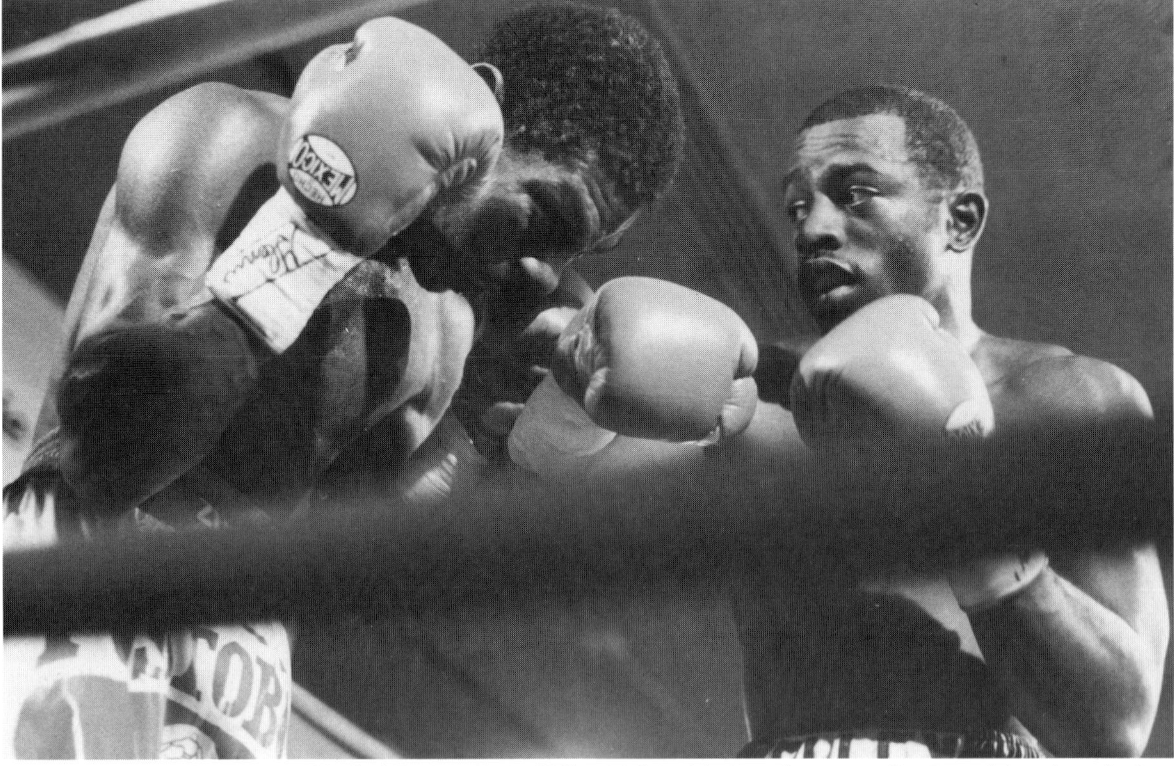

With a fourth round stoppage of Rafael Zuniga, Kevin Kelley (right) picked up the vacant Continental-American featherweight title last December
Chris Farina

Kevin Kelley

New York, USA. *Born* 29 June, 1967
WBC Con Am Featherweight Champion

Two time New York Golden Gloves champion and was undefeated in 14 amateur internationals. Hails from Brooklyn. Southpaw. Managed by the New York Boxing Club and promoted by Madison Square Garden. Had his first professional fight in September 1988. Built up carefully with a number of good tests at the right stages, he has also been exposed to action in Holland and Belgium. Beat Jean DiBateza in 1989 and decisioned tough little Harold Warren in March 1991. Won the New York State title in June 1991 by halting Job Walters and the WBC Continental Americas crown in November with a fourth round stoppage of Rafael Zuniga. Had a real war with Troy Dorsey in a title defence in February 1992 and after a close fight the judges gave Kevin a unanimous verdict. Good boxer with a fine punch, he has registered 21 stoppages.

23.07.91	James Pipps W CO 4 Monticello
31.08.91	Juan Gomez W RSC 2 Curacao
05.10.91	Rafael Almonte W RSC 2 Waregem
12.11.91	Rafael Zuniga W RSC 4 Las Vegas *(Vacant WBC Con Am Featherweight Title)*
31.01.92	Hector Padilla W RSC 2 Waregem
18.02.92	Troy Dorsey W PTS 12 New York *(WBC Con Am Featherweight Title Defence)*
21.05.92	Tomas Valdez W RSC 2 New York
02.06.92	Aldrich Johnson W PTS 10 Rotterdam

Career: 29 contests, won 29.

Napa Kiatwanchai

Nakonratchasima, Thailand. *Born* 27 July, 1967
Former WBC M. Flyweight Champion. Former Undefeated WBC International M. Flyweight Champion

Former kickboxer who made a quick conversion to international style boxing. 5'3" tall, southpaw. Had one six round bout in August 1987 and then lifted the WBC International mini-flyweight title by outpointing the champion Nico Thomas in Indonesia in January 1988. Defended the crown with a points victory over Gim Suryaman in April 1988 to earn a shot at the WBC world title. Had to travel to Osaka in June 1988 to face Hiroki Ioka. In the last round he had Ioka out on his feet, only to have the round ended 32 seconds early. The resulting draw looked to be a hometown decision. Napa gained the title and revenge as he returned to Osaka in November to outpoint Ioka. Defended his title with a points win over Indonesian John Arief in February 1989 and then settled his series with Ioka by battering him to defeat in June. Increasing weight problems finally caught up with Napa and he lost his title on a last round stoppage against Jum-Hwan Choi in Seoul in November. Came back in 1990 with a victory over Rolando Pascua, but lost on points to Hideyuki Ohashi in an attempt to regain his title in June 1990. Was inactive from July 1990 until

December 1991 when he returned as a light-flyweight.

24.12.91	Sugar Ray Mike W RSC 7 Bangkok

Career: 16 contests, won 13, drew 1, lost 2.

Yong-Kang Kim

Hwasoon, South Korea. *Born* 3 January, 1965
WBA Flyweight Champion. Former WBC Flyweight Champion. Former Undefeated OPBF & South Korean L. Flyweight Champion

Tall for a flyweight at 5'7". Fast hands, good boxer, but not a hard puncher. First professional fight in April 1985. Won the South Korean light-flyweight title in January 1987 by decisioning world rated Ha-Shik Kim. Added the OPBF crown in December 1987 when halting Putt Ohyuthanakorn for the vacant title. Registered a big upset in July 1988 as he outpointed Sot Chitalada to become WBC flyweight champion in his first fight at the higher poundage. Made two defences, outpointing Emil Romano and Leopard Tamakuma, but dropped the title in a return with Chitalada, being outpointed in Thailand in June 1989. Suffered a couple of set backs as he lost on points to Yul-Woo Lee and was knocked out by Kaosai Galaxy in a challenge for the WBA super-flyweight title in September 1990. Came back in fine style in June 1991 to decision Colombian Elvis Alvarez to win the WBA flyweight title. Outpointed Leo Gamez on a close decision in a title defence in October and knocked out Jon Penalosa in March this year. Has halted ten opponents.

05.10.91	Leo Gamez W PTS 12 Inchon *(WBA Flyweight Title Defence)*
24.03.92	Jon Penalosa W CO 6 Inchon *(WBA Flyweight Title Defence)*

Career: 28 contests, won 25, lost 3.

Muangchai Kitikasem

Chainart, Thailand. *Born* 6 May, 1968
Former WBC Flyweight Champion. Former IBF L. Flyweight Champion

Real name Nathavudh Janthavimol. Former Muay-Thai champion. His first international style bout was a ten rounder in June 1988 when he outpointed the experienced Indonesian Udin Baharudin. Won the WBC light-flyweight title in only his sixth fight, decisioning Filipino Tacy Macalos in May 1989. Stopped Macalos in his first defence in October 1989. Retained his title with wins over Jeu-Chung Lee and Abdi Pohan early in 1990, but weight reducing weakened him and he was floored four times and halted in the seventh round by Michael Carbajal in Phoenix in July for the title. He moved up to flyweight and sprang a big surprise by halting Sot Chitalada in six rounds in February 1992 to become WBC champion. Scored a big victory in May 1991 when he came off the deck three times to batter the great South Korean, Jung-Koo Chang, to defeat in the twelfth round. Had a tough time in retaining his title again when he clashed with Mexican Alberto Jimenez. Muangchai was on the floor in the third, but boxed his way out of trouble to a controversial points decision. Effectively ended Sot Chitalada's career by flooring and halting Sot in nine rounds, but lost his title to the Russian, Yuri Arbachakov. Stopped eleven opponents.

06.08.91	Lito Gonzaga W PTS 10 Bangkok
25.10.91	Alberto Jimenez W PTS 12 Bangkok *(WBC Flyweight Title Defence)*
28.02.92	Sot Chitalada W RSC 9 Samut Prakan *(WBC Flyweight Title Defence)*
15.05.92	Tarman Gazrim W PTS 10 Patumtani
23.06.92	Yuri Arbachakov L CO 8 Tokyo *(WBC Flyweight Title Defence)*

Career: 22 contests, won 20, lost 2.

Nana Yaw Konadu

Sunyani, Ghana. *Born* 14 February, 1965
IBC S. Flyweight Champion. Former WBC S. Flyweight Champion. Former Undefeated WBC International S. Flyweight Champion. Former Undefeated Commonwealth & ABU Flyweight Champion

Started boxing at the age of ten, but is an all round athlete, also being good at football and track events. Turned professional in May 1985 and fought a draw with Ebo Danquah in only his second fight. Collected the African Boxing Union flyweight crown in December 1986 by knocking out Steve Muchoki in twelve rounds. Added the Commonwealth title in October 1987 with a sixth round demolition of Albert Musankabala. Moved up to take the ABU bantamweight title in December 1988 by flattening Mike Mukenge in the first round and then moved down to super-flyweight and became WBC International champion with a decision over Cesar Polanco in March 1989. Won the WBC world title in impressive style in Mexico City in November when he floored champion Gilberto Roman five times on the way to a wide decision victory. Lost the title in his first defence in January 1990 in controversial circumstances as South Korean Sung-Il Moon was badly cut and won a technical decision. Both fighters were on the floor and the cut did not appear serious. Failed in an attempt to regain the title in March 1991 when he was halted by Moon in four rounds. Won the vacant IBC title last October by decisioning Juan Polo Perez. Has halted 18 opponents.

25.10.91	Juan Polo Perez W PTS 12 Zaragoza *(Vacant IBC S. Flyweight Title)*
17.01.92	Angel Rosario W RSC 7 Bilbao
30.05.92	Luis Ramos W RSC 2 Oviedo

Career: 26 contests, won 23, drew 1, lost 2.

Alfred Kotei

Accra, Ghana. *Born* 3 June, 1968
Commonwealth Flyweight Champion

Hard punching little fighter. Fisherman's son from the same tribe that has produced David Kotey and Azumah Nelson. He represented Ghana all around the world before competing in the 1988 Olympic Games. Won 51 of his 55 amateur fights. Turned professional in November 1988 and won the West African title in his fourth bout. Became Commonwealth flyweight champion in October 1989 by halting fellow-countryman George Foreman in three rounds. Defended the title in Brentwood in July 1990 with a clear points victory over Danny Porter. Ran out of competition and moved his base to Philadelphia in 1991 where he has stopped six opponents and been taken the distance by experienced Mexicans, Francisco Montiel and Armando Diaz. A cool ring general and a very hard puncher, he could fight for the world title in 1993, if not earlier, but he also needs better opposition to prepare him as he has not yet really been tested. Only three opponents have lasted the distance with Alfred.

09.07.91 Kenny Butts W CO 1 Philadelphia
10.09.91 Pop Robinson W RSC 7 Philadelphia
19.11.91 Nelson Vicioso W RSC 2 Atlantic City
14.01.92 Antonio Gastelum W RSC 2 Philadelphia
16.04.92 Francisco Montiel W PTS 10 Philadelphia
25.06.92 Armando Diaz W PTS 10 Philadelphia
Career: 15 contests, won 15.

Don (Golden Boy) Lalonde

Winnipeg, Canada. *Born* 12 March, 1960

Former WBC L. Heavyweight Champion. Former Undefeated WBC Con Am & Canadian L. Heavyweight Champion

Blonde movie star looks earned him his Golden Boy nickname. Had his first professional fight in 1980, losing an early decision to Wilbur Johnson, but capturing the Canadian light-heavyweight title in 1983 by beating Roddie McDonald on a tenth round retirement. Failed in an attempt to win the NABF crown in May 1985 when he was halted by Willie Edwards and took two years to re-establish himself. Succeeded in May 1987 when he won the vacant WBC Continental Americas title with a points victory over veteran Mustafa Hamsho. Won the vacant WBC title in November 1987 by halting Eddie Davis in two rounds and defended it in May 1988 with a fifth round stoppage of Leslie Stewart. Had his big moment in November 1988 when defending his title against Sugar Ray Leonard. Had Leonard on the floor, but was knocked out in the ninth round. A purse of $5.2 million provided some consolation. Donny retired for a short period, but after announcing his comeback he suffered a damaged larynx and retired again. Returned as a cruiserweight in September 1991 and challenged Bobby Czyz for the WBA title last May, losing clearly on points. Stopped 30 victims.

Don Lalonde

05.09.91 Darryl Fromm W RSC 3 Kitchener
20.09.91 Bert Gravely W RSC 7 Tampa
03.12.91 David Bates W CO 4 Memphis
17.12.91 Dave Fiddler W RSC 2 Winnipeg
08.05.92 Bobby Czyz L PTS 12 Las Vegas *(WBA Cruiserweight Title Challenge)*
Career: 39 contests, won 35, lost 4.

Jeff Lampkin

Youngstown, USA. *Born* 21 September, 1961

Former Undefeated IBF Cruiserweight Champion. Former Undefeated USBA Cruiserweight Champion

National AAU champion at light-heavyweight in 1980, he turned professional in June of that year, halting his first 16 opponents. After that bright start he slipped away, losing to Willie Edwards and Willie Starling in 1982, Richie Kates, John Davis and Fulgencio Obelmejias in 1983, Tony Witherspoon and Jerome Clouden in 1984 and Cedric Parsons and Charles Williams in 1985. Moved up to cruiserweight, but still found life tough as he lost successive fights to Ramzi Hassan, Sherman Griffin, Lottie Mwale and Patrick Lumumba. The turning point came in July 1988 when he knocked out the South African Fred Rafferty. Followed this up with a fifth round stoppage of Alfonzo Ratliff to win the USBA title and quick victories over Wali Muhammad and Elvis Parks in title defences. Challenged Glenn McCrory for the IBF crown in March 1990 and took the title on a third round knockout with a brutal body punch. Retained the title in July by knocking out Siza Makhatini in eight rounds, but relinquished it when he signed with Don King as part of King's war with the IBF. Was then inactive for almost two years. Heavy puncher who has finished 32 victims inside the distance.

29.05.92 Larry Davis W RSC 1 Struthers
Career: 50 contests, won 36, drew 1, lost 13.

Yong-Hoon Lee

Sangmun-Dong, South Korea. *Born* 31 March, 1967.

Former Undefeated South Korean Bantamweight Champion

Turned professional in June 1987 and was voted Prospect of the Year in South Korea in 1988. Became the national bantamweight champion in December with a points verdict against Chong-Pil Park, but never defended the title as he always had his eyes on a world crown. Showed how dangerous he could be when he flattened the world rated Argentinian Adrian Roman in the first round. From then on he marked time with only two fights in 1990. Picked it up again in 1991 with a technical decision over highly rated Eun-Shik Lee and a points victory against Rey Paciones. Received his world title shot in March 1992 when he faced Victor Rabanales for the vacant WBC crown. Lee was floored in the second round and this made the difference when Rabanales was cut and the technical decision went to the Mexican. Holds wins over Edgar Apatan and Sombat Eausampan. Has halted eleven opponents.

28.07.91 Rey Paciones W PTS 10 Seoul
07.12.91 Suk-Ha Yoon W CO 2 Wondang
30.03.92 Victor Rabanales L TD 9 Los Angeles *(Vacant WBC Bantamweight Title)*
Career: 21 contests, won 20, lost 1.

(Jesse) James Leija

San Antonio, USA. *Born* 8 July, 1966
NABF Featherweight Champion

Turned professional in October 1988 after a short period as an amateur. His father Jesse, was also a professional. 5'5" tall and managed by Lester Bedford. Lost in the Olympic trials to Kelcie Banks. Not really tested until October 1990 when he faced experienced Ed Parker. A good scrap saw James finish strongly to hurt Parker in the ninth, but the decision was a draw. James came in as a late substitute against Mark Fernandez in February 1991 and floored him twice on the way to a unanimous points victory. He decisioned former top amateur Steve McCrory in October and then won the NABF crown from Jose Martinez in March 1992. James suffered a bad cut from a clash of heads and as he was in front at the time was given a technical decision. A sharp puncher, he has eleven inside the distance wins and has beaten Bob McCarthy, Ricky Alvarez and Miguel Arrozal.

30.08.91	Silvestre Castillo W CO 2 Corpus Christi
18.10.91	Steve McCrory W PTS 10 Houston
03.03.92	Jose Martinez W TD 9 San Antonio *(NABF Featherweight Title Challenge)*

Career: 23 contests, won 22, drew 1.

Genaro Leon

Culiacan, Mexico. *Born* 10 August, 1960
WBC Con Am Welterweight Champion. Former Undefeated WBO Welterweight Champion

Hard puncher, but not a great boxer and has a questionable chin. Won a silver medal in the Central American championships and a bronze in the Pan American Games, but was destroyed by Mark Breland in the 1984 Olympic Games. Turned professional the same year and stopped eleven opponents, before being beaten in five rounds in December 1985 by Ruben Villaman. Ran up another 14 quick wins, but was then caught cold and stopped in a round by club fighter David Taylor in Paris in February 1988. Bounced back with a points victory over Young Dick Tiger in September. Won the vacant WBO welterweight title in May 1989 by knocking out Danny Garcia in one round. Relinquished the title later in the year and won the vacant WBC Continental Americas championship in December by stopping Sulio Sanchez, the brother of Salvador, in one round. Revenged his loss to Villaman with a fifth round stoppage in April 1990. Was held to a draw by Judas Clottey in December 1990. Has defended his WBC Continental title against Miguel Dominguez and Ramon Ramos, but is flattered by his No. 1 rating by the WBC. Has beaten Charlie Brown and Saoul Mamby. Stopped 37 victims.

13.07.91	Newton Barnett W CO 2 Forges les Eaux
24.10.91	Saoul Mamby W PTS 8 Paris
30.01.92	Charles Duffy W RSC 7 Paris
16.03.92	Ramon Ramos W RSC 2 Mexico City *(WBC Continental Americas Welterweight Title Defence)*
22.05.92	Jerry Grant W RSC 1 Mexico City

Career: 46 contests, won 42, drew 2, lost 2.

Tim (Doc) Littles

Flint, USA. *Born* 2 November, 1964
USBA S. Middleweight Champion

5'11" tall, southpaw. Lanky loose armed fighter with plenty of lateral movement and fast hands. Former amateur international who is now part of the very successful Main Events team. Had his first professional bout in November 1989 and halted his first six opponents. Not really tested until he challenged Antoine Byrd for the USBA super-middleweight title in March 1992. It was Tim's first fight over eight rounds, but he outboxed the experienced Byrd and hurt him on a couple of occasions on the way to a very clear decision and the title. His form showed he is a real threat in the division and with more experience will be ready for a world title shot in 1993. Byrd is the only real name on his record. He has stopped thirteen of his victims, nine within the first three rounds.

27.07.91	Ernie Perry W RSC 1 Norfolk
17.09.91	Jerome Kelly W RSC 5 Detroit
23.11.91	Ken Payne W RSC 4 Atlanta
18.01.92	Willie Douglas W PTS 6 Philadelphia
03.03.92	Antoine Byrd W PTS 12 San Antonio *(USBA S. Middleweight Title Challenge)*

Career: 18 contests, won 18.

Daniel Londas

Martinique, France. *Born* 17 May, 1954
WBO S. Featherweight Champion. Former Undefeated European S. Featherweight Champion. Former Undefeated French S. Featherweight Champion

Great battler for whom success has come late in a long career. Turned professional in 1980 after competing for France in the 1980 Olympic Games. Was unbeaten until 1982, winning the French super-featherweight title for the first time that year when knocking out Francis Bailleul in one round. Finally met defeat in November 1982 when he lost on a ninth round retirement to Roberto Castanon for the vacant European title. Failed in another shot at a European title in May 1984, losing on points to Rene Weller. A third attempt also ended in frustration when he was held to a draw by super-featherweight champion Jean-Marc Renard in December 1986 and a fourth try saw a disaster as he was halted in one round by Salvatore Curcetti for the vacant title in May 1987. A points loss to Brian Mitchell in October 1987 for the WBA super-featherweight title seemed to indicate that Daniel would have to settle for national honours. He persevered and in June 1989 halted Racheed Lawal in ten rounds to finally win the European crown. Proved a dominant champion once he was there, with five defences, but in November 1991 lost on a ninth round stoppage to Genaro Hernandez for the vacant WBA crown. Gained a worthy reward in March this year with a victory against Kamel Bou Ali for the WBO title. Has beaten Mark Reefer, Gianni di Napoli and Jacobin Yoma. Stopped 23 opponents.

22.11.91	Genaro Hernandez L RTD 9 Epernay *(Vacant WBA S. Featherweight Title)*
21.03.92	Kamel Bou Ali W PTS 12 San Rufo *(WBO S. Featherweight Title Challenge)*

Career: 65 contests, won 56, drew 1, lost 8.

Fahlan Lukmingkwan

Mahasarakam, Thailand. *Born* 10 April, 1968
IBF M. Flyweight Champion

Former Muay-Thai fighter. Real name Pahlangnum Sorborikara. A southpaw, he lost his first fight in June 1988 to fellow prospect Chana Porpaoin. Made steady progress until winning the Thai mini-flyweight title in July 1989 with a second round blast out of Ded Donjaedee. Took the IBF title with a controversial victory over Eric Chavez in February 1990. Chavez suffered a cut from a clash of heads, but instead of going to the judges for a technical decision, the referee ruled Fahlan the winner on a stoppage. Made three defences in 1990, outpointing Joe Constantino and Chavez, but being held to a draw by Pretty Boy Lucas. In his subsequent defences against Pohan, Tabanas Naranjo and Iskander he has shown steady progress with an improved technique and a strong body punching attack. Halted nine victims.

02.07.91	Abdy Pohan W PTS 12 Bangkok *(IBF M. Flyweight Title Defence)*
21.10.91	Andy Tabanas W PTS 12 Bangkok *(IBF M. Flyweight Title Defence)*
23.02.92	Felix Naranjo W CO 2 Bangkok *(IBF M. Flyweight Title Defence)*
14.06.92	Said Iskander W RSC 8 Bangkok *(IBF M. Flyweight Title Defence)*

Career: 23 contests, won 21, drew 1, lost 1.

Ricardo (Finito) Lopez

Cuernavaca, Mexico. *Born* 25 July, 1967
WBC M. Flyweight Champion.
Former Undefeated WBC Con Am M. Flyweight Champion

Wonderful little box puncher. Stylish, but a sharp hitter with an excellent chin. Won ten titles as an amateur, but was too young for the big tournaments. Captured the Mexican Golden Gloves crown in 1984 and became a professional with the legendary manager Arturo "Cuyo" Hernandez in 1985. Halted his first eight opponents as he learned the game on the Mexican circuit. Did not win his first title until November 1989 when he halted Rey Hernandez in twelve rounds for the WBC Continental Americas crown. Defended the title in March 1990 by halting Jorge Rivera and then travelled to Japan in October to kayo Hideyuki Ohashi for the WBC crown. Ricardo put Ohashi down three times and outclassed him. He returned to Japan in May 1991 and was again in impressive form as he destroyed Kimio Hirano in eight rounds. Was given a better test by South Korean Kyung-Yun Lee in December. After a slow start and despite a cut, Ricardo came on strong to win a unanimous decision. Last March he toyed with Pretty Boy Lucas in his third defence. With his skill and power he could rule for a long time. Also has wins over Jose Luis Zepeda and Francisco Montiel and has halted 20 opponents.

22.12.91	Kyung-Yun Lee W PTS 12 Inchon *(WBC M. Flyweight Title Defence)*
16.03.92	Domingo Lucas W PTS 12 Mexico City *(WBC M. Flyweight Title Defence)*

Career: 29 contests, won 29.

Tony (Tiger) Lopez

Sacramento, USA. *Born* 24 February, 1963
Former IBF S. Featherweight Champion

Son of a professional fighter. Always seems to be in wars, which makes him a big crowd puller. After turning professional in May 1983, Tony ran up 26 straight wins before he lost his unbeaten record in September 1987 for hitting Ramon Rico when he was on the canvas. Tony knocked out Rico a few weeks later. Sprang an upset when outpointing Rocky Lockridge in July 1988 to take the IBF super-featherweight crown. In his first defence, Tony had to climb off the floor and stage a strong finish to outpoint John John Molina. Outpointed Lockridge and stopped Tyrone Jackson in title defences, but against Molina, again in October 1989, he took a bad beating and was halted in the tenth round to lose his crown. Regained the title in May 1990 when he floored Molina and won a split decision. Retained the title with a points win over Jorge Paez and then drew with Brian Mitchell in a fight for both the IBF and WBA titles. Had an easy defence against Lupe Gutierrez, but lost to Mitchell for his IBF crown and moved up to lightweight where he is looking for a title shot. With his style he will always be an attraction, so should get his title match, but his many hard fights may soon catch up with him. Halted 28 opponents.

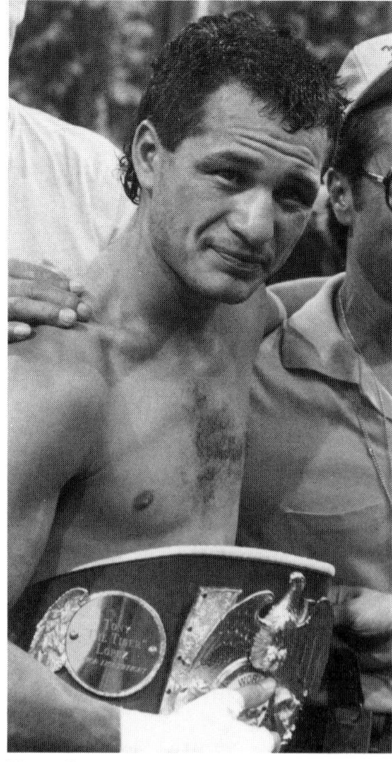

Tony Lopez Chris Farina

12.07.91	Lupe Gutierrez W RSC 6 Lake Tahoe *(IBF S. Featherweight Title Defence)*
13.09.91	Brian Mitchell L PTS 12 Sacramento *(IBF S. Featherweight Title Defence)*
15.11.91	Ditau Molefyane W RSC 8 Sacramento
20.04.92	Narcisco Valenzuela W CO 2 Sacramento
30.06.92	Andres Sandoval W RSC 2 Sacramento

Career: 44 contests, won 40, drew 1, lost 3.

Domingo (Pretty Boy) Lucas

Norzagaray, Philippines. *Born* 20 December, 1965
Former Undefeated Philippines M. Flyweight Champion

Trained by former world champion Erbito Salavarria. A professional since November 1983, he has had no luck at all in attempts at the world title. Became the Philippines mini-flyweight champion in November 1986 with a points victory against Jun Afable. Remained unbeaten until March 1988 when he challenged for the IBF title. Domingo was very much in the fight against Samuth Sithnaruepol until he was cut and stopped, when in fact the rules called for a technical decision. He defended his national title against Boy Dignos and Elson Duran and then challenged Fahlan Lukmingkwan for the IBF crown. This time he had to settle for a draw in the other man's hometown. Suffered first loss to one of his own countrymen in December, when he was outpointed by Manny Melchor. Had his third world title shot in March 1992, but was easily beaten by the talented WBC champion, Ricardo Lopez. Stopped only nine of his victims.

04.10.91	Finito Lopez W PTS 10 Honolulu
13.12.91	Manny Melchor L PTS 10 Quezon City
16.03.92	Ricardo Lopez L PTS 12 Mexico City *(WBC M. Flyweight Title Challenge)*

Career: 32 contests, won 27, drew 2, lost 3.

Mike (The Body Snatcher) McCallum

Kingston, Jamaica. *Born* 7 December, 1956
Former Undefeated WBA Middleweight Champion. Former WBA L. Middleweight Champion

Took up boxing in Jamaica against the wishes of his parents. Great amateur career, winning American Golden Gloves and AAU titles and a Commonwealth gold medal. Lost only ten of 250 amateur fights. 5'11" tall, a professional since 1981. Stopped Ayub Kalule in November 1982. Easily outclassed Sean Mannion for a points verdict in October 1984 in a fight for the vacant WBA light-middleweight title.

Mike McCallum

Made six title defences, including stoppage wins over Julian Jackson in two rounds in 1980, a tenth round stoppage of Milton McCrory in April 1987 and a fifth round kayo of Don Curry in July. Relinquished the WBA title, but was then unsuccessful in a challenge for the WBA middleweight crown, losing on points to Sumbu Kalambay in March 1988. Finally collected the WBA title in May 1989 when he jabbed his way to a split decision victory over Herol Graham. Defended the title with a points win over Steve Collins and a brutal kayo of Michael Watson in 1990. Made a third defence and gained revenge with a split verdict over Kalambay in April 1991. Was stripped of the title by the WBA in November 1991 for failing to defend against Steve Collins, preferring instead to challenge James Toney for the IBF title. Had a good lead over Toney, but a strong finish by the champion saw the bout declared a controversial draw. Is an excellent ring mechanic who wears the opposition down. Has halted 34 opponents.

29.08.91	Carlos Cruz W PTS 10 Reno
10.10.91	Nicky Walker W RSC 5 Las Vegas
13.12.91	James Toney DREW 12 Atlantic City *(IBF Middleweight Title Challenge)*
21.05.92	Fermin Chirino W PTS 10 Las Vegas

Career: 45 contests, won 43, drew 1, lost 1.

Gerald McClellan

Freeport, USA. *Born* 23 October, 1967
WBO Middleweight Champion

American ABF champion 1987, beating Tom Littles in the final and voted "Amateur of the Year" by them that year. Lost only ten of 82 amateur fights. 6'0" tall. Fearsome puncher with both hands, which is reflected in the number of first round wins on his record. First professional bout in August 1988 and none of his first ten opponents lasted beyond the second round. Was outboxed in successive fights in 1989 by Dennis Milton and Ralph Ward when his lack of dedication and his habit of loading up for every punch let him down. Showed improved patience in points victories over Sanderline Williams and Charles Hollis in 1990. Continued to meet only very modest opposition, but his membership of the influential Kronk gym helped him land a fight with John Mugabi for the vacant WBO middleweight title in November 1991. Gerald destroyed a shot Mugabi with three knockdowns in the first round. Now has 16 first round victories and looked very impressive in putting away useful Carl Sullivan last May. Still largely untested against real class middleweights, but has a punchers

Gerald McClellan

chance with anyone. Halted 23 opponents.

27.07.91	Ivory Teague W RSC 3 Norfolk
13.08.91	Sammy Brooks W RSC 1 Detroit
20.11.91	John Mugabi W RSC 1 London *(Vacant WBO Middleweight Title)*
24.02.92	Lester Yarborough W RSC 1 Detroit
15.05.92	Carl Sullivan W RSC 1 Atlantic City

Career: 27 contests, won 25, lost 2.

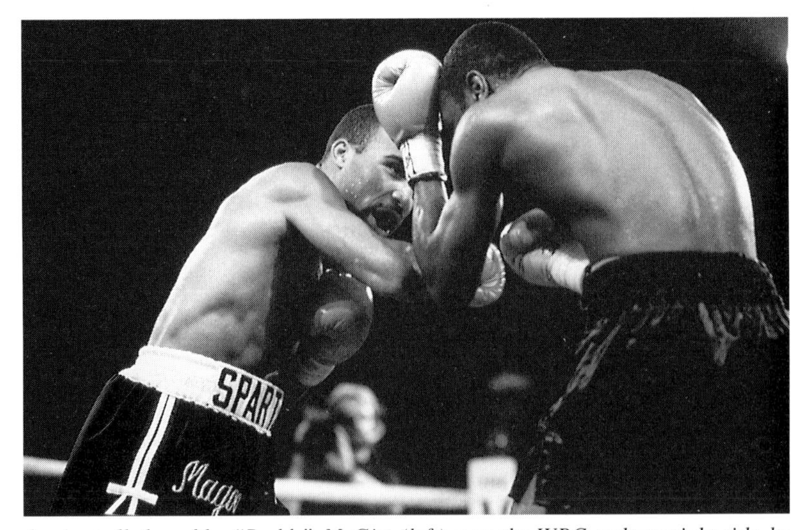

Against all the odds, "Buddy" McGirt (left) won the WBC welterweight title by outpointing Simon Brown Tom Casino

James (Buddy) McGirt

Brentwood, USA. *Born* 17 January, 1964

WBC Welterweight Champion. Former IBF L. Welterweight Champion. Former Undefeated WBC Con Am L. Welterweight Champion

5'6" tall. Good amateur career, but had to settle for minor titles as boxing politics kept him out of the big tournaments. Still ran up a 54-9 record before turning professional at the age of 18 in March 1982. Was held to a draw by Lamont Haithcoach in his first fight, but then won his next 28. Took the vacant WBC Continental Americas light-welterweight title in December 1985 by halting Sugar Boy Nando and retained it in May 1986 by stopping Ricky Young. Lost his unbeaten record on a points decision to Frankie Warren in July 1986. Met Warren again in February 1988 for the vacant IBF title and this time floored Frankie and battered him to a stoppage defeat. His first defence, in July that year, saw him knock out Howard Davis in one round, but a below par performance in September cost him his title as he was stopped in the last session by Meldrick Taylor. Buddy moved up to welterweight in 1989 and scored wins over Tony Baltazar, Gary Jacobs and Joe Manley. 1990 saw him register another four wins, including a second round destruction of Tommy Ayers and in November 1991, Buddy upset the odds by totally outboxing Simon Brown to win the WBC title. He is a talented, classy boxer who may not yet have shown us his best. Stopped 44 victims.

04.10.91	Alfredo Ramirez W RSC 5 Atlantic City
29.11.91	Simon Brown W PTS 12 Las Vegas *(WBC Welterweight Title Challenge)*
02.05.92	Delfino Marin W CO 5 Fort Worth
25.06.92	Patrizio Oliva W PTS 12 Naples *(WBC Welterweight Title Defence)*

Career: 60 contests, won 57, drew 1, lost 2.

Kennedy McKinney

Killeen, USA. *Born* 10 January, 1966

USBA S. Bantamweight Champion

Former truck driver who made his name as an amateur whilst in the US Army. Lost in the US Olympic Trials, but still made it to Seoul where he became the first American to win the bantamweight gold medal. After 255 victories in 266 fights he turned professional with the Las Vegas Golden Gloves team under the Top Rank banner. Apart from a technical draw in an early bout, due to a cut, it has been success all the way for Kennedy in the ring. The story outside has been different. He has disappeared twice from the scene due to a drugs problem and his career was in serious danger with Top Rank threatening to drop him if he did not kick the drugs. Scored a good win at the end of 1990 by halting veteran Adrian Arreola in five rounds. In May 1991 he came from behind to floor experienced Jerome Coffee twice for a sixth round kayo victory. Collected the USBA super-bantamweight title when he overcame a closing right eye to decision the former world champion, Sugar Baby Rojas. Defended his title by battering another former world champion, Paul Banke, to defeat, flooring Banke twice and forcing him to retire in the sixth round. Has talent, good mobility and an excellent jab, but the drugs past still hangs as a threat over his future. Halted thirteen opponents.

13.09.91	Mauro Montes W RSC 1 Las Vegas
24.09.91	Vicente Gonzalez W PTS 10 Reseda
09.02.92	Sugar Baby Rojas W PTS 12 Atlantic City *(USBA S. Bantamweight Title Challenge)*
20.03.92	Paul Banke W RTD 6 Las Vegas *(USBA S. Bantamweight Title Defence)*

Career: 22 contests, won 21, lost 1.

Henry Maske

Trevenbrietzen, Germany. *Born* 6 January, 1964

L. Heavyweight

Outstanding amateur when representing East Germany. Won Olympic and world titles and was twice European champion. A 6'3" tall, southpaw, stand up boxer, but not a big puncher. Had his first paid fight at Wembley in May 1990 when he knocked out Teo Arvizu in one round. Also defeated Sean Mannion, Cordwell Hylton and Glazz

Campbell in the same year. Earned a world rating with a points victory over Yawe Davis in May 1991 and halted a fading Tom Collins in December. A knockout victory over the former WBA champion Leslie Stewart in March 1992 put Henry in the frame for a title shot against Charles Williams, but it was postponed due to an injury to Williams. Has only halted seven victims.

13.09.91	Rodrigo Benech W PTS 8 Dusseldorf
12.10.91	Mike Peak W CO 9 Halle
08.11.91	Darryl Fromm W RSC 2 Paris
06.12.91	Tom Collins W RSC 8 Dusseldorf
06.03.92	Leslie Stewart W CO 7 Berlin
04.04.92	Steve McCarthy W DIS 9 Dusseldorf
27.06.92	Lenzie Morgan W PTS 10 Halle

Career: 17 contests, won 17.

Andy Maynard

Maryland, USA. *Born* 8 April, 1964
Former NABF L. Heavyweight Champion

6'0" tall. Starting boxing in the US Army and won a gold medal in the 1988 Olympic Games. Lost only four of 50 amateur fights and then signed up with the Sugar Ray Leonard team and turned professional in February 1989. Won the vacant NABF light-heavyweight title in April 1990 with a points victory over Mike Sedillo. His progress came to a halt in June when he was knocked out in seven rounds by Bobby Czyz. Retained his NABF title in February 1991 by halting Lenzie Morgan in April, by climbing off the floor to stop Govenor Chavers and in June by battering Ed Mack in ten rounds. Lost his title and his chance at the world crown when he faced fellow Olympic gold medal winner, Frank Tate. Andy was floored twice and stopped in the eleventh round. Holds wins over the Art Jimmerson, Keith McMurray and Mike de Vito and has fifteen stoppages, but may not have the chin to make it to the top.

29.10.91	Matthew Saad Muhammad W RSC 3 Washington
10.01.92	Frank Tate L RSC 11 New York *(NABF L. Heavyweight Title Defence)*

Career: 20 contests, won 18, lost 2.

Roger (Black Mamba) Mayweather

Grand Rapids, USA. *Born* 24 April, 1961
Former WBC L. Welterweight Champion. Former WBA S. Featherweight Champion. Former Undefeated WBA Americas L. Welterweight Champion. Former Undefeated WBC Con Am Lightweight Champion. Former Undefeated USBA S. Featherweight & Lightweight Champion

One of three boxing brothers. Suspended for two years when an amateur for showboating. He was only 16 and never fought again as an amateur. 5'7½" tall, 74" reach. Managed by professional gambler Billy Baxter. Turned professional July 1981. Won the USBA super-featherweight title in October 1982 from Ruben Muniz on points. In January 1983, he ended the long reign of Sammy Serrano by knocking out the Puerto Rican in eight rounds to take the WBA crown. Made two defences and then lost the title on a first round knockout to Rocky Lockridge. Lost to Julio Cesar Chavez in two rounds in July 1985 in a challenge for the WBC title. Moved up to lightweight briefly, losing to Pernell Whitaker on points in March 1987 for the vacant NABF title. Only two fights later, in November 1987, Roger knocked out Rene Arredondo to become WBC light-welterweight champion. Made four successful defences and then dropped the title to Chavez on a tenth round retirement in May 1989. Suffered an upset seventh round stoppage against Rafael Pineda for the vacant IBF crown in December 1991. Talented, but unpredictable fighter. Stopped 25 opponents.

07.12.91	Rafael Pineda L RSC 9 Reno *(Vacant IBF L. Welterweight Title)*

Career: 47 contests, won 40, lost 7.

(Juan) Manuel (Mantecas) Medina

Tecuala, Mexico. *Born* 30 March, 1967
IBF Featherweight Champion. Former Undefeated IBC S. Featherweight Champion. Former Undefeated WBA Intercontinental S. Featherweight Champion

It could not happen here, but Medina actually turned professional in October 1985 when only 14 years of age. Lost on points to Gerardo Martinez in his third fight and was halted by Alex Madrid in his fourth, but then won his next 27 bouts. Was halted again in July

Although he is on the receiving end of this shot, Manuel Medina (left), won the IBF featherweight title by defeating the champion, Troy Dorsey Chris Farina

1989 by Juan Carlos Salazar. Won the vacant WBA Intercontinental title at super-featherweight in December 1989 when Venezuelan Edgar Castro was thrown out in the seventh round for low blows. Retained the title with impressive stoppage victories against Rafael Ortega and Ben Lopez and then became IBC world champion by decisioning Tyrone Jackson in May 1990. By the end of the year he had outpointed Steve Cruz, Bruno Rabanales and Ed Parker to establish himself as a real threat. Despite this, he was not expected to hold off the aggression of Troy Dorsey when he challenged him for the IBF featherweight title. It looked all over when Manuel was floored twice and badly cut, but he outworked Dorsey for the rest of the fight to take the decision and the crown. Retained his title in November 1991 on a technical decision when challenger Tom Johnson was cut with Manuel ahead on points. Took his title to France to face European champion Fabrice Benichou in March 1992 and came away with a clear decision win. Still only 22 years old so he may yet outgrow the division. No punch, but inexhaustable stamina. Stopped 20 victims.

12.08.91	Troy Dorsey W PTS 12 Los Angeles *(IBF Featherweight Title Challenge)*
18.11.91	Tom Johnson W TD 9 Los Angeles *(IBF Featherweight Title Defence)*
14.03.92	Fabrice Benichou W PTS 12 Antibes *(IBF Featherweight Title Defence)*

Career: 46 contests, won 43, lost 3.

Luis (Chicanero) Mendoza

San Onofre, Colombia. Born 7 April, 1965
Former WBA S. Bantamweight Champion. Former Undefeated Colombian Bantamweight & S. Bantamweight Champion

5'8½" tall. Won a bronze medal in the World Junior championships in 1983 and won 78 of 88 amateur fights before moving into the professional ranks in March 1985. Had three fights at the end of that year in Miami and lost the last one on points to Jesse Williams. Won the vacant Colombian bantamweight title in October 1986 by stopping Miguel Ariza in one round. Registered good wins over Daniel Blanco, Enrique Sanchez, Manuel Vilchez and Azael Moran before challenging Juan Jose Estrada for the WBA super-bantamweight title in July 1989. Had Estrada cut and hurt, but missed his chance and was beaten on a unanimous decision. Faced Ruben Dario Palacios for the vacant WBA crown in May 1990, but the fight ended in a draw. Tackled Palacios again in September and this time Luis scored a third round stoppage to win the title. Retained his title in October with a split decision over Fabrice Benichou in Paris. Made successful defences in 1991 against Noree Jockygym, Carlos Uribe and Joao Cardoso, but was outboxed and dropped his crown to Raul Perez in October. Stopped 18 opponents.

07.10.91	Raul Perez L PTS 12 Los Angeles *(WBA S. Bantamweight Title Defence)*

Career: 36 contests, won 31, drew 2, lost 3.

Jean-Baptiste Mendy

France. *Born* Senegal, 16 March, 1963
European Lightweight Champion

5'9¾" tall. Southpaw. Born in Dakar but is now a French citizen. Had his first professional bout in February 1983, but hit a bad spell at the end of the year, winning only one of five fights. From then he ran up 22 victories before being stopped in February 1988 in Puerto Rico by Angel Luis Garcia. The result was changed to a no contest and Mendy knocked out Garcia in three rounds a month later. Suffered a big set-back when he was knocked out by Lofti Ben Sayel in November 1988. He took French citizenship in 1990, but lost on points in March to Christian Merle in the annual French championship tournament. Jean-Baptiste bounced back in 1991 by knocking out Merle and halting Angel Mona in one round to win the French lightweight title. Collected the European title with a controversial stoppage of Antonio Renzo and retained the crown by beating Stefano Cassi in three rounds. Is punching harder now, with 24 stoppages in all, but his own chin remains suspect.

10.01.92	Jeff Roberts W CO 5 Vitroles
27.03.92	Antonio Renzo W RSC 9 Creil *(European Lightweight Title Challenge)*
28.05.92	Stefano Cassi W RTD 3 Creil *(European Lightweight Title Defence)*

Career: 46 contests, won 39, drew 2, lost 4, no contest 1.

Ray (Merciless) Mercer

Jacksonville, USA. *Born* 4 April, 1961
Former Undefeated WBO Heavyweight Champion

Spent nine years in the US Army. Started boxing in 1983. 6'1" tall. Won the heavyweight gold medal in Seoul by knocking out a South Korean in the first round and had a 64-6 amateur record. Ray was paid a $300,000 sign-

Ray Mercer

ing fee to join the Triple Threat Enterprises team. Had his first fight in February 1989 and twelve fights in the following ten months, ending the year with a split points win over the former cruiserweight champion, Puerto Rican, Osvaldo Ocasio. Won the vacant IBF Intercontinental title with a points victory over Kimmuel Odum in March 1990 and retained the title by halting

Lionel Washington in May. Suffered a badly split lip and an injured arm in taking a unanimous decision over Bert Cooper for the NABF crown in August 1990. Became WBO champion in January 1991 when he came from behind to halt Italian Francesco Damiani in nine rounds and retained the title with another come from behind showing as he brutally battered Tommy Morrison to defeat in five rounds in October. The WBO stripped Ray of his title when he chose to fight Larry Holmes rather than a challenger nominated by them and he had his limitations exposed as Larry easily won a unanimous decision. Strong fighter with a good punch, but little skill.

18.10.91	Tommy Morrison W RSC 5 Atlantic City *(WBO Heavyweight Title Defence)*
07.02.92	Larry Holmes L PTS 12 Atlantic City

Career: 19 contests, won 18, lost 1.

Frankie Mitchell

Philadelphia, USA. *Born* 17 April, 1959

NABF Lightweight Champion

Born Georgia. Finished as runner-up in the 1982 National Golden Gloves championships and became a professional the following year, fighting mainly in Ohio. Moved to Philadelphia in 1987 and remained unbeaten until 1990. Scored wins over Billy Young, Robert Byrd and Ed Parker. Challenged Brian Mitchell for the WBA super-featherweight title in September 1990 and it was a close fight until the ninth when Frankie began to fade and the South African took control to retain his title on a clear decision. Frankie moved up to lightweight and in his first fight in July 1991, halted Kenny Vice in two rounds to win the NABF title. Retained the title in a local war with tough Bryant Paden, finishing strongly to take the decision. Halted Roberto Medina in March 1992 in his second title defence. Smooth, fast boxer and a skilled mechanic, but sometimes only does enough to win. Made news when it was discovered that, even as NABF champion, he was living rough on the streets of Philadelphia and fighting a drug addiction problem. Halted twelve opponents.

09.07.91	Kenny Vice W RSC 2 Philadelphia *(Vacant NABF Lightweight Title)*
14.01.92	Bryant Paden W PTS 12 Philadelphia *(NABF Lightweight Title Defence)*
10.03.92	Roberto Medina W RSC 10 Philadelphia *(NABF Lightweight Title Defence)*
16.06.92	Anthony Boyle W RSC 11 Philadelphia *(NABF Lightweight Title Defence)*

Career: 30 contests, won 29, lost 1.

Sharmba Mitchell

Tacoma Park, USA. *Born* 27 August, 1970

Lightweight

5'6" tall, talented boxer, who is naturally right handed, but boxes as a southpaw. Started boxing at eight years old. Won local and national junior titles, but joined the professionals in 1988 after failing to earn a spot on the US Olympic team. Had 148 amateur fights. Trained by former professional Adrian Davis. Came through strongly in 1990 with victories over Rafael Limon, Billy Young and Nigel Wenton and continued the progress in 1991, beating Kevin Marston, Miguel Santana and Felix Gonzalez. Was too fast and young for former world champion Rocky Lockridge and won a unanimous decision over Rocky in April. Still largely untested, but shows so much natural talent that he is highly rated by most of the bodies. Flashy style. Studying for a college degree in his spare time. Halted 16 opponents.

23.07.91	Miguel Santana W RSC 3 Atlantic City
29.10.91	Keeley Thompson W RSC 7 Washington
14.01.92	Leonardo Martinez W RSC 1 Atlantic City
15.02.92	Gilberto Flores W RSC 5 Las Vegas

Career: 28 contests, won 28.

Juan (John John) Molina

Fajardo, Puerto Rico. *Born* 17 March, 1965

IBF S. Featherweight Champion. Former Undefeated WBO S. Featherweight Champion

Real name Juan Molina. Competed for Puerto Rico in the 1984 Olympics Was voted "Athlete of the Year" in 1985 after winning a gold medal in the World Amateur championships. Received a $100,000 signing fee for joining the Main Events team in 1986 Won twelve fights that year, including an impressive points victory over useful Kevin Marston. Lost his unbeaten tag in May 1987 after a great fight against Lupe Suarez. John was floored twice and halted in the ninth round. Challenged Tony Lopez for the IBF super-featherweight title in October 1987 and had Lopez on the floor, before slowing over the last couple of rounds and losing a very close decision. Won the vacant WBO title in April 1989 with a points victory over Juan Laporte, but never defended the title. Instead, he faced Lopez again in October 1989 and this time gave him a one-sided battering before stopping him in the tenth round to take the IBF title. Gained revenge on Suarez in a title defence in January 1990, putting Lupe down twice and halting the Texan in the sixth. A third match with Lopez saw him on the floor in the eleventh and that was enough to swing a split decision to Lopez. Juan regained the IBF title last February with an easy fourth round victory over Jackie Gunguluza. Halted 19 opponents.

Juan Molina

13.09.91	Rowdy Welch W PTS 10 Sacramento
14.01.92	Francisco Ortiz W RSC 2 San Juan
22.02.92	Jackie Gunguluza W RSC 4 Sun City *(Vacant IBF S. Featherweight Title)*

Career: 30 contests, won 27, lost 3.

Sung-Il Moon

Yeoung-Am, South Korea. *Born* 20 July, 1963

WBC S. Flyweight Champion. Former WBA Bantamweight Champion

Oustanding amateur fighter. Stopped John Hyland and knocked out American Robert Shannon in the 1984 Olympic Games, but was eliminated in the quarter-finals. Won the World Amateur championships bantamweight title in 1985. Ended with 115 wins in 127 fights, with 72 stoppages. Started straight into the ten round class as a professional in March 1987. Won the WBA bantamweight title in only his seventh fight on a controversial technical decision against Kaokor Galaxy. Retained the title with stoppages of Edgar Monserrat and Chiaki Kobayashi. Lost the title on a unanimous decision to Galaxy in Bangkok in July 1989. Won the WBC title from Nana Yaw Konadu in January 1990. Both fighters were on the deck in the first round and both were on the floor again in later rounds and badly cut. The fight was stopped due to the cuts in the ninth and Moon given a technical decision. Retained his title when a fading Gilberto Roman retired at the end of the eighth round of their fight in June. Cuts to Moon again brought a halt to his defence against Kenji Matsumura in October and again he won a technical decision. Since then his defences have been less controversial and he has halted Konadu, Ernesto Ford and Torsak Pongsupa. Known as the "Korean Hands of Stone", Moon's fights tend to be wars, but he cuts easily and only the technical decisions have kept him as champion A brave fighter and a very hard puncher.

20.07.91	Ernesto Ford W CO 5 Seoul *(WBC S. Flyweight Title Defence)*
22.12.91	Torsak Pongsupa W RSC 6 Inchon *(WBC S. Flyweight Title Defence)*

Career: 17 contests, won 16, lost l.

Rodney (Rockin) Moore

Philadelphia, USA. *Born* 21 February, 1965

L. Welterweight

Tall, tough box-puncher, but sometimes he only does enough to win and no more. Had a bad start to his professional career in 1983 as he lost his first two fights, while losing three of his first five. Found some form and remained unbeaten again until losing to the late Brian Baronet in February 1986. Reached the finals of the ESPN tournament, but lost to Miguel Santana in July 1986. Started well against Terrence Alli in their May 1987 fight, but then lost his way and was halted in the ninth. Fought a good draw with Bryant Paden at the end of 1988, and in August 1989 floored Santana twice on the way to a revenge points victory. Outpointed Olympic gold medal winner Jerry Page in September 1990 and halted dangerous Sammy Fuentes in two rounds in June 1991. Had to survive two visits to the canvas in the first round against Tony Baltazar and was seconds away from defeat, but boxed his way to a split decision. Suffered a set back with a disappointing loss to journeyman Ramon Zavala. Has stopped fifteen opponents. Also holds wins over Anthony Williams and Alfredo Rojas.

22.10.91	Alfredo Rojas W RSC 9 Philadelphia
26.11.91	Greg Cadiz W RSC 5 Philadelphia
18.01.92	Tony Baltazar W PTS 10 Philadelphia
25.06.92	Ramon Zavala L PTS 10 Philadelphia

Career: 39 contests, won 30, drew 2, lost 7.

Michael Moorer

Detroit, USA. *Born* 12 November, 1967

WBO Heavyweight Champion. Former Undefeated WBO L. Heavyweight Champion

6'2" tall, southpaw, born in Brooklyn. Started boxing when he was twelve. Won the 1986 National Golden Gloves championship and represented the US as an international. Had a 48-16 amateur record. Member of the Kronk team in Detroit. Halted his first professional victim in one round in March 1988 and went on to stop his next 25 opponents. In December 1988, he collected the vacant WBO light-heavyweight title with a fifth round stoppage of Ramzi Hassan. Defended his title five times in 1989, including a spell of

Michael Moorer

two defences in five weeks. Was hurt by Frankie Swindell and was behind on points against Leslie Stewart, but stopped them both. Jeff Thompson lasted only 106 seconds. Added another three defences in 1990. Relinquished the WBO title in 1991, due to weight problems and moved up to heavyweight. Was shaken by Alex Stewart, but came back to floor Alex three times and halt him in four rounds. Was finally taken the distance for the first time by Everett Martin in March. Won the WBO title in a wild fight with Bert Cooper that saw Michael on the floor twice before halting Bert in the fifth. Has not looked so impressive as a heavyweight and struggled against Martin and Mike White. Halted 27 victims.

27.07.91	Alex Stewart W RSC 4 Norfolk
23.11.91	Bobby Crabtree W RSC 1 Atlanta
01.02.92	Mike White W PTS 10 Las Vegas
17.03.92	Everett Martin W PTS 10 Detroit
15.05.92	Bert Cooper W RSC 5 Atlantic City *(Vacant WBO Heavyweight Title)*

Career: 29 contests, won 29.

Charles (The Natural) Murray

Rochester, USA. Born 18 August, 1968

Former USA L. Welterweight Champion

Lost to Todd Foster in the US Olympic Trials and was an alternate choice for the team at the 1988 Games. Won 65 of 70 amateur fights. Signed with the

Triple Threat team, alongside Ray Mercer and Alfred Cole. Had his first professional bout in February 1989 and won ten fights in that year. Took the

Charles Murray

vacant USBA light-welterweight crown with a points victory against Mickey Ward in October 1990. Decisioned David Taylor and halted Bernard Gray in title defences in early 1991, but lost the crown to Terrence Alli. Murray won the early rounds, but Alli out-worked him and then hurt him in the last round to clinch a split verdict and also to retain his NABF title. Since that defeat, Charles has come back with four wins, including a unanimous verdict over experienced Livingstone Bramble. He is a classy boxer with good combination punching and has stopped or knocked out 16 opponents.

25.07.91	Norman Bates W CO 1 Atlantic City
25.09.91	Manuel Salas W RSC 3 Stanhope
13.12.91	Livingstone Bramble W PTS 10 Atlantic City
08.02.92	Alberto Alcaraz W RSC 9 Atlantic City

Career: 25 contests, won 24, lost 1.

Vincenzo Nardiello

Milan, Italy. *Born* 11 June, 1966
S. Middleweight

Tough, good boxing southpaw. Born in Germany, but was Italian amateur champion in 1984, 86 and 87 and lost in quarter-finals of the 1988 Olympics to a South Korean on a disputed decision. Managed by Umberto Branchini. Had his initial professional fight in December 1988. Won his first three fights on points and stopped each of his next three opponents in the first round. Halted useful Jean-Paul Roux in May 1990. Beat Argentinians Jorge Morello, Miguel Maldonado, Miguel Mosna and Edmundo Diaz in successive fights in 1991 and then halted Tony Burke with hard right-hooks in October. Gave Victor Cordoba a fright in their all-southpaw battle for the WBA crown. Vincenzo was down in the second, but boxed with confidence and looked well ahead when floored and halted in the eleventh round. Hard puncher, but is really just a built-up middleweight. Stopped twelve opponents.

20.07.91	Edmundo Diaz W RSC 4 Palermo
12.10.91	Tony Burke W RSC 2 Monaco
13.12.91	Victor Cordoba L RSC 11 Paris *(WBA S. Middleweight Title Challenge)*
12.03.92	Troy Watson W PTS 8 Paris
25.06.92	Eladio Centurion W CO 1 Naples

Career: 20 contests, won 19, lost 1.

Welcome Ncita

Mdantsane, South Africa. *Born* 21 October, 1965
IBF S. Bantamweight Champion. Former Undefeated South African Flyweight Champion

Followed his elder brother Mzandwile into boxing and had over 100 amateur fights. Initially a light-flyweight when he became a professional in March 1984. Collected the South African flyweight title with a decision over experienced Johannes Miya in March 1986 and retained it with victories over Kirk Morris, Victor Sonaba and Miya, before relinquishing the crown to move up in weight. Fought at super-flyweight and bantamweight for two years before challenging Fabrice Benichou for the IBF super-bantamweight title in March 1990. It was the first world title fight held in Israel and Welcome suprised the experts by winning a points verdict. Had a couple of easy defences, halting Ramon Cruz and Gerardo Lopez. Found life a lot tougher in his defence against Jesus Rojas in February 1991. Welcome was on the canvas in the eleventh round and the split decision in his favour was hotly disputed. Easily outpointed Hurley Snead in a defence in June and then retained the title in a return with Rojas. Again the decision was split, but this time Welcome seemed to have won clearly. Really established himself as a worthy champion with a unanimous decision in his defence against dangerous Jesus Salud, building an early lead and holding off a strong finish by the American. Fast, smart boxer with good jab, but not a puncher, with fourteen stoppage victories.

28.09.91	Jesus Rojas W PTS 12 Sun City *(IBF S. Bantamweight Title Defence)*
18.04.92	Jesus Salud W PTS 12 Treviolo *(IBF S. Bantamweight Title Defence)*

Career: 31 contests, won 31.

Azumah Nelson

Accra, Ghana. *Born* 19 July, 1958
WBC S. Featherweight Champion. Former Undefeated WBC Featherweight Champion. Former Undefeated Ghanaian, ABC & Commonwealth Featherweight Champion

5'5" tall. One of the modern greats. Won African, Commonwealth and World Military titles as an amateur, before becoming a paid fighter in December 1979. Became the featherweight champion of Ghana in only his second fight, the African Boxing Union champion in his sixth and Commonwealth champion in his tenth. Came in as a late substitute to challenge Salvador Sanchez for the WBC title in July 1982 and put up a magnificent performance, before tiring and being halted in the fifteenth round. Became WBC champion in December 1984 by knocking out Wifredo Gomez. Made six defences of the title before relinquishing it in 1988. The highlights were a first round kayo of Pat Cowdell in October 1985 and two points wins against Marcos Villasana. Won the vacant WBC super-featherweight title in February 1989 by decisioning Mario Martinez, but Azumah was on the floor and a spirited finish by Martinez convinced many that he deserved the title. Azumah halted Lupe Suarez and Sidnei dal Rovere in defences in 1988. Settled the dispute with Martinez in another hard fight in February 1989 by flooring and halting the Mexican in the twelfth round. Scored a brutal stoppage over Jim McDonnell in a November title fight, but in May 1990 lost a clear points decision to Pernell Whitaker for the WBC and IBF lightweight titles. Was uninspired in a points victory over Juan Laporte in an October title fight and then looked fortunate to remain champion with a draw against Jeff Fenech in June 1991. It was considered a sure thing for Fenech when they met again last March, but Azumah put Jeff down three times and halted him in the eighth round for a great win. Stopped 26 opponents.

01.03.92 Jeff Fenech W RSC 8 Melbourne *(WBC S. Featherweight Title Defence)*

Career: 38 contests, won 35, drew 1, lost 2.

Eric Nicoletta

Sete, France. *Born* 26 August, 1960
Former European L. Heavyweight Champion. Former Undefeated French L. Heavyweight Champion

Tough docker, 5'11" tall. Some of his earlier bouts were as an "independent" against other semi-professional fighters, but they are generally included in his record. Won his first fight in November 1986, but suffered losses against Didier Macrez, Lumbala Tshibamba and Mike Ouattara. In the annual French tournament in 1988 and 1989 he was the big surprise as he decisioned Macrez, halted Richard Caramanolis and outpointed Serge Bolivard to become French champion. Added the European title in October 1989 with a tenth round stoppage of Jan Lefeber and made successful defences by beating Pedro van Raamsdonk and Jose Seys, before being knocked out in nine rounds by Tom Collins in August 1990. A loss to Fabrice Tiozzo in June 1991 seemed to indicate he was slipping, but he has come back with five stoppages, including an eighth round win over useful Eddie Mack. Has also beaten Mike Peak, Tony Larosa and Frank Minton. Halted fifteen victims.

15.11.91 Tony Larosa W RSC 8 Nimes
20.12.91 Frank Minton W CO 3 Canillo
14.02.92 Clemente Ortiz W RSC 3 Antibes
01.05.92 Eddie Mack W RSC 8 Sete
29.05.92 Dawud Shaw W CO 1 Amneville

Career: 29 contests, won 24, lost 5.

Franck Nicotra

Grenoble, France. *Born* 24 October, 1965
European S. Middleweight Champion

Tall, upright style with a hard right hand punch, but limited mobility. Came into the professional ranks in October 1987 without gaining any big titles as an amateur, but has shown steady improvement against not too demanding opposition. Scored two victories in 1987, five in 1988, eight in 1989 and five in 1990, ending with a points win over Ray Webb in December. Added another six wins in 1991 without really being tested and for that reason was a slight outsider against James Cook in April 1992. Franck shocked Cook with the first real punch he threw and kayoed the champion in just 63 seconds to win the European title. Has stopped 16 opponents, but is still an unknown quantity and will have to meet better opposition now.

10.08.91 Hector Rosario W PTS 10 Digne
28.09.91 Diosmel Anaya W CO 5 St Martin
12.12.91 Humberto Jimenez W RSC 1 Massy
10.01.92 Ralph Ward W RSC 2 Vitrolles
03.04.92 James Cook W CO 1 Vitrolles *(European S. Middleweight Title Challenge)*

Career: 28 contests, won 28.

Orlin (Boscoe Bear) Norris

Lubbock, USA. *Born* 4 October, 1965
NABF Cruiserweight Champion. Former NABF Heavyweight Champion

Elder brother of Terry Norris. 5'9" tall. Started boxing at eleven years of age. Won 1986 National Golden Gloves title at heavyweight and lost only ten of 320 amateur fights. Turned professional in June 1986 as a cruiserweight and lost in his second fight to Olian Alexander. Moved up to heavyweight and won the NABF heavyweight crown with a points verdict over Larry Alexander. Registered a good victory in a title defence in March 1988 by decisioning experienced Renaldo Snipes, despite a hand injury and outpointed Dwain Bonds and Jesse Ferguson in other title bouts in 1988. Moved into the world ratings by decisioning Greg Page in a title defence in April 1989, but in November lost the crown on a hairline decision to Tony Tubbs. The fight was later ruled a no decision after Tubbs failed a drugs test. Orlin challenged Bert Cooper for the title in February 199O, but was halted in eight rounds. Wins over Oliver McCall and Tony Willis kept him in the picture and he regained the NABF title by knocking out Leonel Washington for the vacant crown in April 1991. Gave away too much height to the 6'5" Tony Tucker in June and lost his title on a 2-1 decision. Moved down to cruiser-weight and took the vacant NABF title with a technical verdict over Jesse Shelby and floored Anthony Hembrick three times on the way to an eighth round stoppage in his first defence. Halted 17 opponents.

16.08.91 Jesse Shelby W TD 10 San Diego *(Vacant NABF Cruiserweight Title)*
13.12.91 James Pritchard W PTS 10 Paris
25.03.92 Anthony Hembrick W RSC 8 San Diego *(NABF Cruiserweight Title Defence)*
27.05.92 Keith McMurray W CO 2 San Diego

Career: 37 contests, won 33, lost 3, no dec. 1.

Terry Norris

Lubbock, USA. *Born* 17 June, 1967
WBC L. Middleweight Champion. Former Undefeated NABF L. Middleweight Champion

Recommended to manager Joe Sayatovich by his elder brother Orlin and turned professional at the age of 19. Won his first twelve fights before losing on points in the Strohs Tournament at the Inglewood Forum to Derrick Kelly. Lost on a disqualification to Joe Walker in November

1987, but showed his potential in August 1988 by giving previously unbeaten Quincy Taylor a boxing lesson and outpointing him easily. Won the vacant NABF light-middleweight title in December with a sixth round

Terry Norris

kayo of Steve Little and floored and outpointed Buster Drayton in a title defence in March 1989. Challenged Julian Jackson for the WBA crown in July and hurt Jackson in the first round. In the second, Jackson exploded a right hand which put Terry down and forced a stoppage later in the round. Terry bounced back with a points win over Tony Montgomery in a defence of his NABF crown and then took the WBC title in dramatic fashion by flattening John Mugabi in one round. Made one defence that year, allowing Rene Jacquot to last the distance and in February 1991 outclassed Sugar Ray Leonard with one judge giving Terry a 16 points margin. Another former champion, Don Curry, was knocked out in eight rounds in June, Brett Lally was destroyed in one round in August and Terry finished 1991 with a points win over useful Jorge Castro. Carl Daniels and Meldrick Taylor have been stopped in 1992, as Terry continues to look an unbeatable champion. Halted 18 opponents.

16.08.91	Brett Lally W RSC 1 San Diego *(WBC L. Middleweight Title Defence)*
13.12.91	Jorge Castro W PTS 12 Paris *(WBC L. Middleweight Title Defence)*
22.02.92	Carl Daniels W RSC 9 San Diego *(WBC L. Middleweight Title Defence)*
09.05.92	Meldrick Taylor W RSC 4 Las Vegas *(WBC L. Middleweight Title Defence)*

Career: 35 contests, won 32, lost 3.

Michael Nunn

Davenport, USA. *Born* 14 April, 1963
NABF S. Middleweight Champion. Former IBF Middleweight Champion. Former Undefeated NABF Middleweight Champion

6'2" tall. Classy, cocky fighter with a flamboyant style. Was inspired to start boxing after watching Sugar Ray Leonard in the 1976 Olympics. Lost to Virgil Hill in trials for the 1984 Olympic team and turned professional the same year, going on to win his first 36 fights. Came through into the world ratings in 1986 with points wins over Mike Tinley and Alex Ramos. Collected his first title in October 1987 by halting Darnell Knox in four rounds for the vacant NABF middleweight crown. Decisioned Kevin Watts and knocked out Curtis Parker in title defences and in July 1988 outclassed and halted Frank Tate in nine rounds to win the IBF crown. Retained the title in November with an eighth round kayo of Argentinian Juan Domingo Roldan. Not really thought of as big puncher, he sprang a shock by knocking out Sumbu Kalambay in one round in March 1989. Still looked good in beating Iran Barkley in August, but had to settle for a majority decision. Made two defences in 1990, outpointing Marlon Starling and stopping Don Curry. Just when he was begining to look unbeatable, Michael succumbed to the pressure of James Toney and was stopped in eleven rounds in their fight in May 1991. Has now moved up to super-middleweight, but is almost the forgotten man with only one fight in thirteen months. It remains to be seen how much the loss to Toney has dented his confidence and problems out of the ring are casting a cloud over his future. Stopped 25 victims.

29.11.91	Randall Yonker W CO 10 Las Vegas *(NABF S. Middleweight Title Challenge)*

Career: 38 contests, won 37, lost 1.

Hideyuki Ohashi

Yokohama, Japan. *Born* 6 March, 1965
Former WBC M. Flyweight Champion. Former Undefeated Japanese L. Flyweight Champion

5'5" tall. Former university student. Managed by ex-world champion, Kenji Yonekura. Recorded 47 amateur bouts, winning 44 and halting 27 opponents. Had his first paid fight in February 1985 as a light-flyweight. Lost on points in his fifth fight to future champion, Bong-Jun Kim, but despite this was pushed into a title shot with Jung-Koo Chang for the WBC crown only two fights later in December 1986. Took a beating before being halted in the fifth round. Won the Japanese light-flyweight title in January 1988 and was then thrown in with Chang again in June and stopped in eight rounds. Moved down to mini-flyweight in 1989 and in February 1990 put the WBC champion Jum-Hwan Choi down

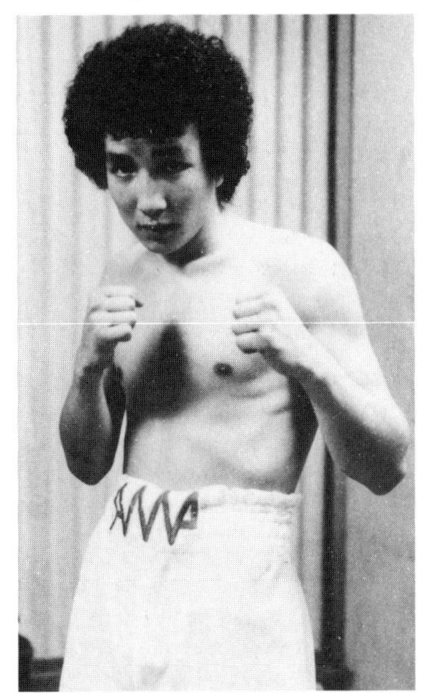

Hideyuki Ohashi

twice with body punches and halted him in nine rounds. Retained his title with a unanimous decision over Napa Kiatwanchai, flooring the former mini-flyweight champion on the way. Had his lack of mobility exposed by classy Ricardo Lopez in October 1990 and lost his title on a unanimous decision. Scored three wins in 1991 to remain in the picture. Good single shot hitter with the right hand, but not fast or mobile. Halted twelve victims.

20.08.91	Rico Macaubos W CO 5 Tokyo
17.12.91	In-Kyu Hwang W PTS 10 Tokyo
02.06.92	Joe Constantino W CO 6 Tokyo

Career: 22 contests , won 18, lost 4.

Patrizio Oliva

Naples, Italy. *Born* 28 January, 1959
Former Undefeated European Welterweight Champion. Former WBA L. Welterweight Champion. Former Undefeated European & Italian L. Welterweight Champion

Was proceeded into boxing by his brother Mario Oliva. Started boxing in 1972. Was Italian featherweight champion as an amateur in 1976 and lightweight champion in 1977 and 1978. Was robbed of the gold medal in the 1979 European Games, but put things right by winning the gold at the 1980 Olympic Games. Had his first professional fight in October 1980. Took the Italian light-welterweight title in November 1981 by knocking out Giuseppe Rosi and made four defences before winning the European title in January 1983 with a points victory over Robert Gambini. Retained the crown through seven defences and in March 1986 decisioned the Argentinian Ubaldo Sacco to take the WBA title. Halted Brian Brunette and outpointed Rodolfo Gonzalez in title bouts, but in July 1987 lost for the first time after 48 wins as he was knocked out in three rounds by Juan Coggi and dropped the WBA crown. Patrizio then retired for two years. In November 1990 he decisioned Kirkland Laing for the European welterweight title and beat Errol McDonald and Antoine Fernandez in defences. Challenged Buddy McGirt for the WBC title in June 1992, but was clearly outpointed and announced his retirement. Never a pretty fighter to watch, he had style that worked and his record speaks for itself. Halted only 20 opponents.

05.10.91	Juan C. Ortiz W PTS 8 Laiguegi
04.12.91	Jose Saldiva W PTS 8 San Pellegrino
19.02.92	Antoine Fernandez W PTS 12 San Pellegrino *(EBU Welterweight Title Defence)*
25.06.92	James McGirt L PTS 12 Naples *(WBC Welterweight Title Challenge)*

Career: 59 contests, won 57, lost 2.

Scotty (Toy Bulldog) Olson

Edmonton, Canada. *Born* 26 February, 1968
USBA Flyweight Champion

Former top amateur. Competed for Canada in the World Cup, World championships and Pan American Games. Won a gold medal in 1986 Commonwealth Games, but lost to Michael Carbajal in the 1988 Olympics. Also holds a win over Carbajal as an amateur. Managed by former boxer Bruce Strauss and trained by former world champion Richie Sandoval. 5'1" tall. Turned professional in January 1990 and registered ten wins that year. Had eight more victories in 1991, but the standard of the opposition was very mixed. Toughest fight was in August in a war with Dadoy Andujar, which saw Scotty settle for a split decision. Won the USBA flyweight title in January 1992 by outclassing and halting little Pedro Feliciano in nine rounds. Had an easy defence in February as he beat Louis Curtis on a fifth round retirement. Tough battler who always seems to turn his fights into wars. Fast hands and hits hard with either one. Well guided by the Top Rank team. Halted 17 opponents.

01.08.91	Dadoy Andujar W PTS 10 Great Falls
29.08.91	Jose de Jesus Gomez W CO 1 Reno
28.09.91	Anthony Griego W RSC 3 Leftbridge
10.10.91	Juventino Delgado W RSC 2 Las Vegas
05.01.92	Pedro Feliciano W RSC 9 Reno *(USBA Flyweight Title Challenge)*
28.02.92	Louis Curtis W RSC 5 Las Vegas *(USBA Flyweight Title Defence)*
10.04.92	Abraham Garcia W PTS 10 Montreal

Career: 22 contests, won 22.

Katsuya Onizuka

Fukuoka, Japan. *Born* 12 March, 1970
WBA S. Flyweight Champion. Former Undefeated Japanese S. Flyweight Champion

5'8" tall. Good amateur career with a 38-5 score and 20 opponents stopped. Won the All-Japan title whilst still a High School student. First professional fight in April 1988 and in 1989 was crowned as Shinjin-o champion in the Japanese novices tournament. Made a big impression with his hard punching, knocking out each of his first three opponents in the opening round. Collected the Japanese super-flyweight title in October 1990 by over-powering the more experienced Shunichi Nakajima in the tenth round. Established his superiority in the division as he knocked out Tomohiko Yokoyama and Suzuharu Kitazama and decisioned Nakajima in title defences in 1991. Also halted the tough South Korean Chan-Woo Park. Looked very lucky to win the vacant WBA title with a hotly disputed decision over Thalerngsak Sitbobay, as even Japanese observers thought that the Thai had won. Very hard puncher, but defence is not too sound. Stopped 16 victims.

04.11.91	Chan-Woo Park W RSC 7 Kitakyushu
10.04.92	Thalerngsak Sitbobay W PTS 12 Tokyo *(Vacant WBA S. Flyweight Title)*

Career: 19 contests, won 19.

Jorge (Maromero) Paez

Mexicali, Mexico. *Born* 27 October, 1965
Former Undefeated WBO & IBF Featherweight Champion

Flamboyant character. Born into a circus family and worked as an acrobat, a clown and a trapeze artist. Moved into the paid ranks in November 1984 and lost a couple of early fights in tough battles in Mexicali and Tijuana. A run of 18 straight wins put him in line for a shot at Calvin Grove for the IBF featherweight title, but he was a long odds outsider. Grove made the odds look right for most of the fight, but Jorge came up with three knockdowns in the

Jorge Paez Chris Farina

last round to win a majority decision. Came from behind to stop Grove again in March 1989 to retain his title. Fought a war with Louie Espinosa in May, but again kept his crown, although this time the judges saw it as a draw. Was very active champion, beating Steve Cruz, Jose Maria Lopez and Lupe Gutierrez in other defences in 1989. An even tougher defence had Jorge go toe-to-toe for twelve rounds to decision Troy Dorsey in February 1990 and then he settled the score with Espinosa with a points win in a bout that was for both Jorge's title and the WBO crown. Met Dorsey in second exciting battle in July 1990, and this time held on to his title with a draw. After battling against weight problems, he relinquished his featherweight titles and challenged Tony Lopez for the IBF Super-Featherweight crown in September 1991, losing on points. Moved up to lightweight to challenge Pernell Whitaker, but was easily outpointed. Has plenty of skill, but rarely uses it fully and is not the best behaved of fighters. Halted 26 opponents.

05.10.91	Pernell Whitaker L PTS 12 Reno *(IBF, WBC & WBA Lightweight Title Challenge)*
17.02.92	Benny Medina W PTS 10 Tijuana
27.03.92	Johnny de la Rosa W PTS 10 Mexico City
29.05.92	Eduardo Perez W PTS 10 Mexicali

Career: 49 contests, won 41, drew 4, lost 4.

Kyun-Yung Park

Seoul, South Korea. *Born* 16 August, 1967
WBA Featherweight Champion. Former Undefeated OPBF Featherweight Champion. Former Undefeated South Korean Featherweight & S. Bantamweight Champion

Gene Fullmer type, but a southpaw, who made no real impression as an amateur. Had his first professional fight in December 1986 and drew with Jung-Woo Park for the Korean super-bantamweight title in October 1987. Won the vacant crown in July 1988 with a decision over Young-Duk Park, but lost it in his first defence to fellow-unbeaten Jae-Won Choi in November. Moved up to featherweight and won his second South Korean national title with a points verdict over Yung-Man Chun. Became OPBF champion in January 1990 as he overpowered Filipino southpaw Jo Jo Cayson and halted him on his feet in the eighth round. Made successful defences against Jimmy Sithfaidang and Cris Saguid and then sprang a major upset by winning the WBA title with a points win over Venezuelan Antonio Esparragoza. Had an easy defence in disposing of Masuaki Takeda in six rounds, but then proved his right to the title with a strong performance to clearly outpoint the dangerous Eloy Rojas. Had little trouble in knocking out Seiji Asakawa in January and stopping Matsumoto in April, 1992. Whirlwind style and iron-chinned. Stopped twelve opponents.

14.09.91	Eloy Rojas W PTS 12 Mokpo *(WBA Featherweight Title Defence)*
25.01.92	Seiji Asakawa W CO 9 Seoul *(WBA Featherweight Title Defence)*
25.04.92	Koji Matsumoto W RSC 11 Ansan *(WBA Featherweight Title Defence)*

Career: 23 contests, won 21, drew 1, lost 1.

Kyun-Yung Park

Lamar (Kid Fire) Parks

Greensville, USA. *Born* 17 March, 1970
NABF, USBA & WBC Con Am Middleweight Champion

Born Henderson, North Carolina. Started boxing at thirteen after losing a street fight. Lost in the semi-finals of the 1988 National Golden Gloves to John Scully. Won 175 of 188 amateur fights. Managed and trained by his father who boxed as an amateur. Promoted by the Madison Square Garden boxing team. 5'9" tall, muscular build. His first professional fight in October 1988 saw him win on points, but he stopped his next thirteen opponents. Faced some good tests in those early fights, including Fabian Williams, Chris Sande and Brinatty Maquilon. Showed his potential and his strength when he proved too strong for Lenzie Morgan and won the vacant WBC Continental Americas title with a points victory in July 1991. Added the NABF crown by halting Donny Giron and the USBA title with a hard-earned victory over Percy Harris. Lamar overcame a huge swelling under an eye, to floor and halt Harris. Excellent prospect with a good punch. Stopped 18 victims.

06.07.91	Lenzie Morgan W PTS 12 Greenville *(Vacant WBC Con Am Middleweight Title)*
15.11.91	Ken Hulsey W RSC 1 Charleston
05.12.91	Donny Giron W RSC 6 Greenville *(Vacant NABF Middleweight Title)*
18.02.92	Francisco de Jesus W CO 3 New York
16.04.92	Percy Harris W RSC 10 New York *(Vacant USBA Middleweight Title & NABF Title Defence)*
26.06.92	Jose L. Lopez W CO 1 Charleston

Career: 22 contests, won 22.

Rolando (Jo Jo) Pascua

Talisay City, USA. *Born* 19 November, 1965
Former WBC L. Flyweight Champion

Southpaw. Real name Rolando Tumongtong, but he took his manager's name to box as a professional. 5'5" tall. His father fought as a professional at featherweight under the name of Vic Tumulak. Former drug addict. Won 29 of 30 amateur fights and had his first professional bout in August 1986, winning 14 in a row. First defeat came in January 1988 in Seoul when he was outpointed by Jum-Hwan Choi. Slipped badly at the end of the year with consecutive points defeats against Paul

Badilla and Rolando Protacio. Took off weight in 1989 as he moved down from super flyweight to light-flyweight. Made a big impression when he fought Napa Kiatwanchai in Bangkok in January 1990 and lost a disputed decision. Was considered a safe opponents for Humberto Gonzalez in December 1990, but cut up the champion and took all of his best punches before wearing him down and knocking him out in the sixth round to take the WBC crown. Had to shed lots of weight for his defence against Melchor Cob Castro in March 1991 and was no match for the Mexican, losing on a tenth round stoppage. He has now moved up to flyweight and scored five wins. Stopped eleven opponents.

25.07.91	Rocky Marcial W PTS 10 Tacloban
21.09.91	Mario Parcon W CO 2 Urdaneta
26.10.91	Kart Charbandit W PTS 10 Baguio City
18.01.92	Chong-Kyu Chang W TD 8 Quezon City

Career: 36 contests, won 30, lost 6.

Tracy Harris Patterson

New Paltz, USA. *Born* 26 December, 1964

WBC S. Bantamweight Champion. Former Undefeated NABF S. Bantamweight Champion

Adopted son of the former world heavyweight champion, Floyd Patterson. He has lived with Floyd since he was fourteen years of age. Had over 100 amateur fights and was New York Golden Gloves champion in 1984. Turned professional in June 1985 and was unbeaten until losing a close decision to Jeff Franklin in a great learning fight. Halted eight of his next nine opponents, before losing a split verdict to world champion Steve Cruz in May 1989. He had to climb off the floor but fought back well to run Cruz close. Had fought as high as super-featherweight, but settled down to super-bantamweight in 1990 and won the vacant NABF title by flooring and knocking out tough George Garcia in February. Carefully protected, whilst waiting for his title shot, but when it came he took his chance in style by crushing Thierry Jacob in two rounds. Stopped 34 opponents.

Tracy Harris Patterson (left), the current WBC super-bantamweight champion, seen losing a close fight to Steve Cruz back in 1989

Tom Casino

03.08.91 Gerardo Sanchez W RSC 4 Columbus
15.11.91 Fernando Ramos W CO 1 Charleston
11.03.92 Angel Mayor W RSC 1 New York
23.06.92 Thierry Jacob W RSC 2 Albany *(WBC S. Bantamweight Title Challenge)*

Career: 47 contests, won 45, lost 2.

Vinnie Pazienza

Cranston, USA. *Born* 16 December, 1962
WBA L. Middleweight Champion. Former IBF Lightweight Champion. Former Undefeated USBA L. Middleweight Champion

Colourful, brave battler, who is rarely in a bad fight and is a huge draw in his local town of Providence. Promoted by Main Events. Scored 100 wins in 112 amateur fights. 5'7" tall. Joined the paid ranks in May 1983 and made rapid progress. His only early loss was in December 1984, a cut eye stoppage against Abdel Marbi. Scored good wins over Melvin Paul , Hector Frazier, Harry Arroyo and Roberto Elizondo. Challenged Greg Haugen for the IBF lightweight title in June 1987 and was given a debatable decision after a bloody, bitter battle. Faced Haugen again in February 1988 and lost his title on a clear decision. Went up to light-welterweight to challenge Roger Mayweather for the WBC crown, in November 1988, but was floored and outpointed. Tried for the WBO title in February 1990, but was outboxed by Hector Camacho and beaten on points. Met Haugen for a third time in August 1990 and won a unanimous decision. Failed in an attempt to win the WBA light-welterweight title against Loreto Garza. Vinnie was taking a beating when he was disqualified for dirty tactics. Jumped up to light-middleweight, and won the USBA crown with a decision over Ron Amundsen. Upset Gilbert Dele for the WBA title in October 1991. Dele was badly hurt in the ninth and in the twelfth turned his back on the fight. Vinnie was badly injured in a car crash in December and is fighting to regain his health. Stopped 24 opponents.

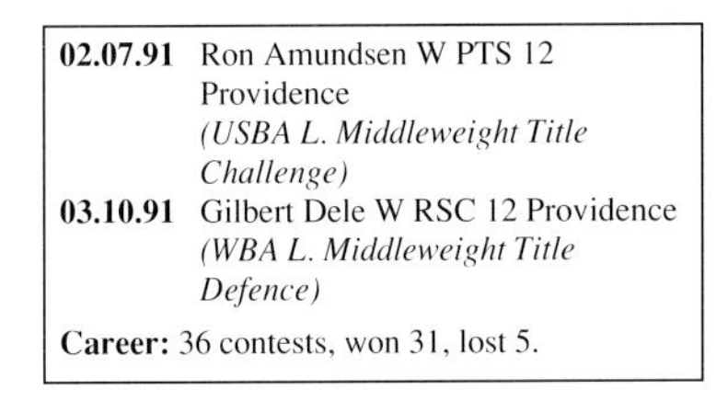
02.07.91 Ron Amundsen W PTS 12 Providence *(USBA L. Middleweight Title Challenge)*
03.10.91 Gilbert Dele W RSC 12 Providence *(WBA L. Middleweight Title Defence)*

Career: 36 contests, won 31, lost 5.

Fred Pendleton

Philadelphia, USA. *Born* 5 January, 1963
Former Undefeated USBA Lightweight Champion

Unpredictable journeyman who has improved with age. Was only 18 when he turned professional in November 1981. Started badly with three losses in his first four fights and he also hit a spell in 1984 and 1985 when he lost six out of seven fights. It would have been all seven, but the loss to Marvin Garris was changed to a win. Despite the seemingly poor form, he was learning and under new management was about to turn his career around. In March 1986 he was matched with Roger Mayweather and caused a major surprise by knocking out the former world champion in six rounds. Four months later he fought an excellent draw with Frankie Randall for the vacant USBA lightweight title. He slipped again in 1986 with losses to Joey Olivera and Shelton LeBlanc, but came back in April 1987 with a draw against Livingstone Bramble. He showed how dangerous he was with a first round stoppage of Sammy Fuentes in February 1988 and halted Bramble on a cut in July to win the USBA crown. John Montes halted Freddie in ten rounds to put him out of the Inglewood tournament, but he was given a shot at Pernell Whitaker for the IBF and WBC titles in February 1990. Pernell won a unanimous decision. Freddie has been keeping busy until Whitaker moved up. Stopped 22 opponents.

20.07.91 Felix Dubray W CO 1 San Remo
22.11.91 Edison Martinez W CO 1 Miami

Career: 52 contests, won 32, drew 3, lost 17.

Isidro (Sid) Perez

Puerto Marquez, Mexico. *Born* 24 May, 1962
Former WBO Flyweight Champion. Former Undefeated Mexican L. Flyweight Champion

Tough, aggressive little battler, who has had very little luck in his career. Turned professional in February 1979 at the age of 17. Won his first 17 fights and then lost in September 1980 to future world champion, Pedro Flores. Worked his way to the top of the Mexican ratings with wins over Aaron Garcia, Emilio Santos and the former world champion, Amado Ursua, but suffered a set back when beaten by Francisco Montiel in December 1984. Won the Mexican light-flyweight title with a close points win over Jorge Cano in May 1986. Was inactive for ten months and when he returned had his jaw broken in a fifth round stoppage loss to Wilibaldo Salazar. He did not fight for nine months and when he did it was a world title match against the great Jung-Koo Chang. Sid almost put Chang away, but the South Korean survived to retain his title on a unanimous decision. This time Sid was inactive for fifteen months and then lost a technical verdict to Jae-Suk Park. A second shot at the world title followed, but he was easily outpointed by Jose de Jesus in October 1989 for the WBO flyweight crown. The little Mexican finally won a title in August 1990 as he halted Angel Rosario in twelve rounds for the vacant WBO flyweight title. Made two successful defences against Chilean Alli Galvez and last March dropped the title to Pat Clinton on a close decision.

10.08.91 Alli Galvez W PTS 12 Santiago *(WBO Flyweight Title Defence)*
18.03.92 Pat Clinton L PTS 12 Glasgow *(WBO Flyweight Title Defence)*

Career: 58 contests, won 47, drew 3, lost 8.

Raul (Jibaro) Perez

Tijuana, Mexico. *Born* 14 February, 1967
Former WBA S. Bantamweight Champion. Former WBC Bantamweight Champion

Known as "The Thin One". 5'10" tall. His real family name is Ruiz, but he fights under the name of his mother's family. Followed his brother Hugo into boxing. Was runner-up in the Mexican national championships at 16 and had his initial paid fight at the age of 17 in March 1984. Halted 18 of his first 21 opponents. Scored a big win in September 1985 when he outpointed the former world flyweight champion, Eleoncio Mercedes. Had his unbeaten record ended after 25 fights when he lost a bad decision to Rafael Ortega in May 1986. Proceeded to turn in some impressive performances as he beat Diego Avila, Prudencio Cardona, James Manning, Gaby Canizales and Wilfredo Vasquez. Had little trouble in taking the WBC bantamweight title from Miguel Lora as he decisioned the Colombian in October 1988. Made three defences in 1989, outpointing Lucio Lopez and Diego Avila and stopping Cardenio Ulloa. In 1990 he defended the title four times, with impressive victories against Gaby Canizales, Gerardo Martinez and Candelario Carmona and a draw with Jose "Pepillo" Valdez. Lost the title in disappointing fashion when he could not handle the speed of Greg Richardson in their bout in February 1991. After an eight month break, Raul came back in style to easily outpoint Luis Mendoza for the WBA super-bantamweight title. Reigned for only five months and was caught cold and blasted out in three rounds by former victim, Vasquez. Halted 31 opponents.

07.10.91	Luis Mendoza W PTS 12 Los Angeles *(WBA S. Bantamweight Title Challenge)*
27.03.92	Wilfredo Vasquez L RSC 3 Mexico City *(WBA S. Bantamweight Title Defence)*

Career: 54 contests, won 49, drew 2, lost 3.

Vince Pettway

Baltimore, USA. *Born* 9 November, 1965
USBA L. Middleweight Champion

5'8½" tall. Hard puncher, but his defence and chin are not too good. Started to box when he was just nine-years-old. Turned professional in February 1984 and won his first 17 bouts, stopping fifteen victims. His vulnerability came through in April 1986 when he was halted by George Leach. Vince came back with seven quick wins and a points victory over Horace Shufford, but in April 1988 was knocked out by Javier Suazo. Established himself again by beating Hugh Kearney, and Luis Santana, but tripped over once more in 1990, being halted by Victor Davis and Steve Johnson. Vince has managed the rubber ball trick again, bouncing back with four victories, including a win over Gilbert Baptist for the USBA crown. Has accounted for 27 quick wins which shows his power, but all of his losses have come by the short route.

09.10.91	Juan Rondon W RSC 8 Pikesville
04.12.91	Frank Montgomery W PTS 10 Pikesville
19.02.92	Gilbert Baptist W PTS 12 Baltimore *(Vacant USBA L. Middleweight Title)*

Career: 39 contests, won 34, lost 4, 1 no contest.

Vince Phillips

Pensacola, USA. *Born* 23 July, 1963
IBF Intercontinental L. Welterweight Champion

Brilliant amateur. Won the National Golden Gloves and US championships in 1985. Competed in the 1986 World Cup and was US champion again that year at super-featherweight. Served in the US Army and was Inter-Services champion. 5'8" tall, trained by Ken Adams and promoted by the Top Rank group. Became a professional in February 1989 and stopped his first six opponents. Beat reasonable tests such as Martin Quiroz, William Hernandez and Victorio Belcher, but then showed class in destroying Mike Johnson in five rounds in April 1991. Collected the IBF intercontinental title with a comprehensive victory over veteran Harold Brazier in April 1992 and destroyed Tyrone Downes, flooring him four times, in June. Talented with potential, but has suffered drug problems and is under threat from Top Rank to drop him if he regresses. Halted 17 opponents.

07.12.91	Jesus Rojas W RSC 6 Reno
26.01.92	Tim Brooks W RSC 3 Indianapolis
09.04.92	Harold Brazier W PTS 12 Las Vegas *(IBF Intercontinental L. Welterweight Title Challenge)*
11.06.92	Tyrone Downes W RSC 7 Atlantic City

Career: 25 contests, won 25.

Rafael (Bombacional) Pineda

Barranquilla, Colombia. *Born* 12 January, 1966
IBF L. Welterweight Champion.
Former Undefeated Colombian L. Welterweight Champion

Born San Cristobal. Trained by the great Argentinian Amilcar Brusa. As an amateur, he halted 50 opponents in winning 96 of his 100 fights, including stopping his last 20 in a row. He continued in the same vein as a professional stopping his first twelve victims between April 1986 and July 1987. Collected the Colombian light-welterweight title in July 1987, stopping Andres Ramos in three rounds. After another run of victories he unwisely stepped up to challenge Mark Breland for the WBA welterweight title. Had Breland hurt early, but could not handle his jabs and turned away and spat out his gumshield, surrender-

Rafael Pineda

ing in the fifth round. Back at light-welterweight he was more comfortable and after chasing for seven rounds, he produced one of his bombs to flatten Roger Mayweather in December 1991 to collect the IBF title. Has the punching power to put any opponent away, but has still to be really tested in a very tough division. His list of 26 stoppages attests to his power.

24.09.91 Gerald Shelton W RSC 7 New Orleans
07.12.91 Roger Mayweather W RSC 9 Reno *(Vacant IBF L. Welterweight Title)*
22.05.92 Clarence Coleman W RSC 7 Mexico City *(IBF L. Welterweight Title Defence)*
Career: 29 contests, won 28, lost 1.

Torsak Pongsupa

Bangkok, Thailand. *Born* 25 November, 1968
WBC International S. Flyweight Champion

Name changes are not uncommon in Thai boxers and Torsak first fought as Torsak Osodspa. Came from the amateur game and not kick boxing and was one of Thailand's best amateur fighters. Southpaw with an aggressive style. Had his first paid fight in December 1988 and knocked out the former Thai flyweight champion Fetch Donjaedee in only his his fourth fight. Clashed with fellow prospect Thalerngsak Sitbobay in August 1989 and lost a close decision in a good scrap. Won the vacant WBC International super-flyweight title by knocking out the tough Filipino Dadoy Andujar in eight rounds in December 1989. Floored and outpointed Romeo Opriasa in May 1990 to retain his title and then scored good wins in decisioning Romy Navarrete and halting Ebo Danquah in non-title bouts. Challenged South Korean Sung-Il Moon for the WBC title in a brutal battle in December 1991. Torsak was on the floor in the first, but fought back bravely, until stopped by body punches in the sixth round. Halted ten opponents.

17.09.91 Chung-Ki Chang W PTS 10 Bangkok
22.12.91 Sung-Il Moon L RSC 6 Inchon *(WBC S. Flyweight Title Challenge)*
Career: 17 contests, won 15, lost 2.

Chana Porpaoin

Petchaboon, Thailand. *Born* 25 March, 1966
Former Undefeated Thai M. Flyweight Champion

5'3" tall. Was a stablemate to the great Kaosai Galaxy. Short, sturdy, methodical fighter. Strong, but tends to throw single shots and lacks mobility. First professional fight in May 1988 and still unbeaten. Took the vacant Thai mini-flyweight title in only his seventh fight by outpointing Ded Donjaedee. Beat the useful South Korean, In-Kyu Hwang, in December 1988. Came through in 1989 as he outpunched former world rated Filipino, Max Forrosuelo, knocked out Silvano Jimenez and decisioned Sammy Tyson. Continued his progress in 1990 with victories over Jun-Bok Koh, Manny Melchor, John Medina, Nikki Maca and Memo Flores. Was given a tough fight by Ric Magramo and had to overcome a bad cut to win a clear decision. Has stopped ten opponents. Holds an early career win over Fahlan Lukmingkwan.

20.07.91 Ric Magramo W PTS 10 Bangkok
13.11.91 Jong-Il Koh W PTS 10 Bangkok
22.12.91 Armando Tenoria W PTS 10 Bangkok
21.06.92 Al Parasona W PTS 10 Bangkok
Career: 24 contests, won 24.

Ludovic Proto

Pointe-A-Pitre, France. *Born* 30 April, 1965
Former Undefeated French Welterweight Champion

Started boxing in April 1983. Met with major success whilst serving with the French Army, winning a gold medal in the world military championships and competing in the 1988 Olympic Games. Rough, tough, hard-hitting southpaw. Turned professional in March 1989 and beat Rawl Frank and Tony Banks that year. Continued his progress with six victories in 1990, including wins over Madjid Madhjoub and Juan Rondon. Showed his power in crushing Chris Blake in one round in May 1991 and in June won the final of the annual tournament in France to become national champion. had a tough scrap in the final with Faouzi Hattab, but just deserved the decision. Scored an impressive win in December by knocking out the world rated Argentinian, Jorge Bracamonte, in the first round. Took out Bracamonte with just one punch. He either lands in the first three rounds or has to go the distance. Halted fifteen rivals.

19.09.91 John Garner W RSC 3 Paris
01.12.91 Mario Salazar W RSC 3 Saint Romain
19.12.91 Jorge Bracamonte W CO 1 Paris
30.01.92 Henry Hughes W CO 8 Paris
12.03.92 Edwin Curet W PTS 10 Paris
18.04.92 Roque Montoya W PTS 8 Hyeres
30.04.92 Unknown Hernandez W RSC 5 Pointe-A-Pitre
Career: 24 contests, won 24.

Dwight Muhammad Qawi

Lindenwold, USA. *Born* 5 January, 1953
Former WBC L. Heavyweight Champion. Former WBA Cruiserweight Champion. WBC Con Am Cruiserweight Champion

Started fighting under his old name of Dwight Braxton. His brother Tony was also a professional. Dwight did not turn professional until he was 25, due to an eight year term in jail. Squat, sturdy fighter, only 5'6½" tall. Started as a light-heavyweight and had his first fight in April 1978, which ended in a draw. Lost in his third fight to John Davis. Crashed the world ratings in 1981 with victories over Mike Rossman and James Scott. Won the WBC light-heavyweight title in December by wearing down and halting Matthew Saad Muhammad in ten rounds. Retained his title with victories over Jerry Martin, Saad Muhammad and Eddie Davis, before giving away almost eight inches in height to Mike Spinks in March 1983 and losing on points. Moved up to cruiserweight and won the WBA title by knocking out Piet Crous in July 1985. Stopped Leon Spinks in March 1986 in his first title defence, but lost a split decision and his crown to Evander Holyfield in July. Failed in a challenge to Holyfield in December 1987, being knocked out in four rounds. Lost on a stoppage to

George Foreman in March 1988. Won the vacant WBC Con Am title in April 1989 with a decision over Andre McCall. Lost successive fights to Robert Daniels for the vacant WBA light-heavyweight crown and to Mike Hunter for the vacant WBA intercontinental title. Recently suffered a big set back in losing to unrated Arthur Williams. Halted 23 opponents.

23.07.91	Young Joe Louis W RTD 4 Atlantic City
07.11.91	Ricky Parkey W RSC 8 Washington
07.04.92	Ric Lainhart W RSC 1 Atlantic City
08.05.92	Arthur Williams L PTS 10 Las Vegas

Career: 48 contests, won 38, drew, 1, lost 9.

Ike (Bazooka) Quartey

Ghana. *Born* 27 November, 1969
WBC International & ABC L. Welterweight Champion. Former Undefeated Ghanaian L. Welterweight Champion

Won a bronze medal in the world junior championships and represented Ghana in the 1988 Olympic Games. Finished with a 50-4 record as an amateur. 5'8" tall, devastating puncher and could be the next African superstar. A professional since 1988 and has not yet been taken the distance. Won the Ghanaian title in October 1989 and flattened Tubor Briggs in December for the West African crown. Appeared in the United States in November 1991 and knocked out the former top amateur Kelcie Banks in seven rounds. Halted Filipino Dindo Canoy in one round for the then vacant WBC International crown and retained the title by defeating unbeaten Juan Carlos Villarreal and Argentinian champion, Alfredo Jaurena. Has eight first round wins in 17 consecutive victories.

02.11.91	Kelcie Banks W CO 7 San Bernardino
07.03.92	Dindo Canoy W RSC 1 Accra *(Vacant WBC International L. Welterweight Title)*
14.04.92	Juan Carlos Villarreal W RSC 5 San Pellegrino *(WBC International L. Welterweight Title Defence)*
25.06.92	Alfredo Jaurena W CO 1 Licola *(WBC International L. Welterweight Title Defence)*

Career: 17 contests, won 17.

Jose (Gallito) Quirino

Tijuana, Mexico. *Born* 19 April, 1968
WBO S. Flyweight Champion

Turned professional at the age of 17 in January 1986. Very active in his first year with fourteen wins. Suffered his initial set back in March 1987 when he faced Tony de Luca in San Diego and was out-hustled on the way to a points defeat. Returned to San Diego again four months later and this time found Ricky Romero too clever and lost the decision. Had a bad time in 1988, losing to Martin Cardenas, Joey Olivo and in a Mexican super-flyweight title shot against Jose Felix Montiel. Turned things around in 1989 as he finally won in San Diego, ending Romero's unbeaten record with a split points verdict in March. Evened the score with de Luca in May 1990 as he floored Tony in the second round and halted him on a cut. Fought a great battle with top prospect Cuahtemoc Gomez in December 1990, but lost on points in a split decision. Challenged Armando Castro for the Mexican super-flyweight title in September 1991, but was halted in nine rounds. Despite this loss, he was given a shot at the WBO crown and took his chance by sweeping the last four rounds to lift the title from the favourite, Jose Ruiz. Good boxer , but not a puncher, as his eleven stoppages show.

08.07.91	Eliseo Illesca W CO 3 Tijuana
30.09.91	Armando Castro L RSC 9 Tijuana *(Mexican S. Flyweight Title Challenge)*
22.02.92	Jose Ruiz W PTS 12 Las Vegas *(WBO S. Flyweight Title Challenge)*

Career: 38 contests, won 31, lost 7.

Robert (Pikin) Quiroga

San Antonio, USA. *Born* 10 October, 1969
IBF S. Flyweight Champion. Former Undefeated WBC Con Am & USBA S. Flyweight Champion

First fighter from San Antonio to win a world title. Started to box in 1983. Turned professional when he was just 17, in March 1987. 5'4" tall. Tireless fighter with a high workrate, but not really a big one shot puncher. Excellent chin and good defence. Was a super-featherweight for his first fight, but soon moved down to super-flyweight. Collected his first title in July 1989 as he floored the former world champion, Joey Olivo, on the way to a unanimous decision for the WBC Con Am crown. Added the USBA title with an easy points win over fellow Texan Ray Medal in December 1989. Came to England in April 1990 to challenge the Colombian Juan Polo Perez for the IBF crown and was a popular winner as he pressured his way to a points victory. Defended his title in Italy in October 1990, putting South African Vuyani Nene on the floor twice and forcing him to retire in the third round. Had more difficulty with the style of Italian Vincenzo Belcastro in January 1991 and had to settle for a split decision, although two of the officials saw him as a clear winner. Fought a brutal battle with unbeaten Akeem Anifowoshe in June 1991. Both fighters took a lot of punishment, but Roberto retained his title with a close but unanimous decision. Akeem collapsed after the fight and required an operation to relieve pressure on his brain. Robert did not fight again until February 1992 when he floored and easily outpointed Carlos Mercado. Has stopped eleven victims.

15.02.92	Carlos Mercado W PTS 12 Salerno *(IBF S. Flyweight Title Defence)*

Career: 19 contests, won 19.

Victor Rabanales

Hidalgo, Mexico. *Born* 23 December, 1962
WBC Bantamweight Champion

One of three fighting brothers, Bruno and Porfirio are still active. 5'5" tall. Lives in Mexico City. Tough, busy fighter. Made a bad start after turning professional in August 1983, losing three of his first four fights and being stopped twice. Took a tough route to the top with plenty of hard fights in the Arena Coliseo. Ran up some good wins beating Arturo Mendoza, Octavio Santos and Armando Castro, but hit a bad spell in late 1987 and early 1988 when he lost four out of five bouts. Burst back into the picture in June

1988 with a points win over rated Armando Salazar and went on to defeat Fernando Varguez, Efrain Pintor, Jose Vegagil and Cesar Soto. Entered the prestigious Inglewood tournament and beat Cardenio Ulloa, Soto again and Javier Leon. Challenged Greg Richardson for the WBC bantamweight title and most observers had him an easy winner. The split decision went to Richardson and Victor was promised an early return. He established his right to a title fight with a points win over Jose Valdez and became WBC interim champion on a technical decision over South Korean Yong-Hoon Lee, after Victor suffered a bad cut. Had an easy defence in halting Argentinian Luis Ocampo. Stopped 17 opponents.

03.08.91 Luis Espinoza W RSC 9 Campeche
30.11.91 Jose Valdez W PTS 12 Tijuana
30.03.92 Yong-Hoon Lee W TD 9 Los Angeles
(Vacant WBC Bantamweight Title)
16.05.92 Luis Ocampo W RSC 4 Tuxtla
(WBC Bantamweight Title Defence)

Career: 43 contests, won 31, drew 2, lost 10.

Jorge (Coca's) Ramirez

Hermosillo, Mexico. *Born* 23 January, 1965

Former Undefeated Mexican S. Featherweight Champion. WBA Intercontinental S. Featherweight Champion

Dangerous Mexican "sleeper". Has spent almost all of his career fighting in the provinces since turning professional in December 1982. He lost two of his 20 amateur bouts. Has three brothers who are boxers. Every one of his first 30 fights ended inside the distance, with Jorge stopping 28 victims and being halted twice. Won the Mexican title in September 1988 by stopping Roger Arevalo, but dropped the crown to Rodolfo Gomez in three rounds in June 1989. Won the WBA Intercontinental title with a seventh round kayo of Robert Byrd in December. Regained the Mexican crown by defeating Bruno Rabanales in June 1990, but lost on points to Jorge Paez in March 1991 in a non-title fight. Tough, methodical battler, who wears the opposition down. His nickname means a drink like coke. Has halted 51 opponents.

01.08.91 Javier Pichardo W RSC 8 Hermosillo
(Mexican S. Featherweight Title Defence)
20.11.91 Ed Parker W CO 6 Hermosillo
07.04.92 Craig Pevy W RSC 3 Los Angeles
02.05.92 Jorge Palomares W RSC 2 Reno
01.06.92 Gilberto Flores W RSC 5 Los Angeles
19.06.92 Omar Catari W CO 6 Hermosillo

Career: 72 contests, won 62, drew 3, lost 7.

Greg (The Flea) Richardson

Youngstown, USA. *Born* 7 February, 1958

Former WBC Bantamweight Champion. Former Undefeated USBA S. Bantamweight & Bantamweight Champion. Former Undefeated NABF Bantamweight Champion

Another one from a boxing family as he is one of three brothers who all boxed as professionals. Started boxing at the age of fifteen. Became the 1974 Golden Gloves flyweight champion and won 260 of 275 amateur fights. Gave up amateur fighting in 1980 when the USA boycotted the Olympics and did not fight again until he turned professional in February 1982. Lost a couple of fights in his first year, but was then unbeaten until 1987. Made his mark in 1984 as he beat Harold Petty on a unanimous decision to win the NABF bantamweight title. Retained the title in 1985 with a victory over James Manning and won the USBA super-bantamweight crown by outpointing Oscar Muniz. Gave up the NABF title in 1986, but retained his USBA crown with subsequent wins over Robert Shannon and Darryl Thigpen. Found Jeff Fenech too strong for him in a challenge for the WBC super-bantamweight title in July 1987 and was halted in six rounds. Lost his USBA title on a split decision to Jesse Benavides in November 1987, but collected the USBA bantamweight crown in November 1990 with a verdict over Eddie Rangel. Upset Raul Perez in February 1991 to take the WBC title on a unanimous verdict. Looked lucky to retain his title against Victor Rabanales in May 1991, but failed to match the strength of Joichiro Tatsuyoshi and retired after eleven rounds, four months later. Fast, slick boxer, but no punch. Halted four opponents.

19.09.91 Joichiro Tatsuyoshi L RSC 11 Tokyo
(WBC Bantamweight Title Defence)

Career: 34 contests, won 29, lost 5.

Edwin (Chapo) Rosario

Toa Baja, Puerto Rico. *Born* 15 March, 1963

Former WBA L.Welterweight Champion. Former WBA & WBC Lightweight Champion

Exciting, but vulnerable fighter, who has had no trouble winning titles, but has found it hard to hold on to them and may now be fading. His elder brother, Luis, was also a good professional. 5'6" tall, had his first paid fight at the age of just 16, and won eleven in a row on stoppages. Became WBC lightweight champion by outpointing tough Jose Luis Ramirez for the vacant crown in May 1983. Halted Roberto Elizondo and won a split decision over Howard Davis in title defences in 1984, before losing to Ramirez. A dramatic fight saw the Mexican roar back from the edge of defeat to halt Edwin in the fourth round. Challenged Hector Camacho for the WBC lightweight title in June 1986. Had Camacho badly shaken, but lost a split decision. In his next fight, in September 1986 he overwhelmed Livingstone Bramble in two rounds to win the WBA lightweight title. Retained his title with a stoppage of Juan Nazario in August 1987, but was halted by the great Julio Cesar Chavez in November. Regained the WBA crown in July 1989 by coming from behind to halt Anthony Jones in six rounds, but dropped the title in his first defence in April 1990 when Juan Nazario halted him on a cut. Became champion yet again in June 1991 as he floored Loreto Garza in the first 30 seconds of their fight and put him down three more times before halting him in the third round to lift the WBA lightwelterweight title. Once again he failed to hold on to the title, being blasted out in a huge upset by Akinobu Hiranaka. Stopped 32 opponents.

10.04.92	Akinobu Hiranaka L RSC 1 Mexico City *(WBA L. Welterweight Title Defence)*
Career: 42 contests, won 37, lost 5.	

Gianfranco Rosi

Perugia, Italy. *Born* 5 August, 1957
IBF L. Middleweight Champion. Former WBC L. Middleweight Champion. Former Undefeated European L. Middleweight Champion. Former EBU Welterweight Champion. Former Undefeated Italian Welterweight Champion

Won Italian amateur titles in 1976 and 1977 at light-welterweight and welterweight, respectively and lost only a handful of his 100 fights. Turned professional in September 1979, but was halted on a cut in his sixth fight. Won the Italian welterweight title in April 1982 by stopping Giuseppe di Padova in seven rounds and retained the title with inside the distance victories over Antonio Torsello, Everaldo Azvedo, Pierangelo Pira and Francesco Gallo. Collected the vacant European crown by decisioning Perico Fernandez in July 1984, but saw his run of 27 wins and his title disappear in January 1985 when Lloyd Honeyghan knocked him out in three rounds. Put on weight and became European light-middleweight champion by outboxing Chris Pyatt in January 1987. Defended his title twice and then decisioned Lupe Aquino in October 1987 to win the WBC title. Managed only one defence of the WBC crown against Duane Thomas and was then floored five times and forced to retire in the ninth round as Don Curry relieved him of the title in July 1988. Gianfranco bounced back in dramatic form in July 1989 by flooring and outpointing the previously unbeaten Darrin van Horn to take the IBF title. Has retained the title with victories against Troy Waters, Kevin Daigle, van Horn, Rene Jacquot, Ron Amundsen, tough Glenn Wolfe, Gilbert Baptist and Angel Hernandez to equal the Italian record of twelve world title fights. Tall, awkward fighter, with a style that is not pretty, but effective. Stopped 17 opponents.

Gianfranco Rosi

13.07.91	Glenn Wolfe W PTS 12 Avezzano *(IBF L. Middleweight Title Defence)*
21.11.91	Gilbert Baptist W PTS 12 Perugia *(IBF L. Middleweight Title Defence)*
30.01.92	Alfredo Ramirez W PTS 10 Salerno
09.04.92	Angel Hernandez W RSC 6 Celano *(IBF L. Middleweight Title Defence)*
Career: 57 contests, won 54, lost 3.	

Donovan (Razor) Ruddock

Canada. *Born* Jamaica 21 December, 1963
Former Undefeated Canadian & WBA Intercontinental Heavyweight Champion

6'3" tall with an 82" reach. Although born in Jamaica, he moved to Canada at the age of four. Started boxing at 16 and was Canadian amateur champion, losing two of his 19 fights. Turned professional in March 1982 and was held to a draw in his sixth fight by spoiler Phil Brown. Suffered an amazing defeat in April 1985 when he retired in the seventh round against travelling loser David Jaco. Razor claimed he was suffering from an asthma attack. Did not fight again for almost a year and beat John Westgarth in seven rounds in London in May 1986. Broke into the ratings with a split verdict over the former WBA champion Mike Weaver in August 1986. Won the Canadian title in May 1988 with a first round knockout of Ken Lakusta. Had to climb off the floor in order to knock out another ex-champion, "Bonecrusher Smith", in seven rounds in July 1989 and then won the WBA intercontinental crown with an impressive fourth round knockout of a third former WBA champion, Mike Dokes, in four rounds in April 1990. Gave Mike Tyson a hard fight in March 1991, despite being floored twice. The referee's decision to stop the bout in the seventh round was hotly disputed by Ruddock. Lost on points to Tyson in a return in June 1991, again being floored twice. Returned with a crushing victory over Phil Jackson last June.

26.06.92	Phil Jackson W RSC 4 Cleveland

Career: 30 contests, won 26, drew 1, lost 3.

Gabriel (Gabe) Ruelas

Arleta, USA. *Born* 23 July, 1970
NABF S. Featherweight Champion

Comes from a fighting family with his younger brother Rafael a top lightweight and elder brother Juan, now retired. managed by the Ten Goose group. Won a number of junior titles as an amateur before handing in his vest in September 1988. Halted five of his initial seven opponents in the first round. Very active fighter who scored eleven wins in 1989. lost his unbeaten record in an unfortunate manner against Jeff Franklin in April 1990. Gabriel had Franklin down in the fifth round, but badly damaged his arm in the sixth. He came out for the seventh round, but was obviously in pain and retired. It was later revealed he had suffered a broken elbow. Gabriel had an operation, but then injured the arm again and did not fight for fourteen months. In only his third comeback fight, he won the vacant NABF super-featherweight title by decisioning Aaron Lopez in July 1991. He has defended the title with wins over Alvaro Bohorquez and Jorge Palomares and also beaten Fred Hernandez, Dana Roston, Fili Montoya and Tomas Valdez. Stopped fourteen opponents.

30.07.91	Aaron Lopez W PTS 12 Reseda *(Vacant NABF S. Featherweight Title)*
16.08.91	Alvaro Bohorquez W PTS 12 San Diego *(NABF S. Featherweight Title Defence)*
26.11.91	Asencion Lugo W CO 1 Reseda
30.01.92	Jorge Palomares W PTS 12 Reseda *(NABF S. Featherweight Title Defence)*
22.02.92	Tommy Valdez W PTS 8 San Diego
02.04.92	Moises Martinez W RSC 1 Reno
27.06.92	Paul Molefyane W PTS 10 Reseda

Career: 30 contests, won 29, lost 1.

Rafael Ruelas

Arleta, USA. *Born* Mexico 26 April, 1971
Former Undefeated NABF Featherweight Champion

His elder brother Gabriel is also a professional. 5'10" tall, loose limbed fighter with a good punch, but leaves himself open with his attacking style. Is part of the Ten Goose team. His

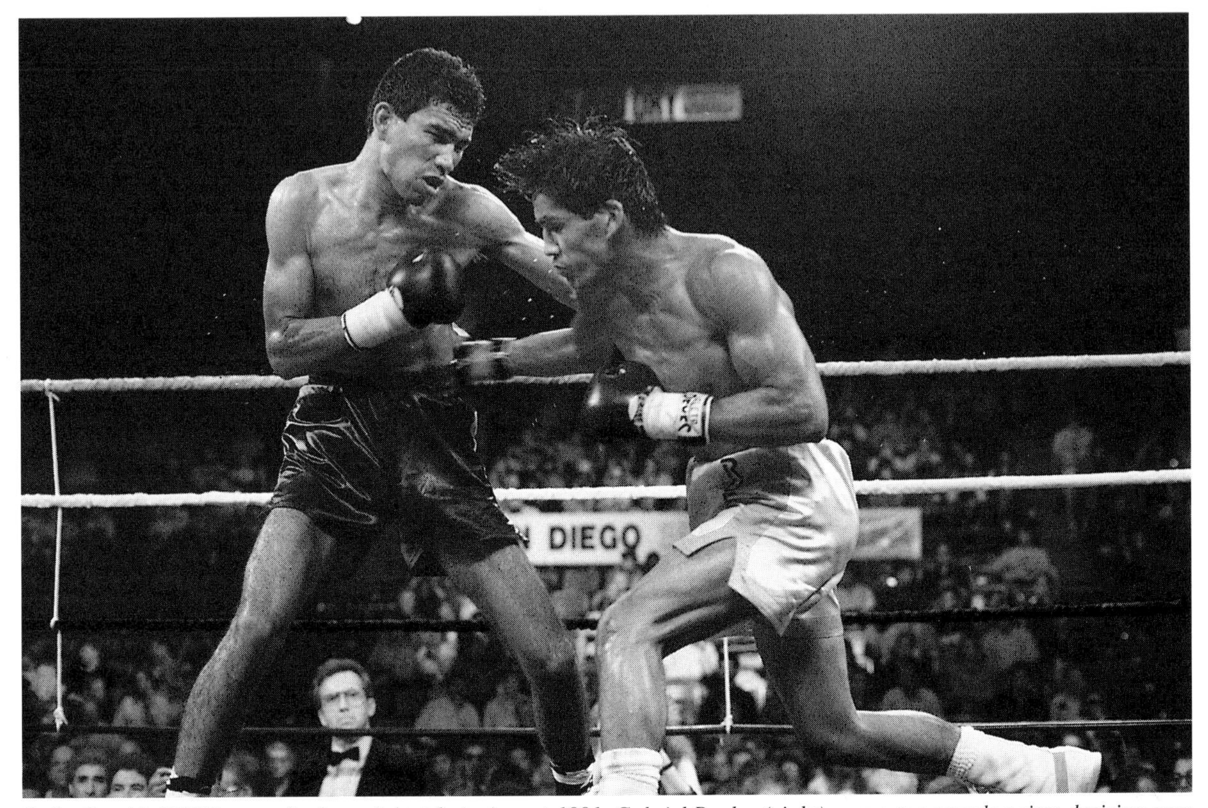

Defending his NABF super-featherweight title in August 1991, Gabriel Ruelas (right) won a ten rounds points decision over tough Alvaro Bohorquez
Chris Farina

first year as a professional was 1989 and after his debut in January he scored eleven other victories. Had nine more wins in 1990, beating good opponents such as Abe Gomez and Job Walters. Won the vacant NABF crown in March 1991 by knocking out the former WBA champion Steve Cruz in three rounds, but moved up to lightweight without defending his title. Challenged Mauro Gutierrez for the WBC Con Am title in July. Rafael was floored in the second round and appeared to be awaiting instructions from his corner to rise, but was counted out. Has won four fights since then, including a points victory against Rocky Lockridge. Has accounted for 24 victims inside the distance.

30.07.91	Mauro Gutierrez L CO 2 Reseda *(WBC Con Am Lightweight Title Challenge)*
26.11.91	Juan de la Paz W RSC 2 Reseda
30.01.92	Rocky Lockridge W PTS 10 Reseda
22.02.92	Tommy Valdez W PTS 8 San Diego
03.04.92	Panchito Lopez W RSC 1 Reno

Career: 32 contests, won 31, lost 1.

Jose (Cheito) Ruiz

Trujillo Alto, Puerto Rico. *Born* 22 October, 1966
Former WBO S. Flyweight Champion

Slick boxing switch-hitter. Started out in July 1984 as a light-flyweight with tough matches from the outset. Beat Luis Monzote and won and lost against Pedro Feliciano. Showed his potential in a close points defeat by Jose de Jesus in April 1987. After that loss he ran up victories over Feliciano, Angel Rosario, Prudencio Cardona and Bernardo Mendoza to earn a shot at the WBO super-flyweight title. Lifted the crown with an upset points victory over Colombian Sugar Baby Rojas in April 1989. Made an impressive first defence in September by halting the former WBC champion Juan Carazo in one round and also stopped Angel Rosario in a title bout in October and Marcos Claudio in December. Retained his crown in fights with Wilfredo Vargas and the tough Mexican, Armando Velasco, in 1990, but did not put his crown on the line in 1991. Unexpectedly dropped his title to late substitute Jose Quirino in February 1992 in a disappointing performance. Has only stopped nine opponents.

06.09.91	Luis Monzote W CO 3 Miami
22.02.92	Jose Quirino L PTS 12 Las Vegas *(WBO S. Flyweight Title Defence)*

Career: 25 contests, won 22, lost 3.

Armando (Jaiba) Salazar

Mexico City, Mexico. *Born* 1968
Former WBC Con Am S. Flyweight Champion. Former Undefeated Mexican S. Flyweight Champion

One of those fighters whose popularity far exceeds his achievements to date. A big draw card in Mexico City. Followed his uncle Clemente into boxing. Turned professional at the age of 18 in September 1986 and was given hard matches all the way in learning fights against Julio Pliego, Josefino Suarez and Juan Chavez. Lost for the first time in June 1988, being outpointed by the current WBC bantamweight champion, Victor Rabanales. Suffered another set back in November 1988, when he was stopped in two rounds by Jose Luis Vegagil, but came back with victories over Artemio Ruiz and Gonzalo Villalobos. Lost on points to Pedro Rabago in June 1989, but halted Rabago in nine rounds in March 1990 to win the Mexican super-flyweight title. Retained the crown with a decision over Gabriel Bernal in May 1990 and four months later took the vacant WBC Con Am title by outpointing Miguel Mercedes. Lost his chance of a shot at the world title and his Con Am crown when he was halted in four rounds by Jose Luis Bueno in September 1991, but can come again. His 22 stoppages show why the Mexican fans like him.

28.09.91	Jose Luis Bueno L RSC 4 Mexico City *(WBC Con Am S. Flyweight Title Defence)*
20.12.91	Betillio Cantu W CO 3 Mexico City

Career: 36 contests, won 28, drew 4, lost 4.

Jesus Salud

Phillipines. *Born* 3 May, 1963
NABF S. Bantamweight Champion. Former Undefeated WBA S. Bantamweight Champion. Former Undefeated IBC S. Bantamweight Champion

Born Sinait, Ilocos Sur in the Philippines, but moved to Hawaii when he was only seven years old. 5'6" tall, former baker. Crisp puncher with a jarring jab. Turned professional in June 1983 in Honolulu and quickly built up a big following, scoring 20 straight wins, including impressive victories over Alfredo Rangel, Joe Hiyas, Mike Phelps and Kenny Mitchell. Fought Frankie Duarte for the vacant NABF bantamweight title in July 1986, but after nine tight rounds Jesus could not continue when his left eye was totally closed. Came back with wins over Edel Geronimo and Allan Makitoki, but was halted in five rounds in September 1987 when he suffered a broken collar bone against Mario Gomez. Lost a disputed decision to Carlos Romero in the semi-finals of the Stroh's tournament in July 1988, but then moved into title contention with seven wins in a row. Collected the WBA super-bantamweight title in December 1989 with a disqualification victory over Juan Jose Estrada. The Mexican had been floored and had two points deducted for low blows, when another punch to the groin saw him thrown out. Salud's management refused to allow him to go to Colombia for a mandatory defence against Luis Mendoza in 1990 and Jesus was stripped of the title. Lost a clear decision to Jesse Benavides in March 1990, but won the vacant IBC crown by halting Martin Ortegon in June and the NABF title with a decision over Darryl Pinckney in September 1991. Failed in a challenge for the IBF title last April, losing on points to Welcome Ncita. Stopped 21 victims.

05.07.91	Vicente Gonzalez W PTS 10 Del Mar
14.09.91	Darryl Pinckney W PTS 12 Maui *(NABF S. Bantamweight Title Challenge)*
17.12.91	Pablo Valenzuela W RSC 5 Honolulu
18.04.92	Welcome Ncita L PTS 12 Treviolo *(IBF S. Bantamweight Title Challenge)*

Career: 46 contests, won 41, lost 5.

Thalerngsak Sitbobay

Mahasarakem, Thailand. *Born* 5 April, 1965
Former OPBF Flyweight Champion. Former Undefeated Thai Flyweight Champion

Started as a kickboxer at the age of nine and became one of Thailand's top performers. His ring name has changed since he entered international style fighting, from Singborbe through Sisborbay to Sitbobay or Sithbobay and his first name has changed from Tanomsak to Thalerngsak. Under any of these names he has established himself as a world class fighter. Moved over from kickboxing in June 1985 and won the Thai flyweight crown in March 1986 with a points verdict against Nongbird Napataya. Became OPBF flyweight title holder in October 1986 by stopping Anburi Sanusi in four rounds and outpointed Choon-Jung Kang to retain his title in March 1987. Lost the OPBF title, and his unbeaten record to Kenji Matsumura in May 1987. The Thai struggled to make the weight and faded in the late rounds, but still looked very unlucky to lose on a split decision. Thalerngsak moved up and scored 17 wins, beating opponents such as Torsak Pongsupa, Cho-Woon Park and Seung-Kwan Lee. Failed in a challenge for the WBA bantamweight title in November 1990, losing on points to Luisito Espinosa. Came down to super-flyweight and after six wins, fought Katsuya Onizuka for the vacant WBA super-flyweight title, but the decision went against him even though he seemed to have won clearly. Good, stylish boxer. Halted 22 opponents.

06.07.91	Santiago Caballero W PTS 10 Bangkok
28.08.91	Chan-Woo Park W CO 4 Bangkok
10.11.92	Romero Oprisa W CO 7 Bangkok
22.12.91	Ricarte Kainira W RSC 3 Bangkok
10.04.92	Katsuya Onizuka L PTS 12 Tokyo *(Vacant WBA S. Flyweight Title)*

Career: 40 contests, won 37, lost 3.

Tracy (Slam Bam) Spann

Piscataway, USA. *Born* 7 April, 1963
Former Undefeated IBF Intercontinental Lightweight Champion

Southpaw, good boxer with a hard punch. Had his first professional bout in October 1984 and won both of his initial contests in the first round. Scored a fine win over Anthony Andrews in 1987 and David Taylor in 1988. Was badly cut in the first round against Miguel Santana in April 1989, but put the Puerto Rican down twice and halted him in round two. Won the vacant IBF intercontinental title in November 1989 with an impressive second round stoppage of tough Bryant Paden. Faced Jorge Paez in an IBF title eliminator in June 1991. Had Paez down and badly hurt in the third round, but let the chance slip and finally lost a majority decision. Inactive until his January 1992 win over Darryl Richardson. has beaten Felipe Julio, Elvis Perez, Ildemar Paisan and Bernard Gray. Stopped 21 victims.

16.01.92	Darryl Richardson W RSC 3 Elizabeth

Career: 28 contests, won 27, lost 1.

Eugene Speed

Palmer Park, USA. *Born* 18 July, 1963
IBC S. Featherweight Champion

Former National Golden Gloves champion. Originally managed by the Sugar Ray Leonard team as a professional. Stopped James Mouzone in five rounds in December 1985 and also halted his next five opponents. Beat good quality opponents, such as Kent Hardee, Luis Andino and former world amateur champion, Floyd Favors. Floored Irving Mitchell three times and stopped him in the third round, halted Kenny Baysmore on a cut and outpointed Kenny Marston on a good run. Took a split decision over former IBF champion Jose Sanabria to win the vacant IBC super-featherweight title in August 1991. Also looked good in stopping Alberto Mercado and Joey Negron, but failed in a challenge for the USBA super-featherweight title, losing on a split decision to veteran, Bernard Taylor. Slick boxer with talent, but has had a problem with drugs in the past. Stopped 16 opponents.

26.08.91	Jose Sanabria W PTS 12 Lanham *(Vacant IBC S. Featherweight Title)*
16.11.91	Alberto Mercado W RSC 3 Alexandria
18.01.92	Joey Negron W RSC 8 Alexandria
28.03.92	Bernard Taylor L PTS 12 Washington *(USBA S. Featherweight Title Challenge)*

Career: 23 contests, won 22, lost 1.

Maurizio Stecca

San Arcangelo, Italy. *Born* 9 March, 1963
Former WBO Featherweight Champion

One of Italy's most successful amateurs. Won a gold medal in the 1983 World Cup, beating the current WBC super-flyweight champion, Sung-Il Moon, on the way. Also took the gold medal at bantamweight in the 1984 Olympic Games. His brother Loris was the WBA super-bantamweight champion for a short spell in 1984. Maurizio turned professional in December 1984 and was unbeaten for almost five years. He was built-up carefully against selected opposition,

Maurizio Stecca

until winning the vacant WBO featherweight title by halting Pedro Nolasco in January 1989. Made only one defence, stopping Angel Mayor in June, but lost the title to Luis Espinosa in November. Maurizio started well, but was floored by a body punch in round seven and refused to fight on. Regained the WBO crown by stopping Armado Reyes for the vacant title in January 1991 and beat Fernando Salas and Tim Driscoll in defences in 1991. Lost the title again when he was outpointed by Colin McMillan in an excellent boxing match in May 1992. Classy box-fighter, but not a puncher as his 20 stoppages show.

09.11.91 Tim Driscoll W RTD 9 Campione d'Italia
(WBO Featherweight Title Defence)
25.03.92 Roy Muniz W RSC 6 Dagenham
16.05.92 Colin McMillan L PTS 12 London
(WBO Featherweight Title Defence)

Career: 46 contests, won 44, lost 2.

Akim Tafer

La Tronche, France. *Born* 27 August, 1967
European Cruiserweight Champion. Former Undefeated French Cruiserweight Champion

Comes from a fighting family. His brother Hocine was French light-heavyweight champion. 6'2" tall, upright stylist. French amateur champion in 1987 and 1988 at heavyweight. Made a bad start as a professional in October 1988, fighting at light-heavyweight he was stopped in three rounds by Norbert Ekassi. Lost again in his sixth fight on points to Christophe Girard in February 1989 and was also stopped by Mohamad Zaoui in November. Moved up to cruiserweight and in May 1990, halted Siriki Sanogo in five rounds to win the vacant French title. Retained the title in April 1991, this time by knocking out Sanogo in two rounds. Took the vacant European crown last February by decisioning Dennis Andries. One judge voted for a draw, but Tafer was too young and strong. Defended his crown in June with an easy victory over Fernando Aiello. Stopped nine opponents.

24.01.92 Butch Kelly W RSC 2 Paris
27.02.92 Dennis Andries W PTS 12 Beausoleil
(Vacant European Cruiserweight Title)
12.06.92 Fernando Aiello W RTD 6 Alencon
(European Cruiserweight Title Defence)

Career: 18 contests, won 15, lost 3.

Frank Tate

Detroit, USA. *Born* 27 August, 1964
NABF & IBF Intercontinental L. Heavyweight Champion. Former IBF Middleweight Champion

6'0" tall, 75" reach. Won a gold medal at the Olympic Games in 1984. His brother Thomas Tate is also fighting as a professional. Signed-up with the now defunct Houston Boxing Association and had his first paid fight in December 1984. Made good progress, defeating fighters such as Curtis Parker and Kevin Watts and collected the vacant USBA middleweight title in July 1987 with a unanimous decision over Troy Darrell. Won the vacant IBF crown in October 1987 by flooring Michael Olajide twice and easily outpointing the Canadian. Made his first title defence in England in February 1988 and knocked out Tony Sibson in ten rounds. Blew his title in 1988 when the speed of Michael Nunn and weight problems proved too much for Frank and he was stopped in nine rounds. Faced Lindell Homes for the vacant IBF super-middleweight crown in January 1990, but lost on a majority decision and climbed up to light-heavyweight. Won the IBF inter-continental title with a decision over Uriah Grant in February 1991. Retained the title by outpointing Yawe Davis and then added the USBA crown by putting Andy Maynard down twice and stopping him in eleven rounds. Strong fighter who looks comfortable at the higher poundage. Stopped 17 opponents.

03.08.91 Yawe Davis W PTS 12 Selvino
(IBF Intercontinental L. Heavyweight Title Defence)
10.01.92 Andy Maynard W RSC 11 New York
(NABF L. Heavyweight Title Challenge)
27.03.92 Tim Johnson W RSC 6 St Louis

Career: 32 contests, won 30, lost 2.

Joichiro Tatsuyoshi

Kurashiki, Japan. *Born* 15 May, 1970
Former Undefeated WBC & Japanese Bantamweight Champion

Known as the "Japanese Olivares" because of his exciting style. The biggest draw card in Japan right now. Renowned street fighter before being introduced to boxing. Became all Japanese champion at 17 and won 18 of his 19 fights, stopping all of his victims. Lost in the Olympic trials, due to a knee injury and disappeared for a while. Returned to the gym in 1989 and had his first paid fight in September, knocking out South Korean Sang-Myon Choi in two rounds. Fought on the Douglas-Tyson show in February 1990 and paid for over-confidence when he was floored in the first round by Chucherd Eausampan, but finished the Thai in round two. Moved up in class to knock out tough Filipino Sammy Durran in seven rounds in June and three months later stopped Shigeru Okabe in four to win the Japanese bantamweight title. Easily knocked out Jun Cardinal in December, but in February 1991, needed some generous home officials to help him get a draw after being out-boxed by the clever Venezuelan, Abraham Torres. Outpointed useful Rey Paciones in May and then set a Japanese record by winning a world title in only his eighth fight, battering the WBC bantamweight champion Greg Richardson to defeat in eleven rounds in September. After the fight he was found to have a problem with his eyes and required surgery. The WBC held eliminators to find an "interim" champion, and Joichiro will fight that champion, Victor Rabanales, when he returns.

19.09.91 Greg Richardson W RSC 11 Tokyo
(WBC Bantamweight Title Challenge)

Career: 8 contests, won 7, drew 1.

Bernard Taylor

Charlotte, USA. *Born* 26 June, 1957
USBA S. Featherweight Champion. Former Undefeated NABF Featherweight Champion

Brilliant stylist. Probably one of the greatest amateur fighters produced by America, but lost the chance of an Olympic gold medal due to the boycott of the 1980 Games. Bernard won eight national titles and in 1979 won gold medals in the World Cup and the Pan American Games. Became a professional in October 1980 and after 18 victories fought a draw with Eusebio Pedroza for the WBA featherweight title in October 1982. Registered fifteen more wins and then challenged Barry McGuigan for the WBA crown in September 1985. After boxing well for six rounds, Bernard suddenly fell apart and retired at the end of round eight. Took the NABF title in September 1986 with a points victory over Baby

Meldrick Taylor

Joe Ruelas. Defended the title in 1987 with a win over Javier Marquez and a draw with Jeff Franklin and halted Marquez in a title bout in September 1988. Bernard was inactive until February 1990 when he returned in style to stop Calvin Grove in eleven rounds for the USBA super-featherweight title. Retained his crown with a close points win over IBC champion Eugene Speed last March in an upset. 5'7" tall, still a good stylist, but needs to be more active if he is to get a third world title chance. Halted 21 opponents.

28.03.92 Eugene Speed W PTS 12 Washington *(USBA S. Featherweight Title Defence)*

Career: 48 contests, won 44, drew 2, lost 2.

Meldrick Taylor

Philadelphia, USA. *Born* 19 October, 1966

WBA Welterweight Champion. Former IBF L. Welterweight Champion

Brilliant as a young amateur. Won the US/ABF title at 17 and the featherweight gold medal in the 1984 Olympic Games at 18. Signed up with Main Events and was obvious world title material from the outset. Was well matched with plenty of good learning fights. Decisioned Robin Blake in February 1986 and "went to school" in outpointing experienced Harold Brazier in May. Disappointed in a draw with Howard Davis in August. Continued to progress in 1987 by taking verdicts over Primo Ramos and Irleis Perez and in September 1988 claimed his first world title by halting Buddy McGirt in twelve rounds for the IBF light-welterweight crown. Stopped John Meekins and decisioned Courtney Hooper in title defences in 1989 and in March 1990 faced Julio Cesar Chavez with the IBF and WBC titles on the line. A great battle saw Meldrick using his tremendous hand speed to build-up an unassailable lead, only to be floored and halted on his feet with just two seconds remaining in the last round. The stoppage was heavily criticised, but, instead of waiting for a return with Chavez, Meldrick challenged for the WBA welterweight title in January 1991 and outpointed Aaron Davis. He decisioned Luis Garcia to retain his title in June 1991, but in his second defence had to climb off the floor twice before winning a unanimous decision over Glenwood Brown in a gusty performance. Made an unsuccessful try at adding a third world title when the WBC light-middleweight champion Terry Norris had too much power and stopped him in four rounds. It remains to be seen how much the loss to Norris has taken out of him. Halted fifteen opponents.

13.09.91 Ernie Chavez W RSC 6 Sacramento
18.01.92 Glenwood Brown W PTS 12 Philadelphia
(WBA Welterweight Title Defence)
09.05.92 Terry Norris L RSC 4 Las Vegas
(WBC L. Middleweight Title Challenge)

Career: 32 contests, won 29, drew 1, lost 2.

Francisco Tejedor

Palenque, Colombia. *Born* 26 July, 1967
Former Undefeated Fecarbox L. Flyweight Champion

Tall, stylish boxer, but not a heavy puncher. Started out as a light-flyweight in January 1986 and became Fecarbox champion in his tenth bout by stopping Panamanian, Leonardo Paredes, in November. Scored nine victories in 1987, beating useful opponents such as Hermogenes Murillo and Victor Sierra inside the distance. With four wins in 1988 and five in 1989, he took his victory total to 28 and put himself in line for a shot at the world title. Challenged Humberto Gonzalez for the WBC crown in Mexico City in March 1990, but after two even rounds was knocked cold by a brutal left uppercut. Has now gone up to flyweight and remains unbeaten at the higher poundage, although he was disappointing in a draw with Guido Trivino and could struggle against the top contenders. Also has victories against Uriel Londono, Roy Thompson and Augustin Garcia. Stopped 23 opponents.

23.08.91 Robinson Quiroz W PTS 10 Cartagena
22.11.91 Antonio Zappa W CO 2 Barranquilla
31.01.92 James Guevara W CO 2 Barranquilla
13.03.92 Guido Trivino DREW 8 Cartagena
28.03.92 Ramiro Carvajal W CO 6 Barranquilla
08.05.92 Saul Guaza W PTS 10 Barranquilla

Career: 37 contests, won 35, drew 1, lost 1.

Dingaan (The Rose of Soweto) Thobela

Johannesburg, South Africa. *Born* September, 1966
WBO Lightweight Champion. Former Undefeated South African S. Featherweight Champion

5'7" tall. Taught to box by his father who fought as an amateur. Had 83 fights in three years and won 80 before becoming a professional in June 1986. Was held to a draw by lightweight Peter Mpikashe in December, the only fight he has failed to win so far. Voted "Prospect of the Year" in 1988 and in October halted Mpisakhaya Mbaduli to lift the South African super-featherweight title. Registered an impressive victory in January 1989 by outpointing the current WBO super-featherweight champion Daniel Londas and also knocked out the former world title challenger Danilo Cabrera in July. Had his first fight outside South Africa in April 1990 when he stopped the WBO lightweight title holder Mauricio Aceves in seven rounds in Biloxi, USA. Came back to the States in September to challenge Aceves for the crown. Although he dropped the Mexican in the second round, Dingaan tired in the 100 degree heat. Aceves made up ground, but Dingaan held out to earn the decision and the title. Has made two defences, decisioning Mario Martinez in March 1991 and Antonio Rivera in September. Fast hands and feet, tight defence and a good puncher, he has yet to be tested against the best in the division. Halted fourteen victims.

13.07.91 Amancio Castro W PTS 10 Pretoria
14.09.91 Antonio Rivera W PTS 12 Johannesburg
(WBO Lightweight Title Defence)

Career: 27 contests, won 26, drew 1.

Tony (The Postman) Thornton

Glassboro, USA. *Born* 8 November, 1959
Former USBA Middleweight Champion

Works as a postman in New Jersey. Outstanding athlete at school and has a big local following. Good boxer and a hard puncher. First professional fight in June 1983 and halted 16 of his first 17 opponents, before being held to a draw by Stacy McSwain in August 1987. Fought Doug de Witt for the vacant USBA light-middleweight title in November 1987. They finished even after twelve rounds, so had to fight a decider and de Witt won round thirteen and the decision. Tony grew into a middleweight and in January 1989 took a unanimous verdict over Mike Tinley to lift the vacant USBA crown. Only ruled for two months and then lost the title to Kevin Watts on a clear decision. Challenged Steve Collins for the same title in July 1989, but was outboxed and dropped a majority decision to the Irishman. Climbed off the floor to take a lead over Ismael Negron in November 1989, but was cut and could not continue in the seventh. Tony is now fighting at super-middleweight and has nine consecutive wins, including stoppages against Dave Tiberi, Kamara Leota and Carl Sullivan and a points victory over Merqui Sosa. Has stopped 23 opponents.

19.11.91 Fermain Chirinos W PTS 10 Atlantic City
22.03.92 Danny Mitchell W PTS 8 Atlantic City
11.06.92 Khalif Shabazz W CO 1 Atlantic City

Career: 36 contests, won 31, drew 1, lost 4.

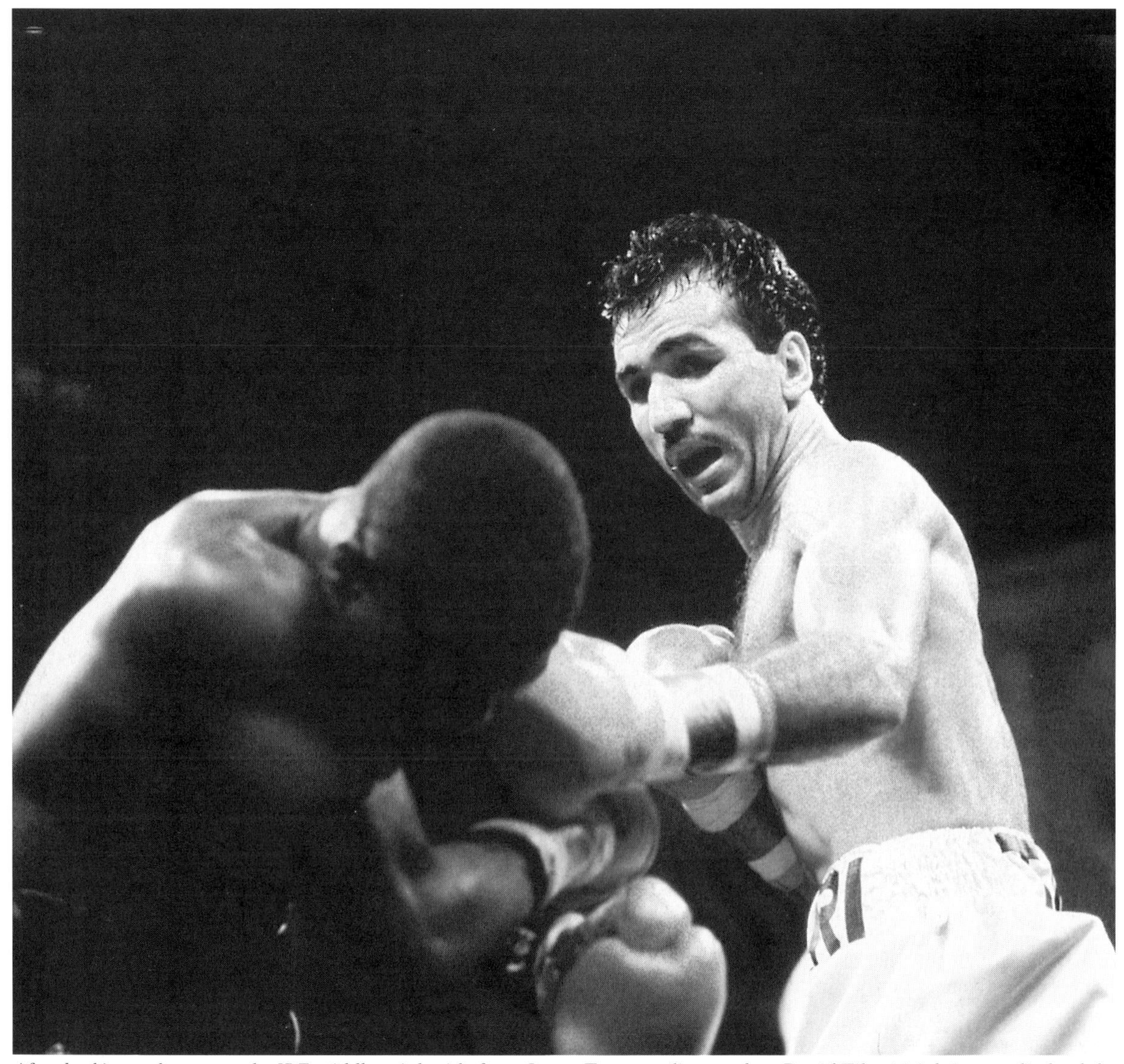

After looking to have won the IBF middleweight title from James Toney, a disconsolate David Tiberi (right) was adjudged the loser on a split decision

Tom Casino

David Tiberi

Newcastle, USA. *Born* 12 September, 1966

IBC S. Middleweight Champion

Comes from a big family and three of his brothers also boxed as professionals. Hosts his own chat show and works as Executive Director at a Youth Centre. Turned professional in July 1985 and drew in three of his first eight fights. Lost his unbeaten record in October 1987, being outpointed by Ronnie Essett. Scored nine wins, but was then halted by a cut in four rounds against Tony Thornton in May 1990. Tried his hand at super-middleweight for a while and won the IBC super-middleweight title in July 1991 by stopping Eddie Hall in four rounds. Was then selected as an easy challenger for the IBF middleweight champion James Toney in February 1992. Dave was hurt in the first round but stayed right in front of Toney and, despite a strong finish by the champion, looked to have won a close contest. The judges disagreed and gave Toney a split decision. The IBF mandated a return, but Tiberi foolishly rejected it. Holds wins over Jerome Kelly, Ken Shannon and Troy Watson. Has only seven stoppage wins.

01.07.91	Eddie Hall W RSC 4 Cheyne *(Vacant IBC S. Middleweight Title)*
08.02.92	James Toney L PTS 12 Atlantic City *(IBF Middleweight Title Challenge)*

Career: 28 contests, won 22, drew 3, lost 3.

Christophe Tiozzo

St Denis, France. *Born* 1 June, 1963
Former WBA S. Middleweight Champion. Former Undefeated European Middleweight Champion

Former Police Officer. His brother Fabrice is a leading contender for the European light-heavyweight title. Outstanding as an amateur. Won French titles in 1982 and 83 at light-middleweight and in 1985 at middleweight. Won a bronze medal in the 1984 Olympic Games and looked unlucky to lose there to Shawn O'Sullivan. Won 86 of 94 bouts. Turned professional in October 1985. Overcame good tests by decisioning Andre Mongalema and knocking out Jimmy Cable and Carlos Title. Easily won the European middleweight title in April 1988 by outpointing Pierre Joly and made two defences, halting Andreas Proux and Alfonso Redondo, before relinquishing the crown at the end of the year. Beat James Kinchen on points in March 1989 and one year later halted In-Chul Baek to win the WBA super-middleweight title. Baek was down twice and badly cut when the referee crowned Christophe in the sixth round. Made two successful defences, stopping Paul Whitaker and Danny Morgan later in 1990, but was battered to defeat in nine rounds by Panamanian Victor Cordoba in a title bout in April 1991. Christophe moved up to light-heavyweight, but found Jeff Harding too tough in a challenge for the WBC title and was stopped in eight rounds. Has halted 21 opponents.

02.08.91	Lenzie Morgan W PTS 10 Cannes
08.11.92	Kenny Schaefer W RSC 2 Paris
05.06.92	Jeff Harding L RSC 8 Marseille *(WBC L. Heavyweight Title Challenge)*

Career: 32 contests, won 30, lost 2.

James (The Michigan Hurricane) Toney

Ann Arbor, USA. *Born* 24 August, 1968
IBF Middleweight Champion

The angry young man of boxing. Almost as aggressive at press conferences as he is in the ring. Had his first paid fight in October 1988, but did not really get any attention until he destroyed fellow prospect Philip Morefield in one round in March 1990. Four months later wasted an early lead against veteran Sanderline Williams and had to settle for a draw. Took on tough Dominican Merqui Sosa in January 1991 and put his man on the floor on the way to a split decision. Sprang a major upset in May when he ripped the IBF middleweight title from unbeaten Michael Nunn. Was behind in the early rounds, but took the eighth, ninth and tenth and

James Toney, the IBF middleweight king and his manager, Jackie Kalen

Chris Farina

floored then stopped Nunn in the eleventh. Had a tough first defence against Reggie Johnson in June, being floored in round two and retaining his title on a split decision. Failed to make the weight for a defence against Francesco dell'Aquila in October, but dell'Aquila's camp agreed to overlook this and Toney easily halted the Italian in the fourth round. Retained his title in a controversial draw with Mike McCallum in December. McCallum built an early lead, but was out on his feet at the finish and both parties felt they had done enough to win. Took what should have been an easy defence against Dave Tiberi last February, but fought badly and looked lucky to win and failed to impress in decisioning Glenn Wolfe in April. Has not dominated in the way he looked capable of doing after the victory over Nunn. Stopped 21 opponents.

12.10.91	Francesco dell'Aquila W RSC 4 Monaco *(IBF Middleweight Title Defence)*
13.12.91	Mike McCallum DREW 12 Atlantic City *(IBF Middleweight Title Defence)*
08.02.92	Dave Tiberi W PTS 12 Atlantic City *(IBF Middleweight Title Defence)*
11.04.92	Glenn Wolfe W PTS 12 Las Vegas *(IBF Middleweight Title Defence)*
26.05.92	Ricky Stackhouse W CO 3 Detroit

Career: 33 contests, won 31, drew 2.

Tony (TNT) Tucker

Grand Rapids, USA. *Born* 27 December, 1958
NABF Heavyweight Champion. Former IBF Heavyweight Champion. Former Undefeated USBA Heavyweight Champion

6'5" tall, 82" reach. As an amateur, Tony won gold medals at the World Cup and Pan American Games and was also national AAU champion. Scored 96 victories in 102 bouts. His father fought also as a professional. After becoming a paid fighter in November 1980, he stopped his first fifteen opponents. Suffered a knee injury in a bout with Danny Sutton in August 1982, but remained unbeaten as it was called a no contest. Scored wins against Eddie Lopez, Jimmy Young and Sutton and beat James Broad on points in September 1986 to win the vacant USBA crown. Became IBF champion when he wore down big James Douglas and halted him in the tenth round of their fight for the vacant title in May 1987. Rocked Mike Tyson a couple of times in the early rounds of their unification fight in August 1987, but then settled for lasting the distance and lost on points. Drug problems and contract disputes kept him out of the ring until December 1989. Won the NABF title in June 1991 by outpointing Orlin Norris, but Tony appeared lucky to get the verdict. Had reconstruction surgery on his right hand which was originally broken shortly before the Tyson fight and was not properly diagnosed over the years since then. Could still be a force in the division. Stopped 36 opponents.

15.02.92	Kimmuel Odum W CO 2 Las Vegas
10.04.92	Mike Faulkner W CO 2 Mexico City
22.04.92	Manny Contrerras W RSC 6 East Rutherford
26.06.92	Oliver McCall W PTS 12 Cleveland *(NABF Heavyweight Title Defence)*

Career: 47 contests, won 45, lost 1, 1 no contest.

Roger Turner

Lansing, USA. *Born* 9 July, 1963
WBF Welterweight Champion. Former NABF Welterweight Champion

Clever switch-hitter. As an amateur won the ABF title in 1987 and was State Golden Gloves champion five times. Lost only five of around 100 amateur fights. Did his early paid fighting in the sticks after turning professional in January 1988. Stopped eight of his first nine opponents, but did not face real tests until he outpointed Floyd Mayweather and Anthony Williams at the end of 1990. Won the World Boxing Federation welterweight title in February 1991 with a points win over Darryl Lattimore and in July scored an impressive victory, decisioning the Olympic bronze medallist, Kenny Gould. Lifted the vacant NABF title in February 1992 by outpointing veteran Tyrone Moore, but looked unlucky to lose in his first defence to the unbeaten Mexican hope, Luis Ramon Campas. Not a big puncher, he has only eleven stoppage wins.

16.07.92	Kenny Gould W PTS 10 Lansing
08.02.92	Tyrone Moore W PTS 12 Lansing *(Vacant NABF Welterweight Title)*
19.06.92	Luis Ramon Campas L PTS 12 Las Vegas *(NABF Welterweight Title Defence)*

Career: 23 contests, won 22, lost 1.

Regilio Tuur

Surinam, Dutch West Indies. *Born* 12 August, 1967
S. Featherweight

Started boxing as a fourteen-year-old in Holland. Really hit the headlines as an amateur when he knocked out the favourite for the gold medal, Kelcie Banks, in the 1988 Olympics. 5'7" tall, he had his first paid fight in New York in July 1989 and with his exciting style has been in demand and kept active. The only blemishes on his early record came within a couple of weeks of each other. In January 1990 he was outpointed by clever Fernando Rodriguez and in the following month was held to a draw by fellow prospect, Jacobin Yoma. Fighting in both the United States and Europe, he countered his bad start to 1990 with eleven wins in the year. Made good progress in 1991 with his most important victory coming against the former IBF champion, Jose Sanabria. Suffered a set-back in March 1992 when he lost on points to another former IBF title holder, Calvin Grove, in a fight that could have gone either way. Bounced back with a brutal fifth round knock out of Paul Harvey. Also has beaten Moussa Sangare, Jean di Bateza and Danilo Cabrera. 21 of his fights have ended early.

23.07.91	Jose Sanabria W PTS 10 Monticello
30.08.91	Wilson Fontalvo W PTS 10 Curacao
05.10.91	Danilo Cabrera W RSC 7 Waregem
05.12.91	Bobby Brewer W PTS 10 Greenville
31.01.92	Tchoza Mukuta W RSC 2 Waregem
03.03.92	Armand Morales W CO 2 Amsterdam
27.03.92	Calvin Grove L PTS 10 Catskills
02.06.92	Paul Harvey W CO 5 Rotterdam

Career: 32 contests, won 29, drew 1, lost 2.

Darryl Tyson

Darryl (Terrible "T") Tyson
Washington, USA. *Born* 17 October, 1960
Former Undefeated NABF & WBC Con Am Lightweight Champion

Started boxing at fourteen after watching Muhammad Ali fight Joe Frazier. Had 60 amateur fights, losing ten. Made his professional debut in September 1982. Stopped his first five opponents, but was outpointed by Dave Grayton in March 1983. Came to prominence in October 1983 with a decision over Jimmy Paul. Won the vacant WBC Con Am lightweight title in July 1985 with a points victory against Melvin Paul and defended it by beating Nick Parker and Freddie Roach. Challenged Jimmy Paul for the IBF crown in August 1986, but lost a unanimous decision in a close fight. Suffered further set-backs as he dropped a disputed verdict to Chil-Sung Chun in Korea in 1987 and was outpointed by Terrence Alli in 1988. That was Darryl's last defeat. He signed-up with Dave Gorman and came under the Madison Square Garden banner, registering fifteen wins in a row. Collected the vacant NABF crown in July 1990 with a split decision against Rocky Balboa. Very good technician, but not a big puncher. Also has wins against Vinnie Costello, Anthony English and Lupe Suarez and has stopped 20 opponents. Relinquished the NABF title to concentrate on landing a shot at the world crown.

24.07.91	Alfredo Rojas W PTS 10 Washington
16.08.91	Lupe Suarez W PTS 10 Charleston
05.12.91	Thomas Quinones W RSC 4 Greenville
11.01.92	Leobardo Mancillas W CO 5 Washington
28.02.92	Eduardo Jacques W PTS 10 Charleston
04.06.92	Roberto Medina W RSC 3 Atlantic City

Career: 44 contests, won 40, lost 4.

Darrin van Horn

Lexington, USA. *Born* 7 September, 1968
Former IBF S. Middleweight Champion. Former IBF L. Middleweight Champion

Born in Morgan City, Louisiana. Began to box at the age of fourteen and turned professional at just 16, under the autocratic management of his father. Did much of his early fighting out of Lexington, where he was studying at the University of Kentucky. His good looks and exciting style attracted TV and in 1987 he impressed the viewers with points wins over Elio Diaz and Luis Santana. Despite having 38 wins behind him, he was a big outsider when he challenged Robert Hines for the IBF light-middleweight title in February 1989. Darrin started fast and never let Hines into the fight, winning a unanimous decision. He reigned for only five months and then dropped his title in July 1989 to the awkward, but effective, Italian, Gianfranco Rosi. Darrin was floored and lost a clear decision. A return with Rosi in July 1990 saw Darrin beaten on points, again in a bad tempered match. In May 1991 he made an unexpected jump as he challenged Lindell Holmes for the IBF super-middleweight title. A big upset saw Darrin knock out Holmes with a body punch in the eleventh round. He retained his title with a third round kayo of John Jarvis, but was floored three times and battered to defeat by Iran Barkley. Halted 27 opponents.

17.08.91	John Jarvis W RSC 3 Irvine *(IBF S. Middleweight Title Defence)*
10.01.92	Iran Barkley L RSC 2 New York *(IBF S. Middleweight Title Defence)*

Career: 50 contests, won 47, lost 3.

Wilfredo Vasquez

WBA S. Bantamweight Champion. Former WBA Bantamweight Champion. Former Undefeated Puerto Rican & IBF Intercontinental Bantamweight Champion

Had only thirteen amateur fights before turning professional in January 1981. Lost his first fight, but was then unbeaten until 1986. Managed by Jim Jacobs and Bill Clayton. Won the Puerto Rican title in March 1984 by stopping Juan Torres in four rounds. Challenged Miguel Lora for the WBC crown in February 1986, but lost on points. Came back with wins over Jose Cervantes, Antonio Avelar and Juan Carazo, to gain a shot at the WBA title. Took the crown in October 1987 by halting Chan-Yong Park in ten rounds in Seoul. Held onto the crown with a draw in a defence in Osaka against Takuya Muguruma, but dropped the title in his next bout, being decisioned by Kaokor Galaxy in Bangkok in May 1988. Lost his next fight to Raul Perez in August and in June 1990 suffered a bad defeat when he was knocked out in a round by Israel Contrerras. Really came into the picture again in March 1992 when he overwhelmed Raul Perez in three rounds to win the WBA world super-bantamweight title. Retained the title with a controversial decision over Freddy Cruz. Stopped 28 opponents.

27.03.92	Raul Perez W RSC 3 Mexico City *(WBA S. Bantamweight Title Challenge)*
01.05.92	Juan Bisono W RSC 3 Miami
27.06.92	Freddy Cruz W PTS 12 Gorle *(WBA S. Bantamweight Title Defence)*

Career: 43 contests, won 34, drew 3, lost 6.

Julio Cesar Vazquez

Santa Fe, Argentina. *Born* 13 July, 1966
L. Middleweight

Tough, very hard punching southpaw. Started boxing in Santa Fe when he was fifteen and was unbeaten as an amateur, with 25 wins and five draws. Fought as a welterweight when he became a professional in June 1986. Had most of his early bouts in Santa Fe, beating useful opponents such as Simon Escobar and Ranon Abeldano. Appeared in Las Vegas in November 1989 and stopped world rated Troy Wortham in six rounds. Next time he came out of Argentina was in May 1991 when he appeared in Paris and knocked out Judas Clottey in one round. He returned home, but had his 30 bout unbeaten streak broken when he lost on a sixth round disqualification against Vernon Phillips. Julio was floored in the sixth round, but his seconds invaded the ring, claiming the punch had landed after the bell. At first it was ruled a no-decision, but the commission later disqualified Julio due to the action of his seconds. He has re-established himself with stoppage wins over Tyrone Trice and Louis Howard. Is not a stylish fighter, but can certainly punch. 5'9" tall, he has finished 29 victims early and halted 20 of his last 22.

27.07.91	Eduardo Contreras W RTD 2 Buenos Aires
19.09.91	Tyrone Trice W RSC 9 Paris
21.11.91	Louis Howard W CO 3 Paris
27.02.92	Sergio Arreola W RSC 1 Paris
18.04.92	Daniel Dominquez W CO 1 Buenos Aires
08.05.92	Jorge Morello W CO 2 Santa Fe
06.06.92	Francisco Bobadilla W RSC 7 Buenos Aires

Career: 38 contests, won 37, lost 1.

David Vedder

San Jose, USA. *Born* 21 July, 1964
WBC Con Am and IBF Intercontinental L. Heavyweight Champion. Former Undefeated USBA L. Heavyweight Champion

San Jose bus driver. Slippery, mobile boxer. Has been a professional since September 1984. Started badly with only one victory in his first five bouts and in fact won just five of his initial fourteen fights. The opposition was pretty tough, including Virgil Hill, Ricky Womack and Jerry Okorodudu. Lost to Antoine Byrd on a very tight majority decision for the Californian State super-middleweight title in June 1989, but beat Sean Mannion in September and took the vacant USBA light-heavyweight crown with a split decision against Uriah Grant. Found Virgil Hill too strong for him in a WBA title challenge in February 1990, losing clearly on points. Added the IBF intercontinental title in May 1990 with a majority verdict over Nigerian Joe Lasisi. Was outboxed by Jeff Harding and lost on points in December 1990. Had only one fight in 1991, but collected the vacant WBC Con Am crown by knocking out Ramzi Hassan in April. Only has three stoppage wins.

29.04.92	Ramzi Hassan W CO 8 San Diego *(Vacant WBC Con Am L. Heavyweight Title)*

Career: 28 contests, won 15, drew 3, lost 10.

Jose Concepcion Vidal

Santo Domingo, Dominican Republic. *Born* 18 May, 1961
Former Undefeated Fecarbox & WBA Americas S. Featherweight Champion

Talented, but erratic performer. Turned professional in Puerto Rico in May 1978 and fought around the Caribbean for a few years before coming to Atlantic City in April 1982. Won the Latin American super-featherweight crown in December 1982 by decisioning Ezequiel Mosquera, but dropped the title in March 1984, being stopped in nine rounds by Juan Nazario. Gained the Fecarbox crown in April 1987 with a seven round victory over Angel Garcia, but was outpointed by Manuel Batista in September 1987. Moved to the Bronx in 1988 and scored a good points victory against Bernard Gray. Won the vacant WBA Americas super-featherweight title by decisioning Delio Palacios in March 1989. Entered the Inglewood Forum tournament later in the year, but was beaten on points in the quarter-finals by Robert Byrd. Slipped out of the picture after being stopped by Bryant Paden in September 1990. Came back in style last March by catching Ricardo Cepeda cold and battered him to defeat in three rounds. Stopped 20 opponents.

11.03.92	Ricardo Cepeda W RSC 3 New York
10.06.92	Albert Rendon W PTS 10 New York

Career: 44 contests, won 33, drew 2, lost 9.

Edito (Ala) Villamor

Cebu City, Philippines. *Born* 12 October, 1970
Philippines M. Flyweight Champion

Born Magsaysay. Began boxing at the age of 16 and suffered only one defeat as an amateur before turning professional at 18. Uses the initials of his manager Antonio L Aldeguer as a ring name. Only one of his first fourteen opponents lasted the distance as he beat good quality fighters such as Max Forrosuelo, Ponidi and Nico Thomas. Won the vacant Philippines mini-flyweight title by halting Rico Macaubos in November 1990. Had to climb off the floor to knock out Yasuo Yogi in December 1990 in Tokyo. Was held to a draw by Yuichi Hosono in October 1991, but looked to have won a close fight. Halted world title challenger Said Iskandar in January 1992 and retained his national crown by stopping the very good Ronnie Magramo in eight rounds. Exciting young southpaw fighter. Very fast with a punch that has accounted for 19 of his victims by the quick route.

08.07.91	Sugar Ray Mike W RSC 8 Cebu City
14.10.91	Yuichi Hosono DREW 10 Tokyo
10.01.92	Said Iskander W RSC 3 Cebu City
04.04.92	Jae-Woon Kim W CO 1 Cebu City
13.06.92	Ronnie Magramo W RSC 8 Cebu City *(Philippines M. Flyweight Title)*

Career: 22 contests, won 21, drew 1.

Marcos Villasana

Acapulco, Mexico. *Born* 18 June, 1960
Former WBC Featherweight Champion. Former Undefeated Mexican Featherweight Champion

Tough, durable veteran with an iron chin. Won the Mexican Golden Gloves title in 1977 and had his first professional bout in December of that year. Did his early fighting in the tough school of the Arena Coliseo in Mexico City. Won his first title in December 1981 by decisioning Justo Garcia for the Mexican featherweight crown. Lost a crucial bout in June 1982 when he was halted in eight rounds in Colombia by Mario Miranda, but came back with thirteen wins and twelve stoppages, including six Mexican title defences. Was outpointed by Lenny Valdez in July 1985, but in February 1986 he challenged Azumah Nelson for the WBC title and only lost on a majority decision. Faced Nelson again in August 1987, but this time was clearly beaten over twelve rounds. Tried for the WBA crown in June 1988 against Antonio Esparragoza, but a point deducted for low blows cost him the title in a drawn verdict. A fourth world title challenge ended in failure in April 1989 when he lost a unanimous decision to Jeff Fenech. It was fifth time lucky in June 1990 when a closed eye forced Paul Hodkinson out of their fight in the eighth round and Marcos took the vacant WBC title. Made successful defences against Javier Marquez, Rafael Zuniga and Ricardo Cepeda, before losing to Hodkinson on points last November. His relentless pressure tactics have halted 46 foes, but the end is near for this gritty competitor.

19.07.91	Ulises Chong W PTS 10 Juarez
16.08.91	Ricardo Cepeda W PTS 12 Marbella *(WBC Featherweight Title Defence)*
13.11.91	Paul Hodkinson L PTS 12 Belfast *(WBC Featherweight Title Defence)*

Career: 65 contests, won 54, drew 3, lost 8.

Anaclet Wamba

Saint Brieuc, France. *Born* Congo 6 January, 1960
WBC Cruiserweight Champion. Former Undefeated European Cruiserweight Champion

6'2¾" tall. Born Luranga in the Congo and represented his country in the 1980 Olympic Games, after only one year as a boxer, losing to Australian Geoff Pike. Anaclet is now a French citizen. Moved to France and had his initial paid bout there in November 1982. Tried his hand as a heavyweight beating Winston Allen, Rocky Burton, Andy Gerrard and Dave Garside. Lost his unbeaten record when he was defeated on points by Horace Notice in London in October 1985. Continued as a heavyweight in 1986 with victories over John Westgarth, Chris Jacobs and Stewart Lithgo, but moved down to cruiserweight in 1988. Won the European crown in November 1989 by decisioning Angelo Rottoli, but relinquished the title without making a defence. Challenged Massimiliano Duran for the WBC title in December 1990, but lost his temper with the spoiling tactics of the Italian and was disqualified in the last round. Faced Duran in another bad tempered match in July 1991 and halted the Italian in round eleven. Stopped Duran in the eleventh round again in December and halted Russian Andrei Rudenko last June. Stopped 18 victims.

20.07.91	Massimiliano Duran W RSC 11 Palermo *(WBC Cruiserweight Title Challenge)*
13.12.91	Massimiliano Duran W RSC 11 Paris *(WBC Cruiserweight Title Defence)*
04.04.92	Ricky Parkey W CO 8 Levallois
30.04.92	Unknown Polanco W CO 2 Pointe a Pitre
13.06.92	Andrei Rudenko W RSC 5 Levallois *(WBC Cruiserweight Title Defence)*

Career: 39 contests, won 37, lost 2.

James Warring

Miami, USA. *Born* 26 November, 1958
IBF Cruiserweight Champion. Former Undefeated NABF Cruiserweight Champion

Has done more kickboxing than ordinary boxing. Started as a kickboxer then had three amateur fights before going back to kickboxing. Returned to boxing, going straight into the professional ranks in January 1985 at the age of 26. His second fight was a ten rounder against experienced Pat Strachan and James tired and was stopped in the eighth round. Won his next six bouts, but in 1986 went back to kickboxing. Won world titles at light-heavyweight, cruiserweight and super-heavyweight, before giving boxing another shot in 1989. In November he took an upset decision over Craig Bodzianowski, but did not fight again for a year, winning the NABF cruiserweight crown with a points victory over Nate Miller. Was then inactive for nine months. He returned to knock out James Pritchard in just 24 seconds in September 1991, the fastest ever finish to a world title fight, to lift the vacant IBF crown. Has defended his title with wins over Donnell Wingfield and Johnny Nelson. 6'4" tall. Appeared with Ernest Borgnine in the film "The Opponent". Not a polished fighter, but he is big and strong. Has nine early finishes.

06.09.91	James Pritchard W CO 1 Salemi *(Vacant IBF Cruiserweight Title)*
15.11.91	Donnell Wingfield W CO 5 Roanoke *(IBF Cruiserweight Title Defence)*
16.05.92	Johnny Nelson W PTS 12 Fredericksburg *(IBF Cruiserweight Title Defence)*

Career: 15 contests, won 14, lost 1.

Guy Waters

Sydney, Australia. *Born* London 25 May, 1964
Commonwealth L. Heavyweight Champion. Former Undefeated OPBF & Australian L. Heavyweight Champion

One of three fighting brothers who have suffered from eccentric management by their father. An over ambitious first professional fight in March 1985 saw him knocked out in two rounds by Geoff Peate. Won the Australian and OPBF titles in only his fifth bout when he decisioned Gary Hubble in February 1987. Collected the Commonwealth crown in April 1989 with a points win against Willie Featherstone. Defended the title with a decision over Roy Skeldon in September and a very close victory on points over the top rated Ugandan Yawe Davis in January 1990. Challenged Dennis Andries for the WBC crown in January 1991, but found Dennis too strong for him and lost a clear points decision. Returned in September with a good win as he retained the Commonwealth crown by outpointing the veteran, Leslie Stewart. Strong, but not a puncher, with only four stoppages.

13.09.91	Leslie Stewart W PTS 12 Melbourne *(Commonwealth L. Heavyweight Title Defence)*

Career: 17 contests, won 14, drew 1, lost 2.

Troy Waters

Sydney, Australia. *Born* London 23 April, 1965
Australian L. Middleweight Champion. Former Undefeated Commonwealth L. Middleweight Champion

5'10" tall. Comes from a fighting family. His brother Guy is the Commonwealth light-heavyweight champion and Dean is a former Australian heavyweight champion. Troy was Australian and Oceania welterweight champion before turning professional in October 1984. Challenged for the OPBF light-middleweight title in only his sixth bout and lost a close decision to In-Chul Baek in March 1986. Won the vacant Australian crown in November and halted Lloyd Hibbert for the Commonwealth title in August 1987. Retained the Commonwealth crown with victories over Gilbert Josamu, Michael Harris and Judas Clottey and then had a shot at the IBF title against Gianfranco Rosi in October 1989. Troy had Rosi badly hurt in the last round, but it was not enough and he lost on points. Defended the Commonwealth crown by knocking out Ronald Doo in April 1990, but was sidelined by an injury, and stripped of the title in 1991. Retained his Australian crown by halting Chris Seng and Craig Trotter. Has twelve quick wins.

06.12.91	Chris Seng W RSC 3 Ettalong *(Australian L. Middleweight Title Defence)*
31.01.92	Craig Trotter W RSC 3 Melbourne *(Australian L. Middleweight Title Defence)*

Career: 20 contests, won 18, lost 2.

Pernell Whitaker (left) looks set to counter a Policarpo Diaz left-hook, while making a successful defence of his world lightweight title
Tom Casino

Pernell (Sweet Pea) Whitaker

Norfolk, USA. *Born* 2 January, 1964
Former Undefeated IBF, WBC & WBA Lightweight Champion. Former Undefeated NABF & USBA Lightweight Champion

Brilliant southpaw with dazzling hand and foot speed. Generally regarded as the best boxer in the world today. 5'9" tall. Won a gold medal at featherweight in the 1984 Olympics and signed-up with Shelly Finkel and the Duva family. From his first paid fight in November 1984 he has grown in stature to totally dominate the lightweight title for three years. Won the vacant NABF title in March 1987 with a unanimous decision over Roger Mayweather, after both fighters were on the deck. Added the vacant USBA crown in July 1987, flooring Miguel Santana twice and halting him in round six with body punches. Should have become WBC champion in March 1988 when he looked to have outclassed the title holder, Jose Luis Ramirez, but two of the officials somehow voted for the Mexican. Received his just reward in February 1989 as he easily decisioned Greg Haugen to win the IBF title. One judge had Pernell fourteen points ahead. Stopped Louie Lomeli in his first defence in April 1989 and then gained revenge against Ramirez and won the vacant WBC crown, with two judges giving it to him by twelve points in a unanimous verdict. Decisioned Freddy Pendleton and Azumah Nelson in title defences and then added the WBA crown by flattening Juan Nazario with a left hook in the first round of their fight in August 1990. Made three more defences, outpointing Anthony Jones, Poli Diaz and Jorge Paez, but has now relinquished all three titles to fight at light-welterweight. Sharp puncher who has halted fourteen opponents.

27.07.91	Policarpo Diaz W PTS 12 Norfolk *(IBF, WBA & WBC Lightweight Title Defence)*
05.10.91	Jorge Paez W PTS 12 Reno *(IBF, WBA & WBC Lightweight Title Defence)*
18.01.92	Harold Brazier W PTS 10 Philadelphia
22.05.92	Jerry Lee Smith W RSC 1 Mexico City

Career: 30 contests, Won 29, Lost 1.

Arthur Williams

Pensacola, USA. *Born* 12 November, 1964
Cruiserweight

Now based in Las Vegas, he made his professional debut in November 1989. Knocked out his first three victims, but was then held to a draw in May 1990 by Sylvester White. Scored six wins before suffering a shock loss to club fighter Sim Warrior in July. Arthur had Warrior down twice in the first round, but was himself knocked out in the third. Gained revenge by stopping Sim two months later and then halted Terry Verners, Keith McMurray, Randy Leaks and Sean McClain. Registered his biggest victory in May 1992 when he decisioned Veteran Dwight Muhammad Qawi. Good puncher with thirteen stoppages.

06.07.91	Sim Warrior L CO 3 Las Vegas
13.09.91	Sim Warrior W RSC 2 Las Vegas
11.10.91	Terry Verners W CO 1 Las Vegas
12.11.91	Keith McMurray W RSC 2 Las Vegas
26.11.91	Randy Leaks W RSC 3 Reseda
28.03.92	Sean McClain W RSC 1 Las Vegas
08.05.92	Dwight Muhammad Qawi W PTS 10 Las Vegas
26.06.92	Jorge Chong W RSC 1 Las Vegas

Career: 19 contests, won 17, drew 1, lost 1.

(Prince) Charles Williams

Grand Rapids, USA. *Born* 2 June, 1962
IBF L. Heavyweight Champion.
Former Undefeated USBA L. Heavyweight Champion

Born Columbus, Mississippi. 6'1" tall. Boxed as an amateur from 1977 until 1978 and lost two of his 25 bouts, being beaten by Tony Ayala in the 1977 Junior Olympics. Turned professional when he was only 16 and was beaten by Henry Bunch in his fight in June 1978. Was thrown-in over his head in his early years, also losing to Jeff Lampkin and Marvin Johnson and being stopped in a round by Reggie Gross. A change of management in 1984 turned his career around and he has not lost since. Beat Lampkin in a return in 1985 and won the vacant USBA light-heavyweight title by outpointing James Salerno in September 1986. Sprang a major upset by forcing Bobby Czyz to retire in the ninth round of a challenge for the IBF crown in October 1987. Charles was floored in the second and only saved in the third by a standing count, which was not in the rules, but recovered to force a win. Halted Richard Caramanolis and Rufino Angulo in defences in 1988. Settled the controversy with Czyz by flooring Bobby twice and forcing him to retire after ten rounds in June 1989. Made only one defence in 1990, halting Frankie Swindell and beat Mwehu Beya, James Kinchen, Vince Boulware and Freddie Delgado in title fights in 1991. Charles has missed out on the big pay days, because he is too tough an opponent and has been avoided by the leading names. Has won his last 22 fights, with 24 inside the distance victories.

20.07.91	Vince Boulware W CO 3 San Remo *(IBF L. Heavyweight Title Defence)*
19.10.91	Freddie Delgado W RSC 2 Williamsburg *(IBF L. Heavyweight Title Defence)*

Career: 39 contests, won 33, drew 2, lost 4.

Tim (Terrible) Witherspoon

Philadelphia, USA. *Born* 27 December, 1957
USBA Heavyweight Champion.
Former WBA & WBC Heavyweight Champion. Former Undefeated NABF Heavyweight Champion

6' 3" tall, 76" reach. Turned professional in October 1979 after only six amateur fights. Was given his nickname by Muhammad Ali when acting as a sparring partner to Ali. Came to prominence in June 1982 with a points win over Renaldo Snipes, but was a 6 to 1 outsider when he challenged Larry Holmes in May 1983 for the world title. Had Holmes out on his feet in the ninth round, but lost on a split decision. Won the vacant WBC title in March 1984 by outpointing Greg Page, but lost it five months later on a decision to Pinklon Thomas. Knocked out James Broad in April 1985 for the NABF crown and retained it two months later when decisioning "Bonecrusher" Smith. Became WBA champion by outpointing Tony Tubbs in a dreary fight in January 1986 and failed a post-fight drugs test. Halted Frank Bruno in a title defence at Wembley in July 1986, but lost it in shocking fashion in December, folding in one round against Smith. He claimed he was distracted by a contract dispute with Don King for which legal action is still pending. Took eight months off and then came back to halt Mark Wills in one round. Won the USBA crown in March 1991 by outpointing Carl Williams. Slow and ponderous now, but still a dangerous puncher. Has 24 stoppages and has won his last twelve fights.

10.09.91	Art Tucker W RSC 3 Philadelphia *(USBA Heavyweight Title Defence)*
04.02.92	Jimmy Lee Smith W CO 1 Atlantic City
23.03.92	James Pritchard W PTS 10 Atlantic City

Career: 40 contests, won 37, lost 3.

Myung-Woo Yuh

Seoul, South Korea. *Born* 10 January, 1964
Former WBA L. Flyweight Champion.
Former Undefeated OPBF L. Flyweight Champion

Started boxing in 1982 and had only five amateur fights before turning professional in March that year. 5'3" tall, baby-faced fighter, who won his first thirteen fights on points before finally recording a stoppage victory against Little Bagio in April 1984. Decisioned future IBF flyweight champion Bi-Won Chung in May and in December 1984, halted Edwin Inocencio to become OPBF light-flyweight title holder. Yuh was doing his compulsory military service in December 1985 when he chased the WBA champion Joey Olivo for fifteen rounds to win a split decision and the title. Had a tough first defence against the future WBO champion Jose de Jesus in March 1986, but held on to his crown with a split decision. Halted Tomohiro Kiyuna in June, but then had a real war with Mario de Marco, before outpointing the Argentinian in November. Halted Panamanians Eduardo Tunon and Benedicto Murillo and flattened the current IBF flyweight champion, Rodolfo Blanco, in 1987. In 1988 he decisioned Willy Salazar, had his hardest defence in another split decision over de Jesus, then knocked out Putt Ohyuthanakorn and Bahar Udin. There were three more victorious defences against Katsumi Komiyama, de Marco and Kebun Taiho in 1989 and three more in 1990 against Hisashi Takashima, plus two tough battles with Leo Gamez. A tenth round stoppage of Kajkong Danphoothai in April 1991 saw Yuh reach 17 defences, but he lost the title to Hiroki Ioka in December. Never floored, he has a tight defence and limitless stamina, but only halted thirteen opponents. His 17 defences is a record for the division.

17.12.91	Hiroki Ioka L PTS 12 Osaka *(WBA L. Flyweight Title Defence)*

Career: 37 contests, won 36, lost 1.

Ysaias Zamudio

Blythe, USA. *Born* 10 May, 1969
NABF Flyweight Champion. Former Undefeated WBA Americas Flyweight Champion

Good defensive boxer, but not a heavy puncher. As an amateur his best effort was to reach the semi-finals of the 1986 United States championships. Moved into the professional ranks in August 1987 and won his first eleven bouts before being controversially disqualified against former world champion German Torres in August 1988. Was stopped in nine rounds by Willy Salazar in a challenge for the NABF light-flyweight title in September 1988, but collected the vacant WBA Americas title by knocking out Jose Diaz in April 1989. Added the NABF crown with a points win over Javier Diaz in April 1990 and has retained the title with victories in defences against Tony de Luca, Jesus Chong, Francisco Montiel and Richard Clark. Stopped only nine opponents. Unbeaten in his last eleven fights.

22.07.91	Francisco Montiel W PTS 12 Los Angeles *(NABF Flyweight Title Defence)*
21.09.91	Juan Akira W PTS 10 Indio
21.10.91	Edgar Decenas W PTS 10 Los Angeles
13.01.92	Abselon Briceno W PTS 10 Los Angeles
21.04.92	Richard Clarke W TD 8 Los Angeles *(NABF Flyweight Title Defence)*
30.06.92	Hector Diaz W RSC 2 Los Angeles

Career: 33 contests, won 29, drew 1, lost 3.

Daniel Zaragoza

Daniel Zaragoza

Mexico City, Mexico. *Born* 11 December, 1957
Former WBC Bantamweight & S. Bantamweight Champion. Former Undefeated NABF S. Bantamweight Champion. Former Undefeated Mexican Bantamweight Champion

Rock-hard, gutsy, southpaw, but prone to cuts. Won a gold medal in the 1979 Pan American Games, but was eliminated in the quarter-finals of the 1980 Olympic Games. Moved straight into the ten round class in October 1980 and scored fourteen wins before being outboxed by Harold Petty in July 1982. Collected the Mexican bantamweight title in September 1989 by decisioning Chuyin Lopez, but was beaten on points again by Petty in a challenge for the NABF crown in August 1983. Made six more defences of his Mexican title and in May 1984 he beat Freddie Jackson on a disqualification to take the vacant WBC crown. Dropped the title in his first defence to Miguel Lora on a points decision in August 1985. He moved up to super-bantamweight, losing to Jeff Fenech in April 1986, but won the NABF crown with a seventh round stoppage of Mike Ayala in December. Retained the NABF title with victories over Aaron Lopez and Darryl Thigpen in 1987 and in February 1988, halted Carlos Zarate to become WBC champion. Held on to his title with a draw against Seung-Hoon Lee in May 1988 and followed with successful defences in bouts with Valerio Nati, Paul Banke, Frankie Duarte and Chan-Yong Park. Lost the title in a war with Banke in April 1990 when Daniel was badly cut and down twice, before being halted in round nine. Regained his title in June 1991 by decisioning Kiyoshi Hatanaka and beat Chun Huh and Banke, before losing on points to Thierry Jacob. Has 20 inside the distance victories.

24.08.91	Huh Chun W PTS 12 Seoul *(WBC S. Bantamweight Title Defence)*
09.12.91	Paul Banke W PTS 12 Los Angeles *(WBC S. Bantamweight Title Defence)*
20.03.92	Thierry Jacob L PTS 12 Calais *(WBC S. Bantamweight Title Defence)*

Career: 51 contests, won 44, drew 1, lost 6.

Joel Luna Zarate

Mexico City, Mexico.
Bantamweight

As the nephew of the great Carlos Zarate he has a lot to live up to. Managed by Jorge Zarate, the brother of Carlos. As an amateur he claims 37 wins in 38 bouts, all inside the distance, with his only loss coming in a tournament in France. Turned professional in September 1988 and was voted "Newcomer of the Year" in 1989 in Mexico. Scored a notable victory in April 1991 when he won a split decision over the former IBF super-flyweight champion, Juan Polo Perez. In March 1992, he halted Colombian veteran Oscar Bolivar, who was fresh from a win over ex-world champion, Jesus Rojas. Joel has made steady progress and his fifteen stoppage wins attest to his punching power.

09.09.91	Juan Aguilar W RSC 3 Tijuana
30.09.91	Francisco Gonzalez W RSC 6 Tijuana
24.01.92	Alejandro Valenzuela W PTS 10 Hermosillo
27.03.92	Oscar Bolivar W RSC 3 Mexico City
15.06.92	Alejandro Valenzuela W RSC 8 Tijuana

Career: 20 contests, won 20.

BILLY AIRD PROMOTIONS LTD
B
A
B
A
Western House, 14 Western Road, Plaistow, London, E13 9JF
Tel: 081-552 3002/081-503 4616 Fax: 081-470 7057
TOMORROWS CHAMPIONS
DARRON GRIFFITHS
MIDDLEWEIGHT
Future world champion
BARRY THOROGOOD
LIGHT-MIDDLEWEIGHT
Ex ABA finalist
JERRY MORTIMER
LIGHT-MIDDLEWEIGHT
Always gives his best
LEE "TIGER" TAYLOR
LIGHT-WELTERWEIGHT
Young prospect who needs experience
MERVYN BENNETT
LIGHTWEIGHT
Strong fighter who wants Welsh title
BARRIE KELLEY
SUPER-FEATHERWEIGHT
Will challenge for the British title this season
KEVIN MIDDLETON
FEATHERWEIGHT
Looking for the Southern Area title this season
BARRY "BABY" JONES
FEATHERWEIGHT
The darling of Welsh boxing, another "Howard Winstone"
Trainers: Pat Thomas (Cardiff) and Jimmy Bennett (London)
WE HAVE OUR OWN TRAINING FACILITIES IN LONDON AND CARDIFF

World Title Bouts, 1991-92

2 July, 1991 Fahlan Lukmingkwan 7.7 (Thailand) W PTS 12 Abdy Pohan 7.5½ (Indonesia), Bangkok, Thailand. IBF Mini-Flyweight Title Defence.

Although successfully defending his title for the fourth time, Lukmingkwan once again made heavy weather of what should have been a formality. After the challenger was put down in the third round, the recipient of a big left-hook, he rallied well enough to last the distance, without unduly troubling the Thai. The contest itself fell well short of championship standard and neither fighter enhanced his reputation. *Judges Scorecards:* 116-110, 115-111, 116-110.

12 July, 1991 Tony Lopez 9.4 (USA) W RSC 6 Lupe Guttierez 9.4 (USA), Lake Tahoe, USA. IBF Super-Featherweight Title Defence.

In a most one-sided, yet very exciting and bloody contest, Lopez retained his title at two minutes, 42 seconds of the sixth round when the referee rescued the brave challenger from further punishment. Right from the first bell, Lopez got to work, but both men were badly cut over their left eyes during an all-action second round. Lopez continued to pound away, round after round, forcing the challenger against the ropes, setting him up with jabs and firing in punches over the top. Guttierez tried everything he knew in trying to stem the tide, but was outgunned and further cuts on the left eye meant he was almost blind on that side. The champion then went into top gear, sending Guttierez crashing through the ropes at which juncture the fight was stopped.

13 July, 1991 Gianfranco Rosi 10.13½ (Italy) W PTS 12 Glenn Wolfe 10.13¾ (USA), Avezzano, Italy. IBF Light-Middleweight Title Defence.

Fighting a predictable campaign, Rosi got off to a good start throwing clusters of jabs, leads and hooks and mixing them up cleverly. However, he received a shock in the third when Wolfe put him down for the mandatory eight count, but he quickly recovered to take the play away from the 29-year-old challenger. And, apart from another left-hook in the fifth which buckled his knees, Rosi was very much in the driving seat. With the American's eyes swelling alarmingly under the constant attention of the champion's fists, Rosi cruised to an easy points victory. *Judges Scorecards:* 118-109, 118-110, 119-109.

20 July, 1991 Kaosai Galaxy 8.3 (Thailand) W RSC 5 David Griman 8.2 (Venezuela), Bangkok, Thailand, WBA Super-Flyweight Title Defence.

After making a useful start, Griman was forced to the ropes in the second round where he was battered from head to body. This was the sign of things to come as Galaxy's sustained aggression continually forced the challenger backwards. In the fifth the champion really cut loose with big combination punches, flooring Griman for a count of eight. On regaining his feet, the referee came to the challenger's rescue, following three or four heavy blows delivered without reply. Galaxy, thus retained his title for the 18th time, having been champion since 1984.

20 July, 1991 Charles Williams 12.6¼ (USA) W CO 3 Vince Boulware 12.6¼ (USA), San Remo. Italy. IBF Light-Heavyweight Title Defence.

Boulware certainly made the champion think he was going to be in a battle for the opening two rounds, but from thereon it was all one way traffic. Coming out for the third like a train, Williams blasted the challenger to the canvas with an old fashioned one-two and on rising, Boulware was given no respite, being decked again from a big right to the head. This time he had no hope of getting up and the referee completed the count at two minutes, 49 seconds of the round.

20 July, 1991 Anaclet Wamba 13.7 (France) W RSC 11 Masimilliano Duran 13.1¾ (Italy), Palermo, Italy. WBC Cruiserweight Title Challenge.

Making a good start, Duran soon got behind the left-jab, but before the end of the second round he was badly cut over the right eye. From then on he decided to negate his opponent's work by holding whenever the opportunity arose and generally messing him around. By the eleventh, Duran was so tired from his exertions that he tripped over himself and with Wamba now in full flow, he appeared to walk back to his corner, as if to retire. Wamba was having none of it and Duran was soon put down on his knees where the referee waved it over with only 42 seconds of the round gone.

20 July, 1991 Sung-Il Moon 8.2½ (South Korea) W CO 5 Ernesto Ford 8.2½ (Panama), Seoul, South Korea. WBC Super-Flyweight Title Defence.

The challenger made an excellent start, nailing Moon with heavy punches from both hands. But after being warned to keep his punches up in the third, he lost his way. Struggling to get past the jab and cut over the right eye, Moon switched his attack to the body with immediate results. By now Ford was also cut over the right eye and beginning to fight a rearguard action as the punches continued to get through. After suffering a short spell on the deck in the fifth, Ford was immediately put down again and, on failing to get to his feet, was counted out at two minutes, 35 seconds of the round.

20 July, 1991 John David Jackson 10.13 (USA) W PTS 12 Tyrone Trice 11.0 (USA), McKee City, USA. WBO Light-Middleweight Title Defence.

Backpeddling furiously for the duration of the contest, the champion left nothing to chance as he pushed out the jab and moved, leaving the challenger chasing shadows for

The southpaw WBO light-middleweight champion, John David Jackson (left), retained his title against Tyrone Trice, despite suffering a knockdown in the final round Tom Casino

most of the time. Flicking southpaw jabs from Jackson did no real damage, but were effective point scorers, while Trice methodically walked forward, failing to cut the ring off, round after round and was unable to land any telling blows of his own. Trice had some success in the sixth, when a cluster of right hands stunned Jackson, but that was to be his last real opportunity until the final round. In the twelfth, after being caught by two thudding right hands, Jackson was finally toppled over. He beat the referees count with a bit to spare and clutched and sped out of range for the remainder of the round in order to foil the by now charged up Trice, who simply ran out of time. *Judges Scorecards:* 116-111, 116-111, 117-110.

27 July, 1991 Mauro Galvano 11.12½ (Italy) W PTS 12 Ronnie Essett 11.13¼ (USA), Capo d'Orlando, Italy. WBC Super-Middleweight Title Defence.

Very even for the first seven rounds, Galvano began to assert himself in the eighth, hurting Essett badly with a couple of solid punches. At this stage, super-fit Galvano went into another gear, moving on his toes, keeping the left-jab in Essett's face continuously and landing several solid rights without reply. Earlier in the contest, Essett had some success with body shots, but had not been able to slow Galvano enough to stop him staging a grandstand finish. *Judges Scorecards:* 116-114, 117-115, 118-115.

27 July, 1991 Pernell Whitaker 9.9 (USA) W PTS 12 Policarpo Diaz 9.7¾ (Spain), Norfolk, USA. World Lightweight Title Defence.

In a battle between the bull and the matador, Whitaker, reckoned by many to be the best pound for pound fighter about, found the Spaniard not only elusive, but as tough as nails. The champion stuck with the jab and fired in punches over the top, but Diaz, so often unpredictable, threw overarm punches from inconceivable angles with a fair bit of success and would not give in, despite obvious rib damage. It was untidy and often a scramble, but you could take nothing away from the Spaniard who was given no chance at all at the start and who gave Whitaker his toughest fight to date. At the finish, the scorelines did not accurately portray Diaz's performance. *Judges Scorecards:* 120-108, 120-106, 120-107.

9 August, 1991 Bobby Czyz 13.6 (USA) W PTS 12 Bash Ali 13.6 (Nigeria), Atlantic City, USA. WBA Cruiserweight Title Defence.

Facing a challenger who never even looked like winning a round. Czyz refused to inject any fire into the contest, being happy instead to keep out of trouble and to control matters from distance. As durable as they come, Ali tried his hardest, but with very limited resources the best he could do was to bravely stay the course and soak up the punches. Lacking balance, the Nigerian was always easy to find and Czyz, although his blows lacked any real snap, took full advantage and coasted to a very easy points win. *Judges Scorecards:* 120-108, 120-108, 120-108.

10 August, 1991 Isidro Perez 7.13 (Mexico) W PTS 12 Alli Galvez 7.13 (Chile), Santiago, Chile. WBO Flyweight Title Defence.

In what ultimately turned out to be a tough defence, Perez began well by getting his jab working to outbox his tough rival over the first few rounds and in doing so built up a solid lead. But by the middle rounds, Galvez was beginning to come more into the action as he took the fight to the champion and cut down the ring space. With the contest drawing towards its conclusion and with both men still having every chance of victory, Perez came with a late charge to put the decision beyond doubt, his cleaner punching winning the day. *Judges Scorecards:* 118-112, 115-113, 116-117.

12 August, 1991 Manuel Medina 8.13¾ (Mexico) W PTS 12 Troy Dorsey 8.13¾ (USA), Los Angeles, USA. IBF Featherweight Title Challenge.

Despite being floored in both the second and third rounds, the challenger came right back into the fight, effectively using his five inch reach advantage and gradually turned Dorsey's features into a bloody mess. Making his first championship defence, Dorsey had the dynamite to finish the job, but found it difficult to nail such an elusive moving target and by the seventh his right eye was cascading blood. Medina, who up to that point had picked up points with fast cuffing blows that lacked any real power, had suddenly become the predator. From then on Dorsey struggled desperately to stem the flow of leather coming his way as cuts over both eyes almost blinded him, but he bravely stuck to his guns to last the distance. *Judges Scorecards:* 115-112, 115-111, 114-111.

16 August, 1991 Marcos Villasana 9.0 (Mexico) W PTS 12 Ricardo Cepeda 9.0 (Puerto Rico), Marbella, Spain. WBC Featherweight Title Defence.

Cepeda made a good start with his hand speed dominating the early rounds. Then slowly, but surely, Villasana began to get going as he pressured his opponent and started to land punches with both hands blazing away. From then on the New York based challenger lost his composure and early sparkle as he rapidly tired. Villasana now had the bit between the teeth and was hardly likely to relinquish his hold on the bout as he remorselessly pushed on to a points victory. *Judges Scorecards:* 117-110, 116-114, 118-112.

16 August, 1991 Terry Norris 10.13 (USA) W RSC 1 Brett Lally 11.0 (USA), San Diego, USA. WBC Light-Middleweight Title Defence.

What on paper appeared to be a reasonable match turned into the division's third quickest victory. The rugged Lally came to fight, attacking wildly from the onset, while Norris tentatively bobbed and weaved from distance. Suddenly, after freeing himself from a clinch, Norris detonated his first punch of the fight, a sweeping left-hook. Lally went down hard, but on rising found the champion biding his time, picking his shots and waiting for the opening to present itself. A series of blows put the challenger on the deck again and when getting up on rubbery legs a cracking right to the jaw floored him for the third time. The referee didn't even bother to count, calling it off at two minutes, 40 seconds of the first round.

17 August, 1991 Darrin van Horn 12.0 (USA) W RSC 3 John Jarvis 12.0 (USA), Irvine, USA. IBF Super-Middleweight Title Defence.

In an impressive first defence, van Horn sensed that Jarvis, who hadn't fought for over a year, would be ring rusty. Getting to work quickly, he soon realised that the challenger did not have the equipment to bother him too much and set about dismantling him. Jarvis had no answer to the bombardment, looking worn and bereft of how to turn the course of the fight and succumbed to a big right in the third round. The referee called it off, without completing the count, with only 71 seconds of the round completed.

24 August, 1991 Daniel Zaragoza 8.9¾ (Mexico) W PTS 12 Huh Chun 8.9¾ (South Korea), Seoul, South Korea. WBC Super-Bantamweight Title Defence.

Zaragoza dominated throughout, despite receiving a badly cut forehead in the sixth round, while the negative South Korean did very little scoring of his own, relying on the champion's cut to worsen. Instead, the 26-year-old Chun was repeatedly forced on the back foot by southpaw punches that found the mark with regular monotony. By the tenth, Chun had received a cut eye himself, but although it was not that serious, he was unable to pick up the pace, thus allowing Zaragoza to cruise home to an easy points victory. *Judges Scorecards:* 118-108, 118-107, 119-106.

31 August, 1991 Jesse Benavides 8.10 (USA) W RSC 5 Fernando Ramos 8.9 (Mexico), Corpus Christi, USA. WBO Super-Bantamweight Title Defence.

Although biding his time, Benavides handed his challenger a steady battering as he got down to work right from the opening bell. Ramos was not in the same league as the American for skill, but proved his toughness in withstanding the heavy bombardment of punches delivered by the confident Benavides, who currently looks better than any of the other champions in the division. By the fifth, the fight had become so one-sided that the champion obviously felt that the time was right to end the contest there and then and he unloaded a brutal barrage of head blows, before the referee jumped in to rescue a very game challenger indeed with 55 seconds of the round remaining.

6 September, 1991 James Warring 13.4½ (USA) W CO 1 James Pritchard 13.7¾ (USA), Salemi, Italy. Vacant IBF Cruiserweight Title.

When Jeff Lampkin vacated the title he would have scarcely believed that a twelve-bout novice would not only be nominated to contest the crown, but would actually go on to win it inside 24 seconds, especially against a seasoned campaigner. Warring didn't even take a punch as he produced a couple of left-jabs, followed by a stunning right which left Pritchard flat on the canvas where the referee counted him out. The 32-year-old, a late arrival on the scene after years of kick-boxing activity, promised he would make up for time lost by becoming a busy champion.

7 September, 1991 Dave McAuley 7.13 (GB) W CO 10 Jacob Matlala 7.11¾ (South Africa), Belfast, Northern Ireland. IBF Flyweight Title Defence.

The tiny challenger, standing only 4' 9½", was not powerful enough to unduly worry the Irishman who was defending his title for the fifth time in just over two years. Matlala's only real chance to win was by getting inside with his short arm punching, even though he lacked any real power and work away. Occasionally, McAuley allowed himself to be taken to the ropes, but in the main he controlled the fight at distance with the left hand. However, in the tenth round the champion delivered a perfect one-two combination which sent Matlala crashing to the canvas where he was counted out in the act of rising at two minutes, 23 seconds of the round.

11 September, 1991 Jeff Harding 12.5 (Australia) W PTS 12 Dennis Andries 12.7 (GB), London, England. WBC Light-Heavyweight Title Challenge.

Recovering from a fearful battering in the first round, Harding came right back matching Andries blow for blow. Neither fighter was decked, although you have to wonder how and the only real surface damage suffered by either man was a cut right eye for Andries. For courage, determination and valour, this was one of the greatest fights ever seen in a British ring, as both fighters landed with punches that would have shattered normal men. How they sustained such workrate and power over twelve rounds was beyond comprehension and the only sadness at the end had to be when two judges decided on Harding as a very narrow winner. The other judge got it right as neither fighter deserved to leave the ring a loser. *Judges Scorecards:* 115-114, 115-113, 114-114.

12 September, 1991 Duke McKenzie 8.6 (GB) W PTS 12 Cesar Soto 8.5¼ (Mexico), London, England. WBO Bantamweight Title Defence.

Constantly making the running, the challenger made a good fight of it but he did not have the know-how to be able to draw McKenzie into an out and out battle, although the champion was forced on occasion to absorb some heavy blows to the head. McKenzie was more than capable of countering with the jab, but as he tired he resorted to holding and tying the challenger up. In the tenth, the champion was badly hurt for the first time in the fight when a right hand bounced off his head, but he weathered the storm out well before getting back on his toes in round eleven. Soto kept trying to the last, but McKenzie made sure that he did not get another opportunity and was well worth the points decision that went his way. *Judges Scorecards:* 117-114, 118-110, 117-113.

13 September, 1991 Brian Mitchell 9.3 (South Africa) W PTS 12 Tony Lopez 9.4 (USA), Sacramento, USA. IBF Super-Featherweight Title Challenge.

Unfortunately, this return match never lived up to expectations with Mitchell climbing all over the champion, never missing with the jab and effectively slipping any leather coming his way. The only time that Lopez had any real success was when he occasionally swamped the South African with punches. Although cut on the side of his right eye as early as the third round, Mitchell was not perturbed and weathered any mini-storm that occured by controlling the fight on the front foot with that unerringly accurate jab. That was the general pattern of the bout, Mitchell scoring, while Lopez wasted too many punches on thin air, resulting in the unanimous decision going to the South African. *Judges Scorecards:* 116-112, 115-113, 117-111.

14 September, 1991 Julio Cesar Chavez 10.0 (Mexico) W PTS 12 Lonnie Smith 10.0 (USA), Las Vegas, USA. WBC Light-Welterweight Title Defence.

From the first bell to last, "Lightnin'" Lonnie Smith showed where he had picked up his nickname; not for his fast hands, but more for his running ability. Chavez at least tried to make a fight of it, but was thwarted by the challenger who got on his skates the moment the two got within distance. Punching from out of range, Smith just wasn't in it. As the contest wore on and Smith tired, Chavez started to get to grips with his man. The last round saw Chavez hitting his opponent at will on his way to an easy points decision. *Judges Scorecards:* 118-106, 119-107, 118-109.

14 September, 1991 Julian Jackson 11.4 (USA) W CO 1 Dennis Milton 11.5 (USA), Las Vegas, USA. WBC Middleweight Title Defence.

Making a fast start, Jackson moved straight into the challenger, whose only immediate answer was to grimly hold on for dear life. As the referee broke them from a clinch, Jackson exploded a right on Milton's head. Milton desperately tried to remain upright by firstly clutching at the ropes and then pushing Jackson across the ring. The champion merely bided his time, before landing a short right to Milton's jaw, which sent him to the canvas, almost in slow motion. Gamely he tried to make it upright before being counted out at two minutes, ten seconds of the first round.

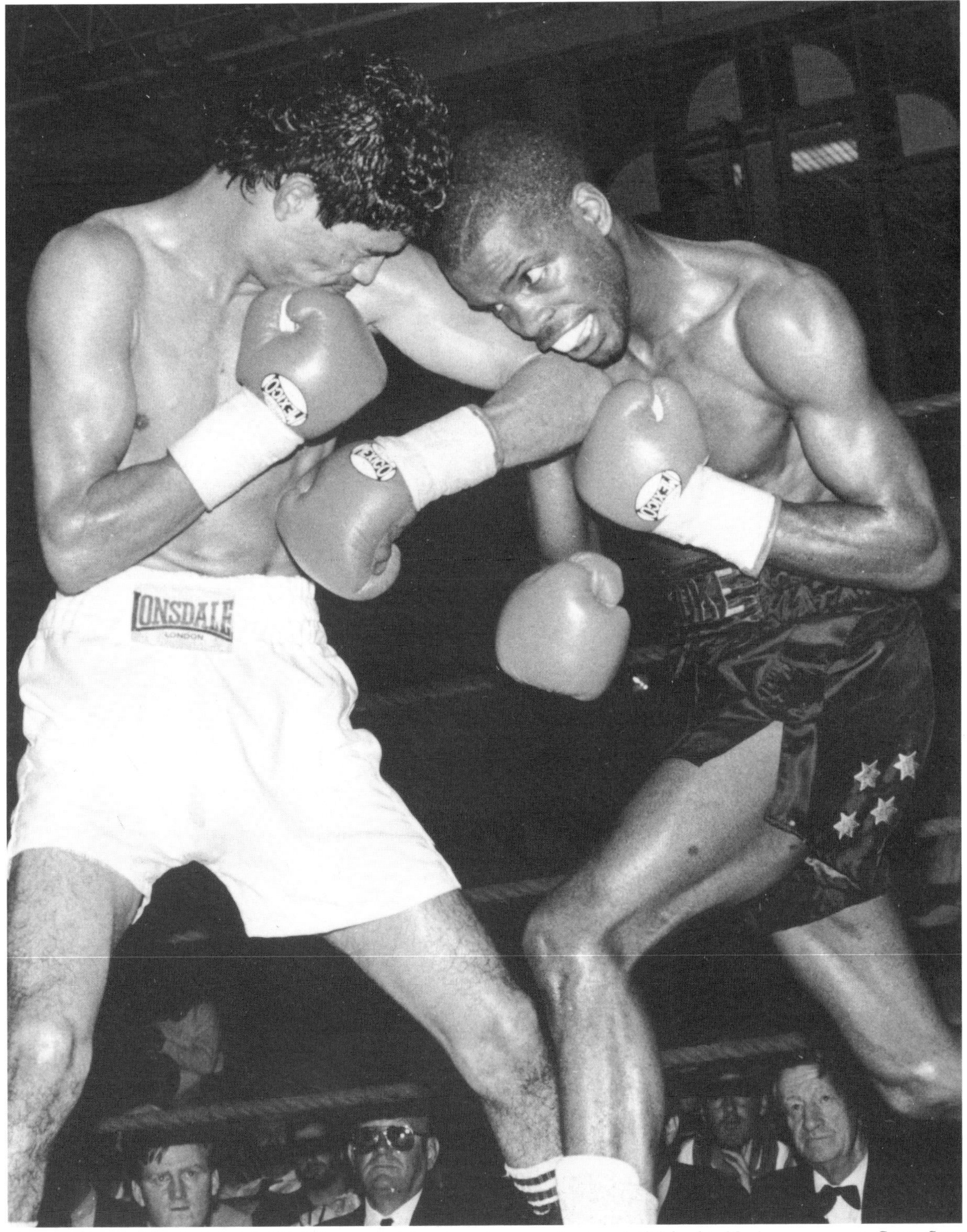

Duke McKenzie (right), Britain's WBO bantamweight champion, was far too skilful for his Mexican opponent, Cesar Soto and won going away

Tony Fitch

14 September, 1991 Kyun-Yung Park 8.13½ (South Korea) W PTS 12 Eloy Rojas 8.12½ (Venezuela), Mokpo, South Korea. WBA Featherweight Title Defence.

Making an impressive start, Park floored Rojas with a right-hook in the first round. The challenger, on getting up, did well to survive the champion's non-stop attack and countered effectively off the back foot to hear the bell. As the bout progressed, Park continued to push Rojas back, dominating with fast hooking punches. In the sixth both men received eye damage and Rojas from that point on looked to exact some pressure of his own as the champion appeared to tire. However, Park cleverly held on, thwarting the challenger's attacking firepower to gain a clear points verdict. *Judges Scorecards:* 118-110, 116-111, 118-113.

14 September, 1991 Dingaan Thobela 9.8¼ (South Africa) W PTS 12 Antonio Rivera 9.8¾ (Puerto Rico), Johannesburg, South Africa. WBO Lightweight Title Defence.

Following a slow start, the pace picked up in the fifth when Thobela was caught with a cracking left-hook to the jaw, which left him exposed to a further barrage of blows to the head. The champion then showed his true mettle by pushing Rivera against the ropes and evading the ensuing punches until his head had cleared. Thobela got back in control in the sixth and backed Rivera up with solid punches to the head and although there was very little activity during the next two rounds, the ninth saw plenty of give and take action. The final three sessions were a bit of an anti-climax with both men tiring rapidly, which enabled Thobela to showboat his way to a clear points victory. *Judges Scorecards:* 117-112, 115-113, 118-112.

15 September, 1991 Manning Galloway 10.7 (USA) W PTS 12 Jeff Malcolm 10.5½ (Australia), Broadbeach, Australia. WBO Welterweight Title Defence.

While always punching faster than Malcolm, the champion often fought in spurts, only doing what he had to do to remain in control. Galloway's southpaw jab had opened up quite a lead by the end of the fourth and from then on the Australian was always playing second fiddle as the champion dictated the pace. Although Malcolm often got home with useful looking punches, it was noticeable that Galloway was still in full control, even when boxing in a negative fashion. The extremely skilful champion was always several moves ahead of his rival and was rarely under pressure as he cruised an easy victory. *Judges Scorecards:* 118-110, 118-109, 118-112.

19 September, 1991 Joichiro Tatsuyoshi 8.5¼ (Japan) W RSC 11 Greg Richardson 8.4 (USA), Tokyo, Japan. WBC Bantamweight Title Challenge.

After a fairly measured start by both fighters, the challenger decided in the third round that he had to absorb Richardson's jab if the need be in order to concentrate on the body to slow the older man down. The plan began to

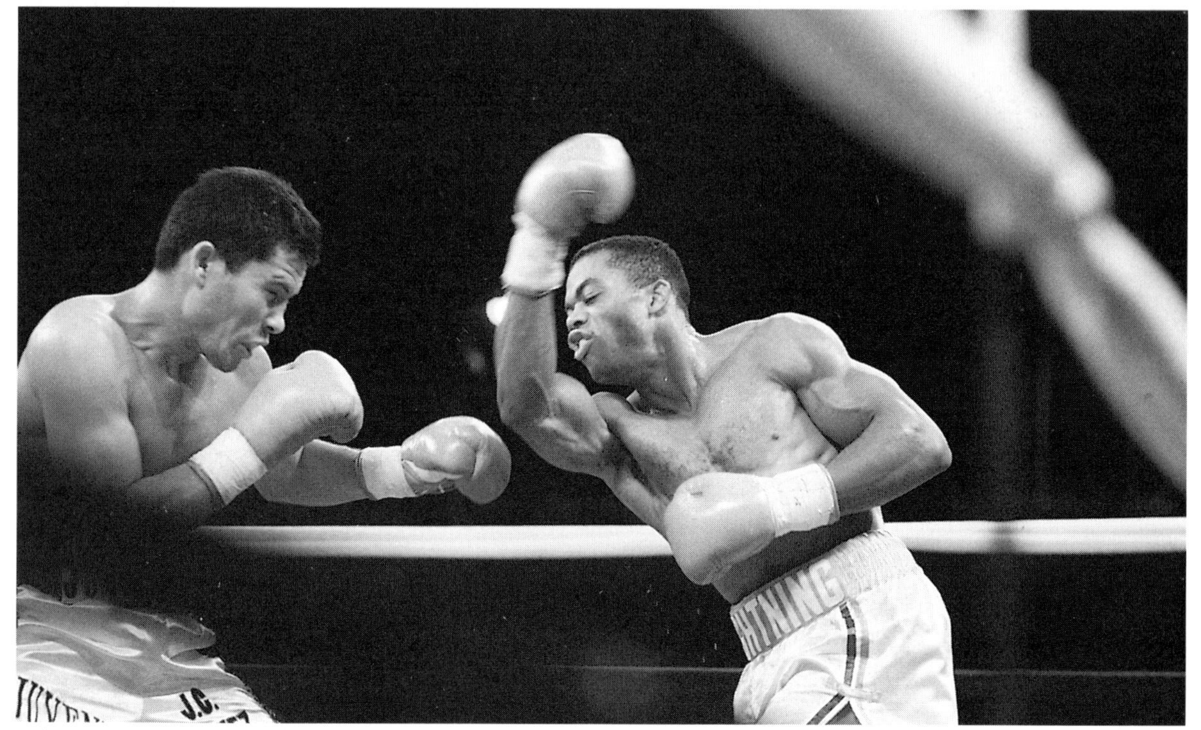

Julio Cesar Chavez (left) successfully defended his WBC light-welterweight title against Lonnie Smith, who kept on the run to go the distance

Chris Farina

The fight is nearly over for Dennis Milton as WBC middleweight champion, Julian Jackson, sends his rival to the floor

pay dividends with Richardson forced to retreat, but in the seventh the champion had his best round to date as he battered Tatsuyoshi with great head punches. Somehow, the Jap stayed errect and it was he not Richardson who came forward incessantly in the eighth, mixing straight punches up with hooks and uppercuts to befuddle the champion. Again in the ninth the pattern was repeated, with Richardson under intense pressure and by now a long way behind on points. The American, a well and truly beaten fighter in the tenth, was subjected to vicious attacks to both head and body and looked to be on the verge of going down several times. Somehow he made it back to the corner at the end of the round, whereupon the third man was called over and told of his retirement.

21 September, 1991 Chris Eubank 11.13 (GB) W RSC 12 Michael Watson 11.12 (GB), London, England. Vacant WBO Super-Middleweight Title.

Michael Watson was just over a round away from scoring a sensational victory over his old adversary, Chris Eubank, when tragedy struck in the shape of a crunching right-uppercut bang on the jaw, which ultimately left him in hospital suffering from severe brain damage. Until that moment, Watson had appeared to be well on the road to victory, having continuously been on the attack, after being stung by remarks made following their earlier contest that he had been too negative. The punch that sealed Watson's fate came immediately after he had sent Eubank sprawling on the deck in the eleventh, the recipient of two good right hand deliveries. Getting off the floor, a desperate Eubank caught Watson by surprise and while the latter got to his feet at the count of eight and somehow stayed upright until the bell, he was gone. Allowed out for the twelfth and under intense pressure, Watson was rescued by the referee, Roy Francis, just two minutes and 31 seconds of the round remaining.

22 September, 1991 Orlando Canizales 8.6 (USA) W PTS 12 Fernie Morales 8.6 (USA), Indio, USA. IBF Bantamweight Title Defence.

Canizales controlled the fight from beginning to end, counter-punching his way to a conclusive points win. The challenger was floored twice, once in the second from a left-right combination and again in the twelfth, from a left-hook. The upright style of Morales was much to the champion's liking and Canizales took full advantage. Although Morales shipped heavy punishment he finished the contest upright, but was later admitted to hospital after collapsing in a critical condition on leaving the arena. *Judges Scorecards:* 116-111, 118-109, 119-107.

28 September, 1991 Welcome Ncita 8.10 (South Africa) W PTS 12 Jesus Rojas 8.10 (Colombia), Sun City, South Africa. IBF Super-Bantamweight Title Defence.

A bad tempered contest was witnessed between two very different styles of opponent when the referee lost control very early on. Using a flashy jab and move routine, Ncita gradually built up a solid points lead over the tough challenger, who persisted with foul blows as his timing continuously let him down. Time and time again Rojas tried to rough the champion up, mainly on the inside, and occasionally Ncita responded with a blatant butt, or two of his own. When discovering that his punching power did not bother Rojas too much, Ncita merely responded by dancing

Michael Watson (left) sends Chris Eubank, floundering against the ropes during their battle for the vacant WBO super-middleweight title

Action Images

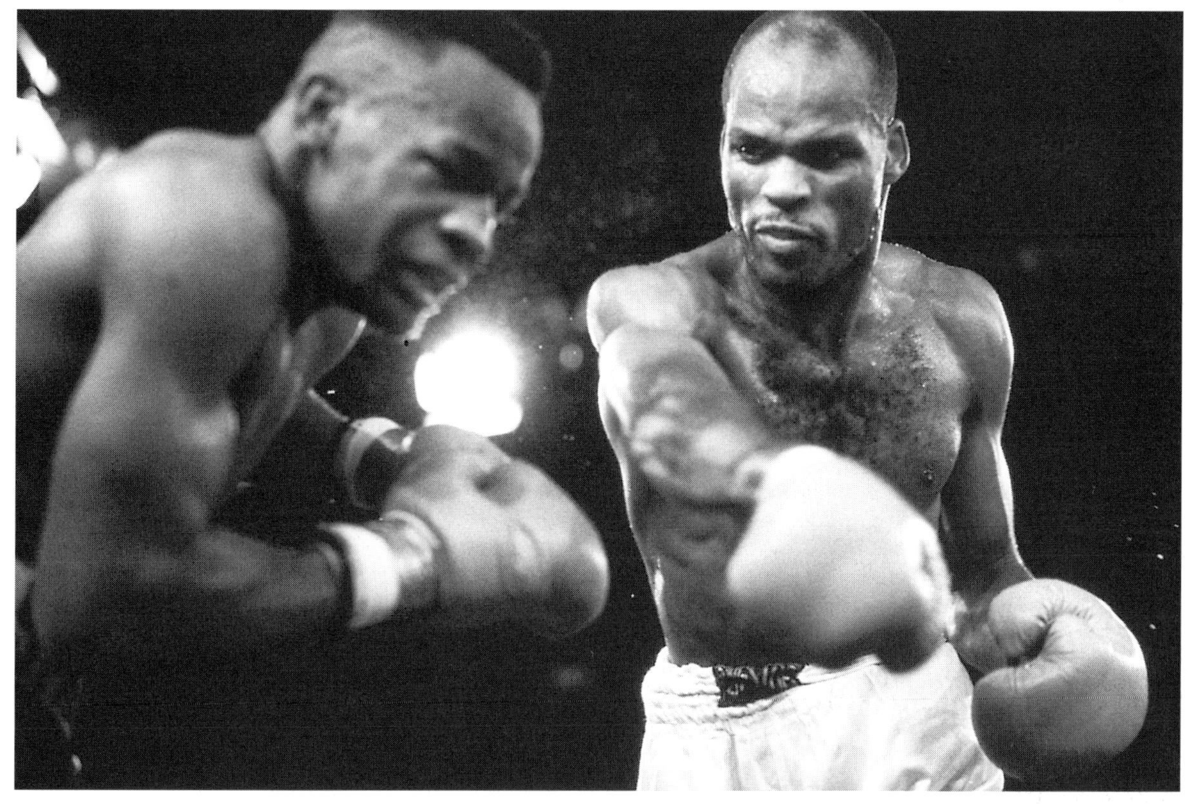

In a war for the vacant IBF welterweight title, Maurice Blocker (right) outsmarted the younger Glenwood Brown to take the crown
Tom Casino

his way backwards to an inevitable points win. *Judges Scorecards:* 115-113, 115-113, 109-119.

3 October, 1991 Vinnie Pazienza 11.0 (USA) W RSC 12 Gilbert Dele 11.0 (France), Providence, USA. WBA Light-Middleweight Title Challenge.

Even with his huge reach advantage, Dele was unable to make use of his jab as Pazienza, arms held low and switching from side-to-side, completely bemused the Frenchman throughout. The champion was unable to find any rhythm and any room to fire his much vaunted big right hand punches, seeming slow and ponderous by comparison to Pazienza, who had moved up two weights in his bid to become a world champion again. After two minutes, ten seconds of the last round, with Dele under pressure against the ropes taking punches without reply, he suddenly turned and walked to his corner, obviously disorientated, claiming temporary blindness, whereby the referee halted the contest in Pazienza's favour.

4 October, 1991 Maurice Blocker 10.7 (USA) W PTS 12 Glenwood Brown 10.7 (USA), Atlantic City, USA. Vacant IBF Welterweight Title.

The much taller Blocker had far too much height and reach and ring savvy over his aggressive rival, who at the end of the day received a lesson in the art of boxing. Brown soon made the running, but was consistently picked off by the jab and found it difficult to make anything count as Blocker either held, used the shoulder, or rode with the blows. Had Brown been able to work steadily on the inside, the result could have been reversed, while he should be thankful that Blocker is only a moderate puncher. Towards the end both men were tired, but continued to maintain their workrate. *Judges Scorecards:* 117-111, 117-111, 114-115.

5 October, 1991 Pernell Whitaker 9.9 (USA) W PTS 12 Jorge Paez 9.9 (Mexico), Reno, USA. World Lightweight Title Defence.

As much as he tried to stamp his mark on the contest, Paez just did not carry the weight well enough, looking soft around the middle and not having the reach to do any real work on the outside. Whitaker, for his part, slotted in the southpaw jab cleverly, while Paez desperately tried to get the inside position, without too much success. Towards the end of the sixth, a collision of heads gashed Paez's right eye and from then on it was really a matter of whether the challenger would go the distance. That he did was a credit to his bravery, but at the finish he had been well outscored. *Judges Scorecards:* 115-112, 115-111, 116-110.

5 October, 1991 Yong-Kang Kim 7.13¾ (South Korea) W PTS 12 Luis Gamez 7.12¾ (Venezuela), Inchon, South Korea. WBA Flyweight Title Defence.

Although the challenger showed plenty of aggression from start to finish, it was not enough as he was more often than not outpunched by the harder-hitting Kim. Cuts over both eyes in the early stages of the contest also hampered Gamez, a former mini-flyweight champion back in 1988, but he gamely continued to take the contest to the champion, before eventually going down narrowly on points. *Judges Scorecards:* 116-114, 116-114, 115-113.

7 October, 1991 Raul Perez 8.9¾ (Mexico) W PTS 12 Luis Mendoza 8.9½ (Colombia), Los Angeles, USA. WBA Super-Bantamweight Title Challenge.

Carrying a huge reach advantage, the challenger immediately found the range with the jab as Mendoza looked for his own counter punches to take effect. Both men proved to be cagey in a clash of styles and both knew how to take care of themselves in tight corners, but because of that the contest did not take off. The champion had some brief success when concentrating on Perez's body, but those attacks were only sporadic and Mendoza often appeared to be idling the time away. As the fight drew to a close with the champion coming more and more into it, it could be noticed that Perez was tiring, but he was still good value for his victory. *Judges Scorecards:* 116-114, 115-114, 111-117.

12 October, 1991 James Toney 11.6 (USA) W RSC 4 Francesco dell'Aquila 11.4¾ (Italy), Monaco, Monte Carlo. IBF Middleweight Title Defence.

Amidst amazing pre-fight scenes, the IBF allowed Toney's title defence to go ahead as planned even though the champion could not officially make the weight. Toney quickly got to work, dropping dell'Aquila for a count of three in the first round, but the Italian cleverly covered up to get through to the bell. Rounds two and three saw the challenger prodding away with short arm punches without any real effect, although it was noticeable that Toney was blowing hard. With weight making obviously beginning to take its toll, Toney gave it everything in the fourth, winging in punches from every conceivable angle. Finally, lefts and rights sent dell'Aquila down against the ropes where the referee dispensed with the count and brought the contest to a halt.

Seconds before the finish. Ray Mercer (left) takes Tommy Morrison to the ropes in defence of his WBO heavyweight title
Tom Casino

18 October, 1991 Ray Mercer 16.1 (USA) W RSC 5 Tommy Morrison 15.11¾ (USA), Atlantic City, USA. WBO Heavyweight Title Defence.

After repeatedly beating Mercer to the punch during the first three rounds, it looked extremely likely at that stage that the title would almost certainly end up in the challenger's hands. But in the fourth the tide began to turn as the champion finally found the range for some awesome right hand punches, which would have knocked lesser men out. At this stage both men had shown great resilience and courage, but the end was nigh. Early in the fifth, Mercer connected with a heavy right-left which sent the challenger veering along the ropes, before six more crushing blows landed on the defenceless Morrison who finally toppled to the canvas. The referee who had been "trying" to stop the fight a punch or two earlier, called it off without a count, 28 seconds into the round.

19 October, 1991 Israel Contrerras 8.5½ (Venezuela) W CO 5 Luisito Espinosa 8.6 (Philippines), Manila, Philippines. WBA Bantamweight Title Challenge.

Right from the off, Contrerras took the fight to the champion, but in a hectic second session he was decked twice and only just made it back to his corner. Changing tactics, the challenger began to concentrate on Espinosa's body. Espinosa had had great difficulty making the weight and this ploy soon began to pay off. In the fifth, a flurry of punches toppled the Filipino over and on rising he was floored for the second time. Even when Espinosa managed to get up yet again it was to no avail as a big left-hook smashed him to the canvas where he was counted out at two minutes, 16 seconds of the round.

19 October, 1991 Charles Williams 12.4 (USA) W RSC 2 Freddie Delgado 12.5 (Puerto Rico), Williamsburg, USA. IBF Light-Heavyweight Title Defence.

It was clear from the start that Delgado was not going to be a good match for Williams, especially as he had already been stopped in a round by Michael Moorer for the WBO title two years earlier. Within a minute of the opening bell, combination punches to the head had forced the challenger to take a standing count and while Delgado did well to get through to the interval, the writing was on the wall. As the second got under way the two fighters collided, leaving Williams with a cut above the left eye. Sensing it was time to go to work and stepping up a gear, Williams took Delgado to the ropes where he hit him with several solid shots to the head without reply. The now defenceless challenger was rescued by the referee at two minutes, 24 seconds of the round.

21 October, 1991 Fahlan Lukmingkwan 7.7 (Thailand) W PTS 12 Andy Tabanas 7.5 (Philippines), Bangkok, Thailand. IBF Mini-Flyweight Title Defence.

In an untidy maul of a contest, Tabanas was extremely dubious about taking any initiative, preferring to stand off and occasionally bundle in head down. The challenger was floored twice by left-hooks, in the eighth and again in the tenth. Both fighters lost their balance many times and in several instances both were wrestled to the canvas. The fight went the distance mainly because Lukmingkwan, instead of standing back and picking his punches with effect, seemed at loss what to do with an awkward opponent, who seemed intent on survival. *Judges Scorecards:* 115-112, 115-112, 116-112.

25 October, 1991 Muangchai Kitikasem 8.0 (Thailand) W PTS 12 Alberto Jimenez 8.0 (Mexico), Bangkok, Thailand. WBC Flyweight Title Defence.

In a battle of varying fortunes, the champion just about got home following a last round finish that must have influenced at least two of the judges. Kitikasem also had to climb off the floor in the third after being nailed by the strong Mexican. To his credit, however, he fought back resolutely, his conditioning paying off. Round after round as Jimenez came forward unremittingly in his bid to take the title back home, he found the Thai equal to the task. And when the bell rang for the last time and the judges scorecards had been totted up, it was the cleaner, more correct punching Kitikasem who was adjudged the winner. *Judges Scorecards:* 117-110, 115-114, 114-114.

26 October, 1991 Hi-Yon Choi 7.6¾ (South Korea) W PTS 12 Bong-Jun Kim 7.6½ (South Korea), Seoul, South Korea. WBA Mini-Flyweight Title Defence.

Choi repeated his title winning performance over fellow-countryman, Kim, when again collecting a clear points win on all three judges scorecards. The champion got off to a sound start, picking up the points with good stiff jabs, until Kim took up the pace in the middle rounds and made a fight of it. *Judges Scorecards:* 118-111, 117-112, 117-112.

9 November, 1991 Maurizio Stecca 8.13½ (Italy) W RTD 9 Tim Driscoll 8.13¾ (GB). Campione d'Italia, Italy. WBO Featherweight Title Defence.

Boxing in a much higher class than that which he had previously been accustomed to, Driscoll started off in confident mood and quickly gained the respect of the champion. After shading the first round, the Englishman continued to box well, but by the fourth, Stecca began to find the range for punches of his own and in the fifth, Driscoll picked up a cut left eye as both men exchanged right hands. Following a couple of fairly quiet rounds, Stecca landed several heavy rights to the challenger's face in the eighth, one of which brought blood gushing from Driscoll's by now broken nose. Bravely coming out for the ninth, Driscoll actually shaded the round, but with his eye and nose injuries rapidly deteriorating, his corner wisely pulled him out before the tenth could get underway.

13 November, 1991 Paul Hodkinson 8.13¾ (GB) W PTS 12 Marcos Villasana 9.0 (Mexico), Belfast, Northern Ireland. WBC Featherweight Title Challenge.

This time there was to be no hard luck story for Hodkinson;

this time his right eye, although cut in the fourth, held up and this time round the Englishman stayed in the driving seat to win the coveted title. How Villasana remained on his feet on the many occasions he was tagged heavily was truly amazing as he once again proved himself to be a genuine "iron-man" of the ring. Switching punches from head to body with great fluidity, Hodkinson opened up a cut over Villasana's right eye in the fifth, while the champion continuously strayed south of the border with his blows. But at the finish Hodkinson was a wide points winner, heralding yet another great night for British boxing. *Judges Scorecards:* 119-109, 119-111, 119-114.

15 November, 1991 James Warring 13.6½ (USA) W CO 5 Donnell Wingfield 13.3¾ (USA), Roanoke, USA. IBF Cruiserweight Title Defence.

It is only recently that James Warring has been devoting his every moment to full-time boxing and at 6' 4" he is certainly powerful enough, even without all the necessary skills, to dominate a division that tends to be completely overshadowed by the heavyweights. The challenger made a fair start, moving in behind a cross-armed defence and for three rounds gave Warring plenty of trouble with wide swings from both hands to the body. But once Warring had picked up the pace in the fourth round, there was only going to be one winner. Finding the range with his jab, the champion began to set his rival up. In the fifth, while pressing in head down, Wingfield was met with a terrific right-hand-uppercut which felled him like a log, splitting his right eye into the bargain. The referee did no more than count the man from Cleveland, Ohio out with one minute, five seconds of the round gone.

18 November, 1991 Manuel Medina 8.13¾ (Mexico) W TD 9 Tom Johnson 8.13¼ (USA), Los Angeles, USA. IBF Featherweight Title Defence.

During the early stages of the fight it appeared that the bigger-hitting challenger would win convincingly as Medina slid around the ring pushing out punches only in retaliation. But gradually Medina got himself into the fray, whacking away desperately with both hands to Johnson's body. In the sixth Johnson nearly went down, while the champion seemed impervious to heavy punches that came his way. A low blow decked Johnson in the seventh, but, following another borderline shot, Medina backed off. In the ninth, as Johnson took Medina to the ropes under a bombardment of punches, a clash of heads left him badly cut over the left eye. The referee immediately called a halt under IBF rules, allowing the scorecards to be totted up and Medina was adjudged the winner by way of a technical decision. *Judges Scorecards:* 78-73, 76-75, 77-74.

20 November, 1991 Gerald McClellan 11.6¾ (USA) W RSC 1 John Mugabi 11.3½ (Uganda), London, England. Vacant WBO Middleweight Title.

With both men noted as powerful punchers, it was expected to be an early night's work. And so it proved to be as McClellan got home with his first right hand, a punch that left Mugabi almost out on his feet. With Mugabi still distinctly wobbly, although still looking to get one across himself, McClellan's follow-up right crashed onto the ex-champion's jaw. The Ugandan dropped to the floor and after taking a standing eight count he was soon back into the fray, looking to land bombs of his own. McClellan, however, had ideas of his own and a range finding left lead opened the way for yet another crunching right which sent Mugabi sliding to the floor for the second time. Up at seven, Mugabi continued to mix it with the younger man, before being pitched face down on the canvas from a further right and succumbing to the three knockdowns in a round ruling.

21 November, 1991 Gianfranco Rosi 11.0 (Italy) W PTS 12 Gilbert Baptist 10.12¾ (USA), Perugia, Italy. IBF Light-Middleweight Title Defence.

Once again, Rosi defended his title with consummate ease against lesser American opposition. Using the jab, coupled with the right-cross, he stayed well on top throughout and Baptist as much as he tried had no real answers. On the occasions the challenger broke through, Rosi's speed ensured that there was never any damage done as he would move out of reach, effortlessly. Making his seventh defence, Rosi, as always, delighted the crowd with his exhibition, being good value for his shut-out points victory. *Judges Scorecards:* 120-108, 120-108, 118-111.

22 November, 1991 Genaro Hernandez 9.2½ (USA) W RTD 9 Daniel Londas 9.3¾ (France), Epernay, France. Vacant WBA Super-Featherweight Title.

When fighting for the crown vacated by Joey Gamache, local hero, Daniel Londas, found himself substantially outreached, outboxed and ultimately outpunched. Hernandez dominated throughout with jabs and chopping rights to the head as the Frenchman sought to get to work on the body. In the fourth, Londas who was having no success at all, picked up a cut on his left eye and did well to survive a torrid seventh round after being dumped by a glancing right-uppercut. Survive he did, but then in the ninth Hernandez dropped him heavily with a left-right for a count of nine. On getting to his feet, Londas signalled his retirement.

23 November, 1991 Evander Holyfield 15.0 (USA) W RSC 7 Bert Cooper 15.5 (USA), Atlanta, USA. WBC, WBA and IBF Heavyweight Title Defence.

In what nearly turned out to be one of great heavyweight shock results of all-time, a 22-1 underdog, "Smokin'" Bert Cooper, who was only brought in as a last minute substitute, had the fans on the edges of their seats. Showing tremendous aggression, Cooper continuously made Holyfield fight his way and although being floored himself in the first, he forced the champion to take a standing count in an unforgettable third round. Holyfield did not go down under the barrage of leather and before long had got himself together and was fighting back. By the seventh he was totally in control and Cooper's time was nearly up. Driving the challenger around the ring, he sent in 20 to 30 punches that went unanswered, before the referee rescued Cooper from taking any further punishment in what had now become a lost cause.

29 November, 1991 James McGirt 10.5 (USA) W PTS 12 Simon Brown 10.7 (USA), Las Vegas, USA. WBC Welterweight Title Challenge.

Right from the opening bell the challenger got into his stride, jabbing, ducking and sliding away from the powerful Brown. By breaking up the champion's rhythm and not allowing him the chance to get set, McGirt negated his opponent's number one asset. At the same time McGirt was not only piling up points, but getting some powerful punches of his own on target. As the fight progressed, Brown's right eye began to close and then, in the tenth, McGirt got home with a tremendous left-hook right on the button. Brown crashed face down and although he somehow got to his feet before the final count, he was a spent force. In one of the great modern upsets, McGirt cruised through the final two rounds to cop both the decision and the title. *Judges Scorecards:* 117-110, 117-110, 119-108.

7 December, 1991 Rafael Pineda 9.13 (Colombia) W RSC 9 Roger Mayweather 10.0 (USA), Reno, USA. Vacant IBF Light-Welterweight Title.

Prior to the ninth round it looked as if Mayweather was on his way to victory as he probed Pineda's defences with the occasional jab, before skating away out of danger. During that time, Pineda had not thrown much leather himself, other than a couple of big left-hooks that caught Mayweather off guard in round six. But after two minutes of the ninth everything changed and all that had gone before counted for nothing, when a huge left-hook flattened Mayweather, leaving him spreadeagled on the canvas. The referee stopped the contest without even bothering to start the count as the new champion celebrated in style.

9 December, 1991 Daniel Zaragoza 8.10 (Mexico) W PTS 12 Paul Banke 8.10 (USA), Los Angeles, USA. WBC Super-Bantamweight Title Defence.

In a gruelling battle of southpaws, Zaragoza, to use his own words, stayed on the outside as the former champion Banke flailed away with shorter arm punches. The champion utilised the reach factor throughout, showing better all-round quality as the younger man continued to press for an

The 22-1 outsider, Bert Cooper (right), gave Evander Holyfield, the world heavyweight champion in the eyes of all but the WBO, all the trouble he could handle until running out of steam in the seventh

Tom Casino

inside the distance win. Occasionally, Banke would get lucky, but Zaragoza was still able to prove what a good champion he is by firing back on all cylinders. Both fighters were dead tired coming into the last round and at the bell lurched into each others arms. *Judges Scorecards:* 117-113, 116-112, 116-112.

13 December, 1991 Victor Cordoba 12.0 (Panama) W RSC 11 Vincenzo Nardiello 11.11½ (Italy), Paris, France. WBA Super-Middleweight Title Defence.

This all-southpaw title fight ended in some controversy in the eleventh round when, with Nardiello on his knees, the referee called the contest off without administering a count. Cordoba had made a good start, staggering the Italian badly in the second and then immediately putting him down with a heavy left-cross. But, showing great defensive skills, Nardiello steadily boxed his way back into contention, boxing, moving and out-thinking Cordoba. By the end of the tenth, Nardiello appeared to be way out in front, almost, at times, having become the aggressor and certainly brimming with confidence on the outcome. Unfortunately for him, Cordoba hadn't read the script and sprang at the challenger from the moment the bell rang for the eleventh round, landing solid punches from both hands until Nardiello crashed to the floor to be rescued by the referee.

13 December, 1991 Anaclet Wamba 13.7½ (France) W RSC 11 Masimilliano Duran 13.2½ (Italy), Paris, France. WBC Cruiserweight Title Defence.

In the main, Wamba used his superior height and reach advantage to consolidate his supremacy over old rival, Duran, in this their rubber match. Working well behind the jab, he gradually built up a solid points lead and apart from sporadic moments of aggression from Duran, he never looked like relinquishing his hold on the title. By the tenth, however, both men were tired, but Duran appeared dejected when he was cut between the eyes and when he was cut over the left eye in the eleventh, he just fell apart. Wamba sensing victory, sent him reeling to the ropes where he was quickly rescued by the referee.

13 December, 1991 James Toney 11.5 (USA) DREW 12 Mike McCallum 11.3¾ (Jamaica), Atlantic City, USA. IBF Middleweight Title Defence.

For once, the fans were fortunate to witness a fight that lived up to all of its pre-match expectations. Both fighters had their moments, but neither was decked and while it was noticeable that Toney had faster hands, it was equally noticeable that whenever McCallum worked the body, the younger man looked vulnerable. Round after round the

After skating the fight for the vacant IBF light-welterweight title for eight rounds, Roger Mayweather (right) was flattened by a big Rafael Pineda left-hook and all that had gone before suddenly counted for nothing Tom Casino

action flowed with varied successes until both men had virtually fought themselves into a state of utter exhaustion. In the final round, Toney came closest to finishing the job when he was within a punch or two of bringing McCallum down, but it would have been an injustice at that stage for the fight not to have gone to a decision. *Judges Scorecards:* 116-112, 114-114, 113-115.

13 December, 1991 Terry Norris 10.11¼ (USA) W PTS 12 Jorge Castro 11.0 (Argentine), Paris, France. WBC Light-Middleweight Title Defence.

Typical of most Argentinian world class fighters, Castro showed that he had the ability to take a punch well and also had the power to cause maximum damage when he landed. Bearing this in mind, Norris took no real risks, as he completely outscored his number one challenger. Boxing with great speed and precision, the champion went on the offensive right from the start, not giving his rival many chances to get set, keeping him off balance with jabs and executing a whole range of combinations on his hapless opponent. With a round or two to go, the referee would have been excused had he pulled Castro out, but although all hope of victory had long departed, the challenger was still upright at the final bell. *Judges Scorecards:* 117-111, 118-110, 120-112.

14 December, 1991 Manning Galloway 10.7 (USA) W PTS 12 Nika Khumalo 10.5¾ (South Africa), Cape Town, South Africa. WBO Welterweight Title Defence.

Following their earlier meeting, it was expected that Khumalo would pressurise the southpaw champion from start to finish and not give the faster man the opportunity to use his better boxing skills. However, once again he made the mistake of standing back throughout in order to unload single punches. After hurting the champion in the third and putting him down in the eighth for a count of eight and again doing some damage in the ninth, the South African still failed to ignite. As before, Galloway fiddled his way to a points win, although his narrow margin of victory was mainly due to his inability to punch correctly with the right, while hardly ever bringing his left into play. *Judges Scorecards:* 116-113, 115-113, 112-115.

17 December, 1991 Hiroki Ioka 7.10 (Japan) W PTS 12 Myung-Woo Yuh 7.10 (South Korea), Osaka, Japan. WBA Light-Flyweight Title Challenge.

In what might have been seen by many as a hometown split decision, the former WBC mini-flyweight champion, Hiroki Ioka, beat the long term titleholder, Myung-Woo Yuh, in front of his ecstatic local fans. Yuh, who first won the crown in 1986 and had 17 successful defences to his

Mike McCallum (right) throws a big right-hand at James Toney during their drawn battle for the latter's IBF middleweight title

Tom Casino

credit, was generally beaten to the jab by the taller man. *Judges Scorecards:* 115-113, 117-112, 113-115.

21 December, 1991 Orlando Canizales 8.6 W RSC 11 Ray Minus 8.5¼ (Bahamas), Laredo, USA. IBF Bantamweight Title Defence.

As in recent defences, Canizales once again was happy to counter and move, a routine he has perfected over the years. It was apparent at an early stage that Minus did not have the artillery to unduly trouble the champion, but to his credit he showed good hand speed and took a punch well. Finally, Canizales got himself cranked up and in the eleventh he beat Minus to the punch with a cracking right hand which left him badly shaken. Although the challenger did not go down, the referee had seen enough and rescued him at one minute, 45 seconds of the round.

22 December, 1991 Kaosai Galaxy 8.3 (Thailand) W PTS 12 Armando Castro 8.3 (Mexico), Bangkok, Thailand. WBA Super-Flyweight Title Defence.

Refusing to be intimidated, Castro hustled into the champion right from the word go and after an even first round put Galaxy down heavily. Fortunately for the local man, the bell came to his aid and thereafter, way into the middle rounds, he boxed effectively on the retreat. But although rocking the Mexican, Galaxy was unable to halt his forward march. In the tenth, however, Galaxy floored the challenger, who also sustained a badly cut right eye in the process, for eight. The final two rounds were fought out bitterly with Galaxy getting the verdict and later announcing his reitrement from the ring after 19 successful defences. The scorecards did not do justice to the durable Castro, whose turn will surely come again. *Judges Scorecards:* 117-109, 117-109, 117-111.

22 December, 1991 Sung-Il Moon 8.3 (South Korea) W RSC 6 Torsak Pongsupa 8.2 (Thailand), Inchon, South Korea. WBC Super-Flyweight Title Defence.

The champion got on the offensive from the opening bell and dropped Pongsupa in the first round with a terrific right. However, the southpaw challenger fought back well under pressure, connecting with several powerful punches of his own and never let Moon totally control the action. But once the champion went to work on the midsection in the fourth round it took the sting out of Pongsupa, who began to show no lateral movement. After continuing where he left off in the fifth, Moon ripped in some heavy uppercuts in the sixth which had the desired effect. Following a knockdown, the brave challenger was finally rescued by third man, having nothing left to offer.

22 December, 1991 Ricardo Lopez 7.5½ (Mexico) W PTS 12 Kyung-Yun Lee 7.7 (South Korea), Inchon, South Korea. WBC Mini-Flyweight Title Defence.

The 23-year-old Mexican once again dominated a championship contest, only this time round he was forced to travel the full course. The challenger, Lee, although putting up game resistance, ultimately went down on points by a wide margin. *Judges Scorecards:* 118-110, 116-112, 120-107.

7 January, 1992 Leonzer Barber 12.4 (USA) W PTS 12 Anthony Hembrick 12.6 (USA), Detroit, USA. WBO Light-Heavyweight Title Defence.

Right from the opening bell it was clear for all to see that Hembrick, whose best weapon is the jab, would have some difficulty getting inside the 6' 3" tall champion's guard. However, it turned into a good match between two good men, with Barber's added fire-power ultimately proving to be the deciding factor. The fight was extremely close for ten rounds and could have gone either way, with Barber often scoring well only to be countered by the jab himself. Then, in the eleventh, with both men tired, Hembrick was floored by a solid right to the jaw. On getting up, he lurched dazedly through the remaining round on heavy legs, but Barber was too tired himself to nail his rival and had to settle for the split decision. *Judges Scorecards:* 114-113, 115-113, 113-115.

10 January, 1992 Iran Barkley 11.13 (USA) W RSC 2 Darrin van Horn 12.0 (USA), New York, USA. IBF Super-Middleweight Title Challenge.

Toe-to-toe from the opening bell, van Horn very nearly went over from a left-hook after only 25 seconds had elapsed, but as the bell rang to end the session he was still in there slugging away. Still throwing caution to the wind, van Horn simply tore into Barkley on the resumption, but was immediately decked following another left-hook. Rising at the count of six, the champion still tried to take the initiative, but was soon under fire again and a left-right dropped him in a heap. Van Horn made it to his feet again only to be blasted along the ropes by a now rampant Barkley, sensing the kill and found himself on the floor for the third time. At one minute, 33 seconds of round two the referee finally brought this uneven contest to a halt.

18 January, 1992 Meldrick Taylor 10.6¼ (USA) W PTS 12 Glenwood Brown 10.6½ (USA), Philadelphia, USA. WBA Welterweight Title Defence.

In what was very nearly another major shock among the welters, Taylor, in falling short with his left leads, was countered and floored by a sweet left-hook to the jaw just before round one ended. The champion got up and continued to go on the offensive, but received another rude awakening when touching down again in the fourth. But from then on Taylor began to assert more control on the fight and, although Brown often fired right back, the champion produced the better quality more often than not. However, Brown was never disheartened and carried on plugging away right up until the final bell, receiving a great ovation for his sterling display. *Judges Scorecards:* 116-113, 116-113, 114-113.

25 January, 1992 Kyun-Yung Park 8.13¾ (South Korea) W CO 9 Seiji Asakawa 8.13¾ (Japan), Seoul, South Korea. WBA Featherweight Title Defence.

It was the champion who made the better start, using the jab effectively and generally controlling the contest. Asakawa was dropped in the second round, but came back well with both hands and drawing blood from Park's nose. Eventually Park got back in the driving seat as he punished his man with solid punches. The pressure finally took its toll and in the ninth, Park spotted an opening to launch a cracking left-hook which left Asakawa flat out on the canvas where he was counted out.

27 January, 1992 Humberto Gonzalez 7.9¾ (Mexico) W PTS 12 Domingo Sosa 7.9 (Dominican Republic), Los Angeles, USA. WBC Light-Flyweight Title Defence.

Hard-hitting Gonzalez incurred the wrath of the referee, with four points being deducted for low blows, but still won clearly on all three judges' scorecards. The taller Sosa, his eye cut in the first, darted around the ring to avoid the punishing fists of the champion. But in the third, Gonzalez was also cut and to add to his woes, suffered a broken left hand sometime during the middle rounds. This allied to his general immobility denied the crowd an inside the distance finish. The low punches certainly took the steam out of the challenger and almost anywhere else in the world Gonzalez would have disqualified. *Judges Scorecards:* 115-107, 115-109, 114-109.

1 February, 1992 Chris Eubank 12.0 (GB) W PTS 12 Thulani Malinga 11.13 (South Africa), Birmingham, England. WBO Super-Middleweight Title Defence.

Making a slow start, Eubank seemed content to counter the South African challenger as he edged forward, but it was soon apparent that the champion had the extra power, even though his punches were often wild. However, by the fifth round Eubank had settled down and had found the range when out of the blue he brought a right-hand crashing down on Malinga's unprotected jaw. Somehow, the challenger got to his feet and took a count of eight, before resuming and surviving the remaining ten seconds of the round. He even wobbled Eubank in the sixth, but was still on unsteady legs two rounds later. By this time, the champion had decided to showboat as Malinga kept coming forward, still looking to make a fight of it, although not quick enough to take advantage of any openings. Eubank had tired by the eleventh and several times threw himself over with wild punches that missed the target, but remained well in control to justify the split decision. *Judges Scorecards:* 116-113, 115-113, 112-115.

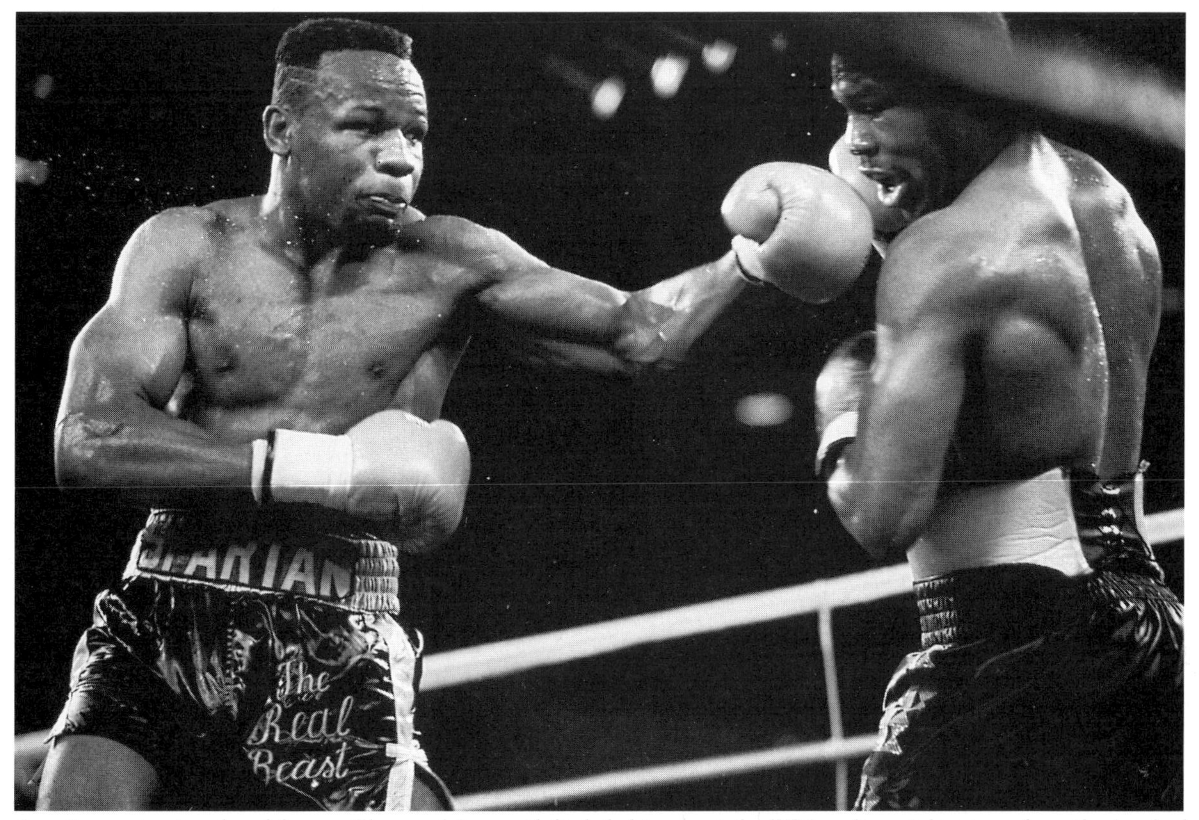

Despite scoring two knockdowns, Glenwood Brown (left) failed to wrest the WBA welterweight crown from the head of Meldrick Taylor

Tom Casino

6 February, 1992 Mauro Galvano 11.13¼ (Italy) W PTS 12 Juan Carlos Gimenez 11.13¾ (Paraguay), Marino, Italy. WBC Super-Middleweight Title Defence.

After three close rounds, Galvano began to find the range with the jab and settled down into a monotonous rhythm, beating out a steady tattoo on his opponent's features. The Paraguayan challenger tried hard to get to close quarters, but to no avail, as he was tied up again and again whenever he managed to find the inside track. Although the rough, tough, dangerous Gimenez kept on coming forward, by midway the fight had turned into a dull mauling affair as the champion decided to concentrate on nullifying the challenger's work, rather than keeping him at distance with the jab which had been so effective earlier on. The contest was refereed by Britain's Larry O'Connell. *Judges Scorecards:* 119-115, 116-114, 116-114.

8 February, 1992 James Toney 11.5¾ (USA) W PTS 12 Dave Tiberi 11.4½ (USA), Atlantic City, USA. IBF Middleweight Title Defence.

Coming out at the opening bell, Tiberi immediately took the fight to the champion, getting himself on the inside track and firing in short slugging punches to head and body. Although Toney carried the heavier armoury, as the fight wore on he was often being outworked and even when he caught the challenger with the occasional mighty wallop he could not totally suppress him. The crowd were loving every minute as the big underdog just kept the punches flowing. But from the eleventh through to the final bell, Tiberi's blows were beginning to lose their snap, while Toney desperately tried to influence the judges by upping his workrate. The decision was controversial to say the least, many believing that Tiberi had done more than enough to win, even allowing for a point being deducted from him for low blows. *Judges Scorecards:* 115-112, 115-111, 111-117.

15 February, 1992 Michael Carbajal 7.10½ (USA) W PTS 12 Marcos Pacheco 7.10 (Mexico), Phoenix, USA. IBF Light-Flyweight Title Defence.

While dictating the fight, Carbajal very seldom exploited his majestic reach advantage and heavy artillery, looking only a shell of the fighter he once was. The crafty southpaw challenger, although totally lacking in power, began to grow in confidence as the bout progressed, especially when he realised that Carbajal was finding him difficult to set up for his big bombs. Continually missing opportunities and not taking advantages of the openings that did come his way, Carbajal finished up not only with a bad gash over his left eye, but also with damaged pride. *Judges Scorecards:* 117-113, 117-110, 116-111.

"Sugar Boy" Malinga is knocked down for the second time by Chris Eubank during the Englishman's successful defence of his WBO super-middles title
Action Images

15 February, 1992 Robert Quiroga 8.3 (USA) W PTS 12 Carlos Mercardo 8.3 (Colombia), Salerno, Italy. IBF Super-Flyweight Title Defence.

Making a great start, Quiroga floored the challenger twice during a hectic first stanza, a left-hook doing the damage first time round with the second knockdown coming from a right to the head. Allowing for that and for the fact that he shipped considerable punishment throughout, Mercardo should not have survived, but survive he did, even coming on strong through the middle rounds and cutting Quiroga's right eye in the sixth. The game Colombian was staggering badly in the latter stages of the fight, but cheered on by the locals, made it to the final bell. *Judges Scorecards:* 116-111, 117-109, 118-109.

15 February, 1992 Julian Jackson 11.5 (USA) W CO 1 Ismael Negron 11.6 (USA), Las Vegas, USA. WBC Middleweight Title Defence.

In what, hardly surprisingly, turned out to be a dreadful mismatch, the American journeyman, Negron, who had been stopped by Britain's Herol Graham, two years earlier, was matched against a man considered to be the hardest puncher, pound-for-pound, in the world today. Straight from the opening bell, Jackson was on top of his lanky opponent, hammering in punches to head and body. Desperate to hold and look for some respite, Negron was like a calf being led to the slaughter. By now, the champion could not miss his target and when Negron threw a feeble jab, he was countered by an awesome left-hook which sent him crashing to the deck. As the challenger lay writhing on his back, with no hope of being able to continue, he was counted out on the 50 second mark.

22 February, 1992 Terry Norris 10.12 (USA) W RSC 9 Carl Daniels 10.12 (USA), San Diego, USA. WBC Light-Middleweight Title Defence.

Showing great patience and taking no extra risks, Norris allowed Daniels to blow himself out before really working him over. The challenger proved to be much better than he looked on paper, presenting Norris with quite a few problems to solve before he could get down to real business. Daniels, fast, clever and elusive, and a southpaw to boot, started the first three or four rounds as if there was going to be an upset on the cards. But at the end of the eighth, Daniels left eye was completely closed and he was beginning to take a shellacking. The end was nigh and Norris came out steaming. Rights and lefts pounded into the challenger's head as Norris opened up and following a short burst of punches, a short left to the head pitched Daniels face first on to the canvas. At that point the referee stopped the contest in Norris' favour.

22 February, 1992 Juan Molina 9.3½ (Puerto Rico) W RSC 4 Jackie Gunguluza 9.3½ (South Africa), Sun City, South Africa. Vacant IBF Super-Featherweight Title.

Gunguluza was in trouble as early as the opening session and just never got into the fight. The Puerto Rican, who was bidding to regain the title he once held, held all the aces in the pack and used them to great advantage. Controlling the action from the centre of the ring, Molina used the left-jab not just as a scoring blow, but also as a damaging weapon. In the fourth round, a left-hook floored Gunguluza for an eight count and on rising a heavy right to the head put him down for another eight seconds. When the South African got to his feet for the second time, Molina struck with deadly venom. A series of punches dropped Gunguluza on all fours and the referee, not even bothering to take up the count, called it off after two minutes, 56 seconds of the fourth round.

22 February, 1992 Jose Quirono 8.3 (Mexico) W PTS 12 Jose Ruiz 8.3 (Puerto Rico), Las Vegas, USA. WBO Super-Flyweight Title Challenge.

The challenger took control of the contest right from the off, cutting down Ruiz's space and landing the better quality punches. Although a clash of heads caused a cut over Quirino's left eye in the sixth, it didn't stop him from keeping control and he even increased the pressure from that moment on. Relentlessly, he continued to track Ruiz, who looked almost out on his feet in the tenth, until somehow calling on extra reserves and even hitting back to good effect before the final bell rang to end his torment. *Judges Scorecards:* 116-112, 116-111, 115-112.

22 February, 1992 Hi-Yon Choi 7.7 (South Korea) W RSC 10 Ryuichi Hosono 7.6¼ (Japan), Seoul, South Korea. WBA Mini-Flyweight Title Defence.

Right from the opening bell Choi swarmed all over the nervous challenger and knocked him down with a vicious left-hook. After regaining his feet, Hosono was immediately floored again by a flurry of blows, but gamely got up and continued. Although the next few rounds were dominated by the champion, Hosono fought well when he could get inside, but in the fifth he was dropped once again by a left-right. Despite the knockdowns, the challenger hit back strongly to have Choi in some difficulty over the next few rounds, but at the end of the ninth he appeared to have tired himself out by his exertions. In the tenth, the champion gained his second wind and hit back with a vengeance, flooring his man with a solid body shot, whereupon the British referee, John Coyle, called it off with one minute, 33 seconds of the round gone.

23 February, 1992 Fahlan Lukmingkwan 7.6 (Thailand) W CO 2 Felix Naranjo 7.4 (Colombia), Bangkok, Thailand. IBF Mini-Flyweight Title Defence.

The first round's action saw Naranjo moving adroitly around the ring seeking to come in behind the left-jab, while the champion appeared happy to bide his time. However, the second round had barely begun when Lukmingkwan began to impose his will on his unfortunate challenger. Switching his attack downstairs, he pursued Naranjo, who was now in full flight, to the ropes where he blasted in a series of vicious blows without return, followed by a left-hook to the body. Naranjo sunk to the canvas where he was counted out at one minute, 49 seconds of the round.

24 February, 1992 Genaro Hernandez 9.0½ (USA) W PTS 12 Omar Catari 9.3½ (Venezuela), Los Angeles, USA. WBA Super-Featherweight Title Defence.

With only thirteen contests behind him and seemingly headed for an early shower, the Venezuelan proved himself to be a tough customer, while at the same time making a mockery of the form book. Although Hernandez shook the inexperienced challenger occasionally, he never really came close to stopping his man, ultimately having to be satisfied with a hard-fought distance victory. Working well to the body, Catari was equally adept with his head, butting throughout and after an early clash had left Hernandez with blood seeping from a head wound, the champion made sure from that moment on to jerk out of harm's way in the clinches. If it wasn't head butts, it was low blows as Catari craftily continued to wage war and towards the finish the refereeing was almost non-existant. But while the third man was losing control, Hernandez was finally beginning to assert his authority in the ring. The twelfth round saw Catari hurt for the first time, but although he rallied well enough, Hernandez pressed on to a close verdict. *Judges Scorecards:* 115-112, 116-112, 116-111.

28 February, 1992 Muangchai Kitikasem 8.0 (Thailand) W RSC 9 Sot Chitalada 7.13½ (Thailand), Samut Prakan, Thailand. WBC Flyweight Title Defence.

After having to shed some 23 pounds in the two weeks prior to the contest, the former champion, Chitalada, was only a shell of his once great self as it became painfully clear for all to see when he was put down for a short count in round two. Somehow, he survived the ordeal, but in the long term it would have almost been a blessing if the fight had come to an end there and then. Cut over the right eye, Chitalada put everything into one great final effort in the sixth when he pounded Kitikasem around the ring non-stop. But it wasn't to be as the champion weathered the storm and hit back. By now, Chitalada was fighting on instinct alone and in the seventh his left eye went. In the ninth, with Chitalada on the verge of going down, blood pouring from his injuries, the referee finally brought matters to a close and almost certainly brought a great career to an end.

1 March, 1992 Azumah Nelson 9.3 (Ghana) W RSC 8 Jeff Fenech 9.3 (Australia), Melbourne, Australia. WBC Super-Featherweight Title Defence.

There were no arguments this time as Azumah Nelson laid the ghost of their previous meeting to rest and at the same time proved himself to be a great champion. Nelson took hold of the fight from the opening bell, decking Fenech for a count of five inside the first two minutes and again dishing out more of the same medicine in the second. Although the challenger effectively pressured the champion in the third, there was to be no respite and early into the fourth a stream of jabs opened up a cut over Fenech's right eye. There was more sustained aggression from the Aussie in the sixth, but the round ended with Nelson blasting back with heavy punches of his own, leaving Fenech defenceless on the ropes. The seventh was a quiet round as Fenech circled away from further trouble, but the eighth proved to be the last as Nelson cornered his man and nailed him with three left-hooks and a heavy right. Fenech slumped down for a count of three, but on rising he was again put under siege and the referee called a halt with two minutes, 20 seconds of the round gone.

14 March, 1992 Manuel Medina 9.0 (Mexico) W PTS 12 Fabrice Benichou 9.0 (France), Antibes, France. IBF Featherweight Title Defence.

As early as round one, dangerous headwork by Benichou had already inflicted cuts on the champion and from then on, Medina boxed warily, using his height and reach to keep away from disaster. But Benichou was unable to take proper advantage of the situation unfurling itself, mainly because of his inability to come in behind the jab, which often left him exposed as he charged in. In the fifth, however, Benichou's great determination finally got some reward as Medina was half pushed, half punched to the canvas and took an eight count into the bargain. But the Frenchman was far too predictable and Medina was able to stave him off with clever boxing, although he showed little of the power that one normally associates with a world champion. Because Medina was unable to totally subdue Benichou, who came forward at every opportunity, the result was close and for those in favour of aggression, left a lot to be desired. *Judges Scorecards:* 115-112, 114-113, 114-115.

15 March, 1992 Eddie Cook 8.6 (USA) W CO 5 Israel Contrerras 8.5½ (Venezuela), Las Vegas, USA. WBA Bantamweight Title Challenge.

Coming in as a substitute, southpaw Eddie Cook completely bamboozled the champion right from the off, spearing him with jabs and keeping him off balance with smart combinations. Trying hard to get to work, Contrerras, recognised as one of the biggest bangers in the division, could not find the range for his mighty wallops and found himself steadily outboxed and outfought, along with superb counters and by the fourth round it had already begun to dawn on the locals that his reign as champion was almost history. In the fifth, Cook was almost disdainfully picking his punches as the champion came apart at the seams. Contrerras was belted along the ropes by the faster punching challenger and although he fired back occasionally, he could make no impression. Following an exchange on the ropes, Cook moved inside a right-uppercut with a left-right to the jaw and the champion hit the deck face down. As the referee tolled off the count, Contrerras desperately tried to get to his feet, but at one minute, 37 seconds of the round he was an ex-champion.

16 March, 1992 Ricardo Lopez 7.6¼ (Mexico) W PTS 12 Domingo Lucas 7.6 (Philippines), Mexico City, Mexico. WBC Mini-Flyweight Title Defence.

Defending his title for the third time, Lopez soon had his

challenger on the back foot after a series of left-hooks to the head paved the way. Lucas was cut as early as the second and after sampling some heavy blows, decided that caution rather than valour was the best way to survive. Although the champion was well on top he couldn't put his man away and during the middle rounds he began to concentrate more on the body in an effort to force Lucas to trade. The Filipino, however, continued with his jab and move routine, much to the dissatisfaction of Lopez, simply refusing to be lulled into any exchange whatsoever. At the final bell there was only one winner, but Lucas received warm praise for an extremely game performance. *Judges Scorecards:* 120-104, 120-104, 120-106.

18 March, 1992 Pat Clinton 8.0 (GB) W PTS 12 Isidro Perez 8.0 (Mexico), Glasgow, Scotland. WBO Flyweight Title Challenge.

The Mexican made an aggressive start, but his longer punches were not accurate enough to unduly trouble Clinton, who was able to block or counter effectively with the southpaw jab. Apart from the second, the little Scot had gone well clear with his better boxing by the seventh, but it was in that round that Perez finally got to grips with his challenger as he thudded in blows from both hands. Clinton had now tired somewhat and with the champion in full cry he did well to ride out the storm over the next few rounds. Hurt early in the tenth, he fought back tenaciously to take the round, but with both men flagging neither was strong enough to mount a winning attack and at the final bell it appeared to be desperately close. The decision in favour of Clinton, although he landed less punches than Perez overall, almost certainly reflected the better quality of his work and his will to win. *Judges Scorecards:* 115-113, 115-114, 113-116.

20 March, 1992 Thierry Jacob 8.9½ (France) W PTS 12 Daniel Zaragoza 8.10 (Mexico), Calais, France. WBC Super-Bantamweight Title Challenge.

This all-southpaw battle saw Jacob make a great start as he quickly got down to work with his relied and trusted right-jab, dominating the action and never letting Zaragoza get settled. It wasn't until the fifth round that the champion showed the crowd a glimpse of his ability, but after producing a little of what he was capable of, he could not sustain the pressure and by the seventh, Jacob was back in command. Jacob was even confident enough to trade punches in an absorbing ninth round, which ended with the champion badly cut by the side of his right eye. In the tenth, Zaragoza was downed for a count of seven and in the following round he was cut again, this time over the left eye. The champion made a grandstand finish, but Jacob was not going to be denied, dancing around the ring to keep out of harm's way, and deservedly received the verdict to rapturous applause. *Judges Scorecards:* 115-112, 118-113, 119-108.

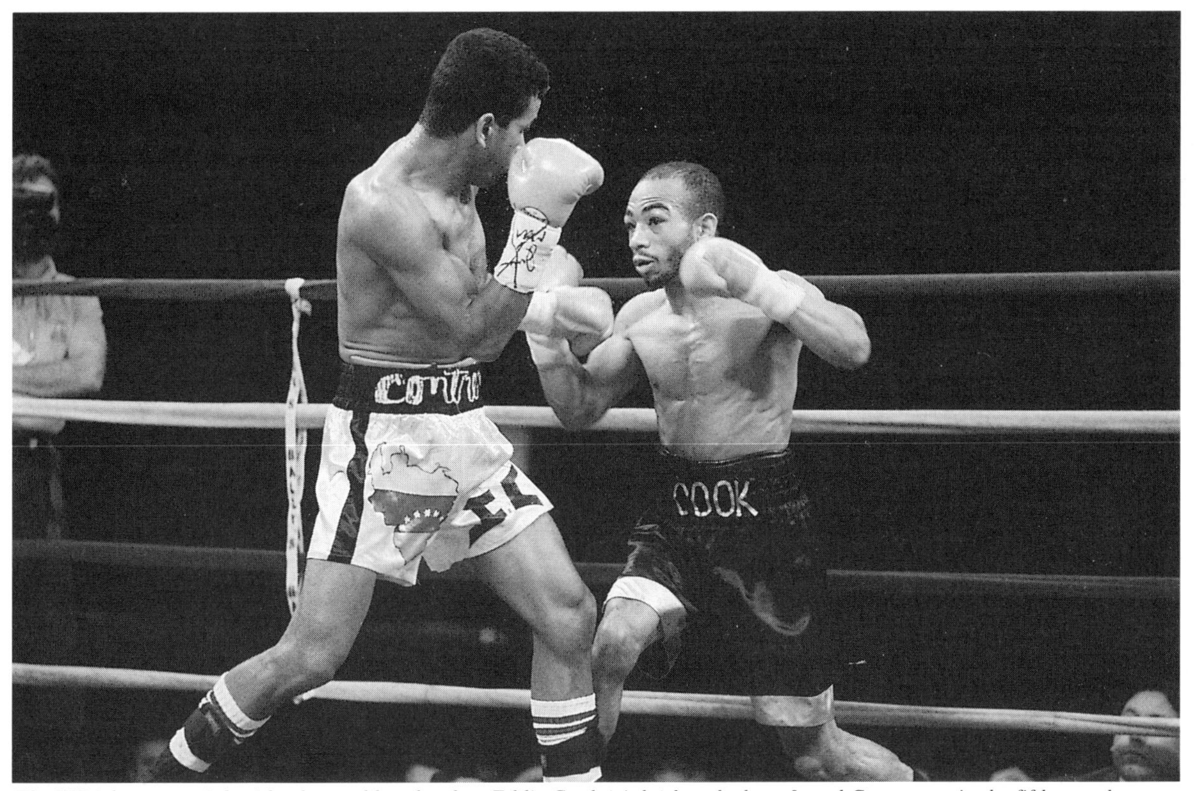

The WBA bantamweight title changed hands when Eddie Cook (right) knocked out Israel Contrerras in the fifth round
Chris Farina

20 March, 1992 Iran Barkley 12.6 (USA) W PTS 12 Thomas Hearns 12.6½ (USA), Las Vegas, USA. WBA Light-Heavyweight Title Challenge.

Iran Barkley's unquenchable will to win was the deciding factor in his thrilling victory over the famous "Hitman" Hearns, who admitted after the contest that he had tactically fought the wrong fight. The challenger, who had a previous victory over Hearns, quickly decided that by staying on top of his opponent, he would be better placed to use his strength and at the same time suffocate the boxing ability of Hearns. It proved to be an excellent move, as it wasn't until the latter stages that Hearns was able to get any leverage for heavy blows and to pick up with his jab. The only knockdown of the fight came in the fourth when Barkley floored Hearns with a venomous left-hook for a count of four, but by the end of the session the champion was firing back well. The last few rounds were fought out toe-to-toe, with neither fighter giving ground and Hearns possibly edged the majority of them to give himself a fighting chance of the verdict. But at the finish two of the judges voted for Barkley, thus making him a double champion. *Judges Scorecards:* 115-113, 114-113, 113-114.

21 March, 1992 Daniel Londas 9.3¼ (France) W PTS 12 Kamel Bou Ali 9.3¾ (Tunisia), San Rufo, Italy. WBO Super-Featherweight Title Challenge.

Over twelve dull rounds, the veteran Frenchman, Londas, finally won a version of the world title, having been stopped last time out at the hands of Genaro Hernandez in a battle for the WBA crown. Londas gradually built up a good lead, scoring points from range, while at the same time keeping well clear of Bou Ali's heavier punches at close-quarters. However, in the middle rounds, the champion tried hard to get back into the contest with solid uppercuts, but was unable to draw the challenger into a punch-up. With time running out and in sight of certain defeat at the hands of the judges, Ali, with cuts over both eyes, mounted his final attack, only to receive an official warning for "rabbit" punching for his pains. *Judges Scorecards:* 116-112, 114-113, 115-115.

24 March, 1992 Yong-Kang Kim 7.13¾ (South Korea) W CO 6 Jon Penalosa 7.13 (Philippines), Inchon, South Korea. WBA Flyweight Title Defence.

On paper, Penalosa presented a tough defence for Kim, as the number two contender, but in the ring it was a far different story. The champion seemed to bide his time in feeling out Penalosa, almost to the point of being too wary, but in the sixth he really began to get the bit between the teeth. Sensing that he had nothing left to fear, he fairly exploded on Penalosa, felling his man with a tremendous right-uppercut to the jaw. The contest was over the moment Penalosa hit the deck, out to the world and the referee was left with the straightforward task of completing the count.

Despite the fact that he already held a previous victory over his famous rival, Iran Barkley (left) still shook the fight public when he captured Thomas Hearns' WBA light-heavyweight crown last March Chris Farina

25 March, 1992 Duke McKenzie 8.5¼ (GB) W RSC 8 Wilfredo Vargas 8.6 (Puerto Rico), London, England. WBO Bantamweight Title Defence.

Content to made a slow start, McKenzie spent the first round "sussing" out his rival, before getting down to business. With a steady stream of left-jabs and the occasional right-cross getting through his defences, Vargas became flustered and his only answer was to reply with wild punches from both hands which scarcely ruffled the champion as they invariably missed the target. Cut by the side of the left eye in the fifth, the challenger continued to march forward, but was unable to get inside to land his shorter punches effectively and was subjected to a steady flow of jabs and crosses. After taking a bit of a breather early in the seventh, McKenzie really got down to work and four consecutive right-handers dropped Vargas on all fours. Although he managed to climb to his feet and answer the bell for the eighth, with 58 seconds of the round gone and Vargas still somehow upright, the referee had seen enough and rescued the brave challenger from further punishment.

27 March, 1992 Wilfredo Vasquez 8.9 (Puerto Rico) W RSC 3 Raul Perez 8.8 (Mexico), Mexico City, Mexico. WBA Super-Bantamweight Title Challenge.

The former WBA bantamweight champion and wide underdog in the betting, Wilfredo Vasquez, stunned the large crowd as he moved onto the attack right from the opening bell. And as early as the second round, a big left-hook had Perez on the floor for a count of eight. There was to be no respite for the champion, as he found himself continuously under the cosh and having no answer to Vasquez's fire power. Vasquez, a loser on points to Perez in a 1988 non-title bout, was not intent on going the distance this time round and early in the third another left-hook put his man down again. Up at eight, Perez was immediately placed in dire trouble and another big left smashed him to the canvas. By this time the referee had seen enough and with two minutes, 27 seconds of the round gone, he brought proceedings to a halt.

30 March, 1992 Victor Rabanales 8.6 (Mexico) W TD 9 Yong-Hoon Lee 8.6 (South Korea), Los Angeles. Vacant WBC Bantamweight Title.

Earlier in some quarters, it had been mooted that this match was merely for the WBC interim title when it was discovered that the champion, Joichiro Tatsuyoshi of Japan, was having eye trouble. However, further examinations ruled Tatsuyoshi out due to a detached retina and the fight went ahead as for the vacant title. The unbeaten Lee, who was fighting outside of South Korea for the first time, was not intimidated by his rival's partisan fans, but an unfortunate clash of styles saw both men constantly cracking heads as they sought to get inside. This

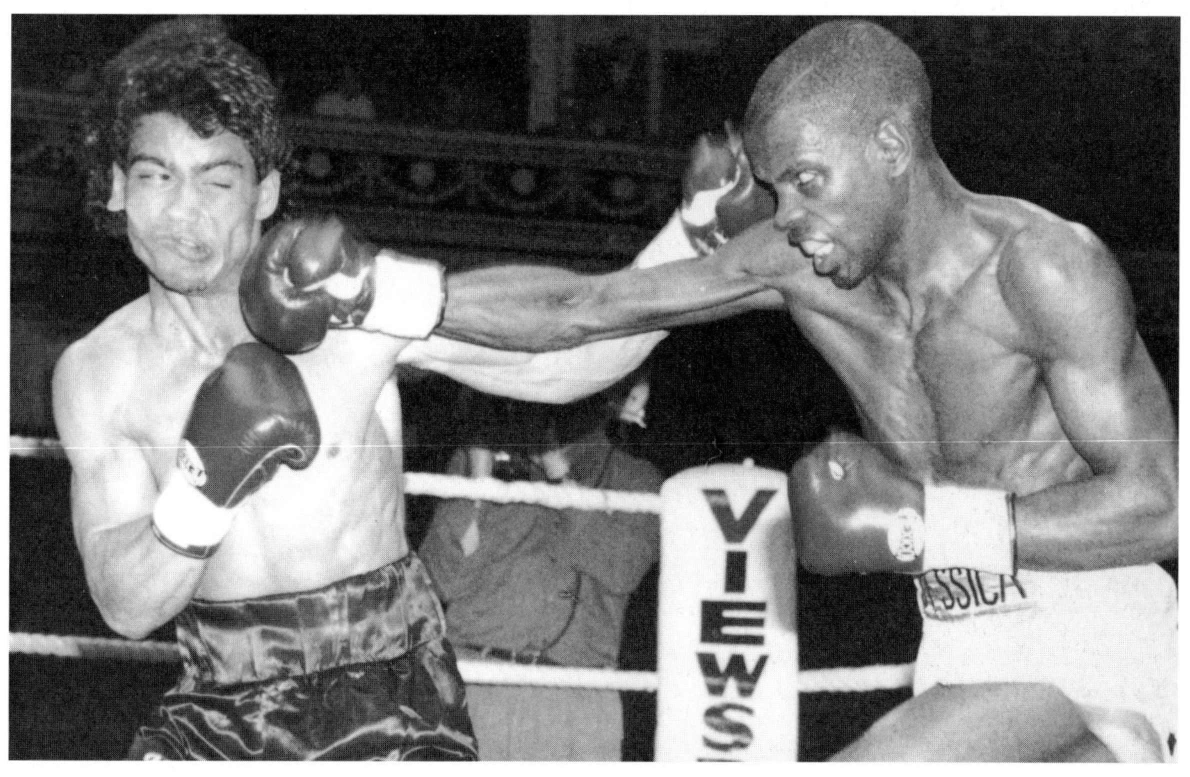

Duke McKenzie (right), making a successful defence of his WBO bantamweight title, thumps in a powerful fight-cross that distorts Wilfredo Vargas' features

inevitably led to cutting up and when another accidental clash of heads occurred at one minute, 21 seconds of the ninth, it unfortunately left Rabanales too badly damaged to continue, according to the ringside doctor. Up to that point there had been a distinct lack of quality punches thrown throughout, making the fight a difficult one to score, but two of the judges cards showed Rabanales to be ahead and he was proclaimed champion. *Judges Scorecards:* 87-84, 85-84, 85-85.

31 March, 1992 Hiroki Ioka 7.10 (Japan) W PTS 12 Noel Tunacao 7.8½ (Philippines), Osaka, Japan. WBA Light-Flyweight Title Defence.

After taking the title from the great Myung-Woo Yuh, Ioka could not get himself up for his first defence and laboured to a boring points victory over a comparatively inexperienced opponent. Tunacao tried hard throughout the fight, but lacked the strength to capitalise on any advantages that came his way. Up until the fifth round, the champion was purely content to prod away with the jab, mainly keeping out of distance and not exposing himself against Tunacao, who came into the ring with eight inside the distance wins behind him. However, between the fifth and eighth, the crowd were finally treated to some vintage Ioka as he let fly with left and right combinations, but it was too little and not often enough to bring Tunacao down. The crowd became increasingly restless with Ioka as he switched back into his negative jab and move routine in the ninth and for a great many fans, the final bell came with some relief. *Judges Scorecards:* 119-111, 117-111, 117-114.

9 April, 1992 Gianfranco Rosi 10.13¼ (Italy) W RSC 6 Angel Hernandez 10.12½ (Spain), Celano, Italy. IBF Light-Middleweight Title Defence.

Controlling the fight from the off, Rosi initially kept the aggressive challenger at bay with his proven left lead, before opening up with both hands as Hernandez looked to get inside. Continuing to ship punches from head to body as he marched forward, by the fourth round the challenger was showing signs of wear, while bleeding copiously from the mouth. Hernandez was systematically being worked over and a left-hook finally sent him toppling early in the sixth. On getting to his feet at the count of eight, he walked back to his corner where he appeared to retire himself, whereupon the referee immediately brought the proceedings to a halt and declared Rosi the winner.

10 April, 1992 Katsuya Onizuka 8.3 (Japan) W PTS 12 Thalerngsak Sitbobay 8.3 (Thailand), Tokyo, Japan. Vacant WBA Super-Flyweight Title.

Sitbobay made a great start, mixing his punches up well and looking to get to work at close quarters, while for his part, Onizuka merely seemed content to cover up on the ropes in peek-a-boo fashion. The Thai continued to dominate and in the fifth, Onizuka was gashed over the right eye and the fight at that stage looked as good as over. Unfortunately, in the sixth, Sitbobay suffered a hand injury and Onizuka was back in the fight. By the ninth, Sitbobay was fading badly and the young Jap attacked with lefts and rights, but was never able to totally dominate his rival. The final three rounds saw both men tiring as Sitbobay got back into the fray by dint of clever defensive skills and clean accurate punches. At the final bell most ringsiders had the Thai out in front, but to his dismay, the judges were the odd men out. *Judges Scorecards:* 115-114, 115-114, 116-114.

10 April, 1992 Julian Jackson 11.4¾ (USA) W RSC 5 Ron Collins 11.5½ (USA), Mexico City, Mexico. WBC Middleweight Title Defence.

Off his stool like greased lightening, Collins actually took the fight right from the opening bell to one of the hardest hitting middles of all time. In a 16' ring there was nowhere for Collins to hide and soon the pair were slugging it out tooth and nail. The challenger appeared out on his feet in the second, but somehow remained erect and was actually fighting back as the round ended. Collins shipped some terrific shots in the third, but yet again he remained upright. After getting through the fourth, Collins was soon under attack in the fifth as heavy punches rained in on him from all angles, both to head and body. Finally a brutal right sent him sliding to the floor in delayed action and after just beating the count, but with legs still twitching, the referee wisely called a halt to the proceedings, 97 seconds into the round.

10 April, 1992 Akinobu Hiranaka 9.13¾ (Japan) W RSC 1 Edwin Rosario 10.0 (Puerto Rico), Mexico City, Mexico. WBA Light-Welterweight Title Challenge.

Both men came out throwing caution to the wind right from the off and it was Rosario who was nailed first from a good right, before hitting back with two solid lefts of his own. This only served to spur Hiranaka into action and two more big rights sent the champion crashing against the ropes. With Rosario drunkenly lurching around the ring, the Jap pursued his prey with a whole battery of blows. At first it appeared that Hiranaka was beginning to punch himself out as Rosario, although swaying against the ropes, would not go down. Finally, following a left-right combination to Rosario's defenceless jaw, the referee stepped in and called a halt with one minute, 28 seconds of the first round still remaining.

10 April, 1992 Julio Cesar Chavez 9.12¾ (Mexico) W RSC 5 Angel Hernandez 9.13 (Puerto Rico), Mexico City, Mexico. WBC Light-Welterweight Title Defence.

At 5' 10", the tall southpaw, Hernandez, posed plenty of problems during the first three rounds for the local hero, Chavez. The champion often looked amateurish as the awkward Puerto Rican first slid one way and then another, often turning up behind his opponent. Finding it difficult to hit the target, Chavez was obviously biding his time and towards the end of the third round he landed some useful blows for the first time in the fight. By now cut over the left eye, Hernandez was subjected to solid rib-benders in the fourth as Chavez finally found the range and the end began to look in sight. Setting his rival up in the fifth, Chavez cracked home nine well placed shots without return, before the referee humanely called a halt with one minute, 39 seconds still left on the clock.

11 April, 1992 James Toney 11.6 (USA) W PTS 12 Glenn Wolfe 11.6 (USA), Las Vegas, USA. IBF Middleweight Title Defence.

Proving to be a very busy champion, Toney merely went through the motions in this defence against a man who was really no more than a blown up light-middle. Having nothing to fear from his rival, the champion fought sporadically, only occasionally unleashing a whole range of combination punches on his luckless foe, but in the main content to preserve the injuries to both hands that he picked up early in the fight. Wolfe's left eye was closed from the seventh onwards, but he managed to last the course, while for Toney it was just another useful payday, following a landslide points victory. *Judges Scorecards:* 117-111, 119-109, 118-110.

18 April, 1992 Welcome Ncita 8.9 (South Africa) W PTS 12 Jesus Salud 8.9 (USA), Treviolo, Italy. IBF Super-Bantamweight Title Defence.

In retaining his title for the sixth time, Ncita got off to a flyer against the former WBA champion with his accurate jab paving the way for a well earned victory. Although the champion finished the fight with a badly swollen left eye, he was never really hurt and was in total control right up to the tenth round. It was at that point that Salud mounted a major attack, catching Ncita with a variety of good hooks and uppercuts, but the champion never wilted and as always relied on his excellent boxing skills to get him out of trouble. Salud gave it everything he had during those last three rounds, but Ncita weathered the storm and came back with his left hand to take the play away from the challenger on the final bell. *Judges Scorecards:* 116-112, 116-112, 115-113.

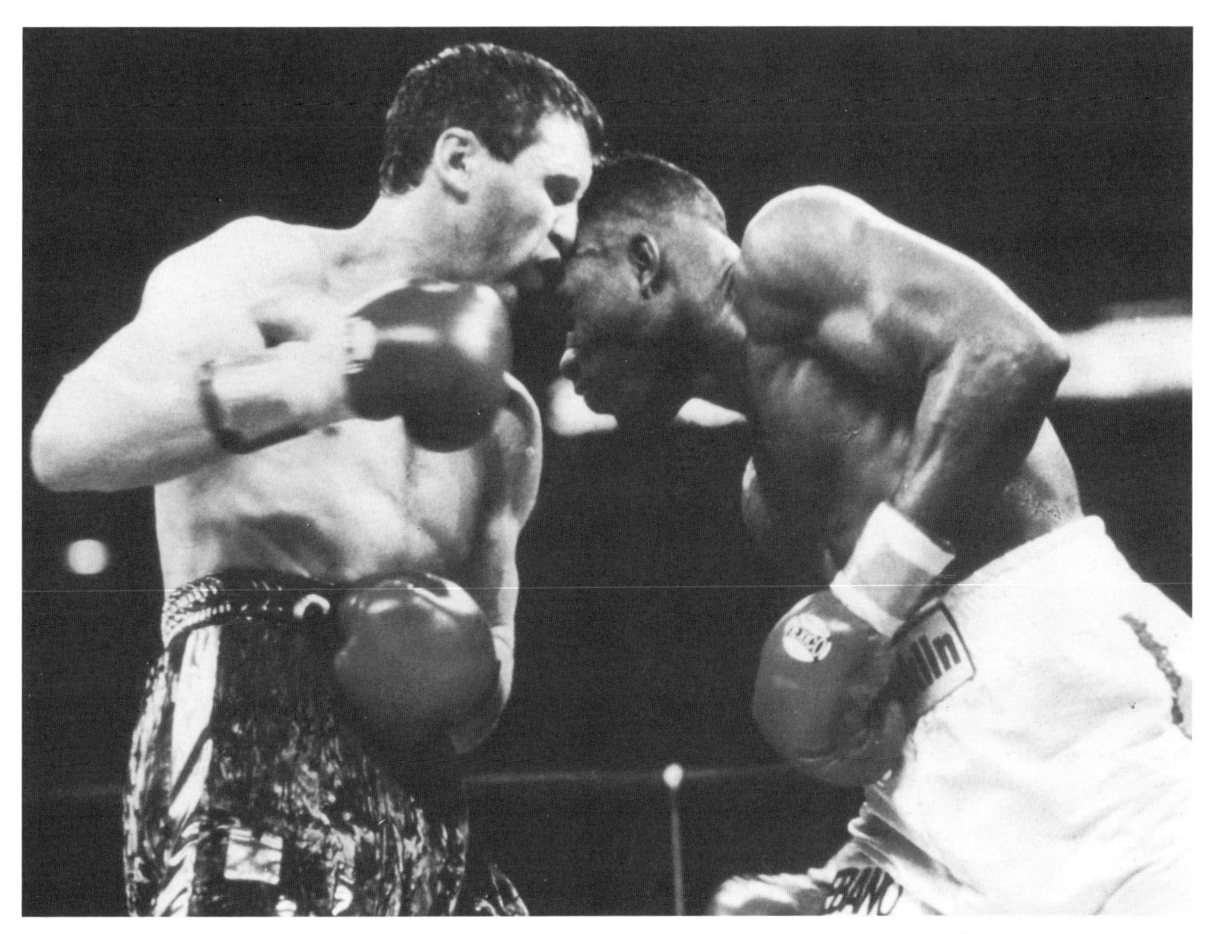

In a good match-up for the vacant WBA middleweight title, Reggie Johnson (right) won over Ireland's Steve Collins

Tom Casino

22 April, 1992 Reggie Johnson 11.5 (USA) W PTS 12 Steve Collins 11.6 (Ireland), East Rutherford, USA. Vacant WBA Middleweight Title.

It was unfortunate that both men were counter punchers, which would explain why on several occasions neither fighter took up the initiative and when Collins marched forward he more often than not found the American's southpaw boxing skills and punching power too much of a hurdle to overcome. Also, it was unfortunate that their styles often resulted in head clashes, which left the Irishman cut over both eyes at the finish. Collins pressed for most of the fight, trying to get the inside track, but in the main Johnson denied him the opportunity to unload. The American fought a very smart fight and apart from a spell in the middle rounds, he was in control for most of the time. The final round saw Collins, who must have recognised that he was a round or so behind, continuing to press forward, while Johnson appeared content to showboat the last 30 seconds to the title. *Judges Scorecard:* 115-113, 115-114, 114-114.

23 April, 1992 Orlando Canizales 8.6 (USA) W PTS 12 Francisco Alvarez 8.6 (Colombia), Paris, France. IBF Bantamweight Title Defence.

The very experienced champion didn't take too long to grab the fight by the scruff of the neck, coming straight out at the first bell and getting his left hand going to beat a steady tattoo on the challenger's face. Alvarez proved to be a tough hombre and would not be intimidated by the superior ability of the champion, who was soon banging in left-hooks to head and body in an effort to bring his challenger down. How Alvarez survived the terrific pounding he received in the sixth was amazing, but after failing to finish his man off, Canizales seemed content to box his way to a comprehensive points victory without taking any further risks. The referee for the contest was England's Roy Francis. *Judges Scorecards:* 119-110, 120-110, 120-108.

25 April, 1992 Chris Eubank 12.0 (GB) W CO 3 John Jarvis 12.0 (USA), Manchester, England. WBO Super-Middleweight Title Defence.

Matched against the third choice 35-year-old challenger from America, Eubank made a cautious start, setting his own pace with good left-jabs and keeping plenty of distance between himself and his rival. The second round saw no real upsurge in pace as Eubank seemed quite happy to pick his shots and wait for the openings to present themselves. Coming out for the third, there was a general air of expectancy from the crowd, but still neither fighter delivered. Suddenly, from out of nowhere, Eubank, in beating Jarvis to the punch, landed a terrific right hand that found its target like a guided missile. The challenger crashed to the canvas as though he had been shot and while in the act of rising, was counted out with one minute and 20 seconds of the round still remaining.

25 April, 1992 Kyun-Yung Park 8.13½ (South Korea) W RSC 11 Koji Matsumoto 9.0 (Japan), Ansan, South Korea. WBA Featherweight Title Defence.

The southpaw Matsumoto made a good start that lasted just one minute before Park fathomed out his style and began to get going himself. In the second round, the challenger was caught by a battery of blows to the head and went down with a thud. But, somehow, he made it to his feet, only to be put under pressure immediately. Round after round followed the same pattern as Park unmercifully battered the game Jap on the ropes from head to body and it was only his lack of sharpness that prevented a count-out. The ninth round witnessed the second knockdown of the fight as another barrage of blows put Matsumoto down and only the bell saved him. Surviving a purgatorial round in the tenth, it only seemed a matter of time with Matsumoto's ear terribly swollen and Park swarmed all over his rival at the start of the eleventh, finally dropping the challenger face down in the neutral corner where the third man called a halt with only 45 seconds of the round gone.

25 April, 1992 Paul Hodkinson 8.13¾ (GB) W RSC 3 Steve Cruz 9.0 (USA), Belfast, Northern Ireland. WBC Featherweight Title Defence.

In making the first defence of his title against a man who has gone back a long way since his glorious victory over Barry McGuigan in 1986, Hodkinson merely did all that was necessary. As early as the first round, Cruz was deposited on the canvas by a left-hook for the mandatory eight count and the writing was already on the wall. On resuming the action, the American was driven to the ropes by a series of lefts and rights, but somehow survived to the bell. It was already clear that Cruz's left lead was not going to deter Hodkinson and he was forced to withstand further heavy shots in the second round. However, it was all over in the third as Hodkinson cracked in a left-hook to the body and doubled up to the jaw, before missing with a follow through right. Cruz sank to his knees, but was up at the count of eight without much fight left in him and the referee called it off with one minute and 55 seconds of the round remaining.

8 May, 1992 Bobby Czyz 13.5 (USA) W PTS 12 Don Lalonde 13.2½ (Canada), Las Vegas, USA. WBA Cruiserweight Title Defence.

With both men looking extremely fleshy, it was Czyz who made the more positive start, as he tracked the Canadian around the ring. After throwing a couple of wild, awkward looking punches, the champion smashed home an explosive left-hook to the jaw which sent Lalonde crashing to the deck. Somehow, Lalonde climbed to his feet and somehow he survived as the champion failed to set him up. At the end of the first, Lalonde had picked up a cut left eye and in the fifth another left-hook opened up scar tissue over his right eye. Lalonde continued to survive as tiredness set in and Czyz was unable to pin point his blows accurately enough to bring his man down as he had done earlier.The contest ended with both fighters stumbling around the ring, hands down and defenceless and although Lalonde showed great bravery in surviving the course, now is the time to pay some thought to his future. *Judges Scorecards:* 116-113, 116-110, 111-111.

9 May, 1992 Terry Norris 10.9 (USA) W RSC 4 Meldrick Taylor 10.9 (USA), Las Vegas, USA. WBC Light-Middleweight Title Defence.

In moving up a weight to contest the title, the WBA welterweight king, Meldrick Taylor, once again proved the old adage that a good "little un" will always have great difficulty in beating a good "big un". After a blistering start, Taylor soon found out that he would have great difficulty with his opponent's longer reach, but instead of resorting to his boxing skills he continued to rush in where "Angels fear to tread". By continuing in this vein he played right into Norris' hands. After being on the receiving end of some solid blows in the earlier rounds, a barrage of punches in the fourth session sent Taylor slithering down and when he regained his feet at the count of six, the champion bided his time before picking quality shots that dumped the challenger on his knees. When Taylor rose, Norris really began to let the punches go. Lefts and rights crashed in on the by now defenceless Taylor and when he was put down by a corner post, the referee rescued him with just five seconds of the fifth round left on the clock.

13 May, 1992 Rafael del Valle 8.5½ (Puerto Rico) W CO 1 Duke McKenzie 8.5 (GB), London, England. WBO Bantamweight Title Challenge.

Catching his opponent cold, brought the inexperienced del Valle, with only twelve previous bouts under his belt, the title in one minute, 56 seconds and surely ranks as one of the biggest upsets ever within the division. The fight started as one would have expected with McKenzie holding the centre of the ring with the jab, while the challenger, gloves held high, moved around looking to lead with either hand. Suddenly, a stiff left-jab put McKenzie down for a count of nine. On the instruction to box on, del Valle moved in with a big right, a short left-hook and another right to send McKenzie crashing to the canvas where he was counted out flat on his back.

15 May, 1992 Michael Moorer 15.7 (USA) W RSC 5 Bert Cooper 16.0½ (USA), Atlantic City, USA. Vacant WBO Heavyweight Title.

Straight from the opening bell, the two fighters were at each other's throats and the fight was barely underway when punches from both hands sent Moorer to the floor. A minute later and back in action, on the ropes, Moorer caught Cooper flush from a southpaw stance. This time it was Cooper's turn to hit the deck. Throughout the rest of the round and then the second and into the third, punches flew fast and furious without respite. Smashed to the floor yet again in the third, Moorer rose at the count of five and was still on the receiving end when the bell rang. By now Cooper had a bad cut over his left eye and it was noticeable in the fourth that Moorer was at last beginning to control the action. The fifth round saw no let up as both men fought as though there was no tomorrow, before a series of punches, but predominately a searing right-uppercut, draped Cooper over the bottom rope in his own corner. Amazingly, he rose at nine, but the referee had seen enough and called the proceedings to a halt with 39 seconds of the round remaining.

16 May, 1992 Colin McMillan 8.13¼ (GB) W PTS 12 Maurizio Stecca 8.13 (Italy), London, England. WBO Featherweight Title Challenge.

For all his "silky" skills, many thought that McMillan would be found wanting at the highest level. The doubters were proved wrong as the British and Commonwealth champion simply outclassed former Olympian, Stecca, to win widely; but to be fair he will face stronger tests when he has to come up against the men from across the Atlantic. McMillan's left jab continuously struck the champion, who lacked the necessary firepower to turn the fight around, being unable to change his game plan. The scintillating speed of the challenger's punches often bewildered Stecca, although it was noticeable in the later rounds that McMillan was beginning to stand his ground in order to get more weight behind his blows. At the final bell there was only one winner - McMillan. *Judges Scorecards:* 116-114, 118-110, 119-110.

16 May, 1992 James Warring 13.6 (USA) W PTS 12 Johnny Nelson 13.7¼ (GB), Fredricksburg, USA. IBF Cruiserweight Title Defence.

As in his earlier challenge for the WBC version of the title against Carlos de Leon, Nelson boxed in a precautionary fashion, not risking anything and generally keeping out of range and certainly not looking like a man who wanted to become a world champion. At least Warring tried to make a fight of it as Nelson continuously drifted away from any prospective action, but unfortunately, for the fans, the champion didn't have the technique to be able to cut the ring space down and force the challenger to stand and deliver. Round after round of the same boring spectacle ensued as Warring chased and Nelson ran and when it was all over the lopsided judges' scorecards told the story. *Judges Scorecards:* 120-108, 118-111, 117-111.

16 May, 1992 Victor Rabanales 8.6 (Mexico) W RSC 4 Luis Ocampo 8.5¼ (Argentine), Tuxtla, Mexico. WBC Bantamweight Title Defence.

This first defence of the title by Rabanales was put on as part of the celebrations to commemorate the 100th anniversary of the founding of the city of Tuxtla Gutierrez in Mexico. Rabanales, a battle scarred veteran of the ring, got down to business from the opening bell, throwing wide left hooks and follow up punches to put the Argentinian challenger immediately under pressure. Ocampo proved a game, but limited fighter, who although never decked, took a steady beating at the hands of the Mexican until he was rescued at two minutes, 41 seconds of the fourth round when he was unable to fight back after shipping a great deal of punishment.

22 May, 1992 Rafael Pineda 9.13 (Colombia) W RSC 7 Clarence Coleman 9.13 (USA), Mexico City, Mexico. IBF Light-Welterweight Title Defence.

It didn't take the audience too long to realise that the challenger, Coleman, who was fighting outside the States for the very first time following bad defeats at the hand of Charles Murray and Mickey Ward, had no right to be sharing the same ring as Pineda. The champion was in complete control all the way and at times he was almost carrying his limited club-fighting opponent. However, Coleman still managed to cut Pineda's mouth in the fifth and inflict a cut over the right eye a round later, so it was probably just as well that the champion did not risk his title against a more worthy opponent. Early into the seventh, Pineda decided that he had better finish the job in case further injuries were sustained and floored his rival twice before the referee waved it off with just 28 seconds on the clock.

5 June, 1992 Jeff Harding 12.6¾ (Australia) W RSC 8 Christophe Tiozzo 12.6¾ (France), Marseille, France. WBC Light-Heavyweight Title Defence.

Tiozzo got off to a flying start, moving well and throwing nice long jabs to unbalance the champion, who although blocking much of the leather that came his way, returned to his corner at the end of the second with blood seeping from a cut over his right eye. Stepping up the pace, Harding at last began to get into the fight with good punches of his own and Tiozzo was cut early in the fourth. The Frenchman came back strongly in the fifth, but it was noticeable that Harding had plenty in hand and looked ominously strong. As the pace hotted up over the next couple of rounds, with Tiozzo out in front and both men cut up around the eyes, the Frenchman appeared to tire rapidly after Harding's bodywork started to take effect. The eighth round saw both men trading and suddenly, as Tiozzo missed with a right, he was immediately countered by a left-hook which sent him crashing on his back. Getting up at the count of eight he was allowed to carry on momentarily, before being rescued by the third man.

7 June, 1992 Humberto Gonzalez 7.10 (Mexico) W RSC 12 Kwang-Sun Kim 7.10 (South Korea), Seoul, South Korea. WBC Light-Flyweight Title Defence.

After a successful amateur career, including winning an Olympic gold medal in 1988, the challenger, who was having only his sixth pro fight, made a very good start, ripping punches in from both hands. Gonzalez, who was coming back after a broken left hand, was understandably nervous earlier on and was unable to strike up any rhythm in his work. Coming into the eleventh, Kim was out in front, but near the end of the round he was floored by a heavy left-hook and was lucky to survive to the bell. Gonzalez was not going to miss the golden opportunity that had presented itself and moved in for the kill. After being floored for a further two counts, Kim was rescued by the referee in the final round to save him from further punishment.

9 June, 1992 John David Jackson 11.0 (USA) W RTD 9 Pat Lawlor 10.11 (USA), San Francisco, USA. WBO Light-Middleweight Title Defence.

Assuming control from the very first round, Jackson had the easiest of title defences as he used the unfortunate Lawlor as a punch bag for most of the night. Slipping inside the Irish-American's blows, the champion worked from head to body as he pleased and it was only the challenger's extraordinary ability to assimilate punishment and the fact that Jackson is not a heavy puncher that kept Lawlor going for so long. However, in the ninth, the champion really cut loose and with Lawlor subjected to a fierce battering it began to look as though the end was nigh. At the bell it was obvious that the local man was in dire straits and with a serious cut over his left eye, his corner called the referee over and the fight was brought to a close.

11 June, 1992 Rodolfo Blanco 8.0 (Colombia) W PTS 12 Dave McAuley 8.0 (GB), Bilbao, Spain. IBF Flyweight Title Challenge.

Showing the challenger far too much respect, McAuley didn't really get his act together until the fifth round when he hurt Blanco with a couple of hard left-hooks. Unfortunately, over the next three rounds, McAuley allowed the challenger to dictate and it was clear then that the title was slipping from his grasp. It was only later, in the tenth, that he launched one of his famous comebacks, as he marched forward for the first time in the fight, nailing Blanco several times and forcing him back on his heels. But the challenger came right back at him in the eleventh and McAuley, with his right eye almost closed, ended the round against the ropes and under attack. Looking for one big punch in the last round, the Irishman rocked Blanco badly with a left-right, but the challenger weathered the storm and the title changed hands. *Judges Scorecards:* 114-113, 114-113, 115-112.

12 June, 1992 Joey Gamache 9.9 (USA) W RSC 8 Chil-Sung Chun 9.8¾ (South Korea), Portland, USA. Vacant WBA Lightweight Title.

With a big local following, Gamache came straight out trying to work off the jab, while the Korean looked to counter any mistakes. In the second round after a flurry of blows, Chun suddenly turned away badly cut over the left eye and the fight looked as good as over. But somehow he survived to hit back on his own account in the third, although his eye damage was worsening with a swelling now appearing underneath the cut. Incredibly, the corner ignored the blood and treated the swelling with the endswell. In the fifth, Chun's right eye went and from then on it was all one-way traffic as Gamache began slicing the jab home again and again as the by now half-blind Korean had great difficulty in picking up the punches. Fighting on borrowed time in the eighth, the brave Chun gave it one last shot, but he was now ready to be taken and as the bell rang to end the round he was finally rescued by the referee who had at last seen enough.

13 June, 1992 Anaclet Wamba 13.7¾ (France) W RSC 5 Andrei Rudenko 13.4½ (CIS), Levallois, France. WBC Cruiserweight Title Defence.

From the bell, the first modern Russian to fight for a title, Rudenko, forced the pace throughout the opening round as Wamba held his ground and scored well with jabs, while also landing some solid combinations to both head and body. Countering admirably, through rounds two to four, Wamba continued to pick off the challenger with good shots, still biding his time and still punching with greater effect than his rival. The Russian only knew one way to fight and that was going forward and in the fifth he was caught squarely on by a battery of lefts and rights, before crashing down for a count of nine. On his feet at ten, the referee stopped the action when the towel came fluttering in from the challenger's corner.

13 June, 1992 Hi-Yon Choi 7.7 (South Korea) W CO 3 Rommel Lawas 7.4½ (Philippines), Inchon, South Korea. WBA Mini-Flyweight Title Defence.

Lawas, a short, sturdy challenger, walked straight into the champion from the off, showing no signs of apprehension whatsoever. That aside, it was Choi who threw the most accurate punches of the opening two rounds as he met the headstrong Filipino with solid combination punches to head and body. Steaming out for the third, the challenger amazed the crowd and certainly confused Choi when he landed several powerful punches. Not to be deterred, the champion dug deep and hit back hard with good blows of his own and a solid right-hook to the side of the ribcage sent Lawas crashing to the canvas in some agony and unable to beat the count with just one second left on the clock.

14 June, 1992 Fahlan Lukmingkwan 7.7 (Thailand) W RSC 8 Said Iskander 7.5 (Indonesia), Bangkok, Thailand. IBF Mini-Flyweight Title Defence.

From the first round when the southpaw champion connected solidly with his favourite right-hook, straight-left combinations, it became a totally one sided contest. In the second, Iskander was floored four times; firstly by a smashing left, secondly by a right-hook following a straight left, thirdly from another solid left and for the fourth time after a short burst of punches. How he got through the round was a miracle. Both men were bleeding badly from the third round on, but somehow, the Indonesian, although still being outpunched, was proving durable and was often coming back for more. The next four rounds were still all Lukmingkwan, with the challenger being nailed by big rights and lefts without reply. Midway through the eighth, the referee was called to the ring apron by the doctor and the fight was stopped to save Iskander from shipping further unnecessary punishment.

15 June, 1992 Hiroki Ioka 7.9½ (Japan) W PTS 12 Bong-Jun Kim 7.9¾ (South Korea), Osaka, Japan. WBA Light-Flyweight Title Defence.

Both fighters made a reasonable start to the contest, with the champion using his extra reach to score with the jab, but before the round ended he was unfortunately cut in the corner of his left eye by a butt. The eye damage did not unduly concern Ioka and he moved into a good lead over the early rounds. Cut over the right eye in the sixth, Kim tried hard to stage a recovery from the seventh onwards as Ioka tired and he had some success, although frequently the pair fell into clinches. It was now most noticeable that Ioka was using his right hand sparingly, due to injury and Kim put in a charge over the last three rounds, but to no avail as the champion held on to run out a unanimous points winner. *Judges Scorecards:* 116-112, 116-114, 117-112.

19 June, 1992 Evander Holyfield 15.0 (USA) W PTS 12 Larry Holmes 16.6 (USA), Las Vegas, USA. WBC, WBA & IBF Heavyweight Title Defence.

The 42-year-old Holmes surprised many by going the distance with a champion 13 years younger than himself, but at the end of the night he had covered himself in glory, while Holyfield had set the division back several rungs. Chasing Holmes to the ropes, the champion's instructions had been to dart in and out and avoid the challenger's right hand at all costs. It worked up to a point, but Holyfield's own heavy artillery had no real effect on the former champion and worse still, he picked up a bad cut over his right eye after being clobbered accidentally by Holmes' elbow at the end of the sixth. With Holmes absorbing Holyfield's best shots and the champion protecting his damaged eye, the contest became almost uneventful and while the verdict was never beyond doubt, the older man even took the last two rounds, twice wobbling his foe into the bargain. *Judges Scorecards:* 117-111, 116-112, 116-112.

23 June, 1992 Yuri Arbachakov 7.13¾ (CIS) W CO 8 Muangchai Kitikasem 8.0 (Thailand), Tokyo, Japan. WBC Flyweight Title Challenge.

The Russian born fighter made a very fast start and showed he meant business when he dropped the champion on the bell to end the first round. However, after taking charge in the second he became careless himself and received a mandatory eight count a round later. On getting back into the fray, Arbachakov immediately landed a cracking right, forcing the champion to take an eight count and on the resumption, Kitikasem was lucky to last the round out. Although the challenger was on top from that moment on, the weight drained Kitikasem tried to punch with him all the way, making it a thrilling contest. In the eighth, Arbachakov finally gained total control and a burst of around 20 punches without reply set Kitikasem up for a bludgeoning right-hander which sent the champion crashing to the boards, out to the world.

23 June, 1992 Tracy Harris Patterson 8.10 (USA) W RSC 2 Thierry Jacob 8.8½ (France), Albany, USA, WBC Super-Bantamweight Title Challenge.

Boxing carefully for the first few minutes, the southpaw Jacob made a cautious start in order to feel his rival out. Suddenly, things took a dramatic turn. After receiving a warning to keep his punches up, the champion was immediately caught by a heavy right which sent him stumbling into the ropes. Patterson chased him and fired in at least eight undefended right hands, the last of which sent Jacob down in a heap. Getting up inside the count, he was saved by the bell, but at the start of the second round, Patterson closed in quickly for the kill. A string of left-hooks put Jacob down in his own corner and when he got to his feet he was mercilessly attacked from both hands and toppled over by the ropes, before the referee humanely came to his rescue.

25 June, 1992 James McGirt 10.3¾ (USA) W PTS 12 Patrizio Oliva 10.6¼ (Italy), Naples, Italy. WBC Welterweight Title Defence.

As awkward as ever, the Italian presented McGirt with a few problems early on in the fight as he closed him down and tied him up constantly. At close quarters, the American was invariably warned for misuse of the head and in the fourth round Oliva picked up a long vertical cut over the left eye and was buckled by a heavy right until the bell gave him some much needed respite. Oliva came back momentarily, rocking McGirt in the eighth with a right to the head, before the champion took over the reigns, making the challenger's body a non-stop target. But the Italian stuck to his guns and although well beaten he finished on a more positive note than the arm weary McGirt, who was glad to hear the final bell. *Judges Scorecards:* 119-111, 118-110, 116-112.

27 June, 1992 Wilfredo Vasquez 8.10 (Puerto Rico) W PTS 12 Freddy Cruz 8.8¾ (Dominican Republic), Gorle, Italy, WBA Super-Bantamweight Title Defence.

Controversy surrounded the verdict at the end of a scrappy contest which had always been close with both men negating much of each others work. The Italian-based Cruz was angry that he had been given a count after being forced to the ropes by a succession of rabbit punches, without ever being on the floor. Although Cruz threw more leather than Vasquez, one of the judges decided that the better quality of the latter's work had won the day, while the other two would have had the fight even if the knockdown had not been taken into account. *Judges Scorecards:* 117-111, 115-114, 115-114.

27 June, 1992 Chris Eubank 12.0 (GB) W PTS 12 Ronnie Essett 11.12½ (USA), Quinta do Lago, Portugal. WBO Super-Middleweight Title Defence.

After winning the first two rounds clearly, while both men were still finding their way around the ring, Eubank allowed the American to shade the next three as he continuously stalked and postured. Right from the off, Essett had fought in reverse gear, obviously not keen to sample the power of Eubank's heavy blows and he carried on in this vein, occasionally countering when the opportunity presented itself. Eubank, for his part, failed in the main to take the initiative by not cutting the ring space down and forcing Essett to fight. But when he was able to corner the challenger he seemed unable to land the solid punches that were needed to take his man out as Essett covered up and waited for the storm to subside. At least Eubank upped the pace to win the final round of a fight that for many resembled nothing more than a glorified sparring session. *Judges Scorecards:* 117-112, 117-112, 118-110.

30 June, 1992 Carlos Gonzalez 9.13½ (Mexico) W RSC 2 Jimmy Paul 10.0 (USA), Los Angeles, USA. Vacant WBO Light-Welterweight Title.

Initially, when Hector Camacho relinquished his WBO crown, "Bolillo" Gonzalez was matched to fight Oba Carr for the vacant title. Unfortunately, for the paying public, Carr was injured and was replaced by his stablemate, Jimmy Paul. After holding his own in the first round, Paul was soon reeling under heavy pressure in the second as the powerful Gonzalez began to unload big punches. Unbeaten in 32 contests, Gonzalez really got the bit between the teeth as he chased the old-stager to the ropes and pounded him with lefts and rights. Finally, a big left-uppercut unhinged Paul and although not going down, he was being battered unmercifully when the referee came to his rescue after two minutes, twelve seconds of the round had elapsed.

World Champions, 1890-1992

The following records attempt to set out by weight division every champion under Queensberry Rules since the beginning of gloves (2 oz minimum).

Boxing grew up in Great Britain and quickly spread to the USA, but it was not until the champions of these two countries came together in the latter part of the last century that it developed on an international scale. Organisations then came into existence solely for the purpose of controlling professional boxing. The National Sporting Club of Britain was formed in 1891, later to be amalgamated into the British Boxing Board of Control during 1929. By the early part of the century the sport had also begun to boom among the French, who in 1911 were instrumental in setting up the International Boxing Union to look after the interests of boxing in Europe. Following World War II the body became known as the European Boxing Union. In America many states had allowed boxing to take place, but in 1920 the New York State Athletic Commission was legally constituted under the Walker Law to govern the sport. Also, at the same time, several of the independent states of America became affiliated to form the National Boxing Association, which by 1962 was re-named the World Boxing Associaion. In an effort to create a balance of power, Britain supported the setting up of the World Boxing Council, formed in 1963, which brought together New York and its satellite states, with the BBBC, the Commonwealth and the EBU. Recently the International Boxing Federation, an offshoot of the WBA, has sprung into prominence on the world boxing stage, along with the World Boxing Organisation.

Over the years many new weight divisions have been formed and original classes have been restructured. For example the bantamweight division limit, which in 1890 stood at 112 lbs, was gradually increased until it reached an internationally accepted 118 lbs in 1909. Similarly other weight limits rose, e.g. featherweight: 1890 (118 lbs) - 1909 (126 lbs); welterweight: 1892 (142 lbs) - 1909 (147 lbs); middleweight: 1891 (154 lbs) - 1909 (160 lbs).

Championship Status Code:

AUST = Australia; CALIF = California; EBU = European Boxing Union; FR = France; GB = Great Britain; IBF = International Boxing Federation; IBU = International Boxing Union; LOUIS = Louisiana; MARY = Maryland; MASS = Massachusetts; NBA = National Boxing Association; NY = New York; PEN = Pennsylvania; USA = United States; WBA = World Boxing Association; WBC = World Boxing Council; WBO = World Boxing Organisation.

Champions in **bold** are accorded universal recognition.

* Undefeated champions.

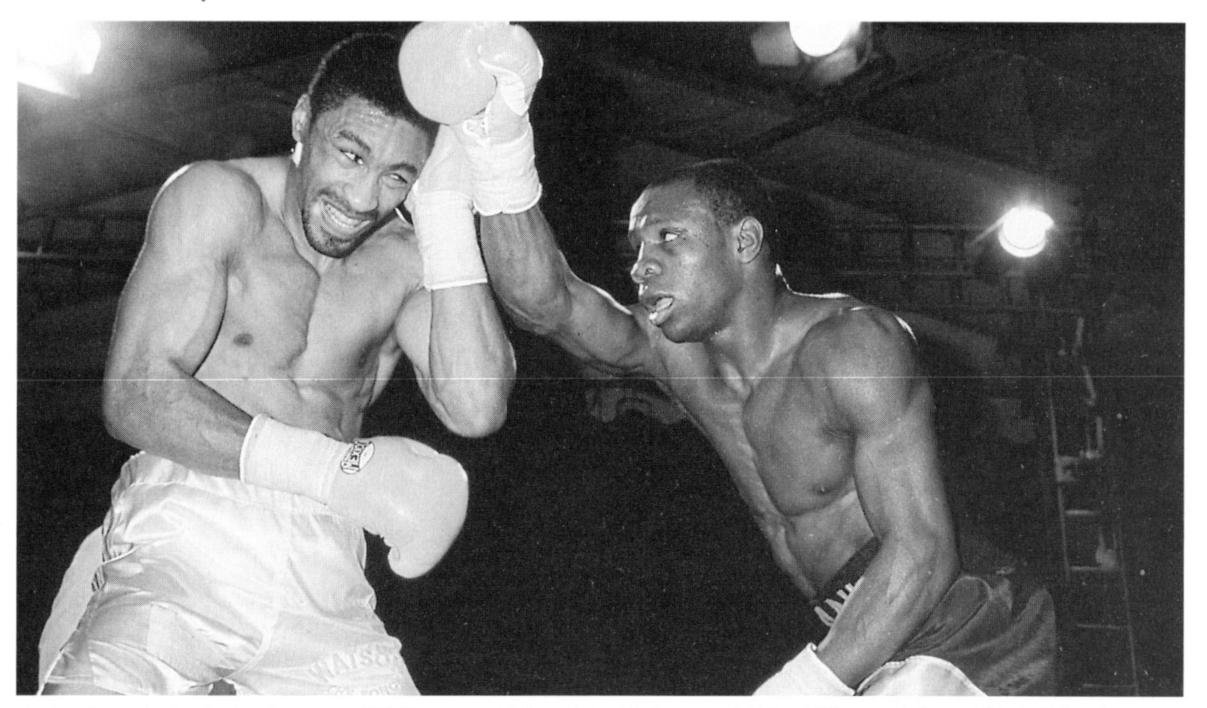

Action from the battle for the vacant WBO super-middleweight title between Michael Watson (left) and Chris Eubank, won by the latter

Action Images

Title Holder	Birthplace	Tenure	Status
M. Flyweight (105 lbs)			
Kyung-Yung Lee*	S. Korea	1987-1988	IBF
Hiroki Ioka	Japan	1987-1988	WBC
Luis Gamez*	Venezuela	1988-1989	WBA
Samuth Sithnaruepol	Thailand	1988-1989	IBF
Napa Kiatwanchai	Thailand	1988-1989	WBC
Bong-Jun Kim	S Korea	1989-1991	WBA
Nico Thomas	Indonesia	1989	IBF
Rafael Torres	Dom Republic	1989-	WBO
Eric Chavez	Philippines	1989-1990	IBF
Jum-Hwan Choi	S Korea	1989-1990	WBC
Hideyuki Ohashi	Japan	1990	WBC
Fahlan Lukmingkwan	Thailand	1990-	IBF
Ricardo Lopez	Mexico	1990-	WBC
Hi-Yon Choi	S Korea	1991-	WBA
L. Flyweight (108 lbs)			
Franco Udella*	Italy	1975	WBC
Jaime Rios	Panama	1975-1976	WBA
Luis Estaba	Venezuela	1975-1978	WBC
Juan Guzman	Dom Republic	1976	WBA
Yoko Gushiken	Japan	1976-1981	WBA
Freddie Castillo	Mexico	1978	WBC
Sor Vorasingh	Thailand	1978	WBC
Sun-Jun Kim	S Korea	1978-1980	WBC
Shigeo Nakajima	Japan	1980	WBC
Hilario Zapata	Panama	1980-1982	WBC
Pedro Flores	Mexico	1981	WBA
Hwan-Jin Kim	S Korea	1981	WBA
Katsuo Tokashiki	Japan	1981-1983	WBA
Amado Ursua	Mexico	1982	WBC
Tadashi Tomori	Japan	1982	WBC
Hilario Zapata	Panama	1982-1983	WBC
Jung-Koo Chang*	S Korea	1983-1988	WBC
Lupe Madera	Mexico	1983-1984	WBA
Dodie Penalosa*	Philippines	1983-1986	IBF
Francisco Quiroz	Dom Republic	1984-1985	WBA
Joey Olivo	USA	1985	WBA
Myung-Woo Yuh	S Korea	1985-1991	WBA
Jum-Hwan Choi	S Korea	1987-1988	IBF
Tacy Macalos	Philippines	1988-1989	IBF
German Torres	Mexico	1988-1989	WBC
Yul-Woo Lee	S Korea	1989	WBC
Muangchai Kitikasem	Thailand	1989-1990	IBF
Jose de Jesus	Puerto Rico	1989-	WBO
Humberto Gonzalez	Mexico	1989-1990	WBC
Michael Carbajal	USA	1990-	IBF
Rolando Pascua	Philippines	1990-1991	WBC
Melchor Cob Castro	Mexico	1991	WBC
Humberto Gonzalez	Mexico	1991-	WBC
Hiroki Ioka	Japan	1991-	WBA
Flyweight (112 lbs)			
Sid Smith	England	1913	GB/IBU
Bill Ladbury	England	1913-1914	GB/IBU
Percy Jones*	Wales	1914	GB/IBU
Tancy Lee	Scotland	1915	GB/IBU
Joe Symonds	England	1915-1916	GB/IBU
Jimmy Wilde	Wales	1916	GB/IBU
Jimmy Wilde	Wales	1916-1923	
Pancho Villa*	Philippines	1923-1925	
Fidel la Barba*	USA	1925-1927	
Johnny McCoy	USA	1927-1928	CALIF
Frenchy Belanger	Canada	1927-1928	NBA
Izzy Schwartz	USA	1927-1929	NY
Newsboy Brown	Russia	1928	CALIF
Frankie Genaro	USA	1928-1929	NBA
Johnny Hill	Scotland	1928-1929	GB/CALIF
Emile Pladner	France	1929	NBA/IBU
Frankie Genaro	USA	1929-1931	NBA/IBU
Willie la Morte	USA	1929-1930	NY
Midget Wolgast	USA	1930-1935	NY
Young Perez	Tunisia	1931-1932	NBA/IBU
Jackie Brown	England	1932-1935	NBA/IBU
Benny Lynch*	Scotland	1935-1937	NBA
Small Montana	Philippines	1935-1937	NY/CALIF
Valentin Angelmann	France	1936-1937	IBU
Benny Lynch*	Scotland	1937	
Peter Kane	England	1938-1940	NY/IBU
Young Dado	Philippines	1938-1940	NBA/CALIF
Peter Kane	England	1940-1943	
Jackie Paterson	Scotland	1943-1947	
Jackie Paterson	Scotland	1947-1948	GB/NY
Rinty Monaghan	Ireland	1947-1948	NBA
Rinty Monaghan*	Ireland	1948-1950	
Terry Allen	England	1950	
Dado Marino	Hawaii	1950-1952	
Yoshio Shirai	Japan	1952-1954	
Pascual Perez	Argentine	1954-1960	
Pone Kingpetch	Thailand	1960-1962	
Fighting Harada	Japan	1962-1963	
Pone Kingpetch	Thailand	1963	
Hiroyuki Ebihara	Japan	1963-1964	
Pone Kingpetch	Thailand	1964-1965	
Salvatore Burruni	Italy	1965	
Salvatore Burruni	Italy	1965-1966	WBC
Horacio Accavallo*	Argentine	1966-1968	WBA
Walter McGowan	Scotland	1966	WBC
Chartchai Chionoi	Thailand	1966-1969	WBC
Efren Torres	Mexico	1969-1970	WBC
Hiroyuki Ebihara	Japan	1969	WBA
Bernabe Villacampo	Philippines	1969-1970	WBA
Chartchai Chionoi	Thailand	1970	WBC
Berkerk Chartvanchai	Thailand	1970	WBA
Masao Ohba*	Japan	1970-1973	WBA
Erbito Salavarria*	Philippines	1970-1971	WBC
Betulio Gonzalez	Venezuela	1972	WBC
Venice Borkorsor*	Thailand	1972-1973	WBC
Chartchai Chionoi	Thailand	1973-1974	WBA
Betulio Gonzalez	Venezuela	1973-1974	WBC
Shoji Oguma	Japan	1974-1975	WBC
Susumu Hanagata	Japan	1974-1975	WBA
Miguel Canto	Mexico	1975-1979	WBC
Erbito Salavarria	Philippines	1975-1976	WBA
Alfonso Lopez	Panama	1976	WBA
Guty Espadas	Mexico	1976-1978	WBA
Betulio Gonzalez	Venezuela	1978-1979	WBA
Chan-Hee Park	S Korea	1979-1980	WBC
Luis Ibarra	Panama	1979-1980	WBA
Tae-Shik Kim	S Korea	1980	WBA
Shoji Oguma	Japan	1980-1981	WBC
Peter Mathebula	S Africa	1980-1981	WBA
Santos Laciar	Argentine	1981	WBA
Antonio Avelar	Mexico	1981-1982	WBC
Luis Ibarra	Panama	1981	WBA
Juan Herrera	Mexico	1981-1982	WBA
Prudencio Cardona	Colombia	1982	WBC
Santos Laciar*	Argentine	1982-1985	WBA
Freddie Castillo	Mexico	1982	WBC
Eleoncio Mercedes	Dom Republic	1982-1983	WBC
Charlie Magri	Tunisia	1983	WBC
Frank Cedeno	Philippines	1983-1984	WBC
Soon-Chun Kwon	S Korea	1983-1985	IBF
Koji Kobayashi	Japan	1984	WBC
Gabriel Bernal	Mexico	1984	WBC
Sot Chitalada	Thailand	1984-1988	WBC
Hilario Zapata	Panama	1985-1987	WBA
Chong-Kwan Chung	S Korea	1985-1986	IBF
Bi-Won Chung	S Korea	1986	IBF
Hi-Sup Shin	S Korea	1986-1987	IBF
Fidel Bassa	Colombia	1987-1989	WBA
Dodie Penalosa	Philippines	1987	IBF

Title Holder	Birthplace	Tenure	Status
Chang-Ho Choi	S Korea	1987-1988	IBF
Rolando Bohol	Philippines	1988	IBF
Yong-Kang Kim	S Korea	1988-1989	WBC
Elvis Alvarez*	Colombia	1989	WBO
Duke McKenzie	England	1988-1989	IBF
Sot Chitalada	Thailand	1989-1991	WBC
Dave McAuley	Ireland	1989-1992	IBF
Jesus Rojas	Venezuela	1989-1990	WBA
Yul-Woo Lee	S Korea	1990	WBA
Isidro Perez	Mexico	1990-1992	WBO
Yukihito Tamakuma	Japan	1990	WBA
Muangchai Kitikasem	Thailand	1991-1992	WBC
Elvis Alvarez	Colombia	1991	WBA
Yong-Kang Kim	S Korea	1991-	WBA
Pat Clinton	Scotland	1992-	WBO
Rodolfo Blanco	Colombia	1992-	IBF
Yuri Arbachakov	Russia	1992-	WBC

Tracy Harris Patterson, the reigning WBC super-bantamweight champion

Title Holder	Birthplace	Tenure	Status
S. Flyweight (115 lbs)			
Rafael Orono	Venezuela	1980-1981	WBC
Chul-Ho Kim	S Korea	1981-1982	WBC
Gustavo Ballas	Argentine	1981	WBA
Rafael Pedroza	Panama	1981-1982	WBA
Jiro Watanabe*	Japan	1982-1984	WBA
Rafael Orono	Venezuela	1982-1983	WBC
Payao Poontarat	Thailand	1983-1984	WBC
Joo-Do Chun	S Korea	1983-1985	IBF
Jiro Watanabe	Japan	1984-1986	WBC
Elly Pical	Indonesia	1985-1986	IBF
Kaosai Galaxy*	Thailand	1984-1991	WBA
Cesar Polanco	Dom Republic	1986	IBF
Gilberto Roman	Mexico	1986-1987	WBC
Elly Pical*	Indonesia	1986-1987	IBF
Santos Laciar	Argentine	1987	WBC
Tae-Il Chang	S Korea	1987	IBF
Jesus Rojas	Colombia	1987-1988	WBC
Elly Pical	Indonesia	1987-1989	IBF
Gilberto Roman	Mexico	1988-1989	WBC
Jose Ruiz	Puerto Rico	1989-1992	WBO
Juan Polo Perez	Colombia	1989-1990	IBF
Nana Yaw Konadu	Ghana	1989-1990	WBC
Sung-Il Moon	S Korea	1990-	WBC
Robert Quiroga	USA	1990-	IBF
Jose Quirino	Mexico	1992-	WBO
Katsuya Onizuka	Japan	1992-	WBA
Bantamweight (118 lbs)			
George Dixon*	Canada	1890-1892	
Billy Plimmer	England	1892-1895	
Pedlar Palmer	England	1895-1899	
Terry McGovern*	USA	1899-1900	
Dan Dougherty	USA	1900-1901	
Harry Forbes	USA	1901-1903	
Frankie Neil	USA	1903-1904	
Joe Bowker*	England	1904-1905	
Jimmy Walsh*	USA	1905-1907	
Owen Moran*	England	1907	GB
Johnny Coulon	Canada	1908-1909	USA
Monte Attell	USA	1909-1910	CALIF
Johnny Coulon	Canada	1909-1911	LOUIS
Frankie Conley	Italy	1910-1911	CALIF
Digger Stanley	England	1910-1912	GB/IBU
Johnny Coulon	Canada	1911-1914	USA
Charles Ledoux	France	1912-1913	GB/IBU
Eddie Campi	USA	1913-1914	GB/IBU
Kid Williams	Denmark	1914	GB/IBU
Kid Williams	Denmark	1914-1917	
Pete Herman	USA	1917-1920	
Joe Lynch	USA	1920-1921	
Pete Herman	USA	1921	
Johnny Buff	USA	1921-1922	
Joe Lynch	USA	1922-1923	
Joe Lynch	USA	1923-1924	NBA
Abe Goldstein	USA	1923-1924	NY
Abe Goldstein	USA	1924	
Eddie Martin	USA	1924-1925	
Charlie Rosenberg*	USA	1925-1927	
Bud Taylor*	USA	1927-1928	NBA
Teddy Baldock	England	1927	GB
Willie Smith*	S Africa	1927-1929	GB
Bushy Graham*	Italy	1928-1929	NY
Al Brown	Panama	1929-1931	NY/IBU
Pete Sanstol	Norway	1931	NBA
Al Brown	Panama	1931-1934	
Sixto Escobar	Puerto Rico	1934-1935	NBA
Al Brown	Panama	1934-1935	NY/IBU
Baltazar Sangchilli	Spain	1935-1936	NY/IBU
Lou Salica	USA	1935	NBA
Sixto Escobar	Puerto Rico	1935-1936	NBA

Title Holder	Birthplace	Tenure	Status
Tony Marino	USA	1936	NY/IBU
Sixto Escobar	Puerto Rico	1936-1937	
Harry Jeffra	USA	1937-1938	
Sixto Escobar*	Puerto Rico	1938-1939	
Lou Salica	USA	1940-1942	
Manuel Ortiz	USA	1942-1947	
Harold Dade	USA	1947	
Manuel Ortiz	USA	1947-1950	
Vic Toweel	S Africa	1950-1952	
Jimmy Carruthers*	Australia	1952-1954	
Robert Cohen	Algeria	1954-1956	NY/EBU
Raton Macias	Mexico	1955-1957	NBA
Mario D'Agata	Italy	1956-1957	NY/EBU
Alphonse Halimi	Algeria	1957	NY/EBU
Alphonse Halimi	Algeria	1957-1959	
Joe Becerra*	Mexico	1959-1960	
Alphonse Halimi	Algeria	1960-1961	EBU
Eder Jofre	Brazil	1960-1962	NBA
Johnny Caldwell	Ireland	1961-1962	EBU
Eder Jofre	Brazil	1962-1965	
Fighting Harada	Japan	1965-1968	
Lionel Rose	Australia	1968-1969	
Ruben Olivares	Mexico	1969-1970	
Chuchu Castillo	Mexico	1970-1971	
Ruben Olivares	Mexico	1971-1972	
Rafael Herrera	Mexico	1972	
Enrique Pinder	Panama	1972	
Enrique Pinder	Panama	1972-1973	WBC
Romeo Anaya	Mexico	1973	WBA
Rafael Herrera	Mexico	1973-1974	WBC
Arnold Taylor	S Africa	1973-1974	WBA
Soo-Hwan Hong	S Korea	1974-1975	WBA
Rodolfo Martinez	Mexico	1974-1976	WBC
Alfonso Zamora	Mexico	1975-1977	WBA
Carlos Zarate	Mexico	1976-1979	WBC
Jorge Lujan	Panama	1977-1980	WBA
Lupe Pintor*	Mexico	1979-1983	WBC
Julian Solis	Puerto Rico	1980	WBA
Jeff Chandler	USA	1980-1984	WBA
Albert Davila*	USA	1983-1985	WBC
Richard Sandoval	USA	1984-1986	WBA
Satoshi Shingaki	Japan	1984-1985	IBF
Jeff Fenech*	Australia	1985-1987	IBF
Daniel Zaragoza	Mexico	1985	WBC
Miguel Lora	Colombia	1985-1988	WBC
Gaby Canizales	USA	1986	WBA
Bernardo Pinango*	Venezuela	1986-1987	WBA
Takuya Muguruma	Japan	1987	WBA
Kelvin Seabrooks	USA	1987-1988	IBF
Chan-Yung Park	S Korea	1987	WBA
Wilfredo Vasquez	Puerto Rico	1987-1988	WBA
Kaokor Galaxy	Thailand	1988	WBA
Orlando Canizales	USA	1988-	IBF
Sung-Il Moon	S Korea	1988-1989	WBA
Raul Perez	Mexico	1988-1991	WBC
Israel Contrerras*	Venezuela	1989-1991	WBO
Kaokor Galaxy	Thailand	1989	WBA
Luisito Espinosa	Philippines	1989-1991	WBA
Greg Richardson	USA	1991	WBC
Gaby Canizales	USA	1991	WBO
Duke McKenzie	England	1991-1992	WBO
Joichiro Tatsuyushi*	Japan	1991-1992	WBC
Israel Contrerras	Venezuela	1991-1992	WBA
Eddie Cook	USA	1992-	WBA
Victor Rabanales	Mexico	1992-	WBC
Rafael del Valle	Puerto Rico	1992-	WBO

S. Bantamweight (122 lbs)

Title Holder	Birthplace	Tenure	Status
Jack Kid Wolfe*	USA	1922-1923	NY
Rigoberto Riasco	Panama	1976	WBC
Royal Kobayashi	Japan	1976	WBC
Dong-Kyun Yum	S Korea	1976-1977	WBC
Wilfredo Gomez*	Puerto Rico	1977-1983	WBC
Soo-Hwan Hong	S Korea	1977-1978	WBA
Ricardo Cardona	Colombia	1978-1980	WBA
Leo Randolph	USA	1980	WBA
Sergio Palma	Argentine	1980-1982	WBA
Leonardo Cruz	Dom Republic	1982-1984	WBA
Jaime Garza	USA	1983-1984	WBC
Bobby Berna	Philippines	1983-1984	IBF
Loris Stecca	Italy	1984	WBA
Seung-In Suh	S Korea	1984-1985	IBF
Victor Callejas*	Puerto Rico	1984-1986	WBA
Juan Meza	Mexico	1984-1985	WBC
Ji-Won Kim*	S Korea	1985-1986	IBF
Lupe Pintor	Mexico	1985-1986	WBC
Samart Payakarun	Thailand	1986-1987	WBC
Louie Espinosa	USA	1987	WBA
Seung-Hoon Lee*	S Korea	1987-1988	IBF
Jeff Fenech*	Australia	1987-1988	WBC
Julio Gervacio	Dom Republic	1987-1988	WBA
Bernardo Pinango	Venezuela	1988	WBA
Daniel Zaragoza	Mexico	1988-1990	WBC
Jose Sanabria	Venezuela	1988-1989	IBF
Juan J. Estrada	Mexico	1988-1989	WBA
Fabrice Benichou	Spain	1989-1990	IBF
Kenny Mitchell	USA	1989	WBO
Valerio Nati	Italy	1989-1990	WBO
Jesus Salud*	USA	1989-1990	WBA
Welcome Ncita	S Africa	1990-	IBF
Paul Banke	USA	1990	WBC
Orlando Fernandez	Puerto Rico	1990-1991	WBO
Luis Mendoza	Colombia	1990-1991	WBA
Pedro Decima	Argentine	1990-1991	WBC
Kiyoshi Hatanaka	Japan	1991	WBC
Jesse Benavides	USA	1991-	WBO
Daniel Zaragoza	Mexico	1991-1992	WBC
Raul Perez	Mexico	1991-1992	WBA
Thierry Jacob	France	1992	WBC
Wilfredo Vasquez	Puerto Rico	1992-	WBA
Tracy Harris Patterson	USA	1992-	WBC

Featherweight (126 lbs)

Title Holder	Birthplace	Tenure	Status
Billy Murphy	New Zealand	1890	AUST
Young Griffo*	Australia	1890-1891	AUST
George Dixon	Canada	1891-1892	USA
George Dixon	Canada	1892-1897	
Solly Smith	USA	1897-1898	
Solly Smith	USA	1898	USA
Ben Jordan	England	1898-1899	GB
Dave Sullivan	Ireland	1898	USA
George Dixon	Canada	1899-1900	USA
George Dixon	Canada	1899-1900	
Terry McGovern	USA	1900-1901	
Young Corbett II*	USA	1901-1903	
Abe Attell	USA	1903-1904	
Tommy Sullivan*	USA	1904-1905	
Abe Attell	USA	1906-1912	
Abe Attell	USA	1912	USA
Jim Driscoll*	Wales	1912-1913	GB/IBU
Johnny Kilbane	USA	1912-1913	USA
Johnny Kilbane	USA	1913-1922	
Johnny Kilbane	USA	1922-1923	NBA
Johnny Dundee*	Italy	1922-1923	NY
Eugene Criqui	France	1923	
Johnny Dundee*	Italy	1923-1924	
Kid Kaplan*	Russia	1925-1926	
Honeyboy Finnegan	USA	1926-1927	MASS
Benny Bass	Russia	1927-1928	NBA
Tony Canzoneri	USA	1927-1928	NY
Tony Canzoneri	USA	1928	
Andre Routis	France	1928-1929	

Title Holder	Birthplace	Tenure	Status
Bat Battalino*	USA	1929-1932	
Tommy Paul	USA	1932-1933	NBA
Kid Chocolate*	Cuba	1932-1933	NY
Freddie Miller	USA	1933-1936	NBA
Baby Arizmendi	Mexico	1934-1935	NY
Baby Arizmendi	Mexico	1935-1936	CALIF
Petey Sarron	USA	1936-1937	NBA
Henry Armstrong*	USA	1936-1937	CALIF
Mike Belloise	USA	1936	NY
Maurice Holtzer*	France	1937-1938	IBU
Henry Armstrong*	USA	1937-1938	NBA/NY/CALIF
Leo Rodak	USA	1938-1939	NBA
Joey Archibald	USA	1938-1939	NY
Joey Archibald	USA	1939-1940	
Joey Archibald	USA	1940	NY
Jimmy Perrin	USA	1940	LOUIS
Petey Scalzo	USA	1940-1941	NBA
Harry Jeffra	USA	1940-1941	NY
Joey Archibald	USA	1941	NY
Richie Lemos	USA	1941	NBA
Chalky Wright	Mexico	1941-1942	NY
Harry Jeffra	USA	1941-1942	MARY
Jackie Wilson	USA	1941-1943	NBA
Willie Pep	USA	1942-1946	NY
Jackie Callura	Canada	1943	NBA
Phil Terranova	USA	1943-1944	NBA
Sal Bartolo	USA	1944-1946	NBA
Willie Pep	USA	1946-1948	
Sandy Saddler	USA	1948-1949	
Willie Pep	USA	1949-1950	
Sandy Saddler*	USA	1950-1957	
Hogan Kid Bassey	Nigeria	1957-1959	
Davey Moore	USA	1959-1963	
Sugar Ramos	Cuba	1963-1964	
Vicente Saldivar*	Mexico	1964-1967	
Raul Rojas	USA	1967-1968	WBA
Howard Winstone	Wales	1968	WBC
Jose Legra	Cuba	1968-1969	WBC
Shozo Saijyo	Japan	1968-1971	WBA
Johnny Famechon	France	1969-1970	WBC
Vicente Saldivar	Mexico	1970	WBC
Kuniaki Shibata	Japan	1970-1972	WBC
Antonio Gomez	Venezuela	1971-1972	WBA
Clemente Sanchez	Mexico	1972	WBC
Ernesto Marcel*	Panama	1972-1974	WBA
Jose Legra	Cuba	1972-1973	WBC
Eder Jofre*	Brazil	1973-1974	WBC
Ruben Olivares	Mexico	1974	WBA
Bobby Chacon	USA	1974-1975	WBC
Alexis Arguello*	Nicaragua	1974-1977	WBA
Ruben Olivares	Mexico	1975	WBC
David Kotey	Ghana	1975-1976	WBC
Danny Lopez	USA	1976-1980	WBC
Rafael Ortega	Panama	1977	WBA
Cecilio Lastra	Spain	1977-1978	WBA
Eusebio Pedroza	Panama	1978-1985	WBA
Salvador Sanchez*	Mexico	1980-1982	WBC
Juan Laporte	Puerto Rico	1982-1984	WBC
Min-Keun Chung	S Korea	1984-1985	IBF
Wilfredo Gomez	Puerto Rico	1984	WBC
Azumah Nelson*	Ghana	1984-1987	WBC
Barry McGuigan	Ireland	1985-1986	WBA
Ki-Yung Chung	S Korea	1985-1986	IBF
Steve Cruz	USA	1986-1987	WBA
Antonio Rivera	Puerto Rico	1986-1987	IBF
Antonio Esparragoza	Venezuela	1987-1991	WBF
Calvin Grove	USA	1988	IBF
Jeff Fenech*	Australia	1988-1989	WBC
Jorge Paez*	Mexico	1988-1990	IBF
Maurizio Stecca	Italy	1989-1992	WBO
Louie Espinosa	USA	1989-1990	WBO

Title Holder	Birthplace	Tenure	Status
Jorge Paez*	Mexico	1990-1991	IBF/WBO
Marcos Villasana	Mexico	1990-1991	WBC
Kyun-Yung Park	S Korea	1991-	WBA
Troy Dorsey	USA	1991	IBF
Maurizio Stecca	Italy	1991-1992	WBO
Manuel Medina	Mexico	1991-	IBF
Paul Hodkinson	England	1991-	WBC
Colin McMillan	England	1992-	WBO

S. Featherweight (130 lbs)

Title Holder	Birthplace	Tenure	Status
Johnny Dundee	Italy	1921-1923	NY
Jack Bernstein	USA	1923	NBA/NY
Johnny Dundee	Italy	1923-1924	NBA/NY
Kid Sullivan	USA	1924-1925	NBA/NY
Mike Ballerino	USA	1925	NBA/NY
Tod Morgan	USA	1925-1929	NBA/NY
Benny Bass	Russia	1929	NBA/NY
Benny Bass	Russia	1929-1931	NBA
Kid Chocolate	Cuba	1931-1933	NBA
Frankie Klick*	USA	1933-1934	NBA
Sandy Saddler*	USA	1949-1950	OHIO
Harold Gomes	USA	1959-1960	NBA
Flash Elorde	Philippines	1960-1967	NBA
Yoshiaki Numata	Japan	1967	WBA
Hiroshi Kobayashi	Japan	1967-1971	WBA
Rene Barrientos	Philippines	1969-1970	WBC
Yoshiaki Numata	Japan	1970-1971	WBC
Alfredo Marcano	Venezuela	1971-1972	WBA
Ricardo Arredondo	Mexico	1971-1974	WBC
Ben Villaflor	Philippines	1972-1973	WBA
Kuniaki Shibata	Japan	1973	WBA
Ben Villaflor	Philippines	1973-1976	WBA
Kuniaki Shibata	Japan	1974-1975	WBC
Alfredo Escalera	Puerto Rico	1975-1978	WBC
Sam Serrano	Puerto Rico	1976-1980	WBA
Alexis Arguello*	Nicaragua	1978-1980	WBC
Yasutsune Uehara	Japan	1980-1981	WBA
Rafael Limon	Mexico	1980-1981	WBC
Cornelius Boza-Edwards	Uganda	1981	WBC
Sam Serrano	Puerto Rico	1981-1983	WBA
Roland Navarrete	Philippines	1981-1982	WBC
Rafael Limon	Mexico	1982	WBC
Bobby Chacon*	USA	1982-1983	WBC
Roger Mayweather	USA	1983-1984	WBA
Hector Camacho*	Puerto Rico	1983-1984	WBC
Rocky Lockridge	USA	1984-1985	WBA
Hwan-Kil Yuh	S Korea	1984-1985	IBF
Julio Cesar Chavez*	Mexico	1984-1987	WBC
Lester Ellis	England	1985	IBF
Wilfredo Gomez	Puerto Rico	1985-1986	WBA
Barry Michael	England	1985-1987	IBF
Alfredo Layne	Panama	1986	WBA
Brian Mitchell*	S Africa	1986-1991	WBA
Rocky Lockridge	USA	1987-1988	IBF
Azumah Nelson	Ghana	1988-	WBC
Tony Lopez	USA	1988-1989	IBF
Juan Molina*	Puerto Rico	1989	WBO
Juan Molina	Puerto Rico	1989-1990	IBF
Kamel Bou Ali	Tunisia	1989-1992	WBO
Tony Lopez	USA	1990-1991	IBF
Joey Gamache*	USA	1991	WBA
Brian Mitchell*	S Africa	1991-1992	IBF
Genaro Hernandez	USA	1991-	WBA
Juan Molina	Puerto Rico	1992-	IBF
Daniel Londas	France	1992-	WBO

Lightweight (135 lbs)

Title Holder	Birthplace	Tenure	Status
Jack McAuliffe*	Ireland	1890-1895	USA
George Lavigne	USA	1896-1899	
Frank Erne	Switzerland	1899-1902	
Joe Gans*	USA	1902-1904	

Title Holder	Birthplace	Tenure	Status
Jimmy Britt	USA	1904-1905	
Battling Nelson	Denmark	1905-1906	
Joe Gans	USA	1906-1908	
Battling Nelson	Denmark	1908-1910	
Ad Wolgast	USA	1910-1912	
Willie Ritchie	USA	1912-1914	
Freddie Welsh	Wales	1914-1917	
Benny Leonard*	USA	1917-1925	
Jimmy Goodrich	USA	1925	NY
Rocky Kansas	USA	1925-1926	
Sammy Mandell	USA	1926-1930	
Al Singer	USA	1930	
Tony Canzoneri	USA	1930-1933	
Barney Ross*	USA	1933-1935	
Tony Canzeroni	USA	1935-1936	
Lou Ambers	USA	1936-1938	
Henry Armstrong	USA	1938-1939	
Lou Ambers	USA	1939-1940	
Sammy Angott*	USA	1940-1941	NBA
Lew Jenkins	USA	1940-1941	NY
Sammy Angott*	USA	1941-1942	
Beau Jack	USA	1942-1943	NY
Slugger White	USA	1943	MARY
Bob Montgomery	USA	1943	NY
Sammy Angott	USA	1943-1944	NBA
Beau Jack	USA	1943-1944	NY
Bob Montgomery	USA	1944-1947	NY
Juan Zurita	Mexico	1944-1945	NBA
Ike Williams	USA	1945-1947	NBA
Ike Williams	USA	1947-1951	
Jimmy Carter	USA	1951-1952	
Lauro Salas	Mexico	1952	
Jimmy Carter	USA	1952-1954	
Paddy de Marco	USA	1954	
Jimmy Carter	USA	1954-1955	
Wallace Bud Smith	USA	1955-1956	
Joe Brown	USA	1956-1962	
Carlos Ortiz	Puerto Rico	1962-1965	
Ismael Laguna	Panama	1965	
Carlos Oritz	Puerto Rico	1965-1968	
Carlos Teo Cruz	Dom Republic	1968-1969	
Mando Ramos	USA	1969-1970	
Ismael Laguna	Panama	1970	
Ken Buchanan	Scotland	1970-1971	
Ken Buchanan	Scotland	1971-1972	WBA
Pedro Carrasco	Spain	1971-1972	WBC
Mando Ramos	USA	1972	WBC
Roberto Duran	Panama	1972-1978	WBA
Chango Carmona	Mexico	1972	WBC
Rodolfo Gonzalez	Mexico	1972-1974	WBC
Guts Ishimatsu	Japan	1974-1976	WBC
Esteban de Jesus	Puerto Rico	1976-1978	WBC
Roberto Duran*	Panama	1978-1979	
Jim Watt	Scotland	1979-1981	WBC
Ernesto Espana	Venezuela	1979-1980	WBA
Hilmer Kenty	USA	1980-1981	WBA
Sean O'Grady*	USA	1981	WBA
Alexis Arguello*	Nicaragua	1981-1983	WBC
Claude Noel	Trinidad	1981	WBA
Arturo Frias	USA	1981-1982	WBA
Ray Mancini	USA	1982-1984	WBA
Edwin Rosario	Puerto Rico	1983-1984	WBC
Charlie Brown	USA	1984	IBF
Harry Arroyo	USA	1984-1985	IBF
Livingstone Bramble	USA	1984-1986	WBA
Jose Luis Ramirez	Mexico	1984-1985	WBC
Jimmy Paul	USA	1985-1986	IBF
Hector Camacho*	Puerto Rico	1985-1987	WBC
Edwin Rosario	Puerto Rico	1986-1987	WBA
Greg Haugen	USA	1986-1987	IBF
Vinnie Pazienza	USA	1987-1988	IBF

Title Holder	Birthplace	Tenure	Status
Jose Luis Ramirez	Mexico	1987-1988	WBC
Julio Cesar Chavez*	Mexico	1987-1988	WBA
Greg Haugen	USA	1988-1989	IBF
Julio Cesar Chavez*	Mexico	1988-1989	WBA/WBC
Maurizio Aceves	Mexico	1989-1990	WBO
Pernell Whitaker*	USA	1989	IBF
Edwin Rosario	Puerto Rico	1989-1990	WBA
Pernell Whitaker*	USA	1989-1990	IBF/WBC
Juan Nazario	Puerto Rico	1990	WBA
Pernell Whitaker*	USA	1990-1992	IBF/WBC/WBA
Dingaan Thobela	S Africa	1990-	WBO
Joey Gamache	USA	1992-	WBA

L. Welterweight (140 lbs)

Title Holder	Birthplace	Tenure	Status
Mushy Callahan	USA	1926-1929	NBA/NY
Mushy Callahan	USA	1929-1930	NBA
Jackie Kid Berg	England	1930-1931	NBA
Tony Canzoneri	USA	1931-1932	NBA
Johnny Jadick	USA	1932-1933	NBA
Battling Shaw	Mexico	1933	NBA
Tony Canzoneri	USA	1933	NBA
Barney Ross*	USA	1933-1935	NBA
Tippy Larkin*	USA	1946-1947	MASS/NY
Carlos Oritz	Puerto Rico	1959-1960	NBA
Duilio Loi	Italy	1960-1962	NBA
Eddie Perkins	USA	1962	NBA
Duilio Loi*	Italy	1962-1963	NBA
Roberto Cruz	Philippines	1963	WBA
Eddie Perkins	USA	1963-1965	WBA
Carlos Hernandez	Venezuela	1965-1966	WBA
Sandro Lopopolo	Italy	1966-1967	WBA
Paul Fujii	Hawaii	1967-1968	WBA
Nicolino Loche	Argentine	1968-1972	WBA
Pedro Adigue	Philippines	1968-1970	WBC
Bruno Arcari*	Italy	1970-1974	WBC
Alfonso Frazer	Panama	1972	WBA
Antonio Cervantes	Colombia	1972-1976	WBA
Perico Fernandez	Spain	1974-1975	WBC
Saensak Muangsurin	Thailand	1975-1976	WBC
Wilfred Benitez*	USA	1976-1977	WBA
Miguel Velasquez	Spain	1976	WBC
Saensak Muangsurin	Thailand	1976-1978	WBC
Antonio Cervantes	Colombia	1977-1980	WBA
Wilfred Benitez*	USA	1977	NY
Sang-Hyun Kim	S Korea	1978-1980	WBC
Saoul Mamby	USA	1980-1982	WBC
Aaron Pryor*	USA	1980-1983	WBA
Leroy Haley	USA	1982-1983	WBC
Bruce Curry	USA	1983-1984	WBC
Johnny Bumphus	USA	1984	WBA
Bill Costello	USA	1984-1985	WBC
Gene Hatcher	USA	1984-1985	IBF
Aaron Pryor*	USA	1984-1986	IBF
Ubaldo Sacco	Argentine	1985-1986	WBA
Lonnie Smith	USA	1985-1986	WBC
Patrizio Oliva	Italy	1986-1987	WBA
Gary Hinton	USA	1986	IBF
Rene Arredondo	Mexico	1986	WBC
Tsuyoshi Hamada	Japan	1986-1987	WBC
Joe Manley	USA	1986-1987	IBF
Terry Marsh*	England	1987	IBF
Juan M. Coggi	Argentine	1987-1990	WBA
Rene Arredondo	Mexico	1987	WBC
Roger Mayweather	USA	1987-1989	WBC
James McGirt	USA	1988	IBF
Meldrick Taylor	USA	1988-1990	IBF
Hector Camacho	Puerto Rico	1989-1991	WBO
Julio Cesar Chavez*	Mexico	1989-1990	WBC
Julio Cesar Chavez*	Mexico	1990-199	IBF/WBC
Loreto Garza	USA	1990-1991	WBA
Greg Haugen*	USA	1991	WBO

Title Holder	Birthplace	Tenure	Status
Hector Camacho*	Puerto Rico	1991-1992	WBO
Edwin Rosario	Puerto Rico	1991-1992	WBA
Julio Cesar Chavez	Mexico	1991-	WBC
Rafael Pineda	Colombia	1991-	IBF
Akinobu Hiranaka	Japan	1992-	WBA
Carlos Gonzalez	Mexico	1992-	WBO

Welterweight (147 lbs)

Title Holder	Birthplace	Tenure	Status
Mysterious Billy Smith	USA	1892-1894	
Tommy Ryan*	USA	1894-1898	
Mysterious Billy Smith	USA	1898-1900	
Matty Matthews	USA	1900-1901	
Eddie Connolly	USA	1900	
Rube Ferns	USA	1900	
Matty Matthews	USA	1900-1901	
Joe Walcott	Barbados	1901-1904	
Dixie Kid*	USA	1904-1905	
Honey Mellody	USA	1906-1907	
Mike Twin Sullivan*	USA	1907	
Mike Twin Sullivan*	USA	1907-1908	CALIF
Frank Mantell	USA	1907-1908	OHIO
Harry Lewis	USA	1908-1910	OHIO
Jimmy Gardner	USA	1908-1910	LOUIS
Harry Lewis	USA	1910-1912	GB/FR
Jimmy Clabby	USA	1910-1912	USA/AUSTR
Waldemar Holberg	Denmark	1914	AUSTR
Tom McCormick	Ireland	1914	AUSTR
Matt Wells	England	1914-1915	AUSTR
Mike Glover	USA	1915	USA
Jack Britton	USA	1915	USA
Ted Kid Lewis	England	1915-1916	
Jack Britton	USA	1916-1917	
Ted Kid Lewis	England	1917-1919	
Jack Britton	USA	1919-1922	
Mickey Walker	USA	1922-1926	
Pete Latzo	USA	1926-1927	
Joe Dundee	Italy	1927-1929	
Joe Dundee	Italy	1929	NY
Jackie Fields	USA	1929	NBA
Jackie Fields	USA	1929-1930	
Young Jack Thompson	USA	1930	
Tommy Freeman	USA	1930-1931	
Young Jack Thompson	USA	1931	
Lou Brouillard	Canada	1931-1932	
Jackie Fields	USA	1932-1933	
Young Corbett III	Italy	1933	
Jimmy McLarnin	Ireland	1933-1934	
Barney Ross	USA	1934	
Jimmy McLarnin	Ireland	1934-1935	
Barney Ross	USA	1935-1938	
Henry Armstrong	USA	1938-1940	
Fritzie Zivic	USA	1940-1941	
Red Cochrane	USA	1941-1946	
Marty Servo*	USA	1946	
Sugar Ray Robinson*	USA	1946-1951	
Johnny Bratton	USA	1951	NBA
Kid Gavilan	Cuba	1951-1952	NBA/NY
Kid Gavilan	Cuba	1952-1954	
Johnny Saxton	USA	1954-1955	
Tony de Marco	USA	1955	
Carmen Basilio	USA	1955-1956	
Johnny Saxton	USA	1956	
Carmen Basilio*	USA	1956-1957	
Virgil Akins	USA	1958	
Don Jordan	Dom Republic	1958-1960	
Benny Kid Paret	Cuba	1960-1961	
Emile Griffith	Virgin Islands	1961	
Benny Kid Paret	Cuba	1961-1962	
Emile Griffith	Virgin Islands	1962-1963	
Luis Rodriguez	Cuba	1963	
Emile Griffith*	Virgin Islands	1963-1966	
Curtis Cokes	USA	1966-1967	WBA
Charley Shipes	USA	1966-1967	CALIF
Curtis Cokes	USA	1967-1969	
Jose Napoles	Cuba	1969-1970	
Billy Backus	USA	1970-1971	
Jose Napoles	Cuba	1971-1975	
Jose Napoles	Cuba	1972-1974	WBA/WBC
Hedgemon Lewis	USA	1972-1974	NY
Jose Napoles	Cuba	1974-1975	
Jose Napoles	Cuba	1975	WBC
Angel Espada	Puerto Rico	1975-1976	WBA
John H. Stracey	England	1975-1976	WBC
Carlos Palomino	Mexico	1976-1979	WBC
Pipino Cuevas	Mexico	1976-1980	WBA
Wilfred Benitez	USA	1979	WBC
Sugar Ray Leonard	USA	1979-1980	WBC
Roberto Duran	Panama	1980	WBC
Thomas Hearns	USA	1980-1981	WBA
Sugar Ray Leonard*	USA	1980-1981	WBC
Sugar Ray Leonard*	USA	1981-1982	
Don Curry	USA	1983-1984	WBA
Milton McCrory	USA	1983-1985	WBC
Don Curry	USA	1984-1985	WBA/IBF
Don Curry	USA	1985-1986	
Lloyd Honeyghan	Jamaica	1986	
Lloyd Honeyghan	Jamaica	1986-1987	WBC/IBF
Mark Breland	USA	1987	WBA
Marlon Starling	USA	1987-1988	WBA
Jorge Vaca	Mexico	1987-1988	WBC
Lloyd Honeyghan	Jamaica	1988-1989	WBC
Simon Brown	Jamaica	1988-1991	IBF
Tomas Molinares*	Colombia	1988	WBA
Mark Breland	USA	1989-1990	WBA
Marlon Starling	USA	1989-1990	WBC
Genaro Leon*	Mexico	1989	WBO
Manning Galloway	USA	1989-	WBO
Aaron Davis	USA	1990-1991	WBA
Maurice Blocker	USA	1990	WBC
Meldrick Taylor	USA	1991-	WBA
Simon Brown	Jamaica	1991	WBC/IBF
Simon Brown	Jamaica	1991	WBC
Maurice Blocker	USA	1991-	IBF
James McGirt	USA	1991-	WBC

L. Middleweight (154 lbs)

Title Holder	Birthplace	Tenure	Status
Denny Moyer	USA	1962-1963	WBA
Ralph Dupas	USA	1963	WBA
Sandro Mazzinghi	Italy	1963-1965	WBA

Meldrick Taylor (left), the WBA welterweight champion, is all smiles at the end of his successful defence against Glenwood Brown

Tom Casino

Title Holder	Birthplace	Tenure	Status
Nino Benvenuti	Italy	1965-1966	WBA
Ki-Soo Kim	S Korea	1966-1968	WBA
Sandro Mazzinghi*	Italy	1968-1969	WBA
Freddie Little	USA	1969-1970	WBA
Carmelo Bossi	Italy	1970-1971	WBA
Koichi Wajima	Japan	1971-1974	WBA
Oscar Albarado	USA	1974-1975	WBA
Koichi Wajima	Japan	1975	WBA
Miguel de Oliveira	Brazil	1975	WBC
Jae-Do Yuh	S Korea	1975-1976	WBA
Elisha Obed	Bahamas	1975-1976	WBC
Koichi Wajima	Japan	1976	WBA
Jose Duran	Spain	1976	WBA
Eckhard Dagge	Germany	1976-1977	WBC
Miguel Castellini	Argentine	1976-1977	WBA
Eddie Gazo	Nicaragua	1977-1978	WBA
Rocky Mattioli	Italy	1977-1979	WBC
Masashi Kudo	Japan	1978-1979	WBA
Maurice Hope	Antigua	1979-1981	WBC
Ayub Kalule	Uganda	1979-1981	WBA
Wilfred Benitez	USA	1981-1982	WBC
Sugar Ray Leonard*	USA	1981	WBA
Tadashi Mihara	Japan	1981-1982	WBA
Davey Moore	USA	1982-1983	WBA
Thomas Hearns*	USA	1982-1986	WBC
Roberto Duran*	Panama	1983-1984	WBA
Mark Medal	USA	1984	IBF
Mike McCallum*	Jamaica	1984-1987	WBA
Carlos Santos*	Puerto Rico	1984-1986	IBF
Buster Drayton	USA	1986-1987	IBF
Duane Thomas	USA	1986-1987	WBC
Matthew Hilton	Canada	1987-1988	IBF
Lupe Aquino	Mexico	1987	WBC
Gianfranco Rosi	Italy	1987-1988	WBC
Julian Jackson*	Virgin Islands	1987-1990	WBA
Don Curry	USA	1988-1989	WBC
Robert Hines	USA	1988-1989	IBF
John David Jackson	USA	1988-	WBO
Darrin van Horn	USA	1989	IBF
Rene Jacqot	France	1989	WBC
John Mugabi	Uganda	1989-1990	WBC
Gianfranco Rosi	Italy	1989-	IBF
Terry Norris	USA	1990-	WBC
Gilbert Dele	France	1991	WBA
Vinnie Pazienza	USA	1991-	WBA

Middleweight (160 lbs)

Title Holder	Birthplace	Tenure	Status
Nonpareil Jack Dempsey	Ireland	1890-1891	
Bob Fitzsimmons*	England	1891-1897	
Kid McCoy*	USA	1897-1898	
Tommy Ryan*	USA	1898-1907	
Stanley Ketchel	USA	1907-1908	
Billy Papke	USA	1908	
Stanley Ketchel*	USA	1908-1910	
Billy Papke	USA	1911-1912	GB
Frank Mantell	USA	1912-1913	USA
Billy Papke	USA	1912-1913	IBU
Frank Klaus	USA	1913	IBU
George Chip	USA	1913-1914	USA
Eddie McGoorty	USA	1914	AUSTR
Jeff Smith	USA	1914	AUSTR
Al McCoy	USA	1914-1917	USA
Mick King	Australia	1914	AUSTR
Jeff Smith	USA	1914-1915	AUSTR
Les Darcy*	Australia	1915-1917	AUSTR
Mike O'Dowd	USA	1917-1920	
Johnny Wilson	USA	1920-1923	
Bryan Downey	USA	1922	OHIO
Dave Rosenberg	USA	1922	NY
Jock Malone	USA	1922-1923	OHIO
Mike O'Dowd*	USA	1922-1923	NY
Lou Bogash*	USA	1923	NY
Harry Greb	USA	1923-1926	
Tiger Flowers	USA	1926	
Mickey Walker*	USA	1926-1931	
Gorilla Jones	USA	1931-1932	NBA
Marcel Thil	France	1932	NBA/IBU
Marcel Thil	France	1932-1937	IBU
Ben Jeby	USA	1933	NY
Gorilla Jones*	USA	1933	NBA
Lou Brouillard	Canada	1933	NY/NBA
Vince Dundee	USA	1933-1934	NY/NBA
Teddy Yarosz	USA	1934-1935	NY/NBA
Babe Risko	USA	1935-1936	NY/NBA
Freddie Steele	USA	1936-1937	NY/NBA
Freddie Steele	USA	1937-1938	NBA
Fred Apostoli	USA	1937-1938	IBU
Fred Apostoli	USA	1937-1939	NY
Edouard Tenet	France	1938	IBU
Al Hostak	USA	1938	NBA
Solly Krieger	USA	1938-1939	NBA
Al Hostak	USA	1939-1940	NBA
Ceferino Garcia	Philippines	1939-1940	NY
Ken Overlin	USA	1940-1941	NY
Tony Zale	USA	1940-1941	NBA
Billy Soose	USA	1941	NY
Tony Zale	USA	1941-1947	
Rocky Graziano	USA	1947-1948	
Tony Zale	USA	1948	
Marcel Cerdan	Algeria	1948-1949	
Jake la Motta	USA	1949-1950	
Jake la Motta	USA	1950-1951	NY/NBA
Sugar Ray Robinson	USA	1950-1951	PEN
Sugar Ray Robinson	USA	1951	
Randy Turpin	England	1951	
Sugar Ray Robinson*	USA	1951-1952	
Randy Turpin	England	1953	EBU
Carl Bobo Olson	Hawaii	1953-1955	
Sugar Ray Robinson	USA	1955-1957	
Gene Fullmer	USA	1957	
Sugar Ray Robinson	USA	1957	
Carmen Basilio	USA	1957-1958	
Sugar Ray Robinson	USA	1958-1959	
Sugar Ray Robinson	USA	1959-1960	NY/EBU
Gene Fullmer	USA	1959-1962	NBA
Paul Pender	USA	1960-1961	NY/EBU
Terry Downes	England	1961-1962	NY/EBU
Paul Pender*	USA	1962-1963	NY/EBU
Dick Tiger	Nigeria	1962-1963	NBA
Dick Tiger	Nigeria	1963	
Joey Giardello	USA	1963-1965	
Dick Tiger	Nigeria	1965-1966	
Emile Griffith	Virgin Islands	1966-1967	
Nino Benvenuti	Italy	1967	
Emile Griffith	Virgin Islands	1967-1968	
Nino Benvenuti	Italy	1968-1970	
Carlos Monzon*	Argentine	1970-1974	
Carlos Monzon*	Argentine	1974-1976	WBA
Rodrigo Valdez	Colombia	1974-1976	WBC
Carlos Monzon*	Argentine	1976-1977	
Rodrigo Valdez	Colombia	1977-1978	
Hugo Corro	Argentine	1978-1979	
Vito Antuofermo	Italy	1979-1980	
Alan Minter	England	1980	
Marvin Hagler	USA	1980-1987	
Marvin Hagler	USA	1987	WBC/IBF
Sugar Ray Leonard*	USA	1987	WBC
Frank Tate	USA	1987-1988	IBF
Sumbu Kalambay*	Zaire	1987-1989	WBA
Thomas Hearns	USA	1987-1988	WBC
Iran Barkley	USA	1988-1989	WBC
Michael Nunn	USA	1988-1991	IBF

Title Holder	Birthplace	Tenure	Status
Roberto Duran*	Panama	1989-1990	WBC
Doug de Witt	USA	1989-1990	WBO
Mike McCallum	Jamaica	1989-1991	WBA
Nigel Benn	England	1990	WBO
Chris Eubank*	England	1990-1991	WBO
Julian Jackson	Virgin Islands	1990-	WBC
James Toney	USA	1991-	IBF
Gerald McClellan	USA	1991-	WBO
Reggie Johnson	USA	1992-	WBA

S. Middleweight (168 lbs)

Title Holder	Birthplace	Tenure	Status
Murray Sutherland	Scotland	1984	IBF
Chong-Pal Park*	S Korea	1984-1987	IBF
Chong-Pal Park	S Korea	1987-1988	WBA
Graciano Rocchigiani*	Germany	1988-1989	IBF
Fully Obelmejias	Venezuela	1988-1989	WBA
Sugar Ray Leonard*	USA	1988-1990	WBC
Thomas Hearns*	USA	1988-1991	WBO
In-Chul Baek	S Korea	1989-1990	WBA
Lindell Holmes	USA	1990-1991	IBF
Christophe Tiozzo	France	1990-1991	WBA
Mauro Galvano	Italy	1990-	WBC
Victor Cordoba	Panama	1991-	WBA
Darrin van Horn	USA	1991-1992	IBF
Chris Eubank	England	1991-	WBO
Iran Barkley	USA	1992-	IBF

L. Heavyweight (175 lbs)

Title Holder	Birthplace	Tenure	Status
Jack Root	Austria	1903	USA
George Gardner	Ireland	1903	USA
Bob Fitzsimmons	England	1903-1905	
Jack O'Brien*	USA	1905-1912	
Jack Dillon	USA	1912-1916	
Battling Levinsky	USA	1916-1920	
Georges Carpentier	France	1920-1922	
Battling Siki	Senegal	1922-1923	
Mike McTigue	Ireland	1923-1925	
Paul Berlenbach	USA	1925-1926	
Jack Delaney*	Canada	1926-1927	
Jimmy Slattery	USA	1927	NBA
Tommy Loughran*	USA	1927	NY
Tommy Loughran*	USA	1927-1929	
Jimmy Slattery	USA	1930	NY
Maxie Rosenbloom	USA	1930-1933	NY
George Nichols	USA	1932	NBA
Bob Godwin	USA	1933	NBA
Maxie Rosenbloom	USA	1933-1934	
Bob Olin	USA	1934-1935	
John Henry Lewis*	USA	1935-1938	
Tiger Jack Fox	USA	1938-1939	NY
Melio Bettina	USA	1939	NY
Len Harvey	England	1939-1942	GB
Billy Conn*	USA	1939-1940	NY/NBA
Anton Christoforidis	Greece	1941	NBA
Gus Lesnevich	USA	1941-1946	NY/NBA
Freddie Mills	England	1942-1946	GB
Gus Lesnevich	USA	1946-1948	
Freddie Mills	England	1948-1950	
Joey Maxim	USA	1950-1952	
Archie Moore*	USA	1952-1961	
Archie Moore*	USA	1961-1962	NY/EBU
Harold Johnson	USA	1961-1962	NBA
Harold Johnson	USA	1962-1963	
Willie Pastrano	USA	1963-1965	
Jose Torres	Puerto Rico	1965-1966	
Dick Tiger	Nigeria	1966-1968	
Bob Foster*	USA	1968-1971	
Bob Foster*	USA	1971-1972	WBC
Vicente Rondon	Venezuela	1971-1972	WBA
Bob Foster*	USA	1972-1974	
John Conteh*	England	1974-1977	WBC
Victor Galindez	Argentine	1974-1978	WBA
Miguel Cuello	Argentine	1977-1978	WBC
Mate Parlov	Yugoslavia	1978	WBC
Mike Rossman	USA	1978-1979	WBA
Marvin Johnson	USA	1978-1979	WBC
Victor Galindez	Argentine	1979	WBA
Matt Saad Muhammad	USA	1979-1981	WBC
Marvin Johnson	USA	1979-1980	WBA
Mustafa Muhammad	USA	1980-1981	WBA
Michael Spinks	USA	1981-1983	WBA
Dwight Muhammad Qawi	USA	1981-1983	WBC
Michael Spinks*	USA	1983-1985	
J. B. Williamson	USA	1985-1986	WBC
Slobodan Kacar	Yugoslavia	1985-1986	IBF
Marvin Johnson	USA	1986-1987	WBA
Dennis Andries	Guyana	1986-1987	WBC
Bobby Czyz	USA	1986-1987	IBF
Thomas Hearns*	USA	1987	WBC
Leslie Stewart	Trinidad	1987	WBA
Virgil Hill	USA	1987-1991	WBA
Charles Williams	USA	1987-	IBF
Don Lalonde	Canada	1987-1988	WBC
Sugar Ray Leonard*	USA	1988	WBC
Michael Moorer*	USA	1988-1991	WBO
Dennis Andries	Guyana	1989	WBC
Jeff Harding	Australia	1989-1990	WBC
Dennis Andries	England	1990-1991	WBC
Thomas Hearns	USA	1991-1992	WBA
Leonzer Barber	USA	1991-	WBO
Jeff Harding	Australia	1991-	WBC
Iran Barkley*	USA	1992	WBA

The WBC welterweight king, James "Buddy" McGirt

Title Holder	Birthplace	Tenure	Status
Cruiserweight (190 lbs)			
Marvin Camel	USA	1979-1980	WBC
Carlos de Leon	Puerto Rico	1980-1982	WBC
Ossie Ocasio	Puerto Rico	1982-1984	WBA
S. T. Gordon	USA	1982-1983	WBC
Marvin Camel	USA	1983-1984	IBF
Carlos de Leon	Puerto Rico	1983-1985	WBC
Lee Roy Murphy	USA	1984-1986	IBF
Piet Crous	S Africa	1984-1985	WBA
Alfonso Ratliff	USA	1985	WBC
Dwight Muhammad Qawi	USA	1985-1986	WBA
Bernard Benton	USA	1985-1986	WBC
Carlos de Leon	Puerto Rico	1986-1988	WBC
Rickey Parkey	USA	1986-1987	IBF
Evander Holyfield*	USA	1986-1987	WBA
Evander Holyfield*	USA	1987-1988	WBA/IBF
Evander Holyfield*	USA	1988	
Taoufik Belbouli*	France	1989	WBA
Carlos de Leon	Puerto Rico	1989-1990	WBC
Glenn McCrory	England	1989-1990	IBF
Robert Daniels	USA	1989-1991	WBA
Boone Pultz	USA	1989-1990	WBO
Jeff Lampkin*	USA	1990-1991	IBF
Magne Havnaa*	Norway	1990-1992	WBO
Masimilliano Duran	Italy	1990-1991	WBC
Bobby Czyz	USA	1991-	WBA
Anaclet Wamba	France	1991-	WBC
James Warring	USA	1991-	IBF
Heavyweight (190 lbs +)			
James J. Corbett	USA	1892-1897	
Bob Fitzsimmons	England	1897-1899	
James J. Jeffries*	USA	1899-1905	
Marvin Hart	USA	1905-1906	
Tommy Burns	Canada	1906-1908	
Jack Johnson	USA	1908-1915	
Jess Willard	USA	1915-1919	
Jack Dempsey	USA	1919-1926	
Gene Tunney*	USA	1926-1928	
Max Schmeling	Germany	1930-1932	
Jack Sharkey	USA	1932-1933	
Primo Carnera	Italy	1933-1934	
Max Baer	USA	1934-1935	
James J. Braddock	USA	1935-1937	
Joe Louis*	USA	1937-1949	
Ezzard Charles	USA	1949-1950	NBA
Lee Savold	USA	1950	GB/EBU
Ezzard Charles	USA	1950-1951	
Jersey Joe Walcott	USA	1951-1952	
Rocky Marciano*	USA	1952-1956	
Floyd Patterson	USA	1956-1959	
Ingemar Johansson	Sweden	1959-1960	
Floyd Patterson	USA	1960-1962	
Sonny Liston	USA	1962-1964	
Muhammad Ali*	USA	1964-1965	
Muhammad Ali*	USA	1965-1967	WBC
Ernie Terrell	USA	1965-1967	WBA
Muhammad Ali*	USA	1967	
Joe Frazier	USA	1968-1970	WBC
Jimmy Ellis	USA	1968-1970	WBA
Joe Frazier	USA	1970-1973	
George Foreman	USA	1973-1974	
Muhammad Ali	USA	1974-1978	
Leon Spinks	USA	1978	
Leon Spinks	USA	1978	WBA
Larry Holmes*	USA	1978-1983	WBC
Muhammad Ali*	USA	1978-1979	WBA
John Tate	USA	1979-1980	WBA
Mike Weaver	USA	1980-1982	WBA
Michael Dokes	USA	1982-1983	WBA
Gerrie Coetzee	S Africa	1983-1984	WBA
Tim Witherspoon	USA	1984	WBC
Pinklon Thomas	USA	1984-1986	WBC
Larry Holmes	USA	1984-1985	IBF
Greg Page	USA	1984-1985	WBA
Tony Tubbs	USA	1985-1986	WBA
Michael Spinks*	USA	1985-1987	IBF
Tim Witherspoon	USA	1986	WBA
Trevor Berbick	Jamaica	1986	WBC
Mike Tyson	USA	1986-1987	WBC
James Smith	USA	1986-1987	WBA
Mike Tyson	USA	1987	WBA/WBC
Tony Tucker	USA	1987	IBF
Mike Tyson	USA	1987-1989	
Mike Tyson	USA	1989-1990	IBF/WBA/WBC
Francesco Damiani	Italy	1989-1991	WBO
James Douglas	USA	1990	IBF/WBA/WBC
Evander Holyfield	USA	1990-	IBF/WBA/WBC
Ray Mercer	USA	1991-1992	WBO
Michael Moorer	USA	1992-	WBO

Iran Barkley (left) on his way to the WBA Light-heavyweight title and victory over Thomas Hearns

Chris Farina

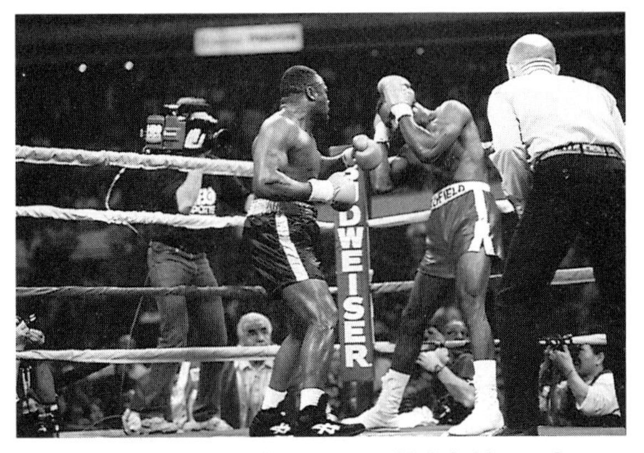

More action from the recent Holyfield v Cooper heavyweight clash as the champion covers up against the ropes

Tom Casino

Highlights From The 1991-92 Amateur Season

by Chris Kempson

The 1991-92 season, which culminated with the Olympic Games in Barcelona, started badly for amateur boxing in this country, both inside and outside the ring.

First, the ABA was reported to be in severe financial difficulties and as a result, England's trip to the junior multi-nations tournament in Izmir, Turkey, from 22-28 September was cancelled. The Sports Council who provide a substantial annual grant to the ABA were understood to be totally dissatisfied with the overall performance of the association and called for a fundamental review of the whole operation. Fortunately, the situation improved somewhat as the season progressed. It is to be hoped that the discussion document, entitled "Review of Amateur Boxing", prepared during the season by the Sports Council, after consultation with the ABA hierarchy, will eventually lead to various changes for the overall benefit of the sport.

Second, the England senior squad suffered a disappointing start to the Olympic season when they went down 8-3 to a strong and experienced Polish team in Kielce on 25 August, only Paul Ingle, Neil McCallum and Adrian Stone emerged as winners.

Then, more financial misery was heaped on the WBA when it was announced that the 1992 ABA championships would be the last event under the sponsorship of George Wimpey Plc. The ABA's successful partnership with Wimpey dated back to October 1980, when both bodies celebrated their joint centenaries and marked the occasion with a multi-nations tournament at the Wembley Arena.

However, performances on the international stage soon improved. Exciting young Lynn heavyweight prospect, Danny Williams, continued his excellent international form when he won a gold medal in the junior multi-nations tournament in Salonica, Greece from 3-8 October. Light-heavyweight Kelly Oliver from the Bracebridge Club in Lincoln and Suffolk's David Starie from the Hurstlea Club, boxing at light-middleweight, returned home with silver medals, while light-flyweight, Michael Brodie, from the Ancoats and Miles Platting Club in Manchester got a bronze. Moving on to Tampere, Finland, in mid-October, it was the turn of England's senior boxers to triumph in the annual Tammer tournament. The English team of five boxers returned home with two gold and two bronze medals. 1991 ABA light-heavyweight champion Anthony Todd (Darlington) and light-welterweight Peter Richardson (Phil Thomas SOB) each won a gold, while 1991 ABA heavyweight champion, Paul Lawson (Newco-Repton) and light-flyweight Rowan Williams of Small Heath ABC, both secured bronze medals.

A month later, we approached the sixth world senior championships at the Sydney Sports Centre in Australia with some cautious optimism. Although England, Ireland and Scotland returned home without any medals, the performances of the first two countries were commendable.

England got three of their five man team through to the quarter-finals where Peter Richardson and light-middleweight Robin Reid (Warrington Cambrian) lost to the eventual runners-up. 1991 ABA flyweight champion Paul Ingle (Scarborough) also made it through to the last eight, as did Ireland's Wayne McCullough at bantamweight and reigning European featherweight champion, Paul Griffin, who were eliminated by the eventual silver and gold medal winners, respectively. Cuba dominated the championships with four gold medals.

England's senior squad drew both their international matches against Scandinavian opposition. First, they entertained Denmark at the Bletchley Leisure Centre in Milton Keynes on 4 December and wound-up with a 6-6 draw, only after a disgraceful decision which went in Danish heavyweight Mark Hulstrom's favour, over Newco-Repton's Paul Lawson, in the last bout of the night. Lawson looked a convincing winner. A week later, England drew five-a-piece with Sweden in Stockholm, in which Adrian Carew (now known as Dodson) from St Pancras and Adrian Stone (Empire) performed particularly well. England, however, managed to notch up a crushing 10-1 victory over the "auld enemy", Scotland at the Everton Park Sports Centre in Liverpool on 17 January. Scotland's only win came via lightweight Malcolm Gowans (Selkirk), who outpointed Andy Green (Phil Thomas SOB). Scotland are now without a win over England since 1975, a situation they will wish to try and rectify as soon as they possibly can.

However, Scotland had the honour of staging the twelfth European junior championships, at the Meadowbank Sports Centre in Edinburgh in April. It is extremely disappointing to record that so few fans attended such a major tournament and amateur boxing's days as a mass spectator sport in these islands seem to be numbered, if not already over. However, there were some good things to cheer about inside the ring where England and Wales each won a silver medal, with the Principality gaining a bronze as well for good measure.

The host nation failed miserably on this occasion, all eight boxers crashed out in the first two days. Darlington lightweight Michael Hall won a silver medal, eventually losing out 12-3 to the vastly more experienced Sergei Shcherbakov (CIS) in the final. Cardiff featherweight Barry Jones (Highfields) also came home with a silver medal, going down 16-7 in the final to Mikhail Silantiev (CIS), while Welsh middleweight Chris Davies secured a bronze medal. Ireland captured two bronze medals through the efforts of bustling Francis Slane at bantamweight and Glen Stevens at lightweight. Overall the championships were dominated by CIS (formally the Soviet Union), who won no fewer than six gold medals.

On the domestic front, the 104th ABA championships dominated the proceedings. There were the usual shocks and upsets along the championship path which only added to the excitement and romance of this prestigious annual event. Peter Culshaw (Huyton), the 1991 light-flyweight title holder, failed to make the weight at the all - England semi-final stage, where dual ABA light-middleweight champion, Tim Taylor (Newco-Repton), was narrowly outpointed by Basingstoke's Dean Francis. Much fancied Manchester middleweight Eric Noi (Moss Side) was knocked out in the third round of the British semi-final at Gateshead by the aggressive punching of Scotland's John Connelly (Renton). Richard Fenton (Pentwyn) was astonishingly given the "nod" over north London's Chris Henry (New Enterprise) in the heavyweight division at Gateshead, where Newbridge's Joseph Calzache, now campaigning at light-middleweight, stopped Dean Francis in two rounds to become the only 1991 champion to return to the Kensington venue on finals night. Entry into the four Olympic Games' qualifying tournaments prevented some of the top boxers in the three countries from participating in their national championships, including 1991 champions, Paul Ingle, John Irwin, Mark Edwards, Anthony Todd and Paul Lawson. Reigning lightweight title holder Paul Ramsey did not enter, while the 1990 champion at this weight, the Angel's Patrick "Blue Boy" Gallagher, was again sidelined due to a knuckle injury. 1991 super-heavyweight champion, Kevin McCormack, was deemed ineligible under the rule that all servicemen must enter through the Combined Services route.

All in all, finals night on Wednesday 6 May at the Royal Albert Hall had a very refreshing "open look" about them as the opening bell sounded. The evening started well with Darren Fifield (Henley) stopping Lennie Woodcock (Royal Navy) in the third round of the light-flyweight final. Woodcock, who had reached the final through a series of walkovers, performed well, but eventually the power and experience of Fifield proved too much for him.

Scotland's only success came at flyweight when Keith Knox (Bonnyrigg) squeezed home on a tight majority decision against a somewhat disappointing Michael Horobin (St Pancras). It was close, but Knox's work-rate and enthusiasm just saw him home.

Southpaw Patrick Mullings (St Patrick's), runner-up in 1990, won the bantamweight crown with a unanimous decision over Michael Alldis (Crawley). The Londoner's quick-silver punches proved to be the decisive factor, although Alldis pushed him all the way.

The featherweight clash between Marlon Ward (Newco-Repton) and the talented teenage southpaw Alan Temple (Hartlepool Boys Welfare) was really one to savour. Temple was undoubtedly the best stylist of the night and he won the crown with a close, but unanimous decision over the east Londoner. I felt a little sorry for Ward, who boxed well throughout and the decision and the title seemed to rest on the third round which was very tight. In the event, the judges went for the educated left-hand work of Temple, who appears to have all the credentials to go far in the amateur game.

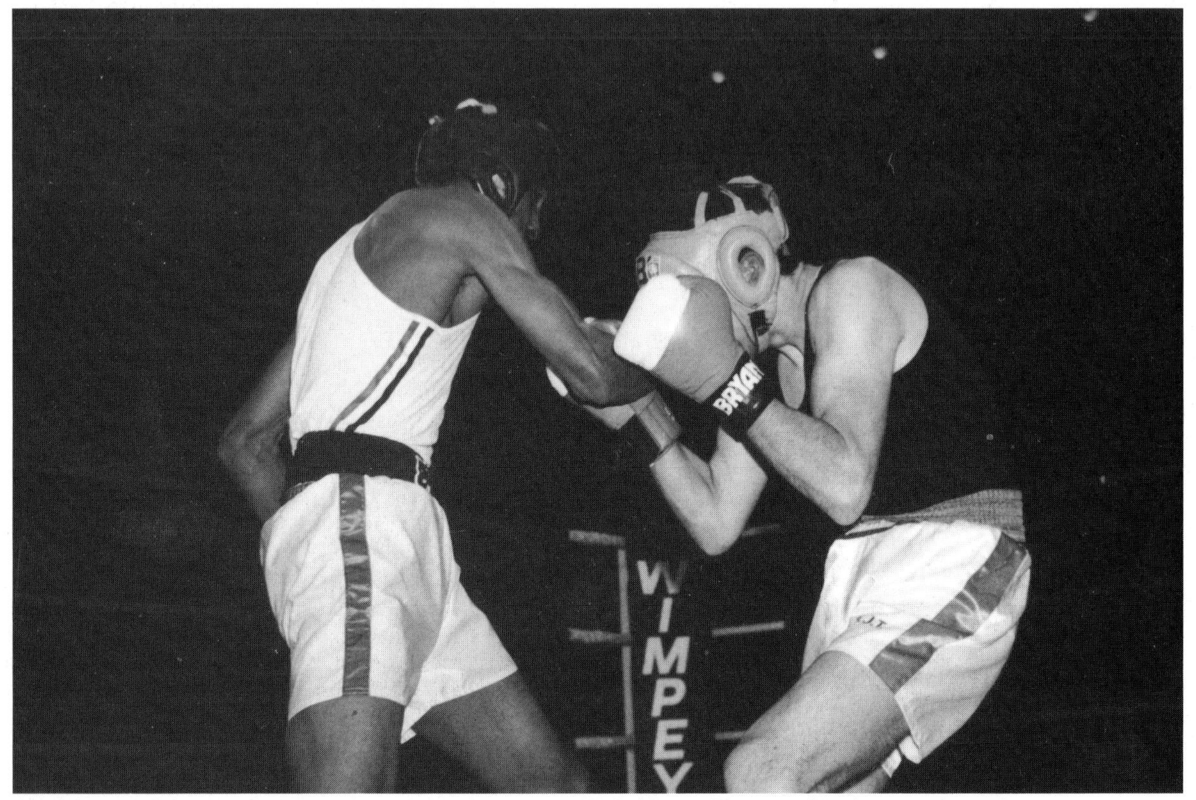

Mark Santini (left) wins the ABA welterweight title, stopping Wales' Barry Thorogood in the second round Les Clark

Up at lightweight Dean Amory (Kingshurst) took the title back to the Midlands for the third time in four years with a well deserved unanimous decision over Coed Eva's Mark Newton. Amory's better work-rate always gave him the edge over the courageous Welshman.

The light-welterweight final proved to be an explosive affair, with Darren McCarrick (Boarshaw) blasting out Empire's Adrian Stone after just 110 seconds of the first round. Stone was decked twice before being rescued by referee Ken Gray. McCarrick thus gained "sweet revenge", following his disputed split decision loss to Stone at Gloucester two years ago.

Twenty nine-year-old Mark Santini (Birmingham City), the "oldest man on show", made light of this when he won the welterweight title, stopping Barry Thorogood (Highfields) in the second round. Santini's right hand punching power was just too much for the Welshman to handle.

Classy Newbridge southpaw, Joseph Calzache, the 1991 welterweight champion, stepped up a weight to win the light-middleweight title, stopping Glen Catley (Empire) towards the end of the third round. The young Welshman, who shrugged off his disappointment at not being selected for the Olympic qualifying tournament in San Pellegrino, was always in charge and had already built up a commanding points lead when his brave opponent was finally rescued by referee Ken Dry.

The middleweight crown was claimed by southpaw Lee Woolcock (Canvey Island) with a runaway points verdict over the crude and inexperienced Scot, John Connelly, from the Renton Club. The skilful Woolcock completely dominated this one-sided contest and all three scores in his favour of 60-53, 60-54 and 60-55 were a clear reflection of the considerable "gap" in class between the two finalists.

Eighteen-year-old Kelly Oliver (Bracebridge) deservedly won his tremendous light-heavyweight "showdown" with Paul Rogers (Penhill). The young Lincoln man took the title with three identical scores of 59-58. The action was fast and furious in each round, with Oliver having to weather a torrid second round to eventually triumph over a determined and very dangerous opponent.

Welsh southpaw Richard Fenton (Pentwyn) was a mere 25 seconds away from being acclaimed the 1992 George Wimpey ABA heavyweight champion when Hove's Scott Welch put him down and out with a final left-hook, after a series of blistering rights to the head. Welch had indeed left it "late" and Fenton was left to reflect on what might have been had he evaded the Sussex man's swinging blows as he had done successfully in the two previous sessions.

The final contest of the evening was the rather disappointing all southpaw super-heavyweight clash

The ABA light-heavyweight title went to Kelly Oliver (right), an exciting young prospect from the Midland Counties, who outpointed the tough Paul Rogers

Les Clark

between Michael Hopper (Spennymoor) and Donovan Holness (St Pancras). The majority decision in Hopper's favour seemed to flatter the North-East Counties man.

I felt that the Londoner had done just enough to win over the first two rounds, although Hopper's work-rate certainly gave him the third. Two officials gave it to Hopper with identical scores of 59-58, while the other judge went for Holness in a "big way" with a score of 60-57.

It is time now to focus our attention on our achievements at the four Olympic qualifying tournaments held in Europe during February and March. Although there were the usual heated arguments over selection and non-selection, our boxers performed magnificently and surpassed all reasonable expectations of qualification. Eight Englishmen and two Scots represented Great Britain in Barcelona, while Ireland felt justifiably proud with their six representatives bound for Spain.

Flyweight Paul Ingle (Scarborough) and middleweight Mark Edwards (Royal Navy) both reached the semi-final stage in Copenhagen to ensure their qualifying places. In Halle, in Germany, light-flyweight Rowan Williams (Small Heath) and heavyweight Paul Lawson (Newco-Repton) booked their tickets to Spain, while Paul Lloyd (Vauxhall Motors) earned a "reserve place" in the bantamweight division. In Berck sur Mer in France, lightweight Alan Vaughan (Huyton) and the two Scots, featherweight Brian Carr (Auchengeich) and light-heavyweight Stephen Wilson (Haddington), all won through. Carr reached the semi-finals, while in the final, Wilson was stopped in the first round by Patrice Aouissi of France. England got all three representatives through in the final qualifying tournament held in Italy at San Pellegrino at the end of March. Peter Richardson (Phil Thomas SOB), our light-welterweight, booked his passage, as did Adrian Dodson (St Pancras) at welterweight. Dodson won a fine gold medal with four emphatic victories, three inside the distance. Robin Reid (Warrington Cambrian) reached the semi-final stage in the light-middleweight division to make the Olympic finals as well.

Paul Ingle, Robin Reid and bantamweight "reserve" Paul Lloyd, tuned up for Barcelona by winning gold medals in the annual prestigious Canada Cup competition held in Ottawa in mid-May.

The Irish squad of six for Barcelona was as follows:- flyweight Paul Buttimer (Sunnyside, Cork), bantamweight Wayne McCullough (Albert Foundry, Belfast), reigning European featherweight champion, Paul Griffin (Drimnagh, Dublin), welterweight Michael Carruth (Irish Army and Drimnagh, Dublin), heavyweight Paul Douglas (Holy Family, Belfast) and Kevin McBride (Smithboro, Monaghan) at super-heavyweight. A truly magnificent achievement for a small country.

As always, the future strength of our sport rests in the hands of our schoolboy and junior boxers. In the "Daily Star" sponsored ABA national junior championships staged at the York Hall, Bethnal Green on 14 December, London boys dominated the proceedings, capturing no fewer than nine titles.

Impressive winners for the capital included George Robshaw (Dale Youth), Daniel Happe (Honor Oak), Benny May (Lynn), Spencer Oliver (Finchley) and West Ham's Guy Wild, all fine young prospects. North-East Counties' Steven Richardson (Sunderland) was also in fine form, winning his first-ever national title.

The national schoolboy finals held at the Assembly Rooms in Derby on 28 March, provided their usual degree of skill, thrills and surprises. Outstanding performances came notably from Delroy Price (Newbridge), Steven Wilson (St Paul's) and Stuart Bendall (Triumph) in the "Junior A" division. In the "Junior B" division, unbeaten Ned Lee (Newco-Repton), Francis Doherty (Angel) and Merseysider Mark Reppion (Gemini), all won with something to spare. In the intermediates, West Ham's Kevin Lear and north-easterners, John Lee (Darlington) and Shildon's Craig Wake, particularly caught the eye. Steven Murray (West Ham), Craig Spacie (St Michael's) and Billy Robertson, (Slough) were the pick of the seniors on show.

The annual trio of NABC championships provided their own special brand of entertainment and spectators at the venues in Bristol, London and Newcastle upon Tyne witnessed some good class fare for their enjoyment. Lee Eedle (Gemini) and schoolboy champion Billy Tyrrell (Sunderland), along with Guy Corbyn (Phil Thomas SOB) and Ryan Rhodes (Unity) were the pick of the "Class A" championships. Another current schoolboy champion Steven Murray (West Ham), impressed in the "Class B" championships, as did Mark Smith (Hartlepool Catholic Boys) and Humeran Sheeraz (Pinewood Starr). Completing the NABC championships, Darren Williams (Fisher, Downside), Jason Sawicki (Eltham and District) and David Starie (Hurstlea) performed particularly well in the "Class C" finals.

Of course, there were the usual string of defections to the paid ranks and in particular it was disappointing to lose the talents of the likes of Mark Bowers, 1991 champions David Hardie and Jason Matthews, Peter Waudby, Gary Delaney, the Newco-Repton duo of Mark Baker and Steve McNess and the multi-titled Sheffield youngster, Nassem Hamed.

However, the sport is still remarkably strong at both senior, junior and schoolboy level as our journey through the 1991-92 season has clearly shown and that can only be for the overall benefit of amateur boxing in these islands. Long may this situation continue.

Note: This article was written before the Olympic Games started, but for the British and Irish boys' results, see under sections: British and Irish International Matches, 1991-92 and International Amateur Champions, 1904-1992.

The George Wimpey ABA National Championships, 1991-92

Combined Services v Western Counties

Combined Services

Combined Services Championships RAF Station, St Athan - 26 & 27 February
L.Fly: *final:* L. Woodcock (RN) wo. **Fly:** *final:* O. Spencely (RN) wo. **Bantam:** *final:* T. Rajcoomar (Army) wo. **Feather:** *final:* C. McCauley (RAF) w pts J. Basford (Army). **Light:** *final:* D. Rudd (RAF) w pts T. Winspear (Army). **L. Welter:** *final:* L. Roche (Army) w pts R. Goodsell (RAF). **Welter:** *final:* C. Bessey (Army) w pts T. French (RN). **L. Middle:** *final:* J. Ollerhead (Army) wo. **Middle:** *final:* G. Grounds (RN) w pts J. Dowling (Army). **L. Heavy:** *semi-finals:* L. Ramsey (RN) w pts P. Treslove (Army), J. Gosling (RAF) wo; *final:* J. Gosling w pts L. Ramsey. **Heavy:** *final:* D. Abbott (Army) w rsc 1 P. Fiske (RAF). **S. Heavy:** no entries.

Western Counties

Western Counties Northern Division Championships British Legion Hall, Penhill - 15 February
L. Fly: no entries. **Fly:** no entries. **Bantam:** no entries. **Feather:** *final:* D. Thompson (Empire) wo. **Light:** *final:* S. Cole (Penhill RBL) wo. **L. Welter:** *final:* A. Stone (Empire) wo. **Welter:** *final:* J. Wrona (Penhill RBL) w pts D. Nardiello (Reckleford). **L. Middle:** *semi-finals:* G. Catley (Empire) w rsc 3 S. Baker (Broad Plain), P. Richards (Penhill RBL) wo; *final:* G. Catley w rsc 3 P. Richards. **Middle:** *semi-finals:* M. Bailey (Avalon) w rsc 1 N. Bullock (Empire), D. Dorrington (National Smelting) wo; *final:* D. Dorrington w rsc 3 M. Bailey. **L. Heavy:** *semi-finals:* P. Rogers (Penhill RBL) w co 2 P. Lewis (Taunton), C. Kerr (Bronx) wo; *final:* P. Rogers w rtd 2 C. Kerr. **Heavy:** *final:* D. Poulson (Taunton) w co 1 H. Williams (Bronx). **S. Heavy:** *final:* K. Oputu (St George) w co 1 S. Woolaston (Lydney).

Western Counties Southern Division Colfox School, Bridport - 8 February
L. Fly: *final:* N. Tooley (Torbay) wo. **Fly:** *final:* D. Lawson (Devonport) wo. **Bantam:** *final:* G. Nicette (Torbay) w rsc 1 M. Stuckey (Apollo). **Feather:** *semi-finals:* K. Hodkinson (Leonis) w rsc 1 P. Hardcastle (Devonport), D. Jeffrey (Poole) w rsc 1 J. Phillips (Ottery St Mary); *final:* K. Hodkinson w rsc 2 D. Jeffrey. **Light:** *final:* D. Saunders (Dawlish) w rsc 3 L. Willcock (Torbay). **L. Welter:** *quarter-finals:* G. Ambrose (Poole) w rsc 2 S. Weekes (Sturminster), P. Gauge (Camborne) wo, I. Lewis (Paignton) wo, A. Beadman (Pisces) wo; *semi-finals:* G. Ambrose w rsc 2 A. Beadman, P. Gauge w pts I. Lewis; *final:* G. Ambrose w pts P. Gauge. **Welter:** *final:* G. Edwards (Devonport) w rsc 2 R. Daniels (Camborne). **L. Middle:** *quarter-finals:* P. Norris (Paignton) w pts A. Castell (Purbeck), D. Norris (Paignton) w rsc 2 J. Nettley (Sturminster), P. Lepage (Dorchester) w rsc 2 T. Houghton (Camborne), D. Roache (Poole) w rsc 1 M. Franklin (Exeter); *semi-finals:* D. Roache w pts P. Norris, P. Lepage wo D. Norris; *final:* D. Roache w pts P. Lepage. **Middle:** *final:* E. Stuart (Leonis) wo. **L. Heavy:** *prelims:* J. McNaught (Devonport) w rsc 2 B. Law (Apollo), L. Rousseau (Pisces) wo, S. Jehu (Camborne) wo, D. Watts (Camborne) wo, M. Hickey (Barnstaple) wo, D. Keenor (Barnstaple) wo, R. Carless (Ax Valley) wo, G. Hyde (Leonis) wo; *quarter-finals:* L. Rousseau w rsc 2 S. Jehu, D. Watts w rsc 2 D. Hickey, D. Keenor w pts R. Carless, G. Hyde w rsc 3 J. McNaught; *semi-finals:* G. Hyde w pts L. Rousseau, D. Watts w pts D. Keenor; *final:* D. Watts w rsc 1 G. Hyde. **Heavy:** *semi-finals:* J. Teaves (Torbay) w rsc 3 N. Kendall (Apollo), N. Hosking (Devonport) wo; *final:* N. Hosking w rsc 1 J. Teaves. **S. Heavy:** *final:* L. Harriott (Purbeck) wo.

Western Counties Finals City Hall, Salisbury - 7 March
L. Fly: N. Tooley (Torbay) wo. **Fly:** D. Lawson (Devonport) wo. **Bantam:** G. Nicette (Torbay) wo. **Feather:** K. Hodkinson (Leonis) w pts D. Thompson (Empire). **Light:** D. Saunders (Dawlish) w pts S. Cole (Penhill RBL). **L. Welter:** A. Stone (Empire) w co 3 G. Ambrose (Poole). **Welter:** J. Wrona (Penhill RBL) w co 2 G. Edwards (Devonport). **L. Middle:** G. Catley (Empire) w pts D. Roache (Poole). **Middle:** D. Dorrington (National Smelting) w pts E. Stuart (Leonis). **L. Heavy:** P. Rogers (Penhill RBL) w pts D. Keenor (Barnstaple) - replaced D. Watts (Camborne). **Heavy:** N. Hosking (Devonport) w co 3 D. Poulson (Taunton). **S. Heavy:** K. Oputu (St George) wo L. Harriott (Purbeck).

Combined Services v Western Counties

RAF Halton, Aylesbury - 21 March
L. Fly: L. Woodcock (RN) wo N. Tooley (Torbay). **Fly:** O. Spencely (RAF) w pts D. Lawson (Devonport). **Bantam:** G. Nicette (Torbay) w pts T. Rajcoomar (Army). **Feather:** K. Hodkinson (Leonis) w co 3 C. McCauley (RAF). **Light:** D. Rudd (RAF) w pts D. Saunders (Dawlish). **L. Welter:** A. Stone (Empire) w rsc 2 L. Roche (Army). **Welter:** C. Bessey (Army) w pts J. Wrona (Penhill RBL). **L. Middle:** G. Catley (Empire) w pts J. Ollerhead (Army). **Middle:** G. Grounds (RN) w pts D. Dorrington (National Smelting). **L. Heavy:** P. Rogers (Penhill RBL) w pts J. Gosling (RAF). **Heavy:** N. Hosking (Devonport) w rsc 3 D. Abbott (Army). **S. Heavy:** K. Oputu (St George) wo.

Eastern Counties v Home Counties v Midland Counties v Southern Counties

Eastern Counties

Essex Division Civic Hall, Grays - 18 January
L. Fly: no entries. **Fly:** *final:* M. Reynolds (Colchester) wo. **Bantam:** *final:* D. Dainty (Canvey) wo. **Feather:** *final:* B. Saich (Canvey) w pts P. Bates (Billericay). **Light:** *final:* G. Newcome (Canvey) w rsc 2 C. Rance (Belhus Park). **L. Welter:** *final:* G. Smith (Canvey) w rsc 1 G. Dunbar (Chelmsford). **Welter:** *final:* A. Sims (Canvey) w rsc 1 L. Clarke (Chadwell & Tilbury). **L. Middle:** *final:* M. Whitbread (Canvey) wo. **Middle:** *final:* L. Woolcock (Canvey) w rsc 1 P. Turner (Castle). **L. Heavy:** *final:* D. Weaver (Canvey) w dis 1 D. Hirons (Rochford. **Heavy:** *final:* G. Cox (Canvey) wo. **S. Heavy:** *final:* J. Jones (Belhus Park) wo.

Mid-Anglia Division GER Club, March - 11 January
L. Fly: no entries. **Fly:** no entries. **Bantam:** *final:* S. Singh (Aldermans) wo. **Feather:** no entries. **Light:** no entries. **L. Welter:** *final:* P. Gill (Chatteris) wo. **Welter:** *final:* L. Baxter (Chatteris) wo. **L. Middle:** no entries. **Middle:** no entries. **L. Heavy:** no entries. **Heavy:** no entries. **S. Heavy:** *final:* M. Dear (Soham) wo.

Norfolk Division Manor Hall, Upwell - 10 January
L. Fly: no entries. **Fly:** no entries. **Bantam:** no entries. **Feather:** no entries. **Light:** no entries. **L. Welter:** *final:* J. Thaxton (Norwich) w rsc 1 M. Green (Thetford). **Welter:** *final:* G. Barker (Norwich) w rsc 1 G. Hewitt (North Lynn). **L. Middle:** *final:* A. Gray (Yarmouth) wo. **Middle:** *final:* S. Smith (Yarmouth) wo. **L. Heavy:** *final:* D. Brunning (Norwich) w pts J. Allard (Yarmouth). **Heavy:** *final:* J. Rouse (Yarmouth) wo. **S. Heavy:** *final:* N. Sturman (Dereham) wo.

Suffolk Division Corn Exchange, Ipswich - 10 January
L. Fly: no entries: **Fly:** no entries. **Bantam:** no entries. **Feather:** no entries. **Light:** *final:* M. Hawthorne (Lowestoft) wo. **L. Welter:** no entries. **Welter:** *final:* F. Bacon (Ipswich) w pts D. Reeve (Lowestoft). **L. Middle:** *final:* A. Ewen (Arcade) w rsc 1 A. Lionnett (Bury RBL). **Middle:** no entries. **L. Heavy:** K. Potter (Ipswich) wo. **Heavy:** *final:* D. Brade (Ipswich) w co 1 P. Byrne (Haverhill). **S. Heavy:** no entries.

Eastern Counties Semi-Finals & Finals Civic Hall, Grays - 1 February
L. Fly: no entries. **Fly:** *final:* M. Reynolds (Colchester) wo. **Bantam:** *final:* D. Dainty (Canvey) w rsc 3 S. Singh (Aldermans). **Feather:** *final:* B. Saich (Canvey) wo. **Light:** *final:* G. Newcome (Canvey) w rsc 3 M. Hawthorne (Lowestoft). **L. Welter:** *semi-finals:* G. Smith (Canvey) w pts J. Thaxton (Norwich), P. Gill (Chatteris) wo; *final:* G. Smith w rsc 2 P. Gill. **Welter:** *semi-finals:* L. Baxter (Chatteris) w rsc 3 F. Bacon (Ipswich), G. Barker (Norwich) w pts A. Sims (Canvey); *final:* G. Barker w rtd 1 L. Baxter. **L. Middle:** *semi-finals:* A. Ewen (Arcade) w pts A. Gray (Yarmouth), M. Whitbread (Canvey) wo; *final:* A. Ewen w pts M. Whitbread. **Middle:** *final:* L. Woolcock (Canvey) w pts S. Smith (Yarmouth). **L. Heavy:** K. Potter (Ipswich) withdrew; *final:* D. Weaver (Canvey) w pts D. Brunning (Norwich). **Heavy:** *semi-finals:* G. Cox (Canvey) w pts D. Brade (Ipswich), J. Rouse (Yarmouth) wo; *final:* G. Cox w rsc 2 J. Rouse. **S. Heavy:** J. Jones (Belhus Park) withdrew; *final:* N. Sturman (Dereham) w co 1 M. Dear (Soham).

Home Counties

Home Counties Championships Bletchley Leisure Centre, Milton Keynes - 15 February
F. Fly: *final:* D. Fifield (Henley) wo. **Fly:** *final:* J. Locke (Reading) wo. **Bantam:** *final:* S. Collar (Dunstable) wo. **Feather:** *final:* J. Gynn (Stevenage) w pts M. Chilton (Milton Keynes). **Light:** *quarter-finals:* J. Wilson (Abingdon) w pts M. Smyth (Milton Keynes), M. Leonard (South Oxhey) wo, M. Fattore (Bushey) wo, J. White (Aylesbury) wo; *semi-finals:* J. White w pts M. Leonard, J. Wilson w pts M. Fattore; *final:* J. Wilson w pts J. White. **L. Welter:** *quarter-finals:* P. Gibbs (Oxford YMCA) w pts S. Ellis (Bedford), K. Marner (Bracknell) wo, M. Flynn (Aylesbury) wo, A. Dozzini (Pinewood Starr) wo; *semi-finals:* K. Marner w pts M. Flynn, P. Gibbs w pts A. Dozzini; *final:* K. Marner w pts P. Gibbs. **Welter:** *quarter-finals:* A. Smith (Chesham) w pts M. Bowers (Pinewood Starr), A. Chase (St Albans) wo, M. Dick (Aylesbury) wo, I. Swaysland (Willy Freund) wo; *semi-finals:* A. Chase w rsc 2 M. Dick, A. Smith w pts I. Swaysland; *final:* A. Smith w pts A. Chase. **L. Middle:** *quarter finals:* N. Reynolds (Dunstable) w co 2 G. Lucas (Slough), L. Pugh (Oxford YMCA) w rsc 3 L. McGuire (Chesham), O. Newman (Aylesbury) wo, R. Harbord (Thames Valley) wo; *semi-finals:* O. Newman w pts N. Reynolds, L. Pugh w pts R. Harbord; *final:* L. Pugh w pts O. Newman. **Middle:** *semi-finals:* M. Hilding (Pinewood Starr) w co 2 A.Wright (Newport Pagnell), R. Baptiste (Lewsey Centre) w rsc 3 D. Warren (Oxford YMCA); *final:* M. Hilding w co 1 R. Baptiste. **L. Heavy:** *semi-finals:* P. Watts (Reading) w pts J. Swabey (Slough), S. Lawlor (Luton Irish) w pts T. March (Chesham); *final:* S. Lawlor w pts P. Watts. **Heavy:** *final:* A. Barnes (Aylesbury) w pts C. Brock (Henley). **S. Heavy:** no entries.

Midland Counties

Derbyshire Division Social Club, Buxton - 16 January
L. Fly: no entries. **Fly:** *final:* M. Davies (Royal Oak) wo. **Bantam:** *final:* C. Robson (Royal Oak) wo. **Feather:** *final:* V. Broomhead (Buxton) wo. **Light:** *final:* S. Rafferty (Trinity) w pts D. Ashley (Merlin). **L. Welter:** *final:* S. Williamson (Merlin) wo. **Welter:** *final:* G. Lowe (Derby) w rsc 2 D. Butterworth (Chesterfield). **L. Middle:** *semi-finals:* S. Goodwin (Merlin) w rtd 2 K. Gibbons (Derby), C. Harrison (Royal Oak) wo; *final:* S. Goodwin w pts C. Harrison. **Middle:** *final:* E. Parsons (Chesterfield) w pts T. Watson (Merlin). **L. Heavy:** no entrries. **Heavy:** no entries. **S. Heavy:** no entries.

Leicester, Rutland & Northants Division Friendlies WMC, Northampton - 14 January
L. Fly: *final:* K. Hassell (Braunstone) wo. **Fly:** no entries. **Bantam:** *final:* P. Neale (Alexton) wo. **Feather:** *final:* A. Thomas (Wellingborough) wo. **Light:** *final:* D. Kehoe (Kingsley Park) w pts L. Revill (Wellingborough). **L. Welter:** *semi-finals:* I. Carroll (Kingsley Park) w pts A. Bosworth (Far Cotton), C. Kerr (Far Cotton) wo; *final:* C. Kerr w co 1 I. Carroll. **Welter:** *final:* S. Metherell (Keystone) w pts P. Bench (Wellingborough). **L. Middle:** *semi-finals:* J. Maxwell (Belgrave) w co 3 B. Sutton (Central), C. Williams (Belgrave) wo; *final:* C. Williams w pts J. Maxwell. **Middle:** *final:* A. McDonald (Venture) wo. **L. Heavy:** *final:* O. Mintus (Braunstone) w pts J. Plant (Central). **Heavy:** no entries. **S. Heavy:** D. McCafferty (Keystone) wo.

Notts & Lincs Division Phoenix ABC Gym, Nottingham - 11 Janaury
L. Fly: no entries. **Fly:** no entries. **Bantam:** *final:* C. Slatcher (Phoenix) wo. **Feather:** *final:* R. Brotherhood (Radford) wo. **Light:** no entries. **L. Welter:** no entries. **Welter:** *final:* K. Buxton (Radford) w pts R. Watson (Grantham). **L. Middle:** *final:* D. Tring (Eastwood) w pts B. Exton (Bracebridge). **Middle:** *final:* A. Capewell (Radford) wo. **L. Heavy:** *final:* K. Oliver (Bracebridge) wo. **Heavy:** *final:* M. Langtree (Bracebridge) wo. **S. Heavy:** *final:* C. Brogan (Harworth Colliery) wo.

Warwickshire Division Builders Club, Coventry - 16 January
L. Fly no entries. **Fly:** *final:* D. Pithie (Willenhall) wo. **Bantam:** no entries. **Feather:** *final:* Y. Vorajee (Triumph) wo. **Light:** no entries. **L. Welter:** *final:* J. Scanlon (Coventry Colliery) wo. **Welter:** no entries. **L. Middle:** no entries. **Middle:** *final:* D. Bendall (Triumph) w pts D. Eales (Bedworth). **L. Heavy:** *final:* N. Simpson (Willenhall) w pts J. Cooke (Coventry Colliery). **Heavy:** *final:* T. Grant (Coventry Boys) wo. **S. Heavy:** no entries.

Midland Counties (North Zone) Semi-Finals & Finals Coventry Colliery, Coventry - 24 January, Leisure Centre, Swadlincote - 29 January & Albion Leisure Centre, Derby - 7 February
L. Fly: *final:* K. Hassell (Braunstone) wo. **Fly:** *final:* D. Pithie (Willenhall) wo M. Davies (Royal Oak). **Bantam:** *semi-finals:* C. Slatcher (Phoenix) w pts C. Robson (Royal Oak), P. Neale (Alexton) wo; *final:* C. Slatcher w pts P. Neale. **Feather:** *semi-finals:* R. Brotherhood (Radford) w co 1 V. Broomhead (Buxton),

The first ABA title for 1992 was decided when Darren Fifield (right) of Henley outpointed the Royal Navy's Lennie Woodcock Les Clark

Y. Vorajee (Triumph) w pts A. Thomas (Wellingborough); *final:* Y. Vorajee w pts R. Brotherhood. **Light:** *final:* D. Kehoe (Kingsley Park) w pts S. Rafferty (Trinity). **L. Welter:** *semi-finals:* J. Scanlon (Coventry Colliery) w pts C. Kerr (Far Cotton), S. Williamson (Merlin) wo; *final:* J. Scanlon w rtd 2 S. Williamson. **Welter:** *semi-finals:* G. Lowe (Derby) wo K. Buxton (Radford), S. Metherell (Keystone); *final:* S. Metherell w pts G. Lowe. **L. Middle:** *semi-finals:* S. Goodwin (Merlin) wo D. Tring (Eastwood), C. Williams (Belgrave) wo; *final:* S. Goodwin w pts C. Williams. **Middle:** *semi-finals:* D. Bendall (Triumph) w rsc 2 A. McDonald (Venture), E. Parsons (Chesterfield) w pts A. Capewell (Radford); *final:* D. Bendall w rsc 1 E. Parsons. **L. Heavy:** *semi-finals:* N. Simpson (Willenhall) w rsc 1 O. Mintus (Braunstone), K. Oliver (Bracebridge) wo; *final:* K. Oliver w pts N. Simpson. **Heavy:** *final:* M. Langtree (Bracebridge) w pts T. Grant (Coventry Boys). **S. Heavy:** *final:* C. Brogan (Harworth Colliery) w co 2 D. McCafferty (Keystone).

Birmingham Division Rover Centennial Hall, Longbridge - 17 January
L. Fly: *final:* R. Williams (Small Heath) wo. **Fly:** no entries. **Bantam:** no entries. **Feather:** *final:* D. Holt (Nechells) w pts M. Hermon (Small Heath). **Light:** *final:* D. Amory (Kingshurst) wo. **L. Welter:** *final:* L. Willis (Small Heath) w rtd 3 P. Clegg (Birmingham). **Welter:** *final:* M. Santini (Birmingham) wo. **L. Middle:** *final:* L. White (Small Heath) w pts S. Levene (Birmingham). **Middle:** *final:* R. Golding (Kingshurst) w rsc 3 O. Cunningham (Hardy Spicer). **L. Heavy:** *final:* L. Page (Birmingham) wo. **Heavy:** *final:* T. Small (Kingshurst) w pts K. Hitchin (Birmingham). **S. Heavy:** *final:* M. McKenzie (Handsworth Police) w pts K. Norville (Birmingham).

South Staffs Division Gala Baths, West Bromwich - 17 January & Rover Centennial Hall, Longbridge - 18 January
L. Fly: no entries. **Fly:** *final:* A. Bickley (Wednesbury) wo. **Bantam:** no entries. **Feather:** no entries. **Light:** *semi-finals:* M. Harris (Walsall Wood Police) w pts F. Smith (Wolverhampton), C. Allen (Scotlands) wo; *final:* M. Harris w pts C. Allen. **L. Welter:** *final:* P. Nightingale (Wednesbury) w pts G. Reid (Wolverhampton). **Welter:** *semi-finals:* A. Houldey (Wednesbury) w pts F. Halls (Bloxwich), C. Barnett (Wolverhampton) wo; *final:* A. Houldey w pts C. Barnett (Wolverhampton). **L. Middle:** *semi-finals:* D. Bain (Wolverhampton) w pts T. Marshall (Wednesbury), A. Peach (Pleck) w co 3 P. Lewis (Scotlands); *final:* D. Bain w pts A. Peach. **Middle:** *final:* S. Martin (Wolverhampton) w pts T. Williams (Wolverhampton). **L. Heavy:** *final:* R. Norton (Silver Street) wo. **Heavy:** *semi-finals:* A. Leddington (Pleck) w pts M. Pugh (Silver Street), B. Summers (Wednesbury) w dis 2 T. Wilson (Wolverhampton); *final:* A. Leddington w pts B. Summers. **S. Heavy:** *final:* C. Brown (Wolverhampton) wo.

Staffordshire Division Brownhills ABC, Stoke - 11 January
L. Fly: no entries. **Fly:** no entries. **Bantam:** *final:* D. Simpkin (Brownhills) wo. **Feather:** *final:* G. Marsden (Queensberry) wo. **Light:** *final:* K. Price (Orme) wo. **L. Welter:** *final:* S. Wooliscroft (Queensberry) w pts S. Cartwright (Stoke). **Welter:** *final:* C. Astbury (The George) wo. **L. Middle:** *final:* M. Lee (Burton) wo. **Middle:** *final:* Darren Ashton (Brownhills) wo. **L. Heavy:** *final:* Dean Ashton (Brownhills) wo. **Heavy:** *final:* S. Murray (Stafford) wo. **S. Heavy:** no entries.

West Mercia Division Northwick Centre, Worcester - 16 January
L. Fly: no entries. **Fly:** no entries. **Bantam:** no entries. **Feather:** no entries. **Light:** *final:* J. Gonzales (Warley) wo. **L. Welter:** *final:* P. Found (Satellite) wo. **Welter:** *final:* W. Clayton (Worcester) w pts S. Hanley (Warley). **L. Middle:** *final:* A. McFarlane (Bennetts Bank) w pts R. Doran (Shrewsbury). **Middle:** *final:* T. Broadbridge (Warley) wo. **L. Heavy:** *final:* S. Richards (Ludlow) w pts D. Baker (Kidderminster). **Heavy:** *final:* F. Woodrow (Hereford) wo. **S. Heavy:** no entries.

Midland Counties (South Zone) Semi-Finals & Finals Northwick Centre, Worcester - 22 January & Hardy Spicer Social Club, Birmingham - 25 January & 1 February
L. Fly: *final:* R. Williams (Small Heath) wo. **Fly:** *final:* A. Bickley (Wednesbury) wo. **Bantam:** *final:* D. Simpkin (Brownhills) wo. **Feather:** *final:* D. Holt (Nechells) wo G. Marsden (Queensberry). **Light:** *semi-finals:* J. Gonzales (Warley) w pts C. Allen (Scotland) - replaced M. Harris (Walsall Wood Police), D. Amory (Kingshurst) w dis 3 K. Price (Orme); *final:* D. Amory w pts J. Gonzales. **L. Welter:** *semi-finals:* P. Nightingale (Wednesbury) w pts P. Found (Satellite), L. Willis (Small Heath) wo S. Wooliscroft (Queensberry); *final:* P. Nightingale w pts L. Willis. **Welter:** *semi-finals:* A. Houldey (Wednesbury) w pts W. Clayton (Worcester), M. Santini (Birmingham) wo C. Astbury (The George); *final:* M. Santini w pts A. Houldey. **L. Middle:** *semi-finals:* A. McFarlane (Bennetts Bank) w pts D. Bain (Wolverhampton), M. Lee (Burton) w pts L. White (Small Heath); *final:* M. Lee w pts A. McFarlane. **Middle:** *semi-finals:* T. Broadbridge (Warley) w pts S. Martin (Wolverhampton), R. Golding (Kingshurst) w pts Darren Ashton (Brownhills: *final:* R. Golding w pts T. Broadbridge. **L. Heavy:** *semi-finals:* R. Norton (Silver Street) w rsc 1 S. Richards (Ludlow), L. Page (Birmingham) wo Dean Ashton (Brownhills); *final:* L. Page w dis 2 R. Norton. **Heavy:** *semi-finals:* F. Woodrow (Hereford) w pts B. Summers (Wednesbury) - replaced A. Leddington (Pleck), T. Small (Kingshurst) w pts S. Murray (Stafford); *final:* T. Small w pts F. Woodrow. **S. Heavy:** *final:* C. Brown (Wolverhampton) w pts M. McKenzie (Handsworth Police).

Midland Counties Finals Daines Camp Leisure Centre, Northampton - 22 February
L. Fly: K. Hassell (Braunstone) wo R. Williams (Small Heath). **Fly:** D. Pithie (Willenhall) wo A. Bickley (Wednesbury). **Bantam:**

C. Slatcher (Phoenix) w pts D. Simpkin (Brownhills). **Feather:** Y. Vorajee (Triumph) w pts M. Hermon (Small Heath) - replaced D. Holt (Nechells). **Light:** D. Amory (Kingshurst) w pts D. Kehoe (Kingsley Park). **L. Welter:** J. Scanlon (Coventry Colliery) w pts L. Willis (Small Heath) - replaced P. Nightingale (Wednesbury). **Welter:** M. Santini (Birmingham) w rsc 3 S. Metherell (Keystone). **L. Middle:** M. Lee (Burton) w pts S. Goodwin (Merlin). **Middle:** R. Golding (Kingshurst) w pts D. Bendall (Triumph). **L. Heavy:** K. Oliver (Bracebridge) wo L. Page (Birmingham). **Heavy:** T. Small (Kingshurst) w pts M. Langtree (Bracebridge). **S. Heavy:** C. Brogan (Harworth Colliery) w pts C. Brown (Wolverhampton).

Southern Counties

Southern Counties Championships South Parade Pier, Southsea - 8 & 15 February

L. Fly: no entries. **Fly:** *final:* J. Murphy (Hove) w pts J. McLean (Basingstoke). **Bantam:** *final:* M. Alldis (Crawley) w pts M. Wright (St Mary's). **Feather:** *semi-finals:* M. Walsh (Portsmouth) w pts P. Cooper (Woking), B. Urquhart (Westree) w pts A. Michaels (Titchfield); *final:* M. Walsh w rsc 3 B. Urquhart. **Light:** *quarter-finals:* M. Castleton (Titchfield) w rsc 3 A. Elcock (Camberley), A. Hayes (Red Ensign) w pts M. Bloomfield (West Hill), D. Sowden (Wecock Farm) wo, N. Chalcroft (Crawley) wo; *semi-finals:* D. Sowden w dis 2 N. Chalcroft (Crawley), M. Castleton w rsc 2 A. Hayes; *final:* D. Sowden w pts M. Castleton. **L. Welter:** *quarter-finals:* W. Rothwell (Tunbridge Wells) w rsc 3 T. Bayracil (Crawley), G. Gates (West Hill) w pts J. Bloomfield (West Hill), G. Spiers (Red Ensign) wo, S. Tonkiss (Ramsgate); *semi-finals:* G. Spiers w dis 1 S. Tonkiss, G. Gates w rsc 1 W. Rothwell; *final:* G. Spiers w pts G. Gates. **Welter:** *quarter-finals:* S. Sheeran (Crawley) w pts D. Brennan (Portsmouth), S. Jenkinson (Onslow) w pts D. Johnson (Red Ensign), S. Small (Fareham) wo, R. Head (Westree) wo; *semi-finals:* S. Small w rsc 2 R. Head, S. Sheeran w pts S. Jenkinson; *final:* S. Jenkinson - replaced S. Sheeran w rsc 2 S. Small. **L. Middle:** *prelims:* D. Francis (Basingstoke) w rsc 3 O. Bello (Parade), P. de Santos (Woking) w pts M. Ballard (Portsmouth), B. Brooks (Westree) w pts S. Small (Fareham), R. Blair (Gosport) wo, K. Fenton (Camberley) wo, D. Quacoe (Horsham) wo, K. Lamley (Birchington) wo, C. Vassillou (Birchington) wo; *quarter-finals:* F. Blair w pts K. Fenton, D. Quacoe w pts K. Lamley, D. Frances w co 2 C. Vassillou, B. Brooks w pts P.de Santos; *semi-finals:* D. Quacoe w rsc 3 R. Blair, D. Francis w rsc 2 B. Brooks; *final:* D. Francis w rsc 1 D. Quacoe. **Middle:** *quarter-finals:* L. Morris (Basingstoke) w pts S. Day (Fareham), W. Sutherland (Smarden) w co 3 S. Fletcher (Woking), R. Dehara (Ashford) w rsc 1 N. Hunt (Ramsgate), D. Douglas (Hove) wo; *semi-finals:* D. Douglas w rsc 1 L. Morris, W. Sutherland w co 1 R. Dehara; *final:* D. Douglas w co 2 W. Sutherland. **L. Heavy:** *semi-finals:* G. Donaldson (Basingstoke) w rsc 3 A. Knight (Ashford), M. Snipe (Brighton) wo; *final:* G. Donaldson w rsc 3 M. Snipe. **Heavy:** *final:* S. Welch (Hove) w rsc 1 C. Little (Sandwich). **S. Heavy:** *final:* C. Parsons (Brighton) w rsc 1 J. Hughes (Ryde).

Regional Semi-Finals & Finals

St Ivo Centre, Huntingdon - 29 February, Daines Camp Leisure Centre, Northampton - 9 March & Bewbush Leisure Centre, Crawley - 21 March

L. Fly: *final:* D. Fifield (Henley) w pts K. Hassell (Braunstone). **Fly:** *semi-finals:* D. Pithie (Willenhall) w pts J. Murphy (Hove) , M. Reynolds (Colchester) w co 1 J. Locke (Reading); *final:* J. Murphy - replaced D. Pithie w pts M. Reynolds. **Bantam:** *semi-finals:* M. Alldis (Crawley) w pts C. Slatcher (Phoenix), D. Dainty (Canvey) w pts S. Collar (Dunstable); *final:* M. Alldis w pts D. Dainty. **Feather:** *semi-finals:* Y. Vorajee (Triumph) w co 2 M. Walsh (Portsmouth), J. Gynn (Stevenage) w rtd 2 B. Saich (Canvey); *final:* Y. Vorajee w co 2 J. Gynn. **Light:** *semi-finals:* D. Amory (Kingshurst) w rsc 1 D. Sowden (Wecock Farm), J. Wilson (Abingdon) w pts G. Newcome (Canvey); *final:* D. Amory w pts J. Wilson. **L. Welter:** *semi-finals:* J. Scanlon (Coventry Colliery) w pts G. Spiers (Red Ensign), K. Marner (Bracknell) w pts G. Smith(Canvey); *final:* J. Scanlon w pts K. Marner. **Welter:** *semi-finals:* M. Santini (Birmingham) w rsc 2 S. Jenkinson (Onslow), A. Smith (Chesham) w pts G. Barker (Norwich); *final:* M. Santini w pts A. Smith. **L. Middle:** *semi-finals:* D. Francis (Basingstoke) wo M. Lee (Burton), L. Pugh (Oxford YMCA) w pts A. Ewen (Arcade); *final:* D. Francis w rsc 1 L. Pugh. **Middle:** *semi-finals:* R. Golding (Kingshurst) w rsc 2 D. Douglas (Hove), L. Woolcock (Canvey) w co 2 M. Hilding (Pinewood Starr); *final:* L. Woolcock w pts R. Golding. **L. Heavy:** *semi-finals:* K. Oliver (Bracebridge) w pts G. Donaldson (Basingstoke), S. Lawlor (Luton Irish) w pts D. Weaver (Canvey); *final:* K. Oliver w pts S. Lawlor. **Heavy:** *semi-finals:* S. Welch (Hove) w rsc 3 T. Small (Kingshurst), G. Cox (Canvey) w rsc 2 A. Barnes (Aylesbury); *final:* S. Welch w dis 3 G. Cox. **S. Heavy:** *semi-finals:* C. Parsons (Brighton) w co 1 C. Brogan (Harworth Colliery), N. Sturman (Dereham) wo; *final:* C. Parsons w rsc 1 N. Sturman.

London

North-East Division York Hall, Bethnal Green - 20 February

L. Fly: *final:* J. Borg (Lion) wo. **Fly:** *final:* J. Green (Repton) wo. **Bantam:** *final:* M. Jones (Repton) wo. **Feather:** *final:* M. Ward (Repton) w rsc 2 G. Andrews (Lion). **Light:** *semi-finals:* M. Holgate (St Monica's) w pts G. Loblack (Newham), S. Smith (Repton) wo; *final:* S. Smith w pts M. Holgate. **L. Welter:** *semi-finals:* S. Bromley (West Ham) w pts P. Wright (Repton), A. Hennessey (West Ham) w pts K. Asare (Lion); *final:* A. Hennessey w pts S. Bromley. **Welter:** *semi-finals:* A. Wilton (West Ham) w pts J. Beard (Newham), W. Dorking (Repton) w pts J. Tokeley (West Ham); *final:* W. Dorking w rsc 2 A. Wilton. **L. Middle:** *quarter-finals:* J. Branch (Repton) w pts S. Smith (Gator), T. Taylor(Repton) wo, F. Farquhar (County) wo, C. Marshall (West Ham) wo; *semi-finals:* J. Branch w pts C. Marshall, T. Taylor w rsc 2 F. Farquhar; *final:* T. Taylor wo J. Branch. **Middle:** *final:* J. Matthews (Crown & Manor) w pts R. Arthey (Newham). **L. Heavy:** *semi-finals:* M. Wright (Repton) w pts D. Kiely (Five Star), M. Delaney (West Ham) wo; *final:* M. Delaney w pts M. Wright. **Heavy:** *final:* T. Dunstan (St Monica's) w rsc 2 S. Lukacs (West Ham). **S. Heavy:** *final:* K. Fletcher (Dagenham) wo.

North-West Division Porchester Hall, Queensway - 13 February

L. Fly: *final:* N. Persaud (St Pancras) wo. **Fly:** *final:* M. Horobin (St Pancras) wo. **Bantam:** *semi-finals:* B. Smith (St Pancras) w rsc 3 J. Simpson (Hayes), P. Mullings (St Patrick's) w rsc 1 M.Khan (Islington); *final:* P. Mullings w rsc 1 B. Smith. **Feather:** *final:* J. Weatherman (St Pancras) w pts S. McNamara (Finchley). **Light:** *final:* P. J. Gallagher (Angel) w pts N. King (St Patrick's). **L. Welter:** *quarter-finals:* A. Brown (Middle Row) w rsc 2 B. Patrick (St Pancras), D. Ahearne (St Pancras) wo, R. Edwards (St Patrick's) wo, S. Bardoville (All Stars) wo; *semi-finals:* A. Brown w pts D. Ahearne, R. Edwards w rsc 1 S. Bardoville; *final:* R. Edwards w co 1 A. Brown. **Welter:** *quarter-finals:* J. Paul (Islington) w pts A. Noonan (St Pancras), V. Rose (New Enterprise) w pts A. Katerega (Gainsford), E. Diedrick (St

Pancras) w rsc 2 W. Dunn (Northolt), G. McCabe (Hanwell) wo; *semi-finals:* J. Paul w pts G. McCabe, V. Rose w pts E. Diedrick; *final:* V. Rose w rsc 1 J. Paul. **L. Middle:** *semi-finals:* R. Colbeck (Gainsford) w pts T. O'Donoghue (St Pancras), M. Edwards (St Pancras) wo; *final:* R. Colbeck w dis 2 M. Edwards. **Middle:** *semi-finals:* A. King w rsc 2 B. Allen (Islington), E. O'Riordan (Angel) w rsc 3 G. Potter (New Enterprise); *final:* E. O'Riordan w co 1 A. King. **L. Heavy:** *quarter-finals:* F. Yemofio (Hanwell) w pts S. Miller (Angel), K. Nevers (Islington) w rsc 1 G. Walters (All Stars), M. Prince (New Enterprise) wo, D. Gibbs (Trojan Police) wo; *semi-finals:* M. Prince w rsc 3 D. Gibbs, K. Nevers w rsc 2 F. Yemofio; *final:* M. Prince w rsc 3 K. Nevers. **Heavy:** *semi-finals:* C. Henry (New Enterprise) w rsc 2 B. Cornwall (Trojan Police), S. Erhahon (Gainsford) w rsc 1 M. Witter (Uxbridge); *final:* C. Henry w rsc 2 S. Erhahon. **S. Heavy:** *final:* D. Holness (St Pancras) w pts D. Gascoyne (Finchley).

South-East Division Crooklog Sports Centre, Bexleyheath - 22 February
L. Fly: *final:* L. Harris (Lynn) wo. **Fly:** *final:* T. Rossiter (St Joseph's) wo. **Bantam:** *semi-finals:* P. Cooper (Fisher) w pts D. Easton (New Addington), I. Sodhi (Lynn) wo; *final:* P. Cooper w pts I. Sodhi. **Feather:** *final:* M. McCrae (Fitzroy Lodge) w pts M. Brown (Lynn). **Light:** *semi-finals:* L. Reynolds (Fitzroy Lodge) w co 3 S. Jean-Paul (Fitzroy Lodge), A. Rossiter (St Joseph's) w pts W. Singh (Eltham); *final:* L. Reynolds w rtd 3 A. Rossiter. **L. Welter:** *quarter-finals:* T. Hearn (St Joseph's) w pts P. Belmar (Fitzroy Lodge), P. Holden (Honor Oak) wo, L. Lingard (BK Movers) wo, D. McGovern (Fitzroy Lodge) wo; *semi-finals:* P. Holden w co 3 L. Lingard, D. McGovern w rsc 1 T. Hearn; *final:* P. Holden w pts D. McGovern. **Welter:** *semi-finals:* A. Schembri (New Addington) w pts N. Appiah (Lynn), M. Edwards (Fitzroy Lodge) wo; *final:* M. Edwards wo A. Schembri. **L. Middle:** *final:* J. Banjo (Lynn) w pts D. Long (Honour Oak). **Middle:** *final:* A. Taiwo (Fisher) w pts B. Galloway (BK Movers). **L. Heavy:** *semi-finals:* T. Banton (Lynn) w pts V. Clarke (BK Movers), C. Okoh (Lynn) w pts D. Archibald (Lynn); *final:* C. Okoh w co 3 T. Banton. **Heavy:** *final:* D. Williams (Lynn) w pts J. Quayson (Lynn). **S. Heavy:** J. Francis (St Peter's) w pts H. Senior (Lynn).

South-West Division Town Hall, Battersea - 24 February
L. Fly: no entries. **Fly:** *final:* P. Mukasa (Old Actonians) wo. **Bantam:** no entries. **Feather:** *final:* D. Oliver (Met Police) w pts A Graham (Battersea). **Light:** *final:* P. Hersey (Battersea) wo. **L. Welter:** *semi-finals:* A. Campbell (Battersea) w pts J. Hemmings (Earlsfield), C. Joof (Battersea) wo; *final:* C. Joof w pts A. Campbell. **Welter:** *final:* S. Prendergast (Earlsfield) w pts A. Gray (Roehampton). **L. Middle:** *final:* H. Eastman (Battersea) w rsc 3 R. Williams (Earlsfield). **Middle:** *final:* D. Cranston (Battersea) wo. **L. Heavy:** *final:* A. McDonald (Balham) wo. **S. Heavy:** no entries.

London Semi-Finals & Finals York Hall, Bethnal Green - 5 & 19 March
L. Fly: *semi-finals:* L. Harris (Lynn) w pts J. Borg (Lion), N. Persaud (St Pancras) wo; *final:* L. Harris w pts N. Persaud. **Fly:** *semi-finals:* P. Mukasa (Old Actonians) wo J. Green (Repton), M. Horobin (St Pancras) wo T. Rossiter (St Joseph's); *final:* M. Horobin w pts P. Mukasa. **Bantam:** *semi-finals:* P. Mullings (St Patrick's) w co 1 P. Cooper (Fisher), M. Jones (Repton) wo; *final:* P. Mullings wo M. Jones. **Feather:** *semi-finals:* M. McCrea (Fitzroy Lodge) w rsc 3 J. Weatherman (St Pancras), M. Ward (Repton) w rsc 1 D. Oliver (Met Police); *final:* M. Ward w pts M. McCrea. **Light:** *semi-finals:* P. J. Gallagher (Angel) w rtd 2 P. Hersey (Battersea), L. Reynolds (Fitzroy Lodge) wo S. Smith (Repton); *final:* P. J. Gallagher w pts L. Reynolds. **L. Welter:** *semi-finals:* P. Holden (Honour Oak) w rsc 3 A. Hennessey (West Ham), C. Joof (Battersea) w rsc 3 R. Edwards (St Patrick's); *final:* C. Joof w rsc 2 P. Holden. **Welter:** *semi-finals:* S. Prendergast (Earlsfield) w dis 3 V. Rose (New Enterprise), W. Dorking (Repton) w pts M. Edwards (Fitzroy Lodge); *final:* W. Dorking w pts S. Prendergast. **L. Middle:** *semi-finals:* T. Taylor (Repton) w pts H. Eastman (Battersea), R. Colbeck (Gainsford) and J. Banjo (Lynn) dis 3; *final:* T. Taylor wo. **Middle:** *semi-finals:* J. Matthews (Crown & Manor) w rsc 3 E. O'Riordan (Angel), A. Taiwo (Fisher) w pts D. Cranston (Battersea); *final:* J. Matthews w pts A. Taiwo. **L. Heavy:** *semi-finals:* C. Okoh (Lynn) w pts H. Benn (Earlsfield), M. Prince (New Enterprise) w co 2 M. Wright (Repton) - replaced M. Delaney (West Ham); *final:* M. Prince w rsc 3 C. Okoh. **Heavy:** *semi-finals:* C. Henry (New Enterprise) w rsc 1 A. McDonald (Balham), T. Dunstan (St Monica's) wo D. Williams (Lynn); *final:* C. Henry w pts T. Dunstan. **S. Heavy:** *semi-finals:* D. Holness (St Pancras) w pts J. Francis (St Peter's), K. Fletcher (Dagenham) wo; *final:* D. Holness w rsc 2 K. Fletcher.

Northern Counties

North-East Counties

North-East Division Leisure Centre, Gateshead - 7 & 14 February
L. Fly: no entries. **Fly:** *final:* S. Parry (Lambton Street) w pts D. Noble (Ocean Road). **Bantam:** *final:* A. Martin (Hartlepool Catholic) w pts S. Newman (South Bank). **Feather:** *final:* A. Temple (Hartlepool BW) w rsc 1 S. Hurcombe (Lambton Street). **Light:** *quarter-finals:* A. Green (Phil Thomas SOB) w pts J. Kelly (Hartlepool BW), I. Walker (Newbiggin) wo, M. Teasdale (Wellington) wo, A. Graham (Grainger Park) wo; *semi-finals:* A. Green w pts A. Graham, I. Walker w rsc 2 M. Teasdale; *final:* A. Green w pts I. Walker. **L. Welter:** *final:* S. Armstrong (Hartlepool BW) w rsc 2 T. George (Marley Hill). **Welter:** *semi-finals:* B. Wright (Shildon) w pts G. Smith (Hartlepool Catholic), J. Green (Phil Thomas SOB) w rtd 2 M. McLean (Durham); *final:* J. Green w rsc 3 B. Wright. **L. Middle:** *prelims:* W. Neil (Sunderland) w pts A. Lee (Birtley), M. Chickocki (Hartlepool Catholic) w rsc 3 M. Lumley (Lambton Street), M. Johnson (Grainger Park) wo, H. Davey (Benfield) wo, J. Pearse (Wellington) wo, D. Curry (Birtley) wo, J. Mett (Phil Thomas SOB) wo, G. Kirby (Blackhall) wo; *quarter-finals:* M. Chickocki w pts W. Neil, M. Johnson w pts H. Davey, J. Pearse w rsc 3 D. Curry, J. Mett w rsc 1 G. Kirby; *semi-finals:* J. Mett w dis 3 M. Chickocki, J. Pearse wo M. Johnson; *final:* J. Pearse w pts J. Mett. **Middle:** *quarter-finals:* S. Bellfield (Sunderland w pts T. Cook (Grangetown), G. Newton (Teams) wo, C. Bedinson (Birtley) wo, A. Exley (Grainger Park) wo; *semi-finals:* A. Exley w pts S. Bellfield, G. Newton w pts C. Bedinson; *final:* A. Exley w rsc 1 G. Newton. **L. Heavy:** *semi-finals:* K. Duke (Sunderland) w co 1 S. Cowlem (Manor), I. Meredith (Newbiggin) w pts S. Bowes (Consett); *final:* K. Duke w pts I. Meredith. **Heavy:** *quarter-finals:* I. Laskey (Teams) w rsc 3 J. Storey (Sunderland), D. McFarlane (Birtley) wo, M. McGuinness (Spennymoor) wo, J. Greenwell (Shildon) wo; *semi-finals:* D. McFarlane w rsc 3 M. McGuinness, I. Laskey w pts J. Greenwell; *final:* D. McFarlane w pts I. Laskey. **S. Heavy:** *final:* M. Hopper (Spennymoor) w rsc 1 M. Rowe (Teams).

Yorkshire & Humberside Divisions Metrodome, Barnsley - 7 February & Liberal Club, Barnsley - 11 February
L. Fly: no entries. **Fly:** *final:* K. Sheridan (Doncaster) wo. **Bantam:** *final:* L. Crosby (St Paul's) w co 1 M. Hopkinson (Bradford Police). **Feather:** *semi-finals:* A. Benton (Batley & Dewsbury) w pts J. Barker (Hull Fish Trades), J. Stovin (Hull Boys) wo; *final:* A. Benton w pts J. Stovin. **Light:** *semi-finals:* J.

Phelan (St Paul's) w rsc 1 A. Leach (Hull Fish Trades), T. Whitaker (Grimethorpe) w pts R. Lattiebaudiere (Meanwood); *final:* J. Phelan w pts T. Whitaker. **L. Welter:** *semi-finals:* M. Barker (St Paul's) w pts F. Hogg (St Patrick's), R. Ali (Kingston) w co 3 J. Bretton (Grimethorpe); *final:* M. Barker w rsc 2 R. Ali. **Welter:** *quarter-finals:* J. Herridge (Hull Fish Trades) w rsc 2 L. Jenkins (Heeley Bank), M. Stones (Hull Fish Trades) w pts S. Tuckett (Sharlston), D. Harper (Grimethorpe) wo, P. Waudby (St Paul's) wo; *semi-finals:* J. Herridge w rsc 3 D. Harper, P. Waudby w pts M. Stones; *final:* P. Waudby w rsc 3 J. Herridge. **L. Middle:** *quarter-finals:* L. Moorhouse (St Patrick's) w pts K. Kaihau (Tom Hill), C. Manterfield (Grimethorpe) w pts D. Larkin (Bentley Miners), S. Hendry (Burmantofts) w co 1 J. Stronach (Keighley), B. Dunn (Grimsby) w pts S. Cassidy (Grimethorpe); *semi-finals:* L. Moorhouse w pts B. Dunn, S. Hendry w pts C. Manterfield; *final:* S. Hendry w pts L. Moorhouse. **Middle:** *quarter-finals:* J. Sharp (Sharlston) w rsc 1 M. Reynolds (Stainland), G. Dunbar (St Paul's) w rsc 3 T. Robinson (Grimsby), J. Lumsden (Hunslet) wo, D. Laban (Grimethorpe) wo; *semi-finals:* J. Sharp w co 1 J. Lumsden, G. Dunbar w rsc 2 D. Laban; *final:* J. Sharp w dis 2 G. Dunbar. **L. Heavy:** *semi-finals:* C. Joseph (Sedbergh) w rsc 2 M. Thompson (Wombwell), R. Atkinson (Batley & Dewsbury) w pts A. Call (Grimsby); *final:* C. Joseph w pts R. Atkinson. **Heavy:** *final:* N. Kirkwood (Grimethorpe) w pts N. Whitelam (Humberside Police). **S. Heavy:** no entries.

North-East Counties Finals The Pavilion, Thornaby - 28 February
L. Fly: no entries. **Fly:** S. Parry (Lambton Street) w rsc 1 K. Sheridan (Doncaster). **Bantam:** L. Crosby (St Paul's) w rsc 3 A. Martin (Hartlepool Catholic). **Feather:** A. Temple (Hartlepool BW) w pts A. Benton (Batley & Dewsbury). **Light:** A. Green (Phil Thomas SOB) w rsc 3 J. Phelan (St Paul's). **L. Welter:** S. Armstrong (Hartlepool BW) w pts M. Barker (St Paul's). **Welter:** P. Waudby (St Paul's) w pts J. Green (Phil Thomas SOB). **L. Middle:** S. Hendry (Burmantofts) w pts J. Pearse (Wellington). **Middle:** A. Exley (Grainger Park) w rsc 3 J. Sharp (Sharlston). **L. Heavy:** C. Joseph (Sedbergh) w pts K. Duke (Sunderland). **Heavy:** N. Kirkwood (Grimethorpe) w pts D. McFarlane (Birtley). **S. Heavy:** M. Hopper (Spennymoor) wo.

North-West Counties

East Lancs & Cheshire Division The Forum, Wythenshawe - 4 & 18 February
L. Fly: no entries. **Fly:** no entries. **Bantam:** no entries. **Feather:** *semi-finals:* B. Alston (Sale West) w pts M. Chambers (Preston Red Rose), J. Roche (Bredbury) w pts C. Rourke (Droylsden); *final:* J. Roche w pts B. Alston. **Light:** *semi-finals:* B. Connolly (Sandygate) w pts S. Walker (Boarshaw), M. Wainwright (Arrow) wo; *final:* M. Wainwright w pts B. Connolly. **L. Welter:** *final:* D. McCarrick (Boarshaw) w co 2 J. Barrow (Preston & Fulwood). **Welter:** *final:* A. Thompson (Hensingham) w rsc 2 B. Gonzales (Preston Red Rose). **L. Middle:** *semi-finals:* J. Whiteside (Preston Red Rose) w rsc 3 D. Richards (Barrow), J. Alston (Preston & Fulwood) w pts C. Walker (Ardwick); *final:* J. Alston w pts J. Whiteside. **Middle:** *semi-finals:* G. Williams (Louvolite) w rsc 1

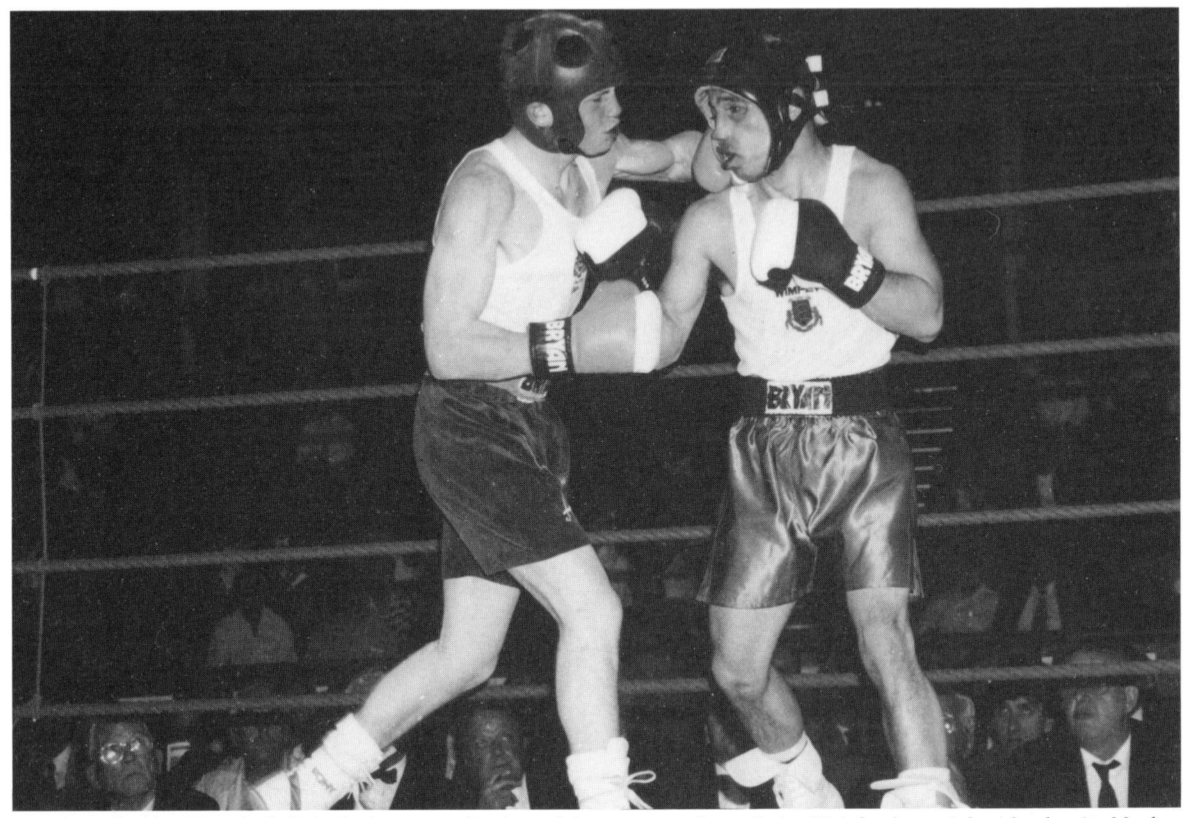

Hartlepool's Alan Temple (left) looked an exceedingly useful prospect as he took the ABA featherweight title, despite Marlon Ward's strong challenge
Les Clark

D. Muir (Droylsden), E. Noi (Moss Side) wo; *final:* E. Noi w pts G. Williams. **L. Heavy:** *semi-finals:* L. Whitehead (Arrow) w rsc 1 D. Magiotta (Droylsden), S. Wood (Currock House) w pts P. Gregory (Sale West); *final:* S. Wood w rtd 1 L. Whitehead. **Heavy:** *final:* M. Levi (Collyhurst & Moston) w pts W. Gibbs (St Boniface). **S. Heavy:** *final:* R. Allen (Preston & Fulwood) wo.

West Lancs & Cheshire Division Everton Park Sports Centre, Liverpool - 7, 14 & 21 February
L. Fly: *final:* P. Culshaw (Huyton) wo. **Fly:** no entries. **Bantam:** *final:* A. Mulholland (Transport) w co 1 P. Wright (Everton). **Feather:** *quarter-finals:* J. Mellor (Transport) w pts A. Moon (Kirkby), T. Peacock (Salisbury) w pts C. Ainscough (Transport), J. Heyes (Salisbury) wo, E. Roberts (Gemini) wo; *semi-finals:* J. Heyes w rsc 2 E. Roberts, J. Mellor w dis 1 T. Peacock; *final:* J. Mellor w pts J. Heyes. **Light:** *final:* G. Ryder (Kirkby) w pts G. Thornhill (Transport). **L. Welter:** *quarter-finals:* J. Neary (Golden Gloves) w pts G. Naylor (Transport), J. Vlasman (Everton) w rsc 2 A. Mason (Wavertree), L. Rimmer (Salisbury) wo, S. Floyd (Roseheath) wo; *semi-finals:* J. Neary w co 1 J. Vlasman, L. Rimmer w co 1 S. Floyd; *final:* L. Rimmer w pts J. Neary. **Welter:** *semi-finals:* J. Jones (Sefton) w pts G. Beadman (Transport), P. Burns (Gemini) w co 1 N. Whelan (Transport); *final:* P. Burns w rsc 3 J.Jones. L. Middle: *quarter-finals:* D. Peters (Golden Gloves) w pts A. Walker (Sefton), R. Murray (Roseheath) wo, P. Stocks (Roseheath) wo, P. McGeady (Golden Star) wo; *semi-finals:* R. Murray w pts P. Stocks, D. Peters w rsc 2 P. McGeady; *final:* D. Peters w pts R. Murray. **Middle:** *semi-finals:* L. Blundell (Warrington) w pts R. Burns (Gemini), J. Naylor (Rotunda) wo; *final:* L. Blundell w pts J. Naylor. **L. Heavy:** *semi-finals:* P. Craig (Knowsley Vale) w rsc 3 P. Addison (Wavertree), D. Kehoe (Gemini) w co 3 B. Jones (Willaston); *final:* P. Craig w rsc 2 D. Kehoe. **Heavy:** *semi-finals:* D. Chubbs (Kirkby) w rsc 2 P. McCormick (Transport), A. Whelan (Transport) wo; *final:* D. Chubbs w dis 2 A. Whelan. **S. Heavy:** *final:* S. Bristow (Rotunda) wo.

North-West Counties Finals The Forum, Wythenshawe - 28 February
L. Fly: P. Culshaw (Huyton) wo. **Fly:** no entries. **Bantam:** A. Mulholland (Transport) wo. **Feather:** J. Mellor (Transport) w pts J. Roche (Bredbury). **Light:** G. Ryder(Kirkby) w pts M. Wainwright (Arrow). **L. Welter:** D. McCarrick (Boarshaw) w pts L. Rimmer (Salisbury). **Welter:** P. Burns (Gemini) w pts A. Thompson (Hensingham). **L. Middle:** D. Peters (Golden Gloves) w pts J. Alston (Preston & Fulwood). **Middle:** E. Noi (Moss Side) w dis 2 L. Blundell (Warrington). **L. Heavy:** S. Wood (Currock House) w pts P. Craig (Knowsley Vale). **Heavy:** M. Levi (Collyhurst & Moston) w co 1 D. Chubbs (Kirkby). **S. Heavy:** R. Allen (Preston & Fulwood) wo S. Bristow (Rotunda).

Northern Counties Finals

Leisure Centre, Gateshead - 13 March
L. Fly: P. Culshaw (Huyton) wo. **Fly:** S. Parry (Lambton Street) wo. **Bantam:** A. Mulholland (Transport) w pts L. Crosby (St Paul's). **Feather:** A. Temple (Hartlepool BW) w pts J. Mellor (Transport). **Light:** A. Green (Phil Thomas SOB) w pts G. Ryder (Kirkby). **L. Welter:** D. McCarrick (Boarshaw) w rsc 3 S. Armstrong (Hartlepool BW). **Welter:** P. Burns (Gemini) w pts P. Waudby (St Paul's). **L. Middle:** D. Peters (Golden Gloves) w pts S. Hendry (Burmantofts). **Middle:** E. Noi (Moss Side) w pts A. Exley (Grainger Park). **L. Heavy:** C. Joseph (Sedbergh) w pts S. Wood (Currock House). **Heavy:** M. Levi (Collyhurst & Moston) w pts N. Kirkwood (Grimethorpe). **S. Heavy:** M. Hopper (Spennymoor) w pts R. Allen (Preston & Fulwood).

British ABA Quarter-Finals

English Semi-Finals Bletchley Leisure Centre, Milton Keynes - 1 April
L. Fly: D. Fifield (Henley) w pts L. Harris (Lynn), L. Woodcock (RN) wo P. Culshaw (Huyton). **Fly:** S. Parry (Lambton Street) w dis 1 J. Murphy (Hove), M. Horobin (St Pancras) w pts O. Spencely (RN). **Bantam:** P. Mullings (St Patrick's) w pts G. Nicette (Torbay), M. Alldis (Crawley) w pts A. Mulholland (Transport). **Feather:** A. Temple (Hartlepool BW) w pts Y. Vorajee (Triumph), M. Ward (Repton) w pts D. Thompson (Empire) - replaced K. Hodkinson (Leonis). **Light:** D. Amory (Kingshurst) w pts P. J. Gallagher (Angel), A. Green w pts D. Rudd (RAF). **L. Welter:** A. Stone (Empire) w pts C. Joof (Battersea), D. McCarrick (Boarshaw) w rsc 2 J. Scanlon (Coventry Colliery). **Welter:** P. Burns (Gemini) w pts C. Bessey (Army), M. Santini (Birmingham) w rtd 3 W. Dorking (Repton). **L. Middle:** G. Catley (Empire) w pts D. Peters (Golden Gloves), D. Francis (Basingstoke) w pts T. Taylor (Repton). **Middle:** E. Noi (Moss Side) w pts G. Grounds (RN), L. Woolcock (Canvey) w co 3 J. Matthews (Crown & Manor). **L. Heavy:** K. Oliver (Bracebridge) w rsc 3 C. Joseph (Sedbergh), P. Rogers (Penhill RBL) w rsc 3 M. Prince (New Enterprise). **Heavy:** S. Welch (Hove) w rsc 3 M. Levi (Collyhurst & Moston), C. Henry (New Enterprise) w rtd 2 N. Hosking (Devonport). **S. Heavy:** D. Holness (St Pancras) w pts K. Oputu (St George), M. Hopper (Spennymoor) w rsc 2 C. Parsons (Brighton).

Scottish Championships

Meadowbank Stadium, Edinburgh - 28 February & Fairfield Social Club, Govan - 16 March & Sports Centre, Grangemouth - 26 March
L. Fly: *final:* S. Robertson (Lanarkshire Welfare) w pts A. Mooney (Sydney Street). **Fly:** *final:* K. Knox (Bonnyrigg) w pts J. Miller (Bannockburn). **Bantam:** *semi-finals:* S. Anderson (Sydney Street) w pts R. Silverstein (Selkirk), J. Murray (Royal Albert) w rsc 2 W. Mguli (Glasgow University); *final:* J. Murray w pts S. Anderson. **Feather:** *semi-finals:* C. Melucci (Calton) w pts I. McLeod (Croy), B. Carr (Auchengeich) w rsc 2 K. Armstrong (Hastie); *final:* B. Carr w pts C. Melucci. **Light:** *quarter-finals:* G. Docherty (Newarthill) w co 3 E. Barclay (Kingcorth), G. Hughes (Drumchapel) w pts W. Leckie (Haddington), M. Gowans (Selkirk) wo, J. Gardner (Paisley) wo; *semi-finals:* M. Gowans w pts J. Gardner, G. Hughes w rsc 2 G. Docherty; *final:* M. Gowans w pts G. Hughes. **L. Welter:** *prelims:* B. Welsh (Dumfries) w pts A. Sung (Meadowbank), W. Leitch (Bellahouston) w pts T. Harrison (Springside), L. McBride (Elgin) w rsc 2 M. Breslin (Croy), J. Townsley(Cleland) wo, T. Kennedy (Barn) wo, J. Black (Blantyre) wo, W. Menzies (Arbroath) wo, S. McLevy (Clydeview) wo; *quarter-finals:* S. McLevy w dis 2 B. Welsh, J. Townsley w rsc 2 T. Kennedy, L. McBride w rsc 1 W. Leitch, W. Menzies w co 3 J. Black; *semi-finals:* J. Townsley w pts W. Menzies, S. McLevy w rsc 3 L. McBride; *final:* S. McLevy w rsc 2 J. Townsley. **Welter:** *quarter-finals:* A. Ingle (Haddington) w dis 3 T. Jolly (Whithorn), A. Craig (Aberdeen) w rsc 2 H. Wood (Chirnside), J. Gilheaney (Cleland) w rsc 1 S. Magee (Rosyth), T. Gonsalves (St Francis) wo; *semi-finals:* A. Ingle w rsc 2 T. Gonzalves, A. Craig w pts J. Gilheaney; *final:* A. Craig w pts A.

Ingle. **L. Middle:** *quarter-finals:* P. Dolan (Gartcosh) w rsc 2 W. McPhee (Huntley), C. Wallace (Lanarkshire Welfare) wo, S. Morrison (Zetland) wo, J. Townsley (Cleland) wo; *semi-finals:* C. Wallace w pts J. Townsley, S. Morrison w pts P. Dolan; *final:* S. Morrison w pts C. Wallace. **Middle:** *quarter-finals:* A. Docherty (Kirkintilloch) w pts J. Daley (Bannockburn), J. Wilson (Leith) wo, J. Jenner (Meadowbank) wo, J. Connelly (Renton) wo; *semi-final:* J. Wilson w pts J. Jenner, J. Connelly w pts A. Docherty; *final:* J. Connelly w pts J. Wilson. **L. Heavy:** *semi-finals:* W. Cane (Four Isles) w rsc 2 R. Lillie (Larkhall), S. Wilson (Haddington) wo; *final:* S. Wilson w pts W. Cane. **Heavy:** *quarter-finals:* N. Taggart (Bellahouston) w pts B. Quinn (Bannockburn), M. Neil (Clydebank) w pts E. Carlon (Perth Railway), S. Aitken (Meadowbank) wo, A. Caulfield (St Francis) wo; *semi-finals:* A. Caulfield w rsc 3 N. Taggart, S. Aitken w pts M. Neil; *final:* A. Caulfield w pts S. Aitken. **S. Heavy:** *semi-finals:* C. Brown (Gartcosh) w pts J. Cowie (Camelon), S. Docherty (Bellahouston) w pts J. Akinlami (Larkhall); *final:* C. Brown w pts S. Docherty.

Welsh Championships

Afan Lido, Aberavon - 15 February, Penylan Club, Swansea - 25 February, Social Club, Merthyr - 27 February & National Sports Centre, Cardiff - 2 April

L. Fly: no entries. **Fly:** *semi-finals:* M. Hughes (Gwent) w rsc 3 P. Crewe (Wrexham), N. Swain (Gilfach Goch) wo; *final:* N. Swain w pts M. Hughes. **Bantam:** *quarter-finals:* R. Keenan (Coed Eva) w dis 3 O. Omar (Prince of Wales), P. Janes (Highfield) wo, N. Birch (Ynysybwl) wo, R. Vowles (Llanharan) wo; *semi-finals:* P. Janes w pts N. Birch, R. Vowles w dis 3 R. Keenan; *final:* R. Vowles w rsc 3 P. Janes. **Feather:** *quarter-finals:* D. Jay (Trelewis) w pts S. Boyce (Pontypridd), B. Jones (Highfield) w rsc 2 A. Fletcher (Newtown), P. Samuels (Crindau) wo, K. Lowie (Red Dragon) wo; *semi-finals:* P. Samuels w co 1 K. Lowie, B. Jones w rsc 3 D. Jay; *final:* B. Jones w pts P. Samuels. **Light:** *semi-finals:* M. Newton (Coed Eva) w dis 2 L. Butler (Llanharan), J. Leto (Splott Adventure) wo; *final:* M. Newton w rsc 2 J. Leto. **L. Welter:** *prelims:* P. Feal (Prince of Wales) w rtd 2 D. Holmes (Cinderford), B. Pritchard (Llangefni) w pts N. Boyce (Pontypridd), A. Arish (Prince of Wales) wo, J. Jones (Rhondda) wo, J. Williams (Gwent) wo, S. Cook (Newbridge) wo, C. Thomas (Pentwyn) wo, M. Isaac (Pontypool) wo; *quarter-finals:* A. Arish w rtd 2 J. Jones, J. Williams w dis 2 S. Cook, C. Thomas w pts M. Isaac, P. Feal w rsc 1 B. Pritchard; *semi-finals:* P. Feal w rsc 3 C. Thomas, J. Williams w co 2 A. Arish; *final:* J. Williams w rsc 3 P. Feal. **Welter:** *Prelims:* A. Law (Carmarthen) w rsc 2 D. Matthews (Heads of Valley), L. Taylor (Gilfach Goch) wo, B. Ahmed (Prince of Wales) wo, B. Thorogood (Highfield) wo, B. Jones (Llangefni) wo, M. Ficiccha (Pontypool & Panteg) wo, J. Reynolds (Newport SC) wo, P. Chapell (Porthcawl) wo; *quarter-finals:* L. Taylor w rsc 3 B. Ahmed, B. Thorogood w rsc 1 B. Jones, M. Ficiccha w rsc 2 J. Reynolds, P. Chapell w rsc 3 A. Law; *semi-finals:* B. Thorogood w pts L. Taylor, P. Chapell w pts M. Ficiccha; *final:* B. Thorogood w pts P. Chapell. **L. Middle:** *quarter-finals:* P. Williams (Cardigan) w co 1 C. Thomas (Deeside), C. Winter (Denby) w co 1 D. Fulton (Splott Adventure), J. Calzache (Newbridge) w rtd 2 C. Onytwu (Premier), A. Langley (Wrexham) w pts D. Williams (Red Dragon); *semi-finals:* J. Calzache w rsc 1 A. Langley, C. Winter wo P. Williams; *final:* J. Calzache w rsc 2 C. Winter. **Middle:** *prelims:* C. Winstone (Pontypool & Panteg) w pts G. Neal (Heads of Valley), S. Stradling (Rhoose) w pts R. Whitehouse (City), L. Hogan (Duffryn) w pts A. Maguire (Red Dragon), A. Kearle (Cardiff YMCA) w pts P. Matthews (Trostre), G. Boddy (St Joseph) w pts P. Watkins (Penarth), P. Hawkesby (Crindau) w pts S. Dennis (Montanna), H. Price (Roath) wo, C. Thomas (Pot Black) wo; *quarter-finals:* C. Winstone w dis 3 H. Price, L. Hogan w co 2 S. Stradling, G. Boddy w rsc 3 A. Kearle, C. Thomas w pts P. Hawkesby; *semi-finals:* C. Winstone w pts L. Hogan, G. Boddy w pts C. Thomas; *final:* C. Winstone w dis 3 G. Boddy. **L. Heavy:** *prelims:* D. Brown (Blaen-y-Maes) w co 1 P. Barnett (Gwent), A. Holloway (Rhoose) w dis 3 T. Brown (Idris), C. Beck (Cymmer Afan) wo, J. David (St Joseph) wo, I. Bishop (Rhoose) wo, N. Ralphs (Rhoose) wo, D. Hitchings (Pontypridd) wo, N. Jones (Porthcawl) wo; *quarter-finals:* C. Beck w pts J. David, I. Bishop w rsc 3 N. Ralphs, D. Hitchings w dis 1 N. Jones, A. Holloway w rsc 1 D. Brown; *semi-finals:* C. Beck w pts I. Bishop, D. Hitchings w rsc 3 A. Holloway; *final:* D. Hitchings w rsc 3 C. Beck. **Heavy:** *quarter-finals:* H. Hartt (Preselli) w pts G. Davies (Gilfach Goch), R. Fenton (Pentwyn) wo, T. Redman (Idris) wo, K. Mumford (Fleur-de-Lys) wo; *semi-finals:* R. Fenton w rsc 3 T. Redman, H. Hartt w dis 3 K. Mumford; *final:* R. Fenton w rsc 1 H. Hartt. **S. Heavy:** *semi-finals:* K. McCormack (Coed Eva) w rsc 1 H. Jokarzadeh (Roath), N. Harvey (Heads of Valley) w rsc 1 J. Davidson (Trostre); *final:* K. McCormack w co 1 N. Harvey.

British ABA Semi-Finals & Finals

Leisure Centre, Gateshead - 13 & 14 April & Royal Albert Hall, Kensington - 6 May

L. Fly: *semi-finals:* L. Woodcock (RN) wo S. Robertson (Lanarkshire Welfare), D. Fifield (Henley) wo; *final:* D. Fifield w rsc 3 L. Woodcock. ***Fly:*** *semi-finals:* K. Knox (Bonnyrigg) w pts S. Parry (Lambton Street), M. Horobin (St Pancras) w pts N. Swain (Gilfach Goch); *final:* K Knox w pts M. Horobin. **Bantam:** *semi-finals:* M. Alldis (Crawley) wo J. Murray (Royal Albert), P. Mullings (St Patrick's) w rsc 1 R. Vowles (Llanharan); *final:* P. Mullings w pts M. Alldis. **Feather:** *semi-finals:* M. Ward (Repton) w pts C. Melucci (Calton) - replaced B. Carr (Auchengeich), A. Temple (Hartlepool BW) w pts B. Jones (Highfield); *final:* A. Temple w pts M. Ward. **Light:** *semi-finals:* D. Amory (Kingshurst) w pts M. Gowans (Selkirk), M. Newton (Coed Eva) w pts A. Green (Phil Thomas SOB); *final:* D. Amory w pts M. Newton. **L. Welter:** *semi-finals:* D. McCarrick (Boarshaw) w pts S. McLevy (Clydeview), A. Stone (Empire) w rsc 2 J. Williams (Gwent); *final:* D. McCarrick w rsc 1 A. Stone. **Welter:** *semi-finals:* M. Santini (Birmingham City) w rtd 3 A. Craig (Aberdeen), B. Thorogood (Highfield) w pts P. Burns (Gemini); *final:* M. Santini w rsc 2 B. Thorogood. **L. Middle:** *semi-finals:* G. Catley (Empire) w pts J. Townsley (Cleland) - replaced S. Morrison (Zetland), J. Calzache (Newbridge) w rsc 2 D. Francis (Basingstoke); *final:* J. Calzache w rsc 3 G. Catley. **Middle:** *semi-finals:* J. Connelly (Renton) w co 3 E. Noi (Moss Side), L. Woolcock (Canvey) wo C. Winstone (Pontypool & Panteg); *final:* L. Woolcock w pts J. Connelly. **L. Heavy:** *semi-finals:* P. Rogers (Penhill RBL) w rsc 2 W. Cane (Four Isles) - replaced S. Wilson (Haddington), K. Oliver (Bracebridge) w rsc 1 D. Hitchings (Pontypridd); *final:* K. Oliver w pts P. Rogers. **Heavy:** *semi-finals:* S. Welch (Hove) w pts A. Caufield (St Francis), R. Fenton (Pentwyn) w pts C. Henry (New Enterprise); *final:* S. Welch w co 3 R. Fenton. **S. Heavy:** *semi-finals:* M. Hopper (Spennymoor) w pts C. Brown (Gartcosh), D. Holness (St Pancras) wo K. McCormack (Coed Eva); *final:* M. Hopper w pts D. Holness.

Irish Championships, 1991-92

Senior Championships

The National Stadium, Dublin - 10 & 17 January

L. Fly: *semi-finals:* P. O'Halloran (St Munchin's, Limerick) w pts P. Brannigan (Dockers, Belfast), M. McQuillan (Holy Family, Drogheda) wo; *final:* M. McQuillan w co 1 P. O'Halloran. **Fly:** *quarter-finals:* T. Wait (Cairn Lodge, Belfast) w pts S. McMahon (Bracken, Dublin), G. Griffin (Drimnah, Dublin) w pts A. Brannigan (Dockers, Belfast), D. Kelly (Holy Trinity, Belfast) w pts D. Hosford (Greenmount, Cork), P. Buttimer (Sunnyside, Cork) wo; *semi-finals:* P. Buttimer w pts T. Waite, D. Kelly w pts G. Griffin; *final:* P. Buttimer w pts D. Kelly. **Bantam:** *semi-finals:* J. Lawlor (Darndale, Dublin) w pts P. Norton (Hillview, Belfast), W. McCullough (Albert Foundry, Belfast) wo; *final:* W. McCullough w pts J. Lawlor. **Feather:** *final:* P. Griffin (Drimnagh, Dublin) w pts C. Notarantonio (Newhill, Belfast). **Light:** *quarter-finals:* P. Ireland (St George's & St Malachy's, Belfast) w pts J. Breen (St Jude's, Wexford), F. Carruth (Drimnagh, Dublin) w pts T. Lawlor (Kilcullen, Kildare), M. Winters (Antrim) w pts J. Blanche (St Michael's, Wexford), E. Bolger (CBS, Wexford) w pts M. Kelly (Phoenix, Dublin); *semi-finals:* P. Ireland w pts F. Carruth, M. Winters w rsc 3 E. Bolger; *final:* M. Winters w pts P. Ireland. **L. Welter:** *quarter-finals:* E. Magee (Sacred Heart, Belfast) w pts S. McCloskey (Dockers, Belfast), G. Ormonde (Donore, Dublin) w pts T. Hennessey (Glasnevin, Dublin), N. McGough (St Paul's, Waterford) wo, B. Geraghty (Mount Tallant, Dublin) wo; *semi-finals:* N. McGough w pts B. Geraghty, E. Magee w pts G. Ormonde; *final:* E. Magee w pts N. Gough. **Welter:** *quarter-finals:* W. Walsh (St Ibar's, Wexford) w pts M. Roche (Sunnyside, Cork), S. Gibson (Immaculata, Belfast) w pts J. Webb (Holy Trinity, Belfast), M. Carruth (Drimnagh, Dublin) w pts M. McBride (Edenderry, Offaly), J. McCormack (St Saviour's, Dublin) w pts E. Fisher (Holy Trinity, Belfast); *semi-finals:* W. Walsh w pts S. Gibson, M. Carruth w pts J. McCormack; *final:* M. Carruth w pts W. Walsh. **L. Middle:** *semi-finals:* J. Lowe (Holy Trinity, Belfast) w pts A. Wilson (Ledley Hall, Belfast), G. Joyce (Sunnyside, Cork) w pts P. McCullagh (Immaculata, Belfast); *final:* J. Lowe w pts G. Joyce. **Middle:** *quarter-finals:* H. Byrne (St Munchin's, Limerick) w pts T. Brady (Angel, London), D. Galvin (Moate, Westmeath) wo, J. Mills (Drimnagh, Dublin) wo, T. Daly (Edenmore, Dublin) wo; *semi-finals:* D. Galvin w rsc 1 J. Mills, H. Byrne w pts T. Daly; *final:* D. Galvin w pts H. Byrne. **L. Heavy:** *quarter-finals:* M. Delaney (Holy Trinity, Belfast) w dis 2 D. Lawlor (Grangecon, Kildare), D. Griffin (Drimnagh, Dublin) w pts B. Ward (Olympic, Galway), P. Lawlor (Edenderry, Offaly) w pts S. Dawson (Edenmore, Dublin), D. Curran (CIE, Dublin) w pts G. Crichton (Donore, Dublin); *semi-finals:* P. Lawlor w pts D. Curran, M. Delaney w rsc 1 D. Griffin; *final:* M. Delaney w pts P. Lawlor. **Heavy:** *semi-finals:* T. Currie (St Agnes', Belfast) w rtd 1 W. Burke (Innisfree, Sligo), P. Douglas (Holy Family, Belfast) wo; *final:* T. Currie w pts P. Douglas. **S. Heavy:** *semi-finals:* C. Robinson (Antrim) w rsc 2 F. Curran (St Luke's, Dublin), K. McBride (Smithboro, Monaghan) w pts W. Clyde (Ballyclare, Antrim); *final:* K. McBride w pts C. Robinson.

Intermediate Championship Finals

The National Stadium, Dublin - 7 & 14 December, 1991

L. Fly: D. McKenna (Holy Family, Drogheda) w pts J. Prior (Darndale, Dublin). **Fly:** A. Brannigan (Dockers, Belfast) w pts B. Walsh (St Colman's, Cork). **Bantam:** F. Slane (Immaculata, Belfast) w rsc 2 J. Feeney (Inner City, Dublin). **Feather:** S. Redmond (Kilmount, Dublin) w pts L. O'Brien (Tramore, Waterford). **Light:** F. Carruth (Drimnagh, Dublin) wo N. Sinclair (Holy Family, Belfast). **L. Welter:** G. Ward (Darndale, Dublin) w pts T. Tolan (St Agnes', Belfast). **Welter:** R. O'Connor (St Canice's, Derry) w pts B. Walsh (St Colman's, Cork). **L. Middle:** S. Gibson (Immaculata, Belfast) w rsc 3 N. Moore (Galway). **Middle:** J. Rock (CIE, Dublin) w pts S. Power (Tramore, Waterford). **L. Heavy:** B. Ward (Olympic, Galway) w rsc 3 M. Sutton (St Saviour's, Dublin). **Heavy:** L. Capper (Philsboro, Dublin) w pts M. Okasill (Clonoe, Tyrone). **S. Heavy:** J. Connolly (St Jude's, Wexford) wo.

Junior Championship Finals

The National Stadium, Dublin - 14 & 20 March

L. Fly: D. McKenna (Holy Family, Drogheda) w pts J. Prior (Darndale, Dublin). **Fly:** A. Patterson (St Patrick's, Armagh) wo J. Moore (St Francis', Limerick). **Bantam:** F. Slane (Immaculata, Belfast) w rsc 2 M. Reneghan (Keady, Armagh). **Feather:** M. Sutcliffe (Drimnagh, Dublin) w rtd 2 P. Williams (St Luke's, Dublin). **Light:** G. Stephens (Drimnagh, Dublin) w pts S. Berkley (Golden Cobra, Dublin). **L. Welter:** N. Sinclair (Holy Family, Belfast) w pts G. Ward (Darndale, Dublin). **Welter:** R. Quigley (Darndale, Dublin) w rsc 2 S. McKenna (Omagh, Tyrone). **L. Middle:** K. Walsh (St Colman's, Cork) w co 3 M. Rock (CIE, Dublin). **Middle:** V. Carroll (St Mary's, Kildare) w rsc 1 A. Sheerin (Swinford, Mayo). **L. Heavy:** R. Dawson (Freshford, Kilkenny) wo. **Heavy:** B. Devine (Dockers, Belfast) w pts M. Hillferty (Carrigart, Donegal). **S. Heavy:** A. Ward (Olympic, Galway) wo.

Pat O'Halloran, runner-up in the Irish Senior championships at light-flyweight

British and Irish International Matches, 1991-92

Internationals

Poland (8) v England (3) Kielce, Poland - 25 August, 1991
(English names first): **L. Fly:** R. Williams l pts R. Niedbalski, P. Culshaw l pts A. Rzany. **Fly:** P. Ingle w rsc 2 L. Olszewski. **Bantam:** M. Alldis l pts P. Dolinski, N. McCallum l pts A. Flakiewicz. **Feather:** A. Vaughan l rsc 1 D. Kasprzak. **Light:** P. Ramsey l pts D. Snarski. **L. Welter:** P. Richardson l pts D. Czernij, A. Stone w pts J. Zietek. **Welter:** S. McNess l pts D. Wasiak. **Middle:** M. Edwards l pts R. Buda.

Scotland (3) v Ireland (6) Angus Hotel, Dundee - 31 October, 1991
(Scottish names first): **L. Fly:** P. Weir w rsc 3 M. McQuillan. **Fly:** J. McLean w pts P. O'Halloran. **Feather:** I. McLeod l pts P. Ferris. **Light:** T. Ahmed l pts M. Winter. **L. Welter:** A. MacDonald l pts B. Geraghty. **Welter:** A. Craig l rsc 1 E. Fisher. **L. Middle:** M. Inglis l rsc 2 G. Joyce. **Middle:** S. Wilson w rsc 2 C. Cullen. **L. Heavy:** J. McCluskey l pts M. Delaney.

Young Scotland (5) v Young Ireland (5) Fairfield Social Club, Glasgow - 14 November, 1991
(Scottish names first): **Fly:** J. Mellon w pts F. Enright. **Bantam:** S. Hay w pts R. Farrell, J. Miller w pts D. O'Connor. **Feather:** S. Burnett l pts S. Murray. **Light:** R. Beattie l pts A. Dunne. **L. Welter:** G. McLevy w rsc 1 J. Honnan, D. Brown l pts T. Logan. **Welter:** A. Wolecki w rsc 2 E. Barker. **L. Middle:** M. Pinkin l pts S. Crompton, S. Coughtree l co 1 V. Carroll.

Young England (3) v Young Ireland (5) Hilton Hotel, Mayfair - 25 November, 1991
(English names first): **L. Fly:** P. Culshaw w rsc 2 D. McKenna. **Fly:** M. Broadie l co 2 O. Duddy. **Bantam:** C. Slatcher l pts J. Feeney. **Feather:** R. Jeffrey l pts S. Redmond. **Light:** S. Smith l pts T. Lawlor. **L. Welter:** P. Wright l pts J. McBride. **Welter:** S. Bendall w pts B. Campbell. **L. Heavy:** K. Oliver w rsc 3 P. Deane.

England (6) v Denmark (6) Bletchley Leisure Centre, Milton Keynes - 4 December, 1991
(English names first): **Fly:** I. Sodhi l pts J. Jensen. **Bantam:** P. Lloyd l pts D. Pedersen. **Feather:** J. Irwin w pts B. Lamina. **Light:** P. Ramsey l pts T. Damgaard. **L. Welter:** A. Stone w rtd 1 T. Frederickson, D. McCarrick w pts A. Hassan. **Welter:** T. French w co 2 P. Pedersen, P. Waudby l pts I. Fidan. **L. Middle:** T. Taylor w pts K. Munika, A. Dodson w rtd 2 J. Winter. **L. Heavy:** M. Wright l pts M. Ibsen. **Heavy:** P. Lawson l pts M. Hulstrom.

Ireland (6) v Wales (3) Donegal Social Club, Belfast - 7 December 1991
(Irish names first): **Fly:** O. Duddy w pts J. Davies. **Bantam:** M. Heneghan w rsc 1 R. Rees. **Feather:** P. Griffin w pts P. Samuels. **Welter:** J. Webb w pts J. Samuels, E. Fisher l pts B. Thorogood. **L. Middle:** J. Lowe w pts M. Turner. **Middle:** D. Ryan w pts K. Thomas. **L. Heavy:** M. Delaney l dis 3 C. Beck. **Heavy:** M. Telford l rsc 1 T. Redmond.

Sweden (5) v England (5) Stockholm, Sweden - 12 December, 1991
(English names first): **Feather:** M. Ward l rtd 1 W. Sabuni. **Light:** J. Phelan l pts Z. Sarossy. **L. Welter:** A. Stone w rsc 1 M. Nilsson. **Welter:** M. Santini l co 3 R. Welin. **L. Middle:** A. Dodson w pts S. Antman, R. Reid w pts J. Gustavsson. **Middle:** E. Noi l pts A. Bredler. **L. Heavy:** A. Todd w pts L. Keiski. **Heavy:** D. Abbott l rsc 1 S. Gaspar. **S. Heavy:** C. Brown w pts M. Lindstrom.

England (10) v Scotland (1) Everton Park Sports Centre, Liverpool - 17 January
(English names first): **L. Fly:** P. Culshaw w pts A. Mooney. **Fly:** P. Ingle w pts K. Knox, M. Horobin w rsc 2 J. Miller. **Bantam:** P. Lloyd w pts S. Anderson. **Feather:** A. Temple w rsc 3 C. Melucci. **Light:** A. Green l pts M. Gowans. **Welter:** S. McNess w rsc 3 L. McBride. **L. Middle:** R. Reid w rsc 2 C. Wallace. **Middle:** M. Edwards w rsc 2 J. Daley. **Heavy:** D. Williams w rsc 1 M. Neil. **S. Heavy:** C. Brown w rsc 1 J. Akinlami.

Ireland (4) v USA (5) National Stadium, Dublin - 24 January
(Irish names first): **L. Fly:** M. McQuillan w pts D. Davis. **Fly:** P. Buttimer l pts J. Fields. **Feather:** P. Griffin w pts K. Friday. **Light:** M. Winters l pts P. Brooks. **L. Welter:** E. Magee l pts S. Mosley. **Welter:** M. Carruth w pts D. Hutchinson. **L. Middle:** G. Joyce w pts T. Harris. **L. Heavy:** D. Curran l pts H. McKee. **Heavy:** P. Douglas l pts S. Briggs.

Young England (4) v Young Italy (4) Royal Lancaster Hotel, Queensway - 3 February
(English names first): **Bantam:** N. Smith w pts P. Campete. **Feather:** D. Holt w pts G. Verga. **Light:** M. Hall l pts V. Oi, N. Secker l pts E. Filippi. **L. Welter:** M. Jones l pts U. Merrola. **L. Middle:** J. Branch w pts A. Brancalion, D. Starie w pts G. Mocerino. **Middle:** M. Ellis l pts F. Bugada.

Ireland (7) v Scotland (2) National Stadium, Dublin - 7 February
(Irish names first): **Fly:** P. Buttimer w pts J. McLean, D. Kelly w rsc 2 K. Knox. **Bantam:** P. Norton l pts S. Anderson. **Light:** M. Winters w rtd 2 M. Gowans. **L. Welter:** E. Magee w pts J. Pender. **Welter:** S. Gibson w rtd 3 S. McGee, R. O'Connor w pts L. McBride. **L. Heavy:** D. Curran l rsc 3 S. Wilson, M. Delaney w rsc 1 J. McCluskey.

Ireland (6) v Scotland (3) Jury's Hotel, Cork - 9 February
(Irish names first): **Fly:** P. Buttimer w pts J. McLean, D. Hosford l pts K. Knox. **Bantam:** G. Griffin l pts S. Anderson. **Feather:** L. O'Brien l pts C. Melucci. **Light:** P. Ireland w pts M. Gowans. **L. Welter:** N. Gough w pts J. Pender. **Welter:** D. Higgins w rsc 2 L. McBride. **L. Middle:** K. Walsh w rtd 2 B. Laidlaw. **L. Heavy:** D. Cowman w pts S. Kerr.

Young Wales (4) v Young England (2) City Hall, Cardiff - 6 March
(Welsh names first): **Fly:** J. Davies l pts J. Squires. **Feather:** G. Lawrence w rtd 1 M. Hicklin. **L. Welter:** J. Morgan w pts W. Robertson. **Welter:** D. Williams l pts G. Matsell, D. Jenkins w pts M. Takolobighasi. **Middle:** C. Davies w pts A. Lowe.

Spain (7) v Ireland (2) Santa Cruz, Canary Islands - 29 April
(Irish names first): **L. Fly:** M. McQuillan l pts R. Lozano. **Fly:** P. Buttimer w pts J. Sosa. **Feather:** P. Griffin l pts M. Calvo, P. Ireland w pts O. Garcia. **Light:** M. Winters l pts O. Palomino. **L. Welter:** E. Magee l rsc 2 V. Bauto, N. Gough l pts S. Sergio. **L. Middle:** G. Joyce l pts J. Barrautabena. **Heavy:** A. Currie l pts J. Ortega.

Spain (3) v Ireland (4) Las Palmas, Canary Islands - 30 April
(Irish names first): **Fly:** P. Buttimer w dis 2 E. Villega. **Bantam:** W. McCullough w rsc 2 O. Vega. **Light:** M. Winters w pts O. Palomino. **L. Welter:** N. Gough 1 pts S. Sergio. **L. Middle:** G. Joyce 1 dis 3 J. Barrautabena, T. Mullen 1 pts J. Navare. **L. Heavy:** M. Delaney w pts J. Pena.

Scotland (3) v Ireland (2) Angus Hotel, Dundee - 28 May
(Scottish names first): **Fly:** K. Knox w rsc 1 D. McAree. **Bantam:** S. Hay 1 pts R. Bowe. **L. Welter:** R. Hay 1 pts R. Brannigan. **Welter:** L. McBride w co 2 S. Gibson, A. Wolecki w pts B. McGee.

Ireland (2) v Hungary (8) Templemore Sports Complex, Derry - 2 June
(Irish names first): **Fly:** P. Buttimer 1 pts I. Kovaks. **Bantam:** C. Notarantino 1 pts L. Bognor. **Feather:** R. Nash 1 rsc 1 Z. Kalocsai. **Light:** M. Winters w pts J. Petrovics. **L. Welter:** S. McCloskey 1 pts L. Szocs. **Welter:** J. McCormack 1 pts L. Rezes. **L. Middle:** J. Webb 1 pts G. Mizsei. **Middle:** D. Ryan 1 rsc 1 F. Schubert. **L. Heavy:** B. Ward 1 rsc 2 Z. Beres. **Heavy:** P. Douglas w pts S. Deak.

Championships

World Championships Sydney, Australia - 15 to 18 November, 1991
L. Fly: P. Weir (Scotland) 1 pts A. Nalbandian (URS). **Fly:** J. McLean (Scotland) 1 rsc 2 H. Avila (Dominican Republic); P. Ingle (England) w pts E. Villegas (Spain), w pts V. Naynan (Israel),1 pts M. Hassan (Egypt). **Bantam:** W. McCullough (Ireland) w rsc 2 F. Costa (Portugal), w pts J. Zabakly (Austria), 1 pts E. Carrion (Cuba). **Feather:** J. Irwin w pts M. Yamoto (Japan); P. Griffin (Ireland) w co 1 A. Ullah (Bangladesh), w pts J. Irwin (England), 1 pts K. Kirkorov (Bulgaria). **L. Welter:** P. Richardson (England) w pts S. Rey (Spain), w pts A. Zuelow (Germany), 1 pts V. Forrest (USA). **Welter:** W. Walsh (Ireland) w pts M. Bajrovic (Yugoslavia), 1 pts S. Scriggens (Australia). **L. Middle:** R. Reid (England) w rsc 1 C. Karnhsupan (Thailand), 1 pts I. Akopkokhian (URS). **Middle:** S. Wilson (Scotland) 1 pts J. Crawford (Australia); M. Edwards (England) 1 rsc 2 T. Russo (Italy); D. Galvin (Ireland) w pts J. Larvea (Ghana), 1 rsc 3 R. Garbey (Cuba). **L. Heavy:** J. McCluskey (Scotland) 1 pts B. Guang (Chile).

European Junior Championships Meadowbank Stadium, Edinburgh - 6 to 11 April
L. Fly: D. McKenna (Ireland) 1 pts M. Velicu (Romania); S. Robertson (Scotland) 1 pts C. Molaro (Italy). **Fly:** J. Miller (Scotland) 1 pts M. Gobak (Turkey); D. Pithie (England) 1 rsc 2 V. Vasilev (Bulgaria). **Bantam:** N. Smith (England) 1 rsc 2 T. Olah (Hungary); F. Slane (Ireland) w rsc 2 L. Sharpe (Scotland), 1 rsc 3 T. Olah (Hungary). **Feather:** D. Holt (England) 1 rsc 2 M. Silantiev (URS); R. Hay (Scotland) 1 co 1 F. Reyes (Spain); M. Sutcliffe (Ireland) 1 rsc 2 P. Soltys (Poland); B. Jones (Wales) w pts M. Eraslem (Turkey), w pts P. Soltys (Poland), w pts A. Styve (Norway), 1 pts M. Silantiev (URS). **Light:** R. Beattie (Scotland) 1 rtd 1 R. Suzlekov (Bulgaria); G. Stephens (Ireland) w pts F. Barbero (Spain), w pts M. Varga (Hungary), 1 pts S. Shcherbakov (URS); M. Hall (England) w pts J. Halvarsson (Sweden), w pts I. Hazsaros (Czechoslovakia), w pts M. Yagli (Turkey), 1 pts S. Shcherbakov. **L. Welter:** M. Jones (England) 1 pts F. Us (Turkey); G. McLevy (Scotland) 1 rsc 3 O. Saitov (URS); N. Sinclair (Ireland) w pts I. Meszaros (Hungary), 1 pts O. Saitov (URS). **Welter:** G. Matsell (England) 1 pts P. Palakovic (Czechoslovakia); D. Jenkins (Wales) 1 pts R. Nordman (Sweden); R. Quigley (Ireland) w pts A. Wolecki (Scotland), 1 pts H. Kurtlumaz (Turkey). **L. Middle:** J. Branch (England) 1 pts S. Munno (Italy); A. Wright (Scotland) 1 pts O. Knabe (Germany); K. Walsh (Ireland) w pts M. Demir (Turkey), 1 pts S. Munno (Italy). **Middle:** C. Davies (Wales) w pts A. Lowe (England), 1 pts S. Samilsan (Turkey).

Stop Press:
Olympic Games Barcelona, Spain - 26 July to 8 August
L. Fly: R. Williams (England) w pts S. Ahialey (Ghana), 1 pts R. Velasco (Philippines). **Fly:** P. Buttimer (Ireland) 1 pts M. Malagu (Nigeria); P. Ingle (England) w pts A. Baba (Ghana), 1 pts C-C. Su (North Korea). **Bantam:** W. McCullough (Ireland) w pts F. Muteweta (Uganda), w pts A. Ghmim (Iraq), w pts M. Sabo(Nigeria), w pts G-S. Li (North Korea), 1 pts J. Casamayor (Cuba). **Feather:** P. Griffin (Ireland) 1 rsc 2 S. Chungu (Zambia); B. Carr (Scotland) 1 pts F. Reyes (Spain). **Light:** A. Vaughan (England) 1 rsc 3 B. Irwin (Canada). **L. Welter:** P. Richardson (England) w pts V. Forrest (USA), w pts N. Alankhuyeg (Mongolia), 1 pts L. Doroftei (Romania). **Welter:** A. Dodson (England) w rsc 2 M. Kawakami (Japan), 1 pts F. Vastag (Romania); M. Carruth (Ireland) w pts M. Tuifao (Western Samoa), w pts A. Otto (Germany), w pts A. Chenglai (Thailand), w pts J. Hernandez (Cuba). **L. Middle:** R. Reid (England) w co 1 M. Thomas (Barbados), w pts L. Maleckis (Lithuania), w pts O. Klemetsen (Norway), 1 pts O. Delibas (Holland). **Middle:** M. Edwards (England) 1 pts C. Byrd (USA). **L. Heavy:** S. Wilson (Scotland) w pts M. Masoe (Samoa), 1 pts R. Zaulitschny (URS). **Heavy:** P. Lawson (England) 1 pts D. Nicholson (USA); P. Douglas (Ireland) w pts J. Pettersson (Sweden), w pts A. Tchudinov (URS), 1 rsc 1 A. Vanderlijde (Holland).

Peter Waudby (left) and Jimmy Phelan of St Paul's Hull, both represented England during 1991-92

British Junior Championship Finals, 1991-92

National Association of Boy's Clubs

Mayfair Suite, Newcastle - 15 May

Class A: 42 kg: R. Sheehan (Lion) w pts J. Davies (Pontypool & Panteg). 45 kg: D. Curran (Luton Irish) w pts M. Hillard (Pontypool & Panteg). 48 kg: G. Corbyn (Phil Thomas SOB) w pts M. Bush (West Ham). 51 kg: L. Eedle (Gemini) w pts B. May (Lynn). 54 kg: W. Tyrell (Sunderland) w rsc 1 A. Moss (Bury St Edmunds). 57 kg: J. Hare (Batley & Dewsbury) w pts S. Sargent (Foley). 60 kg: S. Gardner (Trowbridge) w pts D. Kenneally (Luton Irish). 63.5 kg: G. Lockett (Pontypool& Panteg) w co 1 D. Doyle (Belhus Park). 67 kg: B. Rhodes (Unity) w rsc 2 D. Bailey (Hollington). 71 kg: G. Johnson (Bracebridge) w pts S. Wilton (Aylsham).

Holiday Inn, Bristol - 8 May

Class B: 45 kg: K. Roberts (Gemini) w pts S. Chinnock (Rugeley Police). 48 kg: D. Costello (Hollington) w pts D. Ward (Small Heath). 51 kg: S. Murray (West Ham) w rsc 3 A. Lewis (Radcliffe). 54 kg: A. McLean (Simonside) w pts M. Bowden (Honour Oak). 57 kg: S. White (Medway Golden Gloves) w pts K. Bennett (Warley). 60 kg: H. Sheeraz (Pinewood Starr) w pts A. Knight (West Gorton). 63.5 kg: P. Larner (Bognor) w pts M. Scotland (Wednesbury). 67 kg: J. Guest (Belgrave) w pts G. Wild (West Ham). 71 kg: M. Smith (Hartlepool Catholic) w pts C. Howarth (Crown Wood). 74 kg: L. Stevens (Pinewood Starr) and T. Dowling (St Giles') both disqualified. 77 kg: P. Anderson (Medway Golden Gloves) w pts A. Smith (Poplar).

Grosvenor House, Mayfair, London - 11 May

Class C: 48 kg: G. Jones (Knowsley Vale) wo S. Duncan (Army). 51 kg: D. Williams (Fisher) w pts A. Bickley (Wednesbury). 54 kg: D. Burrows (Wythenshawe) w pts M. Wright (St Mary's). 57 kg: K. Roberts (Gemini) w pts D. Adams (Repton). 60 kg: M. Fennell (Humberside Police) w pts S. Wills (Hanwell). 63.5 kg: C. Stanley (Hanwell) w pts R. Vanzie (Karmand Centre). 67 kg: P. Miles (Foley) w pts J. Witter (Bradford Police). 71 kg: D. Starie (Hurstleigh) w pts L. Murtagh (Hunslet). 75 kg: J. Sawicki (Eltham) w rsc 3 J. Whiteside (Preston Red Rose). 81 kg: D. Littlewood (Parsons Cross) w pts J. Frankham (Tilehurst Mo's).

Schools

Assembly Rooms, Derby - 28 March

Junior A: 32 kg: D. Price (Newbridge) w rtd 2 L. Buckley (Sparrow Farm). 34 kg: S. Wilson (St Paul's) w pts V. Lynes (Hornchurch & Elm Park). 36 kg: T. Driscoll (Newham) w pts M. Woodward (Channel View). 39 kg: B. Doherty (Dale) w pts S. Hodgson (Shildon). 42 kg: R. Hatton (Sale West) w rsc 2 M. Geary (Dale). 45 kg: L. Maltby (Focus) w pts S. Swales (Lingdale). 48 kg: A. Larkins (Bracknell) w pts K. Mitchell (Splott). 51 kg: S. Bendall (Triumph) w pts R. Beck (Repton). 54 kg: T. Eastwood (Foley) w pts E. Savage (Prince of Wales).

Junior B: 36 kg: G. Dove (West Ham) w pts M. Stanfield (St Paul's). 39 kg: D. Price (Repton) w pts A. Kelly (Darlington). 42 kg: N. Lee (Repton) w pts J. Rooney (Hartlepool Catholic). 45 kg: D. McDermott (Dudley) w pts A. Vine (Medway Golden Gloves). 48 kg: S. Rees (Gilfach Goch) w pts J. Cole (Camberley). 51 kg: M. Reppion (Gemini) w pts W. Nuurah (Devonport). 54 kg: C. Lynes (Hornchurch & Upminster) w pts D. Bardavskas (Durham Miners). 57 kg: F. Doherty (Angel) w pts J. Donkin (Hylton Castle). 60 kg: M. Jennings (Chorley) w pts J. Stannard (Malmesbury). 63 kg: W. Smith (Foley) w pts B. Ogden (South Normanton).

Intermediate: 39 kg: A. Rossiter (St Joseph's) w pts J. Nightingale (Wednesbury). 42 kg: K. Lear (West Ham) w pts J. Rogers (Priory Park). 45 kg: J. Lee (Darlington) w pts R. Robshaw (Dale). 48 kg: J. Thomas (Merthyr) w pts N. Coe (Hornchurch & Elm Park). 51 kg: F. Luke (Highfield) w pts L. Hill (Rover). 54 kg: W. Tyrell (Sunderland) w co 2 R. Warman (Woodham & Wickford). 57 kg: K. Fessey (Sefton) w pts S. Sargent (Foley). 60 kg: J. Smith (Darlington) w pts D. Coates (Highfield). 63 kg: A. Reeves (Kirkdale) w pts B. Stevens (Pinewood Starr). 66 kg: C. Wake (Shildon) w pts R. Campbell (Portsmouth Golden Gloves).

Senior: 42 kg: L. Rees (Gilfach Goch) w rsc 1 R. Myatt (Gloucester). 45 kg: P. Brady (St Pancras) w pts W. Toohey (Gemini). 48 kg: B. Pollard (Gemini) w pts R. Havill (St George's). 51 kg: S. Murray (West Ham) w rsc 1 M. Payne (Bell Green). 54 kg: C. Wall (Gemini) w pts G. Robshaw (Dale). 57 kg: J. Hare (Batley & Dewsbury) w pts S. White (Medway Golden Gloves). 60 kg: C. Spacie (St Michael's) w pts D. James (Bury St Edmunds). 63.5 kg: W. Robertson (Slough) w pts B. Kilbride (Willaston). 67 kg: D. Rhodes (Hunslet) w pts N. Gambell (King George's). 71 kg: A. Dowling (St Giles') w pts R. Beck (Stalham).

ABA Youth

York Hall, Bethnal Green, London - 14 December, 1991

Class A: 42 kg: S. Stocking (Haverhill) w rsc 2 C. Brown (Lynn). 45 kg: P. Brady (St Pancras) w pts G. Corbyn (Lingdale). 48 kg: B. May (Lynn) w co 1 J. Ollerhead (Barton). 51 kg: G. Robshaw (Dale) w pts C. Wall (Gemini). 54 kg: S. Richardson (Sunderland) w pts T. Bruns (West Ham). 57 kg: D. Happe (Honour Oak) w pts J. Hare (Batley & Dewsbury). 60 kg: P. Larner (Bognor) w pts C. Spacie (St Michael's). 63.5 kg: G. Behan (Leamington Spa) w rsc 1 D. Loft (West Hill). 67 kg: C. Wake (Shildon) w rsc 3 N. Haynes (Kingswood). 71 kg: R. Hayes-Scott (Brixton) w pts A. Dowling (St. Giles').

Class B: 42 kg: D. Burke (Salisbury) w pts S. Chinnock (Rugeley Police). 45 kg: D. Costello (Hollington) w pts C. Toohey (Gemini). 48 kg: N. Bell (Brighton) w pts T. Feecham (Coventry). 51 kg: J. Squires (Belgrave) w pts S. Murray (West Ham). 54 kg: S. Oliver (Finchley) w pts A. Lewis (Bury). 57 kg: G. Hibbert (Gallagher) w co 2 E. Kahlow (West Hill). 60 kg: D. James (Bury St Edmunds) w rtd 1 C. Pitman (Frome). 63.5 kg: G. Wild (West Ham) w pts J. Guest (Belgrave). 67 kg: G. Matsell (Hull Fish Trades) w pts M. Takalobighasi (Margate). 71 kg: G. Mayor (Nottingham Golden Gloves) w pts M. Smith (Hartlepool Catholic). 74 kg: D. Lynes (Hornchurch & Elm Park) w rsc 3 J. Young (Birtley). 77 kg: M. Johnson (Grimsby SOB) w pts J. Carter (Callowland).

ABA Champions, 1881-1992

L. Flyweight
1971 M. Abrams
1972 M. Abrams
1973 M. Abrams
1974 C. Magri
1975 M. Lawless
1976 P. Fletcher
1977 P. Fletcher
1978 J. Dawson
1979 J. Dawson
1980 T. Barker
1981 J. Lyon
1982 J. Lyon
1983 J. Lyon
1984 J. Lyon
1985 M. Epton
1986 M. Epton
1987 M. Epton
1988 M. Cantwell
1989 M. Cantwell
1990 N. Tooley
1991 P. Culshaw
1992 D. Fifield

Flyweight
1920 H. Groves
1921 W. Cuthbertson
1922 E. Warwick
1923 L. Tarrant
1924 E. Warwick
1925 E. Warwick
1926 J. Hill
1927 J. Roland
1928 C. Taylor
1929 T. Pardoe
1930 T. Pardoe
1931 T. Pardoe
1932 T. Pardoe
1933 T. Pardoe
1934 P. Palmer
1935 G. Fayaud
1936 G. Fayaud
1937 P. O'Donaghue
1938 A. Russell
1939 D. McKay
1944 J. Clinton
1945 J. Bryce
1946 R. Gallacher
1947 J. Clinton
1948 H. Carpenter
1949 H. Riley
1950 A. Jones
1951 G. John
1952 D. Dower
1953 R. Currie
1954 R. Currie
1955 D. Lloyd
1956 T. Spinks
1957 R. Davies
1958 J. Brown
1959 M. Gushlow
1960 D. Lee
1961 W. McGowan
1962 M. Pye
1963 M. Laud
1964 J. McCluskey
1965 J. McCluskey
1966 P. Maguire
1967 S. Curtis
1968 J. McGonigle
1969 D. Needham
1970 D. Needham
1971 P. Wakefield
1972 M. O'Sullivan
1973 R. Hilton
1974 M. O'Sullivan
1975 C. Magri
1976 C. Magri
1977 C. Magri
1978 G. Nickels
1979 R. Gilbody
1980 K. Wallace
1981 K. Wallace
1982 J. Kelly
1983 S. Nolan
1984 P. Clinton
1985 P. Clinton
1986 J. Lyon
1987 J. Lyon
1988 J. Lyon
1989 J. Lyon
1990 J. Armour
1991 P. Ingle
1992 K. Knox

Bantamweight
1884 A. Woodward
1885 A. Woodward
1886 T. Isley
1887 T. Isley
1888 H. Oakman
1889 H. Brown
1890 J. Rowe
1891 E. Moore
1892 F. Godbold
1893 E. Watson
1894 P. Jones
1895 P. Jones
1896 P. Jones
1897 C. Lamb
1898 F. Herring
1899 A. Avent
1900 J. Freeman
1901 W. Morgan
1902 A. Miner
1903 H. Perry
1904 H. Perry
1905 W. Webb
1906 T. Ringer
1907 E. Adams
1908 H. Thomas
1909 J. Condon
1910 W. Webb
1911 W. Allen
1912 W. Allen
1913 A. Wye
1914 W. Allen
1919 W. Allen
1920 G. McKenzie
1921 L. Tarrant
1922 W. Boulding
1923 A. Smith
1924 L. Tarrant
1925 A. Goom
1926 F. Webster
1927 E. Warwick
1928 J. Garland
1929 F. Bennett
1930 H. Mizler
1931 F. Bennett
1932 J. Treadaway
1933 G. Johnston
1934 A. Barnes
1935 L. Case
1936 A. Barnes
1937 A. Barnes
1938 J. Pottinger
1939 R. Watson
1944 R. Bissell
1945 P. Brander
1946 C. Squire
1947 D. O'Sullivan
1948 T. Profitt
1949 T. Miller
1950 K. Lawrence
1951 T. Nicholls
1952 T. Nicholls
1953 J. Smillie
1954 J. Smillie
1955 G. Dormer
1956 O. Reilly
1957 J. Morrissey
1958 H. Winstone
1959 D. Weller
1960 F. Taylor
1961 P. Benneyworth
1962 P. Benneyworth
1963 B. Packer
1964 B. Packer
1965 R. Mallon
1966 J. Clark
1967 M. Carter
1968 M. Carter
1969 M. Piner
1970 A. Oxley
1971 G. Turpin
1972 G. Turpin
1973 P. Cowdell
1974 S. Ogilvie
1975 S. Ogilvie
1976 J. Bambrick
1977 J. Turner
1978 J. Turner
1979 R. Ashton
1980 R. Gilbody
1981 P. Jones
1982 R. Gilbody
1983 J. Hyland
1984 J. Hyland
1985 S. Murphy
1986 S. Murphy
1987 J. Sillitoe
1988 K. Howlett
1989 K. Howlett
1990 P. Lloyd
1991 D. Hardie
1992 P. Mullings

Featherweight
1881 T. Hill
1882 T. Hill
1883 T. Hill
1884 E. Hutchings
1885 J. Pennell
1886 T. McNeil
1887 J. Pennell
1888 J. Taylor
1889 G. Belsey
1890 G. Belsey
1891 F. Curtis
1892 F. Curtis
1893 T. Davidson
1894 R. Gunn
1895 R. Gunn
1896 R. Gunn
1897 N. Smith
1898 P. Lunn
1899 J. Scholes
1900 R. Lee
1901 C. Clarke
1902 C. Clarke
1903 J. Godfrey
1904 C. Morris
1905 H. Holmes
1906 A. Miner
1907 C. Morris
1908 T. Ringer
1909 A. Lambert
1910 C. Houghton
1911 H. Bowers
1912 G. Baker
1913 G. Baker
1914 G. Baker
1919 G. Baker
1920 J. Fleming
1921 G. Baker
1922 E. Swash
1923 E. Swash
1924 A. Beavis
1925 A. Beavis
1926 R. Minshull
1927 F. Webster
1928 F. Meachem
1929 F. Meachem
1930 J. Duffield
1931 B. Caplan
1932 H. Mizler
1933 J. Walters
1934 J. Treadaway
1935 E. Ryan
1936 J. Treadaway
1937 A. Harper
1938 C. Gallie
1939 C. Gallie
1944 D. Sullivan
1945 J. Carter
1946 P. Brander
1947 S. Evans
1948 P. Brander
1949 H. Gilliland
1950 P. Brander
1951 J. Travers
1952 P. Lewis
1953 P. Lewis
1954 D. Charnley
1955 T. Nicholls
1956 T. Nicholls
1957 M. Collins
1958 M. Collins
1959 G. Judge
1960 P. Lundgren
1961 P. Cheevers
1962 B. Wilson
1963 A. Riley
1964 R. Smith
1965 K. Buchanan
1966 H. Baxter
1967 K. Cooper
1968 J. Cheshire
1969 A. Richardson
1970 D. Polak
1971 T. Wright
1972 K. Laing
1973 J. Lynch
1974 G. Gilbody
1975 R. Beaumont
1976 P. Cowdell
1977 P. Cowdell
1978 M. O'Brien
1979 P. Hanlon
1980 M. Hanif
1981 P. Hanlon
1982 H. Henry
1983 P. Bradley
1984 K. Taylor
1985 F. Havard
1986 P. Hodkinson
1987 P. English
1988 D. Anderson
1989 P. Richardson
1990 B. Carr
1991 J. Irwin
1992 A. Temple

Lightweight
1881 F. Hobday
1882 A. Bettinson
1883 A. Diamond
1884 A. Diamond
1885 A. Diamond
1886 G. Roberts
1887 J. Hair
1888 A. Newton
1889 W. Neale
1890 A. Newton
1891 E. Dettmer
1892 E. Dettmer
1893 W. Campbell
1894 W. Campbell
1895 A. Randall
1896 A. Vanderhout
1897 A. Vanderhout
1898 H. Marks
1899 H. Brewer
1900 G. Humphries
1901 A. Warner
1902 A. Warner
1903 H. Fergus
1904 M. Wells
1905 M. Wells
1906 M. Wells
1907 M. Wells
1908 H. Holmes
1909 F. Grace
1910 T. Tees
1911 A. Spenceley
1912 R. Marriott
1913 R. Grace
1914 R. Marriott
1919 F. Grace
1920 F. Grace
1921 G. Shorter
1922 G. Renouf
1923 G. Shorter
1924 W. White

Lee Woolcock (right) was always going too well for the inexperienced Scot, John Connelly and copped a wide points win to take the ABA middleweight honours for 1992 Les Clark

1925 E. Viney
1926 T. Slater
1927 W. Hunt
1928 F. Webster
1929 W. Hunt
1930 J. Waples
1931 D. McCleave
1932 F. Meachem
1933 H. Mizler
1934 J. Rolland
1935 F. Frost
1936 F. Simpson
1937 A. Danahar
1938 T. McGrath
1939 H. Groves
1944 W. Thompson
1945 J. Williamson
1946 E. Thomas
1947 C. Morrissey
1948 R. Cooper
1949 A. Smith
1950 R. Latham
1951 R. Hinson
1952 F. Reardon
1953 D. Hinson
1954 G. Whelan
1955 S. Coffey
1956 R. McTaggart
1957 J. Kidd
1958 R. McTaggart
1959 P. Warwick
1960 R. McTaggart
1961 P. Warwick
1962 B. Whelan
1963 B. O'Sullivan
1964 J. Dunne
1965 A. White
1966 J. Head
1967 T. Waller
1968 J. Watt
1969 H. Hayes
1970 N. Cole
1971 J. Singleton
1972 N. Cole
1973 T. Dunn
1974 J. Lynch
1975 P. Cowdell
1976 S. Mittee
1977 G. Gilbody
1978 T. Marsh
1979 G. Gilbody
1980 G. Gilbody
1981 G. Gilbody
1982 J. McDonnell
1983 K. Willis
1984 A. Dickson
1985 E. McAuley
1986 J. Jacobs
1987 M. Ayers
1988 C. Kane
1989 M. Ramsey
1990 P. Gallagher
1991 P. Ramsey
1992 D. Amory

L. Welterweight
1951 W. Connor
1952 P. Waterman
1953 D. Hughes
1954 G. Martin
1955 F. McQuillan
1956 D. Stone
1957 D. Stone
1958 R. Kane
1959 R. Kane
1960 R. Day
1961 B. Brazier
1962 B. Brazier
1963 R. McTaggart
1964 R. Taylor
1965 R. McTaggart
1966 W. Hiatt
1967 B. Hudspeth
1968 E. Cole
1969 J. Stracey
1970 D. Davies
1971 M. Kingwell
1972 T. Waller
1973 N. Cole
1974 P. Kelly
1975 J. Zeraschi
1976 C. McKenzie
1977 J. Douglas
1978 D. Williams
1979 E. Copeland
1980 A. Willis
1981 A. Willis
1982 A. Adams
1983 D. Dent
1984 D. Griffiths
1985 I. Mustafa
1986 J. Alsop
1987 A. Holligan
1988 A. Hall
1989 A. Hall
1990 J. Pender
1991 J. Matthews
1992 D. McCarrick

Welterweight
1920 F. Whitbread
1921 A. Ireland
1922 E. White
1923 P. Green
1924 P. O'Hanrahan
1925 P. O'Hanrahan
1926 B. Marshall
1927 H. Dunn
1928 H. Bone
1929 T. Wigmore
1930 F. Brooman
1931 J. Barry
1932 D. McCleave
1933 P. Peters
1934 D. McCleave
1935 D. Lynch
1936 W. Pack
1937 D. Lynch
1938 C. Webster
1939 R. Thomas
1944 H. Hall
1945 R. Turpin
1946 J. Ryan
1947 J. Ryan
1948 M. Shacklady
1949 A. Buxton
1950 T. Ratcliffe
1951 J. Maloney
1952 J. Maloney
1953 L. Morgan
1954 N. Gargano
1955 N. Gargano
1956 N. Gargano
1957 R. Warnes
1958 B. Nancurvis
1959 J. McGrail
1960 C. Humphries
1961 A. Lewis
1962 J. Pritchett
1963 J. Pritchett
1964 M. Varley
1965 P. Henderson
1966 P. Cragg
1967 D. Cranswick
1968 A. Tottoh
1969 T. Henderson
1970 T. Waller
1971 D. Davies
1972 T. Francis
1973 T. Waller
1974 T. Waller
1975 W. Bennett
1976 C. Jones
1977 C. Jones
1978 E. Byrne
1979 J. Frost
1980 T. Marsh
1981 T. Marsh
1982 C. Pyatt
1983 R. McKenley
1984 M. Hughes
1985 E. McDonald
1986 D. Dyer
1987 M. Elliot
1988 M. McCreath
1989 M. Elliot
1990 A. Carew
1991 J. Calzache
1992 M. Santini

L. Middleweight
1951 A. Lay
1952 B. Foster
1953 B. Wells
1954 B. Wells
1955 B. Foster
1956 J. McCormack
1957 J. Cunningham
1958 S. Pearson
1959 S. Pearson
1960 W. Fisher
1961 J. Gamble
1962 J. Lloyd
1963 A. Wyper
1964 W. Robinson
1965 P. Dwyer
1966 T. Imrie
1967 A. Edwards
1968 E. Blake
1969 T. Imrie
1970 D. Simmonds
1971 A. Edwards
1972 L. Paul
1973 R. Maxwell
1974 R. Maxwell
1975 A. Harrison
1976 W. Lauder
1977 C. Malarkey
1978 E. Henderson
1979 D. Brewster
1980 J. Price
1981 E. Christie
1982 D. Milligan
1983 R. Douglas
1984 R. Douglas
1985 R. Douglas
1986 T. Velinor
1987 N. Brown
1988 W. Ellis
1989 N. Brown
1990 T. Taylor
1991 N. Taylor
1992 J. Calzache

Middleweight
1881 T. Bellhouse
1882 A. H. Curnick
1883 A. J. Curnick
1884 W. Brown
1885 M. Salmon
1886 W. King
1887 R. Hair
1888 R. Hair
1889 G. Sykes
1890 J. Hoare
1891 J. Steers
1892 J. Steers
1893 J. Steers
1894 W. Sykes
1895 G. Townsend
1896 W. Ross
1897 W. Dees
1898 G. Townsend
1899 R. Warnes
1900 E. Mann
1901 R. Warnes
1902 E. Mann
1903 R. Warnes
1904 E. Mann
1905 J. Douglas
1906 A. Murdock
1907 R. Warnes
1908 W. Child
1909 W. Child
1910 R. Warnes
1911 W. Child
1912 E. Chandler
1913 W. Bradley
1914 H. Brown
1919 H. Mallin
1920 H. Mallin

1921 H. Mallin
1922 H. Mallin
1923 H. Mallin
1924 J. Elliot
1925 J. Elliot
1926 F. P. Crawley
1927 F. P. Crawley
1928 F. Mallin
1929 F. Mallin
1930 F. Mallin
1931 F. Mallin
1932 F. Mallin
1933 A. Shawyer
1934 J. Magill
1935 J. Magill
1936 A. Harrington
1937 M. Dennis
1938 H. Tiller
1939 H. Davies
1944 J. Hockley
1945 R. Parker
1946 R. Turpin
1947 R. Agland
1948 J. Wright
1949 S. Lewis
1950 P. Longo
1951 E. Ludlam
1952 T. Gooding
1953 R. Barton
1954 K. Phillips
1955 F. Hope
1956 R. Redrup
1957 P. Burke
1958 P. Hill
1959 F. Elderfield
1960 R. Addison
1961 J. Caiger
1962 A. Matthews
1963 A. Matthews
1964 W. Stack
1965 W. Robinson
1966 C. Finnegan
1967 A. Ball
1968 P. McCann
1969 D. Wallington
1970 J. Conteh
1971 A. Minter
1972 F. Lucas
1973 F. Lucas
1974 D. Odwell
1975 D. Odwell
1976 E. Burke
1977 R. Davies
1978 H. Graham
1979 N. Wilshire
1980 M. Kaylor
1981 B. Schumacher
1982 J. Price
1983 T. Forbes
1984 B. Schumacher
1985 D. Cronin
1986 N. Benn
1987 R. Douglas
1988 M. Edwards
1989 S. Johnson
1990 S. Wilson
1991 M. Edwards
1992 L. Woolcock

L. Heavyweight
1920 H. Franks
1921 L. Collett
1922 H. Mitchell
1923 H. Mitchell
1924 H. Mitchell
1925 H. Mitchell
1926 D. McCorkindale
1927 A. Jackson
1928 A. Jackson
1929 J. Goyder
1930 J. Murphy
1931 J. Petersen
1932 J. Goyder
1933 G. Brennan
1934 G. Brennan
1935 R. Hearns
1936 J. Magill
1937 J. Wilby
1938 A. S. Brown
1939 B. Woodcock
1944 E. Shackleton
1945 A. Watson
1946 J. Taylor
1947 A. Watson
1948 D. Scott
1949 *Declared no contest*
1950 P. Messervy
1951 G. Walker
1952 H. Cooper
1953 H. Cooper
1954 A. Madigan
1955 D. Rent
1956 D. Mooney
1957 T. Green
1958 J. Leeming
1959 J. Ould
1960 J. Ould
1961 J. Bodell
1962 J. Hendrickson
1963 P. Murphy
1964 J. Fisher
1965 E. Whistler
1966 R. Tighe
1967 M. Smith
1968 R. Brittle
1969 J. Frankham
1970 J. Rafferty
1971 J. Conteh
1972 W. Knight
1973 W. Knight
1974 W. Knight
1975 M. Heath
1976 G. Evans
1977 C. Lawson
1978 V. Smith
1979 A. Straughn
1980 A. Straughn
1981 A. Straughn
1982 G. Crawford
1983 A. Wilson
1984 A. Wilson
1985 J. Beckles
1986 J. Moran
1987 J. Beckles
1988 H. Lawson
1989 N. Piper
1990 J. McCluskey
1991 A. Todd
1992 K. Oliver

Heavyweight
1881 R. Frost-Smith
1882 H. Dearsley
1883 H. Dearsley
1884 H. Dearsley
1885 W. West
1886 A. Diamond
1887 E. White
1888 W. King
1889 A. Bowman
1890 J. Steers
1891 V. Barker
1892 J. Steers
1893 J. Steers
1894 H. King
1895 W. E. Johnstone
1896 W. E. Johnstone
1897 G. Townsend
1898 G. Townsend
1899 F. Parks
1900 W. Dees
1901 F. Parks
1902 F. Parks
1903 F. Dickson
1904 A. Horner
1905 F. Parks
1906 F. Parks
1907 H. Brewer
1908 S. Evans
1909 C. Brown
1910 F. Storbeck
1911 W. Hazell
1912 R. Smith
1913 R. Smith
1914 E. Chandler
1919 H. Brown
1920 R. Rawson
1921 R. Rawson
1922 T. Evans
1923 E. Eagan
1924 A. Clifton
1925 D. Lister
1926 T. Petersen
1927 C. Capper
1928 J. L. Driscoll
1929 P. Floyd
1930 V. Stuart
1931 M. Flanaghan
1932 V. Stuart
1933 C. O'Grady
1934 P. Floyd
1935 P. Floyd
1936 V. Stuart
1937 V. Stuart
1938 G. Preston
1939 A. Porter
1944 M. Hart
1945 D. Scott
1946 P. Floyd
1947 G. Scriven
1948 J. Gardner
1949 A. Worrall
1950 P. Toch
1951 A. Halsey
1952 E. Hearn
1953 J. Erskine
1954 B. Harper
1955 D. Rowe
1956 D. Rent
1957 D. Thomas
1958 D. Thomas
1959 D. Thomas
1960 L. Hobbs
1961 W. Walker
1962 R. Dryden
1963 R. Sanders
1964 C. Woodhouse
1965 W. Wells
1966 A. Brogan
1967 P. Boddington
1968 W. Wells
1969 A. Burton
1970 J. Gilmour
1971 L. Stevens
1972 T. Wood
1973 G. McEwan
1974 N. Meade
1975 G. McEwan
1976 J. Rafferty
1977 G. Adair
1978 J. Awome
1979 A. Palmer
1980 F. Bruno
1981 A. Elliott
1982 H. Hylton
1983 H. Notice
1984 D. Young
1985 H. Hylton
1986 E. Cardouza
1987 J. Moran
1988 H. Akinwande
1989 H. Akinwande
1990 K. Inglis
1991 P. Lawson
1992 S. Welch

S. Heavyweight
1982 A. Elliott
1983 K. Ferdinand
1984 R. Wells
1985 G. Williamson
1986 J. Oyebola
1987 J. Oyebola
1988 K. McCormack
1989 P. Passley
1990 K. McCormack
1991 K. McCormack
1992 M. Hopper

The Billy Walker look-a-like, Scott Welch (left), from Hove, won the ABA heavyweight title when he put the Welshman, Richard Fenton, down and out with just 25 seconds left on the clock Les Clark

International Amateur Champions, 1904-1992

Shows all Olympic, World, European & Commonwealth champions since 1904. British silver and bronze medal winners are shown throughout, where applicable.

Country Code

ARG = Argentine; AUS = Australia; AUT = Austria; BEL = Belgium; BUL = Bulgaria; CAN = Canada; CEY = Ceylon (now Sri Lanka); CUB = Cuba; DEN = Denmark; DOM = Dominican Republic; ENG = England; ESP = Spain; EST = Estonia; FIJ = Fiji Islands; FIN = Finland; FRA = France; GBR = United Kingdom; GDR = German Democratic Republic; GER = Germany (but West Germany only from 1968-1990); GHA = Ghana; GUY = Guyana; HOL = Netherlands; HUN = Hungary; IRL = Ireland; ITA = Italy; JAM = Jamaica; JPN = Japan; KEN = Kenya; MEX = Mexico; NKO = North Korea; NIG = Nigeria; NIR = Northern Ireland; NOR = Norway; NZL = New Zealand; POL = Poland; PUR = Puerto Rico; ROM = Romania; SAF = South Africa; SCO = Scotland; SKO = South Korea; STV = St Vincent; SWE = Sweden; TCH = Czechoslovakia; TUR = Turkey; UGA = Uganda; URS = USSR; USA = United States of America; VEN = Venezuela; WAL = Wales; YUG = Yugoslavia; ZAM = Zambia.

Olympic Champions, 1904-1992

St Louis, USA - 1904
Fly: G. Finnegan (USA). **Bantam:** O. Kirk (USA). **Feather:** O. Kirk (USA). **Light:** H. Spangler (USA). **Welter:** A. Young (USA). **Middle:** C. May (USA). **Heavy:** S. Berger (USA).

London, England - 1908
Bantam: H. Thomas (GBR). **Feather:** R. Gunn (GBR). **Light:** F. Grace (GBR). **Middle:** J.W.H.T. Douglas (GBR). **Heavy:** A. Oldham (GBR).
Silver medals: J. Condon (GBR), C. Morris (GBR), F. Spiller (GBR), S. Evans (GBR).
Bronze medals: W. Webb (GBR), H. Rodding (GBR), T. Ringer (GBR), H. Johnson (GBR), R. Warnes (GBR), W. Philo (GBR), F. Parks (GBR).

Antwerp, Belgium - 1920
Fly: F. Genaro (USA). **Bantam:** C. Walker (SAF). **Feather:** R. Fritsch (FRA). **Light:** S. Mossberg (USA). **Welter:** T. Schneider (CAN). **Middle:** H. Mallin (GBR). **L. Heavy:** E. Eagan (USA). **Heavy:** R. Rawson (GBR).
Silver medal: A. Ireland (GBR).
Bronze medals: W. Cuthbertson (GBR), G. McKenzie (GBR), H. Franks (GBR).

Paris, France - 1924
Fly: F. la Barba (USA). **Bantam:** W. Smith (SAF). **Feather:** J. Fields (USA). **Light:** H. Nielson (DEN). **Welter:** J. Delarge (BEL). **Middle:** H. Mallin (GBR). **L. Heavy:** H. Mitchell (GBR). **Heavy:** O. von Porat (NOR).
Silver medals: J. McKenzie (GBR), J. Elliot (GBR).

Amsterdam, Holland - 1928
Fly: A. Kocsis (HUN). **Bantam:** V. Tamagnini (ITA). **Feather:** B. van Klaveren (HOL). **Light:** C. Orlando (ITA). **Welter:** E. Morgan (NZL). **Middle:** P. Toscani (ITA). **L. Heavy:** V. Avendano (ARG). **Heavy: A.** Rodriguez Jurado (ARG).

Los Angeles, USA - 1932
Fly: I. Enekes (HUN). **Bantam:** H. Gwynne (CAN). **Feather:** C. Robledo (ARG). **Light:** L. Stevens (SAF). **Welter:** E. Flynn (USA). **Middle:** C. Barth (USA). **L. Heavy:** D. Carstens (SAF). **Heavy:** A. Lovell (ARG).

Berlin, West Germany - 1936
Fly: W. Kaiser (GER). **Bantam:** U. Sergo (ITA). **Feather:** O. Casanova (ARG). **Light:** I. Harangi (HUN). **Welter:** S. Suvio (FIN). **Middle:** J. Despeaux (FRA). **L. Heavy:** R. Michelot (FRA). **Heavy:** H. Runge (GER).

London, England - 1948
Fly: P. Perez (ARG). **Bantam:** T. Csik (HUN). **Feather:** E. Formenti (ITA). **Light:** G. Dreyer (SAF). **Welter:** J. Torma (TCH). **Middle:** L. Papp (HUN). **L. Heavy:** G. Hunter (SAF). **Heavy:** R. Iglesas (ARG).
Silver medals: J. Wright (GBR), D. Scott (GBR).

Helsinki, Finland - 1952
Fly: N. Brooks (USA). **Bantam:** P. Hamalainen (FIN). **Feather:** J. Zachara (TCH). **Light:** A. Bolognesi (ITA). **L. Welter:** C. Adkins (USA). **Welter:** Z. Chychla (POL). **L. Middle:** L. Papp (HUN). **Middle:** F. Patterson (USA). **L. Heavy:** N. Lee (USA). **Heavy:** E. Sanders (USA).
Silver medal: J. McNally (IRL).

Melbourne, Australia - 1956
Fly: T. Spinks (GBR). **Bantam:** W. Behrendt (GER). **Feather:** V. Safronov (URS). **Light:** R. McTaggart (GBR). **L. Welter:** V. Jengibarian (URS). **Welter:** N. Linca (ROM). **L. Middle:** L. Papp (HUN). **Middle:** G. Schatkov (URS). **L. Heavy:** J. Boyd (USA). **Heavy:** P. Rademacher (USA).
Silver medals: T. Nicholls (GBR), F. Tiedt (IRL).
Bronze medals: J. Caldwell (IRL), F. Gilroy (IRL), A. Bryne (IRL), N. Gargano (GBR), J. McCormack (GBR).

Rome, Italy - 1960
Fly: G. Torok (HUN). **Bantam:** O. Grigoryev (URS). **Feather:** F. Musso (ITA). **Light:** K. Pazdzior (POL). **L. Welter:** B. Nemecek (TCH). **Welter:** N. Benvenuti (ITA). **L. Middle:** W. McClure (USA). **Middle:** E. Crook (USA). **L. Heavy:** C. Clay (USA). **Heavy:** F. de Piccoli (ITA).
Bronze medals: R. McTaggart (GBR), J. Lloyd (GBR), W. Fisher (GBR).

Tokyo, Japan - 1964
Fly: F. Atzori (ITA). **Bantam:** T. Sakurai (JPN). **Feather:** S. Stepashkin (URS). **Light:** J. Grudzien (POL). **L. Welter:** J. Kulej (POL). **Welter:** M. Kasprzyk (POL). **L. Middle:** B. Lagutin (URS). **Middle:** V. Popenchenko (URS). **L. Heavy:** C. Pinto (ITA). **Heavy:** J. Frazier (USA).
Bronze medal: J. McCourt (IRL).

Mexico City, Mexico - 1968
L. Fly: F. Rodriguez (VEN). **Fly:** R. Delgado (MEX). **Bantam:** V. Sokolov (URS). **Feather:** A. Roldan (MEX). **Light:** R. Harris (USA). **L. Welter:** J. Kulej (POL). **Welter:** M. Wolke (GDR). **L. Middle:** B. Lagutin (URS). **Middle:** C. Finnegan (GBR). **L. Heavy:** D. Poznyak (URS). **Heavy:** G. Foreman (USA).

Munich, West Germany - 1972
L. Fly: G. Gedo (HUN). **Fly:** G. Kostadinov (BUL). **Bantam:** O. Martinez (CUB). **Feather:** B. Kusnetsov (BUL). **Light:** J. Szczepanski (POL). **L. Welter:** R. Seales (USA). **Welter:** E. Correa (CUB). **L. Middle:** D. Kottysch (GER). **Middle:** V. Lemeschev (URS). **L. Heavy:** M. Parlov (YUG). **Heavy:** T. Stevenson (CUB).
Bronze medals: R. Evans (GBR), G. Turpin (GBR), A. Minter (GBR).

Montreal, Canada - 1976
L. Fly: J. Hernandez (CUB). **Fly:** L. Randolph (USA). **Bantam:** Y-J. Gu (NKO). **Feather:** A. Herrera (CUB). **Light:** H. Davis (USA). **L. Welter:** R. Leonard (USA). **Welter:** J. Bachfield (GDR). **L. Middle:** J. Rybicki (POL). **Middle:** M. Spinks (USA). **L. Heavy:** L. Spinks (USA). **Heavy:** T. Stevenson (CUB).
Bronze medal: P. Cowdell (GBR).

Moscow, USSR - 1980
L. Fly: S. Sabirov (URS). **Fly:** P. Lessov (BUL). **Bantam:** J. Hernandez (CUB). **Feather:** R. Fink (GDR). **Light:** A. Herrera (CUB). **L. Welter:** P. Oliva (ITA). **Welter:** A. Aldama (CUB). **L. Middle:** A. Martinez (CUB). **Middle:** J. Gomez (CUB). **L. Heavy:** S. Kacar (YUG). **Heavy:** T. Stevenson (CUB).
Bronze medals: H. Russell (IRL), A. Willis (GBR).

Los Angeles, USA - 1984
L. Fly: P. Gonzalez (USA). **Fly:** S. McCrory (USA). **Bantam:** M. Stecca (ITA). **Feather:** M. Taylor (USA). **Light:** P. Whitaker (USA). **L. Welter:** J.

Page (USA). **Welter:** M. Breland (USA). **L. Middle:** F. Tate (USA). **Middle:** J-S. Shin (SKO). **L. Heavy:** A. Josipovic (YUG). **Heavy:** H. Tillman (USA). **S. Heavy:** T. Biggs (USA).
Bronze medal: B. Wells (GBR).

Seoul, South Korea - 1988
L. Fly: I. Hristov (BUL). **Fly:** H-S. Kim (SKO). **Bantam:** K. McKinney (USA). **Feather:** G. Parisi (ITA). **Light:** A. Zuelow (GDR). **L. Welter:** V. Yanovsky (URS). **Welter:** R. Wangila (KEN). **L. Middle:** S-H. Park (SKO). **Middle:** H. Maske (GDR). **L. Heavy:** A. Maynard (USA). **Heavy:** R. Mercer (USA). **S. Heavy:** L. Lewis (CAN).
Bronze medal: R. Woodhall (GBR).

Barcelona, Spain - 1992
L. Fly: R. Marcelo (CUB). **Fly:** C-C. Su (NKO). **Bantam:** J. Casamayor (CUB). **Feather:** A. Tews (GER). **Light:** O. de la Hoya (USA). **L. Welter:** H. Vinent (CUB). **Welter:** M. Carruth (IRL). **L. Middle:** J. Lemus (CUB). **Middle:** A. Hernandez (CUB). **L. Heavy:** T. May (GER). **Heavy:** F. Savon (CUB). **S. Heavy:** R. Balado (CUB).
Silver medal: W. McCullough (IRL).
Bronze medal: R. Reid (GBR).

World Champions, 1974-1991

Havana, Cuba - 1974
L. Fly: J. Hernandez (CUB). **Fly:** D. Rodriguez (CUB). **Bantam:** W. Gomez (PUR). **Feather:** H. Davis (USA). **Light:** V. Solomin (URS). **L. Welter:** A. Kalule (UGA). **Welter:** E. Correa (CUB). **L. Middle:** R. Garbey (CUB). **Middle:** R. Riskiev (URS). **L. Heavy:** M. Parlov (YUG). **Heavy:** T. Stevenson (CUB).

Belgrade, Yugoslavia - 1978
L. Fly: S. Muchoki (KEN). **Fly:** H. Strednicki (POL). **Bantam:** A. Horta (CUB). **Feather:** A. Herrera (CUB). **Light:** D. Andeh (NIG). **L. Welter:** V. Lvov (URS). **Welter:** V. Rachkov (URS). **L. Middle:** V. Savchenko (URS). **Middle:** J. Gomez (CUB). **L. Heavy:** S. Soria (CUB). **Heavy:** T. Stevenson (CUB).

Munich, West Germany - 1982
L. Fly: I. Mustafov (BUL). **Fly:** Y. Alexandrov (URS). **Bantam:** F. Favors (USA). **Feather:** A. Horta (CUB). **Light:** A. Herrera (CUB). **L. Welter:** C. Garcia (CUB). **Welter:** M. Breland (USA). **L. Middle:** A. Koshkin (URS). **Middle:** B. Comas (CUB). **L. Heavy:** P. Romero (CUB). **Heavy:** A. Jagubkin (URS). **S. Heavy:** T. Biggs (USA).
Bronze medal: T. Corr (IRL).

Reno, USA - 1986
L. Fly: J. Odelin (CUB). **Fly:** P. Reyes (CUB). **Bantam:** S-I. Moon (SKO). **Feather:** K. Banks (USA). **Light:** A. Horta (CUB). **L. Welter:** V. Shishov (URS). **Welter:** K. Gould (USA). **L. Middle:** A. Espinosa (CUB). **Middle:** D. Allen (USA). **L. Heavy:** P. Romero (CUB). **Heavy:** F. Savon (CUB). **S. Heavy:** T. Stevenson (CUB).

Moscow, USSR - 1989
L. Fly: E. Griffin (USA). **Fly:** Y. Arbachakov (URS). **Bantam:** E. Carrion (CUB). **Feather:** A. Khamatov (URS). **Light:** J. Gonzalez (CUB). **L. Welter:** I. Ruzinkov (URS). **Welter:** F. Vastag. **L. Middle:** I. Akopokhian (URS). **Middle:** A. Kurniavka (URS). **L. Heavy:** H. Maske (GDR). **Heavy:** F. Savon (CUB). **S. Heavy:** R. Balado (CUB).
Bronze medal: M. Carruth (IRL).

Sydney, Australia - 1991
L. Fly: E. Griffin (USA). **Fly:** I. Kovacs (HUN). **Bantam:** S. Todorov (BUL). **Feather:** K. Kirkorov (BUL). **Light:** M. Rudolph (GER). **L. Welter:** K. Tsziu (URS). **Welter:** J. Hernandez (CUB). **L. Middle:** J. Lemus (CUB). **Middle:** T. Russo (ITA). **L. Heavy:** T. May (GER). **Heavy:** F. Savon (CUB). **S. Heavy:** R. Balado (CUB).

World Junior Champions, 1979-1990

Yokohama, Japan - 1979
L. Fly: R. Shannon (USA). **Fly:** P. Lessov (BUL). **Bantam:** P-K. Choi (SKO). **Feather:** Y. Gladychev (URS). **Light:** R. Blake (USA). **L. Welter:** I. Akopokhian (URS). **Welter:** M. McCrory (USA). **L. Middle:** A. Mayes (USA). **Middle:** A. Milov (URS). **L. Heavy:** A. Lebedev (URS). **Heavy:** M. Frazier (USA).
Silver medals: N. Wilshire (ENG), D. Cross (ENG).
Bronze medal: I. Scott (SCO).

Santa Domingo, Dominican Republic - 1983
L. Fly: M. Herrera (DOM). **Fly:** J. Gonzalez (CUB). **Bantam:** J. Molina (PUR). **Feather:** A. Miesses (DOM). **Light:** A. Beltre (DOM). **L. Welter:** A. Espinoza (CUB). **Welter:** M. Watkins (USA). **L. Middle:** U. Castillo (CUB). **Middle:** R. Batista (CUB). **L. Heavy:** O. Pought (USA). **Heavy:** A. Williams (USA). **S. Heavy:** L. Lewis (CAN).

Bucharest, Romania - 1985
L. Fly: R-S. Hwang (SKO). **Fly:** T. Marcelica (ROM). **Bantam:** R. Diaz (CUB). **Feather:** D. Maeran (ROM). **Light:** J. Teiche (GDR). **L. Welter:** W. Saeger (GDR). **Welter:** A. Stoianov (BUL). **L. Middle:** M. Franek (TCH). **Middle:** O. Zahalotskih (URS). **L. Heavy:** B. Riddick (USA). **Heavy:** F. Savon (CUB). **S. Heavy:** A. Prianichnikov (URS).

Havana, Cuba - 1987
L. Fly: E. Paisan (CUB). **Fly:** C. Daniels (USA). **Bantam:** A. Moya (CUB). **Feather:** G. Iliyasov (URS). **Light:** J. Hernandez (CUB). **L. Welter:** L. Mihai (ROM). **Welter:** F. Vastag (ROM). **L. Middle:** A. Lobsyak (URS). **Middle:** W. Martinez (CUB). **L. Heavy:** D. Yeliseyev (URS). **Heavy:** R. Balado (CUB). **S. Heavy:** L. Martinez (CUB).
Silver medal: E. Loughran (IRL).
Bronze medal: D. Galvin (IRL).

San Juan, Puerto Rico - 1989
L. Fly: D. Petrov (BUL). **Fly:** N. Monchai (FRA). **Bantam:** J. Casamayor (CUB). **Feather:** C. Febres (PUR). **Light:** A. Acevedo (PUR). **L. Welter:** E. Berger (GDR). **Welter:** A. Hernandez (CUB). **L. Middle:** L. Bedey (CUB). **Middle:** R. Garbey (CUB). **L. Heavy:** R. Alvarez (CUB). **Heavy:** K. Johnson (CAN). **S. Heavy:** A. Burdiantz (URS).
Silver medals: E. Magee (IRL), R. Reid (ENG), S. Wilson (SCO).

Lima, Peru - 1990
L. Fly: D. Alicea (PUR). **Fly:** K. Pielert (GDR). **Bantam:** K. Baravi (URS). **Feather:** A. Vaughan (ENG). **Light:** J. Mendez (CUB). **L. Welter:** H. Vinent (CUB). **Welter:** A. Hernandez (CUB). **L. Middle:** A. Kakauridze (URS). **Middle:** J. Gomez (CUB). **L. Heavy:** B. Torsten (GDR). **Heavy:** I. Andreev (URS). **S. Heavy:** J. Quesada (CUB).
Bronze medal: P. Ingle (ENG).

European Champions, 1924-1991

Paris, France - 1924
Fly: J. McKenzie (GBR). **Bantam:** J. Ces (FRA). **Feather:** R. de Vergnie (BEL). **Light:** N. Nielsen (DEN). **Welter:** J. Delarge (BEL). **Middle:** H. Mallin (GBR). **L. Heavy:** H. Mitchell (GBR). **Heavy:** O. von Porat (NOR).

Stockholm, Sweden - 1925
Fly: E. Pladner (FRA). **Bantam:** A. Rule (GBR). **Feather:** P. Andren (SWE). **Light:** S. Johanssen (SWE). **Welter:** H. Nielsen (DEN). **Middle:** F. Crawley (GBR). **L. Heavy:** T. Petersen (DEN). **Heavy:** B. Persson (SWE).
Silver medals: J. James (GBR), E. Viney (GBR), D. Lister (GBR).

Berlin, Germany - 1927
Fly: L. Boman (SWE). **Bantam:** Dalchow (GER). **Feather:** F. Dubbers (GER). **Light:** H. Domgoergen (GER). **Welter:** R. Caneva (ITA). **Middle:** J. Christensen (NOR). **L. Heavy:** H. Muller (GER). **Heavy:** N. Ramm (SWE).

Amsterdam, Holland - 1928
Fly: A. Kocsis (HUN). **Bantam:** V. Tamagnini (ITA). **Feather:** B. van Klaveren (HOL). **Light:** C. Orlandi (ITA). **Welter:** R. Galataud (FRA). **Middle:** P. Toscani (ITA). **L. Heavy:** E. Pistulla (GER). **Heavy:** N. Ramm (SWE).

Budapest, Hungary - 1930
Fly: I. Enekes (HUN). **Bantam:** J. Szeles (HUN). **Feather:** G. Szabo (HUN). **Light:** M. Bianchini (ITA). **Welter:** J. Besselmann (GER). **Middle:** C. Meroni (ITA). **L. Heavy:** T. Petersen (DEN). **Heavy:** J. Michaelson (DEN).

Los Angeles, USA - 1932
Fly: I. Enekes (HUN). **Bantam:** H. Ziglarski (GER). **Feather:** J. Schleinkofer (GER). **Light:** T. Ahlqvist (SWE). **Welter:** E. Campe (GER). **Middle:** R. Michelot (FRA). **L. Heavy:** G. Rossi (ITA). **Heavy:** L. Rovati (ITA).

Budapest, Hungary - 1934
Fly: P. Palmer (GBR). **Bantam:** I. Enekes (HUN). **Feather:** O. Kaestner GER). **Light:** E. Facchini (ITA). **Welter:** D. McCleave (GBR). **Middle:** S. Szigetti (HUN). **L. Heavy:** P. Zehetmayer (AUT). **Heavy:** G. Baerlund (FIN).
Bronze medal: P. Floyd (GBR).

Milan, Italy - 1937
Fly: I. Enekes (HUN). **Bantam:** U. Sergo (ITA). **Feather:** A. Polus (POL). **Light:** H. Nuremberg (GER). **Welter:** M. Murach (GER). **Middle:** H. Chmielewski (POL). **L. Heavy:** S. Szigetti (HUN). **Heavy:** O. Tandberg (SWE).

Dublin, Eire - 1939
Fly: J. Ingle (IRL). **Bantam:** U. Sergo (ITA). **Feather:** P. Dowdall (IRL). **Light:** H. Nuremberg (GER). **Welter:** A. Kolczyski (POL). **Middle:** A. Raedek (EST). **L. Heavy:** L. Musina (ITA). **Heavy:** O. Tandberg (SWE).
Bronze medal: C. Evenden (IRL).

Dublin, Eire - 1947
Fly: L. Martinez (ESP). **Bantam:** L. Bogacs (HUN). **Feather:** K. Kreuger (SWE). **Light:** J. Vissers (BEL). **Welter:** J. Ryan (ENG). **Middle:** A. Escudie (FRA). **L. Heavy:** H. Quentemeyer (HOL). **Heavy:** G. O'Colmain (IRL).
Silver medals: J. Clinton (SCO), P. Maguire (IRL), W. Thom (ENG), G. Scriven (ENG).
Bronze medals: J. Dwyer (SCO), A. Sanderson (ENG), W. Frith (SCO), E. Cantwell (IRL), K. Wyatt (ENG).

Oslo, Norway - 1949
Fly: J. Kasperczak (POL). **Bantam:** G. Zuddas (ITA). **Feather:** J. Bataille (FRA). **Light:** M. McCullagh (IRL). **Welter:** J. Torma (TCH). **Middle:** **L. Papp (HUN)**. **L. Heavy:** G. di Segni (ITA). **Heavy:** L. Bene (HUN).
Bronze medal: D. Connell (IRL).

Milan, Italy - 1951
Fly: A. Pozzali (ITA). **Bantam:** V. Dall'Osso (ITA). **Feather:** J. Ventaja (FRA). **Light:** B. Visintin (ITA). **L. Welter:** H. Schelling (GER). **Welter:** Z. Chychla (POL). **L. Middle:** L. Papp (HUN). **Middle:** S. Sjolin (SWE). **L. Heavy:** M. Limage (BEL). **Heavy:** G. di Segni (ITA).
Silver medal: J. Kelly (IRL).
Bronze medals: D. Connell (IRL), T. Milligan (IRL), A. Lay (ENG).

Warsaw, Poland - 1953
Fly: H. Kukier (POL). **Bantam:** Z. Stefaniuk (POL). **Feather:** J. Kruza (POL). **Light:** V. Jengibarian (URS). **L. Welter:** L. Drogosz (POL). **Welter:** Z. Chychla (POL). **L. Middle:** B. Wells (ENG). **Middle:** D. Wemhoner (GER). **L. Heavy:** U. Nietchke (GER). **Heavy:** A. Schotzikas (URS).
Silver medal: T. Milligan (IRL).
Bronze medals: J. McNally (IRL), R. Barton (ENG).

Berlin, West Germany - 1955
Fly: E. Basel (GER). **Bantam:** Z. Stefaniuk (POL). **Feather:** T. Nicholls (ENG). **Light:** H. Kurschat (GER). **L. Welter:** L. Drogosz (POL). **Welter:** N. Gargano (ENG). **L. Middle:** Z. Pietrzykowski (POL). **Middle:** G. Schatkov (URS). **L. Heavy:** E. Schoeppner (GER). **Heavy:** A. Schotzikas (URS).

Prague, Czechoslovakia - 1957
Fly: M. Homberg (GER). **Bantam:** O. Grigoryev (URS). **Feather:** D. Venilov (BUL). **Light:** K. Pazdzior (POL). **L. Welter:** V. Jengibarian (URS). **Welter:** M. Graus (GER). **L. Middle:** N. Benvenuti (ITA). **Middle:** Z. Pietrzykowski (POL). **L. Heavy:** G. Negrea (ROM). **Heavy:** A. Abramov (URS).
Bronze medals: R. Davies (WAL), J. Morrissey (SCO), J. Kidd (SCO), F. Teidt (IRL).

Lucerne, Switzerland - 1959
Fly: M. Homberg (GER). **Bantam:** H. Rascher (GER). **Feather:** J. Adamski (POL). **Light:** O. Maki (FIN). **L. Welter:** V. Jengibarian (URS). **Welter:** L. Drogosz (POL). **L. Middle:** N. Benvenuti (ITA). **Middle:** G. Schatkov (URS). **L. Heavy:** Z. Pietrzykowski (POL). **Heavy:** A. Abramov (URS).
Silver medal: D. Thomas (ENG).
Bronze medals: A. McClean (IRL), H. Perry (IRL), C. McCoy (IRL), H. Scott (ENG).

Belgrade, Yugoslavia - 1961
Fly: P. Vacca (ITA). **Bantam:** S. Sivko (URS). **Feather:** F. Taylor (ENG). **Light:** R. McTaggart (SCO). **L. Welter:** A. Tamulis (URS). **Welter:** R. Tamulis (URS). **L. Middle:** B. Lagutin (URS). **Middle:** T. Walasek (POL). **L. Heavy:** G. Saraudi (ITA). **Heavy:** A. Abramov (URS).
Bronze medals: P. Warwick (ENG), I. McKenzie (SCO), J. Bodell (ENG).

Moscow, USSR - 1963
Fly: V. Bystrov (URS). **Bantam:** O. Grigoryev (URS). **Feather:** S. Stepashkin (URS). **Light:** J. Kajdi (HUN). **L. Welter:** J. Kulej (POL). **Welter:** R. Tamulis (URS). **L. Middle:** B. Lagutin (URS). **Middle:** V. Popenchenko (URS). **L. Heavy:** Z. Pietrzykowski (POL). **Heavy:** J. Nemec (TCH).
Silver medal: A. Wyper (SCO).

Berlin, East Germany - 1965
Fly: H. Freisdadt (GER). **Bantam:** O. Grigoryev (URS). **Feather:** S. Stepashkin (URS). **Light:** V. Barranikov (URS). **L. Welter:** J. Kulej (POL). **Welter:** R. Tamulis (URS). **L. Middle:** V. Ageyev (URS). **Middle:** V. Popenchenko (URS). **L. Heavy:** D. Poznyak (URS). **Heavy:** A. Isosimov (URS).
Silver medal: B. Robinson (ENG).
Bronze medals: J. McCluskey (SCO), K. Buchanan (SCO), J. McCourt (IRL).

Rome, Italy - 1967
Fly: H. Skrzyczak (POL). **Bantam:** N. Giju (ROM). **Feather:** R. Petek (POL). **Light:** J. Grudzien (POL). **L. Welter:** V. Frolov (URS). **Welter:** B. Nemecek (TCH). **L. Middle:** V. Ageyev (URS). **Middle:** M. Casati (ITA). **L. Heavy:** D. Poznyak (URS). **Heavy:** M. Baruzzi (ITA).
Silver medal: P. Boddington (ENG).

Bucharest, Romania - 1969
L. Fly: G. Gedo (HUN). **Fly:** C. Ciuca (ROM). **Bantam:** A. Dumitrescu (ROM). **Feather:** L. Orban (HUN). **Light:** S. Cutov (ROM). **L. Welter:** V. Frolov (URS). **Welter:** G. Meier (GER). **L. Middle:** V. Tregubov (URS). **Middle:** V. Tarasenkov (URS). **L. Heavy:** D. Poznyak (URS). **Heavy:** I. Alexe (ROM).
Bronze medals: M. Dowling (IRL), M. Piner (ENG), A. Richardson (ENG), T. Imrie (SCO).

Madrid, Spain - 1971
L. Fly: G. Gedo (HUN). **Fly:** J. Rodriguez (ESP). **Bantam:** T. Badar (HUN). **Feather:** R. Tomczyk (POL). **Light:** J. Szczepanski (POL). **L. Welter:** U. Beyer (GDR). **Welter:** J. Kajdi (HUN). **L. Middle:** V. Tregubov (URS). **Middle:** J. Juotsiavitchus (URS). **L. Heavy:** M. Parlov (BUL). **Heavy:** V. Tchernishev (URS).
Bronze medals: N. McLaughlin (IRL), M. Dowling (IRL), B. McCarthy (IRL), M. Kingwell (ENG), L. Stevens (ENG).

Belgrade, Yugoslavia - 1973
L. Fly: V. Zasypko (URS). **Fly:** C. Gruescu (ROM). **Bantam:** A. Cosentino (FRA). **Feather:** S. Forster (GDR). **Light:** S. Cutov (ROM). **L. Welter:** M. Benes (YUG). **Welter:** S. Csjef (HUN). **L. Middle:** A. Klimanov (URS). **Middle:** V. Lemechev (URS). **L. Heavy:** M. Parlov (YUG). **Heavy:** V. Ulyanich (URS).
Bronze medal: J. Bambrick (SCO).

Katowice, Poland - 1975
L. Fly: A. Tkachenko (URS). **Fly:** V. Zasypko (URS). **Bantam:** V. Rybakov (URS). **Feather:** T. Badari (HUN). **Light:** S. Cutov (ROM). **L. Welter:** V. Limasov (URS). **Welter:** K. Marjaama (FIN). **L. Middle:** W. Rudnowski (POL). **Middle:** V. Lemechev (URS). **L. Heavy:** A. Klimanov (URS). **Heavy:** A. Biegalski (POL).
Bronze medals: C. Magri (ENG), P. Cowdell (ENG), G. McEwan (ENG).

Halle, East Germany - 1977
L. Fly: H. Srednicki (POL). **Fly:** L. Blazynski (POL). **Bantam:** S. Forster (GDR). **Feather:** R. Nowakowski (GDR). **Light:** A. Rusevski (YUG). **L. Welter:** B. Gajda (POL). **Welter:** V. Limasov (URS). **L. Middle:** V. Saychenko (URS). **Middle:** I. Shaposhnikov (URS). **L. Heavy:** D. Kvachadze (URS). **Heavy:** E. Gorstkov (URS).
Bronze medal: P. Sutcliffe (IRL).

Cologne, West Germany - 1979
L. Fly: S. Sabirov (URS). **Fly:** H. Strednicki (POL). **Bantam:** N. Khrapzov (URS). **Feather:** V. Rybakov (URS). **Light.** V. Demianenko (URS). **L. Welter:** S. Konakbaev (URS). **Welter:** E. Muller (GER). **L. Middle:** M.

Perunovic (YUG). **Middle:** T. Uusiverta (FIN). **L. Heavy:** A. Nikolyan (URS). **Heavy:** E. Gorstkov (URS).
Bronze medal: P. Sutcliffe (IRL).

Tampere, Finland - 1981
L. Fly: I. Hristov (BUL). **Fly:** P. Lessov (BUL). **Bantam:** V. Miroschnichenko (URS). **Feather:** R. Nowakowski (GDR). **Light:** V. Rybakov (URS). **L. Welter:** V. Shisov (URS). **Welter:** S. Konakvbaev (URS). **L. Middle:** A. Koshkin (URS). **Middle:** J. Torbek (URS). **L. Heavy:** A Krupin (URS). **Heavy:** A. Jagupkin (URS). **S. Heavy:** F. Damiani (ITA).
Bronze medal: G. Hawkins (IRL).

Varna, Bulgaria - 1983
L. Fly: I. Hristov (BUL). **Fly:** P. Lessov (BUL). **Bantam:** Y. Alexandrov (URS). **Feather:** S. Nurkazov (URS). **Light:** E. Chuprenski (BUL). **L. Welter:** V. Shishov (URS). **Welter:** P. Galkin (URS). **L. Middle:** V. Laptev (URS). **Middle:** V. Melnik (URS). **L. Heavy:** V. Kokhanovski (URS). **Heavy:** A. Jagubkin (URS). **S. Heavy:** F. Damiani (ITA).
Bronze medal: K. Joyce (IRL).

Budapest, Hungary - 1985
L. Fly: R. Breitbarth (GDR). **Fly:** D. Berg (GDR). **Bantam:** L. Simic (YUG). **Feather:** S. Khachatrian (URS). **Light:** E. Chuprenski (BUL) **L. Welter:** S. Mehnert (GDR). **Welter:** I. Akopokhian (URS). **L. Middle:** M. Timm (GDR). **Middle:** H. Maske (GDR). **L. Heavy:** N. Shanavasov (URS). **Heavy:** A. Jagubkin (URS). **S. Heavy:** F. Somodi (HUN).
Bronze medals: S. Casey (IRL). J. Beckles (ENG).

Turin, Italy - 1987
L. Fly: N. Munchyan (URS). **Fly:** A. Tews (GDR). **Bantam:** A. Hristov (BUL). **Feather:** M. Kazaryan (URS). **Light:** O. Nazarov (URS). **L. Welter:** B. Abadjier (BUL). **Welter:** V. Shishov (URS). **L. Middle:** E. Richter (GDR). **Middle:** H. Maske (GDR). **L. Heavy:** Y. Vaulin (URS). **Heavy:** A. Vanderlijde (HOL). **S. Heavy:** U. Kaden (GDR).
Bronze medal: N. Brown (ENG).

Athens, Greece - 1989
L. Fly: I. Hristov (BUL). **Fly:** Y. Arbachakov (URS). **Bantam:** S. Todorov (BUL). **Feather:** K. Kirkorov (BUL). **Light:** K. Tsziu (URS). **L. Welter:** I. Ruznikov (URS). **Welter:** S. Mehnert (GDR). **L. Middle:** I. Akopokhian (URS). **Middle:** H. Maske (GDR). **L. Heavy:** S. Lange (GDR). **Heavy:** A. Vanderlijde (HOL). **S. Heavy:** U. Kaden (GDR).
Bronze Medal: D. Anderson (SCO).

Gothenburg, Sweden - 1991
L. Fly: I. Marinov (BUL). **Fly:** I. Kovacs (HUN). **Bantam:** S. Todorov (BUL). **Feather:** P. Griffin (IRL). **Light:** V. Nistor (ROM). **L. Welter:** K. Tsziu (URS). **Welter:** R. Welin (SWE). **L. Middle:** I. Akopokhian (URS). **Middle:** S. Otke (GER). **L. Heavy:** D. Michalszewski (GER). **Heavy:** A. Vanderlijde (HOL). **S. Heavy:** E. Beloussov (URS).
Bronze medals: P. Weir (SCO). A. Vaughan (ENG).

Note: Gold medals were awarded to the Europeans who went the furthest in the Olympic Games of 1924, 1928 & 1932.

European Junior Champions, 1970-1992

Miskolc, Hungary - 1970
L. Fly: Gluck (HUN). **Fly:** Z. Kismeneth (HUN). **Bantam:** A. Levitschev (URS). **Feather:** Andrianov (URS). **Light:** L. Juhasz (HUN). **L. Welter:** K. Nemec (HUN). **Welter:** Davidov (URS). **L. Middle:** A. Lemeschev (URS). **Middle:** N. Anfimov (URS). **L. Heavy:** O. Sasche (GDR). **Heavy:** J. Reder (HUN).
Bronze medals: D. Needham (ENG), R. Barlow (ENG), L. Stevens (ENG).

Bucharest, Romania - 1972
L. Fly: A. Turei (ROM). **Fly:** Condurat (ROM). **Bantam:** V. Solomin (URS). **Feather:** V. Lvov (URS). **Light:** S. Cutov (ROM). **L. Welter:** K. Pierwieniecki (POL). **Welter:** Zorov (URS). **L. Middle:** Babescu (ROM). **Middle:** V. Lemeschev (URS). **L. Heavy:** Mirounik (URS). **Heavy:** Subutin (URS).
Bronze medals: J. Gale (ENG), R. Maxwell (ENG), D. Odwell (ENG).

Kiev, Russia - 1974
L. Fly: A. Tkachenko (URS). **Fly:** V. Rybakov (URS). **Bantam:** C. Andreikovski (BUL). **Feather:** V. Sorokin (URS). **Light:** V. Limasov (URS). **L. Welter:** N. Sigov (URS). **Welter:** M. Bychkov (URS). **L. Middle:** V. Danshin (URS). **Middle:** D. Jende (GDR). **L. Heavy:** K. Dafinoiu (ROM). **Heavy:** K. Mashev (BUL).
Silver medal: C. Magri (ENG).
Bronze medals: G. Gilbody (ENG), K. Laing (ENG).

Izmir, Turkey - 1976
L. Fly: C. Seican (ROM). **Fly:** G. Khratsov (URS). **Bantam:** M. Navros (URS). **Feather:** V. Demoianeko (URS). **Light:** M. Puzovic (YUG). **L. Welter:** V. Zverev (URS). **Welter:** K. Ozoglouz (TUR). **L. Middle:** W. Lauder (SCO). **Middle:** H. Lenhart (GER). **L. Heavy:** I. Yantchauskas (URS). **Heavy:** B. Enjenyan (URS).
Silver medal: J. Decker (ENG).
Bronze medals: I. McLeod (SCO), N. Croombes (ENG).

Dublin, Ireland - 1978
L. Fly: R. Marx (GDR). **Fly:** D. Radu (ROM). **Bantam:** S. Khatchatrian (URS). **Feather:** H. Loukmanov (URS). **Light:** P. Oliva (ITA). **L. Welter:** V. Laptiev (URS). **Welter:** R. Filimanov (URS). **L. Middle:** A. Beliave (URS). **Middle:** G. Zinkovitch (URS). **L. Heavy:** I. Jolta (ROM). **Heavy:** P. Stoimenov (BUL).
Silver medals: M. Holmes (IRL), P. Hanlon (ENG), M. Courtney (ENG).
Bronze medals: T. Thompson (IRL), J. Turner (ENG), M. Bennett (WAL), J. McAllister (SCO), C. Devine (ENG).

Rimini, Italy - 1980
L. Fly: A. Mikoulin (URS). **Fly:** J. Varadi (HUN). **Bantam:** F. Rauschning (GDR). **Feather:** J. Gladychev (URS). **Light:** V. Shishov (URS). **L. Welter:** R. Lomski (BUL). **Welter:** T. Holonics (GDR). **L. Middle:** N. Wilshire (ENG). **Middle:** S. Laptiev (URS). **L. Heavy:** V. Dolgoun (URS). **Heavy:** V. Tioumentsev (URS). **S. Heavy:** S. Kormihtsine (URS).
Bronze medals: N. Potter (ENG), B. McGuigan (IRL), M. Brereton (IRL), D. Cross (ENG).

Schwerin, East Germany - 1982
L. Fly: R. Kabirov (URS). **Fly:** I. Filchev (BUL). **Bantam:** M. Stecca (ITA). **Feather:** B. Blagoev (BUL). **Light:** E. Chakimov (URS). **L. Welter:** S. Mehnert (GDR). **Welter:** T. Schmitz (GDR). **L. Middle:** B. Shararov (URS). **Middle:** E. Christie (ENG). **L. Heavy:** Y. Waulin (URS). **Heavy:** A. Popov (URS). **S. Heavy:** V. Aldoshin (URS).
Silver medal: D. Kenny (ENG).
Bronze medal: O. Jones (ENG).

Tampere, Finland - 1984
L. Fly: R. Breitbart (GDR). **Fly:** D. Berg (GDR). **Bantam:** K. Khdrian (URS). **Feather:** O. Nazarov (URS). **Light:** C. Furnikov (BUL). **L. Welter:** W. Schmidt (GDR). **Welter:** K. Doinov (BUL). **L. Middle:** O. Volkov (URS). **Middle:** R. Ryll (GDR). **L. Heavy:** G. Peskov (URS). **Heavy:** R. Draskovic (YUG). **S. Heavy:** L. Kamenov (BUL).
Bronze medals: J. Lowey (IRL), F. Harding (ENG), N. Moore (ENG).

Brondy, Denmark - 1986
L. Fly: S. Todorov (BUL). **Fly:** S. Galotian (URS). **Bantam:** D. Drumm (GDR). **Feather:** K. Tsziu (URS). **Light:** G. Akopkhian (URS). **L. Welter:** F. Vastag (ROM). **Welter:** S. Karavayev (URS). **L. Middle:** E. Elibaev (URS). **Middle:** A. Kurnabka (URS). **L. Heavy:** A. Schultz (GDR). **Heavy:** A. Golota (POL). **S. Heavy:** A. Prianichnikov (URS).

Gdansk, Poland - 1988
L. Fly: I. Kovacs (HUN). **Fly:** M. Beyer (GDR). **Bantam:** M. Aitzanov (URS). **Feather:** M. Rudolph (GDR). **Light:** M. Shaburov (URS). **L. Welter:** G. Campanella (ITA). **Welter:** D. Konsun (URS). **L. Middle:** K. Kiselev (URS). **Middle:** A. Rudenko (URS). **L. Heavy:** O. Velikanov (URS). **Heavy:** A. Ter-Okopian (URS). **S. Heavy:** E. Belusov (URS).
Bronze medals: P. Ramsey (ENG), M. Smyth (WAL).

Usti Nad Labem, Czechoslovakia - 1990
L. Fly: Z. Paliani (URS). **Fly:** K. Pielert (GDR). **Bantam:** K. Baravi (URS). **Feather:** Gvasalia (URS). **Light:** J. Hildenbrandt (GDR). **L. Welter:** N. Smanov (URS). **Welter:** A. Preda (ROM). **L. Middle:** A. Kakauridze (URS). **Middle:** J. Schwank (GDR). **L. Heavy:** Iljin (URS). **Heavy:** I. Andrejev (URS). **S. Heavy:** W. Fischer (GDR).
Silver medal: A. Todd (ENG).
Bronze medal: P. Craig (ENG).

Edinburgh, Scotland - 1992
L. Fly: M. Ismailov (URS). **Fly:** F. Brennfuhrer (GER). **Bantam:** S. Kuchler (GER). **Feather:** M. Silantiev (URS). **Light:** S. Shcherbakov (URS). **L. Welter:** O. Saitov (URS). **Welter:** H. Kurlumaz (TUR). **L. Middle:** Z. Erdie (HUN). **Middle:** V. Zhirov (URS). **L. Heavy:** D.

Gorbachev (URS). **Heavy:** L. Achkasov (URS). **S. Heavy:** A. Mamedov (URS).
Silver medals: M. Hall (ENG), B. Jones (WAL).
Bronze medals: F. Slane (IRL), G. Stephens (IRL), C. Davies (WAL).

Note: The age limit for the championships were reduced from 21 to 19 in 1976.

Commonwealth Champions, 1930-1990

Hamilton, Canada - 1930
Fly: W. Smith (SAF). **Bantam:** H. Mizler (ENG). **Feather:** F. Meacham (ENG). **Light:** J. Rolland (SCO). **Welter:** L. Hall (SAF). **Middle:** F. Mallin (ENG). **L. Heavy:** J. Goyder (ENG). **Heavy:** V. Stuart (ENG).
Silver medals: T. Pardoe (ENG), T. Holt (SCO).
Bronze medals: A. Lyons (SCO), A. Love (ENG), F. Breeman (ENG).

Wembley, England - 1934
Fly: P. Palmer (ENG). **Bantam:** F. Ryan (ENG). **Feather:** C. Cattarall (SAF). **Light:** L. Cook (AUS). **Welter:** D. McCleave (ENG). **Middle:** A. Shawyer (ENG). **L. Heavy:** G. Brennan (ENG). **Heavy:** P. Floyd (ENG).
Silver medals: A. Barnes (WAL), J. Jones (WAL), F. Taylor (WAL), J. Holton (SCO).
Bronze medals: J. Pottinger (WAL), T. Wells (SCO), H. Moy (ENG), W. Duncan (NIR), J. Magill (NIR), Lord D. Douglas-Hamilton (SCO).

Melbourne, Australia - 1938
Fly: J. Joubert (SAF). **Bantam:** W. Butler (ENG). **Feather:** A. Henricus (CEY). **Light:** H. Groves (ENG). **Welter:** W. Smith (AUS). **Middle:** D. Reardon (WAL). **L. Heavy:** N. Wolmarans (SAF). **Heavy:** T. Osborne (CAN).
Silver medals: J. Watson (SCO), M. Dennis (ENG).
Bronze medals: H. Cameron (SCO), J. Wilby (ENG).

Auckland, New Zealand - 1950
Fly: H. Riley (SCO). **Bantam:** J. van Rensburg (SAF). **Feather:** H. Gilliland (SCO). **Light:** R. Latham (ENG). **Welter:** T. Ratcliffe (ENG). **Middle:** T. van Schalkwyk (SAF). **L. Heavy:** D. Scott (ENG). **Heavy:** F. Creagh (NZL).
Bronze medal: P. Brander (ENG).

Vancouver, Canada - 1954
Fly: R. Currie (SCO). **Bantam:** J. Smillie (SCO). **Feather:** L. Leisching (SAF). **Light:** P. van Staden (SAF). **L. Welter:** M. Bergin (CAN). **Welter:** N. Gargano (ENG). **L. Middle:** W. Greaves (CAN). **Middle:** J. van de Kolff (SAF). **L. Heavy:** P. van Vuuren (SAF). **Heavy:** B. Harper (ENG).
Silver medals: M. Collins (WAL), F. McQuillan (SCO).
Bronze medals: D. Charnley (ENG), B. Wells (ENG).

Cardiff, Wales - 1958
Fly: J. Brown (SCO). **Bantam:** H. Winstone (WAL). **Feather:** W. Taylor (AUS). **Light:** R. McTaggart (SCO). **L. Welter:** H. Loubscher (SAF). **Welter:** J. Greyling (SAF). **L. Middle:** G. Webster (SAF). **Middle:** T. Milligan (NIR). **L. Heavy:** A. Madigan (AUS). **Heavy:** D. Bekker (SAF).
Silver medals: T. Bache (ENG), M. Collins (WAL), J. Jordan (NIR), R. Kane (SCO), S. Pearson (ENG), A. Higgins (WAL), D. Thomas (ENG).
Bronze medals: P. Lavery (NIR), D. Braithwaite (WAL), R. Hanna (NIR), A. Owen (SCO), J. McClory (NIR), J. Cooke (ENG), J. Jacobs (ENG), B. Nancurvis (WAL), R. Scott (SCO), W. Brown (WAL), J. Caiger (ENG), W. Bannon (SCO), R. Pleace (WAL).

Perth, Australia - 1962
Fly: R. Mallon (SCO). **Bantam:** J. Dynevor (AUS). **Feather:** J. McDermott (SCO). **Light:** E. Blay (GHA). **L. Welter:** C. Quartey (GHA). **Welter:** W. Coe (NZL). **L. Middle:** H. Mann (CAN). **Middle:** M. Calhoun (JAM). **L. Heavy:** A. Madigan (AUS). **Heavy:** G. Oywello (UGA).
Silver medals: R. McTaggart (SCO), J. Pritchett (ENG).
Bronze medals: M. Pye (ENG), P. Benneyworth (ENG), B. Whelan (ENG), B. Brazier (ENG), C. Rice (NIR), T. Menzies (SCO), H. Christie (NIR).

Kingston, Jamaica - 1966
Fly: S. Shittu (GHA). **Bantam:** E. Ndukwu (NIG). **Feather:** P. Waruinge (KEN). **Light:** A. Andeh (NIG). **L. Welter:** J. McCourt (NIR). **Welter:** E. Blay (GHA). **L. Middle:** M. Rowe (ENG). **Middle:** J. Darkey (GHA). **L. Heavy:** R. Tighe (ENG). **Heavy:** W. Kini (NZL).
Silver medals: P. Maguire (NIR), R. Thurston (ENG), R. Arthur (ENG), T. Imrie (SCO).
Bronze medals: S. Lockhart (NIR), A. Peace (SCO), F. Young (NIR), J. Turpin (ENG), D. McAlinden (NIR).

Edinburgh, Scotland - 1970
L. Fly: J. Odwori (UGA). **Fly:** D. Needham (ENG). **Bantam:** S. Shittu (GHA). **Feather:** P. Waruinge (KEN). **Light:** A. Adeyemi (NIG). **L. Welter:** M. Muruli (UGA). **Welter:** E. Ankudey (GHA). **L. Middle:** T. Imrie (SCO). **Middle:** J. Conteh (ENG). **L. Heavy:** F. Ayinla (NIG). **Heavy:** B. Masanda (UGA).
Silver medals: T. Davies (WAL), J. Gillan (SCO), D. Davies (WAL), J. McKinty (NIR).
Bronze medals: M. Abrams (ENG), A. McHugh (SCO), D. Larmour (NIR), S. Oglivie (SCO), A. Richardson (ENG), T. Joyce (SCO), P. Doherty (NIR), J. Rafferty (SCO), L. Stevens (ENG).

Christchurch, New Zealand - 1974
L. Fly: J. Odwori (UGA). **Fly:** D. Larmour (NIR). **Bantam:** P. Cowdell (ENG). **Feather:** E. Ndukwu (NIG). **Light:** A. Kalule (UGA). **L. Welter:** O. Nwankpa (NIG). **Welter:** M. Muruli (UGA). **L. Middle:** L. Mwale (ZAM). **Middle:** F. Lucas (STV). **L. Heavy:** W. Knight (ENG). **Heavy:** N. Meade (ENG).
Silver medals: E. McKenzie (WAL), A. Harrison (SCO).
Bronze medals: J. Bambrick (SCO), J. Douglas (SCO), J. Rodgers (NIR), S. Cooney (SCO), R. Davies (ENG), C. Speare (ENG), G. Ferris (NIR).

Edmonton, Canada - 1978
L. Fly: S. Muchoki (KEN). **Fly:** M. Irungu (KEN). **Bantam:** B. McGuigan (NIR). **Feather:** A. Nelson (GHA). **Light:** G. Hamill (NIR). **L. Welter:** W. Braithwaite (GUY). **Welter:** M. McCallum (JAM). **L. Middle:** K. Perlette (CAN). **Middle:** P. McElwaine (AUS). **L. Heavy:** R. Fortin (CAN). **Heavy:** J. Awome (ENG).
Silver medals: J. Douglas (SCO), K. Beattie (NIR), D. Parkes (ENG), V. Smith (ENG).
Bronze medals: H. Russell (NIR), M. O'Brien (ENG), J. McAllister (SCO), T. Feal (WAL).

Brisbane, Australia - 1982
L. Fly: A. Wachire (KEN). **Fly:** M. Mutua (KEN). **Bantam:** J. Orewa (NIG). **Feather:** P. Konyegwachie (NIG). **Light:** H. Khalili (KEN). **L. Welter:** C. Ossai (NIG). **Welter:** C. Pyatt (ENG). **L. Middle:** S. O'Sullivan (CAN). **Middle:** J. Price (ENG). **L. Heavy:** F. Sani (FIJ). **Heavy:** W. de Wit (CAN).
Silver medals: J. Lyon (ENG), J. Kelly (SCO), R. Webb (NIR), P. Hanlon (ENG), J. McDonnell (ENG), N. Croombes (ENG), H. Hylton (ENG).
Bronze medals: R. Gilbody (ENG), C. McIntosh (ENG), R. Corr (NIR).

Edinburgh, Scotland - 1986
L. Fly: S. Olson (CAN). **Fly:** J. Lyon (ENG). **Bantam:** S. Murphy (ENG). **Feather:** B. Downey (CAN). **Light:** A. Dar (CAN). **L. Welter:** H. Grant (CAN). **Welter:** D. Dyer (ENG). **L. Middle:** D. Sherry (CAN). **Middle:** R. Douglas (ENG). **L. Heavy:** J. Moran (ENG). **Heavy:** J. Peau (NZL). **S. Heavy:** L. Lewis (CAN).
Silver medals: M. Epton (ENG), R. Nash (NIR), P. English (ENG), N. Haddock (WAL), J. McAlister (SCO), H. Lawson (SCO), D. Young (SCO), A. Evans (WAL).
Bronze medals: W. Docherty (SCO), J. Todd (NIR), K. Webber (WAL), G. Brooks (SCO), J. Wallace (SCO), C. Carleton (NIR), J. Jacobs (ENG), B. Lowe (NIR), D. Denny (NIR), G. Thomas (WAL), A. Mullen (SCO), G. Ferrie (SCO), P. Tinney (NIR), B. Pullen (WAL), E. Cardouza (ENG), J. Oyebola (ENG).

Auckland, New Zealand - 1990
L. Fly: J. Juko (UGA). **Fly:** W. McCullough (NIR). **Bantam:** S. Mohammed (NIG). **Feather:** J. Irwin (ENG). **Light:** G. Nyakana (UGA). **L. Welter:** C. Kane (SCO). **Welter:** D. Defiagbon (NIG). **L. Middle:** R. Woodhall (ENG). **Middle:** C. Johnson (CAN). **L. Heavy:** J. Akhasamba (KEN). **Heavy:** G. Onyango (KEN). **S. Heavy:** M. Kenny (NZL).
Bronze medals: D. Anderson (SCO), M. Edwards (ENG), P. Douglas (NIR).

Obituaries, 1991-1992

by Ron Olver

Because of my long link with the various Ex-Boxers' Associations, over a quarter of a century, I am usually among the first to be informed of the demise of former fighters. I imagine that is why editor Barry Hugman has asked me to provide suitable obituaries on those who have died within the last 18 months or so. It is impossible to list everyone, but I have done my best to supply details of as many of the more well-known boxers as I can. I believe this is an essential feature of any Yearbook, a final tribute to those who gave us pleasure and made significant contributions to the sport we all love. We honour them and will remember them.

ARMAH Richard. *Born* 24 April, 1920. *Died* April 1991. Turned pro in his native Gold Coast (now Ghana) in 1939. Won Gold Coast featherweight and welterweight titles. Won West African middleweight title (1946) and West African light-heavyweight title (1947). Came to Britain in 1948 and stayed. Beat Harry Davis, Ron Cooper, Bert Sanders, Bob Cleaver, Doug Mansfield, Wally Beckett, Dick Langley, Jackie Brown, Tom Meli and Empire champion, Bos Murphy. Retired 1955. Was a staunch member of the London Ex-Boxers' Association. In later years he was confined to a wheelchair, but still attended meetings as often as he could. Also met champions Randy Turpin, Alex Buxton and Johnny Sullivan.

ARRENDONDO Ricardo. *Born* 26 May, 1949, at Apatzingan, Michoacan, Mexico. *Died* September 20, 1991. Pro 1966-79. Challenged for world junior-lightweight title in 1971, but was beaten by Hiroshi Kobayashi. Won WBC junior-lightweight title by beating Yoshiaki Numata (1971). Successfully defended title against Jose Isaac Marin, William Martinez, Susumu Okabe, all in 1972, Apollo Yoshio (1973), and Morito Kashiwaba (1973), before losing it to Kuniaki Shibata (1974).

BALDASARA Joe. *Born* February 1913, Haswell, Durham. *Died* 19 May, 1992. Pro 1929-37. Parents were Italian, who came to Sunderland to set up an ice-cream business. First opponent was Mickey McGuire, who went on to become a leading contender for the world flyweight title. Beat Mick Carney, Bobby Thackray, Tommy O'Keefe, Tony Butcher, Bobby Tate, Jack Delaney. Vice-president of Tyneside EBA and Sunderland EBA.

BEALE Barney. *Born* 1 January, 1935, at Lambeth, London. *Died* 28 April, 1992. Pro 1955-59. Beat Jimmy Brown in an eliminator for the British lightweight title, then lost to Billy Kelly in another eliminator, both in 1959. Defeated Dave Stone, Ernie Fossey, Teddy Best, Peter Cobblah, Johnny Kidd, Ron Hinson and Dennis Hinson.

BERG Jack "Kid". *Born* 28 June, 1909, at Whitechapel, London. *Died* 22 April, 1991. Real name Judah Bergman. Known as the "Whitechapel Whirlwind." Pro 1924-45. Won world junior-welterweight title by beating Mushy Callahan (1930). Lost it to Tony Canzoneri (1931). Won British lightweight title by beating Harry Mizler (1934) and lost it to Jimmy Walsh (1936). Was beaten by Laurie Stevens for British Empire lightweight title (1936). Became president of the London Ex-Boxers' Association, a position he held until his death.

BROOKS Harry. *Born* Aldgate, London. *Died* May 1991. Pro 1925-46. Beat Tommy Daly, George Rose, Alby Kestrell, Bugler Lake, Johnny Quill, Bep van Klaveren, Bill Hood, Norman Dale, Tommy John, Packy McFarland, Chuck Parker, Norman Snow, Jimmy Wheeler, Frank

Jack "Kid" Berg

Meacham, Douglas Parker, Robert Disch, Jimmy Stewart, Jimmy Vaughan, Alby Day, George Darlow and Eric Boon. Also met Nel Tarleton, Seaman Watson, Freddie Miller, Ernie Izzard, Johnny Curley and Francois Machtens.

BROWN Tommy. *Born* Hackney, London. *Died* October 1991. Pro 1937. A heavyweight. Beat Tiny Woodhouse, Jack Fox, Dick Allen, Archie Norman, Alf Luxton and Jack Fitzpatrick.

BYGRAVE Doug. *Born* 1919, Norwich. *Died* December 1991. Pro 1937-47. Won Eastern Area bantamweight title by beating Charlie White (1939). Beat Harry Lazar, Pat Palmer, Harry Kid Silver, Johnny Ryan, Billy Stevens, Mickey Martin. Had six fights with Eric Dolby, winning four (three in 29 days) and losing two. Beat Jimmy Brunt, drew with him, then lost to him within seven weeks at London's Queensberry All-Services Club (1944). Also met Dave Crowley, Dave Finn, Johnny Ward, Johnny McGrory and Laurie Buxton. Boxed many exhibitions with Freddie Mills during their RAF days and after the war became Freddie's chief sparring-partner.

CHADWICK Dennis. *Born* 1914, Bridlington. *Died* February 1991. Pro 1931-47. Beat George Marsden, Dan McAllister, Cyril Maudsley. Also went the distance with Ronnie James. As a steeplejack he suffered appalling injuries to both legs when demolishing a building. Was in a wheelchair for two years.

DANAHAR Alf. *Born* 15 March, 1923, Bethnal Green, London. Died January 1991. Pro 1946-55. Won South-Eastern Area welterweight title by beating Jeff Tite (1949). The Areas then changed and he beat Eric McQuade for the Southern Area title (1950), successfully defending it against Bob Frost (1950), Jeff Tite (1951), and Bob Frost (1952). Awarded a Boxing News Certificate of Merit for beating Tite (1949). Was beaten by Wally Thom in an eliminator for the British title (1951). Drew with former British lightweight champion, Billy Thompson (1951). After retiring became a manager and also served on the Southern Area Council for five years.

DAVIS Billy "The Kid". *Born* 11 April, 1943, Bow, London. *Died* 29 December, 1991. Pro 1960-64. Defeated Phil Lundgren, Danny O'Brien, Ron Jones, Jimmy Carson, Peter Lavery, Spike McCormack, Johnny Kidd and Chris Elliott. Also met Howard Winstone and Maurice Cullen. Became a trainer at Poplar & District BC.

DOLBY Eric. *born* 1915, Derby. *Died* February 1991. Pro 1931-45. Beat Pat Butler, Evan John, Eric Boon, Fred Lowbridge, Tommy Jones, Ted Hinton and Herbert Booth. Played cricket for Long Eaton. Former chairman of the North Midlands Area Council.

EBIHARA Hiroyuki. *Born* 26 March, 1940, Nishitama-Gun, Tokyo, Japan. Managed by Masaki Kanehira. *Died* 20 April, 1991. Pro 1959-69. Won world flyweight title in 1963 by stopping Pone Kingpetch in one round. Lost it back to Kingpetch in 1964. Was beaten by Horacio Accavallo in 1966 and 1967 in WBA flyweight title fights. Won the vacant WBA title in 1969 by beating Jose Severino, losing it in the same year against Bernabe Villacampo.

FORAN Gus. *Born* 15 October, 1919, Liverpool. *Died* 24 November, 1991. Real name Gerard Foran. Pro 1939-1951. In 1943 made a guest appearance for Everton Reserves at soccer and ten days later outpointed Ronnie Clayton in an eliminator for the Northern Area bantamweight title. In 1945 was beaten by Joe Curran in a final eliminator for the Northern Area title. Won North Central Area title by beating Billy Tansey (1948) and vacant Central Area title by beating Jimmy Gill (1950). Proudest moment was in beating Jackie Paterson at the Queensberry All-Services Club (1945). Paterson was world flyweight champion at the time and afterwards Lord Alexander, First Lord of the Admiralty, said to him: "Foran, you are the guts of the Navy." Also beat Teddy Gardner and Kid Tanner and went the distance with Peter Kane.

FRANKS Nat. *Born* 1 December, 1911, Shoreditch, London. *Died* November 1991. Real name Nathaniel Franklin. Pro 1927-39. Beat Len Munden, Les Ward, Eddie Maguire, Bob Scally, Tommy Martin, Paul Schaefer, Cock Moffitt, Jack Lord, Jack Aldir, Dixie Cullen, Jack McKnight and Billy Barr. Drew with Freddie Mills and also met Dick Turpin. Became a trainer, looking after Ken Diston and Billy Thompson. Rescued thirteen-year-old invalid Lily Burton from a burning house at Westgate-on-Sea (1936). Was injury prone - injured right hand against Ernie Mason (1932), broke hand against Archie Sexton (1935), collapsed in the ring with a torn neck muscle (1936) and on his way to watch the Derby was knocked down by a car (1937). In the early '30s was knocked out by Red Pullen. The doctor could find no pulse and no heartbeat and said there was nothing more he could do. Whereupon trainer Joe Russell, brother of referee Sam, slammed him against the wall, pummelling his body and eventually he started breathing again. In 1970 he slipped on an icy surface in the street, landed on his back and required an operation. This left a weakness and henceforth he needed the aid of a stick. Was a member of the London Ex-Boxers' Association.

GILL Jimmy. *Born* 5 October, 1917, Nottingham. *Died* 25 September, 1991. Known as the Fighting Jockey. The only man to combine boxing and racing at the same time on a professional level. Pro 1933-50. Beat Rinty Monaghan, Tiny Bostock, Ronnie Bishop, Frank Kid Bonsor, Tommy Farricker, Billy Clinton, Hugh Cameron, Jimmy Thompson, Norman Lewis, Mickey Jones, Billy Hazelgrove, Sammy Reynolds, Eric Jones and European champion, Raoul Degryse. Also met Peter Keenan, Terry Allen and Teddy Gardner . In 1938 went to India, riding many winners for well-known owners, at the same time winning the local flyweight and bantamweight championship. From 1942 to 1945, served in India, riding for the Maharajah of Cooch Behar and winning the All-India fly and bantam titles. Was a member of the Nottingham Ex-Boxers' Association. Beaten by Gus Foran for the vacant Central Area flyweight title (1950).

GRAHAM Billy. *Born* 9 September, 1922, New York. *Died* 22 January, 1992. Pro 1941-55. Twice met Kid Gavilan for the world welterweight title, losing both on points (1951 and 1952). Came to London in 1949 to meet Eddie Thomas, the latter winning on points. Met Gavilan twice in non-title fights, winning one and losing the other, (both in 1950). Met champion Carmen Basilio three times in 1952/3, drawing one and losing the others. Was never beaten inside the distance in 126 bouts.

HAMIA Cherif. *Born* Guergou, Algeria, 23 March, 1931. *Died* 24 June, 1991. Pro 1953-59. Former French and European featherweight champion. Was beaten by Hogan Bassey for the vacant world title 1957. Beat Jean Sneyers, Robert Cohen, Miguel Berrios, Ike Chestnut and Carmelo Costa.

HOLLAND Danny. *Born* 1907, London. *Died* July 1992. One of Britain's most famous trainers. Was an expert "cuts" man, showing his skills on numerous occasions when former heavyweight champion Henry Cooper was in action. Danny trained the Jim Wicks stable, which included Henry, brother George (who boxed as "Jim"), Joe Lucy, Alex Buxton, Vic Andreetti, Jake Tuli and a host of others. He boxed as an amateur, but in 1933 was working on the docks when he fell, in a ship's hold and fractured his skull. Ran the Thomas A'Becket gym for many years and even

Joe Lucy (left) shown in his last professional contest, losing his British lightweight title in a gutsy struggle against the rising young star, Dave Charnley

when he became ill he still enjoyed being taken to the gym, where he sat quietly and chatted with his friends.

HOOD Jack. *Born* 17 December, 1902, Birmingham. *Died* July 1992. Was Britain's oldest surviving ex-champion. Pro 1921-35. Won British welterweight titles by beating Harry Mason (1926). Successfully defended against Mason (1926), Alf Mancini (1928), Stoker Reynolds (1933) and retired still holding the title. Met Len Harvey three times for the British middleweight crown (twice in 1929 and in 1931), drawing one and losing two. The Empire title was also involved. Won European welterweight title by beating Adrian Anneet (1933) and was still holding the crown when he retired. Had two fights with legendary Frenchman Marcel Thil (1927 and 1932), winning the first and losing the return on a stoppage, the only bout Jack lost inside the distance in the whole of his career.

JOHNSON Les. Real name Leslie John Spence. *Born* 26 December, 1911, Hoxton, London. *Died* June 1991. Pro 1937-49. Although not turning pro until 26-years-old, made quite an impact, reaching the top half dozen flyweights in Britain and beating No.1 contender, Charlie Squire. Was beaten by Alf Ward for the Southern Area bantamweight title (1942), reverted to flyweight and beat No. 3 contender Dickie O'Sullivan. He was 37-years-old at the time. Also defeated Pat Palmer, Mickey Jones, Ronnie Bissell, Len Shaw, Jimmy Gill, Billy Hazelgrove and Alf Hughes. Drew with Joe Curran, Johnny Kent and Norman Tennant. Also met Terry Allen and Ronnie Clayton, who outpointed him twice, but he put Ronnie on the canvas. A former committee member of the London Ex-Boxers' Association, Les knocked out Dave Keller, his sister's dancing-partner. Dave is now a LEBA vice-president.

JONES Frankie. *Born* 12 February, 1933, Plean, Scotland. *Died* January 1991. Pro 1955-60. Managed by Joe Gans, father of Walter McGowan. Won British and British Empire flyweight title by beating Len Reece (1957) and successfully defended against Alex Ambrose (1959). Lost Empire title to Dennis Adams (1957) and the British title to John Caldwell (1960). Became a Beefeater at the Tower of London.

KANE Peter. *Born* 28 February, Golborne. *Died* 23 July, 1991. Known as The Man With The Eddie Cantor Eyes. Pro 1934-48. Was beaten by Benny Lynch for the world and British flyweight titles (1937). Won the world title by beating Jackie Jurich (1938), losing it to Jackie Paterson, with the British and Empire titles also involved (1943). Captured the European bantamweight title when beating Theo Medina (1947), successfully defending against Joe Cornelis (1947), before losing it to Guido Ferracin (1948). In a return title fight later that year, Ferracin again won.

LANGFORD Kenny. *Born* 25 March, 1933, Slough. *Died* July 1992. Pro 1955-57. England amateur international. Beat Malcolm McLeod, Dennis Hill, Don Cosheril, Dave Walsh and Dick Currie. Also met Eric Brett, Frankie Jones and John Morrissey. Member of the Slough Ex-Boxers' Association.

LARKIN Tippy. Real name Antonio Pilleteri. *Born* 11 November, 1917. Garfield, New Jersey. Known as The Garfield Gunner. *Died* January 1992. Pro 1935-52. Managed by Angelo Pucci. In 1939 was outpointed by Jack Kid Berg in Garfield. Stopped by Beau Jack in 1942 for the vacant New York version of the world lightweight title. Won the vacant world junior-welterweight title by beating Willie Joyce in 1946 and successfully defended it against Joyce the same year. Retired still holding the title.

LUCY Joe. *Born* 2 February, 1930, Mile End, London. *Died* 21 July, 1991. Pro 1950-57. Won British lightweight title by beating Tommy McGovern (1953). Lost it to Frank Johnson (1955). Regained it from Johnson (1956). Successfully defended it against Sammy McCarthy (1956). Lost it to Dave Charnley (1957). Was beaten by Johnny van Rensburg for the British Empire title (1955). Never knocked out.

McALLISTER Dan. *Born* 1918, Belfast. *Died* May 1991. Pro 1937-47. Beat Johnny King, Frank Kenny, Reg Quinlan, Benny Sharkey, Johnny McManus, Frank Parkes, Frank McCudden, George Marsden and Johnny Cunningham. Also met Chalky Wright, Johnny McGrory and Billy Thompson. Was beaten by Jim "Spider" Kelly for the Northern Ireland featherweight title (1938).

MIDDLETON George. *Died* January 1991, Warwick. One of Britain's most famous managers since 1936, whose stable included world middleweight champion Randy Turpin, Dick Turpin, Jackie Turpin, Maurice Mancini, Mick Leahy, Danny McAlinden, Jack Whittaker, Michael Stack, George Roe, Stan Parkes, Ronnie Vale, Tony French, Dave George, Tommy Icke, Frank Raven, Billy Williams and Maxie Earle.

MILLER Doug. *Born* 6 October, 1926, Johannesburg. *Died* December 1991. Pro 1946-67. Never won a South African title, although one of the best middleweights ever produced there. He stopped reigning champion Bob Bradley in one round (1948), reigning champion George Angelo twice (1950 and 1951), but all were non-title bouts. Came to Britain in 1948, the first of several visits. Beat Jake Kilrain, Jackie Brown, Johnny McGowan, George Dilkes, Michael Stack, George Casson, Bob Cleaver and Les Allen. Also met Dick Turpin, Randy Turpin, Mark Hart, Jean Stock and Bobby Dawson. In 1953 he at last got a shot at the South African middleweight title, but was beaten by Jimmy Elliott. He then went to live and work in Rhodesia, where he promoted, managed, refereed and even carried on boxing, finishing up as Rhodesian heavyweight champion. Eventually returned to South Africa to become a matchmaker.

George Middleton (right) was famous as the man who guided Britain's Randy Turpin (centre) to the world middleweight title and victory over the legendary Sugar Ray Robinson. Promoter, Jack Solomons, is on the left of the picture.

MILLER Tommy. *Born* 1 May, 1929, Blackburn, West Lothian. *Died* April 1992. Pro 1950-58. Was beaten by Freddie King in a final eliminator for the British featherweight title (1952) and the two boxers won the Boxing News Annual Trophy for the "Best Fight In A British Ring" in 1952. The same year he won a Boxing News Certificate of Merit for winning the Scottish title by beating George Stewart. Also beat Jim Kenny, Glyn Evans, Stan Skinkiss, Billy Kelly, Johnny Molloy, Eric Brett, Billy Rafferty, Gene Caffrey and George Lamont.

MONTANE Pierre. *Born* 1 December, 1919, Toulouse, France. *Died* 15 January,1991. Pro 1942-52. Won French lightweight title. Met Billy Thompson for the latter's European title (1948). The result was a draw. They met for the vacant European title in February 1951. Montane won, but lost the title six months later to Elis Ask. He boxed in Australia (1949), winning three and losing five.

NOVA Lou. *Born* 16 March,1915, Los Angeles California. Nationality, German-Irish-American. *Died* 29 September, 1991. National AAU heavyweight champion 1935. Won International amateur heavyweight championship in Paris 1935. Pro 1936-45. In successive fights in December 1938 and June 1939 he outpointed Tommy Farr and stopped Max Baer. In September 1941 he met Joe Louis for the latter's world title, but was beaten in six rounds.

OLEK Stephane. *Born* Poland 15 January, 1920. *Died* 21 January, 1991. Pro 1941-50. Won French heavyweight title. Twice boxed for European title, against Bruce Woodcock (1947) and Joe Weidin (1950), losing both. Besides Woodcock, he boxed in Britain against Freddie Mills, Johnny Williams and Jack Gardner, going the distance on each occasion. He also beat Australian champion Alf Gallagher at Manchester.

PAUL Tommy. Real name Gaetano Alfonso Pappa. *Born* 4 March, 1909, at Buffalo, New York. *Died* April 1991. National AAU bantamweight champion 1927. Pro 1927-36. NBA featherweight champion 1932-33. Won vacant title by beating Johnny Pena and lost it to Freddie Miller.

PRICE Ron. *Born* 19 August, 1922, Bilston. *Died* December 1991. Pro 1944-53. Beat Ron Dennington, Jordan Tarone, Roy Davies, Ginger Ward, Les Rendle and Dick Levers. Drew with Bob Foster.

SADD Arthur "Ginger". *Born* 27 March, 1914, Norwich. *Died* 10 April, 1992. Pro 1932-51. Won Eastern Area welterweight title by beating Seaman Jim Lawlor (1935) and Eastern Area middleweight title by beating Fred Clements (1937). Successfully defended against Joe Beckett (1948), before losing it to Beckett (1949). Was beaten by Jock McAvoy for the British middleweight title (1939). Three weeks later he beat Freddie Mills. Beaten by Bert Gilroy in a final eliminator for the British title (1940), he defeated Dave McCleave in another eliminator (1941), before losing to Ernie Roderick (1942). Besides McAvoy, Mills, McCleave and Roderick, he met several other champions, beating Dick Turpin, Harry Mason and Pat Butler and losing to Vince Hawkins, Albert Finch and Don Cockell. Later coached Norwich Lads' Club and was a member of the Eastern Area EBA.

SALCOMBE Colin. *Born* 10 October, 1940, Smethwick. *Died* August 1991. Won several fights by clean knockouts in the first round. In 1958 he kayoed Lew Devro twice inside a week, each time in round one. In 1960 he met Howard Winstone and Maurice Cullen.

STRIBLING Pat. Real name William Gardner. Took ring name after Young Stribling, heavyweight contender from America. *Born* 26 January, 1926, Croydon. *Died* 28 March, 1992. Pro 1946-51. Beat Ginger Sadd, Jock Taylor, (rated No. 3 light-heavyweight in Britain), Ernie Woodman, Gene Fowler, Trevor Burt, Vic Brooks, Tommy Caswell and Jackie Wilson. When Croydon Ex-Boxers' Association was formed in 1982 he became chairman, a position he held until his death. In 1985 he and his wife Ellie were the guests of the then Speaker of the House of Commons, Bernard Weatherill, MP., at the House of Commons.

TAVAREZ Leonard. *Born* 29 December, 1938. *Died* 20 November,1991. Pro 1967-74. Won French lightweight title by beating Jean Pierre le Jaouen (1969) and successfully defended it against the same man (1970). Was beaten for the European lightweight title by Ken Buchanan (1974) and in a non-title fight by world champion, Roberto Duran (1974).

WARREN Harry. *Born* 27 April, 1924, Bethnal Green. *Died* 1 May, 1991. Pro 1946-52. Beat Billy Pearce, Freddie Hicks, Ted Saunders, Billy Cook and Johnny Rendell. After retiring he went to Canada, finally settling in the United States, where he became a successful sports journalist. Life Member of the APTC, also of Croydon Ex-Boxers' Association. Serving with distinction in World War II, he was boxing coach of the Canadian Army, eventually becoming an actor and stunt man.

WEIR Ike. *Born* February 1920, Belfast. *Died* 19 August, 1991. Real name James Rooney. Took ring name from Ike "Spider" Weir, a Belfast boxer who went to America in 1889 and drew with Frank Murphy for the vacant world featherweight title. Pro 1940-49. Beaten by Bunty Doran for the Northern Ireland flyweight title (1944). Never weighed more than eight stones in the whole of his career. In fact for his final bout against Jimmy Orr he scaled 7st. 5lb. and conceded over ten pounds. Outpointed Rinty Monaghan (1943). Also beat Les Johnson, Billy Nash, Jimmy Quinn, Tommy Madine, Jack McKenzie and Tommy Farricker.

WILDE Jim. *Born* Swansea. *Died* March 1991. Pro 1932-46. Beat Charlie Bundy for the vacant Welsh heavyweight title (1935). Later lost the title to Tommy Farr (1936). Had two title fights with George James, but lost both (1938 and 1939). Beat Norman Baines, Maurice Strickland, Max Hodgetts, Alf Robinson, Robey Leibrandt, Dom Lydon, Alex Bell, Steve McCall, Bill Wainwright, Salah El Din and Manuel Abrew. Drew with Tommy Farr.

WILLIAMS Taffy. *Born* January 1920, Swansea. *Died* March 1992. Pro 1938-46. Real name William McVeigh. Won vacant Welsh welterweight title by beating George Reynolds (1939). Was defeated by Tommy Davies for the Welsh middleweight title (1946). A good soccer player, he was offered terms by the Scottish club St. Johnstone.

Leading BBBoC Licence Holders: Names and Addresses

Licensed Promoters

Michael Andrew
47 New Barn Street
Plaistow
London E13 8JY

Anglo-Swedish Promotions
11 Whitcomb Street
London WC2H 7HA

Graham Baldock
209 Wood Street
London E17 3NU

Mike Barrett
PO Box 1230
London SW7 4QZ

Jack Bishop
76 Gordon Road
Fareham
Hampshire PO16 7SS

Pat Brogan
112 Crewe Road
Haslington
Crewe
Cheshire

Harry Burgess
25 Calthorpe Street
London WC1X 0JX

Ernie Cashmore
18 North Drive
Handsworth
Birmingham B20 3SZ

Annette Conroy
144 High Street
Sunderland
Tyne and Wear

Thomas Cooper
Pen Prys Farm
Bryn
Llanelli
Dyfed

Pat Cowdell
129a Moat Road
Oldbury
Warley
West Midlands

Frank Deans
11 Bedale Court
Simonside
South Shields
Tyne and Wear

Eastwood Promotions
Eastwood House
2-4 Chapel Lane
Belfast 1
Northern Ireland

Evesham Sporting Club
17 Worcester Road
Evesham
Worcestershire
WR11 4JU

Norman Fawcett
10 Fuschia Place
Blackelaw
Newcastle upon Tyne

Douglas Firkin-Flood
Nut Bank House
Blackley
Manchester 9

John Forbes
5 Durham Road
Sedgfield
Stockton on Tees
Cleveland TS21 3DW

Joe Frater
The Cottage
Main Road
Grainthorpe
Louth
Lincolnshire

Joe Foster
4 Denham Avenue
Fulwell
Sunderland

Gardiner & Hayde
587 Cowbridge Road
East
Victoria Park
Cardiff
Wales

Harold Gorton
Gorton House
4 Hollius Road
Oldham
Lancashire

Ron Gray (Boxing) Promotions
Ingrams Oak
19 Hatherton Road
Cannock
Staffordshire

Stephen Griffin
98 Stonehill Avenue
Birstall
Leicester

Graham Grinnell
Pro Sport
2 Riverside
Bridgenorth
Shropshire

David Harris
16 Battle Crescent
St Leonards on Sea
Sussex

Barry Hearn
Matchroom
10 Western Road
Romford
Essex RM1 3JT

Brian Hearn
12 Newnham Road
Colebrook
Plymton
Devon PL7 4AW

Vince Heckman
The Bungalow
Rear of White Widows
Croydon Road
Westerham
Kent

Holiday Inn Promotions
St Nicholas Circle
Leicester LE1 5LX

Harry Holland
12 Kendall Close
Feltham
Middlesex

Terry Holland
29/31 Orchard Road
Stevenage
Hertfordshire SG1 1EQ

Hull & District Sporting Club
25 Purton Grove
Bransholme
Hull HU7 4QD

Alma Ingle
26 Newman Road
Wincobank
Sheffield S9 1LP

K K Promotions
19 Whittington
Off Parnwell Way
Peterborough PE1 4YE

John Levine
38 St Vincent Road
Westcliff on Sea
Essex S50 7PR

Burt McCarthy
Fieldwood House
144 Clerkenwell Road
London EC1R 5DP

Terry McHale
Irish Amateur
Sporting Bar
Lime Street
Liverpool

McMahan Promotions
122 Twinnel House
Easton
Bristol

Frank Maloney
Champion Enterprises
22 Dorset Street
London W1H 3FT

Phil Martin
79 Buckingham Road
Charlton
Manchester
M21 1OT

Matchroom
10 Western Road
Romford
Essex RM1 3TT

Midland Sporting Club
2 Bilton Hall
Church Walk
Old Bilton
Rugby CV22 7LX

Chris Moorcroft
10 Chingall Close
Fir Tree Drive South
Croxteth Country Road
Liverpool L12 0JE

National Promotions
National House
60-66 Wardour Street
London W1V 3HP

North Staffs Sporting Club
J Baddely
29 Redwood Avenue
Stoke
Staffordshire ST15 0DB

North-West Promotions
93 Keir Hardie Avenue
Bootle
Liverpool 20
Merseyside

Prime Promotions
85 Sydney Street
Glasgow

B A Quinn-Reed
Westcliffe House
Madeira Road
Weston super Mare
Avon BS23 1AP

Gus Robinson
Stranton House
Westview Road
Hartlepool TS24 0BB

Steve Robinson
513 Hackney Road
London E2 9ED

Chris Rustage
Riverside House
St Simon Street
Salford
Manchester M3 7ET

St Andrews Sporting Club
c/o Tommy Gilmour
Anderson Suite
Forte Crest Hotel
Bothwell Street
Glasgow G2 7EN

Mike Shinfield
126 Birchwood Lane
Somercotes
Derbyshire
DE55 4NF

James Smith
1 Mainway
Alkington
Middleton
Manchester M24 1LE

Brian Snagg
The Princess
Princess Drive
West Derby
Liverpool 12 6QQ

Jack Solomons Sporting Club
High Beech
Hayway
Rushden
Northamptonshire

John Spensley
1st Floor
339 Linthorpe Road
Middlesbrough
Cleveland TS5 6AD

Stoke European Sporting Club
113 Crewe Road
Haslington
Crewe
Cheshire

Tara Boxing Promotions
Lane End Cottage
Golden Street
Shaw
Oldham
Lancashire OL2 8LY

Team Promotions
Contract House
Split Crow Road
Gateshead
Tyne and Wear

Jack Trickett
Acton Court Hotel
187 Buxton Road
Stockport
Cheshire

Brian Walker
52 Cardiff Street
Aberdare
Wales

WAM Promotions
Victoria Works
Machynys
Llanelli
Dyfed

Frank Warren
18 Tavistock Place
London
WC1H 9RE

Wolverhampton Sporting Club
Centre City Tower
7 Hill Street
Birmingham B5 4OU

Yorkshire Executive Sporting Club
c/o John Celebanski
87 Crowtree Lane
Allerton
Bradford BD8 0AN

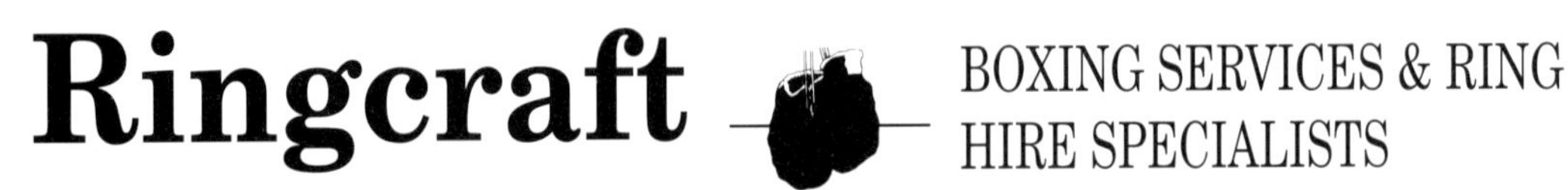

Licensed Managers

Billy Aird
Western House
14 Western Road
Plaistow
London E13 9JF

Isola Akay
129 Portnall Road
Paddington
London W9 3BN

Mike Atkinson
9 Tudor Road
Ainsdale
Southport
Lancashire PR8 2RU

Don Austin
14 Winchat Road
Broadwaters
Thamesmead
London SE28 0DZ

William Ball
6 Copse Close
Marlow
Buckinghamshire
SL7 2NY

Johnny Barclay
3 Newall Close
The Furlongs
Turnfurlong Lane
Aylesbury
Buckinghamshire
HP21 7FE

Mike Barrett
PO Box 1230
London SW7 4QZ

Nat Basso
38 Windsor Road
Prestwich
Lancashire M25 8FF

Bob Batey
243 Ladykirk Road
Newcastle upon Tyne
NE4 8AL

John Baxter
6 Havencrest Drive
Leicester LE5 2AG

Tom Bell
46 Station Road
Laughton Common
Dinnington
Yorkshire

Doug Bidwell
2 De La Warr Road
East Grinstead
West Sussex

Lance Billany
32 Beaconsfield
Carrs Meadow
Withernsea
North Humberside
HU19 2EP

Jack Bishop
76 Gordon Road
Fareham
Hampshire PO16 7SS

Gerald Bousted
46 Coombe Lane
St Mary Church
Torquay
Devon

George Bowes
24 St Mawes Close
Thorston Grange
Hartlepool
Cleveland

Colin Breen
31 Penlan Road
Treboeth
Swansea
West Glamorgan

Mike Brennan
2 Canon Avenue
Chadwell Heath
Romford
Essex

Fred Britton
71 Henrietta Street
Leigh
Lancashire WN7 1LH

Pat Brogan
112 Crewe Road
Haslington
Cheshire

Ron Browne
12 Cromwell Drive
Kates Hill
Dudley DY2 7EU

Dick Brownson
Armada House
Marine Parade
Instow
North Devon EX39 4JJ

Harry Burgess
25 Calthorpe Street
London WC1X 0JX

Alex Buxton
2 Romola Road
London SE24

Paddy Byrne
70 Benfield Way
Portslade by Sea
Sussex BN4 2DL

Pat Byrne
11 Cadman Close
Bedworth
Warwickshire

Trevor Callighan
40 Prescott Street
Halifax
West Yorkshire
HX1 2QW

Harry Carnall
270 Hastilar Road
South Woodthorpe
Sheffield
Yorkshire S13 8EJ

Ernie Cashmore
18 North Drive
Handsworth
Birmingham B20 3SZ

John Celebanski
87 Crowtree Lane
Allerton
Bradford BD8 0AN

Michael Chapman
9 Mill Lane
Farington
Moss
Lancashire PR5 3PS

Nigel Christian
80 Alma Road
Plymouth
Devon PL3 4HU

Peter Coleman
9 Easterly Grove
Leeds
Yorkshire LS8 3AB

Roger Colson
63 Amwell Street
Roseberry Avenue
London EC1

William Connelly
79 Clincart Road
Mount Florida
Glasgow G42

Tommy Conroy
144 High Street East
Sunderland
Tyne and Wear

George Cooper
16 Robin Hood Green
St Mary Cray
Orpington
Kent

Michael Copp
62 Fleet Street
Swansea
West Glamorgan

Pat Cowdell
129a Moat Road
Oldbury
Warley
West Midlands
B68 8EE

John Cox
11 Fulford Drive
Links View
Northampton
NN2 7NX

James Cresswell
3 Williamson Street
Clydebank G81 2AS

Bingo Crooks
37 Helming Drive
Danehust Estate
Wolverhampton
West Midlands
WV1 2AF

David Davies
10 Byrngelli
Carmel
Llanelli
Dyfed SA14 7EL

Glyn Davis
63 Parc Brynmawr
Felinfoel
Llanelli
Dyfed SA15 4PG

Ronnie Davies
3 Vallensdean Cottages
Hangleton Lane
Portslade
Sussex

Frank Deans
11 Bedale Court
Simonside
South Shields
Tyne and Wear

Brendan Devine
12 Birkdale Close
Clubmoor
Liverpool L6 0DL

Jack Doughty
Lane End Cottage
Golden Street
Shaw
Lancashire OL2 8LY

Terry Downes
Milestone
Milespit Hill
London NW7

Phil Duckworth
The Shepherd
96 Pontefract Lane
Leeds
Yorkshire L59 6TG

Mickey Duff
National House
60-66 Wardour Street
London W1V 3HP

Pat Dwyer
93 Keir Hardie Avenue
Bootle
Liverpool 20
Merseyside L20 0DN

Bernard Eastwood
Eastwood House
2-4 Chapel Lane
Belfast 1
Northern Ireland

Billy Evans
18a Yorkaster Road
Allerton
Liverpool L18 9TT

George Evans
14 Donald Street
Abercanaid
Merthyr Tydfil
Glamorgan

Greg Evans
21 Portman Road
Liverpool
Merseyside L15 2HH

Jack Evans
Morlee House
Hanbury Road
Pontypool
Monmouth

Michael Fawcett
44 Rawstone Walk
Plaistow
London E13

Norman Fawcett
4 Wyndsale Place
Gosforth
Newcastle upon Tyne

Collin Flute
84 Summerhill Road
Bilston
West Midlands
WV14 8RE

George Francis
11 Hill Way
Holly Lodge Estate
London N6

Dai Gardiner
13 Hengoed Hall
Drive
Cefn Hengoed
Hengoed
Glamorgan

John Gaynor
7 Westhorne Fold
Counthill Drive
Brooklands Road
Crumpsall
Manchester M8 6JN

Danny Gill
8 Whitehouse Street
Coseley
West Midlands
WV14 8HE

Tommy Gilmour
Forte Crest Hotel
Bothwell Street
Glasgow G2 7EN

Lee Graham
17 Felday Road
Lewisham
London SE13 7HQ

Ben Grant
16 Southgate Street
Neath
Glamorgan

Ron Gray
Ingrams Oak
19 Hatherton Road
Cannock
Staffordshire

Johnny Griffin
98 Stonehill Avenue
Birstall
Leicester

Harry Griver
187 Redbridge Lane
East
Redbridge
Essex IG4 5DF

Dick Gunn
43 Moray Avenue
Hayes
Middlesex OB3 2AY

Carl Gunns
Flat 2
Heathcliffe
469 Loughborough
Road
Birstall
Leicester LE4 0DS

Clive Hall
23 Linnet Drive
Barton Seagrave
Kettering
Northamptonshire

Con Harris
97 Heyford Way
Castle Vale
Birmingham
B35 6JB

David Harris
16 Battle Crescent
St Leonards on Sea
Sussex

Teddy Haynes
The Henry Cooper
516 Old Kent Road
London SE1 5BA

Geoff Hayward
51 Derby Avenue
Tettenhall
Wolverhampton
West Midlands
WV6 9JR

Patrick Healey
1 Cranley Buildings
Brookes Market
Holborn
London EC1

Barry Hearn
Matchroom
10 Western Road
Romford
Essex RM1 3JT

Terry Hernon
Fairview Farm
Penyfed Pembrey
Llanelli
Dyfed SA16 0RJ

George Hill
52 Hathaway
Marton
Blackpool
Lancashire FY4 4AB

Mick Hill
35 Shenstone House
Aldrington Road
London SW16 1TL

Harry Holland
12 Kendall Close
Feltham
Middlesex

Gordon Holmes
Wayland House
Shipdam Road
Scoulton
Norwich
Norfolk

Lloyd Honeyghan
50 Barnfield Wood
Road
Park Langley
Beckenham
Kent BR3 2SU

Ken Honniball
Avon Sporting Club
14 Purewell
Christchurch
Dorset

Brendan Ingle
26 Newman Road
Wincobank
Sheffield S9 1LP

Derek Isaamen
179 Liverpool Road
South
Maghill
Liverpool L31 8AA

Joe Jackson
The Blenheim
Churchfields
Keresley
West Midlands

Colin Jones
1 Brookfield Close
Penyrheol
Gorseinon
Swansea SA4 2GW

Richard Jones
1 Churchfields
Croft
Warrington
Cheshire WA3 7JR

Duncan Jowett
Cedarhouse
Caplethill Road
Paisley
Renfrewshire
Scotland

Billy Kane
17 Bamburn Terrace
Byker
Newcastle upon Tyne
NE6 2GH

Archie Kasler
17 Claude Road
Leyton
London E10 6NG

Johnny Kramer
115 Crofton Road
Plaistow
London E13

Terry Lawless
4 Banyards
Off Nelmes Way
Emerson Park
Hornchurch
Essex

Brian Lynch
53 Hall Lane
Upminster
Essex

Pat Lynch
Gotherinton
68 Kelsey Lane
Balsall Common
Near Coventry
West Midlands

Glenn McCrory
Holborn
35 Station Road
Stanley
Co Durham DH9 0JL

Clinton McKenzie
7 Market Parade
South Norwood
London SE25

James McMillan
21 Langcliffe Road
Preston
Lancashire PR2 6UE

Frank Maloney
Champion Enterprises
22 Dorset Street
London W1H 3FT

Dennie Mancini
16 Rosedew Road
Off Fulham Palace
Road
London W6 9ET

Tony Mancini
3 Guinness Trust
Buildings
Fulham Palace Road
Hammersmith
London W6

Terry Marsh
141 Great Gregorie
Basildon
Essex

Phillip Martin
79 Buckingham Road
Chorlton
Manchester M21 1TQ

Gary Mason
Suite 310
Blackfriars Foundry
156 Blackfriars Road
London SE1 8EN

Teddy Mason
55 Hall Green Lane
Hutton
Brentwood
Essex

Arthur Melrose
85 Sydney Street
Glasgow G31 2ND

Tommy Miller
128 Clapton Mount
King Cross Road
Halifax
West Yorkshire

Achille Mitchell
54 Portland Avenue
Gravesend
Kent

Carl Moorcroft
108 Stuart Road
Crosby
Liverpool 23

Alexander Morrison
39 Armour Street
Glasgow G33 5EX

Graham Moughton
11 Neville Road
Dagenham
Essex

James Murray
87 Spean Street
Glasgow G44 4DS

David Nelson
29 Linley Drive
Stirchley Park
Telford
Shropshire TF3 1RQ

Paul Newman
Flat 7
Selbourne Court
Hove
Sussex

Gary Nickels
36 William Dromey Court
Dyne Road
Kilburn
London NW6 7XD

Norman Nobbs
364 Kings Road
Kingstanding
Birmingham B44 0UG

Bob Paget
8 Masterman House
New Church Road
London SE5 7HU

George Patrick
84 Wooler Road
Edmonton
London N18 2JS

Billy Pearce
Flat C
36 Courtfield Gardens
South Kensington
London SW5 0PT

Terry Petersen
54 Green Leafe Avenue
Wheatley Hills
Doncaster
South Yorkshire
DN2 5RF

Steve Pollard
35 Gorthorpe
Orchard Park Estate
Hull HE6 9EY

John Pook
75 Stapley Road
Hove
Sussex

Ricky Porter
73 County Road
Swindon
Wiltshire

Dennis Read
65 Bridle Road
Shirley
Croydon
Surrey

Ken Richardson
15 East Walk
North Road Estate
Retford
Nottinghamshire
DN22 7YF

Fred Rix
14 Broom Road
Shirley
Croydon
Surrey CR0 8NE

Brian Robinson
6 Fetters Close
Broadlands
Swinton
Lancashire M27 1PD

Gus Robinson
Stranton House
Westview Road
Hartlepool
TS24 0BB

John Rushton
20 Alverley Lane
Balby
Doncaster DN4 9AS

Joe Ryan
22a Glenarm Road
Clapton
London E5 0LZ

Kevin Sanders
19 Whittington
Off Parnwell Way
Peterborough
Cambridgeshire

Chris Sanigar
41 Chaplin Road
Easton
Briston B55 0JT

Eric Secombe
11 Joseph Trotter Close
Myddleton Street
Finsbury
London EC1

Kevin Sheehan
84 Amesbury Circus
Bells Lane Estate
Nottingham NG8 6DH

Mike Shinfield
126 Birchwood Lane
Somercotes
Derbyshire DE55 4 NE

Steve Sims
The Welsh Prince
78 Commercial Street
Newport
Gwent

Len Slater
78 Sutcliffe Avenue
Nunsthorpe
Grimsby
Lincolnshire

Andy Smith
Valandra
19 St Audreys Lane
St Ives
Cambridgeshire

Darkie Smith
21 Northumberland
House
Gaisford Street
London NW5 2EA

John Smith
6 Kildare Road
Chorlton
Manchester 21 1YR

Brian Snagg
The Princess
Princess Drive
West Derby
Liverpool L12 6QQ

Les Southey
Oakhouse
Park Way
Hillingdon
Middlesex

John Spensley
1st Floor
339 Linthorpe Road
Middlesborough
TS5 6AD

Ken Squires
27 University Close
Syston
Leicestershire LE7 8AY

Gregg Steene
11 Whitcomb Street
London WC2H 7HA

Danny Sullivan
29 Mount Gould
Avenue
St Judes
Plymouth
Devon PL4 9HH

Norrie Sweeney
3 Saucehill Terrace
Paisley
Scotland PA2 6SY

Wally Swift
Grove House
54 Grove Road
Knowle
Solihull
West Midlands B93 0PJ

Keith Tate
214 Dick Lane
Tyersal
Bradford BD4 8JH

Glenroy Taylor
95 Devon Close
Perivale
Middlesex

Eddie Thomas
Runnington
Penydarren Park
Merthyr Tydfil
Mid Glamorgan

Andrew Thompson
144 Springvale Road
Upperthorpe
Sheffield S6 3NU

James Tibbs
44 Gylingdune Gardens
Seven Kings
Essex

Terence Toole
8 Conningsby Gardens
South Chingford
London E4 9BD

Mick Toomey
25 Purton Grove
Bransholme
Hull HU7 4QD

Jack Trickett
Acton Court Hotel
189 Buxton Road
Stockport
Cheshire

Noel Trigg
Waterford
The Bridge
Bettws Lane
Newport NP9 6AB

Frankie Turner
Matchroom
10 Western Road
Essex RM1 3JT

Stephen Vaughan
43-45 Pembroke Place
Liverpool L3 5PH

Alan Walker
47 Consett Road
Castleside
Consett
Durham DH8 9QL

Frank Warren
18 Tavistock Place
London WC1H 9RE

Robert Watt
32 Dowanhill Street
Glasgow G11

Gordon White
34 Gaskell Street
London SW4 6NS

Ken Whitney
22 Oundle Road
Weldon
Northamptonshire

Mac Williams
351 Chapelwood
Llanedeyrn
Cardiff CF3 7EQ

Michael Williamson
34a St Marys Grove
Cannonbury
London N1

Tex Woodward
Spanorium Farm
Berwick Lane
Compton Greenfield
Bristol BS12 3RX

Licensed Matchmakers

Don Aagesen
156 Lodge Road
Winson Green
Birmingham B18 5DN

Mike Barrett
PO Box 1230
London SW7 4QZ

Nat Basso
38 Windsor Road
Prestwich
Lancashire M25 8FF

Jack Bishop
76 Gordon Road
Fareham
Hampshire

Harry Burgess
25 Calthorpe Street
London WC1

Paddy Byrne
70 Benfield Way
Portslade by Sea
Sussex BN4 2DL

David Davis
179 West Heath Road
Hampstead
London NW3

David Davies
10 Byrngelli
Carmel
Llanelli
Dyfed SA14 7EL

Mickey Duff
National House
60-66 Wardour Street
London W1 3HP

Ernie Fossey
26 Bell Lane
Brookmans Park
Hertfordshire

John Gaynor
7 Westhorne Fold
Counthill Drive
Brooklands Road
Crumpsall
Manchester M8 6JN

Tommy Gilmour
Fort Crest Hotel
Bothwell Street
Glasgow G2 7EN

Ron Gray
Ingrams Oak
19 Hatherton Road
Cannock
Staffordshire

Patrick Healey
1 Cranley Buildings
Brookes Market
Holborn
London EC1

Steve Holdsworth
85 Sussex Road
Watford
Herts WD2 5HR

Terry Lawless
4 Banyards
Off Nelmes Way
Emerson Park
Hornchurch
Essex

Graham Lockwood
106 Burnside Avenue
Skipton
North Yorkshire
BD23 2OB

Frank Maloney
Champion Enterprises
22 Dorset Street
London W1H 3FT

Dennie Mancini
16 Rosedew Road
Off Fulham Palace Road
London W6 9ET

Tommy Miller
128 Clapton Mount
King Cross Road
Halifax
West Yorkshire

Chris Moorcroft
10 Chignall Close
Fir Tree Drive South
Croxteth Country Road
Liverpool L12 0JE

Alex Morrison
39 Armour Street
Glasgow G33 5EX

Gary Nickels
36 William Dromey Court
Dyne Road
Kilburn
London NW6 7XD

Norman Nobbs
364 Kings Road
Kingstanding
Birmingham B44 0UG

Ricky Porter
Angelique Guest House
73 County Road
Swindon
Wiltshire

Dean Powell
10 Cuddington
Deacon Way
Heygate Estate
Walworth
London SE17 1SP

Len Slater
78 Sutcliffe Avenue
Nunsthorpe
Grimsby
Lincolnshire

Terry Toole
8 Conningsby Gardens
South Chingford
London E4 9BD

Frank Turner
Matchroom
10 Western Road
Romford
Essex RM1 3JT

Stephen Vaughan
276 Aigburth Road
Aigburth
Liverpool L17 9PJ

Tex Woodward
Spanorium Farm
Berwick Lane
Compton Greenfield
Bristol BS12 3RX

Licensed Referees

Class 'B'

Teddy Gardner	Southern Area
Keith Garner	Central Area
Anthony Green	Central Area
Mark Green	Southern Area
Rudi Harders	Welsh Area
Al Hutcheon	Scottish Area
David Irving	Northern Ireland
Marcus McDonnell	Southern Area
Terry O'Connor	Midlands Area
Roy Snipe	Central Area
Grant Wallis	Western Area
Gerald Watson	Northern Area

Class 'A'

Ivor Bassett	Welsh Area
Arnold Bryson	Northern Area
Phil Cowsill	Central Area
Richard Davies	Southern Area
Roddy Evans	Welsh Area
Ron Hackett	Central Area
Michael Heatherwick	Welsh Area
Brian Hogg	Central Area
Michael Jacobs	Southern Area
Wynford Jones	Welsh Area
John Keane	Midland Area
Denzil Lewis	Western Area
Len Mullen	Scottish Area
Fred Potter	Northern Area
James Pridding	Midlands Area
Reg Thompson	Southern Area
Lawrence Thompson	Northern Area
Anthony Walker	Southern Area
Barney Wilson	Northern Ireland

Class 'A' Star

John Coyle	Midlands Area
Roy Francis	Southern Area
Adrian Morgan	Welsh Area
Larry O'Connell	Southern Area
Dave Parris	Southern Area
Billy Rafferty	Scottish Area
Paul Thomas	Midlands Area
Mickey Vann	Central Area

Licensed Timekeepers

Roy Bicknell	Midlands Area
Roger Bowden	Western Area
John Breward	Northern Area
Neil Burder	Welsh Area
Ivor Campbell	Welsh Area
Frank Capewell	Central Area
Robert Edgeworth	Southern Area
Harold Elliott	Northern Ireland
Harry Foxall	Midlands Area
Jack Gidman	Midlands Area
Eric Gilmour	Scottish Area
Brian Heath	Midlands Area
Ken Honiball	Western Area
Lewis G. Hubbard	Southern Area
Albert Kelleher	Northern Area
Peter McCann	Southern Area
Norman Maddox	Midlands Area
Gordon Pape	Welsh Area
Daniel Peacock	Southern Area
Barry Pinder	Central Area
Raymond Preston	Western Area
Raymond Rice	Southern Area
Tommy Rice	Southern Area
Colin Roberts	Central Area
James Russell	Scottish Area
Nick White	Southern Area
Geoffrey Williams	Southern Area

Licensed Inspectors

Alan Alster	Central Area
Ken Barclay	Scottish Area
Michael Barnett	Central Area
Jeffrey Bowden	Western Area
John Braley	Midlands Area
Fred Breyer	Southern Area
Tom Byron	Midlands Area
Ray Chichester	Welsh Area
Geoff Collier	Midlands Area
John Crowe	Midlands Area
Les Dean	Midlands Area
Phil Edwards	Central Area
Vic Edwards	Southern Area
Kevin Fulthorpe	Welsh Area
John Hall	Central Area
Richard Hingston	Western Area
Dennis Kearney	Northern Ireland
Freddie King	Southern Area
Bob Lonkhurst	Southern Area
Ken Lyas	Southern Area
John McMillan	Central Area
Stuart Meiklejohn	Central Area
David Ogilvie	Northern Area
Charlie Payne	Southern Area
Les Potts	Midlands Area
Ron Pudney	Southern Area
Ray Randall	Welsh Area
Ken Rimmington	Southern Area
John S. Shaw	Western Area
Bert Smith	Western Area
Charlie Thurley	Southern Area
John Toner	Northern Ireland
David Venn	Northern Area
Ernie Wallis	Welsh Area
P. J. White	Southern Area
Billy Wilkins	Welsh Area
Geoff Williams	Midlands Area
Harry Woods	Scottish Area
Charlie Wright	Southern Area

Licensed Ringwhips

Robert Ainsley-Mathews	Southern Area
Robert Brazier	Southern Area
Albert Brewer	Southern Area
Steve Butler	Central Area
Theodore Christian	Western Area
Ernie Draper	Southern Area
Danny Gill	Midlands Area
Chris Gilmore	Scottish Area
Mike Goodall	Midlands Area
Peter Gray	Midlands Area
Arran Lee Grinnell	Midlands Area
David Hall	Central Area
Thomas Hallett	Northern Area
John Hardwick	Southern Area
Keith Jackson	Midlands Area
Philip Keen	Central Area
Alun Martin	Welsh Area
Tommy Miller (Jnr)	Central Area
Dennis Pinching	Southern Area
Barry Pinder	Central Area
Sandy Risley	Southern Area
Phillip Thomas	Welsh Area
John Vary	Southern Area
Paul Wainwright	Northern Area
James Wallace	Scottish Area
James Whitelaw	Scottish Area
John Whitelaw	Scottish Area

Legendary referee, Harry Gibbs, now acting as a judge Les Clark